real
flavours

the handbook of gourmet & deli ingredients

Dedication

For Richard Broome, a delicious friend and culinary support for almost 40 years

About the author

TV chef and traveller Glynn Christian is acknowledged as one of Britain's leading experts on delicatessen, gourmet and speciality ingredients. He has cooked on British television for both the BBC and ITV since 1982. Over 1000 live broadcasts include Pebble Mill and Breakfast Time and he also appeared with Cilla Black, Esther Rantzen and Noel Edmonds. His filmed series include those shot on location in the Eastern Mediterranean, New Zealand, California, Sri Lanka, China, Thailand and, most recently, a 26-part series Tasting Australia, for the Travel Channel UK.

Glynn learned much of his ingredient knowledge as a travel writer in the early days of inclusive holidays and in 1974 he opened Mr Christian's, the iconic delicatessen on London's famous Portobello Road market.

He was a founding committee member of the Guild of Food Writers and has written more than 25 food and cookery books including *The Delicatessen Food Handbook* and *Edible France*. Other books include *Fragile Paradise – The Discovery of Fletcher Christian*, *Bounty Mutineer*, which remains the only biography of Glynn's gt gt gt gt grandfather, who led the mutiny on *Bounty* in 1789.

After 10 years in Australia and New Zealand, Glynn has returned to live in London and is pioneering the sale of speciality foods on QVC, the shopping channel.

Published in 2005 by
Grub Street
4 Rainham Close
London
SW11 6SS
Email: food@grubstreet.co.uk
Web: www.grubstreet.co.uk

Text copyright © Glynn Christian 2005
Copyright this edition © Grub Street 2005
Design and jacket design Lizzie Ballantyne
Photographs David Whyte

British Library Cataloguing in Publication Data
Christian, Glynn
Real flavours: the handbook of gourmet and deli ingredients. – 3rd edition
1.   Food
I.   Title II Christian, Glynn. Glynn Christian's new delicatessen food handbook 641.3
ISBN 1 904943 20 9

Printed and bound in India

real flavours

the handbook of gourmet & deli ingredients

Glynn Christian

Grub Street • London

Acknowledgements

Thousands of people and experiences helped write this book originally, and with each new edition thousands more might find nuggets they have given me are now in print. Thanks for all those conversations and observations, for the advice generously given and the opinions passionately imposed.

Many of those who helped with the first edition are still helping, particularly Richard Broome in London, Kurt Weyrauch in New York, and Fr Anthony Parker in Baltimore, to whom Topher and Audra Russo must now be gratefully added. In Australasia the ever-curious Chris Beech made me think more deeply, Professor Laurie Melton enthused, John Prince and his magical garden and mind did both, Noelene Gillies and her unfailing hospitality kept me going, Peter Howard's ever-willing generosity was unwitting fuel: Jacqui, Phil and John of Sabato in Auckland still run one of the best speciality food shops in the world, as generous-spirited as they are.

In London, Maria Jose Sevilla of Food from Spain was quick off the mark to help yet again, and there was great support from Fabrizio Di Clemente and his colleagues at the Italian Trade Centre, and from Catherine Manac'h of Sopexa (Food from France).

Bob Farrand, publisher of *Fine Food* magazine and Supremo of speciality food fairs, the Great Taste Awards, the UK Cheese Guild and the World Cheese Awards, was a brick, delightfully cemented into place by Linda, his equally kind and knowledgeable wife. Mark Steene of The Seasoned Pioneers generously shared amazing information, as did Ian Hemphill, author of the extraordinary *Spice Notes*. Jenni Muir, author of award-winning *A Cook's Guide to Grains* let me into more grain secrets than I had imagined possible, and good old and new friends supported the research, the eating and the arguing that made the book such fun to bring up to date, especially Robin, Louella and Merlin Hanbury Tenison, Richard Patching, Carolyn Cavele, Rosie Stark, Michael Truscott, Kitty van Hagen, George and Anne Andrews, Dinah Morrison, Mattie Wall and Rehan Kularatne.

Nothing would have been possible if my family in NZ had not supported me through some difficult times, especially Dale – big thanks also to Bruce, Faye, Ross and Sheryl, Matt, Jared and Alicja, Natalia and Daniel, who did more than he imagines. Most of all a book like this needs a publisher and an editor who profoundly understands food writing and food writers; in Anne Dolamore I am blessed with both.

Contents

Foreword

Welcome to a book about real flavours and how to recognise and enjoy them.
It won't make you an expert or even tell you everything you might want to know but I hope it will give you enough points of reference and opinions to discover what you like best. The fame of any special food and drink is based on the pleasure principles of the culture in which it developed. If you are from a different culture there's no guarantee you'll like it as much as the locals, and no-one can tell you otherwise. If you don't like something, you don't, and that's that.

Equally, there's no pleasure in making a fool of yourself; it's useful to have some sense of what to expect when confronted by something for the first time. If you expect caviar to be sweet, or that risotto rice should be crunchy or that an unpasteurised Camembert cheese is best when ammoniacal you'll get no pleasure from tasting the real thing – in turn salty, silken and pasture-sweet. But get your mind-set right and the pleasures of fine food are one of our greatest pastimes. Everybody eats and we all eat every day, so good food makes more of each day, at home or travelling.

The particular advantage of great food with full flavour is we eat less of it. Gratify the palate with pleasure and the stomach is replete: starve the palate by eating bland, fatty mush and the stomach demands more and more – more food than we need. My rule is never to put anything in my mouth that doesn't bite back with flavour; that way I get more gratification but actually eat and drink less.

The extraordinary mushrooming of farmers' markets all around the world could only have happened if our palates were not being gratified by honest, bite-back food. They prove monolithic supermarkets know little about food, less about customer satisfaction. They've helped millions realise how much better it is to eat dry-cured bacon only at weekends or a free-range chicken once a fortnight, than it is to eat bland falsely-plumped flesh every day. Of course we need cheaper produce. For most of us food budgets are a way of life, but we want traditional foods cheaper, not larger margins for supermarkets on factory-produced food with no relationship to the originals. Science fiction belongs in comics, not kitchens.

If we are what we eat and drink, we owe it to ourselves to improve both. That's what this book is here for, and to encourage and to congratulate the men and women who have kept the faith, who continue or who plan to produce good foods the good way.

The best diet is variety, and the best variety is the widest. Real gourmets appreciate baked beans on toast just as much as caviar and blinis, but that toast had better not turn to paste, the butter better be unadulterated, and the baked beans cooked without chemicals or added flavours. **Delicious.**

Introduction

Switching the Labels

For all the interest in organics and health foods and nutrition, real flavour is getting harder and harder to find. The dishonest culprits have sneaked into our foods with barely a mention, but can be flushed out simply, by reading labels properly. One of the achievements I most enjoyed during BBC TV Breakfast Time was introducing the 'supermarket switch' that is switching everything you pick up so you can read the label on its back. Here's where you find out how much disguised sugar is there, whether or not hydrogenated oils and trans-fatty acids lurk, and if the flavour you thought you'd bought is a sham.

These are a few of the tricks manufacturers play on food labels. They are jokes at your expense if you don't do the switch and know what you are buying.

Fat: many low-fat products have a greater energy content (calories/kilojoules) than the full-fat original, particularly yoghurts. Fat gives comforting mouth-feel to food, making it seem rich and luxurious to eat. Take away the fat and it often seems thin and miserable. To make up for the reduced fat manufacturers add their other mouth-feel fall-back – sugar, and plenty of it. No wonder so many hips remain hippapotamoid

If you want to control your weight by controlling your energy intake you must look at what the back label says about the calorie/kilojoule content, rather than at what the front label seems to promise.

All fats and oils have the same calorie/kilojoule count. So-called 'good' fats and oils have exactly the same rating as a 'bad' one. The health difference is in their make up.

Simplified, we are recommended to eat less saturated fat, generally made from animals; lard and dripping, fat in sausages or from roasts, butter, cream and milk, and cheese. This is because saturated fats tend to clog the arteries of some people; In others it has little effect and anyway

much if not most cholesterol in bloodstreams is actually manufactured by our own bodies and not directly related to diet at all. Plant-derived oils, like olive oil, have less saturated oil or none at all, and some can also actively reduce saturated fats already in the bloodstream. But this is only while they are in their natural liquid state, and not all plant oils are so useful – palm oil is highly saturated and thus not recommended, even in its liquid form.

The market is overwhelmed with 'spreads', essentially substitutes for butter made from vegetable oils. But to make oils into a solid fat, they must be hydrogenated, and this process creates something called trans-fatty acids. Trans-fatty acids have now been identified as much worse for the human body than any animal fat. Not only do they clog the arteries, like sand in clockwork, they also actively reduce the good cholesterol we have in our veins and arteries. And they are considered to be carcinogenic. It has been estimated 100,000 US citizens each year are hastened to an early death because their doctors have advised them to switch to margarines and spreads made with hydrogenated oils.

This is the food scandal that has been waiting to explode for decades. Food manufacturers have used everything in their power to prevent it being discussed or believed, because hydrogenated oils deep-fry better, keep cakes and pastries seeming fresh longer – in fact they are a major player in modern food production. But their time has come. The US Food and Drug Administration has declared war and soon food labels will have to state hydrogenated oil content. And wouldn't you know it, US companies are already playing the label game, saying on the label they have reduced hydrogenated oils and trans-fatty acids, but failing to point out they are using palm oil instead. Palm oil!

Hydrogenated oils are found in far more places than you would expect. Take an internationally recognised Table Water biscuit. You'd expect to find the ingredients include water. There's not a drop, but there is hydrogenated oil, which will make them last months and months. It must be wrong for a product to pose as something traditional, to use the traditional name, but to be made with modern chemistry, chemistry that can harm each of us.

The rest of the world must follow suit and also start to get rid of hydrogenated vegetable oils. Just as has been suspected, the substitutes for real food are worse for us, in this case killing us. Take off your blinkers. Switch everything you pick up and put it back if it contains hydrogenated oil or vegetable fat – a clever way of saying the same thing but an obvious contradiction in terms. There are now spreads available that clearly say they contain no hydrogenated oils or trans-fatty acids. Well goodie. But why eat a substitute for butter, that could hardly be more pure or more natural?

Buy butter but perhaps eat less of it, or enjoy olive or any other safe plant-based oil and leave 'spreads' where they are. It's not worth killing yourself or your family to save a little – and anyway can you honestly say any of them is as good tasting as butter? Better eat butter. Sugar: a great deal of processed or bought product contains hidden sugar. Oh yes, you may find 'sugar' on the label – but that's not necessarily all the sugar. There's not just one kind of sugar, but many.

White sugar is sucrose, but any other ingredient that ends with 'ose' is also sugar. Glucose, lactose, galactose, levulose and more. Often a manufacturer will use two or more types to hide the actual sugar content – but the information is on the label if you look.

Don't think honey is any better or different. Honey is simply a mixture of simple sugars, a nicely flavoured solution of them, and its concentration makes it very calorific. The worst sinners for presenting honey as a healthy substitute for sugar when it is essentially the same thing are 'health' bars and snacks. Look at the labels; they might self righteously contain no animal fats but have far more sugar content and energy content than many branded bars and snacks. They particularly show just how hollow many 'healthy-eating' claims really are.

But is sugar really bad for you? Of course not. Other than poisons, no food is essentially good for you or bad for you. What counts is how much of them you eat. You'd think water and carrots were both very good for you, but people have died from drinking too much water and from eating too many carrots.

My biggest gripe concerning sugar and energy content is the international switch to publishing kilojoule count rather than calorie count as an indicator of energy content. What the hell is a kilojoule? I reckon it's yet another ploy by manufacturers and nutritionists to bamboozle the public. There's never been a public information or education programme to introduce kilojoules or to publish comparative tables. Most of the world still speaks of the ideal calorie intake per day per man, woman or child, and many of us have some idea of what this should be – but not in kilojoules. But if not just how do you convert from one to another?

In the UK, responsible manufacturers include both calorie and kilojoule counts and there you'll see the relationship is about 4:1. To work out an approximate calorie equivalent, divide the kilojoule count by four: to work out an approximate kilojoule value, multiply the calories by four. So simple when you know how.

Flavours/flavors: the names of many products give you a clue that something is not quite what you might think. Any fruity beverage described as 'drink' rather than as a juice is water based.

Strawberry ice cream will contain real strawberries, but strawberry-flavoured ice cream contains none of the fruit. As obvious as this is, the majority seem never to have thought about it. Still, at least the information is there right on the front label.

There are worse flavouring iniquities that you only find buried deep on back labels.

The culprits are 'nature-identical' oils, a misnomer if ever I heard one. These factory-produced oils, thousands of them, do have an identical chemical make-up to those flavours found naturally. But none of those natural oils occur in isolation. An essential rosemary oil comes with dozens of other aromas when you cook with rosemary leaves, from the twig, from the bark, or from the leaves themselves.

Organics: I could write a million words about organic food, but this isn't the place. What is important is to know that labels guaranteeing organic production are meaningless if you want flavour and quality.

Whatever the organization guaranteeing the organic source of fresh produce – and surely it's suspicious there has to be so many different ones, now we have the official 2004 Organic Produce Regulations - they aren't doing much more than saying the food is grown without artificial fertilizers or insecticides.

What they don't guarantee is that they have chosen fine-flavoured varieties or what happens to the produce after it is harvested. Many worthy organic farms are run on a shoestring, for even though the costs are lower than modern commercial farming, the crops are usually lower, too. Tight budgets do not allow for refrigerated storage and transport and, if there is one universal rule about fresh garden or orchard produce, it is that these deteriorate nutritionally from the moment they are harvested: the only way to slow this and to keep maximum nutrition is to store the produce out of sunlight and as cool as possible.

What actually happens is the produce is driven to shops on the back of open trucks and then displayed in whole food and health stores or at markets, at ambient temperature inside or outside. In mid-summer the deterioration is rapid; you might not be eating fertilizers and sprays but you are eating damned little else either! Oh yes, and paying extra for it.

Infuriatingly to many, this means the supermarket is the most reliable place to buy organic fruit and vegetables if you feel they are important, for at least they will have cooled transport lines and will sell the more fragile produce from chilled displays Or should.

It is true that some organic produce tastes a sight better than mainstream produce. This has nothing to do with the way it is grown but what has been grown, what variety of lettuce or plum or parsnip. Some organic farmers grow old-fashioned or heritage varieties and they will taste great even if grown totally artificially, by hydroponics. They were only superceded because they did not react to modern farming techniques, not because someone produced a better flavoured variety.

Once you know the above, you have choices. One of them is to shop for maximum nutrition and flavour. In this case head for the supermarket and their organic produce or to choose frozen vegetables. Frozen vegetables cooked without added water in the microwave are by far the most nutritious way to eat them: they have been processed and frozen within hours of harvesting, and because you microwave them without water none of the goodness is leached away. Boiling and steaming both give far less nutrition, unless you steam the oriental way, on a plate and in bamboo. Otherwise steaming does give marginally better texture, but the water vapour dripping back onto the food dissolves goodness away and that falls back into the water. A bamboo steamer absorbs the water vapour so this can't happen. Belief in the nutritional superiority of vegetables steamed in colanders or in those expandable French thingies is the single most wide-spread misconception about food.

So, it's frozen vegetables for nutrition but not always flavour (because of the varieties they grow) and perhaps some residues. Or it's residue free produce that will have lost nutrition on its way to you. It's fresh but more expensive organic produce sold by supermarkets, or it's frozen organic produce, which is starting to appear and should be encouraged as much as possible. The American Cancer Society believes use of refrigeration for storage of vegetables and other food was possibly the greatest health advance of the 20th century, not just because fruit and vegetables stored at ambient temperature lose so much nutrition and flavour, but because mouldy food is always a great health risk and associated with many types of cancer. Refrigeration keeps this in check.

So, my advice is not to spend extra on organic fresh produce because you think it's good for the land and for you and because the combination gives you a warm fuzzy feeling. The warm fuzzy feeling might be a symptom of nutrition lack. Stock up on frozen veg the next time you are at the supermarket.

Never put anything ino your mouth that doesn't bite-back

Food that shimmers with flavour, that fills your mouth with gratification, is the only food you should eat. Fatty food coats your taste buds, so they can't assess how much you have eaten, so you eat and eat, both your palate and your stomach waiting for something to happen so they know when to stop. What does happen is you over eat.

The same goes for bland food, like sliced white and a butter substitute - because nothing much happens in your mouth, the stomach thinks it's not getting fed and so hunger pangs continue long after you have had enough nutrition.

The bigger food tastes, the sooner both mouth and stomach agree you have had enough: you eat less but feel more satisfied.

There's a rather nice way to prove this and you have probably done it already. Have you noticed how much you drink of cheap quaffing wines? You never do that when the wine has quality, when it has flavour that lights up your eyes as much as your mouth with sheer pleasure. I've seen four people drink six bottles of cheap wine over dinner. I've also seen eight people take an hour and a half over one exceptional bottle. Guess who actually spent less, and who had a far greater and more gratifying time?

So clever are the manufacturers they even offer variations that will do exactly what a food producer wants – there are more than 300 different strawberry flavours available, for instance. What's the problem? These substitutes are used to trick us, because neither they nor their function are fully described or fully explained on the label.

Buy a pastry or cake that tastes buttery and you'll be delighted (and lucky) – if you could look at the label you will find there's not a dot of butter in it, but there is hydrogenated oil and 'flavour'. I bought some raspberry shortbread recently, fooled by the appearance of raspberry jam: too late I realised there was only a smear, hardly enough to give the over-raspberry flavour I tasted. The label gave it away – the shortbread contained 'flavor'. Note it didn't say what flavour, so there's not the slightest nod to transparency.

This labelling loophole allows manufacturers to sell something that looks and might even taste right, but that isn't.

These introduced flavours always appear way down on the ingredient list, which are always published in descending order of quantity. This means there is very little in your food, and so you could be lulled into not caring. They are there in such small quantity because they are so highly concentrated - another clever disguise by the manufacturers.

I don't buy any food I find with flavour/flavor in the list of ingredients. This iniquitous ploy might well bring us cheaper food, but that's become such a hollow self-justification. Give us real flavours, and if you don't, tell us so on the front label.

To summarise

- Eat as many different things as you can each day -the Japanese try for at least 17 every day
- Eat little and often so you are never hungry
- Ignore anyone who tells you not to eat any food category
- Take note of what you eat today and try not to eat the same thing tomorrow, not the same amount, anyway
- Balance your food over the week, not the meal or the day – except it's good to do the day if you can
- Give yourself treats: there's no point having chocolate in the world if you don't eat it. But eat only the very best, so you eat less of it

There, now you have all you need to know about good diet and weight control.

Welcome to my world of real flavours, and real enjoyment.

Beans and pulses

Beans, peas, and lentils are lumped together under the name 'pulses' when they are dried, but that term is little used outside Britain.

These most ancient of foods, cheap and nourishing, are sadly still looked upon with suspicion in the UK, particularly by the hard-up; those in fact who would most benefit from them. Earnest perpetrators of characterless lentil rissoles have only themselves to blame for the failure of their regimen to grip our imaginations. If only they could be as original with these foods as they are with their clothes.

The other oft-heard complaint against beans is wind. This is a very real and at times painful problem for many people, but sound knowledge will sort it out in most cases. First concentrate on the thin-skinned varieties of pulses, which cook faster, as they cause fewer side effects. Then, although lentils cook well and fast without the added bother of soaking, you do reduce wind-causing content by always soaking, rinsing and parboiling before cooking in yet more fresh water.

The wind problems will not always be lesser, but if you introduce these products to your diet slowly, as side dishes rather than main courses, you will find the bowel will adjust and in a month or so without it going – or blowing – against the grain.

In just a few weeks you will be able to enjoy a red kidney bean stew or a chickpea salad with barely a grumble. Thus with a little care and patience when you begin it is possible to eat spectacularly well as a vegetarian, almost thoughtlessly obtaining the high fibre, low fat, low sugar ideals of modern nutritional theory. Milk, cheese or eggs each day, or some soy product, or a proper mixture of grains and pulses and you are safe and very well indeed.

Beans, peas and pulses are excellent sources of protein and carbohydrate but are not as balanced as animal protein, including eggs, milk and cheese. This does not matter if your diet includes such animal protein but ovo-lactarian vegetarians, who eschew everything from an animal source, should take care to balance the imbalance by also eating grains, done without thought if you pour a lentil dhal onto rice, eat baked beans on toast or scoop up hummus with pitta bread.

None of these ingredients has a fat content but it's difficult to find enjoyable recipes that do not add it in some form. They also have plenty of dietary fibre, and this is most important to those of us getting old, when a general trend towards eating soft food means it might take several days to pass through the alimentary canal, something that exacerbates any illness and contributes to general ill-health, too. Even small amounts of beans, peas, pulses or grains in the diet can make a major difference to the health of the elderly and is a good habit to start young, too.

You could cook these ingredients a different way every day, but I generally end up cooking them the same way – with tomato, lots of garlic, fresh herbs in a bundle and plenty of fat: bacon, olive oil, duck or goose fat. Butter is good but not as good as the less sweet fats and oils.

Often much of the fat, pork and garlic will come largely from chunks of something like Polish boiling sausage q.v. But be brave with peas, beans and lentils. With chickpeas, use cumin and coriander and tomato paste and olive oil when they are warm – just enough tomato paste to bind them together – and serve sprinkled with chopped chives as a salad. But not for me, as I never serve or eat chives because of their dominating onion flavour: I'd sprinkle the chickpeas with toasted cumin seeds. Serve cold tuna fish with cannellini in vinaigrette as a starter. Mix leftover butter beans with chilled orange slices, black olives and segmented tomato. See how easy it is?

To make a succulent sauce for any hot beans, take up to a quarter of cooked ones from the saucepan, add water, stock or tomato purée to them and cook to a mush or purée them. Return to the drained beans and cook on. A real chili should have a sauce of softened purée-like beans like this. Beans in their own sauce are excellent hot or cold, and reheat well, too – witness the famous *refritos* of Mexican and Tex-Mex cooking.

Whenever a bean recipe fails to excite you, and you have added enough salt and extra fat and more garlic, then add red wine vinegar teaspoon by teaspoon. Or sherry or Chinese or balsamic vinegars, of course. The difference will be wondrous, and fast.

Neither should you overlook the flavouring possibilities of oil. Olive oil is almost *de rigueur* unless you have very fatty bacon or a tin of goose fat. But beans cooked simply with tomatoes and then finished with a splash of walnut oil make a superb accompaniment to poultry and, after sitting in a refrigerator overnight, the most memorable cold salad. Better with garlic, it goes without saying.

Lamb, especially the cheaper fattier cuts, goes well with beans. I like to cook neck of lamb in tomato with garlic sausage and some fresh thyme, then to add in cooked haricot or butter beans and cook on for enough time to allow some of the beans to melt into the sauce and absorb the fat. Just put the pot on the table and let your family and friends help themselves.

For all I have said about the boring way these foods are generally seen, nothing can quite equal the feverish grip with which lentils hold our great chefs in thrall. From something to sneer at, lentils have become an essential accompaniment. Their affinity with fish is the most surprising discovery, but pigeon and every type of bird now seem naked without them and even aristocratic beef is served with lentils perfumed with herbs and glistening with pork fat.

Cooked beans in cans are a godsend standby. Heated and drained and dressed with oil and garlic as a salad base, puréed, or drained and reheated with a herb-rich garlic-laden tomato sauce, they make a fast vegetable stew appear to have taken you days to make. Of course, they instantly bulk out a soup, casserole or ready-made salad, too, if someone should come knocking upon your door whom you do not wish to send away. I think beans and lentils are good hot or cold but never at room temperature.

Storing

Although good keepers, all peas, beans and lentils will toughen with age and many reach a stage where even the most determined soaking and cooking will never soften them. It is better to buy them in smallish quantities from shops you expect sell enough to have a regular turnover of stock. Do check, if they are in bulk, for excess dirt or insect contamination, but expect some. Don't bother with stock that is broken. Store cool and dark.

Adzuki/aduki beans: small, ochrous-red and sort of pillow-shaped, these are an Oriental bean and have long been regarded as the best of them all in Japan, China and Thailand.
The bean is the seed of a bushy plant that grows up to about 75cm/30 inches high.
Juice made from the beans is still prescribed by Oriental herbalists to help kidney problems.
Cook at least 30 minutes, perhaps longer.

Unknown to the West until George Ohshawa introduced the macrobiotic diet in the 20th century, they are now much favoured here because they are the most 'yang' of beans, and because they have an appealing, strong, nut-like flavour.

Adzuki are one of the most important ingredients in Oriental sweet cookery. I've always preferred these beans whole, eaten as sweets covered with sugar but they appear far more commonly as a red-bean paste and used as a starchy filling to spoil nice dumplings and steamed buns or to stuff those relentlessly dull and leaden Chinese desserts. But they are also served savoury: the most famed version is Serkhan or Festival Rice from Japan. Rice is tinted with the pink cooking water of adzuki beans, then the two are mixed together.
Begin with a proportion of about one part adzuki to eight of rice. This mixture is similar, of course, to the rice and beans of Jamaican cooking.

In macrobiotic cookbooks you will find suggestions for soups and desserts; I like the sound of one that cooks together adzuki and dried chestnuts, makes a purée of the mixture flavoured with cinnamon, and bakes that in a pie crust that is served with cream and almonds.

Black-eye beans/peas: these beans are actually peas, a variety of cow pea, and this is why they are also called black-eye peas in the United States. To add to the confusion, they are the seeds you find in the yard-long bean. I find I like the rather savoury flavour and interesting appearance of these more than most haricots. They cook comparatively faster too and I believe many people find them lighter on the stomach. Essential to Creole cooking and the related soul food. Soaked beans take 30-45 minutes to cook.

Broad beans: one of the few beans native to the Old World, dried broad beans have kept their honoured place in many Mediterranean and Middle Eastern countries, but are rather over-run by new-comers in the rest of the world. They are different, bigger and with a tendency to flouriness, but that is also their appeal, together with a bit of a chew sometimes, particularly if you leave the tough skins on each individual bean. You either have to skin them after cooking, or buy the more expensive ready-skinned variety.

Easily recognized by being flatter and broader than New World beans, they are the fava bean, the horse bean, the ful and countless other names, and when dried are most often a brownish colour. These should have a good long soak and will then need about 1½ hours cooking – less, of course, if you are using those without skins.

Ful medames, a stew of dried broad beans, has been fundamental to Egypt for countless centuries. Its rough, hearty flavour comes with the welcome vigour of garlic, oil and onion and is usually served topped with hamine eggs, whole eggs simmered in a spicy liquid for many hours so the spices penetrate and colour the egg white, which softens in an especially appealing way.

In some countries of the South Pacific, where frozen vegetables might come from China, I have found packets of gorgeous, small broad beans already shucked of their outer skins. Perfect for adding to salads, for dressing with oil and vinegar or for serving hot any way you can imagine. Triumph.

Butter beans/lima beans: many books divide butter beans from lima beans but I'm sure they are the same thing. If they aren't, it doesn't matter for they are both large, white, flat and aristocratic of flavour. They should not be cooked until pulpy, but must be very well pre-soaked and cooked otherwise they have some rather unpleasant constituents. Smaller ones will take 45-60 minutes to cook; bigger ones will take 15-25 minutes longer.

Baby lima beans are pale green and usually sold fresh or frozen. Fresh baby limas are quite the best for mixing with sweet corn to make succotash, even though I have seen recipes that require cooked, dried ones. In the US you will also find the Chestnut Lima, which has a genuinely nutty flavour and mashes to give the texture of mashed potatoes.

Chickpeas/garbanzos: with their spicy, peppery flavour, appealing golden colour and hazelnut shape, these are amongst the most attractive of all dried pulses from any point of view.

They are the main ingredient in hummus, that standby dip of Middle Eastern, Greek and Cypriot restaurants, but one also found in Spanish and Latin American cooking, and make excellent additions to soups as well as fascinating salads. They mix well with other vegetables, too, and I always like to have some on hand in cans.

Cooking times can vary enormously. Older types may take up to three hours or more but newer varieties, the ones most likely to be bought today, should be cooked in something over an hour. They rarely go out of shape and are much nicer, I think, when rather floury, for then they absorb somewhat more easily the oils, spices and flavours with which they can be mingled.

But a warning if you plan to travel in the Eastern Mediterranean. Hummus has officially been recognised as a major cause of serious stomach upsets – a few years ago it was specially rife in Jerusalem and laid out its victims for almost a week. Best avoided in restaurants unless you know when it was made and that it has been refrigerated since that time.

Kidney beans: this is the biggest group of beans and one that causes much confusion. Simply, all beans that are kidney shaped without being flat are kidney beans. There is a variety of colour and flavour – but they are all kidney beans. The average time for cooking these beans is one hour, but haricots can be stubborn and need longer so be prepared to exercise patience.

Don't be confused if you don't find a bean you know here, throughout the United States there are local names as well as local varieties. When beans first crossed the Atlantic they were given new Spanish or Greek or Italian or anything names, and then when they adapted to their new homes they changed both their characteristics and their names again. Only if you are in pursuit of insanity should you consider tracing each bean to its original name. They won't taste any better when or if you do. Haricots Tarbais IGP are French and found fresh or dried.

Black beans: very popular in the Caribbean and in the southern United States, these shiny, very black beans are the most like better-known red kidney beans. They cook to a firm satisfying texture and have a meaty, full flavour. Used by themselves or with other beans they make an attractive change to the look of your cooking.

Borlotti beans: also known as rose cocoa beans, these are streaked with rose or crimson, and all the better for being pale of colour. These are particularly popular in Italy and excellent tinned examples are available. They seem usually to require little soaking when dried, and they have a rather sweet, soft texture.

Cannellini beans: a small white kidney bean that is absolutely interchangeable with haricots. In Italy cannellini might mean other white beans, too. These are almost always the right bean to use with rugged Italian sausages and with lots of garlic and tomato of some sort and they make excellent cold salads dressed with good olive oil. Sorana beans, *fagioli di Sorana* IGP, are milky white and almost flat or cylindrical and red: both colours have a full, elegant flavour and very tender skins.

Flageolet beans: these are very young haricots removed from the pod before they are ripe. Thus they are a delicate green, sweet and tender. They are far the most expensive of beans and a very special accompaniment to fatty birds, to young lamb or to hot ham.

Great Northern beans: a small white haricot bean that's thought to be the most popular in the US. It could be the navy bean with a different hat.

Haricot beans: these creamy kidney beans are perhaps the best known of all, for they are the beans for baked beans. Extraordinarily adaptable, they are the basis for the varying versions of cas¬soulets in France, cooked with bacon or goose fat. Some say they are called haricot because the French included them in their stews called haricots, but the late food writer Tom Stobart says `haricot' is really a corruption of the Aztec word *ayecotl*, which I am romantically inclined to believe.

In America they are known as navy beans; and just to add to the confusion they are often shaped more like a cushion than a kidney.

Pinto beans: a shorter, fatter, squarer version of the borlotti, speckled and savoury of flavour. Rattlesnake beans are the same bean and so named because their pods grow into snake-shapes. Traditional in the US Southwest and in Mexico, they are the best choice for re-fried beans, *refritos*

Red kidney beans: because delicatessen counters discovered they were nice to eat cold as a salad, and because chili con carne has proliferated, these are as well known as white haricots now. Their rich colour and texture and full flavour make them worth the popularity, but they can kill. Red kidney beans must be very well soaked and very well cooked until really soft; during cooking they should actually boil for 15 minutes or can indeed be fatal.

Their uses abound throughout Central and South America and the Caribbean; they are the basic chili bean and, like their black brothers, add considerable flavour when mixed with white ones.

Lentils: one of the first-ever crops, lentils are richer in protein than other pulses, except for soy. They have a very high calorie content too, so even though lacking some essential amino acids they make an important food staple, especially in Third World countries. There are two basic types but both have many names:

Green or brown lentils: also called continental lentils. It is generally these lentils that are used in European cookbooks, old or new. They keep their shape when cooked and have a stronger, earthier taste than the red ones, which blend very well with smoked meats, fatty pork, herbs and onions, but quickly cook into a mush. Green and brown lentils take about 30-45 minutes to cook.

You would have to be a particularly zealous hermit not to know that from their long-standing association with weirdos, lentils have moved up to spearhead trendy cooking. These will generally be green ones, and inevitably *lentilles de Puy*, a greeney-blue variety from central France that have an especially delicious smokey-sweet tang, plus the snob appeal of DOP/AOC status. Almost the same status are *lentilles vertes du Berry IGP*. Italy offers *Lenticchia di Castelluccio di Norcia IGP*, notably small and with a very fine skin and rich colours in the yellow-brown spectrum. They are grown around Perugia and Macerata, and those lucky enough to have eaten enough of both reckon Norcias are tastier than Puy lentils.

Well-cooked lentils provide a surprising way to make all kinds of fish more gratifying for big eaters, indeed they were always part of the Indian rice dish *kitcheree*, which ended up as kedgeree without lentils. Lentils make far more sense of game than those infuriating potato crisps, and when really soft and lightly puréed make a sensationally good sauce for vegetarian lasagne. But, and it is a big but, they must be well-cooked and not served crisp and individual, no matter how aesthetic this seems. For me, the point of lentils is rich, comforting smoothness, with at least some of them mushed and emulsified with rather more fat or oil than you care to know about; a pile of individual lentils is as pointless as eating dry toast, and sometimes quite as parching unless they have been cooked until each has a moist creaminess.

Perhaps the single most comforting dish I know, Greek in style, is soaked green lentils then cooked in stock with plenty of vegetables, plenty of olive oil and a good handful of fresh mint stalks – mint is very fugitive and so you need masses to get any value. Cooked gently for hours until some of the lentils have mushed and perhaps with separately cooked sweet vegetables added – carrots particularly – it perfectly bridges the gap between a soup and a stew. It's the mint and olive oil that make the difference, so don't stint. Ham, bacon, garlic sausage etc can also be added.

Depending on the texture you prefer and how fresh they are, lentils take from 25 minutes to over an hour. They don't really need soaking and salt or salty bacon should not be added until they are quite well cooked.

Red lentils: also known as Egyptian or Indian lentils. These look reddish but are the ones that cook into a yellow-gold mush, and are the basic dhal of India. They are vital to all sorts of winter soups and go extra well with contrasted sharper vegetables like garlic, onion and green peppers. They take 15-30 minutes to cook.

Mesquite beans: flour is made from the bean pods of this desert tree, the one with the aromatic wood used for aromatic smoking. Harvested by the endangered Seri Indians in late summer and autumn, the beans are dried and ground into naturally sweet flour, increasingly used as an addition to soups, muffins, breads, tortillas, cakes and biscuits. The actual seeds are very high in protein and the flour seems to help stabilise blood sugar in people with diabetes.

Mung beans: entrancing dark, frosted-olive green mung beans are one of the basics for making into bean sprouts but can be cooked as any ordinary pulse. Like the red adzuki, they are quite soft and sweet when cooked. Cook between 25 and 40 minutes.

Peas: provided you can suspend both belief and memories of what other people may have done to them, dried peas can be an excellent, honest and sustaining food. They are available whole or skinned and split, green or yellow; the green seem harder to find but I prefer them. Peas rarely hold their shape, which is why they are put into soups or made into soups. It is always a surprise to taste how sweet they are, a good reason why they have always seemed a natural accompaniment to salted meats.

Cook for about 45 minutes. If you want to keep some semblance of shape, use a minimal amount of water and watch carefully.

Soy beans: God's worst joke. That's the verdict on soy beans by the late Tom Stobart, surely one of the greatest but least rated food writers. In *The Cook's Encyclopedia*, he acutely points out that on the one hand soy beans are the richest and most sustaining vegetable food on earth; on the other they are terminally boring to the point of being inedible. The only exception I ever found were small green ones available for just a few weeks in early July around and about Nanjing, and thus unlikely to change the world's perceptions.

But what I want to know is, who bothered to work out that if you made milk from soy beans you could make almost anything else? Which Chinese person worked out it was so good for you it should be called the 'meat plant'? We'll never know that and are still finding extraordinary facts, most importantly that soy beans are the only vegetable product that exactly replicates the complete spectrum of the proteins (amino acids) of meat. In fact, soy is a far better provider even than meat. Stobart says an acre that grew soy beans would keep a man alive for 2,200 days, but the same acre of grass would sustain him only 75 days if he ate the beef it produced.

The United States is now the world's greatest grower of soy beans and virtually all of it is genetically engineered, something constantly to remember if this is important to you. So also is most of the world's soy crop, and non-GE soy beans are thus particularly hard to source. Most of the US crop is for margarines, after hydrogenation of course, but the East is still the greatest consumer of soy products, as bean curd or tofu and myriad other products including soy sauce. In the West, we are also beginning to take soy milk seriously, use soy flour to add protein to breads and baked goods, make non-dairy ice cream-style products and, less successfully, spin its protein into threads which we stick together and pretend is meat, but less than we used to do, thank goodness.

There are thought to be a thousand varieties of soy beans, in most colours of the rainbow and sized from petits pois to cherry size. Their oily blandness make most of them pretty awful to eat, for they neither absorb other flavours nor contribute anything of their own, no matter what their culinary companions. But once they are cooked (probably after chopping) and then pressed and drained, the result is soy milk and that opens a new world. But before you start on it, beware.

The soy bean harbours the most gas-inducing ingredients of all. Introduce soy bean curd slowly into your diet, over several months, or your good intentions will be just so much hot air.

Soy milk can be made instantly at home from dried pre-cooked soy powder or other products of the beans. The end result will look like milk and should have rather less soy taste than the beans. But not always. Some soy-based products are frankly inedible, too distinctly bean-tasting, others are good enough for second helpings. In some cases the cause of the horrors is bad production technique, but it is much more likely to be the use of inferior bean varieties, which leave a lingering, raw, green bean taste. At least that is how the problem was explained to me in Japan, where I tasted wonderfully creamy tofu, and in Sweden, where an ice cream-type product comes without the slightest clue to its soy bean origin.

Bean curd: probably best known as Japanese tofu, but this is actually an invention of the Chinese, as most things seem to be. They call it *dau fu*. Like dairy milk, soy milk can be curdled with lemon juice or vinegar, giving a slight welcome acidity and flavour. Commercially the curd may be obtained with a whole range of substances. Calcium sulphate, gypsum, usefully increases the calcium content but can give a slightly chalky consistency – hardly surprising as the substance is related to plaster of Paris. Calcium chloride may also be used and this is often accompanied by emulsifiers which bind in the liquid whey that would normally separate out, thus giving a higher yield and softer, wetter curd; the addition of simple sugars (not sucrose) add sweetness and a smoother mouth feel. The Japanese also use an extract of sea water to obtain soy curd, and there are other ingredients which will do the curdling.

As with dairy cheese making, the exact texture and firmness of the curd will be affected both by the amount of curdling agent and by how much pressing and draining there is of the curd. Generally the softer curd is used for steamed dishes or for adding at the last moment to wet dishes. The firmer curd is chosen for frying, often done to give extra strength to pieces of curd before they are added to a braising or boiling stock.

Although made from a liquid which has been boiled, bean curd must be treated as though it were a fresh milk product and kept submerged under water and refrigerated for safety, where it will be fresh and safe for a few days up to a week if the water is changed daily. It should be virtually odourless and tasteless, but has the invaluable chameleon virtue of absorbing other flavours, making it a great extender of other foods. Soy curd/tofu is a complete replacement for animal protein, but is commonly used as a complementary extender of meat, particularly in south-east Asian and Oriental cookery.

Apart from its invaluable protein content, bean curd is high in B vitamins and iron, but the latter is in a form difficult for the body to absorb. Vegetarians are recommended always to eat or drink something containing vitamin C with bean curd, as this helps unlock the iron.

The growing interest in south-east Asian and Oriental produce and flavours has brought tofu firmly out of the cold and into the chilled cabinets of many supermarkets.

It is important to introduce bean curd gradually into your diet and best to mix it with other foods rather than eating it in large quantities or on an empty stomach. When you are used to it, treat it as a bland white cheese, and serve it with bright condiments, or add it to highly flavoured foods, giving it time to absorb its surroundings. It may be fried, deep-fried, roasted, toasted, marinated, microwaved, crumbed, stir-fried, chopped, cubed, sliced, whisked into 'cheesecakes', whipped into creamy desserts, frozen into ices. Frozen tofu/bean curd products run the gamut from beany to amazing.

There are, famously, food writers who claim they would put anything but tofu into their mouths. But as the choice of products and standards grow it is increasingly difficult to avoid doing so. Bean curd is no longer an alternative, but a pleasure to pursue for itself.

Bean curd sheets: also called bean curd skin, because this is how they begin and how they can feel in the mouth – like skin. They are made from soy milk rather the way clotted cream is manufactured; the milk is heated until a skin is formed, which is taken away and dried flat. They must be soaked to soften before being used as a wrapper for other foods, and are then deep-fried or fried and poached in a rich stock of some sort, which is when they soften up to the texture of skin. Funny thing for vegetarians to want in their mouths, but there you are.

Milk: soy milk is a godsend for thousands, for it is cholesterol free and lactose free. But it can have a vegetal flavour that is either disconcerting or downright horrid, to say nothing of the internal problems caused by those indigestible leguminous sugars, problems that are not a million miles away from those of lactose malabsorption, which many are trying to avoid.

A comparative taste test of soy milks in *Good Food Retailing* magazine was not flattering on the whole: many manufacturers over-sweeten their product to counteract the intrusive soy flavour and, unsurprisingly, the soy milks liked best had no soy aftertaste. Still, at least soy milk is taken seriously enough to be listed by supermarkets and manufacturers are trying hard to get it right, offering a choice of organic, sweetened and unsweetened. It's a product worth watching, but in the meantime, you are more likely to enjoy using it in hot drinks only if you also sweeten them.

How anyone believes the difference in fat content – or anything else - between cows' milk and soy milk justifies ordering soy milk in espresso coffee is stratospheres away from my understanding. If you don't like cows' milk, drink black coffee, the way it is supposed to be.

Miso: a Japanese product that looks like thick, dark, grainy honey but is a paste of soy beans fermented with malted grains. The precise grain added determines the colour and flavour of the result, and some versions are traditionally more salted than most. The most important basic use is for miso soup, miso diluted with dashi or plain water, a highly nutritious and delicious soup with a malty, salty flavour, which is basic to the Japanese diet. In my experience, it is much more digestible and causes far fewer intestinal problems than other soy bean products such as bean curd: indeed a bowl of miso soup seems to settle everything down.

The basic flavour of miso is warm and sweet, with overtones of honeyed fermentation and when diluted there is a nuttiness rather than beaniness. Once you discover miso there are thousands of ways to use it to flavour food before, during and after cooking, as well as to enjoy it for itself. Excellent for making marinades. Chinese (brown/yellow) bean paste is related but not as comfortingly flavoured. Miso should be refrigerated when opened.

Aka: a red, rice-based miso, generally highly salted and will last without refrigeration; any mould may be removed and ignored.

Hatcho: made only of soy beans and aged in wood for at least three years. It is rich, dark and complicated in flavour and although it may be mellowed with *shinsu-miso*, q.v. may be used by itself as a tonic drink or in a soup.

Mugi: made with barley to give a peasant and gratifying flavour, but is said to be more popular in the West than in Japan these days, where it is expensive.

Shinsu: yellowish, young, all purpose and cheapest.

Shiro: made with rice, white and rather sweet.

Soy protein: the protein content of soy beans spun into strands, which are like meat fibres and may be shaped this or that way to imitate meats. Like bean curd, TVP is characterless but absorbs any flavours with which it is cooked and thus conveniently extends meat dishes, especially chopped or minced ones, to reduce costs or increase profits. That seems reasonable if labelling rules are strictly observed.

Soy protein mixed with meat in sausages is an important advancement in nutrition for low-income families with children. Vital, accessible protein gets into their bodies without excesses of fat and low-quality meat usually associated with cheap sausages. In fact, if soy protein were used as an extender even in high-quality sausages, we would all win, eating less animal fat, and supporting an agricultural industry that makes far better use of land than meat production.

What makes me uncomfortable is the use of TVP as a meat substitute for vegetarians. You find it flavoured with all manner of manufactured ingredients, as bacon or chicken fillets and commonly in some 'healthy' frozen foods for instance. If you are a vegetarian it follows you are

looking for better nutrition, more honest nutrition. So why would you eat soy masquerading as meat, and only be able to do that because of perfectly unnatural additives? There are hundreds of millions of the world's inhabitants who would share their proper, honest soy-based vegetarian recipes. Why reinvent the wheel if you have to add ingredients from factories?

I encourage both vegetarians and meat eaters to enjoy more soy products of all kinds. Growing soy for human consumption is an excellent and more productive use of natural resources, offers countless fascinating ways to vary the diet, helps balance our budgets – and you do get over the wind problems. But vegetarians eating fake meat? That seems very second rate.

Tempeh: essentially, yet another form of fermented soy bean. Generally made with cubed bean curd injected with a specific yeast that creates a white mould and turns the curd into a creamy texture, like ripening cheese. May also be made with cooked and lightly crushed whole soy beans. Like cheese, it should be avoided if ammoniacal.

Tepary beans: in the legends of the Tohono O'odham peoples of the US South, the Milky Way is made of white tepary beans scattered across the sky by their coyote deity Ban. These small beans, native to the Arizona desert and thereabouts, are one of the most drought and heat resistant crops in the world and varieties are being introduced into Africa to help ease food shortage problems there.

As well as their capability to flourish in blistering desert conditions, the tepary is particularly high in protein, more so size for size than most bigger beans, and so is also valued as a practical food to carry – less is indeed more. The two most valued varieties, marketed throughout the US, are the rich earthy brown bean and the sweeter, lighter white. Both are prepared like other beans and can be used as the basis for stews and casseroles, for bean salads, for soup or in soups, puréed as dips, in fact, can be used wherever any sort of bean would appear.

There are many other colours and flavours of tepary bean, and my bet is this most ancient food is poised to become one of the saviours of the 21st century.

General cooking advice

There is continuing discussion about whether beans, peas and pulses need to be soaked, and certainly if the soaking is not done properly fermentation can begin, which gives an unplea¬sant flavour. My experience is that soaking in cold water can sweeten and enhance the flavour by starting the germination process, the malting process and it certainly cuts down on cooking time, a saving of expensive energy. Generally speaking, overnight, or from morning to afternoon, is enough soaking time – allow plenty of room for expansion, especially for chickpeas, and keep everything fairly cool.

If you have forgotten the cold water soak, it is possible to plump them relatively fast by bringing them up to the boil in water, simmering for five minutes then turning off the heat and leaving until cold – for at least two hours.

It's vital soaking water should not be used for cooking if you are a-feared of digestive wind problems. Drain off the soaking water, rinse under running water and then use fresh cold water for cooking. If you have persistently bad digestive problems you can add a blanching stage, bringing the soaked produce to the boil in fresh water, simmering for five minutes, draining and then rinsing before cooking in more fresh water.

Salt should never be added to the cooking water until everything is thoroughly cooked or they will be tough; this includes not adding bacon. Acid in the water also toughens, making tomatoes or onions in any form a bad choice too. The age-favoured technique is to cook your beans, peas or pulses in plain water. And only then to drain and add them to a rich stock or vegetable-based liquid that has been prepared separately. This is when herbs, onion, tomato, bacon, ham, pancetta or prosciutto shank might be added too, and beans, for instance, would then be baked on for some hours, so some disintegrate to help form a sauce. It is acceptable technique with whatever you are cooking to mash up to a quarter to thicken the sauce.

Pressure cooking gets beans really tender or cooked in a short time. My advice, gleaned from Rose Elliott's *The Bean Book*, is that you should use 6kg/15lb pressure, cook for a third of the usual time and always include a few spoonfuls of oil as this prevents foaming up, which might clog the valve.

Sprouting grains and seeds

Sprouted seeds and grains are invaluable nutritionally, but are no more packed with goodness than the fully matured seed or grain crop. Their real plus is as a reliable crunch when you want texture contrast.

Today mung beans are the most commonly used and you'll also find sprouted alfalfa and adzuki beans. Alfalfa is the finer smaller one, and mung are the ones coarsely used to excess by mean vegetarian restaurants and by Chinese takeaways. Both should be eaten before there is a tinge of green apparent, for at this stage they develop bitterness and lose vitamin vitality.

They are best eaten raw or barely cooked. So add them to soups or stews just before serving. You can add them to nut loaves, omelettes, scrambled eggs, stuffings or vegetable purées – and to salads of course. It's worth trying them tossed in lots of butter with garlic and lemon juice as a vegetable.

It's so easy to sprout your own grains I thought I'd tell you how. As well as the mung, alfalfa and adzuki, you might also experiment with chickpeas, whole lentils, peas, soy beans, beans, whole rices, wheat, fenugreek, barley and sesame seeds. Chickpeas and fenugreek usually give home growers the fastest results.

This is what you do:
- Put 50g/2oz of seeds or grains into a jam jar.
- Cover the seeds with luke-warm water.
- Tie a piece of muslin or very coarse cotton over the mouth of the jar.
- Let the seeds absorb the water overnight, adding more water if required as some seeds will more than double their size. Chickpeas swell so fast they get jammed, so free them gently.
- After eight hours, drain off the excess water and leave the jar to stand.
- Twice a day rinse the seeds with cold water. Then invert the jar and gently shake it to prevent sprouting roots tangling. Leave for a few minutes to allow water to drain thoroughly, then invert again. When the shoots are three times the length of the seeds but before tiny leaves appear, the sprouts are at their peak.
- If you don't want to eat them immediately, put the rinsed sprouts into the refrigerator, which inhibits but doesn't stop further growth.

Bread and baked goods

Bread need only be made from flour, water and salt. Bread
made without a raising agent – unleavened bread – is one of
our oldest foods; even bread raised to lightness by the action
of yeast was possibly discovered in Ancient Egypt.

It is a simple, honest, satisfying food, yet bread represents such an emotive part of our heritage that it is always at the mercy of social fashion. It is a reflection on living standards in much of the western hemisphere that we should have to go to a speciality store or farmers' market to buy bread that is honest, well made and unadulterated. In other parts of the world, sense has long prevailed and bread making is just as it was ten, one hundred or two thousand years ago.

In the villages, towns and cities of India, Pakistan and Bangladesh, for instance, the unleavened *chapatti* and its relatives are still regularly hand-shaped and baked over open fires. The slapping sound of the dough being shaped between the palms of squatting women is an integral part of daily life. Some families may buy the coarse wholemeal chapatti flour but most will grind their own as they need it. Similar breads, sometimes made with flours other than wheat but also baked on griddles, are made further north. In Afghanistan the dough is rolled out to be a metre or more in diameter. Armenians make smaller, even thinner chapatti-type breads and Sardinians still make 'paper bread' in their mountain villages. Further west these thin flat breads have been discovered by sandwich shops, and are now rolled around fillings, cut into smaller sizes and sold as 'wraps'.

In the lands of Islam, yeast has long played a part in bread and pastry making. The most common types of bread there are flattish discs, often spiced, and the oval envelopes known widely in Europe as pitta. These are also common in Greece, Cyprus and have become the national bread of Israel. Eaten fresh and warm – whether Israeli, Greek or Arabic – it is perfectly delicious.

Countries of the eastern and southern Mediterranean still offer the interested tourist a chance to see a sight once familiar throughout Europe. In the tight alleyways and up the steep-stepped lanes of bazaars and medinas you will see single loaves of leavened dough being carried to a central baker. Each family identifies its loaves with its own mark, a custom that prevailed in some areas of England right up to the turn of the 20th century.

Countries with a traditional high regard for their food forbid their flour to be tampered with, by omission or commission. This is certainly true of France and largely why the French enjoy such good breads; there is also a relative absence of large baking combines in France so the independent village baker reigns supreme, and just as well for French bread stales within hours of baking.

Elsewhere the story is rather different. 'Scientific' advances during the last century have changed bread making in some parts of the world more than during the previous 3,000 to 4,000 years. Reliable yeasts, better and cheaper wheat flour and ovens with controllable temperatures all coincided and caused a revolution from which upheaval recovery is still some way off. At first the new-fangled bakeries simply made old-fangled bread faster and cheaper. And then food scientists stuck their deadening hand into the dough and changed expectations from bread forever.

The chemically assisted, fast-rising, sliced white loaf is marketed mainly in the United States, the United Kingdom, the Netherlands and parts of the British Commonwealth and stimulates a continuing controversy. The essential complaint is that the dough for this product is mixed, risen and baked within the hour. The gradual stretching of gluten and maturing of the dough's flavour doesn't happen; the first is achieved by extremely fast, brutally rough beating, the second is forgotten or approximated with additives. The end product, to the scientist who created it, smells right, slices like a dream, does not crumble when spread with butter and keeps well. And that, claim the manufacturers, is all bread is expected to do. The flavour seems not to matter and if it does then it must, by definition, be an accept¬able flavour because everybody buys it. The saddest talent mankind has developed is an ability to like anything if that's all there is.

Then there's the texture, so slight it scrunches to paste with the slightest application of pressure, even when toasted. Western civilization seems not to be civilisation at all when it's difficult to buy bread suited to toasting, difficult to buy bread you can cut yourself, almost impossible easily to buy bread that retains a chew and texture strong enough to absorb butter and jam, rather than collapsing under their weight. There are hundreds of millions of people, over several generations, who have never once held an unsliced loaf of bread, perhaps the worst-ever dumbing down of modern life

Those many millions who think bread only comes sliced have also never eaten decent toast, which Victorian cookery books took seriously enough to give instructions for making – the secret is to ensure the slices are warmed through before they crisp and brown, which you did by first holding the toasting fork away from the fire and then moving it closer. To be scrupulously fair, the modern style of bread is probably quite good for you, even though the long-term effects of some of the additives are unknown.

No evidence exists to support the common assumption that wholemeal bread is good for you while white bread is damaging to your health. Wholemeal bread does contain bran, however, and should offer both vitamin E and a higher proportion of minerals and trace elements than white. In practice, according to some dieticians, wholemeal bread could actually be detrimental to health. It seems we are likely to spread it more thickly with butter, jam and other good-tasting comestibles than we might white bread; arguments exist to show that such excesses are far worse for us than the suspected chemical shortcomings of white bread.

Research in the United States shows that as long as the rest of the diet has a minimal proportion of high quality protein, a white bread diet successfully supports life and encourages excellent growth in 5-15 year olds. But what about good old-fashioned enjoyment of the real thing, white bread that tastes richly of baked flour, that springs back when you bite it and has a crackling crust? And what about the Atkins Diet, that has once more tarred all bread with the feathers of cowardice, so millions actually brag about eating bread no more?

When asked if he also went to bed with men, James Dean is supposed to have said he didn't see why he should go through life with one arm tied behind his back. That's what I think about the Atkins Diet. Variety is the greatest, safest, healthiest most natural diet there is: living without decent bread is hardly life at all.

Yeast leavening

To leaven means to aerate dough or batter. Gas, created as a by-product of a biological or chemical action, is trapped in the elastic gluten of flour in bread dough or as simple bubbles in batter. In the heat of the oven, the gas expands even more; continued heat kills the gas-forming action and hardens the balloons formed by the gas, allowing the baked end product to retain its risen shape.

Without yeasts we would not have beer, wine or bread. Yeasts are an enor¬mous family of minute, single-celled fungi. Each is only about $1/20$th of a millimetre diameter, and there are millions of them in the air, almost everywhere. Some are useful, some not. The most important are those with a special aptitude to convert, by the action of their enzymes, sugar into alcohol and carbon dioxide.

The yeasts on the skins of fruits and vegetables are directly responsible for the fermentation of wines. Yeast for beer making was grown in a sweet liquid mixed with flour and potatoes, hops or both, although in Belgium *kreuze* and *kriek* beers are still made spontaneously, with what ever yeasts are in the air.

A clever brewer's wife would try to use mainly hops with plenty of pollen upon them; she may not have known it, but these supported the strongest colonies of the yeasts she wanted.

The barm, which she also sold to bakers and housewives to leaven their bread, was made and used only within the broadest of guidelines. There was no way of knowing what combination of yeasts had been cultivated or how they would perform in dough. It was this ever-changing broth of many types of yeast that necessitated 'proving' some of the dough in former times – you had to wait for the yeast to prove itself in a small amount of the dough, the sponge, before you used it in the full batch. Then, in 1850, came German or compressed yeast, made of one yeast only – *saccharomy cescerevisiae*. At last bakers had their own yeast. It worked quickly and consistently on the maltose (sugar) in flour and permanently changed the face of yeast cookery, commercial and domestic.

The new yeast went on the market under three different names: German, compressed or dried. This has confused many people who have tried baking from old recipes: the chances are that 'dried' yeast in a 19th century book actually means 'compressed' fresh yeast.

Modern compressed yeast is usually called fresh yeast. It performs consistently if it is in good condition and can be kept in the refrigerator for weeks or deep-frozen for months.

Modern dried yeast, the sort that comes in granules, is much more expensive than compressed yeast but very much more easily obtainable. Dried yeast granules are twice as strong, weight for weight, as fresh yeast, e.g. 15g/$1/2$oz dried yeast equals 25g/1oz fresh yeast. Always use less rather than more dried yeast even if it looks ludicrously little. American recipes usually state the number of packets of yeast required; their packets hold only 7g/$1/4$oz dried yeast, which is the same as 15g/$1/2$oz fresh yeast.

Easy-mix yeast is just what it says. It does not have to be proved or treated separately, but is mixed dry into the flour. You use the same amount as ordinary dried yeast. A boon. Even though you no longer have to prove your yeast is viable in a sponge or in a first rising, it's always best to give bread doughs at least two slow risings, as this is when complicated interactions between yeast and flour give rise to greater flavour. Fresh yeast needs only to come into contact with warm liquid to start reproducing and creating gas and alcohol. Sugar is used for starting dried yeast but must never be added to fresh yeast as it actually enervates its strength; salt also inhibits all yeasts and thus must only ever be added to the flours and not the yeast mixture – that is not a problem with Easy-mix. Adding salt to a yeast mixture or to an old-fashioned and now largely pointless 'sponge' is a common reason for amateur bread makers to produce heavy loaves – most of the yeast was slaughtered before it had drawn breath.

If it is easy for you to buy fresh (compressed) yeast, then buy exactly the quantity you want, when you want it. If you have to store it, use the coldest part of the refrigerator. Provided the yeast was in good condition and you have bought a good-sized piece, it should last a full two weeks.

Some air circulation helps storage of yeast, so either wrap it loosely in greaseproof paper or store it in a fairly close-fitting container with a little ventilation. Keep it away from strong odours. Melon, slices of which are very often put into refrigerators unwrapped, is a particularly bad offender. There are few things that invade other foods quite so vigorously. Even under refrigeration, yeast is prone to self-digestion, making it rather less potent than it might be. A clean smell, light colour and a tendency to crumble rather than collapse are clear indicators fresh yeast is in good condition.

Those who find it difficult to obtain compressed yeast but own a freezer may safely splash out on some when they have the opportunity. Yeast freezes very well, and should produce excellent results for up to three months, possibly longer. Pack the yeast in suitable sizes say 25g/1oz batches – and seal and label it carefully. Allow frozen yeast to thaw slowly, and then dissolve it in lukewarm liquid as usual.

Magical as yeast seems, all types can exceed their usefulness in bread and related baking. The action that creates gas is accompanied by other enzymic actions that ripen the flour and enhance the dough's flavour. But after a certain point bread can be over-yeasted, the risen dough will begin to collapse and if you bake it will taste decidedly wrong. The key is to let dough rise slowly in a cool temperature – even overnight in a refrigerator. Bread yeast dies at a temperature of around 55C/130F. This is a gradual process during baking as the heat penetrates from the crust to the centre. Over-proving bread, proving in a hot place or using too much yeast, will make a loaf heavy and also makes it stale quickly.

Readers who wish to try out recipes printed before the advent of fresh yeast should work backwards from the amount of flour required. For bread dough, 25g/1oz fresh yeast is more than enough for 1.5kg/3lb 5oz. You can double the amount for sweet brioche-type dough and sweet buns and cakes. The old yeasts and barms, measured by the pint or cup, contained liquid, so you may have to add extra water, milk or egg if you are adapting an old recipe and using compressed yeast instead of the old types. In fact, the greatest surprise for amateurs when they see professionals making bread is how wet and sticky the mixture can or should be.

Baked Goods

This is an absolutely idiosyncratic list of what I like and what I think you are most likely to find. It should be enough for you to develop a sense of your own preferences.

Babke: Polish or Russian, with the dense, satisfying texture of a pound cake, baked in a deep decorative ring mould. The mixture usually incorporates beaten egg white, so it is often described as a soufflé cake. It might be leavened with yeast or a chemical agent. Serve plain with coffee when fresh. Babke makes an excellent quick dessert or special teatime treat served with a flavoured cream, doused with syrup or liqueurs, or covered with such cream/fruit mixtures as raspberry fool. Sometimes they are sold covered in chocolate.

Bagel: this yeasted, white dough bread roll is like a doughnut with a hole and varies from 8-12cm/3-6 inches in diameter. Each ring of dough must be poached in water before baking, to give the requisite tough, chewy crust. Associated with kosher food, particularly with that of New York, it is better eaten warm or split and toasted, and is at its most famous when filled with a combination of cream cheese and smoked salmon – the lox and bagel ubiquitous for Sunday breakfast or brunch. Bagels can also be bought sprinkled with caraway seeds, salt, poppy seeds or sesame seeds. Seasoned or garlic salt might be added to the dough. Even raw onion can be sprinkled on top, which bakes to a caramelized brown – not a very social breakfast choice.

Now, as bagels invade muffin land, they even have their own franchises, and in these you find sweet and spiced bagels, although few are flavoured with much courage and can be mistaken one for the other. Spiced bagels are specially good toasted but as with almost everything else baked or cooked – from pancakes to cheesecakes – beware the blueberry for its taste never survives the heat of the kitchen. Cranberry bagels, yes, cinnamon and dried apricot, absolutely, peanut butter and jelly bagels, yes please and the very non-kosher bacon and pineapple bagel is a triumph. In Auckland New Zealand, a whole food bakery, wouldn't you know it, sells bagels without a hole, amidst the usual ever-brown heaps of wheatmeal/date/nut slices. Now usually a bagel without a hole is called a bialy and that's that. But these ones are not only still called bagels but are also made of white flour and then stuffed with lemon curd and cream cheese or with blueberry preserves and cream cheese they fly out of the shop. They might not be true bagels, but are so good I have never heard a complaint, perhaps because this is the only way to make blueberries taste great in a bagel – if they are bagels.

Baklava: for many years this meant a single oblong pastry found in Greek delis, high stacks of buttery phyllo pastry, stuffed with chopped almonds or walnuts and swimming in a syrup. Delicious. Then the Turks and Lebanese and Egyptians and Iranians and everyone else who lives on or close to the Eastern Mediterranean got into the act, selling their versions ever more westerly, particularly in the West End of London to which hundreds of thousands of the richest migrate in the warmer months.

There is little so exotic and moving to the sweet tooth as a window filled with tiered platters of Middle Eastern pastries and I known none as breathtaking anywhere than in Green Valley at the Edgeware Road end of Upper Berkeley Street, W1. The syrup that soaks into most of them prevents staling for weeks, even at room temperature, so they offer better value for money than Frenchy pastries that go soggy in the few hours/days they wait to be sold.

Essentially all baklava, an incorrect but widely used collective name, are variations on a few themes. With few exceptions they are made of paper-thin phyllo pastry or something similar, buttered and piled in many layers. These are cut into squares or circles or oblongs and then stuffed, pinched, piled or layered or folded or rolled up with nuts, sometimes spiced. The nuts might be almonds, cashews, pistachios, walnuts or pine nuts, sometimes singly sometimes mixed together. When they come out of the oven they are drenched in syrup that can be made with honey and are commonly scented with rose water or orange flower water. Each minute variation of the pastry, the nut filling or the syrup gives another type and flavour, and each of these will have a different name, even in neighbouring towns and cities, let alone countries.

They keep very well in the refrigerator, and are a guaranteed talking point at any gathering, for few ever dislike them – those afflicted with low sweet-toothsomeness should pick those with the greatest proportion of nuts on show.

In Perth, Western Australia, I once dined for the camera on sardine sandwiches at a restaurant called Moorish: they had flavoured the local specialty of layered and fried sardines with such Middle Eastern aromatics as *chermoula* and then matched the result with a local beer and wine. No confusion about the fusion here, but better tastes with every mouthful. Just as we were leaving, the cameraman pointed out what I had missed in the chilled display. Chocolate coated baklava! Only in Australia . . .

A few baklava are made with *konafa*, the curious pastry that looks like shredded wheat and which is called *kataifi* by Greeks. If you arrange and bake the buttered shreds into a nest shape, and then drench these while hot with a cool syrup flavoured with orange flower water and rose water, you have the basis of an amazing dessert: the simplest is to stuff them with mixed berries and top with clotted cream.

Batch loaf or loaves: this means bread baked without tins but so close together they touch and must be pulled apart – they will have no crust where this has happened.

Bath buns: a white bread bun, the dough of which should contain egg and milk; must have crushed lump sugar on top. Can contain lemon, chopped peel or sultanas but never currants.

Bialys: the bialy, once a product of Bialystock in Poland and now a great NY favourite, is related to a bagel but instead of having a hole has a central indent. This is filled or scattered with browned onion and, properly, with poppy seeds too. It shouldn't be split, and is best eaten when warm and spread with butter or cream cheese.

Bloomers: these are the oblong, fat and rounded loaves of white bread which are always slashed diagonally and never baked in tins. Often made with a little milk powder, the texture stands up to being used in a summer pudding or a bread and butter pudding; but you should test this first because plastic bread is sometimes made into this shape. The way it collapses when you try to slice it is the usual giveaway.

Brioches: made of light, yeasted dough with a high proportion of egg and butter to give a cake-like texture. Sweetness is variable, but brioches are usually baked in tapering, fluted moulds, large or small, and most often eaten warm for breakfast; sometimes the dough is plaited, and sometimes it's baked in a small loaf tin, so you can slice it neatly.

Unsweetened brioches make an elegant accompaniment to soups and other light first courses, especially if fish of any kind is involved. If the centre is scooped out and replaced with a vegetable or meat purée they make a stunning savoury snack, hot or cold. A big, cake-sized brioche cut into elegant wedges and toasted lightly is nice for tea; these can also be served with light supper dishes such as chicken or fish with a cream sauce if the brioche is not too sweet. In France *brioches vendéennes* are good enough to have IGP status.

If you find a loaf-shaped brioche, it makes heavenly toast but it burns very easily: help it make friends with lots of butter and great apricot or wild strawberry or black cherry preserve, or *visciole al sole* q.v. if you can find it. Otherwise, warm slices of brioche toast are the best possible accompaniment to foie gras.

Brioche dough baked around a whole coarse, pork sausage is a great treat, hot or cold – Fauchon in Paris did this to salmon once and served it in slices with saffron-flavoured butter. I was eating some outside Notre Dame when a congregation spilled out. Once the Fauchon wrappings were espied literally dozens of Parisians wished me an envious *bon appetit*. So that's how to gain the attention of a Parisian!

My favourite way to start Christmas dinner is warm saffron-flavoured brioches served with a bowl of chilled soured cream and a pot of caviare, and it requires great Christian resolve to share, I can tell you.

Brown: this could and can mean white bread that has been coloured with caramel. Today it more often means bread made with 85 per cent extraction flour, what we used to call wheat meal until that was forbidden; apparently this may have some colouring too. The lesson is simply not to say brown when you mean wholemeal.

Brownies: a satisfying but confusing thing, for the name covers a multitude of glorious sinfulness. Brownies can be big, flattish and roundish cookies with a distinct chewiness and are then generally studded with nuts or chocolate. The ones I ate at the New York State Fair that included dollops of crunchy peanut butter were spectacularly good. But brownies are also a type of cake baked in an oblong pan and then cut into squares; they may be moist and chewy or cake-like. Together with muffins, they continue to compete with cheesecakes as staple café fare, and are just as easy to make as to buy in, which you might choose to remember when considering the prices charged.

Bulkas: probably Russian, but certainly a favourite 'coffee-cake' with much of Central and Eastern Europe too. The basis is a rich yeasted dough moistened with soured cream. It's rolled out, sprinkled with cinnamon and sugar, and then rolled up like a sponge roll or jelly roll and sliced thickly. Each slice makes a fragrant swirled bun that's almost certainly the genesis of the most outrageous of the US's cinnamon buns q.v. Cardamom, raisins and nuts might also be added by cooks to express individuality.

Ciabatta: this unquestioned star of the bread basket burst onto the scene in the early 90s with more instant acceptance than a new song by Elvis Presley. It continues its dominance of delis and cafés and, even, Italian bread shops, in spite of a late-century rush by panini. But have you never wondered where something as good as ciabatti could have been hiding before the '90s? The answer is . . . nowhere.

Ciabatta is not Italian. It's a modern construct, actually invented by the British baking industry in the 1980s as a competitor for the French stick. Didn't they do well?

Ideally a ciabatta is a flattish, long rectangle of white dough with rounded corners, a bit of a waist and is made with an element of olive oil; the shape is said to be reminiscent of the sole of a sloppy sort of casual slipper, but seems equally to be that of a steam-rollered bone. Ciabatta dough is made with water rather than anything milky, which encourages the floury flavour, and when properly made should prove for quite a long time, so there are many large air-pockets, each eager to suck in olive oil or butter. Inevitably, ciabatta's great success means many commercialized types are imposters, of the right shape but of ordinary texture and thoroughly disappointing. Often flavoured with such trendy additions as sun-dried tomatoes, herbs, olives or olive pastes, arcane cheeses and the like.

Ciabatta is particularly good when a few days old, split and toasted under a grill or over a barbecue. Its holey texture will gulp oceans of melting butter or of olive oil and also help keep toppings from slipping out or off: one of the split sides makes the best open sandwich, an actual sandwich of hotly-toasted ciabatta with lots of oil-rich salad, sunny tomatoes and a pink, juicy steak is the greatest pleasure imaginable, particularly in the open air and for a sailor home from the sea – even if he's just been paddling.

Chapatti: unleavened Indian flat bread that should be made of wholemeal flour. It should be as fresh as possible and makes a nice wrap as well as its more traditional role as a scooper and plate-wiper – see flatbreads.

Cheesecakes: there is a traditional small English cheesecake containing no cheese at all, but is only a sweet sponge on a pat of raspberry jam, baked in puff or short pastry: I believe it's even wrong to think of them as English and they should properly be called Welsh cheesecakes. Home cookery shops in Australia and New Zealand, which have nothing to do with homes and are more often run by Vietnamese or Chinese, are a reliable preserve of these curious treats.

Real curd cakes, cheesecakes and tarts with curd-based fillings, have been a staple ever since men and women began to write down what they cooked or ate. Once flavoured with rose water, nutmeg, orange, lemon, sherry or dried fruits, or all of them, they were an Everest above the uncooked or cooked but inedible cheesecakes today inflicted on those not infected with dieting.

To try and to buy the real baked thing you need to find a Polish, Russian or Jewish area or a shop run for these people. Austrians and Germans also make them, perhaps the richest versions of all, and most look like a dense-textured cake on a pastry base when cut. If you can bear it, plain baked cheesecakes often mature and sweeten over a few days – the price you pay for this greater flavour is the usual pastry base is no longer crisp and sweet, particularly if it has been spread with a rose petal or raspberry or apricot jam. Who said the cheesecake world was fair?

What I call the 'wet ones' are baked cheesecakes in which fresh white curd, cream or cottage cheese is the major ingredient and flour and eggs are there simply as binders: home-made ones might also include cream or soured cream or yoghurt too. These are the most common commercial cheesecakes, and usually have a biscuit base and a topping of fruit in a thick syrup or sauce. Provided they are slightly chilled they can make a satisfying and attractive snack or pudding, but the cheaper they are, the worse they are and the further they stray from being a good way to get extra animal protein in the diet: before you leap, look at the ingredients in that 'fruit' topping, and consider if a scoop of very fresh cream or curd cheese and some fresh fruit might not be a whole lot nicer to put into your body.

Then there is New York, where cheesecake is close to a religion; and as with any decent religion there are schisms, sects and breakaway movements. The essential New York cheesecake is a baked one, made with ricotta and cream or curd cheese, usually flavoured with cream and vanilla and sitting high on a pastry base. Its antecedents are the cheesecakes of Poland and Germany and Russia and the like, most usually from the Jewish tradition. Sometimes a little shop will still do things the old way – like putting a layer of rose-petal or apricot jam between the cheesecake and the pastry, but that's not really a New York cheesecake. NY cheesecake should be lighter than you expect and have a soothing acidity to balance the sweetness. Except, that's only what some people think of as a real New York cheesecake.

Hot on its heels is the Italian style, made with ricotta and, so, often a little grainy and regularly not made as high or thick. Here the cheese is more a subtle background, in fact proper ricotta is not truly a cheese as it is made from whey and has little casein in it. Its bland sweetness tells you it retains the sugar of milk and none of the fat, but makers of ricotta cheesecake conveniently forget to mention ricotta hurtles up many realms closer to God when mixed with cream and/or with ground almonds. So it's just as rich as the cream-cheese style NY

New York's Magnificent Seven

Ed Levine is a celebrated food writer for the *New York Times*. He decided to settle arguments and find for himself the best cheesecake in New York. He couldn't, and didn't dare choose just one, and so from the 48 he tasted he offered his magnificent seven. What a delicious food trail these addresses might make.

Eileen's Special: 'ethereally light and not too sweet'
17 Cleveland Place at Kenmare St: SoHo
Helen's Fabulous: 'crustless, creamy . . . lovely vanilla accent'
126 Union Street, between Columbia and Hicks, Brooklyn
Mona Lisa Pastry Shoppe: baked in coal-fired brick ovens – an almost 'Italian cheesecake heaven' orange ricotta cheesecake and an excellent traditional one with 'a custardy interior and a perfect crust'
1476 86th St at 15th Avenue, Bay Ridge, Brooklyn
Monteleone: a Sicilian cheesecake with three types of ricotta: 'light, moist, plenty of body and flavour'
355 Court Street at President, Carroll Gardens, Brooklyn
Monte's Venetian Room: a ricotta cheesecake 'so ridiculously good and creamy it's hard to believe it's not made with cream cheese'
451 Carroll Street, between Nevins and Third Ave, Carroll Gardens, Brooklyn
Two Little Red Hens: ' first amongst equals' meriting 'trumpets and shouts . . . the very definition of a phenomenal New York cheesecake, rich, light . . . the perfect balance of sweet and tart'
1652 Second Avenue, between 85th and 86th
Yura & Co. 'wonderfully lemony fluffy cheesecake' and a 'turtle' cheesecake with a caramel top complementing the 'tart sour creamy cheesecake' that is 'one of the great tastes of this city'
1659 Third Avenue at 93rd

To these I would add, for the experience, a terrific Polish shop retaining the atmosphere and amazing range of traditional Ashkenazi Jewish baking, brought to the New World from the Old by 20th century immigrants: Moshe's Home-made Kosher Bake Shop is at 115 2nd Avenue, New York.

cheesecake, but is subtler in flavour. This sublime mixture of ricotta, cream and almonds can be served and eaten fresh pretty much as it is, but for a cheesecake is baked with eggs to set it. The best I ever ate was in Naples, their particular Easter special, studded with cooked wheat grains and candied orange, perfumed with orange flower water and baked in seriously rich pastry. Second best is one I make with a spectrum of orange; candied orange, orange zest, orange juice and orange flower water. The possibility of this sort of baking originating with the Moors seems very likely.

The New York connection with cheesecake works well for the rest of the USA. When Junior's Brooklyn restaurant offered their cheesecake on QVC shopping channel, they sold 70,000 in 24 hours.

A third type of cheesecake is often found in small delicatessens where food is made on the premises. This is the unbaked cheese, often set with gelatine, and they are no bad thing as long as they also contain a measure of whipped cream or yoghurt to give a fluffy, light texture. Those without gelatine often use only flavoured cream cheese, sometimes just whisked up Philadelphia cheese and are thus thin and miserable, scarcely thicker than the biscuit base, a swizz and a disappointment. They make your teeth sticky.

Whatever your delicatessen does, you should always store a wet or a gelatine-based cheesecake in a refrigerator, for even if made with the finest ingredients it will go sour in warmth, or it will dry out, or both.

Quite plain New-York style baked cheesecake can be made special with the accompaniment of a purée of sharp fruit – blackcurrants, gooseberries, red currants with orange, or rhubarb with orange and a touch of green root ginger would all be good. Very special jams or preserves do just as well: think black or red cherry, rose petal, lime marmalade with plenty of peel in it, or apricot, but everything must be well chilled, So, spunkily flavoured ice cream is even better with cheesecake, for everything but your cholesterol count.

Thin slices of chilled cheesecake on beautiful plates are the best way to extend small amounts of exquisite fruits. A slice of lemony cheesecake with just half a scented red or white-fleshed peach, or some passion fruit pulp, or with perhaps a slice of mango, or lime-splashed kiwi fruit slices would leave guests wishing for nothing more – unless of course they knew you had some chilled, well-matured elderflower wine, which goes with all cheesecakes. For a hot drink, coffee is usually favourite, but black rather than one of the milky types. Otherwise anything rosy goes, particularly rose pouchong tea, a mild black China tea infused with the oils from acres of richly scented roses: very good iced, too. So do citric teas like Earl Grey and Lady Grey, but check the flavourings are real and not nature identical flavours.

Chelsea buns: these are a spiral at least 2.5cm/1 inch thick and slightly domed, rather square shaped and with a distinct filling of currants, cinnamon and sugar between the spirals. To be absolutely authentic Chelsea buns should be made from a slightly sweetened, light, white, yeasted dough and must incorporate both lemon zest and mixed spice. The flavoured dough is rolled flat, covered with a mixture of butter, currants, spice and sugar, rolled up and then sliced

– to make spirals of dough. They are laid flat and arranged so when the yeast swells the dough they just touch one another, giving the authentic slightly square shape. Freshly baked Chelsea buns should be glazed with boiled milk and sugar syrup, then sprinkled with caster sugar. There is a fashion for icing them thickly, sometimes with raspberry icing: you decide. Although made to eat just as they are, very fresh Chelsea buns move to higher estate when pulled apart and thickly buttered.

Chollah: a large loaf of yeasted white flour enriched with milk and a little egg, often slightly sweetened too. The usual shape is a plait, sprinkled with poppy seed. Particularly associated with Jewish food and festivals but not that much different from small English milk loaves. At special festivals and in better shops they can look and taste like brioche.

Cinnamon buns: these give over-eating a good name. Particularly American, and specially associated with the coffee carts of Seattle, they are pretty much Chelsea Buns that have gone way over the top, survived and gone for it again. Huge, snowy turbans with the moist cinnamon and sugar filling that only Americans ever seem to get right, and all even better if there is caramel present. You think you couldn't possibly manage a whole one. You manage.

Cob/coburg loaf: the name for any round loaf of leavened white, brown or wholemeal bread. They are sometimes slashed or pricked or topped with whole grains but are never baked in a tin.

Corn breads: because no type of corn contains gluten it cannot make leavened breads by itself. Thus cornmeal, ground from a less sweet relation of sweet corn, is used only to flavour yeast-leavened breads, much the way rye must. More commonly it is made into chemically raised breads that are virtually unsweetened cakes. These are fairly soft and so are commonly known as spoon breads in the USA, because they are served in the baking dish and spooned out as you eat. Pone, Johnny Cakes and a dozen other funny names all mean the same thing. A commercially available sourdough corn-bread mix is terribly good.

The happy golden colour and the inherent sweetness make corn bread particularly good with the robust flavours of barbecued food.

Cottage loaf: bread loaf of any type made of two rounds of unequal size the smaller sitting on top of the bigger. Not often made commercially now.

Crisp bread: unleavened, thin bread from Scandinavia. Made domestically only with rye flour but commercial manufacturing often dictates the addition of wheat and other ingredients.

Croissants: one of the heights of yeast baking, croissants are made by rolling out rich, yeasted dough with a great deal of butter – in fact a yeasted puff pastry. Although now far more easily available, even in supermarkets, many of the mass-produced croissants have a metallic taste induced by the use of fats other than butter and are not worth the money. Croissants are found as a basic throughout Europe, varying mainly in their sweetness – Polish and Austrian are the sweetest.

Several places claim the invention of these crescents of cholesterol – I plump for the Viennese baker who is said first to have fashioned them on the morning the crescent-emblazoned flags of the invading Turkish army were finally repelled from his city gates.

If not too sweet, croissants go surprisingly well with some of the sweeter meats, especially ham; such combinations make a change in a picnic basket. If you make your own croissants, roll the uncooked dough around slices of ham, pancetta or prosciutto or smoked salmon and make the croissants bigger than usual, for a more substantial breakfast croissant; these are good hot or cold with herby, chive or garlic butter or with flavoured cream cheese.

Nothing is quite as restorative as a rich croissant dipped into milky coffee. If you are not a dipper, please refrain from cutting a warm or fresh croissant – if you must add butter or jam they should be pulled gently apart or you end up with clay under your knife, and those in the know will snicker.

Crown loaf: a specialty loaf made by baking a circle of rolls of white dough in a tin – they should only just touch. To make it more crown-like, some bakers use two circles, the top one smaller and joined to the bottom in the same way cottage loaves would be. Great for home bread bakers and feasts, for like monkey bread q.v. the rolls can be pulled apart when wanted.

Danish loaf: a long, oval, crusty loaf of white bread with a central slash, lightly floured. Not baked in a tin. Excellent for all those things where you need a bread with muscle, a bread to make croutons, to fry in bacon fat, to slice into puddings or to toast.

Danish pastries: these are made with rich, yeasted dough similar to that of croissants but the butter is usually incorporated all in one layer and the dough turned and rolled without further additions. The pastry is then cut into decorative shapes, filled, iced or flavoured in dozens of ways and the finished products are served hot or cold at almost any time of the day.

The secret of the fascinating but fugitive flavour of the better ones is ground cardamom. Probably invented in Vienna but particularly associated with Scandinavia – the Danes call Danish pastries *Wienerbrod*! Here and there I find mini-Danish, each just a few mouthsful. They are too girly and bitty for breakfast or brunch, but a wonderfully original thing at tea time or as a dessert with fresh fruit.

Doughnuts: round hunks of leavened white-flour dough, sometimes filled with jam or fruit, then fried in fat or oil and smothered in sugar or a thin icing. Extremely widespread. It is mainly Arabs and Americans who make the ones with holes in the middle and these are just as often chemically leavened. Poles and Russians are addicted to their jam-filled doughnut balls, *ponshki*. The Greeks make them smaller and then soak them in warm honey and call them *loukoumades*. The Dutch, who normally make boring food, make wonderful doughnuts for New Year's Eve, stuffed with grated apple and fruit and spices, and then give them the delightful name *olliebollen*.

Escargots: they hate it when you point and ask for a snail, really hate it when the sign says *pain au raisins*. Better that than they snigger when you can't say escargot or *pain au raisins*. These are a sort of French Danish, a low swirl of yeasted dough, like an ill Chelsea bun, held together with a little pastry cream or custard, with a few raisins or sultanas, and a glazed top. French bakers tend to put rather too many raisins for my taste, for they fall out as you break and eat. Otherwise, variations are enormous, from a little sweet spicing of the filling, to completely over the top slatherings of spice and yummy caramel with pecan nuts from Clarke's in Kensington Church Street, London. Perfect for slowly unswirling as you gossip over coffee. And then there are cinnamon buns q.v.

Farmhouse loaf: a white bread loaf baked in a tin both wider and shallower than the usual tin loaf. The word farmhouse is imprinted on the side of the loaf, which is sometimes slashed lengthwise and floured; sometimes the maquillage of flour is all that distinguishes this from fast-food bread, but more often it indicates a bread at least as good as a Danish or split-tin or Vienna.

Flatbreads: a catch-all name for the many styles of Indian and Middle Eastern breads now so easily available, some leavened, some unleavened. Some leavened flatbreads, like pitta q.v. can be split to make pockets, much appreciated by those who must eat on the go; others like naan q v are torn and used to hoist food from plate to mouth.

The unleavened breads of India, Asia and America are also used more as plates, forks and spoons rather than for open or closed sandwiches. Chapattis, the Indian staple, are well known to devotees of red flock wallpaper throughout Europe and although made just of wholemeal flour and water, are quite tricky to get right. Indian cookbooks will give instructions and introduce you to more adventurous chapattis, including the vegetable-stuffed parathas and the deep-fried pooris.

Other easily available unleavened breads are the Jewish matzos, which are crisp, and the Mexican tortilla, which is not, unless it is a taco, which is a fried tortilla. Swedish crisp breads and the dense German pumpernickel and vollkornbrot, which simply means whole grain bread, are further examples – strange to think these relative exotica are related to the damper, that flour and water paste wrapped around green sticks, baked over fires and called bread by followers of Baden-Powell.

Flatbreads can be just that, a flat round or square of dough, more often than not cooked on a hot flat surface, like a pancake and barely as thick. Some are no bigger than a hand; others could hide a small table top. They are universally delicious, but only when hot and ideally a little charred, as they inevitably are. If they are rolled around sandwich ingredients and then cut at a cheeky angle across into segments, like pretend sushi, and then kept in a fridge or in a cool pack for lunch, these breads can become very ordinary and often rather tough. If you do want to use them like this, it's best to choose very wet and highly flavoured fillings, the first to keep the bread chewable, and the second to override the flavour ennui into which they plunge.

If you can wrap up these flat breads when they are still piping hot and tender, and eat them directly, you are rewarded with a genuine new take on the sandwich, something countless kilometres better than panini.

Anything flat, leavened or unleavened, lends itself most admirably to being lightly flavoured with a sprinkle of something. Oregano and olive oil will give a Greek flavour, so that's also perfect for anything to do with a pizza or pizza-like ingredients. Flavoured salts work well, if used sparingly and so do many seeds. Sumac, the ground smokey-red and acidic berry is very good indeed. Perhaps the best is za'atar, a flavouring particularly associated with Jerusalem: it's simply sesame seeds, dried thyme and sumac. Dukkah, the mix of toasted and spiced nuts and seeds, is meant to be used with oil as a dip for bread, but is terrific when used as a crust-sprinkle for bread you bake yourself.

Focaccia: a thick, light, flat Italian bread, often slightly sweet, dimpled on the top and drizzled with olive oil. Sometimes it also has herbs, tomatoes and the like in the dough or on it. Either way it is thus a sort of thick, naked pizza and can be eaten just as it is. It seems best when split and lightly toasted or grilled and then dressed liberally with olive oil and anything that goes with it you happen to have on hand. The perfectly behaved instant starting point for fast pizzas or toasted, open-face sandwiches.

Friands: these funny little ovals of enriched sponge cake appeared as an up-market challenge to the muffin, something that at least looks elegant on its way to your mouth. When very fresh and warm, and when the high butter content has caramellised a little of the mixture around the bottom edge, they can be good. At room temperature or less they seem heavy and greasy and to cost rather a lot for what they are. The most common one I encounter has a fresh raspberry baked into the top, and just as well. Financiers seem to be the same thing, but who'd trust anything to do with bankers?

French bread: the name generally given to any yeasted bread baked in long rolls, even though French flour or techniques may not have been incorporated. Usually called French sticks, but there are correct names for most types. Properly, baguettes are the crisp, golden, medium-sized sticks that bulge in the middle because they have been baked without confines. If baguettes are baked in roll pans, which gives them straight, even sides, they are properly called *longuets*. The very long or very thin ones are properly called *ficelles*. Large, hand-shaped, cylindrical or round French loaves are usually *pain de campagne* or *pain de ménage*, country or home-style breads

It has long been said French stick breads get their delicious taste from the use of low-gluten soft flour. That's part of it. Far more important is they are proved very much longer than UK or American breads, something you can check by the number of large holes in each loaf, which British bakers think is a sign of badly made bread; if baguettes or longuets don't have those holes they are ordinary bread with an attack of pretension. Additionally, genuine baguettes are baked in specialized ovens that shoot steam onto the loaves from time to time, and thus these loaves never were and never can be made at home.

For years supermarkets tried to foist us off with quickly made breads in long roll shapes; now some have taken the trouble to install proper ovens, and to let the bread prove properly before baking, so some British baguettes are decidedly French. Even so you still commonly buy French sticks that on cutting turn out to be nothing but tasteless froth in a tough crust. To check out what you are buying, the smell should be sweet, the creamy-white crumb should look like bread with windows in it rather than semi-transparent chemical foam, and the crust should just stop short of cutting your gums when you bite. It's that combination of sweet crumb and a crackling golden crust that make the true baguette so filling and satisfying. An elasticized, chewy crust and negligible crumb should be called something else.

True French sticks, made of a soft flour and with a good holey texture, stale very quickly. Next time you put your hand out to buy a French stick and find it has a sell-by day some time in the future, pull that hand back, remembering the French buy bread three or more times a day; in France the sell-by date is always today.

It's great proof of people power that all over the world young men and women can earn a living by baking the old way. And not so young ones, too. In New Norcia, way north of Perth in Western Australia, they've refired the brick ovens of the Benedictine community there and now supply wonderful sourdough breads thereabouts and in Perth. In Greytown, New Zealand's oldest inland town, an inspired Frenchman is so well known for baking the real thing he is whispered of in awe by those who have never been to his shop or eaten his bread. And you can barely move in any of the USA or Britain's farmers' markets without confronting a tumble of crisp-crusted loaves, equally likely to have been baked in a wood-fired oven. Here you are more likely to buy a sourdough baguette, sometimes heavier because of some wholemeal flour and sweeter and chewier because of the sourdough leavening, and thus so much closer to the French bread sticks sorely missed by Marie-Antoinette's subjects.

Gingerbread: you'll find this in several guises these days, both hard and chewy and more cake like. The original is the chewy one and for many centuries was often not much more than honey, flour and ground ginger. It kept for ages and ages, as it still does; you can indeed have gingerbread cookies as Christmas-tree decorations and eat them too. Ditto a gingerbread house. The considerable expense of the ginger did little to make gingerbread attractive, so it was often gilded with gold leaf, hence the common saying. Panforte from Sienna is a survivor of the original gingerbreads.

Granary loaf: a commercial brown loaf to which is added a measure of malted wheat grains for flavour and texture. Very popular as a make-your own bread mix.

Grissini: these are the thin, well-baked breadsticks beloved of Italian restaurants. There is no secret to making them yourself other than rolling your dough evenly and thinly and then baking them long enough.

Gugelhopf: this egg-rich, yeasted cake, also called kugelhopf and related to babke and brioche, and to pannetone, contains chopped peel and other dried fruit. It may be eaten plain but the very high yeast content means it stales too quickly for the taste of those not from Central Europe. Butter, jam or syrup will put that right particularly when warmed. Like babke, gugelhopf may also be covered with chocolate and nuts.

Italian: this is usually the sign of dense, floury white loaves with a robust texture and thick crusts that need a strong jaw. These breads, sometimes with striking names like pugliese, indicating a putative origin, all slice wonderfully and keep their shape, too. They don't usually contain oil, thus dry rather than stale and in a day or two make terrific toast. Crazily, these Italian breads are quite the best for classic British bread puddings, like summer pudding, bread and butter pudding and so on. It's not surprising Italians invented bruschetta and crostini and the like – toasted or grilled slices, scraped with garlic or tomato and topped with Mediterranean goodies.

Italian loaves marked 'integrale' will contain wholemeal flour but often far less than you might think: in Italy wholemeal flour, like wholemeal pasta, is reserved for the sick.

Kaiser rolls: round floury rolls with a chewy rather than crisp crust, the one with a pattern of lumps on top.

Lardy cake: sometimes still available in small, independent baker's shops, this is bread dough rolled and folded like a simple puff pastry, except that instead of butter, pure lard, brown sugar and sultanas or mixed fruit are incorporated. The dough should be scored with a sharp knife and the baked lardy cake broken on these marks rather than sliced. It is better warm than cold but either way is wonderful, because it is so very wicked. If you have access to good lard, lardy bread is a wonderful project for two on a dark and stormy day.

Milk loaf: a generic term for white bread mixed with milk or milk and water, which gives a sweeter flavour, softer texture and longer life. Often made in small sizes and usually glazed. Milk powder can be added to a basic loaf to get the same added sweetness and more cake-like texture. The intoxicating smell and heightened richness of milk loaves makes them specially good for special sandwiches and for toast some days later. Outstanding for summer pudding, smoked salmon, bread and butter pudding and with blue cheeses.

Monkey bread: also commonly known as 'pull-aparts' for these loaves do just that, and need no slicing. The secret, for home bakers anyway, is to divide the dough into more or less even pieces and then lightly to smear each piece with butter or oil, which can be strongly flavoured. When they are put together in some sort of mould they appear to cook into one shape, but then split very easily where they have been joined.

The great fun is to flavour the butter or oil. So, you might actually use an olive paste or a saffron and paprika-heightened butter for a monkey bread to serve with something fishy, or a tomato, anchovy and chilli paste, perhaps with a cheese-spiked dough. Sweet doughs welcome being buttered together with any kind of spice or spiced mixture and fruit breads could be joined with butter into which orange zest had been grated.

Next time you plan to eat outdoors, even if it's a barbecue in the backyard, monkey breads are much easier than having to slice loaves, for even the small amount of oil or butter is enough to make them edible just as you pluck them.

Why is it called monkey bread? No idea. Rude rolls, a smart kid once called them, for they are indeed bread rolls without a crust on.

Muffin, American: like a large cup cake, but rarely seen as plain as these can be. Its most common manifestation once was studded with blueberries, but we eventually latched on – unless they are very fresh and wild, cooked blueberries have virtually no flavour. Now we have cranberry muffins (excellent), banana muffins, courgette (zucchini), chocolate, double chocolate, white chocolate, poached rhubarb and raspberry muffins, and cream-cheese-coconut-pineapple-white-chocolate and macadamia nut muffins – and everything else.

Muffins have moved on since their initial appearance at American breakfasts, for the pioneering ones were, you might remember, bran muffins and touted as being good for us, an asset airily but incorrectly carried over to their sugar and cholesterol descendants.

Some will argue there is a special muffin mixture, and there probably is, but frankly you can bake any cake mixture in suitable tins and call them muffins. The absolute best I ever had were served warm as a lunch time dessert on the terrace of the Hotel Martinez in Cannes; they were almost black with bitter chocolate and just under the top crust were a couple of rum-soaked cherries in syrup. For the days I find myself anywhere but Cannes I have always relied on the comfort of Betty Crocker muffin mixes. If only the world's ever-burgeoning cafes did the same.

What were once 'good for you', have now joined the ranks of the insipid, all made from mixes quite unacquainted with butter or other real ingredients. Fatty, heavy and getting smaller and smaller they are daily closer to signing their own death warrants, and that is a greater comfort. Friands q.v. have been giving them a run for their money, but they are often worse, cheesecakes are out of fashion – so what do the discerning do when they want something with their espresso? I would have said scones – but look what is happening to them! Perhaps we should all heed Queen Marie-Antoinette's advice to eat cake, except she probably meant brioche of which there was a glut in her palace at the time.

If you like to make muffins at home, here is a tip that helps ensure they come out light and well risen. You should only put one dump of batter into each muffin tin – topping up with a second spoonful somehow inhibits the rising. No, I don't understand it either, but Alison Holst told me and that's like being given a graven stone tablet.

Muffin, English: related to the sort muffin men used to hawk through British city streets. Today they are rarely found in England but are very common in the United States and Australasia. Chewy, yeasted and flat, and when split (cutting ruins the texture) they look rather like rag-topped crumpets. Properly, muffins were always toasted whole and then split and buttered on the hot untoasted sides before being put back together again. That might have been acceptable in the good old days but when I did it recently the muffin's interior collapsed into a disgusting paste that got worse when chewed. Honestly, why bother making something so horrid, and so unlike the original?

Naan: a truly delicious yeasted Indian bread traditionally cooked on the searingly-hot inside surface of a tandoori oven and thus they should properly be rather tear-shaped, a result of gravity on the soft, spongey dough, and the force with which they had to be thrown to make them stick to the oven's surface. Available fresh and frozen, and an invaluable way to jazz up any meal, for even from frozen they are crisp outside, chewy and sweet inside, after just a few minutes under the grill; but you must follow the instructions first to sprinkle or quickly rinse them with water.

I use them as a type of pizza base; spread when hot with fromage frais or soured cream and topped with smoked salmon drizzled with truffle oil and scattered with rocket, for instance. Quickly sliced into wedges it's perfect for serving as a first course with drinks before sitting at table. More substantially, I've had much success with hot naan topped with yoghurt, chicken tikka, thick blobs of mango chutney and flat-leaf parsley. Good enough to eat, specially by pop groups and no I won't tell you which one.

Pain d'epices: See gingerbread.

Pains au raisin: See escargots.

Pannetone: an ultra-high-rise yeasted cake from Italy, traditionally found at Christmas time. The basic one might contain delicious sultanas or raisins; others have candied orange or chocolate pellets or swirls of sweetened sauces. It's a sort of brioche, of course, and when very fresh is so addictive you quickly forget how much it might have cost you, for Italian made ones do cost a bit. But here and there is salvation, for in other countries, other bakers, like those of Marks & Spencer, have begun to question why they can't make it themselves. They can and do, sometimes just as wondrously for about 10% of the import price. If they sit around long enough to get a little dry – even if they don't – all sorts of pannetone are great to dip into sweet dessert wine, Port or an Italian vin santo.

Fabulous when cut into robust cubes, split and spread thickly with apricot jam and then used as the base of a trifle. And if you really tire of the pleasure of eating pannetone as is, then use it to make a superior bread and butter pudding with everything else self indulgent – rum-soaked raisins or cherries, candied apricots, elvas plums, chunks of high-cocoa chocolate, toasted walnuts or almonds, all in a wine or liqueur flavoured custard. Goodness, it's enough to make one buy another. And another.

Lightly toasted pannetone is a worthwhile end in itself, and particularly good with lusciously scented fruit.

Panforte: now a specialty of Sienna, this 'strong bread' is a brave survivor of what would be recognized by medieval folks as a type of the original style of gingerbread. Like these, panforte is essentially honey and sugar mixed with nuts and candied fruit, with plenty of sweet spices and flour. It comes in a flat disc, big or small and is usually topped and tailed with edible rice paper, which also helps stop the surfaces becoming sticky. Textures and flavours vary enormously but the one I liked best included black pepper in its spices, exactly as recommended by Elizabeth David. It keeps for ages if kept cool and should be served in thin wedges with coffee or tea or with a fortified wine: it's too gutsy and too sweet to eat with wine or champagne.

Panforte makes a terrific ingredient to serve with or to chuck into or over ice cream, to chop over grilled peaches or nectarines or to bake into big meringues; serve these with fresh fruit and whipped cream for an outrageous end to an otherwise sedate meal. Recently taken up by experimenting chefs all round the world, panforte is encountered in ever more variety. Chocolate panforte can be very good, but seems to need extra spice to make a flavour bridge between the sweet honey and bitter chocolate or cocoa – ginger seems to do it. Those who shop by Internet, or who live in Australia should look for the Sienna-style nut bread baked by the New Norcia Bakery in Western Australia. This mixture of almonds, hazelnuts, dried fruits and spices also includes cocoa and native red gum honey, and is baked in different sizes in the wood-fired ovens of New Norcia's Benedictine monastery, founded in 1846. It is very good.

Panini: this means 'little breads' if you haven't been paying attention in Italian conversazione classes. To observers of culinary fashion it has come to mean a high-profile example of how gullible a ravenous public gets when it's lunchtime.

Panini are quite ordinary, oval shapes of soft, slightly sweet bread, often flavoured with olives or tomato and the like. Sliced in two and stuffed, inevitably, with good Mediterranean things to eat, salads and mozzarella and roasted vegetables at the very least, they look terrific in a deli's refrigerated display. It then takes 10 or more minutes to get one on to your plate because they go off to be toasted, not only toasted but squashed flat by the toasting/pressing/cooking process between two heavy hotplates. Then out it comes, a third or less the size you paid for, and now filled with boiling hot lettuce. Hot squashed lettuce isn't on my must-eat list.

Presumably the idea is based on the toasted Italian sandwiches that are a particular specialty of New York – but there the long crisp rolls are pressed only with the meat, and the salad and mayonnaise are added afterwards.

Like so many novelties, panini only made it because you couldn't get them at home, and someone must have said they were fashionable. Their day is over, except of course in Italy, where panini are only ever served with a slice or two of cheese and ham and the squashing doesn't matter. It rarely pays to do something to a food never done in its country of origin.

Petits pains au chocolat: the ultimate sin in breakfast fare – or at any other time. They are usually made of brioche or croissant dough in which is embedded a chunk of rich dark chocolate, rather like a sweet sausage roll. Such is the sweetness and richness of these delights, those made with a simpler white bread are actually more enjoyable than those made with richer doughs.

Pitta: a flat oval of white or wholemeal bread popularized by the growth of interest in Greek, Turkish and Arabic food. Usually served heated and torn into small squares and used as a scoop. Otherwise it is cut in half and the space inside encouraged to become a pocket, which is then filled with salad and sliced hot meats or kebabs. The flourishing of Middle Eastern shops means we are now seeing many variations, some thinner, some thicker and many scattered with unusual herb or spice mixtures.

Pizza: originally a Neapolitan way to fill hungry stomachs cheaply – now an easy way for restaurateurs to fill bank accounts. True Neapolitan pizza (and the better American type) is a thick slab of yeasted white or part-wholemeal flour dough mixed with oil and/or some milk to give lightness and more sustenance. It should be very crisp underneath and around the edges thanks to the generous application of olive oil to the baking tray.

Originally toppings were simple and yet rich, as concentrated as true pasta dressings should be, and were chosen to blend into the dough rather than curl and crisp on top in the way modern pizza ingredients do. Cheese has become a common ingredient, especially chewy cows' milk mozzarella or grated Cheddar – but neither is originally authentic. Although now essential, tomato as a topping would also have been unknown through most of history.

For a long time after they were introduced to Europe, tomatoes cooked to a pulp were merely one of the optional sauces you smeared onto cooked bread slabs in and around Naples.

Elizabeth David says the absolutely original pizza-type dish is from Armenia and the topping was of minced lamb. The French pissaladi`ere covers dough (or thick slices of bread fried on one side only) with a mush of onion cooked in olive oil and decorated with black olives and anchovy fillets – a tomato-less pizza, in effect.

Arguments rage that thin, crisp bases are the original but the Neapolitan woman who taught me to make pizza scoffs at that, saying bread was what her poor ancestors could afford, not toppings, just as with pasta. But who really cares? You want thin, bendy, unsatisfying crusts so toppings slide off, then you have them, mate, and enjoy making those bankers even richer.

Pumpernickel: the many packaged varieties of these unleavened German wholegrain breads are essentially the same, with slightly different emphasis given to one or the other whole grain. Thus pumpernickel and *vollkornbrot* are much the same and versions from Westphalia and Osnabruck differ on purpose, as both these German areas claim to have created the original as far back as 1400. There is just as much controversy over the origin of the word pumpernickel. Some say it is onomatopoeic for the flatulent effect on the eater. Try saying it with a German accent, and you'll hear what I mean.

It is not easy to make at home; the commercial pumpernickels are often baked for 24 hours at a very low temperature in a closed container. This makes a moist, dense, dark, flat loaf that is now usually bought ready sliced. It should be refrigerated when opened. Pumpernickel and similar unleavened loaves, which might include grains other than rye, are excellent bases for open sandwiches; but as they dry and split easily I find it is better to cut each slice into squares or fingers before they are covered. A thin layer of butter keeps such pumpernickel slices and pieces supple and prevents them either drying out or becoming soggy when on a buffet.

At Kapitea Ridge Lodge on NZ's wild west coast I was once served a fritter of freshly netted whitebait, held together only by beaten egg, on a slice of pumpernickel: not the horrid clash I expected but an epiphany, for its acidity was far more suitable than the usual lemon juice and its sweetness and complicated flavours played with the whitebait in my mouth for ages.

Rolls: once, the creation of ever-more recondite bread roll shapes was quite as important as startling new ways with table napkins. Modern baking practices in supermarkets have reduced this high art to a choice of pap-soft breads that are either thick or thin or round or long and with or without cheese, but universally soft-crusted. Not all supermarkets, of course, but most, and most small bakers too.

Find a baker who still makes crusty rolls, still makes Kaiser rolls that need strong jaws to chew, and who still produces long rolls that splatter shards of crisp crust when you bite into them, and you have a gem. Other than that, all you need to know is never to cut a bread roll if you are sitting at a table, but to pull it apart, particularly if it is hot: if you cut you smear the dough into pap, an insult to the baker, horrid to eat, and it makes you look a klutz.

When filling a roll to eat later, they will be all the easier and less messy to eat if you slice into the top at an acute angle, rather than splitting them on their equator. Don't use any pressure but let the knife do the work, so the roll is not compressed in any way. They look much nicer on a counter or at a buffet too, with their fillings sitting up so proudly to be inspected.

Rum babas: part of the classic French repertoire I have never understood. They are made of savarin dough, a sweet, very highly yeasted dough, and are baked in small ring moulds. They should be saturated with rum-flavoured syrup, which dissuades the growth of mould but which does not always disguise the taste of staleness, precipitated by the high yeast content. If they are nice and fresh they can be decorated with chilled fresh fruit and whipped cream to a meal. The groans of delight evinced by those who buy bottled rum babas in syrup are suspiciously close to groans of displeasure: in my experience most flavour is in the syrup, usually only slightly acquainted with any rum I know, and there is none of the blending or melding of flavours to create something fresh and original. Rum do, altogether.

Rye bread: a generic term for any bread which contains a proportion of rye flour, which itself has a very low gluten content and so cannot make decent bread unless mixed with wheat flour. The actual content varies from as low as 15 per cent, which gives a delicious light-coloured, light-textured loaf, to 100 per cent, which gives a dark, dense loaf of specialist interest only. The light version, sometimes also a sourdough and most often baked in a bloomer shape, with or without caraway seeds, is the classic bread for salt beef sandwiches or for its very big brother the Reuben, a tower of salt beef and sauerkraut amongst other goodies.

With a large potful of long-cooked salt brisket or salt topside, and pre-sliced loaves of a light rye or light rye sourdough, you have the makings of a very good party: simply add salt cucumbers, a choice of mustards and the instruction that people are welcome to make a hot salt beef sandwich whenever they like. Corned beef is the same thing as salt beef: it's an antique name from the time salt came in grains as big as corn and so you added corns of salt to make the brine for the beef.

Sally Lunn: this light, sweet bread was either originally sold in the streets of Bath by a woman of the same name or the name is a corruption of the French *sol et lune*, for these delicacies are supposed to look like the sun and the moon – a rich shining golden top over a pale delicate base. Put more simply, a Sally Lunn loaf is a white flour, yeasted dough bread mixed with full milk or milk and cream, slightly sweetened, perhaps slightly spiced and thus a sort of lesser brioche. It should be glazed with beaten egg yolk and scattered with crushed cube sugar whilst still hot. In Australia and New Zealand they replace the crushed sugar with white icing and desiccated coconut. They would.

Sandwich loaf: white, brown or wholemeal bread baked in an enclosed tin to give a square or rectangular shape. Usually made only with modern fast-rising 'bread' and then sliced and wrapped.

Scones: scones are the sleeping giants of baking, and if produced and marketed properly would soon see off the upstart muffin and greasy friand. For a start, scones are simpler more honest things. Because they are simple, they are easy to glorify with any of the sweet or savoury additions you might add to muffins. They are good hot or cold and virtually demand simply to be split (never cut) and slathered with butter, a very good thing.

The trouble is many scones are not scones at all but a fast-food version of whigs, rich little tea cakes containing egg and lots of butter, that increased in popularity as tea drinking did in Georgian times, and decreased in Victorian times as anything fancy or French or both took over. Whigs were originally yeast raised, and when faster baking powder was introduced the true thing became archaic. To emulate what was indeed something only their 'betters' once ate, ordinary people made similar mixtures, still containing egg and lots of butter but leavened with baking powder and so they were neither one thing nor another. The simpler scone, which had always been with us, settled into continued popularity – without egg in the mixture – mainly in Britain's colonies.

So, no mixture that contains egg can properly be called a scone; it will taste good but is actually a whig. Neither should scones be low mounds, like manicured rock cakes, nor should they be dainty, although these have their place if you are wearing your best and don't want to spill jam and cream. Scones are properly high, wide and handsome, with rough exteriors but sweet soft interiors. And when split in the hands they should look and smell rather more like bread than a cake. Beware also of adding too much fat, which shortens the necessarily firm mixture and encourages them to spread rather than to rise. It's a matter of respecting the how and where and when of scones.

Scones were once made from flour and from milk that had soured – the soured milk was what made one think of making scones. The flour was warmed and then enriched slightly by rubbing in a little butter. Baking soda was added and this was all mixed up with the soured milk, also slightly warmed. The acid of the milk reacted with the soda almost immediately, and so would begin to fizz and create bubbles. It was an imperative to get the mixture into the oven as soon as possible, quickly patted into shape, but mainly around the edges or you would express or burst the very bubbles you had encouraged.

Scones and rolling pins should never keep company. Anything more than the merest pat into shape of a stiff dough that more than holds its own shape risks a heavy end product.

Then you cut quickly with something very sharp, because if you use something blunt you risk smearing the sides together, making it tough for the scones to rise much – that's why fancy cutters can be such a bad idea for scones. Just look at the next scone you see that has risen unevenly or too little: chances are the sides are shiny-smooth, smeared shut by the use of a blunt cutter, and so the scones had no chance to rise and shine.

Put the cut scones into a hot oven on warmed, floured trays, and that's all there is to scones.

In the search for novelty or just to show off, some scone makers have taken to using cream rather than milk, creating flat blobs rather than high and mighty towers. Some roll the mixture and take their time about getting the scones into the oven, both of these mistakes making them dense.

Today's use of sweet milk and baking powder does not start working on contact but only when heat is applied: because you have used warmed flour and warm milk some action is still under way almost at once and should not be wasted, so speed of fashioning is still important.

Oh yes, and then there are those who use lemonade as one of the mixing agents, in belief this gives a lighter scone. Because such recipes often specify cream as well, the end results look like weathered cowpats, low and roundish, with a sweet rich crumb that crumbles when you split it or try to butter it. Sadly the younger café generation will think these are the real thing – their mums are unlikely to be baking them at home – and soon real scones will be mocked for all the factors that once made them so famous.

They still serve hot scones for breakfast in Scotland, and that is a very good idea. Warm and floury and tall and light, with or without all manner of savoury or sweet content mixed into them – but no egg, not too much butter, milk rather than cream, and barely touched between the mixing and the baking. Surely any café owner would rather make and serve these proven favourites? Lemonade scones? What a fizzer.

If you'd like to see how far away from the real thing scones can get, London's Marylebone Farmers' Market is the place. There a local Italian restaurateur, (an urban peasant?), sells what he calls scones but which are bright yellow, smooth sided and thus barely risen, and acidic and dry to eat. If they are a guide to the quality and authenticity of everything else in the market, we are doomed.

Soda breads: any breads leavened with baking soda and something acidic like soured milk or buttermilk, or with baking powder and a sweet milk. Now associated mainly with Ireland soda breads are normally made in a cob shape, sometimes deeply slashed with a cross. It's usual to add a fair bit of wholemeal flour to white flour, making the bread more substantial but in today's plenty you can freely make it only of white flour. They are specially good when made with buttermilk, even though most of this is cultured whey rather than the real thing. Of course, soda breads are really a big, plain scone.

If you score the top of uncooked soda bread into servings with the blunt back of a knife, it then pulls apart when hot – just what you want because slicing will smear it into grey mud.

Sourdough breads: breads leavened by the addition to the dough of some old, soured dough – the souring creates a gas that in turn gives the rise. For continuity, only part of a mother sourdough, or starter, is used to make a new batch, and some of that fresh dough is then mixed back into the original mother, which then grows enough to be used once again, and so on. Some people claim their sourdough mother is many years old, and it can be: having been additionally nourished by the natural yeast cells in the atmosphere of an area for so long, it is also likely to have developed a character no other baker or area can emulate. Regional bread flavours, *terroir* breads, are just as possible as regional cheeses, apples or bacon.

A nicely ripened sourdough mother can smell very close to foul, although there will always be enticing sweet notes behind the first gush of sourness. In our common way of accepting names without questioning it's a surprise to learn 19th-century gold prospectors in California were christened 'sourdoughs' because they carried sourdough mothers with them, and the smell was difficult to hide. San Francisco is still famous for its sourdough breads.

Please don't let the possibility of smelly 'mothers' put you off making your own sourdough bread. Invariably the nastiest sourdoughs make the best breads. You don't actually get a sour taste, but a marvellously rich sweet-acid flavour, varying according to the sourdough itself, the flour or flours used for the bread, how long it took to rise and so on.

Don't feel you have to be clever with ingredients for the greatest surprise is how extraordinarily good otherwise plain white-flour bread can be when raised with a sourdough culture; a plain sourdough rye that's mainly white flour is probably best of all. The chewy texture, excellent keeping qualities and big flavours makes one keenly aware of how it might indeed be possible to live on bread alone.

Good sourdough bread should feel heavy for its size: if it doesn't, and you can squash it easily, the sourdough will have been assisted by yeast and is often not worth your money for it will be bland.

Toasted sourdough is one of life's greatest pleasures. Particularly when used as the basis for something special and savoury: a warm goat cheese with a salad including toasted walnuts and a dressing made with walnut oil gets most people's vote for top place. Me? I can't eat goat cheese so bacon and eggs with hot maple syrup and long-grilled, caramellised tomatoes does it for me. Sourdough breads tend to last well, often maturing to a richer and fuller flavour, so a single loaf can give differing pleasures, first as a fresh loaf, and then cruising on to greater heights as toast.

Once almost forgotten, sourdough breads have become the stage upon which any new or would-be artisan baker must play successfully. M. Poilane's bread factories in Paris can certainly take credit for re-awakening interest but, as any visitor to any farmers' market knows, enthusiastic young bread makers have recaptured the idea and are making something very new of one of bread making's oldest techniques. Long may they rise.

In the Dark Ages, when only rye bread makers and San Francisco kept up the tradition, the simplest and most reliable way to make excellent sourdough breads at home was to fly to San Francisco and stock up on packets of dried sourdough mother mixes. I've not seen them on my recent visits so here's a great marketing chance for someone. Then, these small packets of dried sourdough starter were ahead of the world's tastes: now they would be feeding a huge international hunger.

Split-tin loaf: a tin loaf with a long slash down the middle. They can also be made by placing two long rolls of dough end to end in the tin. Almost always made with white dough and often the top crust is very browned, perhaps even slightly burned. Delicious.

Stollen: a dense, yeasted German specialty for Christmas and which has a very long life. It's made in a flattish oblong and the sweet, spiced and fruited dough is wrapped around a central wodge of marzipan, all meant to resemble the swaddled Christ-child. Serve it sliced thinly. Personally, I can't contain myself; if there is one in the house I must eat it all within hours.

Sweet or savoury breads: at home or in a shop, bakers would usually keep back small amounts of dough from the batch and use these to make fruit breads, cheese breads, lardy cake q.v., herb breads and so on. That all stopped when bread making became centralized and commercialized. Now breads with additions are perhaps the fastest growing baking genre: there are few independent bakers who could survive without offering olive breads, sun-dried tomato breads, olive and sun-dried tomato breads and zillions more, many in increasingly alarming shapes and sizes. Well, good I say, if it gets people used to the idea of always having bread on the table and that bread is an important part of what is served, rather than an afterthought.

The reflection I make on the trend is to wonder whoever persuaded whom that dried rosemary is a good flavour in bread or that mixed herbs, which I had hoped dead, should be resurrected: it is the resinous, dusty rosemary in the latter that usually makes a nasty taste nastier.

There's a sure way to know what works in a bread dough and what does not. Try a bite of the flavouring on a slice of similar bread. Often you need a third flavour to make the flavouring work as well as it might: that trio structure is the key to almost everything good to eat. Thus, chocolate bread does not work unless there is also a good deal of sugar in the bread, orange bread also needs a sweetened dough, perhaps made with milk and with nutmeg or cardamom, black pepper bread might need tomato purée and garlic: fruit breads really must be sweet and most are all the better for spice – dried fruits and toasted nuts (they must first be toasted) are much better than fresh fruits, which work best in cake mixtures.

Quite the best-flavoured loaf of all is the traditional French walnut loaf and as usual its simplicity is deceptive. The walnuts must be fresh and have no hint of acidic rancidity, often the only flavour many of us associate with them, for walnuts do go off very quickly indeed. If you are uncertain, toast the walnuts first – the microwave does this best – indeed I toast all nuts I use in baking so when their flavour is diluted by the dough or cake mixture, there is still something substantial left. Walnut loaves can be and are made with second-rate bread doughs, but when they are made with the real thing nothing beats toasted walnut bread slices with cheese, particularly Cheddars and blue cheeses, or for the best-ever toasted tomato sandwich.

Tarts: these are getting closer to patisserie than baking, I know, but some seem to have established firm footholds in deli and café food around the world. The lemon tart, tarte au citron, is a real winner when it is what it should be. It should be made with butter in the pastry and flavoured only with lemon juice or lemon zest, perhaps with help from an outstanding citrus oil but many are made with non-butter fat and bad citrus oil that lingers as a bitter rather than acidic taste. If you make them, and customers are displeased the pastry softens too quickly, brush melted chocolate onto the cooked pastry tart before adding the filling; it will act as a moisture barrier. Rather more delicious and reliable are two types of egg or custard tart.

The first is Chinese and relies on great sweetness of its custard and the compelling richness of lard in its short, layered pastry. The sweetness of very good pork lard in otherwise unsweetened pastry is transporting, but even in London's central Chinatown I bought egg tarts in over-sweetened pastry that contained no lard, that offered no bridge between the pastry and the egg custard. There was nothing inscrutable here, but a plain-to-taste switch to a pre-mix of some type. Lard pastry for egg tarts is not just a Chinese technique. They also make egg tarts this way in Lecce, that wonder-carved city in southern Italy. They are very tasty with a naturally sweet ristretto, so it's worth looking again in your Italian deli or café.

Better still, and slowly taking over the world it seems, are Portuguese egg tarts, *pasties de nata*, made fantastically in Golbourne Road, way down at the bottom of Portobello Road market, or in the Portuguese bakeries of New Canterbury Road in Petersham, Sydney NSW, and just about everywhere else Portuguese cooks with a yen for home have settled. The filling is very sweet so it does not split or dry in the hot oven, for the more sugar a custard contains the longer it takes to set. The top will invariably caramelise a little and the pastry – well, this is one of the world's most delicious and complicated, properly two pastries, one pocketing the other. The outside can be so crisp and flaky it crackles when you bite into it, and there might even be an ephemeral back-taste of bitterness from some scorching, all the better as a contrast to the centre, which concentrates into a silken, golden, condensed cream. It's impossible to eat just one.

Like all sorts of egg or custard tarts these are best eaten warm; they are tasteless when too hot and too sweet when cold. Gratifyingly outrageous when eaten at the same time as an intoxicating mango.

Tin loaf: generic term for all loaves baked in metal tins, but especially applied to loaves which are long, rectangular and have a markedly high rise.

Vienna loaf: this is a style of bread rather than a shape of loaf and the difference is in the technique used. It is not often made commercially but is essentially milk dough baked in a bloomer shape. The shape has become so associated with the vienna loaf that ordinary bloomers or sourdough loaves are sold as 'viennas'.

Wholemeal bread: the extraordinary difference between domestic and commercial wholemeal loaves is due to ignorance as much as anything else. Dough made with only 100 per cent wholemeal flour should be handled as little as possible or it will not rise very well – yes, kneading dough of wholemeal flour gives worse not better results and is often the reason countless worthy health food shops and independent bakers offer such deadweight doorstoppers. If you like to knead, mix a high proportion of strong white flour with wholemeal flour.

A good 100% wholemeal loaf should feel heavy for its size but not leaden. When you squeeze it a little there should be definite resistance. If it is as soft as sliced bread there seems little point to it. For me the best test of a plain, firm wholemeal loaf is how it tastes and smells when a few days old: really good ones, with a very high or 100% wholemeal content develop a more complex, sweeter flavour.

wholemeal toast needs special care. When toasted enough it must be stood up or put into a toast rack so the outside steams dry and crisps: I can never forget my maternal grandmother eternally sending back wholemeal toast allowed to lie flat and steam soft – 'I asked for toast not sweaty bread', she would say. Quite.

Zwieback. this means 'twice baked' and these are rusks or slices of bread that have been baked dry, but which are usually thicker than commercial French or melba toast made the same way.

Storing

There are two great fallacies about bread storage: one concerns refrigeration and the other concerns air. Although refrigeration will certainly slow down the appearance and growth of mould, it can also hasten the drying process if any plastic storage wrapper or bag is not perforated.

Breads keep better if there is circulation of air. The reason is simple. In a space without an air flow there will be a build-up of the moisture given off by the bread. A moist atmosphere is a basic requirement for the growth of mould: the more tightly the bread is sealed, the better the chances of it going mouldy, and mouldy food is considered a prime encourager of many cancers: in a tightly sealed loaf the mould may simply have grown inwards, unseen.

Any container that can easily be washed and cleaned and is not porous is suitable for bread storage. If you have a bread bin that does not allow circulation of air, prop the lid open with a few pieces of cork.

Simply wrapping bread in a clean tea towel and storing it on a cool, airy shelf is just as effective.

Deep-freezing is the perfect way to maintain the moisture content of bread, provided each item is absolutely fresh. Each loaf must be well wrapped and sealed, and any type can be used, although crusty French loaves tend to crack and must be refreshed in the oven before use.

The dimensions of most domestic freezers dictate square-sided loaves are the most suitable for storing. They stack more easily, with almost no wasted space. Bread can be thawed slowly at room temperature, or finished in the oven, or thawed entirely in the oven.

At room temperature a fairly large loaf will take anything up to four hours to thaw completely. Condensation will form inside the freezer bag and settle on the bread, which will begin to dissolve the crust and this softened crust will shorten the life of the bread. To obtain a better crust, open the bag and take the bread out as soon as you can. Ten minutes in a moderate oven will finish the job and ensure you avoid serving a loaf with an icy heart.

When you need bread quickly, take it directly from the freezer to the oven, unwrapped. Half an hour, at a moderate temperature, is usually enough but use a metal skewer to check for a frigid core. Otherwise I find the automatic defrost programme in most microwaves very reliable and much quicker: but the crust will always be soft and a few minutes in a hot oven will fix that.

If you wish, take the opportunity to glaze or re-glaze your loaf by brushing it over quickly with some milk or cream.

Something Different

Sandwiches don't have to be made from bread: they can be just the filling, the way they are at PRET, aka Pret A Manger, the ubiquitous London sandwich shop and snack chain with outstanding coffee and exceptional food quality and staff standards. They layer sandwich fillings in a square, see-through, sandwich-sized container, say tuna salad on the base, a nicely dressed salad of sweet and bitter salad leaves next, and then some sliced tomato. You eat it with a fork, and they call it a sandwich without bread. Others might call it a layered salad, but it's a fantastic marketing idea and a great success. There is a place for squares in this ever-more hip world.

Sandwiches of sliced smoked salmon, with dill and parsley in a very light, horseradish-scented whipped cream, soured cream, marscapone or ricotta is very superior, but must be cut into very dainty shapes. Caviar in smoked salmon slices should be melded with the same sort of spread, or with soured cream heightened with cut Persian saffron of the very finest. Zest lemon or lime rind over the filling, rather than squeezing juice over the salmon, please.

Halloumi, the cheese from Cyprus you can fry in slices, makes superb hot sandwiches of almost anything, even if you are not a vegetarian: a very good chilled salad or hot, thick ratatouille will be as good as it can get as a one-slice open sandwich you'll have to eat with a knife and fork. A real sandwich of two pieces of fried halloumi filled with a flattened and grilled breast of chicken, rubbed with fresh garlic, dusted with ground Australian lemon myrtle, and finished with a few fresh thyme leaves and plenty of black pepper well rewards elbowing others out of the queue.

The ultimate breadless sandwich for meat eaters was the erstwhile Chateaubriand, the way they used to prepare it at the Savoy: a thick piece of aged fillet steak cooked between slices of sirloin, which were not served. Cooked directly under or over the heat the fillet would have burned before the centre was even restored to blood heat. These days chefs cut out the sirloin and cut the fillet steak thinner, averaging out everything but the price.

Easier is a simpler version of the carpet-bag steak, originally fillet steak slashed into a pocket and stuffed with oysters, the only possible combination of surf and turf. The simpler way is to make sandwiches of good sirloin, cut not too thick, and very fresh oysters, all held together with long, water-soaked bamboo skewers, or your grandmother's hatpins if that is easier. The steaks should be just cooked through but the oysters merely frightened enough by the heat to plump up in anger. Watch for the pins, and try to combine steak and oysters in every mouthful. Veal escallops make a nice change for this, for beaten much thinner, as paillards, they cook faster, are sweeter, and they very much like the lemon juice you should never put onto the beef version.

The Puerto Rican community in Chicago likes to make *jibaritos*, from thick slices of fried or grilled plantains. Thinly sliced steak is the favourite filling but anything Caribbean does nicely too – chicken breast marinaded with honey/lime/chilli perhaps or bean-based vegetarian patties. They are always topped with fried garlic and in neighbourhood restaurants come with lettuce, tomato, fried onion and a side of French fries or more plaintain, deep-fried as chips. Something different when it's your turn to do lunch?

In Australasia your sandwich or sanger is just as likely to be a Jiffy. These toast two pieces of bread with a filling but the pressure is applied only around the crust, sealing the substantial pouch made by the bread. Jiffys can be filled with everything from steak and kidney to chilli beans or a dried-fruit salad in a rose-scented cardamom syrup, and are excellent for eating out of the hand, provided you start to eat with a corner up-top, so the rest of the sandwich forms a sealed pocket. One bright spark is making a commercial go of take-aways selling very creative Jiffys. They deserve to go internationally ballistic.

As usual it's New York that's ahead of the rest of us – now with the Vietnamese *bahn ni*. This is a toasted baguette filled with pork, pickled vegetables, fresh coriander and mayonnaise, and that in turn is a variation of what only the cognoscenti in Dominican and Puerto Rican communities know they can find at a *lechonaria*, a shop selling only pork. Here pork freshly sliced from a roast leg is sliced into a hero roll, and when that's been heated in a sandwich grill, salad and mayonnaise are added. If you order it with a pork chop, they carve the meat away for the sandwich, and serve it with the bone on top so you truly do gnaw what you get for your dollars.

In Italian shops a great favourite is also roast pork, served with salted gravy and freshly made mozzarella; one serves hot Italian sausage sandwiches with *broccolini* (broccoli rabe) and ricotta, most serve sandwiches of pecorino-spiced meatballs, or breadcrumbed chicken – but you might have to wait 30 minutes, because the cutlets are only cooked when you order and then have to be dipped in sauce and served with more fresh mozzarella; the chicken parmigiana sandwich, and utterly unknown in Italy.

Back to the *bahn ni*: the classic starts with Vietnamese pork sausage (luncheon meat, bologna) and pork pâté, to which pickled daikon and carrot might be added, together with fresh coriander and a sweet Japanese mayonnaise. But grilled chicken thighs, pork chop or prawns marinated in fish sauce and lemon grass can take the place of the two porks, and a vegetarian version features Portobello mushrooms.

What's the best way to keep up to date with what New York is doing to sandwiches? Why, reading Ed Levine's column on Wednesdays in the *New York Times*.

Charcuterie

For thousands of years the pig furnished virtually all of the
meat of the European peasant and was prized both for its
ability to prosper where other animals starved and for being
almost totally edible.

For city dwellers, too, the pig was a mainstay. The urban poor scavenged the pigs that scavenged the litter of the filthy streets. Street pigs, which were usually ownerless, were common in New York well into the 19th century and in Naples until even later – they were the only street cleaning service this notoriously grubby city could maintain. All is very different now.

It's just as well the pig is the most prolific animal after the rabbit: one sow is supposed to be able to accumulate almost 6.5 million descendants in a mere 12 years. Even today it is still *the* meat of much of the world, especially about the Pacific and in China and south-east Asia.

Almost every fact about the pig is superlative. For every 45kg/100 lb of feed, a pig will produce 10kg/20 lb of flesh, whereas cattle would struggle to covert the same amount to 3kg/7 lb. Pigs are also the animal world's most efficient converters of carbohydrates into protein and fat.

Neither is any animal easier to preserve. Once their adult pigs had been fattened on the last of the summer's fruits and vegetables each cottager would in turn have hired the slaughterman, and neighbours would come to help preserve quickly the pigs' flesh for sustenance during the winter. The fine rear legs were made into hams, salted and then perhaps air dried or smoked. Some pieces were put into brine-cures until needed – salt pork. Other bits and bobs were minced and flavoured and cooked and put under protective coatings of the pig's fat – the pates and terrines. If you lived somewhere with low humidity, high in the mountains ideally, the same minced flesh and back fat might also have been forced into cleansed intestines to make *saucissons* or salami to be slung from rafters somewhere airy, and air-dried. The belly and loin were salted, dried and sometimes also smoked to make bacon or pancetta and the like, and if your pig was the type that had a long jaw, its cheeks were similarly treated and these would be called chaps. The head was made into brawn or head cheese. The small intestines were chopped and used as stuffing for sausages, chitterlings or *andouilletes*, or they were dried for later use as sausage casings. Even the blood was made into black puddings, thickened with barley or oatmeal and textured with glistening blobs of firm, back fat. Only a few choice pieces, like the liver and the trotters, were enjoyed fresh with the neighbourly helpers – but only if there was a real abundance, for the liver could also be used in faggots and pâtés, and the trotters could be boiled and stuffed and kept for ages in their own jelly or under fat.

Even then the dead pig kept working for you, for its dung is one of the best manures of all and throughout winter the rain would wash the nutrients back into the soil, there to feed new growth in spring. When Mao decreed he wanted there to be one pig per person throughout China, he was more practical than the French king Henri IV who wished there to be a chicken in the pot of each peasant.

Modern husbandry, refrigeration and transport give us fresh pig meat and offal throughout the year, and thus many cured pork products are increasingly difficult to obtain. Those marketed often cut traditional corners and are certainly far less salty or smoked than the originals, for once given the chance, modern palates decided to avoid the high-salt flavour of well-preserved meats. Indeed, nowadays processing methods have so changed the flavour of the pig and its products, the general public tends neither to recognize nor like, say, a genuine ham, which is relatively dry and dense. Instead they prefer the moistness and bright colour of products with artificially high water content, and that have been reformed into a false and often slimy tenderness. It is nothing for that ham in your sandwich to be made from muscles from pigs from three different countries, and for the yield, that is the amount of meat for sale after processing, to be greater than the weight of the original fresh meat.

Even to the uninitiated it must be obvious the avalanches of pork products passing through our shops and supermarkets are largely variations on a very few themes. As with cheese, it is important to be able to recognize those basic groups by sight, to understand the manufacturing process and the ultimate aims and then to be able to judge what is put in front of you. In the end, you should eat whatever you like best. My job is to give you some idea of what you should be getting.

The most exciting thing happening in the pig world is a dawning appreciation that different pigs do better at giving us some products than do others. These specifics were why this or that breed of pig was liked more or less in each geographical area of Europe, or of the USA or Canada or anywhere before modern manufacturing techniques required us all to like the same thing. Some breeds mature early in the season, some have bigger haunches and so make better hams, some eat specially well as pork, some are better or bacon. A pig with a short jaw was no use to people who lived around Bath and liked to make and eat Bath Chaps.

All over the USA, in Europe and Australasia heritage breeds are again being raised for their old specialties though you are still more likely to encounter them at farmers' markets than in shops or supermarkets.

Those you might find in the UK include:
Berkshire: a particularly light and delicate meat from an early maturing pig, originally from around Wantage, Berks.
British Lop: these attractive pigs with the large floppy ears that give them their name are Britain's rarest, with perhaps only a few hundred currently reared, but at least they are being watched and encouraged. The breed originated in Devon and Cornwall, and can be used for both meat and bacon.
British Saddleback: a black pig with a white saddle across its shoulders, and from the Dorset/Hampshire borders and Essex. The mostly black skin means it is protected from sunburn and so happily lives outdoors. The top-quality flesh is full-flavoured.
Essex: another pig we almost lost but that is now looking very secure, thanks to the interest of John Crawshaw and his Essex Pig Company. Direct descendants of the Saxon and Norman pigs that foraged in ancient Epping Forest, these modern ones roam freely in ancient woodland, eating wild garlic, acorns and chestnuts to produce a marbled meat that's particularly sweet and delicious.
Gloucestershire Old Spot: from the Vale of Severn, these delightful pigs were traditionally kept in orchards and fattened on windfalls. Another well-marbled meat, sweet, delicious and tasting the way pork should.

Large Black: a West Country breed, much admired for hardiness and mothering skills, that makes very succulent pork and bacon. Because its black skin protects it from sunburn it's happy to live outdoors with minimal attention from the farmer.

Middle White: an early maturing breed, this time from Yorkshire. Its meat is particularly sweet and the Japanese, who know a good thing when they taste it, have even built a shrine in this breed's honour. Middle White piglets are the preferred choice as suckling pigs.

Tamworth: from the Midlands, it's a ginger-coloured pig particularly prized as a bacon producer, but you'll find the rest of the flesh is deliciously full flavoured.

Of course wherever you go you might find a local breed or variation. In New Zealand watch for any offer to taste *kumi-kumi*. The thin, still largely wild, pigs of NZ introduced by Captain Cook in the late 18th century, are known as Captain Cookers. Once domestic British breeds were brought by later settlers, they interbred to create pigs of monumental fatness and every imaginable colour combination, yet *kumi-kumi* manage to keep a hint of the bigger, richer flavour of wild pig meat. Particularly good when cooked in a *hangi*, the pit oven of the Maori.

While supermarkets worship consistency of shape, size and flavour as retail gods, the public is slowly realizing variety is far worthier of praise. The larger retail world is listening too, and in Britain at least, supermarkets are offering products that detail the type of pig they came from: some are even breeding exclusively for their own customer.

When fresh, the main differences you are likely to find between the flesh of free-range heritage pigs and the modern factory pig are a more savoury flavour and a thicker layer of fat. Then the fun begins, because the same variety of pig fattened on acorns will taste different from a brother or sister fed corn or that has been allowed to rootle, the way pigs should.

Throughout Europe special breeds have been maintained unchanged, the pigs for genuine Parma ham and the Spanish *pata negra* pigs for instance, and those on Corsica and Sardinia: even if just once, you should pay the extra for the real thing, so you have a valid taste reference for the future and so you understand spluttering food writers and super-star chefs are not talking drivel when they complain about factory-produced, supermarket-encouraged pork products.

Charcuterie is widely used to describe the family of pork products that follow. In France you would go only to a *charcutier*, to buy them, and in Italy to a *salumeria*.

Uncooked, Air-dried Meats

The best-known air-dried produce are the 'raw' hams such as the Parma, Bayonne and *Pata Negra*, and the salami of Italy, the *saucissons secs* of France, which are essentially the same thing. Most are meant to be eaten as they are, but English air-dried hams are usually cooked.

Hams

Such sweet, air-dried hams as Parma, thin slices of which are constantly assassinated by luke-warm hunks of dreadful melon, differ from salami in two ways: (a) they are always brined before drying and (b) they are left whole. True hams are made only from the detached rear legs of the pig; if the leg is cured while still attached to the side of the animal it should be called a gammon, and this is how Wiltshire hams are cured.

The traditional way to get fine flavour and texture from an air-dried, uncooked ham is to begin with dry-salting. The raw meat is rubbed with dry salt at regular intervals. This slowly draws the fluids from the flesh that in turn dissolves the salt, which is then absorbed back. The high salt content preserves the flesh, as bacteria cannot flourish in such conditions. There is always the risk the brine will not penetrate right to the bone and the unsalted meat there will go off, causing a very nasty taste and potential danger known as bone taint. The men who traditionally do such salting are great specialists, knowing each leg is different and thus requires more or less salt and might need more or fewer months to cure.

It is by the addition of sugar and spices to the salt that differing styles of cure and flavour are encouraged, and naturally the food eaten by the pig will also have some influence. The famous Virginia hams should be made from pigs fed on peanuts and peaches; the Smithfield (which is in Virginia, not London) pig should dine on acorns and other wild nuts before being fattened on corn and peanuts. Few of the animals responsible for furnishing the 'Virginia' hams sold in the United Kingdom have ever seen a peanut, let alone a peach.

A faster method of salting is simply to soak the meat in a brine bath, but this brand stroke curing always leads to a tougher end product. The newest technology of all automatically weighs each raw ham and then injects it with a predetermined proportion of brine, ideally using a major artery as the main point of entry. By using the animal's own natural channels the brine travels quickly and evenly throughout the flesh. Results seem better than the brine bath, but experts say they can still detect a certain toughness. Today more and more, faster and faster curing techniques are being invented, but none so far has been able to identify the subtle differences recognized by a man rubbing in salt with his hands.

The salting's task is to mix with the liquid content of the meat and then to drain it, leaving a preservative salt content behind. Once the brine has been drained, the hams must be dried further. This can lead to a 'green' or unsmoked ham, or to a smoked ham, and once again the time and type of wood used will influence the flavour. In Ireland peat smoke is used, in Virginia apple and hickory wood are popular, oak is common in the UK and manuka or ti-tree is commonly used in New Zealand.

Smoking and/or further drying allows the final development of flavour, and can take as much as 24 months and this is why real hams are so expensive; the cooked pressed hams, hams for slicing and those sold sliced, will have been salt-cured but neither drained nor dried. Indeed factory curing adds ingredients that retain added water, so virtually all commercial ham and bacon ends up weighing more than they did when they arrived to be cured, and the extra is all water.

Sometimes air-dried hams are boned before curing, some are boned after curing. Beware of boned hams that have too obviously been pressed into an even shape. This is often done after curing but before drying and so some of the liquor is expressed too soon, which is not conducive to the greatest possible development of flavour. If you want a traditional ham that is also boneless, it is better to choose a ham cured whole and then later de-boned. It would be pointless to attempt to estimate the different types of air-dried hams produced, even in Britain, for those who make them on a farm will do it differently each time, and even the well-known ones vary a little. But if you have the inclination, luck (and money) here is the guide to what you may find.

Britain

Up and down the country small producers make an ever-increasing range of air-dried hams, both for cooking and increasingly for eating raw.

In Romsey one company has created a new breed with blood from the wild pig, and is apparently having success converting this lean flesh into very tasty charcuterie of all kinds. Another producer in Ripon offers air-cured, oak-smoked haunches of farmed wild boar. In Cumberland, Ashdown makes very large numbers, comparatively, of both ham types from conventional pigs and to considerable acclaim and are also fighting the battle to re-establish macon hams, made from sheep. Yet, when I wrote in *The Sunday Telegraph* about real ham and gave addresses of suppliers, it generated more complaints than anything else. As far as I can see the produce was probably good, but expectations were for something different – few appreciated the firm texture and saltiness of real ham. Or was it that they did not know how to cook it? I have had ham from the same suppliers and it was almost too good to eat

Still, it is an industry well worth supporting, and whenever you are out and about in the country, do look out for local ham makers and give them a try, as many sell in small portions and sliced packs, too. Apart from Ashdown there are a couple of other names you might expect to find nationally and even the Prince of Wales' Duchy Originals brand has entered the market with products bound to be as good as it gets.

Bradenham: the Bradenham cure includes molasses, and is both smaller and more expensive than most hams. It has a very black skin and a highly individual flavour, drawn both from the molasses and such spices as juniper and needs to be soaked for a good 72 hours before being baked. It has been made in Chippenham for just over two centuries but now is made by one of the big conglomerate companies and may be disappearing.

Suffolk: this is quite sweet and is smoked before being allowed to develop its 'blue bloom'. I rather like this one for it is a rich colour and good full flavour.

York: well-known even in Europe where many an anonymous ham is sold as **Jambon d'York:** some would say the anonymity is a blessing, for otherwise those who know the real thing would do awful things to the manufacturers. A real York ham is blessedly mild and pink and might have been smoked to varying degrees. A dry salt cure is used rather than brine, so any sweetness is due to careful tending during the maturation, which takes three months and should be accompanied by the growth of a green mould. A York needs to be soaked 12-24 hours before cooking, and is always sold cooked.

NB:Britain alone in Europe seems to be preserving the tradition of curing ham on the bone, and long may it last Equally curiously the bullying and insensitivity of supermarkets is increasing the choices of traditional ham and bacon products in Britain. Supermarkets increasingly specify only very young pigs, as young as four to five months, something hardly profitable for the farmer and a disaster as far as the educated public is concerned. At this age the flesh has barely formed texture or flavour; for seven months is traditionally considered the best minimum age. Unable to make ends meet by selling to supermarkets, pig farmers have turned to making and marketing their own products, and have mercifully turned to traditional methods to guarantee individuality to you and better returns for themselves. Everywhere you look – even in the very supermarkets who hastened this revolution – there are more and more dry-cure bacons and more and more farmers are successfully making air-dried ham products, even though Britain's weather is about as unsuitable as possible.

France

It is said the pigs of Corsica are closest to those of the Ancient Romans, and they are still matured on forest-foraged chestnuts and acorns until their haunches give the correct hollow ring when thumped: find Corsican hams, salami and the like on the island, or from countless stalls in markets in the south of France, for a genuine taste across the ages.

Jambon de Bayonne IGP: the best known. This is eaten raw and differs from the air-dried hams of Spain and Italy by being lightly smoked.

Jambons des Campagnes: local variations of the Bayonne and depending on their excellence will be recommended for use as they are, or for cooking. *Jambons sec des Ardennes IGP* and *Noix de Jambon sec des Ardennes IGP* deserve their elevated status.

Germany

One of my favourite hams of all is the **Westphalian**. It is a darker colour than many and quite smoky. I know some experts, such as the late food writer Tom Stobart OBE, believe its smoky taste is better without accompaniments but I think the more assertive flavour is a fine complement to a really succulent pear or syrupy fig, which can sometimes overwhelm the delicate Bayonne or Parma.

Black Forest: is even more highly smoked than Westphalian, and is thus useful as a foil in mixed sandwiches or salads when a subtle product might be overwhelmed. As well as these two, there are many regional smoked hams, often simply called country hams – you can tell at a glance if they are air-dried by the translucency of the flesh – or one of the equally populous cooked hams, some smoked, some not.

Ammerlander Schinken: is made in north-west Germany's Ammerland, close to the North Sea. First dry salted in a mixture that includes brown sugar and spices, it is then cold smoked in beech and oak smoke for around 10 weeks. This superb ham is notably mild in flavour and smokiness and is particularly admired when combined with white asparagus, or fresh breads.

Italy

Prosciutto is Italian for ham; if you want one of her excellent air-dried hams you must ask for prosciutto crudo. But which one? Parma ham, kindly remember is not a collective for all Italian air-dried hams, but a very specific product protected by DOP status. It is breaking the law to sell or to call anything but a genuine Parma ham by this name. It's done every second, all round the world.

Culatello di Zibello DOP: made along the River Po in the Emilia Romagna for many centuries, this is a distinctive string-tied pear shape, aged at least 11 months and is particularly sweet and delicate in flavour.

Prosciutto di Carpegna DOP: the smallest producers and the most expensive prosciutto crudo, produced in a small area between San Marino and Urbino. They are not covered in fat for maturation and come in two versions. **San Leo** is delicate, sweet, and entrancingly balanced on the palate. **La Ghianda** is much more aromatic and intense, having been flavoured with herbs.

Prosciutto di Modena DOP: you should taste nothing of salt in the notably intense sweetness of this ham. The pigs can be grown in a number of regions but the hams must be made and matured at an altitude of around 900 metres in the province of Modena, particularly in the hills and valleys close to the Panaro river.

Prosciutto di Norcia IGP: perhaps the least well-known prosciutto crudo. Made in the districts of Valnerini at about 500 metres above sea level, it has a rather light flavour, and salt should be barely present.

Prosciutto di Parma DOP: around eight million hams are produced from pigs bred and grown all over Italy, but to the same standards. The specially sweet flavour, moistness and light skin colour are a result of their two-step curing: during the second stage the skin is covered in peppered fat, slowing moisture loss and preventing discolouration. Look for the branded ducal crown and the word PARMA: without these they could be made almost anywhere from any sort of pig.

Prosciutto di San Daniele DOP: the hams are flattened and always keep the trotter. The small production area is in the far north east. They are branded with an SD.

Prosciutto Toscano DOP: they've been salt-curing pork in Tuscany since at least the Middle Ages and by the 15th century laid down production regulations. The cool valleys and wooded hills lend a particular discreet savouriness to Tuscan prosciutto, which will be rather round in shape and weigh 8-9 kg.

Prosciutto Veneto Berico-Euganeo DOP: only 400,000 are made in the hills between the provinces of Padova and Vicenza. They are branded VENETO and display the winged lion of Venice.

Valle d'Aosta Jambon de Bosses DOP: by the 13th century the town of Saint-Rhemy-en-Bosses was already known for its air-dried hams. Slightly flattened and tending to red rather than pink flesh it offers a salt tang with gamey nuances and should weigh at least 7 kg. Saint-Rhemy is only 21 kms from Aosta and is where winds from four mountain ranges meet, perfect conditions for safe air-curing.

Speck: you will find this rather like German air-dried hams, for it comes from the Alpine valleys of Bolzano, in other words the South Tyrol. The smoking gives away the connection. Although speck is the German word for bacon, this isn't.

Speck dell'Alto Adige IGP: thought of as a sort of bacon, this is nonetheless made from a boned leg, that is dry cured with such aromatics as pepper, chilli, garlic and juniper berry and then cold smoked. It has been made in the Bolzano region (but without the chilli) since at least the early 14th century.

Spain

Spain claims to be the biggest producer of hams in the world. **Jamon Serrano:** the basic air-dried product, which is guaranteed up to very high standards if stamped with the elaborate 'S' of its consortium and has taken at least nine months to produce. This includes the *calado*, when it is poked in three places by a sharpened horse bone to test for maturity and sweetness by smell. Next up will be **Jamon Iberico**, made with ancient types of pig in the south-western provinces

of Spain, which are finished on acorns and can be air-dried and aged for 24 months.

Grander by far are the *Pata Negra* hams. Produced exclusively from the small black-footed Iberian pigs raised in the west of the country and that are also fattened on acorns, said to give a truffle-like flavour to the flesh. Like cockatoos, they have a riveting ability to take whole acorns into one side of their mouth and to spit out the shells from the other, whilst chewing without cease.

A welcome sign of the real jamon Iberico and *pata negra* hams (often the same thing) is that the cured flesh is streaked with acorn-based fat that's not only high in healthier mono-unsaturates but which also softens or melts at room temperature, giving the palate almost instant access to its truly unique, bigger and more gratifying flavour. You should serve these hams at room temperature and in very thin slices with absolutely no accompaniment other than a chilled fino sherry or a young red wine, a *crianza*. The Spanish believe anything else you might do debases the product. Ferran Adrià, avant-garde chef of Spain's famed El Bulli restaurant is an expected exception and serves what looks like cherries dipped in white chocolate, but the creamy shell is actually the fat from a jamon iberico.

Even the Spanish will admit their system of grading hams is not consistent throughout the country, but there are a couple of clues you should look for. The words *de bellota* mean the pigs put on at least a third of their weight while eating only foraged acorns plus whatever else is on the forest floor: if you find the word *recebo*, this means they are one grade down and were fattened on a diet of rather fewer acorns: *pienso* means they have been fattened only on grains.

Some to look for:

Jamon de Guijuelo: small hams with pink to purple flesh likely to be a little salty and made only from the black-footed Iberian pig or agreed others with 50 per cent of that blood. Class 1 is fattened only on acorns, Class 2 starts with acorns and finishes with fodder, Class 3 is fed on fodder only. These hams are guaranteed under Spain's *Denominacion de Origen* system and are not the real thing if they do not show the symbol, no, not even if your retailer charges three or four times the usual price. The very best Guijelo hams are thought to be those of Joselito.

Jamons de Teruel: also protected by a Spanish DOC, but made from bigger pigs. The meat is sweeter and more delicate, and made from Landrace and related breeds.

Lacon Gallego IGP: not strictly speaking a ham because this is always made with the shoulder or foreleg of pigs; the trotter is always left attached. A label saying Traditional Galician Lacon means the pigs have been fed the old way, on acorns, chestnuts, grain and tubers: if it says only Galician Lacon, the pigs have been raised on approved commercial feeds. The pink to purple-red flesh is sweet but has a definite saltiness.

Other labels with DOC accreditation, or that are expecting it, are **Jamons de Huelva, Dehasa de Extramadura, Sierra de Sevilla** and **Los Pedroches de Cordoba.**

The Rest of Europe

Once you start looking, you will find most European countries also have air-dried hams that are worth exploring. The Dutch have the smoked **Guelder ham** and the **Coburger**, which is only the top part of the ham. The Swiss make an excellent **Rohschinken** , a lovely word that translates as raw ham. The Belgians are justly proud of their **Jambon d'Ardennes** and the **Prague** ham, from what was called Czechoslovakia, of course, is considered the best air-dried ham of all to be cooked and served hot.

Of all the rare and wonderful treats I have enjoyed I specially remember homemade hams on the Isle of Elba, encrusted with peppers and herbs in a way I've seen nowhere else. Almost mahogany in colour, the flesh resisted the teeth but then released a flavour that hung on the tongue for hours. With a glass of chilled Elban wine and a sun-warmed peach direct from the bough, I had lunched enough, and hardly ever better.

Salami and Saucissons

It is a dreadful shock for many to learn that true salami is actually uncooked pig meat, raw pork; even more are mortified to the point of nausea to learn the origin of some salami casings. And almost no one believes the white powder on these skins is not flour or 'preservative' but is an encouraged bacterial mould.

Salami are usually made from raw pork minced with back fat and, sometimes, with a little beef. In France a variety of spices and herbs plus salt and pepper will be added. Italians use fewer spices and herbs but are more likely than the French to incorporate beef, or to use donkey, geese or wild boar.

The flavour of salami is first determined by the proportion of meat to fat and then by the texture to which each ingredient is minced. In my experience the larger the pieces of meat and fat, the sweeter the salami; look for the plump **Jesus de Lyon** if you like this style. If you like strongly flavoured salami, go for those with a fine texture and/or high fat content, both of which can be judged by sight of the cut edge; the Italian Milano and the Hungarian salami are popular examples.

Further effects on eventual flavour can be expected from the casing into which the basic preparation is forced. Ideally they should be the cleansed intestine of the pig. As each part of an intestine harbours or attracts different types of bacteria and accompanying enzymes, so will each part donate a different flavour to a salami. A long thin salame will dry at a different speed from a thicker or shorter one and this will affect the eventual flavour, too. Some of the casings are quite extraordinary; the large *saucisson sec* called **Rose de Lyon**, uses the last few feet of the pig's large intestine, including the puckered sphincter: the saucisson's name has nothing to do with its colour.

Once the prepared mixture is encased it might then be tied overall with string in a traditional manner or simply tied both ends so it may be suspended. With minimum attention in a constant temperature, each salame should lose about 35 per cent of its weight through evaporation of its water content. The time taken may vary from a few weeks to many months depending on the size and the degree of dryness required. Some Italian salami are cured not in air but by being pressed between boards. The boards, which absorb the liquid expressed, are changed at regular intervals and these products, immediately recognizable by their flatness, thus cure faster than those left to evaporate in the air.

During the air curing process some salami will regularly be wiped free of exudate, some will not; some may be dusted with talcum to seal any holes in the casings, others will be dipped into herbs or black pepper. In Hungary and Italy a fine white ambient bacterium is encouraged to grow on the skins, because the enzymic action of its by-products further tenderizes and flavours the meat. Eventually the water content falls below the degree necessary to harbour and encourage harmful bacteria, and then highly specialized and localised bacterial and enzymic agents get to work, developing flavour safely in this benign, raw-meaty environment.

Of course modern techniques have been applied to salami, too. Many have artificial casings and may even contain preservatives. The startling pink of **Danish** salami is due to the meat being pre-salted, a process that incorporates saltpetre, which gives rise to the hue: the meat is lightly cooked, too. In humid areas you simply can't make traditional air-dried salami and saucissons. Instead the mixture must be heat-treated to make it safe and then bacterial action continues, keeping it safe and improving the flavour: smoking usually gives added flavour and protection. Provided the pork is not cut up finely, the texture and flavour can be very like the real thing, and even if not, can be exceptionally good.

The theory behind the preservation and long life of all air-dried products is that all bacteria dangerous to humans require water to flourish. Salami's combination of high fat content and low water level means a properly made and stored salame is impervious to the attention of putrefactive influences. But manufacturing techniques that do not allow proper drying can make a salame very dangerous indeed to eat. When the French government tested salami samples from throughout the country they found only the largest and oldest manufacturers could be relied upon consistently to be absolutely safe. I will never eat salami that is soft or spongy in the centre or that smells sharply; it may simply be too young but it could be incorrect, and then have unpleasant digestive effects.

Essentially salami may be stored for a long time in a cool airy place without refrigeration, indeed they can be left so long they dessicate, but they'll still be safe to eat. Once cut, I reckon they should be treated like a fresh product, with the cut end sealed from air-borne contaminants with paper or film, and also refrigerated. It would be different if you had been brought up eating these products, because your digestive system would have developed any number of protective bacteria to cope with salamis and *saucissons secs* left about in warm temperatures. Not for me though, and certainly a very bad idea for the young and the old: it's still a very bad idea to eat warm salami even if you are somewhere between being young or old.

An Italian salame made only of pork will bear a metal tag stamped with an 'S', if beef is included it says SB. It is a commonly held fallacy that most Italian salami include garlic. Some do, but it is rare, for it is likely to go rancid. There are salami with a garlic-like flavour, but this is rarely induced by garlic itself. One shop where you'll be sure to find specialties is Villandry, in Great Portland Street, London W1. There I found a choice of wild boar *cinghiale* salami, a goose *salame d'oca* that left a discreet sweet goose fat flavour in the mouth and a salame made from the *toros de Chiannina*, and that's some bull! Once kept exclusively for local gourmands, more and more producers are also selling their truffled salamis, expensive of course, but a few slices enliven an *aufschnitt* no end.

If you see salami from Desulo in Sardinia, buy without a second thought. Made high in mountains, these products are made with yet another local breed of pig, the Desulo, and have amongst the biggest, sweetest flavours I've found and that like all quality food, linger on the palate for ages.

For farmers' markets and gourmet shops all round the world, younger butchers, Richard Saunders of Auckland for instance, are managing to combine good traditional techniques with very untraditional meats. He, for example, makes salami from venison or with part venison: he's made salami with wild duck that were superb and actually tasted like duck and he has made some with lamb. He's experimented with using smoked peppercorns, dried orange zest and smoked paprika too. His growing posse of admirers and customers love him to experiment with greater or lesser coarseness of fat, or of peppercorn, more or less chilli, more or less drying time, more or less smoke, thicker or thinner shapes. Richard's regular Saturday tastings draw the crowds at Sabato, a great supporter of new food artisans in Auckland. Believe me, tradition is superb, but these new variations should be encouraged at every turn. Just think, if you will, of what might be the taste of a lightly-smoked salami that includes wild-duck breast, dried mandarin zest, a little juniper berry and coarsely ground, smoked black peppercorns . . .

Cooked Salami

In countries without the right climate, or without the right attitudes, salami are made a modern, slightly different way: they are heat treated, often in conjunction with smoking. The heat must raise them to an officially specified temperature to kill unwanted bacteria, but other flavour-developing bacteria have been introduced; the process is a type of fermentation. The end products are firmer than most air-dried salami, but can be just as remarkable and individual as Richard Saunders is demonstrating. For those who don't like to eat foreign, or for children, cooked salami offers a genuine choice. None can possibly be called traditional, but in a few more decades the good ones should have such a status. It goes without saying you should avoid any that seem to be all chemical, otherwise, don't be a snob.

But, back to tradition. Finely textured **Milano** salami contain garlic and must mature three or four months; **Napoli** is a coarse, lightly smoked type which matures in a couple of months and is rather aromatic; **Felino** is flavoured with white wine and is notably slim, lean and delicate; **Salami di Varzi DOP** made between the Po and the Apennines, are coarse meat with fine fat, garlic and red wine and after four months have a soft texture and sweet taste. **Finocchio** or words like that indicate fennel seed is included, and these are always particularly good to eat. **Salame Brianza DOP**, **Salame Piacentino DOP** and **Salamini alla cacciatora DOP**: ten regions, in the north and centre of Italy, make these air-dried sausages no more than 20cm long and 13-20cm in diameter, called *alla cacciatore* because they were so convenient for hunters to carry.

Salsiccia di Calabria DOP: small sausages made only from shoulder of pork and with no added fat. The fine chopping promotes high flavour, complemented with black pepper or with chilli in lesser or greater (usually) amounts. When still quite fresh they are used in traditional cooking or are grilled: matured, they are sliced for snacks like any other salami. Their delightful dialect name is *sozizzi*.

Nduja sounds African and can be as searingly hot as that continent, but is a curious spreadable salami made in Calabria: essentially a paste of what's left over once the noble cuts have been used for true salami but which is murderously mixed with locally grown chilli pepper, giving intense colour and fire, rather as anti-flavour. It is lightly smoked with both resinous and aromatic woods and can then be stored a year or more.

North of Barcelona they have been making **Salchichon de Vic IGP**, also known as **Llonganissa de Vic IGP** since at least the mid15th century. Made from good lean pork, from the leg, shoulder etc, it has fat and whole, or crushed, peppercorns added to it and then cured in natural casings. The area in which it's cured, 500 metres plus above sea level, has developed a unique fungal flora, and it's this that adds a flavour no other Spanish area can copy.

Both Hungary and Switzerland make salami flavoured with paprika, well worth seeking out, but some are really very hot. Much more easily available is Spanish **Chorizo**, but be certain you are buying a slicing sausage, for the same name is also given to scalded sausages flavoured with paprika, which must be cooked before eating. Chorizos are almost the only sausages that do not use a clear casing for cooked or air-dried and an opaque casing for cooked versions. The paprika content can vary from comforting to corrosive, so take time and good advice when buying, perhaps from Garcia on Portobello Road, one of London's greatest Spanish specialty shops.

Germany makes a swag of salamis, but only the **Greusener** from Thuringia has a DOP: it's a coarsely cut salami with a slight garlic flavour and plenty of chunky black peppercorns and its unique flavour is said to come from the micro-climate of the valley in which it's made.

Other Air-Dried Meats

Some countries go to great lengths to dry mutton and lamb, but these inevitably end up being rather too special in flavour for any but the initiated, the starving or Viking ravishers. There are beef products more worth the exploring. They are **Bresaola** from northern Italy and **Bundnerfleisch** from the Grisons in Switzerland. **Bresaola della Valtellina** from the province of Sondrio is the only one with DOP status and can be made with beef or veal. They should be notably sweet without the slightest touch of acidity. Fatless and very hard, they were originally fillet or some other lean cut and are never chopped or minced. To serve, they must be sliced very thinly indeed, and although constantly served with drinks in super-luxe Gstaad, I always thought these translucent, scarlet slithers tasted of soap – even when served on a plate and moistened with excellent olive oil and a little lemon juice. Recently I discovered a sign for a venison version, at Selfridges Food Hall, but that's all they had, the sign. **Cecina de Leon IGP** is an ancient salted and air-cured beef product from northern Spain, made from a number of good cuts – rump or topside for instance. Once cured it is cold-smoked over oak or holm oak and so comes with a good spectrum of flavours but is not salty and should be very sensuous in texture.

I far prefer **Coppa Cruda**, from Italy. This is a piece of air-dried pork mainly from the neck, pressed into a skin. It has often some quite noticeable runs of fat throughout; *coppa cruda* is essential in antipasto, sweet and satisfying and acceptable to those who do not usually like salami. They also make it on Sardinia, and this is probably the best there is other than **Coppa Piacentina DOP**, made throughout the province of Piacenza, but no higher than 900m above sea level.

From the other end of the pig comes **Capocollo di Calabria DOP**. Made only from home-reared pigs aged two, that have never eaten industrial feed, but have lived on domestic leftovers: for their last several months this also includes acorns, chestnuts, broad beans, chickpeas or whatever their owners grow. It's a type of air-dried ham really, made from the upper part of the loins, which are dry salted for a week and then pressed, peppered and wrapped, and hung to cure for five to 12 months. Thinly sliced, usually as a first course, as snacks or on bread. Some authorities say *capocollo* is made from head (*capo*) and shoulder (*collo*)meat, and that when well matured, this is then coppa; the definition I give is correct and official, and the *capo* (*head*) is actually the top of the rear (*cullo*) i.e. the loin

Soppressata de Calabria DOP is another of the products that straddles several categories; made from the best pork loin meat, which is very finely chopped and then, unusually, cooked with chilli or black pepper. The meat is stuffed into natural intestine, tied and then weighted for a few days, which gives the classic flattened cylinder. Finally they are matured for at least six months. Used as a special treat either to start meals or to honour special occasions or special guests, soppressata is considered one of the very finest of all Italian pork products.

Sobrasada de Mallorca IGP was probably introduced to Mallorca (it has stopped being Majorca) by Romans and was made the same way until the discovery of the New World: by the late 16th century paprika was being added to the rosemary, thyme and oregano which still give it a unique attractiveness to its flavour. Sobrasada de Mallorca can be made with any sort of pork, but *Sobrasada de Mallorca de cerdo negro* can be made only with the indigenous breed that has been fattened traditionally.

Lachsshinken, is a great but increasingly rare German treat. It is lightly-salted, slightly-dried, lightly-smoked loin of pork, wrapped in fine fat. It is soft, meltingly so, and its name means 'salmon ham' for the cure, the texture and the flavour are not a millions miles from a lightly smoked salmon. It should be served just below room temperature in quite thin but not too thin slices, and should never be cooked, although it would be sublime. Spain makes **lomo** air-dried loin of pork that can be further flavoured with herbs and spices.

I suppose **biltong** from South Africa should be included here too. It can be almost any kind of meat but the source makes little difference – it is all pretty filthy except for ostrich biltong and that is absolutely filthyexcept for one I found being made in the UK, which tasted of sweet porcini. **Pemmican** was air-dried buffalo meat, somehow combined with cranberries, and bear fat, too. As well as being a staple of the American Indian, it was popular with early Arctic explorers. The modern equivalent in the United States is something called **jerked beef** or **jerky**; it is strips of sun-dried beef, and last time I was in Los Angeles everyone carried some around as a low calorie way to assuage hunger. Now I understand they eat nothing but strawberries, unless it is Wednesday when they eat nothing but pineapple, and jerky is once again only available where people hunt and shoot and fish.

Swiss **Rospeck** is air-dried belly of pork/ streaky bacon, and thus first cousin of pancetta. **Valle d'Aosta Lardo d'Arnad DOP:** unrendered salt-cured back fat, pinky white, and with a few streaks of meat towards the top. Made only in Arnad in the Aosta region, this lardo has a pedigree documented to 1763.

Serving

Salami and saucissons are made to be eaten simply, with bread, and perhaps some cheese and a few unobtrusive pickles. The Scandinavians, Dutch and Germans tend to serve them for breakfast, with bland sweet cheeses, too.

In general I don't think salamis should be cooked, even those that have been heat-treated rather than air-dried, but a leftover end-piece of salami might be cut into chunks to finish a spaghetti sauce or for inclusion in a salad. Or you can roll slices around a flavoured cream cheese as a snack. They should always be skinned, unless coated with herbs or peppers. If you have a piece that you are to slice yourself, peel it first.

On one of my cruises through Harrods Food Halls I found an exception to the rule about cooking air-dried salamis, the *salama da sugo* of Ferarra. Made with finely chopped meat, spices and red wine since the 14th-century, it is put into a skin and tied with eight lengths of string into a rather pointy Christmas pudding shape. These eighth portions are now vacuum packed, hence their availability in Harrods. It has a big savoury flavour when hot and the sugo which melts into it as you reheat it seems to be pink-tinted fat – certainly tomato isn't or shouldn't be there. Even more suspicious for a 14th century specialty, the manufacturers suggest it be served with mashed potatoes, and even illustrate it like this. Whatever the truth, it is delicious and unusual – an arresting way to start a meal.

Slicing and serving air-dried or cooked ham

There is a proper way to go about slicing ham on the bone, as you might expect, and you should look for this if you're going to spend the money. The technique is sensibly based on what will desiccate soonest. Thus, you should begin with the flesh of the narrow shank and then move on to the shank half, that is the narrower of the two portions on either side of the bone, essentially the upper front when the leg was alive. Only then should you move on to the thicker juicier butt half, as it is the longest lasting portion. Do it the other way round and by the time you get to the shank it will have dried so much it will be inedible.

A serrated knife should never be used and the fat must only be cut away as you go, for it helps protect the uneaten flesh and keep it moist. Each slice should be cut towards the shank,

Pancetta

This is made with the same pork-belly cut that gives us streaky bacon, but the salt-cure is flavoured with such herbs and spices as nutmeg, fennel seeds, pepper and garlic and the result subsequently air-dried for up to four months. There are commercial versions that are heat-cured, giving results faster and more cheaply; I've even known one that included dark rum in the cure and this was exceptionally good.

Pancetta was traditionally cured between boards, *pancetta tesa*, which gives an old-time shape to the slices: as markets for traditional cured products ever expand the flattened version is seen more and more. One version is rather heavily covered with dried rosemary and another made in Sardinia from the Desulo pig is coated in black pepper.

Pancetta is just as likely to be rolled, *pancetta arrotolata*; there is also a *magretta* version, almost totally fat free, a contradiction in terms. There are cheaper pancetti, made by faster, less traditional methods and in my experience these are very good, and here and there have flavour, so it's usually sow meat.

Pancetta is regularly specified instead of bacon in American recipes; but it is really only worth paying the extra money if you are using enough to appreciate the flavour. A few slices or chunks in a large stew are pointless. Quite a lot of pancetta in a simple pasta dish is ambrosial. However, once I discovered you can and should also eat pancetta in its uncooked state, this opened a spectacular new world, for here you really appreciate its subtle extra flavouring. I know the idea of raw bacon sounds worrying but it's more than bacon because of the air-drying: bacon is never air-dried.

Serve pancetta in see-through slices instead of more expensive air-dried Italian prosciutti – with fresh figs or melon, with dark-red plums or perfumed white peaches. When pancetta is wrapped around a chilled lychee or rambutan, the world seems to stand still

Once, I served pancetta as part of a buffet choice with smoked salmon. Many people found the combination wondrous and quite without the slightest prompting from me. But it's quite as memorable with fried eggs, or with scrambled eggs, yes, particularly if it's scrambled eggs with smoked salmon.

Pancetta de Calabria DOP is easily spotted because the skin is red with chilli pepper, and made only in Calabria from piglets four months old. **Pancetta Piacentina DOP** comes rolled into a cylinder weighing between 5 and 8kg. It is noted for a characteristic sweet spiciness and a good aftertaste.

with your left hand behind the knife. Once sliced, or if you have bought slices, I think refrigeration is recommended, but let them warm slightly, still covered, before serving or you will not enjoy the essential sweetness.

I grant great melon is a good accompaniment, but better by far are fresh figs or a juicy pear, or some seriously fragrant mango: fresh lychee or mangosteen or rambutan are more 'creative' accompaniments, and why not? If the Medicis or the Doges of Venice or countless Holy Roman emperors and Popes had known about them, I bet they would have served these tropical flavour bombs with air-dried hams too...

It is also good to serve such a ham sliced onto a plate and scattered with an excellent dressing made with olive oil and lemon juice or a mildly flavoured vinegar, sherry vinegar particularly. As a wrapping of flavour and excellence for special vegetables, whole truffles, even fillets of fish, translucent slices of uncooked ham cannot be bettered. But the more robust flavour of the smoked Westphalian ham is usually more appreciated than the rather fragile unsmoked or lightly smoked varieties.

The end-of-knuckle pieces are delicious diced and thrown into a sauce or pasta dish, or when finely minced as the basis of a stuffing or worked into a Bolognese-style pasta sauce; but do check for rancidity.

Raw beef products are eaten sliced extremely thinly, sometimes also sitting in a little first class olive oil spiked with a little lemon juice, or less wine vinegar.

Storing

Whilst they are still whole, air-dried products are better kept out of the refrigerator and simply hung in a cool, well-ventilated place. But once they have been cut they must be treated with care. They may not go mouldy, but will easily go rancid, particularly if they are already sliced. Even the flavours of the more robust salami are delicate and likely to be swamped by something powerful in a refrigerator, so always wrap these products well in cling film, but let them warm a little before eating, otherwise their essential sweetness will be hidden from your palate.

An unfluctuating room temperature is generally thought more conducive for whole air-dried hams than bringing them in and out of a refrigerator once cut. The tradition is for them to be loosely covered with a light, open-textured cloth, which allows 'breathing'. If you buy sliced ham of any kind it should be refrigerated or vacuum-packed.

Fresh Sausages

These are sausages made for immediate use and thus are usually made from fresh rather than cured meat, and are called **Rohwurst** in Germany.

Sometimes they are rather pink when cooked, a result of the addition of saltpetre, a scourging bactericide of ancient use and that can also give a characteristic flavour. There are those who rail against its use, but I would rather a bright pink sausage safe to eat than a doubtful grey one. All the sausages in this section must be cooked before eating and so should be sold in transparent casings, the world-wide convention of the trade.

In Britain the fresh sausage is lovingly known as the 'banger', perhaps because badly filled ones or ones cooked over too high a heat tend to explode.

British bangers of all kinds have included bread or cereal as part of their fillings for centuries, for their absorbency kept the fat where it should be, making the sausages juicier, tastier and a greater giver of energy, important for low-income workers. It is thought the Industrial Revolution increased the cereal content to today's high level. The need for cheap filling food for the thousands of labourers who left the country for the city meant traditional sausages were extended with all kinds of farinaceous ingredients. But although the contents changed the traditional names did not.

Don't be persuaded by such come-ons as 'all-pork' or 'beef' sausages. The claims might be true at an artisan butcher shop or in some farmers' markets, but generally the rules about names refer to that proportion that must be meat i.e. if a type of sausage is allowed to have 30 per cent filling and 70% pork meat, and if that 70% is indeed all pork it will legitimately be sold as a 100% pork sausage. Naughty, and not really nice.

For a premium and with some effort it is increasingly easier to buy chunky, chewy sausages, and ones with real herbs and spices rather than an infuriating parade of 'flavours' or 'nature-identical' oils that are never natural and rarely identical.

The call is being answered and all round the world you find specialist butchers and specialist sausage shops that do thriving business. With modern machinery and a little imagination there is no reason every butcher can't make his own sausages again: those who do are famed far afield, even when their product is trash.

Beef sausages, which many find a contradiction in terms are turning up again, but these too often contain exotica you might not consider proper to a sausage, like mutton. It is vital to read the names and labels of sausages more and more carefully and always to think twice about anything called something 'flavour', beef flavour sausages, for instance. As with ice cream this means they are not the real thing, but have had those dratted flavourings added. The contents are then likely to be a chemical formula rather than recognizable food. However, there is one ingredient you should not denigrate: soy.

Soy protein has exactly the same protein content as meat, but is without any fat/cholesterol content and is also very much cheaper. For low-income families sausages extended with soy protein are a thrifty way to get protein into themselves and their children. It's just a shame the good qualities of soy protein are so often sold in mixtures with chemical additives with questionable long-term effects.

For those who eat sausages only from time to time, and then fall upon them with great relish, the contents might not be as important as the apparent flavour – but they should be. For connoisseurs, the sausage world is getting more and more thrilling. Kangaroo, wild boar and wild duck sausages are just some I've seen, these fleshes are usually mixed with pork. Venison sausages are fairly common but commonly disappointing, for venison easily dries out, and the flavour is bland and often undetectable when farmed venison has been used.

Experimenters have presented me with paua (NZ abalone) and leek sausages, with goose and pickled plum sausages, with salmon and gherkin sausages and almost every other mixture you can imagine plus, you guessed it, mixtures that should never have been seen and certainly not tasted. Yet nothing is ever better than a well cooked, properly made, generously filled, nicely browned, all-pork sausage, be it traditionally British or German or Polish or newly invented in Australasia. Except . . . well, except for any pork sausage that includes fennel seeds, the classic Italian version. Fennel sausages win almost every sausage competition in Australia, and they usually come from the AC Butchery in Leichardt, Sydney.

And that neatly takes me to the question of pricking. Sausages should never be pricked before being cooked 'to let the fat out and stop them bursting'. Instead you should cook them gently so the melting fat is absorbed by the other sausage contents and everything stays tasty and juicy. Think about it – if the fat can escape so can meat juices and flavour, most of which is in the fat anyway.

The best way by far to cook sausages is at a medium to low heat in an oven: say 325F/170C/gas 3 for around 45 minutes. It's the only way they brown evenly and they never ever burst. Best of all is the gorgeous rich smell they make as they bake, and anticipation has always been the greatest spur to culinary enjoyment. If you don't like fat in your sausages, please go away and eat something else.

When you are buying fresh sausages there are a few things to watch for, indicators of better or worse quality. First, the filling should look consistent from one end to the other, so even if it is a very coarse mixture it must be pretty much the same where ever you look, with no unusual clumps of meat or fat. Second, the filling should be evenly packed with no visible air-bubbles and thicker or thinner parts. Colour should also be even, with no patches or smears and the skins should be rather shiny: a dull skin could mean it's old and getting dangerous. Last of all, trust your nose: if it smells funny it is.

Fresh sausages should be cooked within a couple of days of purchasing. If you don't think you can do this, it is best to freeze them. Defrost them fully, using the automatic defrost programme on your microwave before thoroughly cooking them. And last but certainly not least, cooking fresh sausages from raw on a barbecue is asking for trouble, particularly if they have come directly from a refrigerator. The outside might be burned but the inside will be raw or worse, be lukewarm, just right for rapid growth of bacteria.

Sausages for barbecues should always be pre-cooked, by putting them into cold water, bringing them to the boil and simmering until cooked through. Don't do this much in advance but take them directly from the pot to the barbecue. The point of starting them in cold water is the sausages heat up at the same rate as the water does, and so heat and cook through evenly, without bursting or splitting.

. . . With Casings

American breakfast sausages: generally smaller and slimmer than British sausages, they also contain much less cereal filler, are more coarsely cut and rather peppery with a distinct herbiness. Some are smoked and these are my favourite, particularly with buckwheat pancakes and maple syrup.

You are just as likely to find this mixture sold as skinless patties, which give much more fat in the pan, the basis for a delicious milk gravy made by stirring in flour to create a simple brown roux and then milk.

Bratwurst: meaningless as a definition really, as the word simply means a frying sausage. So, just as in Germany, their country of origin, a bratwurst can and does contain almost anything and they can be shaped like a long thin frankfurter or a thick British pork sausage. They should be sold uncooked and thus have a transparent skin. Generally the fillings will be chunky and have nothing but pork, fat and flavourings inside the casing.

Bratwurst are used in many ways: apart from gently frying or oven-baking they can be boiled in water and served with sauerkraut or slapped into bread rolls or bread. I like them better when having been boiled for five minutes or so they are taken from the water, dried and then fried a rich golden brown in butter or bacon fat.

Sometimes bratwurst are sold 'scalded' to give them a longer life in shops and cafés: you can eat them as they are but they are much better if heated through thoroughly, as above. Some of the variations worth looking for are:

Thuringer Rostbratwurst: 600 years old in 2004, this is one of the great grilling or barbecueing sausages. Up to 150gm each, they should be long and thin, made of pork usually flavoured with caraway, marjoram and garlic, although variations are permitted amongst the 24 companies in Thuringia permitted to make to DOP standards.

Nurnberger Bratwurst: from Nuremburg, these piquant little sausages of coarsely ground pork flavoured with marjoram have a heritage dating back to the late 16th century. Ideally cooked over wood they are eaten with mustard and horseradish if you buy them in the street as *drie in Weckla*, that is three in a bun. In a restaurant they'd be more likely to come with sauerkraut or potato salad. But look also for *Saure Zipfel*, when the sausages are cooked in vinegar with onions, bay, cloves, juniper and black peppercorns.

Chipolata: essentially a smaller English sausage very popular with children and those with barbecues. The name is derived from *cibolla*, Italian for chives, for they should contain some of this member of the onion family, but I'd be amazed if you found any that did. Cook as you would the basic English sausage.

Cotechino: this big Italian sausage generally weighs in around 500g/ 1 lb and is always encased in pig skin, so it's a close relative of *zampone*, which is wrapped in skin from the shank. Cotechino should be pricked slightly and then cooked in simmering water for several hours. I also like to finish it off by browning it in a little butter or fat. Part of the special flavour of a cotechino is that it will – or should – have been air-cured for up to a month before being sold. It is best served with masses of soft, cheesy polenta or buttery mashed potatoes. The Cotechino Modena has IGP status.

Cumberland: one of the few traditional British sausages that remain and taste something like it should. Essentially a pork sausage twisted into a large coil, it should have a minimum of bread or cereal, be coarsely cut and rather peppery. You can still buy it readily in Cumberland, where each good butcher has his own recipe. A Cumberland coil which feeds two or more, should be baked slowly in the oven until golden brown and wallowing wickedly in a pool of excess fat. Its pepperiness and the fat combine marvellously with excellently mashed potatoes and a simple green vegetable like cabbage, which has an affinity with virtually every hot sausage of merit.

English beef: generally a paste of beef and pork with permitted fillers and perhaps a little herby and peppery, sometimes also tomato flavoured. In countries with lax or indifferent food rules they might contain nothing but mutton, fillers, additives and beef 'flavour'.

English pork: there are as many of these as there are manufacturers. Generally made from a paste of pork and other ingredients to enhance flavour, extend and preserve life. Here and there you do find a butcher who will go to some trouble to achieve a degree of authenticity, i.e. to include detectable amounts of sage and a few pieces of meat to chew upon, even if they are gristly.

I'm afraid we put up with bland sausages simply because we put up with them and that's that. The cost of increasing the texture and enhancing the flavour by including some decent herbs is negligible. Indeed decent sausages, with taste and texture seem to be a touchstone for better foods everywhere. For some time it has been possible for sausage-makers to open shops selling nothing else, and farmers' markets where such products can be sold are great hunting grounds for good sausages.

Merguez: thin, very hot pork sausages brought to us from Algeria via France. Nice barbecued or cut up into casseroles, and sometimes sold scalded.

Salsiccia: this is the generic Italian term for all sausages, fresh and cured. You can find them wherever there are Italian immigrants, but the best I've found outside Italy are in Sydney. The best in Italy are thought to be the **Salsiccia di Calabria DOP**.

Amongst the many variations on a simple theme the best and best selling (often judged Australia's best sausage) by far, is the fennel sausage, a chunky pork sausage (made with a little white wine I suspect) and a scatter of fennel seeds – *finocchio* will be somewhere in its name. It's a great sausage anyway but even better when eaten outside, where the palate always appreciates bigger flavours: the sudden burst of savour when you bite into a fennel seed when chewing already delicious sweet pork enlivens eating no end. As fennel also aids digestion there seems never to be a reason not to have another.

Saucisses: French sausages. *Saucissons* or *saucissons secs* are air-dried salami.

Toulouse: this is the most famous French fresh sausage and is available in fairly good versions at specialist butchers. It has a high meat content and is further flavoured with *quatre-epices* and perhaps white wine. All round the world its contents, size and extra flavourings vary enormously.

Whatever sausage you are eating in France someone will tell you it should be called something else. For the French have a huge variety of fresh sausages, all of which contain only pork and natural flavourings but which can be called whatever the maker decides. They are usually thinner and longer than British sausages. The best I ever tasted were offered to me by a four-year-old French girl on a beach by the walled city of Aigues-les-Mortes in the Camargue. They were crammed with chunks of chewy pork, with tiny slices of garlic, leaves of fresh thyme and coarsely ground pepper. The meat had obviously been lightly cured for it was bright red. The little girl's family had cooked the sausages over an open fire and they were quite simply superb. When I asked what name they had, the answer was, 'Oh, no special name – they're just the *saucisses* our local charcutier makes'.

Zampone: this Italian sausage is stuffed into the skin of a pig's trotter. If you find it at all it has probably been scalded to lengthen its life, although modern vacuum packing means that pre-cooking is less important. Cook in the same way as cotechino, perhaps slightly longer, to ensure the skin is deliciously gelatinous. It is especially good with hot pulses and potatoes. **Zampone de Modena** has IGP status.

. . . Without Casings

Some sausage mixtures are sold without the usual skins. In Britain this is simply called sausage meat and is much used, although I wish it were not, as the base for stuffings. If you buy some, mix it with fresh herbs, breadcrumbs, grated lemon rind, some mace, nutmeg and black pepper, and a good slosh of well-flavoured white wine or vermouth, and then bake it in pastry. It makes delicious picnic fare.

Crepinettes: these are usually made from minced pork, but sometimes other meats, seasoned and spiced and wrapped up in a piece of caul fat; thus they are similar to English faggots, which usually include some degree of offal as well. While I was researching my book *Edible France* I discovered parts of northern Provence make the same thing, but call their faggots . . . *gayettes*. Honest.

Keftethes: these Greek uncased sausages are really meat patties, I suppose. Beef or veal is the usual basis and there is always a proportion of breadcrumbs, onion and the obligatory oregano and mint. They are not the same if they are not cooked in very hot olive oil.

Smoked Dried Sausages

Cervelat: this finely minced salami-like sausage, usually a mixture of beef and pork, is packed into a long gut casing and then smoked a golden brown. The texture and mild flavour are popular with those who are not normally keen on charcuterie.

Landjaeger: popular snacks with skiers, these robustly flavoured small sausages usually have a flattened look, as they are pressed between boards for smoking. They should be quite hard and dry and consist mainly of spiced beef. Red wine is incorporated into the mixture too. Excellent with hot wine and with cold beer.

Mett(wurst): this can be many things and each area of Germany will have its own,
i.e Braunschweiger Mettwurst, Berliner Mettwurst, etc. Made from pork and beef, it is air-
dried then cold-smoked. It has a very smoky flavour and all can be heated to eat with, say,
cabbage. Sometimes made as a spread, too.

Tee(wurst): spicy and salmon pink and smooth but available in many variations.

Ruegenwalder Teewurst: is considered the best and is made only of pork and spare rib bacon.
Usually sold in small sizes and is also available as a spread.

Schinken(wurst) or ham sausage: a Westphalian specialty of coarsely chopped or flaked ham,
mild and tender.

Schinkenplockwurst: this has large pieces of fat but is easy to cut. If the colour is dark this
indicates a high beef content, otherwise the meat used for this one is pickled pork.

Scalded Sausages, Smoked and Unsmoked

These are what the Germans would call Briihwurst and what the French call saucisses, not
saucissons. They are usually rather finely minced and sometimes smoked, but always lightly
cooked to prolong their life and preserve their texture. This is by far the largest group of
sausages, and many are for slicing. They are always in a coloured opaque casing, indicating they
do not need cooking.

A curious modern problem is that many if not most butchers don't know what they should be
aiming for because they are simply too young ever to have seen the real thing. As Chief Judge of
the Sausage of the Year in New Zealand I have been appalled at some entries, which were miles
off the mark in their classes – too thick, too long, too short, wrongly flavoured or worse, inedible.
Are there no rules? I asked this in despair as yet another saveloy turned up twice as big as I
remember, knobbled rather than smooth, and a bilious purple rather than a bright cherry red.

Well, there were rules, but only to do with what goes into a sausage and none to do with the
specifications that make a cheerio or a saveloy, poloney or . . . anything. Often the product
offered is very good but because it has nothing to do with the class it won't get an award. That's
very frustrating for enthusiastic butchers and just as bad for judging panels that can't offer
encouragement where it is deserved. And yet again the public misses out.

Bierwurst: a large, German slicing sausage which does not contain beer, but which is excellent
with it. It is always eaten cold and has a peppery flavour.

Bierschinkenwurst: is the same thing with small chunks of ham included.

Bockwurst: this is really a subsection all of its own. The name is used generically for most
sausages that are extremely finely ground, like frankfurters and wieners and knackwurst

Boiling ring: this Polish sausage, which is usually tied into a horseshoe shape and weighs about
500g/1lb is chunky, garlicky pork, sometimes lightly smoked. Basically reheated in boiling water
like the frankfurter, it is invaluable for adding to things in slices, especially cassoulet, bean
casseroles, and rugged poultry dishes – see kielbasa.

Bologna: many things to many people. Known in America as baloney and in Australasia as

Devon or **luncheon sausage**. It is finely minced pork with a peppery taste, sometimes smoked and usually made in a fattish shape. Quite good sliced and fried but usually eaten in bread rolls or as part of a mixed hors d'oeuvre.

Cervelas: not to be confused with **cervelat**, which is German and a type of salami, this French saucisse is not unlike a shorter, thicker frankfurter, but might contain garlic and is often slightly dried. Reheat like the frankfurter and its family. In Switzerland it is also called a **Chlopfer** and served grilled.

Cheerios: always referred to as 'little boys' by my mother. These are 'cocktail-length' saveloys or frankfurters, useful for parties. Usually red-skinned, they are sometimes called 'weenies', which also takes us back to mother, I suppose.

Chorizo: although Spanish by name, this paprika-flavoured sausage is made by a number of countries and is not always scalded, but can be air-dried, as with an Hungarian paprika-flavoured salami. There are hot and sweet versions made in France and in Spain. They may be cooked whole or in slices and make an excellent addition either way to dishes of beans, cassoulets and that sort of thing. Chorizo can be fat and hard and stubby, or they can be a metre long. Chorizo commonly infuriates by not sticking to the international pattern, so opaque skins mean they are cooked or air-dried and can be eaten as is; chorizo that should be cooked, usually with other ingredients, should have a transparent skin

For one of life's great experiences, join the extraordinary queues at Brindisa over lunchtimes at London's Borough Market on Friday and Saturday, when this epicentre of delicious Spanish things sells a split and barbecue-grilled bread roll stuffed with a split and fried chorizo sausage, a handful of zingy rocket leaves and an optional slab of *piquillo* capsicum. The inspiration is that the chorizo is gently flavoured, but the rocket is punchy and the pepper somewhere in between. In spite of insinuating carolling by a Salvation Army band a week before Christmas, I could have believed God was Spanish. And a chef.

Genuine Hungarian paprika sausages are much harder to find nowadays but are always worth the money; they are called **Gyulai** and sometimes found made outside Hungary by Magyars with a hankering.

Fleischwurst/Extrawurst: this is a slicing sausage, one of the nicest of the finely ground types. It is pale, firm but moist, and variations contain garlic, pistachio nuts or pieces of red pepper. Their decorative appearance makes them perfect for *aufchnit*, which means a selection of sliced meats what the Americans call cold cuts. I know the Swiss make excellent sausages of this type.

Frankfurters: these should be made from a paste of fine pork and salted bacon fat and be cold-smoked, which gives a yellowish colour to the skin. Often they are made with whatever is to hand and even in Germany such sausages can have lots of fat or none at all. Frankfurter is now a name for any long thin sausages and in the United States you can buy chicken, turkey, ham or beef frankfurters. Once they get around to making one with fish, that really *will* be a fish finger. To heat these and other similar sausages, put into cold water and bring slowly to the boil – they will burst if you plunge them into hot water. Sliced frankfurter is delicious in hot or cold potato salad or a salad of cold French beans. A frankfurter is what you usually find in a hot dog – except when you find a weiner. In Germany they are always sold in pairs and should be eaten from the hand.

Garlic sausage: one of the best-known slicing sausages and made by most European countries. The French ones are usually fairly fat and in an artificial casing; sometimes they include chunks of ham and thus are simply a ham sausage containing garlic. There are some thinner Polish types that have a wrinkly brown skin and are only a few inches in diameter. I think they are better than most; ask for krakowska q.v.

Ham sausage: the other half, with garlic sausage, of the big two of the slicing sausage world. Chunks of ham in a paste of ground up ham, stablizers etc. If you can find one, the genuine Polish variety is usually a better choice.

Jagerwurst: finely minced veal and pork with a very peppery taste, sometimes with green peppercorns.

Kabanos/kabanossi: piquant, smoked, chewy pork sausages that are very thin and very long, 500mm perhaps. There are two types, the soft and the dried – one is simply older than the other. The soft one makes an excellent snack or, cut into long thick diagonal slices, a good addition to salads. The hard one is popular for chewing but better sliced and cooked, especially in a dish with lots of garlic, tomatoes or beans, or all three: great for meat interest in a tomato-based pasta sauce, or for adding to cooked green lentils. And much better than frankfurters in a potato salad or mixed into a tumble of roasted root vegetables, hot or cold.

Keilbasa: Polish for sausage, and thus for Polish sausage, which is also sold as boiling ring. American food writers tend always to use such foreign terms and names as *keilbasa*, rather than saying Polish sausage, and this makes their usually very good books difficult to use by other than the cognoscenti, which seems to defeat the purpose of writing. See boiling ring.

Knackwurst: short fat frankfurters, really, usually tied together in strings.

Krajana: another Polish one of roasted ham and pork, but without garlic.

Krakowska: an excellent Polish mixture of ham, pork, beef and garlic with a flavouring of nutmeg – you should be able to see big pieces of flesh. The darker, wrinkled, older and drier version is quite different from the fresher one, but both may be enjoyed sliced and cold or cooked in any way you can conceive.

Mazurska: not a dance but music to anyone who is a Polish sausage lover. Like a slightly larger 'banger' in size but filled with chewy pork, garlic and pepper, and smoked. Simply heat in water and serve with buttered cabbage or spiced red cabbage and some good relishes. Perfectly indispensable for cooking in winter dishes but equally wonderful sliced and served cold in summer. One per person is usually more than enough.

Mortadella: the big fat one for slicing. There are many, many, many types and some horrid stories – this is the one that really was once made with donkey meat, I think. The best types should include green pistachios but all have cubes of fat, thus it can be disagreeable if warm Chilled enough to keep the fat solid, it is nice on fresh crusty bread or in mixed platters, but not memorable.

Strangely, true Mortadella is considered a cooked salame, for cured meats are used; bologna is said to have been invented as a simpler and, to American eyes, safer substitute. The best will be a **Mortadella Bologna DOP** which will have a minimum of 15% fat and is made in Emiglia Romagna, Piemonte, Lombardia, Veneto and the provinces of Trento, Toscana, Marche and Lazio.

Mysliewska: a dry short sausage of pork that is heated in water like a frankfurter. Coarse and chewy and quite peppery, but I prefer the *mazurska*.

Saucisson: confusingly, the Swiss name for a delicious smoked sausage containing ham, brandy, leeks and paprika. Served hot.

Saveloys: a corruption of the French *cervelas* as far as etymology goes, and a corruption of most other things as far as the product generally goes. They should be made from finely minced pork and, like a fat frankfurter, should also be cold-smoked, but often the smoke is an artificial added flavour and modern red food colourings will be too fluorescent. Rarely made with any quality these days, but keep asking and they might be.

Schublig: a lightly smoked, fine Swiss sausage with a thick skin. Served hot.

Tuchowska: another slender Polish sausage of pork plus beef and a little garlic, coarse but solid and smoked. Excellent cold but can be sliced into casseroles. Slightly wetter and fatter than *wieska*.

Weinerwurst: first cousin, if not brother, to the frankfurter, but often shorter in length. The *real* 'little boys' and hence weenies, etc.

Weisswurst: varying in size but always very white and firm and sometimes sold as white bratwurst. They should be made of young, pallid-fleshed veal, perhaps with some chicken, and often include parsley. Like bratwurst they are especially good if they are first heated in water and then browned in fat or butter. They should be light, delicate and taste of veal rather than any additives, a common failing. A little gentle French mustard is all they need as an accompaniment. The Wolseley on London's Piccadilly serves them with mashed potatoes and butter-fried apple segments, and there are said to be people who have two servings, instead of one main and a pudding. Sounds right to me

White pudding: is pretty much the same thing in a longer casing.

Wieska: one of the basic Polish sausages, and one which can be eaten sliced and cold, boiled, grilled or stewed or as an ingredient in stews and casseroles. It has a full flavour and coarse-textured mix of pork and beef with a touch of garlic.

Cooked or Boiled Sausages

These nearly always include offal or blood or some such combination, and so these products, such as the German Kochwurst, are steam-cooked in their casings. There is considerable crossover with the previous category.

Black pudding/Blutwurst/Boudin noir: based on blood thickened with cereals like barley or oatmeal and often with cubes of back fat and onion flavouring. Made in many qualities and sizes, black pudding is usually sliced and fried to serve hot, especially for breakfast. Some skin it first, some don't . The French *boudins* are often more delicate, containing cream and spices. Taken from their skin and mixed with grated apple, perhaps some good sausage meat and a lively dash of Calvados, *boudins noirs* make an imaginative stuffing for a chicken or turkey, particularly when slid between the skin and the breast. The most ethereal combination I ever tasted was from the London restaurant Bank, at a food fair in the courtyard of Somerset House, London; an elegant slice of lightly spiced French black pudding, topped with a slice of flash-fried foie gras, topped with a sweet-spiced raisin chutney. The Polish kashanka is rather firm blood sausage, and is usually made in a natural casing. Rotwurst is a German variation, spicier and coarser.

Brawn: made properly, with lots of pepper and *big* pieces of meat, brawn can be the most delicious of charcuterie treats. It should be made from the many contrasting meats of a well-boiled pig's head set in an aspic from its own cooking. English brawn stops there but continentals tend put the whole lot into a gut, or even a stomach – the Poles do this. Brawn is much better if served slightly chilled with a sharpish accompaniment, like a vinaigrette sauce, pickled cucumber, gherkins and olives.

If you make your own, defy tradition and add herbs and spices. Orange and lemon peel, finely chopped garlic, horseradish, chives, mint, thyme, mace, and whole peppercorns – white, black or green – make this normally bland dish into something quite marvellous. It is doubly good, if you have well-flavoured the cooking stock, with vermouth, bay and citrus in particular. Germans call this Sulzwurst and the French Fromage de Tête, which is why it's commonly called head cheese.

Haslet: this is particularly English, a sort of meat loaf made only from offal, which should be cooked in a lace of caul fat… not often available and not often worth eating. But it could be. Eaten cold or hot in slices.

Leber kas: a speciality of Bavaria, but not often special, for it is a baked meat loaf with a high liver content – and meat loaf is nearly always awful unless you make it yourself. Thinly sliced and grilled or fried it can be fine in Bavaria, but those found elsewhere are often crammed with filler and preservative. The Swiss Fleischkaise is also a meat loaf, but contains little liver. It is served sliced, hot or cold.

Liver sausage/leberwurst: the price and quality depends both on the amount of liver actually included and the type of liver used. Generally such sausages are made with pork liver and pork meat. Some are firm enough to slice and are wrapped in fine fat, others are meant to be spread and these are often gratifyingly rich in flavour. There are variations also in the texture of the mixture and the inclusion of spices, onion and so on. The most expensive are made only from calves' liver, Kalbsleberwurst, or from unfattened goose liver. None is usually heated before use, but if they are rich and full-flavoured some of the slicing liver sausages could be fried or grilled or heated on toast, perhaps as an accompaniment to game.

Mix up a serving of a rich, soft liver sausage with a little brandy, ideally a fruit brandy or eau de vie like calvados, poire william or kirsch, and then season with freshly-scraped nutmeg and chopped parsley and you have a very good stuffing for such *petites bouchees* as lightly-excavated cherry tomatoes, or to slide under the skin of a small roasting bird, or of chicken thighs.

Tongue sausage: one of the best-looking sausages for making arrangements of *aufschnitz* or cold cuts. The German tongue sausage Zungenwurst is usually a superior blood sausage in which whole pieces of tongue are suspended. It looks better than it tastes but no-one seems to mind.

Cooked Hams

Cooked hams, boneless and meant for slicing, are the charcuterie counter's equivalent of sliced white bread. There are some exceptions, but this is generally what happens, and it is important you begin this voyage of discovery at the end rather than the beginning. First, most ham is not ham that is, from the rear leg of the animal, not even that in a ham shape, and what you are buying is as much water as anything else.

Pork for such products can come from all parts of the animal, and is always cured in a salt brine that plumps rather than dries out the flesh; those sold as Virginia hams probably have some sweeteners added to the cure. Once this is completed the meat is shredded and tumbled to make it even in texture. Then it is pressed into moulds, either square, 'd' or ham shaped, and steamed to prevent weight or moisture loss. These reconstituted hams are quickly recognizable from small bubbles and air pockets in the meat, where none should be.

All this is done to bring a cheaper product to the market, you understand, and there must be some merit in that. But how sad to see people preferring this literal dilution of one of our oldest foods, thinking real ham too dry or too strongly flavoured. You do get what you pay for with ham, and the bottom end of the scale in cooked hams is tasteless, and barely worth eating nutritionally.

Closer inspection of some cooked ham will reveal they are not reconstituted, as above, but are natural muscle meat. The problem is they are not necessarily the correct muscles for ham, and the ham might even be formed from muscles from different pigs – even from different pigs from different countries.

Wouldn't you rather eat something else?

Other Products

Bacon: not usually thought of as being from a delicatessen (although see Pancetta). Yet sometimes these are the only shops where rare, dry-salted traditional bacons might be obtained. For belly pork is cured just as randomly and with the same additives that turn out ham products weighing much more than the original meat did, through water retention.

Dry-cured bacon is made by rubbing salt into the raw flesh, rather than soaking it in a brine bath. It takes longer but the results are noticeably more tender, sweeter and tastier, and this will only get better as there is a slow move back to heritage and free-range pigs. If you find dry-cure bacon, the rewards are extraordinary. The cooking smell is cleaner and clearer and richer, making people look up to ask what is cooking. There is no white curd in the pan, and the rind goes to a golden crispness rather than a brown toughness: be sure you keep the extra fat for frying eggs or potatoes or tomatoes or bread – or anything.

In some areas bacon is almost always sold smoked, yet unsmoked bacon, known in the UK as green bacon, is a far more useful and delicious and direct flavour altogether. If you are just starting a journey of discovering better foods, there can be no better place to start than with green, dry-cured bacon.

It is worth looking for **Speck**, German bacon, of which there are many varieties. The most useful is probably the type that is simply salted back fat: sometimes this is smoked, or as **Ziguener Speck**, it is coated in paprika. Thinly sliced or cubed, it can be used to add richness to cooking, for rendering or to make crisp lardons. The paprika speck is eaten as is, very thinly sliced, an interesting experience.

Bozcek: is Polish and is lean belly of pork, salted, smoked or unsmoked, cooked or uncooked. The cooked, smoked *bozcek* is delicious sliced and eaten with mustard and can also be fried or grilled. The raw *bozceks* are the best way I know to get a smoky bacon flavour into any dish, from pâté to casseroles.

Chitterlings/ chitlins: however you see this word in the USA's Deep South, it is always pronounced chitlins, and if ever there were a culinary Mason/Dixon line, chitterlings would be it. They are the cooked intestines of piglets and the cause of as much grief as pleasure, because of associated health problems. If not fully and properly cleaned they will harbour salmonella and yersinia, a nasty food-poisoning agent that grows just as nicely in cool conditions. Street stall dining is not recommended, and the administration of many southern States sternly counsel against cleaning and cooking at home.

Once cleansed of everything but globs of intestinal fat, chitterlings are boiled for three or four hours, sometimes only with an onion and black pepper, and then served with a chilli sauce or vinegar, which might be just as well; like France's *andouillettes* they offer a residual sweetness I find nauseating – and I have a sweet tooth. Fancy cooks might add bay leaves, mace, cloves and allspice to the pan, perhaps even garlic. They might then also cut the boiled chitterlings into smaller pieces and fry them in batter or in breadcrumbs and serve them; boiled turnip greens are top accompaniment. Anything to disguise the flavour.

Even now uncooked chitterlings are dirt cheap and it's no surprise they remain a traditional Southern soul-food favourite, a survivor of the bad times when any food was once better than nothing. Like me, you might indeed choose to eat nothing rather than to eat some foods . . .

Fritulli: you'll find these in Calabria. They are the ultimate in pork efficiency, the skin and fat of pigs, scraped, cleaned, boiled in salt water and then sealed under lard. They are eaten hot or cold, in sauces, in omelettes, with vegetables and in soup. Meatless *rillons* q.v., I suppose.

Kassler: is made by various countries. This is the eye of the loin, salted, very lightly smoked and cooked. Cut thin or thick it is succulent and delicious in sandwiches, salads or *aufschnitz*. It can be sliced and grilled or fried, and makes the most superior and attractive ham for ham and eggs.

My friend Nicholas Scott in Melbourne, who has cooked for three duchesses, ('only two of them were royal') roasts kassler whole, to slice at table, a wondrous way to enjoy a pork roast quickly without the fuss, the fat and the leftovers. Take the trouble to serve something specially fruity: lightly spiced cherry compote, deseeded kumquats poached in orange juice, crab apples in cider or very good *mostarda di frutta* q.v., and the best possible baby potatoes boiled whole. The outstanding Polish version of kassler is called Sopocka: this is generally smaller and leaner and gives a more elegant oval-shaped slice.

Pastrami: common enough in the United States but only now beginning to appear elsewhere. It is, or should be, salted, spiced and smoked brisket of beef. Firm of texture and covered with black pepper and other spices, sliced extremely thinly and served cold or hot, especially in sandwiches – who hasn't heard of pastrami on rye? When you are planning a cold buffet, the bite of pastrami can be welcome relief amidst the sweetness of ham, chicken and turkey.

Porchetta: the real thing is a sight to see, a flavour to savour and a particular speciality of Abruzzo; it is a whole pig that's been fully deboned and then put back together with herbs including fennel leaves and spices and then oven roasted, which takes huge skills considering the different muscles, the density and sheer size. Plenty of crackling too. Sliced roast, hot or cold it's always a treat. What a party piece!

Rillettes: fatty belly of pork cooked and cooked until all the fat is rendered and the meat is in strands; and then the meat is pulled apart with two forks to further separate it and even out the texture. It sets to a wicked, thigh-plumping, high-fat pork spread used rather like a meat paste. Also made with goose and its fat.

Rillons: small cubes of pork long-cooked in their own fat and used rather like lardons.

Simple Spiced Salt Beef

Here is an interesting way to enjoy spiced beef, which was long traditional at Christmas time, without first having to brine the meat yourself. Allow about four days before you cook it and, if you can, a couple more after that before you slice and serve it.

To serve 6 generously
75g/3oz dark brown sugar
2 tsp black peppercorns
4 whole cloves
1 tsp ground mace
1 tsp ground nutmeg
1 tsp mustard powder
1 tsp ground coriander
6 dried bay leaves
3-6 garlic cloves
2kg/4 lb lean salt (corned) beef

Pound the sugar with the black peppercorns and cloves: it should be even but does not have to be very fine. Then mix in the spices. Crumble in the bay leaves and then mix in as much garlic as you want – you could just chuck in six whole cloves in their skin once the meat is cooking.

Stand the meat on a substantial plate or dish and press the spice mixture firmly into as much of the surface as you can. Cover the plate and the meat with aluminium foil, perhaps using two layers to ensure the aromas do not escape to invade other goodies. Refrigerate for four to six days.

Put the meat together with all the spices into a large saucepan and cover with cold water. Cook just as it is or add any other flavourings that occur – garlic, onion, juniper berries, carrots, parsnips and so on. Simmer gently for four hours or longer, until it is really tender, but don't boil it ragged.

Spiced beef may be served hot but is perfectly marvellous if left to cool in the liquid and served the next day. The vegetables used in the cooking will be past all revival, no, not even in a soup.

Cheese

'Don't touch the Stilton, it's refrigerated,' hissed the photographer to his editor over a crowded banqueting table. To make it worse he said it in French, `Pas le Stilton, cherie, etc...'

What a stupid poser. If he had really known about cheese he would have welcomed the sense of a banqueting manager in keeping the cheese protected from heat, smoke, insects and airborne bacteria. After a few minutes in the hot room the small portions were at a perfect temperature to enjoy and, more importantly, safe to eat. Nothing is worse for cheese than heat and air, for these encourage rotting rather than ripening and although to the novice they might look and taste somewhat the same, the difference can be deadly.

If cheese didn't exist, you probably couldn't imagine it. Who would believe it possible? Thousands, perhaps tens of thousands these days, of different foods spanning every imaginable taste from savoury to sweet, and most of them made simply by forming solid curds from the casein in milk with rennet or acid. If only it were that simple. The slightest difference in temperature, of fat content, of pressure on the curds – even the time of year – will give you an utterly different result. And that's just with cows' milk. Cheeses are also made from goat milk, sheep milk, buffalo, camel and mares' milk.

There are threads of commonality that, once understood, help even the inexperienced to appreciate the potential a cheese that's new to you offers. Each cheese gives visual clues to judge how it might taste well before you put it in your mouth, and there are simple ways to know if an unfamiliar cheese is in good condition or not when it is smelly, runny or sharp tasting. These facts are obvious once you have a rudimentary understanding of cheese making, which in spite of the huge number of cheeses actually falls into a surprisingly small number of categories.

Each of the categories that follow is based on cheese-making technique that results in a recognizable family of cheeses, with broadly related flavours and appearances.

All casein-based cheese begins with a curd, that is the solidified protein content of milk, and this can be obtained two ways. An acid curd is the original way, simply allowing milk naturally to sour, sometimes called ripening, during which the lactic acid formed will solidify the milk: when this curd is cut it separates into smaller curds and whey. This instant cheese curd can also be achieved by adding vinegar or lemon juice to fresh milk, the way Indian panir is usually made. Such cheeses will always have an acidic bite, refreshing when balanced and new, but quickly turning harsh and unpleasantly sour.

The other curd is sweet and must be obtained from sweet fresh milk with a curding agent like rennet. Rennet is usually obtained from the stomachs of young ruminants and when added to such milk makes curds and whey without adding anything to the milk's natural flavour. This discovery, probably on the Steppes, is really where cheese making began.

Absolutely fresh milk or cream is rarely used, for as it sits and ripens it develops a fuller flavour, which is passed on to the cheese; yet a true mozzarella is made with the freshest milk possible, and so tastes delicately of the most fugitive notes of milk.

Getting a balance of sweet and sharp is the secret of many great cheeses; traditional Lancashire cheese was always made from a mixture of morning milk which had been stored to become riper and sharper, plus fresh and so sweeter evening milk.

These days much cheese-making milk is pasteurised, which kills both the potentially bad bacteria and the good ones that would create the preferred flavour and texture of matured cheeses. You cannot make worthwhile cheese with this sterile milk and so a carefully cultivated mixture of the best bacterial cultures, known as starter, is put back into the milk and allowed to develop and give flavour to the milk before it is then renneted. Even unpasteurised milk can have a starter added, to ensure the proper development of acidity or the development of a favoured flavour. We know better than to leave cheese to chance.

So-called vegetarian cheeses use a curdling agent based on vegetable products; they should not be confused with curds made from soy milk, which can't help being vegetarian because they are not made with animal milk.

Understanding the fat content of cheese is a complicated subject, but very important for those who wish to control energy intake yet include cheese in their diet. The fat content stated is not a percentage of the cheese bulk you see or buy, but is expressed as a percentage of only the cheese's solid matter.

A pressed cheese like Cheddar with 48 per cent fat content or Parmesan at 32 per cent will have very little moisture content so this means that what you eat will be close to the nominal fat content percentage. Yet a creamy tasting but wetter Brie (up to 60 per cent fat) or Camembert (up to 50 per cent fat) will actually be much lower in fat weight for weight, as each mouthful contains rather a lot of moisture and that is not where the fat resides. Portion for portion, soft cheeses, other than enriched triple-cream cheeses, will generally have less fat and calories per mouthful than pressed cheeses. This explains why a 25g/1oz portion of Parmesan made with semi-skimmed milk may have 10% or more fat per portion than the same weight of a full-milk Cheddar and will be almost 20% higher than the same weight of Camembert.

Skimmed milk can be used to make most cheeses but will generally give a meaner, harder cheese than full fat milk. The cream (fat) content of goat and sheep milk cannot be separated and so these are always relatively high in fat, especially those made from ewe milk, which is particularly rich.

Planet Earth is currently enjoying an absolute explosion of cheese making. In every country in the world where there are dairying animals, men and women have turned to it, some to prove you can still live comfortably on a few acres with some milking animals, some because they are besotted by the cheese-making processes and others because they thought they could do better than those they found at shops and markets. So, where it was once possible to give an easy overview of cheese making in, say New Zealand or New England, it is now impossible. Every farmers' market has brand new cheeses and the competition from the new has spurred greater interest in marketing some of the older, rarer traditional cheeses. At London's Fine Food Fair last year, I found some of the most interesting were from the Italian provinces, and a number were flavoured with black truffles. Something new? I asked at several stands, only to be told the cheeses were traditional but the district had only recently decided to share them. You won't find them easily but from what I tasted Italian cheese and black truffle – the true tuber *melanosporum* and not the bland tuber *aestivum* or summer truffle – were meant to be married, and the long time they spend together as a pressed cheese ensures the magical property truffle has to encourage other flavours gets the chance really to show off.

Thus, don't be alarmed or surprised if your favourite cheese is not mentioned. The family to which it belongs is certainly here, and knowing its characteristics will help you decide if a cheese new to you is a success or a failure: more important you can judge if it is safe and good to eat, for not every blue mould you find in a cheese is good mould, not every high smell is good, not every runny cheese is amusing. And you do need to know. There are cheese makers I found in farmers' markets in several countries who need urgent lessons in hygiene, safe storage and even, what good cheese should taste like. Enthusiasm, clean hands and nice cows are not enough.

Learn the characteristics of each cheese type and you will soon be able to judge the sort of flavour to expect from a cheese just by looking at it. If you can, smell it next, judging it only within its own class or family. And finally there's the tasting and here fast judgements are not the thing at all. The fat content of a cheese tends to coat our taste buds, slowing down our assessment. So chew slowly, hold the cheese in your mouth a while until you can taste it all over your palate, and once you have swallowed think about the palate again. As the fat is diluted the taste buds should be presenting you with ever-changing flavours. If the flavours seem to stop half way along your tongue, the cheese has a short finish and so is incomplete and unsatisfying to eat. If it leaves flavours all the way to the back of the tongue and that lingers for some time, it has true quality.

A cheese with a short finish is never good value, no matter how cheap, and a cheese that fills the mouth and leaves flavour after you have swallowed is always good value. You'll probably need less of it to feel satisfied too, for it has fed all your senses and not just answered hunger pangs.

Fresh Cheeses

Fresh cheeses deteriorate and sour exceptionally easily and must be kept chilled at all times. They are the exception to the rule that cheese tastes better when at room temperature – these taste better when below room temperature, but lightly chilled rather than deeply refrigerated.

Curd cheese: although all soft cheese is basically curd, this term is usually used for those not made with full fat milk. Even the lowest fat versions should smell clean, fresh and milky with no sourness, but they may have a chalky graininess. Quark, fromage frais, fromage blanc, q.v., are essentially all the same thing, varying in consistency through the amount of renneting, the commercial addition of stabilizers and emulsifiers or homogenization, which does for curds what the Fairy Godmother did for Cinderella.

Cream cheese: this causes much confusion. You can make a cheese by curdling cream alone, but it is very rich, and you would have to be to buy or make it. A commercial cream cheese is so called because it is rich and creamy, made with full milk. Homogenization of curds and whey means lower fat cheeses can now ape their betters, so cream cheese may simply taste that way but be quite low fat. Read the labels, ask the questions.

Cottage cheese /farmers or pot cheese in the United States: curd cheese which has been drained and washed so there are no remnants of whey, which although fat free does contain lactose, the milk sugar. The richness and calorie content of cottage cheese will depend on the fat content of the milk used, but it is most likely to be made with skimmed or semi-skimmed milk, hence its blandness and thin flavour, which easily sours. Don't you feel sorry for dieters who have so changed normal thought patterns they equate a tasteless scoop of this with real food?

Fromage frais/fromage blanc: these French fresh cheeses are soft curd cheeses but generally have a deceptively rich texture and velvety mouth feel, even those that are absolutely fat free. This is because once made, the curds and whey are forced through fine nozzles to homogenize the mixture, and that gets rid of any grittiness.

NB: mascarpone is NOT a cream cheese or any other sort of cheese, but is an Italian version of soured cream.

Ripened Cheeses

The following broad guide to ripened cheeses is based on how much is done to the curds of the cheese by way of heating, cutting, draining, milling, moulding, pressing, flavouring and so on, including treatment of the surface. These are the things you can identify from the appearance of the cheese, your start to guessing how they should look and taste when in good condition, and your guide to assessing if they are or not.

Soft-paste, with bloomy unwashed rinds: e.g. Brie, Camembert: the curds are sliced into moulds and drain naturally with no pressing. They mature in about a month, developing a characteristic white furry mould on the outside – penicillium candidum. These are mild, buttery cheeses in flavour and appearance, and the rinds should have a mushroomy smell. They ripen from the outside – a chalky centre means immaturity. Cheeses made with unpasteurised milk have much more flavour, a deliciously distinctive lactic farminess and only this type – Brie de Meaux for instance – should have any appreciable brown or red markings on the rind. The rinds may be eaten, but it is eccentric and dangerous to eat these cheeses when runny and ammoniacal, for they are overripe and such flavours were never the target of the makers

Soft-paste, washed or brushed rind: e.g. Pont l'Eveque, Maroilles, St Paulin: the curd is broken up as it is put into moulds but rarely pressed. During the one or two month ripening period the rinds are washed with brine or other liquids which encourages a straw or red coloured bacterial growth on the rind. These are the 'smelly feet' cheeses, but universally have a sweeter and more delicious flavour than you expect. The surface should not be overly sticky; the body is usually buttery and perhaps a little rubbery. The rinds are rarely eaten.

Scalded cheeses/pressed, uncooked cheeses

The biggest range by far:

Lightly pressed: e.g. Caerphilly, Cheshire: the curd is obtained from hotter milk than for bloomy or washed rind cheeses and the curd is cut and drained at a higher temperature again, than scalding. It is lightly pressed in moulds and retained whey shortens the cheese's life. They have no appreciable rind. Expect a clean, slightly lactic flavour, sometimes salty but with underlying creaminess. They sour very easily and should have no moulds on the outside or discolouring on cut surfaces.

Hard-pressed uncooked cheeses: e.g. *Cheddar, Gouda*: the curds are pressed harder and longer, giving a firmer cheese, which takes longer to mature. These cheeses usually have a noticeable rind; Gouda is brined, commercial Cheddar is sprayed with hot water and cheese cloth is used to bind handmade Farmhouse Cheddar. Avoid any such cheeses that are cracked, mouldy or 'oiling' on the cut surface. Acidity on the palate is a good thing but bitterness indicates something has gone wrong, often with the starter culture.

Cooked cheese: e.g. *Swiss Emmental* and *Gruyèrere*: the curd is cooked at a high temperature, to give dry and tough curds that are then pressed very hard indeed. They take a long time to ripen during which they soften and sweeten and then last well. Swiss Gruyère re also has a washed rind and thus a slight stickiness and rich nose is to be expected. Its nutty-tasting body should show small eyes, often with a drop of liquid; Swiss Emmental is the one that has the big holes. Which one goes stringy when you cook it? Emmental.

Plastic-curd cheese: e.g. *Provolone, Cacciotta*: made mostly in Italy except for mozzarella, which is made everywhere there are cows and factories and pizza ovens – *pasta filata* is the Italian name for this family of cheeses. Here 'plastic' refers to the texture of the cheese when still at the curd stage, rather than any reflection on eating texture and taste, but it could for there are two quite distinct types of plastic-curd cheese, the good and the bad going on ugly.

The curd for plastic cheeses is soaked in hot whey, which makes it putty-like, thence it is kneaded, just the way bread dough is, which further develops its particular textures. Then it is teased or rolled into strange shapes, like tops and skittles and sometimes a monstrously big sausage shape, usually a Provolone. The truly plastic-like factory-made mozzarella, often called pizza mozzarella, bears such little resemblance to the real thing – someone should throw a legal case at it.

Provolone is typically aged, giving a delicious acidity to an essentially sweet, smooth body. These are the cheeses you might see up to two metres long and 50cm thick. Sometimes these aged cheeses are lightly smoked and it works better than with many cheeses. All types are good for grating. *Cacciotta con burro* is a small fat gourd shape with a wodge of butter inside, very handy for slicing into sandwiches or rolls when you are away from home.

Whey cheeses: e.g. *ricotta, mızıthra, gjetost*: not strictly cheeses because they are not made from casein. Heating whey makes the available albumen collect in cloudy flakes, a process known rather wonderfully as flocculating: they contain much of the vitamins and virtually all the sugars of the original milk but are fat free. Today milk is often added to the hot whey to increase the yield. Whey cheeses are moist and still relatively low fat cheeses but their sweetness indicates the presence of lactose, milk sugar – if it's not fat it'll be carbohydrates!

Provided it is very fresh, I find decent ricotta one of the most useful of all cooking cheeses, lighter and more biddable than curd or cream cheese for everything from stuffings to cheese-cakes, cooked or otherwise. Try lightening it with cream then firming it to cutting texture with ground almonds and flavouring that with orange flower water and orange zest; serve as is or in pastry. Add eggs and it can be baked. The same basic mixture of ricotta, almonds and cream or milk can be made savoury too, say with chicken flakes, fresh tarragon and toasted almonds. All these cheeses are sometimes dried and grated as a condiment.

In Scandinavia the process of boiling is continued long enough to caramelize the lactose and then to turn the cheese golden brown, and the best known of these is *gjetost*, made with goat's milk whey.

Albumen cheeses, made by heating whole milk until it coagulates are very rare, and include Swiss Schabzeiger.

Blue cheese: e.g. *Stilton, Fourme d'Ambert, Roquefort*: these are invariably made with a scalded, lightly pressed curd which leaves spaces for the moulds to grow. In French the effect is called *persillé*, as the blue veining looks like parsley, it is incorrect, as some text books say, that blue veining was once encouraged by mixing parsley into the curds, although mouldy breadcrumbs were certainly used. Today freshly pressed, moist curds are usually injected with *penicillium roquefortii* or something similar, but the veins in the softer body of Italian Gorgonzola are due to the related *penicillium glaucum*.

In general, the warning signs of a blue that is past its best are browning, unpleasant sourness on the nose rather than a rich acidity, obvious oiliness or weeping oiliness or an excessively moist crust, which will also smell foul. The crusts should never be eaten and nor should they be used for soup, the equivalent of expecting cowhide to make good bouillon.

All blue cheeses are the absolute ground-zero excuse for bringing out your very best sweet dessert wines, including Madeira, sherry and port, which is only a sweet red wine. An interesting exercise is to present a gang of friends with a big piece of a perfect blue cheese, but a choice of pudding wines, varying from the lissome Germans, including an ice wine, through unctuous Bordeaux to the heady muscats of Southern France and then to the chewy masterpieces of Australian and New Zealand vineyards, perhaps even including a liqueur muscat – oh, and a sweetish champagne, *sec* or *riche*. You can also do this the other way around, offer one wine but a choice of blue cheeses. Fewer might accept the invitation. Not always a bad thing.

Goat and sheep milk cheeses: most surviving traditional cheeses in Britain would once have been made with ewe or goat milk, for cows were much more expensive to feed and their cheeses worn in the boss. Perhaps the most important thing to get right about these cheeses is that neither of the milks can be separated from their cream: the fat globules are so small they are, more or less, naturally homogenised milks and this is what makes them so much easier to digest. Indeed, infants who cannot take cows' milk – I was one of them – can almost always tolerate goat milk.

All around the world, goat and sheep farmers are spearheading a huge increase in the interest and enjoyment of cheese made from these milks. It is such a revolution, particularly in sheep milk cheeses, there are several generations growing up to take them for granted, whereas my generation knew about Roquefort only, and was a bit pleased you couldn't get *that* sort of thing in New Zealand. Now, some cheeses, usually pressed ones, made of sheep milk don't even say so on the label; that is you are invited to like it and judge it against everything else on offer, rather than as a novelty. To farmers, the advantages are enormous: they are not obliged or disobliged by milk quota systems and because goats and sheep are free of diseases harmful to humans, the milk does not need to be pasteurised. The only thing you can't do is to make low-fat versions, for which millions give thanks.

The difference between goat and sheep milk cheeses is important. Whereas goat milk invariably has more or less of the musky, some say nutty, goat taste, sheep milk is always sweet.

Thus, a note of warning about goat cheese if you have never eaten it before: take the merest smear or thinnest flake as a first taste. I hope you will find it as wonderful as millions of others, but you might not. Some palates do a very curious thing: they dramatically heighten the flavour of the oil that gives the goaty tang. The minutest amount is blown up to fill the mouth with what you might imagine is the taste of licking between the rear leg and testicles of an aged billy goat on a particularly hot day. Nutty? Gross goes nowhere near it. If it happens to you or someone else, you must quickly get something else fatty into the mouth, milk or cows' milk cheese: as with chillies, water or anything non-fatty can't wash the oil away and makes the effect actually last longer. Please don't laugh at anyone afflicted, for the confrontational taste in their mouth is so horrific they can go into a severe state of panic and shock, which takes some time to subside. I know, believe me, and yet as an infant goat milk saved me. Payback?

Goat milk cheeses were not generally pressed because it takes so much more milk to get a result. Now pressed cheeses are more common and both goat and sheep milk pressed cheeses are amongst the most popular and delicious, and the range burgeons monthly, with hard and soft blue cheeses joining the more traditional small soft and aged cheeses. Some traditional goat milk types are surface ripened with white *candidum* moulds; some are aged in black ash.

The particular appeal of sheep milk is that this milk has the highest fat content of all milks and also gives the greatest yield of curd per measured quantity of milk, hence its age-old appeal to peasants of yore and to smallholders today. Pecorino cheeses from Italy are supposed to be made from sheep milk but are commonly made from that of cows with a special starter culture added to give the acidity and punch needed. Feta should also be made from sheep milk but is much more likely to be made from bleached cows' milk. Sheep cheese should have none of the farmy/nutty taste of goat milk cheeses, and because their richness can stand it, are often quite sharp and salty, too.

Whereas goat milk cheeses can be so white they seem blue, sheep milk cheeses always have a warmer colour, which can become quite benignly golden in pressed cheeses.

Multi-media cheeses: one of the few truly worthwhile experiments of recent decades has been based on the production of soft gorgonzola-type blue cheeses with a white surface mould, blue bries they were often called when they first appeared. Some are more successful than others, as may be imagined, but all are probably preferable to processed cheese, that slowly disappearing triumph of science over conscience – except that such bland products have enormous appeal to children and to unsophisticated palates and so are both an important protein source and an introduction to cheese eating anyway. Soft blue cheeses with white moulds now come in every conceivable shape, size and power of flavour and I've seen but not tasted one made with goat milk. Some, such as the Kaipara blue of Puhoi Cheeses in New Zealand are multi-award prize winners.

Flavoured cheeses: many well-known cheeses also exist in other forms, flavoured with spices or herbs, smoked or marinated in this or that after maturity. Cumin seeds are very common additives, found in Holland and Alsace for instance, and so are nettles. Recently a wicked coven of food scientists and nutritionists, who should know better, have gone ballistic and flooded the world with flavoured cheeses of combinations bordering on the ridiculous: white Stilton with stem ginger, pineapple or apricot may not have lasted, Cheddar with asparagus and leek did for a while, Cheddar and Red Leicester with Marmite, Cheddar with garlic or smoked garlic or cranberry or anything – all those extras are ingredients that should go with cheese, not in to it. Just thinking of what they have to do to perfectly good cheese to get the other stuff into it should make your nose curl. And that's if the cheese were any good to start with. Like mangy dogs they should be ignored, in the hope they'll skulk away. Washing or coating the outside of a cheese is a different thing.

In Burgundy washed cheeses are regularly marinated in alcohol and throughout France many an *affineur* will have his own flavoured version of a local product.

Smoked and coated cheeses: smoking generally ruins a cheese unless it is intrinsically brightly flavoured and savoury, ideally ewe or goat milk; some washed rind cheeses smoke well too, for they have an acidity which balances out the bitterness of smoke residue.

The use of ash as a coating will help dry a cheese and encourage the controlled growth of moulds that will in turn affect the texture and flavour of the body, commonly done with goat cheeses and on the few cheeses made in Champagne, all rather dry and chewy. We should be grateful for some advances away from tradition. Once the *Champenoise* used to mature the same cheeses under the bed, in the wife's urine in a chamber pot – it was called *fromage de cul* or *bum cheese*. A nice wee cheese, I presume.

Serving

Cheese is usually served after the meal in Britain, whereas in Europe, France particularly, it was and is more likely to appear after the main course. This is a reflection of ancient eating habits. The main British meal of dinner was once served as early as 10am, and in the evening a light supper was followed by cheese, believed to seal the stomach while you slept. The unemployed upper classes and emerging middle and merchant classes gradually moved dinner later and later in the day, dining at 3 or 4pm in the 18th century until it eventually became an evening event, when it was neatly joined on to supper, still completed with cheese. Wine was rarely drunk with meals but between them. The invading Norman French did drink wine as they ate and served cheese after the main course to accompany the last of the red wines served, before moving on to sweeter things: but they never changed the cheese habits of the English table.

Take care to eat cheese only in prime condition and a phenomenal world of excitement is guaranteed. A perfect piece of cheese has taken extraordinary care and skill to make. It seems only fair to give it equal respect when it is in your care.

When there is just one or two eating it is probably wasteful and pretentious to serve more than one perfect cheese. For more than that number there should be a maximum of one cheese for every couple of guests – three cheeses for a table of six. On a buffet table the proportion should be less, with a maximum of six for 30 people. This way you will always be displaying large inviting pieces of cheese, rather than small mean pieces, which will quickly crumble and become untidy as they are cut by your guests; even so, it is horrific to discover cheese precut into pieces or portions on a buffet.

It is always better to serve a single perfect cheese to a table, rather than three dodgy ones because you think you need to make up the numbers, something more restaurants should heed.

Storing

This is where most fine cheese is ruined, often by the adherence to old, and new, wives' tales and a misunderstanding of cheese making. The body of a cheese ripens anaerobically, that is without direct contact with air. Once cheeses have been cut they should be stored at a cool temperature with the exposed edges protected from the air until the last minute before eating, and yes that can mean cling film and a refrigerator. For the best flavour, cheese should be at cool room temperature when eaten, but letting cheese 'breathe' unwrapped or storing it in a cheese bell at room temperature – or both – are the worst and most dangerous things imaginable, for both encourage the growth of unwelcome bacteria and this is especially threatening to the very young and the very old. Cheese is the most perfect medium for bacterial culture, but makes no distinction between good and bad.

Those who mock the advantages of cling film as a safe, convenient and airtight storage medium do not understand cheese or cling film. Neither do those who say a refrigerator destroys cheese. Why should it? There is many an old fashioned larder and safe which would have been very much colder in winter than a domestic refrigerator... the widely available cling film designed for fatty foods and the warmest part of a refrigerator are possibly the best friends cheese has ever had.

You will only see cheese 'sweating' in cling film if the cling film is not tight or the temperature is too warm, which would happen whatever the wrapping medium. Greaseproof paper does cheese badly for two reasons: it slowly absorbs the fat content and, being porous, lets air in and out, whilst also keeping a layer of slow moving air trapped against the surface, exactly right for the growth of moulds. Foil is as impervious as cling film, although I have seen one 'expert' quoted as saying it will allow cheese to breathe! *In extremis*, foil might replace cling film, but it can react with acidity and is thus best used only briefly, unless it has been specially coated.

Except where they are part of the manufacturing process, storing whole cheeses wrapped in film or foil would do terrible things to them, as their crusts and skins must breathe; it is through them that moisture and excess gas of maturation must leave, otherwise off flavours, unbalanced moisture and trapped gas cause awful problems, including 'blowing'.

Whole cheeses should never be sealed from the air other than by any process that is part of their manufacture. But *cut* cheese must be properly protected from the air and kept wrapped as it comes back to eating temperature. Let no one tell you otherwise.

The worst posturing of all is a restaurant cheese board with lots of cut cheeses, virtually a guarantee they will universally be too warm, rotting, oxidized and generally absorbing smoke and smells. Far better to have two or three cheeses in superb condition, kept cool and protected until wanted by the customer. Of course, in your own home, you can have as many as you like at once, provided they have been kept in good condition and you rewrap them closely the moment you are satisfied.

A famed cheese shop like Neal's Yard gets away with keeping cut cheese surfaces uncovered simply because they are so busy, and so no major desiccation or contamination is likely. But what should a restaurant do?

There'd be resistance to showing diners an array of cheeses wrapped in cling film, even though I wouldn't mind. You can't really expose cut cheeses in restaurants where there is smoking – New York *has* done the right thing – and anyway restaurants are usually far too hot. There's no easy answer, but I'd rather be served chilled cheese and allow it to warm up on the plate, than be served cheeses collapsing and oiling in heat. So, if it's to be a cheese board, it must be kept somewhere cool – out of the dining area perhaps – and if the cheeses are not individually wrapped the board must be covered and protected from coughs, sneezes, smoke, insects and animals. Between services I'd certainly cover exposed faces of all cheeses, and if not chilled keep them close to floor level which is always coolest and draughtiest. It's a lot of trouble, sure. But think how much trouble the cheese makers have gone to in the first place.

Australia

Once there were only Cheddars, mild or tasty, and exceptionally good they were and are. But when the apron strings were cut by Britain joining the EU both Australia and New Zealand looked inward and discovered ingredients and expertise in almost every aspect of food and drink. Their wines have changed expectations of flavour and value all round the world, and although you may not taste them unless you are there, their cheese making is world class. Australia's King Island brie, Gippsland blue, indeed almost any cheese from this district of Victoria, washed rind Mungabeera and Kervella goats' cheese, have their fan clubs, but tops for me are sheep's milk Meredith blue and Heidi Gruyère from Tasmania, made with pasteurised or unpasteurised milk. There are zillions more and one of the best things you can ever do is to make a pilgrimage to The Richmond Larder in Melbourne, where Stephanie Alexander is one of the partners. In Sydney, Simon Johnson's shops in Paddington and Pyrmont both have outstanding walk-in cheese chillers whose contents will whisk you to cheese heaven.

Canada

Canada makes a slew of cheese including spectacularly good Cheddar-style cheeses and a highly famed washed rind cheese called Oka, first made in an eponymous Trappist monk settlement. It's a very good melter and so used in many startling ways, including in a soup with Canada's other icon, fiddlehead ferns. The cheeses of Canada are judged at the Canadian Cheese Grand Prix, and best cheese in 2004 was also a washed rind cheese, Le Douanier, made in Quebec. Some of the other class winners to include on a Canadian cheese trail include:

La Riopelle de l'Isle: made on an island off the coast of Charlevoix, Quebec, this triple cream cheese has a bloomy rind and flavours of hazelnut, mushroom and butter, but a clean acidic finish.

Balderson 5-year Heritage: champion of the old and extra old Cheddar class, this cheese is made in the Ottawa Valley by one of Canada's oldest cheese factories.

Bleubry: a soft and creamy blue-cheese champion from Montreal and the heritage of six generations of the Cayer family.

Cheddar Britannia doux jaune: judged the best of the 2004 mild Cheddars, this cheese is made by Agropur in Granby, Quebec, owned by more than 4300 dairy producers throughout Canada.

Cheddar Ile-aux-Grues: the medium Cheddar class winner, aged six months, and made on the same island as La Riopelle.

La Douanier: class and overall champion, Le Douanier is a washed-rind cheese that's been a Canadian favourite for some time. It has a central stripe of ash, now purely decorative, and a typical high nose but soft sweet flavour that increases with maturity. From Fromagerie Fritz Kaiser, Noyan, Quebec.

Gouda, Old: produced in Salmon Arm, British Columbia, this aged Gouda is just one of a range from Gort's Gouda Cheese Farm that can be flavoured with ginger, onion or cumin, be young, old or medium, and spiced or natural.

Kingsberg: made in Kingsley Falls, Quebec, Kingsberg won the Swiss-type cheese class, with a sweet ripeness and texture similar to Emmental.

Valbert: a raw milk cheese with an orange-brown washed rind, this won the artisan class, which must be made with milk from the maker's own cows and farm. Based on the traditions of Jura in western France.

Verdelait, cracked pepper: from quite new artisan cheese makers on the east coast of Vancouver Island BC, and one of a range of flavoured cheeses that includes cumin seed, garlic & chive and wasabi cheeses.

France

Although revered as a cheese-making haven, France's claims were once based on making the world's broadest range (almost certainly not true today), and not even the greatest Franco-*fromophile* would claim all those were wonderful. Most were originally made to be eaten fairly soon after they were made, and eaten close by, too. Thus to eat them elsewhere, even in France, often means their natural maturation period has been inhibited or extended or techniques have been changed to make them more robust. As well, modern demands mean many are made at times when the milk is simply not its best; fine if you are experienced and know what not to expect season to season, but a great disappointment if you are not up on such minutiae.

The great French specialties are Brie and Camembert types, and only France makes anything approaching the wonderment of those that begin with unpasteurised milk. The rare fougères, thicker than Camembert and cured in ferns, are worth any trouble to hunt out. The next most famed types are the smelly washed rind cheeses, and once you understand their bark is not as bad as the bite, you are likely to eat them rather more regularly than you imagined. And then come the goat and sheep milk cheeses, the blue cheeses, and the pressed cheeses – France has outstanding examples of most cheese styles.

Eating French cheese abroad can be rewarding but is nothing like the thrills found in France, where most towns have at least one *affineur*, who ripens cheeses so they may be enjoyed on the precise day, even hour, they are perfection.

The *Appellation d'Origine Controllee* (AOC) is a simple guide to the most highly prized French cheeses and is the same status as DOP. Many are not readily available outside France and many that are vary in quality because they were not designed to travel. This is the complete French AOC cheese list in 2004 and a good basis for judging the seriousness of the people behind the counter in specialist shops in any part of the world, and, increasingly, in one or two supermarket chains, although cheeses from these may suffer unduly from the very low storage temperatures required by multiple retailers.

French AOC/DOP Cheeses

Abondance: also Tomme d'Abondance. Made in mountain chalets of partly skimmed milk from the Abondance Valley and the Drosnes. Creamy rich taste varying from subtle to full: best eaten late summer and autumn.

Banon: from Isère, Drme and Vaucluse in Provence, these small, cleanly lactic tasting cheeses should be wrapped in chestnut leaves. In time-honoured fashion they can be made of cow, goat or ewe milk, so be certain which you are buying if this is important. Excellent slightly chilled with fresh or stewed fruit and with chilled Provençal rosé wines.

Beaufort: Brillat-Savarin thought this the best of Gruyère-style cheeses. Made from raw milk in the high Alpine region of Savoy, in discs up to 70kg. Fruity nose and nutty taste.

Bleu d'Auvergne: one of the newest AOC cheeses, only invented in 1875. It has a full savoury flavour, and is perhaps like gentler cows' milk Roquefort, sharp, salty and rich. A foil-wrapped cylinder with a thin pinkish skin, which is at its best after six weeks. Avoid any stickiness or over-blueing that looks grey-green, as this is an over-aged cheese that has been poorly matured. At its best it is light and melting on the tongue.

Bleu des Causses: it comes from further south but this cheese tastes and looks closely related to Bleu d'Auvergne. It's cured in natural caves, and the whiter winter cheese has a more determined flavour.

Bleu de Gex: from the highest pastureland of the Jura, where exceptionally varied flora gives unique flavour, and so this raw milk cheese is at its best from May to October. The flavour is subtle and fascinating, and should always be the first you eat if it's offered on a mixed platter.

Bleu du Vercors-Sassenage: known for its strong, good flavour since the Middle Ages, this cheese has a body that can vary from ivory to orange. It's made with strict controls on three breeds of cow up in the Massif of Vercors, in the departments of Isère and Drome. You'll find it's a flattish cylinder, weighing up to 4.5 kg.

Brie de Meaux: voted King of Cheeses by the Congress of Vienna in 1814. Until you've tasted this unpasteurised brie from Normandy you can't imagine the heights curded and aged milk might reach. A definite farmy nose, and some discolouring of the white bloomy rind are both acceptable: the body should be shiny and lissome – never runny – and the taste rich and full, with the merest whisper of farmyard and raw milk flavours, leading to a full, savoury but clean finish. Like ordinary brie that's lived a little, in Las Vegas. Enjoyable even when slightly young and with a chalky centre. Expect to pay quite a lot, up to 50 per cent more, if and when you can find it, although in recent years even supermarkets have come alive to its existence.

Brie de Melun: the strongest tasting of all unpasteurised-milk brie cheeses, it was probably the original. A Meaux may weigh up to 3kg, but the Melun never exceeds 2kg. When ripe its rind will be more red and brown than white but not sticky or horrid.

Brocciu: these small national cheeses from Corsica are really a sort of ricotta, made by heating whey from sheep or goat's milk, to which full milk is added for a greater yield. When fresh they are eaten with jam or sugar or cooked in cakes, pastries and soups. Older ones *brocciu passu* are aged at least 21 days and their higher flavour and firmer texture are enjoyed as something savoury.

Camembert de Normandie: raw cow milk only, cured 21 days, and must also bear the inscription *lait cru* on its chipboard container. Should not be runny but may be eaten young, when the body or some of it is chalky looking. Big but clean farmyard smell and smooth taste with a perfectly balanced acid finish. Late spring, summer and autumn are when to find the best. Increasingly available, often made with milk from unsprayed grass, like the brie *fermier*, when it is browner and tangier, delicious when slightly young, more expensive but worth every centime. Expect a rather stronger flavour than, say, a Brie de Meaux but nevertheless avoid any suggestion of ammonia or a cheese that is running all over the place – runny means rotting.

AOC Camembert is made in only five Normandy *départements*, but ordinary Camembert is made in almost 70 *départments* around France.

Cantal: they reckon this cheese has been known at least 2000 years. Made in the massif of the Auvergne it has a lighter coloured body than Cheddar but belongs to the same family, including its delicious flavour. Some are still made by hand on farms. Eat or cook with it as though very good Cheddar.

Chabichou du Poitou: small truncated cones of goat milk cheese made around Poitiers.

Chaorce: a cheese from Champagne, known since the 14th century. At 50% fat content it is as rich as it tastes – and with its bloomy white rind that means a gentle nutty taste, accompanied by a light mushroomy nose. It comes in a drum shape and its bulk makes it difficult to mature evenly, but even when a little chalky it will still have a fragrant, sometimes floral flavour overlying the richness, which in turn is balanced by saltiness, making it an excellent accompaniment to other foods.

Chavignol: properly a *crottin de Chavignol*. Made with raw goat milk in the Loire Valley, perhaps since the 16th century, these small balls are white or ivory in colour and come with a fine white mould. Best spring to autumn, their flavour increases dramatically as they age, and this is when they become *crottins*: you know what the name means, don't you? Droppings, that's what, for old ones are dark and sharp and surprising things for anyone to put in their mouth. Used a lot for grilling and cooking, young or old, and may be found marinated in white wine.

Chevrottin: produced in the Bourbonnais, this is a quite fresh truncated cone of goat milk cheese, and is made to be eaten both when mild and creamy or aged and robust.

Comté: sometimes *Gruyère de Comté*, and made for 1000 years. Manufacture is mainly in the *massif* of Jura but spreads into Franche-Comté. Only milk from *montbeliarde* and *pie rouge de l'Est* cows may be used. A cooked and pressed cheese, it should have very little nose and a sumptuous but clean, sweet taste, whether quite new or aged – it's sold both ways. A superb cheese, that's not half appreciated enough.

Epoisses: a small Burgundian cows' milk cheese washed with *marc*, so it develops a powerful penetrating smell and very high flavour, which is nonetheless sweet.

Fourme d'Ambert: taller and thinner than any other blue cheese, it's made mainly in the farms and dairies of Puy-le-Dome and has a history predating the arrival of the Caesars in Gaul. A touch salty but balanced with a fruity flavour that leaves an intriguing aftertaste and which made it the favourite of President Giscard d'Estaing. Often thought of as a French Stilton, it has grey rind: some bitterness is acceptable, and so is a light musty smell, but neither must be pronounced. Avoid sticky, cracked rind, over-blueing or grey/brown appearance. Also known as *Fourme de Montbrison*.

Laguiole: not unlike a Cantal and made with raw milk from the herbier pastures of the Aubrac mountains.

Langres: a strong tasting and smelling disc of washed rind cheese from Champagne, which is at its best for eating from spring to autumn. Ideally eaten fairly soon after its five months maturing.

Livarot: one of the oldest and one of the most popular Normandy cheeses. The washed rind smell has been described as 'town drains running to the sea' but the flavour is deliciously sweet and delicate. Must have three bands of green sedge running around it, and hence the nickname Le Colonel.

Maroilles: invented over 1000 years ago at the Abbey of Maroilles in an area of luxurious pastureland between Hainault and the Ardennes. It's a washed rind cheese that should be supple but not runny, have the usual 'dirty-feet' smell and an earthy, nutty-sweet flavour with no hint of ammonia. *Goyere* (not *gougere*) is a flan made with this cheese.

Mont d'Or: unusual for being a winter cheese. Moulded in a strip of pine, which gives a light resinous flavour, the cheese can be anything from 200g to 3kg in size but all have top skins that crumple when the cheese is ready to eat. It is very rich tasting, a true dessert cheese for a dinner party, when it is correct to remove the upper crust and then spoon out the body. If it is cut into wedges, the remaining paste must be held back with a piece of glass or wood.

Morbier: this is the sweet, pressed cheese with the streak of soot through it – originally to prevent a skin forming while the cheese made in the morning awaited marriage with that made at night. Made in Franche-Comté it is best eaten in spring if you can find the real thing, as it will have been made with the previous summer's lush milk.

Munster: made high in the Vosges mountains of both Alsace and Lorraine this is a famed washed rind cheese with a heritage said to date from the settling of 7th century Irish monks. Round, flat, orange-red rind and rich yellow body. The typical washed rind cheese smell is penetrating and the flavour equally stronger, richer and sweeter when mature. Locally eaten rather young, often accompanied with cumin seeds. Munster *fermier* is best eaten in summer and autumn when the pasture gives a distinct extra flavour. Made as a washed-rind disc it has the typical smell yet is very mild tasting when young. Non-*fermier* and *petits munsters* may be included in the AOC category if made the right way in the right places.

Neufchatel: from Neufchatel-en-Bray and perhaps dating back to the 10th century. There should be a white bloomy rind and a mousse-like texture with a delicate lingering flavour that's very good with soft fruits. Most are creamery made, but if you stop in Neufchatel on your way to Dieppe, a visit to the market will reveal artisan examples, usually presented on straw mats. The heart-shaped version, *Coeur de Neufchatel* is most commonly seen in the UK, but there are also barrels, loafs and squares.

Ossau-Iraty-Brebis: a remarkable cheese made in the Pyrenées from the milk of two local sheep breeds. It's hand-shaped, lightly pressed and has a brushed rather than washed crust, varying from yellow-orange to grey, a creamy body and rich earthy flavour.

Pelardon: small soft goat milk cheeses made in the Cevennes.

Picodon: *St Agreve* in Gascony is the place to buy these rich, nutty small discs of goat milk cheese

Pont l'Eveque: the real one is only about 10cm/4in square, matured in wooden boxes and has been made since the Middle Ages. These washed rind cheeses should have a smooth gold-yellow rind, sometimes with straw indentations, a tangy sweet flavour and a moderately strong smell. Many variations include the larger Pavé, from which better shops will cut a portion; even bigger – 30cm/12in square or more – is the Tour Gris. These are equally expensive as the small ones but you can buy smaller amounts. Even when smelling rather high, the body of this washed-rind cheese will taste surprisingly sweet. It should not, however, be eaten runny, which is over ripe.

Pouligny-Saint-Pierre: these pyramids of goat cheese with a truncated top were the first French cheeses to be awarded an AOC. There are two types, both aged at least 10 days. Those *en blanc* offer a gentle flavour likened to dried fruits and have a melting, tender body: the *bleu* version has a white *penicillium* coating, is drier and has a strong spicy flavour in which its goaty origins and classic hazelnut notes are to the fore. Made in the west of the Indre, around Touraine and Berry.

Reblochon: a fascinating cheese made in the Haute Savoie since the 14th century. A full cream raw milk product properly made with a retained, richer second milking. Always sold in a wooden box, best in summer and autumn: rather a dank smell but a delicate creamy flavour with a distinct hazelnut after taste. It will weigh up to 500g/1lb and be fairly expensive, especially if made with unpasteurised milk, but this really is worth the expense, if only to experience one of the few *gouts verités*.

Rocamadour: made from sheep milk in spring and goat milk in summer, the latter giving a nuttier tang to these tiny discs, from the Dordogne.

Roquefort: the locals have had a royal monopoly on making cheese in Roquefort-sur-Soulzon since 1411. This is the world's most famous sheep's milk cheese, and the most famous blue, too, but don't tell that to Stilton makers.

Sadly, the rest of the world struggles to get Roquefort the way it should be, for there is a tendency to over-salt the ones that are exported. The milk should all come from the Larzac breed of sheep, and although milk used to be imported from other areas, Roquefort currently supplies all it needs. Expect a clean sharp smell and a pronounced but pleasant sheepy flavour that's never musky or unpleasant, and which leaves a rich, salty after-taste.

The blueing should be even and seem more green than blue. The rest of the body is a subtle ivory-like white, rather like some unsalted butters, and that gives a clue to the ideal eating quality, the texture should be buttery, but if you ask for a small portion to be cut from a block expect some crumbling from the edge.

This remains one of the few cheeses matured the way it always was, in the caves of the Combalou mountain, where mechanisation is impossible – every cheese is still wrapped and turned by hand. Each of the caves harbours a slightly different strain of blue mould *penicillium roquefortii*, and experts claim to know from which cave they prefer their cheese to come. You'll see the labels of many whole cheeses reveal the cave in which the cheese has been matured: some to look for are Cave de l'Abeille, Cave Baragnaudes, Cave Arnals, Cave Le Saul, Cave Rodat. The first is the most common and thought a light style suited for everyday eating, the second is considered an exceptional cheese and for great occasions, the third is – no, you eat your way to your own conclusions.

Whilst showing off such information you should add that the fissures that ventilate the caves are *leurines* and the draughts are fiercer the deeper you go. People have won Mastermind on less.

At Christmas Roquefort makers often market a half-moon shaped tin, in which you'll find three cheeses, each matured in a different cave – usually Arnals, Baragnaudes and Arlabosse.

Saint-Nectaire: another ancient cheese, pressed for only 24 hours and then ripened on straw for two to four months. It has a dry, violet-to-pink thin rind with a slightly mouldy smell. There will be a firm texture and fruity flavour with a slight bite. For such an aristocratic cheese it cooks very well; it melts nicely on toast and in the Auvergne, where it is made, they stir it into soup.

Sainte-Maure de Touraine: goat milk cheese with a very high flavour, each is a cylinder and made on a farm, or it's not an AOC cheese.

Salers: made from raw milk deliciously redolent of the grasses, bushes and berries, including bilberries, of the Cantal. The flavours become earthy, strengthening as the cheese is aged anything from three to 12 months.

Selles-sur-Cher: said to recall the sweetness of life in the Loire Valley, these are mild goat milk cheeses with a delightful texture due to especially careful treatment of the curds. Coated in powdered charcoal and best during summer.

Tomme des Bauges: the newest AOC cheese and few details have yet been published by the French. It is a pressed but uncooked cheese made in Savoie and the Haute Savoie. It is likely to have the unctuous smooth body of Tommes, and a sweet nose in which the finer notes of natural pasturing and wild flowers can be detected.

Valencay: another *fermier* goat milk cheese, made as a low truncated pyramid and dusted with charcoal, which controls what grows where. Best from late spring to autumn and can be found macerated in crocks for winter, but only for the very hungry and the distinctly brave.

Almost as treasured are four IGP status cheeses: *Emmental de Savoie, Emmental Francaise Est-Central, Tomme de Savoie* and *Tomme de Pyrenées*.

Germany

The early establishment of international trading centres in Holland and Germany ensured both countries were guaranteed constant exposure to advances in cheese-making techniques which, in some ways, makes it harder to understand why most cheeses from both countries tend to be bland but sweet. The exceptions are a few ripened German cheeses that are so strong they frighten most foreigners. Perhaps it is in direct contrast to the smoked, pickled and salted foods so beloved by both countries, but if you care to look hard enough there are other treasures to be found.

The average German eats more cheese than most and cheese production all over Germany is prolific although much ends up in prepared foods. In recent years the Germans have given us some interesting smoked cheeses, although too many are highly processed, and increasingly they have developed a number of very sweet, fruity cheese confections which arguably should not even be described as cheese. Yet Germany was also first to develop soft blue cheeses with a white moulded rind, so they are top of the class for millions.

Allgauer Emmenthaler DOP: this looks and tastes like a classic Swiss Emmental (note the different spelling) and so after six months will taste quite as sweet and nutty. Must be made from raw cow milk in the districts of Lindau, Oberallgau, Unterallgau, Ravensberg and Lake Constance or the towns of Kaufbeuren, Kempten and Memmingen.

Allgauer Bergkase DOP: because at 20-30 kg it is just half the size of an Allgauer Emmenthaler this is often called its baby brother. Yet Bergkase (sometimes Alpenkase) is more artisan, more intense, and can be aged longer for greater rewards. Made from raw cow milk only in alpine huts or on small mountain farms during late spring and summer between 900m and 1800m. Because it's brought down into the valleys after four weeks it ripens more slowly than the Emmenthaler and has fewer, smaller holes. Enjoyed when three or four months old, its peak is reached after a year, by which time it is intensely aromatic and offers a particularly long finish.

Altenburger Ziegenkase DOP: made with traditions that reach back into the mid 19th century, this cheese mixes cow and goat milk. Produced only in the eastern provinces of Saxony and Thuringia, it almost disappeared while Germany was divided. The goat milk (15%) is added after the cows' milk is homogenized and pasteurised, and a pinch of caraway seed is added to the cut curds, which then mature with both a white *penicillium* surface mould and the red, smelly washed-rind bacteria. A rarity making a comeback, but not easily, because it is notoriously difficult to ripen and maintain. Thus worth pouncing on if you see it and it looks and smells acceptable.

Butterkase: a creamy buttery taste and with almost no odour, this is a favourite breakfast cheese: low-fat versions are pejoratively called Damenkase or women's cheese.

Limburger: is oblong and loaf shaped and bigger than most washed rind cheeses, therefore there is more of the brick-red rind to assail your nostrils. Infuriatingly Limburger is perfect for only a couple of days. Usually foil wrapped. The rind should be smooth and only just moist or sticky rather than slimy; the pale smooth-textured body has a full flavour much less assertive than the ferocious farmyard odour might suggest. Beware of any hint of ammonia, sliminess on the rind or runny paste, which is a sure sign the cheese is tired and way past its best. Also known as Brick cheese, because of its shape.

Munsterkase: these cheeses also come in several sizes, which means different maturing times of five to 13 weeks depending on size. All are flattish discs with a white to yellow body with the occasional hint of red, thin skin rather than rind, a strong smell and a slightly sharp sweetness of flavour. Avoid dryness, cracking or very moist, slimy skins. The name is a reminder that Alsace was German from time to time.

Odenwalder Fruhstuckkase: a specialty breakfast cheese with a washed rind made only in a single cheese dairy in Huttenthal in the South Hessian Odenwald. Although mild the cheese present a complexity only such artisan manufacture could guarantee.

Quark: made from naturally or lactic-acid soured curds, and always sold within two to three days of manufacture, quark can be small discs, long cylinders, small logs and other shapes. Less than 10% fat content by decree and thus high in protein, quark cheeses vary enormously from region to region, from delicate to rumbustious and noisy.

Romadur: a lesser Limburger in every way but quality, which can be superior. It's smaller, eaten younger and has a less challenging nose and flavour but must most particularly be kept cool, or it will spoil within hours.

Sauermilchkase: a group of cheeses that also includes **Handkase, Mainzerkase** and others, all made from lactic or soured milk that's usually skimmed too. Fresh cheeses are quarks *q.v.* Handkase is an all-purpose name for cheeses theoretically still hand-shaped into opaque yellow or buff-coloured bars, discs, rolls or just about any design the maker can conjure up. They can be eaten at all ages and sometimes have red bacterial or white surface moulds. The older ones develop a rather chewy texture. Mainzerkase will always have a bloomy white mould and a mild flavour.

Tilsiter: originally from East Prussia, this cheese is supposed to have been made by Dutch immigrants trying to recreate Gouda. Instead they made a spongy, washed-rind cheese, found as rounds or oblongs, with all sorts of additions and sold either young and spritely or aged and distinctively aromatic.

Weinkase: invented early in the 20th century as the ideal accompaniment to Rhine and Moselle wines, it comes in 75g discs with a lightly pink-washed rind; a treat to find and to drink with the intended wines.

Weiss-Blau: often erroneously called Blue Brie because it's actually a soft cheese with a white Camembert mould on the rind. Usually cut from the disc, the most popular and most copied variety is creamy in texture and flavour, the bite coming from the blue rather than the rind. Inevitably, its success has spawned many 'me-too' cheeses, some better than others. In Germany you will find much stronger versions too.

Weisslackerkase: pungent, powerful and piquant, this is made with skimmed evening milk added to full morning milk. After five to six months of ageing it is ready to announce its presence. A southern specialty, it's particularly good with beer and so might also be found as **Bayerische Bierkase.**

Greece

Yes, there is something more than **feta**, which should properly be made from ewe milk and stored in brine; a delicious cheese for adding savoury bite to baking and firm enough to crumble into salad dressings. In Greece it is used very much like a condiment, even if it has been made from imported powdered cows' milk that had to be bleached.

Halloumi: most often made in Cyprus if seen abroad, this is almost a plastic curd cheese q.v. It should be rinsed clear of any brine before use and may be sliced and lightly fried or grilled with olive oil. This makes a superb basis for anything vegetarian, as the replacement for a piece of meat.

Kasseri: a kneaded, pressed cheese that melts well.

Kefalotiri: a piquant ewe milk cheese used in cooking – a little goes a long way.

Ireland

With untold centuries of dairying on her clean, green pastures Ireland was very early into the eruption of smallholder cheeses, and some of these, like small surface ripened cheeses, have now been around for over 20 years, enough to put them firmly amongst the ranks of significant contributors to better eating.

Cashel Blue: is perhaps the most famous and widely distributed Irish cheese; the Irish enjoy eating this fine cheese in sandwiches, both when quite young and when aged 14 weeks or so.

Coolea: is an Irish cheese made in the Gouda style by the Willems, but the combination of Ireland's untouched, verdant pastures and the devoted individuality of such cheese makers give flavours you won't find elsewhere: a two-year old has been described as 'stunning . . . incredible intensity'.

Ireland seems particularly gifted at making sweetly aromatic, washed rind cheeses and if you are a lover of these high-nose, satin-fleshed cheeses, look out for **Durrus**, which is notably powerful when made with autumn milk and then long matured; **Milleens** is bold and idiosyncratic, varying according to the mood of Veronica Steele, who makes it; **Gubbeen** is made with raw milk in Co Cork and **Ardrahan** from Kanturk, County Cork, wins prizes when it is also smoked.

Over on the Dingle Peninsula Maja Binder combines evening milk and next morning's milk to make **Kilcummin** and prize winning **Beenoskee**, using dark red dillisk seaweed as added flavour.

At the British Cheese Awards 2004, **Cratloe Hills Sheep** cheese was voted best Irish cheese: others that won medals were soft **St Killian**, washed rind **Croghan Goat**, and **Crozier Blue**. Best new Irish cheese was **Croghan's** hard-pressed **Blackwater Goat**.

After 18 months to two years **Doolin**, from Waterford reaches complex, rather caramellised flavours with a notably long finish.

Italy

Very underrated cheeses, with a range running from rich dessert cheeses through challenging blues to the complex piquancy of pecorinos, granas and Parmesans. The north tends towards cows, the south towards goats and sheep, and also favours the water buffalo for the original mozzarella.

No one really knows how many cheeses are made in Italy because almost every farmhouse makes their own, and in their own way. One of the simplest ways to see and enjoy a wide selection of Italian cheeses is in New York's Little Italy. At Di Palo Fine Foods, 200 Grand Street at Mott, the family that has run the shop since 1925 reckons to sell around 300 cheeses made in Italy, as well as huge amounts of mozzarella and ricotta they make fresh on site every day.

A smaller but equally startling introduction to the number of cheeses we known nothing about can be found at the Gastronomica stall at London's Borough Market, where Gian Alberto offers a startlingly unfamiliar range only from Piedmont and thereabouts, including an amazing cone of aged ricotta that's a somewhat translucent khaki, and what look like grubby boulders; all reward explorers wonderfully.

The particular fascination of many Italian cheeses, including the DOP protected varieties, is they are often made with a couple of types or mixtures of milk and in varying sizes, so what is correct about the flavour or appearance of a 2kg cheese is quite different when it's made as 6 or 8kg. That's exciting. It means whatever you thought you knew about an Italian cheese, there's three more coming around the corner with the same name but differing flavours. You'll never be bored exploring Italian cheese. The following list includes all the DOP cheeses, plus some others you'd be pleased to meet.

Asiago DOP: produced in the provinces of Vicenza and Trento and in agreed areas of Treviso and Padova. Asiago is sold both fresh and matured. The fresh cheeses are made from full-cream milk and have an elegant light sweetness: matured asiago will have been made from partly skimmed milk in rounds weighing up to 12kg, and is highly flavoured with a compact body that contains small holes.

Bel Paese: a firm, pearly-white textured cheese with a full, fruity nose and a clean creamy taste that leaves a sweet finish. A mild, washed rind cheese perfected by Galbani in the 20th century and the basis for much of their international fame and fortune. Keeps very well but beware an excess suggestion of paraffin under the foil, a fault easily detected by your nose.

Bitto DOP: from inland areas of the province of Sondrio and neighbouring villages in the province of Bergamo, Bitto is a lightly pressed cheese made unusually from cows' milk mixed with goat milk. A light sweet taste and a body that compacts on aging, when the flavour is noticeably more aromatic and strong.

Bra DOP: made all over the province of Cuneo, but ageing often takes place in the districts of Villafranca Piemonte, near Torino. Raw cows' milk is used to make both semi-hard and hard cheeses in tall cylinders that can weigh 6-8kg. The soft **bra tenero** has a white body and a pale grey skin, giving a light piquancy; harder **bra duro** has a creamier coloured body, an even, dark-grey skin and elevated savouriness.

Caciocavallo Silano DOP: a plastic curd/*pasta filata* cheese, made from cows' milk into an oval shape or an oval with a head that shows the marks of the strings by which it was hung. It always looks very smooth and yellow outside but is white inside. The body is typically very smooth, with a sweet flavour; melting texture when fresh but these cheeses can be matured to a delicious savouriness suited to grating. The areas of production are all regions in the southern Appenines – Basilicata, Calabria, Campania, Molise and Puglia.

Canestrato Pugliese DOP: a hard sheep milk cheese made all over the province of Foggia and in parts of Bari, it shows the characteristic rich savoury flavour of sheep milk when young and matures to a distinct piquancy. Made in cylinders of 7-14kg, it usually displays stamped impressions associated with the area in which it was made.

Casciotta d'Urbino DOP: an unusual mixture of 70% sheep milk and 30% cows' milk made along the borders of Pesaro and Urbino provinces. The matured body is yellowish and malleable, as with all plastic-curd/*pasta filata* cheeses, and it has their classic sweet taste.

Castelmagno DOP: made with cows' milk to which some sheep milk is added, giving a medium-bodied cheese with a delicate but intense herbal quality and that deepens with age. Made in Pradleves, Monterosso Grana and Castelmagno, all in the province of Cuneo.

Dolcelatte: a milder, creamier, commercial version of Gorgonzola, using richer milk. **Dolceverde** is the same thing made by a different manufacturer.

Fiore Sardo DOP: its name means 'the flower of Sardinia' and this raw sheep milk cheese is very fragrant and floral when young, when it is also meltingly tender and might have some holes. Aged Fiore Sardo has a more decisive and pointed flavour, and flakes and grates beautifully. It's made all over Sardinia.

Fontina/Fonta DOP: ripened for three months and sold according to the season in which it was made all over the Valle d'Aosta: that made on alpine pastures during summer is always the best, of course. **Fontal** is the commercialized version made with pasteurised milk. It is a pale yellow cheese with a sweet aroma and delicate, nutty flavour and can be made up to 18kg in size. A few small round eyes in the body are acceptable. It is a good melting and cooking cheese, especially when matured, and is favoured in dishes on which white truffles might be sliced.

Formai de Mut dell'Alta Val Brembana DOP: apart from winning the longest cheese name award, Formai de Mut are famed for their discreet, floral flavours balanced by a distinct but light salt tang. Another that can vary from 8-12 kg, so expect variations of flavour within recognisable bounds from each of the 21 villages that makes the cheese In the Alta Val Brembana in Bergamo province.

Gorgonzola DOP: Italy's best known blue cheese, a world and flavour of its own, for it is one of the few blue cheeses which does not rely on *penicillium roquefortii*, but on *penicillium glaucum*. The original Mountain Gorgonzola has a thousand-year history and was once made only with so called *stracchino*, the 'tired' milk of thinner autumn grass that nonetheless makes terrific cheese. The body is a yellow colour and the veins are green rather than blue. Avoid a brown appearance, bitterness or sourness, but expect a pungent, rich flavour with a definite bite – sometimes the differences between bitterness and acidic bite are hard to spot, and only a great deal of eating will teach you. The 20th century created a mellower Creamy Gorgonzola, and that's what is usually stocked. Made through a largely continuous area inland, in the provinces of Bergamo, Biella, Brescia, Como, Cremona, Cuneo, Lecco, Lodi, Milano, Novara, Pavia, Vercelli, Verbano Cisio Ossola and in Casla Monferrato In Alessandria.

Grana: in fact, the proper name for the type of cheese we call Parmesan, in turn simply the best known member of the family.

All granas are hard pressed cooked cheeses made from semi-skimmed milk and are the salt and pepper of Italian cuisine. They are terrific table and sandwich cheeses, sliced thickly or scraped off with a vegetable peeler. The flavour is sweeter than you expect and as complicated and long-lasting in the mouth as the finest wine. A piece of grana eaten at the end of a meal, perhaps with a pear or apple, is very hard to beat, and the manifold tastes last as long as, well, as long as it takes to persuade yourself one more piece won't hurt. Indeed, it won't.

It is ok to freeze these cheeses, for then you can grate them while still frozen. This should be done along the length of the piece, so you are always incorporating some of the skin, both so it is not an annoying left over and because it has extra piquancy through being washed with brine at an early stage in the manufacture. Italians use grana skins widely in cookery.

Grana Padano DOP is made all over Lombardy from cows fed on grass and hay. On the left bank of the Po river the cheese is made in the provinces of Alesandria, Asti, Cuneo, Novara, Torino, Vercelli, Bergamo, Brescia, Como, Cremona and Mantova; on the right bank of the Reno River it's made in Milano, Pavia, Sondrio, Varese, Trento, Padova, Treviso, Venezia, Verona, Vicenza and Bologna, as well as in Ferrara, Forli, Piacenza, Ravenna, the areas of Antrivio, Lauregno, Proves, Senale-S. Felice and Trodena in Bolzano. They will generally be light in colour, faster to mature than Parmesans, and flakier and cheaper.

Parmigiano Reggiano DOP: the cows whose milk makes Parmesan cheeses are fed only clover and lucerne and only in the provinces of Parma, Reggio Emilio, Modena and Bologna on the left bank of the Reno river, and in Mantua on the right bank of the Po. These regal cheeses take longer to mature than a grana padano, and are also much underrated as a table cheese when young. In Italy, at least, you can buy them as *giovane*, *tipico*, *stravecchio* and *vecchio*, progressively older – and more expensive of course. Italians believe it to be one of the great aids to digestion, long life – and almost everything else I bet. Parmesan is unrecognized as a cheese name in Italy, where it is Parmigiano, or more properly Parmigiano Reggiano. The awful 'parm-uh-zharn', neither Italian nor English, should never be uttered. Parmesan is not so hard to say, is it? See Twineham Grange page 135.

Montasio DOP: produced throughout Friuli Venezia Giulia, the provinces of Belluno and Treviso and in a few areas of Padova and Venezia. Its weight varies between 5kg and 9kg and the body varies from white to pale yellow as it ages, when it becomes a little grainy and develops greater bite, flavour and presence.

Monte Veronese DOP: made throughout the province of Verona in two versions, full cream and semi-skinned. A full-cream Monte Veronese weighs up to 10kg, is up to 11cm thick and has a thin pale yellow crust, a white or cream body with lots of small holes and a gentle, mild flavour: the skimmed-milk variety is shallower, weighs a little less, but develops a bigger more savoury flavour as it matures.

Mascarpone: fooled you – and almost everyone else. This isn't a cheese, but for all that it appears in every list of Italian cheeses. It is an Italian crème fraîche, that is, cream thickened by the action of a lactic fermentation. Thoroughly and wickedly delicious, it is suddenly everywhere, but like ciabatta q.v. was only invented a few decades ago.

You particularly find it in tiramisu, the Italian dessert that layers it with sponge fingers, coffee, chocolate and alcohol and that masquerades as a traditional pick-me-up (which is what the name means) but is yet another modern favourite invented only a few decades ago – hence the hideous, infamous variations, and why there are tiramisu shops in Tokyo that sell tiramisu flavoured with giggles and any and everything except seaweed, so far.

Mozzarella: a plastic curd/ *pasta filata* cheese q.v. originally made to be eaten within hours – a farmer's wife would make it in the morning for their lunch and Italian shops often make it on the premises every morning – they do in New York anyway. Its freshness means it will, or should, have very little smell or flavour other than of the original milk, and should be light and rather sponge-like. The classic technique once the hot curds have been kneaded enough is to pull off portions and to then make them into balls by rolling lightly between your palms, either big blobs the size of your fist or *bocconcini*, little mouthfuls.

Comparison to the yellow slabs commercially made from cows' milk, and sold as pizza mozzarella is pointless – how can such different cheeses be called the same name? True mozzarella is *bufala* q.v. made with buffalo milk. Mozzarella of the blob and *bocconcini* types are also very successfully made with cow's milk as *fior de latte* or flower of the milk, and are almost as light and as white and somewhat richer in flavour, as well as being cheaper. Even cows' milk mozzarella is too special to be cooked. Sliced thickly both are wonderful in sandwiches and wraps and rolls, for the light spongy contrast they offer: in New York's Italian, Dominican and Puerto Rican suburbs you'll find very fresh mozzarella is sliced into sandwiches of hot pork, chicken or beef.

If you want such luxury on your pizza, slice *bufala* or white cows' milk mozzarella, and tuck these well under other ingredients for just the last few minutes of cooking, so the cheese only warms through and none or very little browns or bubbles. Nothing you do to yellow commercial mozzarella matters.

Mozzarella di Bufala Campana DOP: authentic mozzarella made only with the milk of the buffalo, the most common milking animal of southern Italy, and is always stored in whey or light brine. Fresh *mozzarella di bufala* is like eating milky clouds of a newborn's breath. Italians describe the colour of *bufala* as porcelain-white, and if there is any skin at all it must be very thin; a thicker skin means older cheese, and the sniff test will tell if it is souring or soured.

Although the flavour of both *bufala* and *fior de latte* is very light and milky it comes curiously alive when put together with other flavours, absorbing them without alienating its own; not much is better than sliced *bufala* with very good tomato, basil leaves and a somewhat prevailing olive oil, which is partly soaked up by the cheese.

Warm mozzarella curd stays elastic for 8-10 hours and so can be rolled quite thin, and then rolled up with pancetta or prosciutto and fresh basil leaves, that is then cut into slices of white pink and green spirals. Better for being so unsuspected and so indulgent is *straciatelli*; the buffalo milk curd is manipulated and punched and pulled in such a way it can be torn into thin narrow strips about the size of thick spaghetti or tagliatelle, which are then put into tubs of single (light) cows' cream. I was told you eat it on bread, but I wouldn't; some of life's pleasures should not be shared. You probably have to look hard for it even in southern Italy, but it's worth the search. Or, like me, you might get lucky and stumble on to a demonstration in Harrods Food Hall.

Genuine *mozzarella di bufala* is made in the provinces of Caserta, Salerno, Napoli and Benevento as well as Latina, Frosinone and Roma. In Italy you will find more sizes and shapes than the big or small balls you're used to: these will include *treccia, perlina, ciliegina* and *nodino* – tresses, pearls, cherries and nests. Smoking of mozzarella is allowed but only if traditional, 'natural' methods are followed.

Murrazanno DOP: a delicate fresh cheese weighing up to 400g and with no skin, made in 50 districts in the Langhe area.

Pecorino: a unique family of piquant ewe milk cheeses associated with the south of Italy, Sicily and Sardinia. Although the name can be used for any cheese made with this milk, it is specially applied to hard-pressed types, usually made in small drums or wheels with convex rims. The most famous types are Pecorino Romano, traditionally made in Lazio, but much is now made in Sardinia as Pecorino Sardo; frankly, you are just as likely to be buying something made in a factory from cows' milk with a usefully sharp starter added. If you can buy it young, pecorino makes a superb table cheese, and there is a version of pressed pecorino that contains black peppercorns. Otherwise it is an outstanding cooking cheese, a sheepish grana.

Pecorino Romano DOP: produced in three quite distinct areas – Lazio, Sardinia and the province of Grossetto in Tuscany. Made only with sheep milk and varying from 2.5 to 3.5kg, these cheeses are aromatic and delicious to eat as a table cheese when five months old, and once at least eight months old become solid enough for grating and using as a seasoning; the flavour will be more pronounced but never too farmy.

Pecorino Sardo DOP: two types made throughout Sardinia. So-called sweet pecorino Sardo is sold after very little ageing and is very white and with a light acidity that fluctuates according to the cheese's size – from 1 to 2.3kg. Matured pecorino Sardo is more likely to be a creamy yellow and will be firm yet malleable texture and can develop a noticeably strong but never unbalanced or unpleasant flavour. Use with discretion as a seasoning.

Pecorino Siciliano DOP: you'll find this made all over Sicily but few taste alike and you can enjoy the same cheese but a different flavour every day. The weight varies up to 2kg, the colour from white to pale yellow. The fresh and semi-matured cheeses keep a fresh milky taste, and the firmer matured ones are characteristically sharper and deeper in flavour.

Pecorino Toscano DOP: less well known than sheep milk cheeses from Sardinia and Sicily, the Toscano also varies in size from 1 to 3kg and is sold fresh or matured. The fresh cheeses are soft and pale yellow and as the cheese matures the colour deepens as does the fragrant, slightly tangy flavour. Sometimes the crusts are treated and so can be red or even black, and these differences usually mean a variation in flavour too. Made throughout Tuscany and on the borders of Lazio and Umbria.

Provolone Valpadana DOP: the greatest of the great plastic curd or *pasta filata* cheeses, even this DOP version can be made in such shapes as a salami, a melon, a cone or a pear and can have or be without a round head too. These cheeses can be matured for a long time without drying out and still retain their classic smooth texture. Small and fresh ones are notably sweet and benign, and the full-flavoured mature cheeses have a nice bite and delicious long-lasting flavour. The best of Provolone must be made in the central areas of Cremona, Brescia, Verona, Vicenza, Rovigo, Padova and Piacenza, and in some parts of the provinces of Bergamo, Mantova, Lodi and Trento.

Quartirolo Lombardo DOP: an unusual soft cheese made from full or semi-skimmed cows' milk throughout Brescia, Bergamo, Como, Cremona, Lecco, Lodi, Milano, Pavia and Varese. It's square in shape and weighs between 1.5 to 3.5kg. The body can be rather uneven in texture when young, when the coat will be smooth and white-reddish and the flavour nicely acidic: as it matures the skin turns grey-green and fragrant without being piercing or intrusive.

Ragusano DOP: made only from raw, full-cream milk from the province of Ragusa plus the districts of Noto, Palazzolo, Acreide and Rosolini in the province of Siracusa. Like so many Italian cheeses this cheese is sweet and delicate when young and can also be matured long enough to be a robust but non-aggressive grating cheese. It is a long oblong with a skin that darkens from yellow to brown as it ages and has a creamy yellow body.

Raschera DOP: a thin reddish-grey crust cuts to reveal a white body. It can be made in a cylinder weighing up to 8kg or in a rectangle up to 10kg. It has a notably agreeable moderate and well balanced flavour when mature. It's made throughout the province of Cuneo: another version found as *raschera d'Alpeggio* is made and matured more than 900 metres above sea level in the districts of Frabosa Soprana, Frabosa Sottana, Geressio, Magliano Alpi, Montaldo Mondovi, Ormea, Pamparato, Ruburent and Roccaforte Mondovi.

Ricotta: one of the most useful of all dairy products, although not a true cheese in its original form, for it's then made from the albumen content of whey, which retains the sugar of milk but none of its fat. These days it is as likely to be made by adding whole or skimmed milk to whey, which greatly enhances the yield. It has all the clean fresh flavour of milk and when bought from a wicker-impressed cake that is still drooling with excess moisture makes the best cooking cheese of all, perfect for everything from savoury stuffings to sweet cheesecakes. How some supermarkets dare sell tubs of fine-textured, solid white cheese as ricotta beats me.

Robbiola di Rocaverona DOP: made from cows' milk and at least 15% goat or sheep milk in specific districts of the provinces of Asti and Alessandria and in the eastern farms of the Langhe. A skinless small cheese no more than 14cm across and 5cm thick, it can weigh between 250 and 400g. It's distinctly white and with the added goat or sheep milk is discreetly tasty and has a delicious acidity.

Spressa della Giudicare DOP: made with raw milk that must come from the local Rendena cows or from the Bruna, Grigio Alpina, Frisona and Pezzata Rossa breeds. It's a low cylinder 30-35cm in diameter and weighing up to 10kg. Typical of cooked mountain cheeses it has sweet floral and herbal notes that intensify with age and it usually presents an unusual, faint but acceptable residual bitterness. Made in the Giudicare Valley, Chiese, Rendana and Ledro, all mainly in the Trento province.

Taleggio DOP: a flat, square cheese of up to 2.2kg with a lightly acidic and fruity flavour some think like black truffles, created either early in the 20th century or a thousand years ago, depending on your reference book. It is a slab of creamy full fat cheese with a thin rind which should be pinkish-grey, but that is more often seen looking distinctly blue or grey – yet this does not seem to matter. Essentially mild with an attractive acidity, it should also have a distinct fruitiness but can develop a bitterness, which should be firmly rejected if encountered. Excellent examples in perfect condition can be aged twice as long as the recommended six weeks, when they deepen in colour and develop greater aroma and attraction. Made in the provinces of Bergamo, Brescia, Como, Cremona, Lecco, Lodi, Milano, Pavia, Treviso and Novara.

Toma Piemontese DOP: a classic mountain Tomme but this one ranges from a mere 1.8kg to 8kg, and so matures for 15 to 60 days according to size. It is typically sweet and creamy and becomes more intensely fragrant as it ages. Made in Novara, Verbania, Vercelli, Biella, Torino, Cuneo and some districts in the provinces of Asti and Alessandria.

Torta: these layered cheeses look like the invention of a colour-blind marketing man, but they are actually a tradition of the Trieste area. All should be served slightly chilled and the best version layers Gorgonzola with mascarpone, which is outstandingly good with a ripe pear.

Valle d'Aosta Fromadzo DOP: the two versions of this cheese have a fat percentage of 20% or a of 35% and both can be from 1kg to 7kg. Both are naturally sweet and aromatic and become a little salty and more savoury if aged. The crust is pale yellow when relatively young but slowly turns grey, just as the body turns from white to yellow if allowed to age. The milk for this cheese can come from anywhere in the Valle d'Aosta.

Valtelina Cassera DOP: a big low-fat cheese made throughout Sondrio province and which can weight from 7 to 12kg. It is characterised by a special sweetness that is reminiscent of dried fruits and which intensifies with maturity. Typically the body ages from white to yellow and although compact shows fine open lines throughout.

Netherlands

Edam: is a full flavoured cheese despite its lower fat content, but the shame of it is that most is sold and eaten long before its true flavour has had the chance to develop, which is why it is frequently called the cheese for people who hate cheese. It is a medium pressed, ball of a cheese with a distinctive rind that is the result of immersion in whey and brine baths, and salting after it has been pressed. Any sourness tells you it is too immature but a good one is quite useful in cooking with its most notable attribute being its relative cheapness. When you are there, remember the red coat which makes Edam so easily recognized throughout the world is for export and never seen in the Netherlands.

Gouda: is richer, larger and yellower than Edam and has more flavour. Salt rubbed on the rind helps develop the flavour, which continues to develop for well over a year. At a food exhibition in Birmingham we offered tastings of a two-year-old Gouda with a close texture and rich, golden colour that took everyone by surprise with its tangy, full flavour and spicy nose. Honestly, I think a matured Gouda repays exploration more than most cheeses. An excellent cooker whatever the age. When in Holland, look out for the farmhouse versions, Boeren made with unpasteurised milk and often flavoured with nettles, cumin and other spices or herbs.

New Zealand

New Zealand's range has suddenly expanded tremendously. She has long made an excellent blue vein cheese in the Danish Blue/Roquefort style and equivalents of British territorials but now makes outstanding bloomy rind cheeses and ewe milk styles too, all of which must by law only be made with pasteurised milk. Currently, New Zealand suffers a proliferation of evermore arcane flavoured cheeses, sad to see when there is so much scope for making a greater basic variety from its high quality milk, thus complementing some of the world's best natural produce and most worthwhile restaurant cooking; veteran international travellers and eaters regularly tell me their best eating experiences anywhere have been in Auckland or Wellington. And now they include the cheese, for just as with the rest of the world New Zealand has rediscovered good cheese and artisans have been encouraged. At the last cheese awards I judged there were almost 450 cheeses, some very worthwhile copies of European ones – Ferndale raclette was judged overall winner – and many Dutch cheese makers offer truly superlative aged Gouda-style cheeses.

But what thrilled me most of all was the way the commercial cheeses turned out. I wondered what great plastic blocks of Cheddar cheese were doing at a serious competition – well, I did until I tasted some. It felt like biting into rich summer pasture with cream, actually tasting of what it was made from. Then I discovered block cheeses from other factories were as good but had flavour differences – and then I was confronted with a block cheese being in the finals for judging as overall champion. Nothing could have been more wonderful than to be reminded of the extraordinary pleasure there can be in a Cheddar cheese from one's own backyard, even if not made by hand and on a farm in England.

Puhoi Valley cheeses and Kapiti cheeses are big companies that produce prize-winning cheeses of all varieties. Kapiti's Port Nicholson is a robust washed rind cheese that's worth finding, as is Whitestone's brie and Zany Zeus halloumi or ricotta. There's an extraordinary range of soft blue cheeses: Puhoi's Kaipara Blue comes in blue wax – for an amazing treat, slice off the top and dress the exposed blue cheese with lime marmalade, one with plenty of zest. And then do the same with a true rose petal jam. Amazing!

Scandinavia

A bewildering variety of bland, slightly chewy cheeses that look and taste pretty much the same make standing at a cheese counter in Sweden or Denmark a nightmare of yellowness. It is perhaps as well they are unassuming for in these countries cheese is eaten at breakfast, not as noisy as cornflakes but substantially more of a challenge to those used to grains at dawn. The most extraordinary exceptions are whey cheeses, the gjetost and mesost, which are brown because the sugar in the whey is caramelized in the process. There are spiced cheeses, tasty cheeses and supposedly a smoked cheese made from reindeer milk that must be dunked into coffee to make it palatable. I would be surprised to learn it was worth the trouble.

Danablue/Danish Blue: a 20th century invention designed as a substitute for Roquefort, but whilst the young pretender to the crown has been an enormous commercial success, any similarity to Roquefort in its eating characteristics has eluded me. Its sharp saltiness belies its richness, which is due to the use of homogenized milk in the making. Should be white rather than creamy, with blue rather than green veining, and crumbliness is perfectly acceptable if there is plenty of moisture. Much used in cheese mousses, blue cheese dressings and other American-style dishes but mixed with butter it makes an excellent savoury spread.

Gjetost: the cheese that looks like caramel fudge. Made with goat milk whey or a mixture of cows' and goats' milk whey. When pure goat milk is used, it is called ekte (real) gjetost and is even more of an acquired taste than the more commonly found Ski-Queen gjetost. Sliced very thinly, gjetost is said to be a great complement to herring and other fish dishes. Yeah, right.

Havarti: comes in two types, one with a dry rind and one with a washed rind. The dry rind version was once called **Danish Tilsit** and although it is mildly aromatic it is basically a bland tasting cheese. The washed-rind havarti is fairly full flavoured at three months and develops a more pungent taste as it matures further. Made in loaves weighing 4.5kg.

Jarlsberg: was extinct until the 1950s when this old Norwegian recipe was spruced up and given a new lease of life. Now it is widely marketed, particularly in the United States. It has some similarity in texture to Gouda with a paste that is soft, smooth and mildly aromatic.

Munajusto: this Finnish cheese is translated as 'egg cheese' and indeed contains one or two eggs for every six litres of milk. The yolks give the cheese a wonderful colour. Good for melting and grilling.

Mycella: the Danish gorgonzola, with a full but unaggressive flavour, a yellowish, supple body and green, not blue, veins. Steer clear of any brownness or over-blueing, sharp smell or bitter flavour. **Castello** is mycella with a surface, camembert-type mould as well, which is intentional.

Samso: probably the head of Denmark's most important cheese family. All those ending in 'o' of this type are related with the first part of the name indicating the cheese's origin. Samso is firm, yellow and nutty with cherry-sized holes and a flavour which varies from mild sweetness to distinctive strength. Made in a cartwheel shape. Flavour preference is highly personal and rather arbitrary, varying fat content may have some bearing. Useful in cooking. Types include **Danbo**, square shaped and sometimes flavoured with caraway; Elbo, which is firm, loaf-shaped and with holes; and **Tybo**, brick-shaped, very firm and red-rinded.

Ridder is a modern cheese from Norway and similar to Saint Paulin, with an orange, lightly washed rind and a buttery paste.

Spain

Her inclusion in the EU has meant Spain's cheeses are slowly becoming better known but a visit to the country is very rewarding as much cheese-making remains artisanal with only

localized distribution. Ewe milk cheese is the most common, of which the Manchego of
La Mancha is the most famous, sold either young or ripened at least a year in olive oil. Cabrales
is the best-known blue cheese, often made with mixed milks; Spaniards are said by Sandy Carr
to like it almost totally blue and alive with mites and maggots.

Both Manchego and Cabrales have the protected DOP status that guarantees the standards
of the country's most esteemed foods, a project Spain has led Europe in adopting and
promoting.

The 2004 list of DOP Spanish cheeses is:

Queso de l'Alt Urgell and de la Cerdanya DOP: from these two regions in the north-eastern
provinces Lerida and Gerona, both in the central-eastern Catalan Pyrenées, these cheeses are
made only by the CADI cooperative, which has greatly helped maintain rural life in this area
since the early 20th century, before which the cheeses were made domestically. Made from
pasteurised Friesian milk in low, convex cylinders. Surface ripening gives a sometimes sticky,
brown appearance and the classic nose of such cheeses. The body has plenty of irregular but
small holes throughout, the flavour is sweet and mild but with the distinct tang of all surface
ripened cheeses.

Cabrales DOP: from the Alpine pastures of the Picos de Europa in the province of Asturias. A
blue cheese made from raw cow, sheep or goat milk, since the 18th century. The blue is not
injected but invades naturally when the cheeses are aged for 2-5 months in natural caves.

Idiazabal DOP: from Alaya, Vizcaya, Guipuzcoa and Navarre, homes of the Lacha and
Carranzana sheep breeds, and where sheep have been kept since 2200BC. A pressed cheese
aged at least sixty days, which can be natural or smoked over beech or alder wood shortly
before marketing.

Mahon-Menorca DOP: from the Balearic island of Menorca, where cheese making is recorded
since the 5th century. Mahon Arteseno is made from raw milk and must mature at least 60 days

but ordinary Mahon is also made industrially with heat-treated milk. Semi-cured cheeses are aged less than 150 days: cured cheeses must age longer. These cheeses are curious cushion shapes with a yellow to brownish rind, with the marks of cloth folds on the upper faces of the *artesano* cheeses. The flavour is slightly acidic with definite lactic overtones, both of which increase with age.

Picon-Bejes-Tresviso DOP: from the Liebana district in the southwest of the Autonomous Community of Cantabria, where cheese making has been recorded since May 15th 962. A blue cheese made from the milk of cow, sheep, goat or any combination of the two, a thin greyish rind and white body. The blue veins develop naturally in caves with very specific characteristics that enhance their growth.

Queso de Cantabria DOP: from the Autonomous Community of Cantabria except the areas of the Council of Tresviso, and of Bejes in the Council of Cillorigo: records since 1647 show cheese merchants exporting these products to surrounding cities and to the Royal Palace in Madrid 400km away. A lightly pressed, quite fresh cheese made from the milk of Friesian cows and so rather white: in oblongs or drums. The rennet used must be from the stomachs of suckling calves from the local Pintas de Cantabria breed. Sold after a minimum seven days aging.

Queso Ibores DOP: from 35 municipalities in the southeast of the province of Caceres for most of history. Made from the raw milk of designated mountain-goat breeds – Verata, Retinta and their crossbreeds. When the rind is left natural it's a greyish colour, but it's more likely to be reddish, *pimentonados*, due to surface ripening, or yellow if rubbed with oil. The flavour keeps its raw milk edge and leaves a characteristic goat milk taste. An artisan cheese means it's been made by someone with his or her own flocks and has been matured at least 100 days.

Quesecos de Liebana: made in the northern municipal districts of Liebana in Cantabria, which is thought to have smoked cheeses so they could be carried to Ancient Rome. Usually made with the raw milk of highly specialised breeds of cow, sheep and goat, it varies during the seasons, but is a firm compact cheese made in small shallow discs 8-12cm wide, and with distinct marks made by self-draining moulds. Pasteurised milk must be used for cheeses matured for less than 60 days, and around Aliva, Brez and Lomena the cheeses are customarily smoked, to give longer life and different flavours. The smoking medium is usually juniper and the cheese will be cold-smoked for up to 36 hours, according to preference.

Queso de La Serena DOP: from 21 districts in the extreme southeast of the province of Badajoz, where cheese making is recorded since the 16th century. A soft to semi-hard ewes' milk cheese made in discs with flattened tops and bottoms and that must be aged at least 20 days. The rind can be waxy yellow to ochre and the body from ivory white turning to waxy yellow with aging. A low temperature and mild curding means the body can be unevenly distributed with small holes. After 20 days, the body softens and becomes plastic and malleable, so great care must be taken not to split the rind: the cheese then gradually matures and becomes firmer.

Queso Majorero DOP: from the island of Fueteventura, the closest of the Canary Isles to Africa, only 100km away, where goat herding has been known for centuries. A pressed cheese with sides showing the imprints of plaited fibre or of similarly marked moulds imitating these, and made with the raw milk of Majorero goats, occasionally supplemented with up to 15% of milk from Canary sheep. Fresh cheeses are very white, but matured ones can have a surface smeared with paprika, oil or toasted cornmeal and a more ivory-coloured body.

Queso Manchego DOP: one of Spain's best known and made exclusively from a local breed of ewe in the provinces of Albacete, Cuidad Real, Cuenca and Toledo, which together make the vast region known as La Mancha, hence Manchego: Don Quixote certainly knew about manchego, or Cervantes did anyway. It's a pressed cheese aged at least 60 days after pressing: the top and bottom should be impressed with a flower and the sides with the familiar braid pattern. It's a hard cheese that yellows as it gets older and is used a lot in cooking, especially grated.

Queso de Murcia and Queso de Murcia al vino DOP: produced all over the eastern province of Murcia, where fresh goat milk cheese seems always to have been made. Prepared with the milk of a distinct local breed of Murciano-Grandina goat, small, dainty and either black or mahogany. There are three types, all part cured in brine:

Fresh Murcian is cheese where the fresh curds are only lightly processed by shaking to keep a tender texture, lightly pressed if at all and then packed into cylindrical moulds with typical braided esparto grass patterns. Very white and compact but soft.

Cured Murcian is made from cheese curds heated to firm them up and shaken more vigorously and for longer. Packed into straight-sided cylinders and lightly pressed for up to four hours, giving a compact white body with firm texture and virtually no holes.

Murcian Cheese Cured in Wine is worked less than plain cured cheeses but also pressed up to four hours. Washed with concentrated red wine to give characteristic rind colour and developing a creamy, rather elastic texture and recognisable washed-rind flavour. Aged about 30 days.

Queso Palmero DOP: another cheese from the Canary Islands, this time from San Miguel de la Palma, La Palma for short, and has been made since Spaniards introduced the goat in 1493. Produced from raw milk of the La Palma goat, they can be eaten fresh, soft, semi-cured or cured. Some are smoked, over almond shells, prickly pear cactus or Canary Island pine. Only available fresh in season and after that the cheeses are sealed with olive oil, cornmeal or flour and kept in caves or specially ventilated rooms. Ancient ordinances decree these cheeses should be branded, identifying the owner of the herd from which the milk came, and the herd's exact whereabouts on the island.

Queso Roncal DOP: made in the Valle de Roncal in the province of Navarre on Spain's northern border with France. A pressed ewe milk cheese made from Rasa and Lacha breeds since at least the 10th century, when the area had as many as 100,000 sheep all of which migrated back and forth, to and from the mountains, in the famed transhumance. At 50% Roncal is particularly high in fat, and is a hard porous cheese without holes and has a definite tang to its flavour.

Queso de Tetilla DOP: from all the Autonomous Community of Galicia on the north-western tip of the Iberian Peninsula. Made from the mixed milks of three cattle breeds, the Friesian and two local ones, the Parda Alpina and Rubia Gallega. Instantly recognisable for its pear shape, it should have a nice straw-coloured thin rind, with a creamy soft body that's white to ivory, and will have been matured at least seven days.

Queso de Valdeon DOP: from the Posada de Valdeon in the north of the province of Leon, where goat milk cheese was probably made in Roman times. This is a blue cheese made from cows' milk or a mixture with goat or ewe milk, but is sold two ways as the creamy white, blue-veined whole cheese or as 'beaten' Valdeon cheese, made from cheeses that are seen not to be maturing evenly, when they are decrusted and trimmed of problem areas and then the remainder is whisked, giving it a rather more buttery texture and then packed in sizes from 20g to 1.5kg.

Queso Zamorano DOP: from all the districts in the province of Zamora, where cheese making was recorded in the 11th century. A pressed cheese with a definite rind, and made only with the raw milk of two local sheep breeds, the Churra and the Castellana, it has a sweet, distinctive aroma and flavour that lingers on the palate. Curing must be at least 100 days.

Torta del Casar DOP: made in Caceres, a province of the north-western Autonomous Community of Extremadura, where transhumance and sheep have had rights since 1273. The milk comes only from Merino and Entrefino sheep and must be curded with thistle milk. The smallish discs of Casar Cake have yellow to ochre crusts and a soft body that can be white to creamy and with small holes. They have an intense scent and high flavour with an unusual slight bitterness, from the thistle.

Switzerland

Swiss cheese making has a pedigree you can trace directly to Roman heritage and traditions. Some like Sbrinz were actually known and appreciated by the Romans, but others have a relationship linked through monastic Ireland. Let me explain.

It was the Romans and their roads that took civilized eating and sophisticated agriculture westwards, including cheese making. But when the Vandals and Goths took the same route and pulled down the curtains on civilizations, repositories of that knowledge retreated ever westwards, until only the monasteries of western Ireland kept and upheld Roman tradition. When the Dark Ages brightened, barefoot Irish monks took civilization back to Europe and reintroduced cheese making to the country we know as Switzerland. Today the Swiss have still not heard any convincing argument to change the way they make their renowned cheeses, some of which are amongst the very few truly useful to the cook. Indeed Swiss cheese cooking traditions are well worth anyone's interest.

Appenzeller: some 700 years ago a cheese from the Appenzell region was recorded as a tithe payment to the Saint Gall monastery but how much it resembled the cheese of today is not known. Its yellowish brown rind is the result of regular washing with a brine marinade of herbs, spices and frequently wine or cider. At its best after three to four months' maturation, this semi-hard cheese should have a tangy, quite strong flavour. Whole cheeses weigh between 6 and 8kg with a diameter of 30cm. When explorer Tim Severin sailed across the Atlantic in a leather boat to recreate the supposed 6th century discovery of America by Irish monk St Brendan, I supplied him with food of the period. When they used modern foods on the first half of the voyage they were sick and weak, but with the Appenzeller, grains and smoked, salted meats in the 6th century style, they thrived – a lesson for us all.

Emmental: although cheese making in Emmental can be traced back to 1293 the earliest mention of this cheese by name is in a register of donations handed out to the inhabitants of Langenthal whose houses were burnt down in 1542. Since then it has been copied all round the world but in Switzerland, it is made only from unpasteurised milk, of which it takes 1000 litres to make each 80kg cheese. Although such a big cheese, it requires minutely detailed care to get right, which explains the despair of its imitators. The eyes should be fairly evenly distributed, the body a light yellow, the rind smooth and free from mould which may, nonetheless, easily be wiped off, and causes no ill effect. The smell and taste should be sweet and clean, not bitter and assertive in any way. The milk is usually only from the mottled Emmental cows of the Emme valley and hills.

Useful in cooking but will draw threads if heated too highly. Real Emmental always has 'Switzerland' stamped on the rind in red. A drop of moisture or 'tear' in the eyes is a very good sign of a perfectly mature and well-developed cheese. Cheese book author Sandy Carr quotes the makers as saying: 'Anyone can make the holes, only the Swiss can make the cheese.' Note, it is Emmental, not Emmenthal, which is a German cheese.

L'Etivaz AOC: an exceptional cheese that should be far better known and appreciated. Essentially it is a Gruyère cheese made the original way by cheese makers in the small village of L'Etivaz who broke away in the 1930s to protect traditions they thought were in danger of being erased. The cows graze on rare herbs and alpine flowers between 1000 and 2000 metres above sea level and the cheese is handmade in copper cauldrons over wood fires only between May 10th and October 10th. The relationship to Gruyère is apparent, but you'll probably find greater mellowness and butteriness. It is the first Swiss cheese to be given AOC status.

Fribourgeois: See Vacherin Fribourgeois.

Gruyère: another cheese with a tradition dating back to the 12th century

Today around 60 alpine farms make Gruyère during the summer at heights mostly over 1000m/3282 ft, close to Lake Geneva and with milk from black and white cows bred exclusively in the region. Over 400 litres of milk are needed for a cheese weighing 35kg and during the maturing process the rind is wiped with salt water to encourage a briny, dry sharpness. Firmer than Emmental and only half the size, the development of the rind flora gives a fuller, fruitier flavour which is notably sweeter and has a hint of nuttiness. The texture is supple with very few holes, no larger than a cherry. Check for the 'Switzerland' stamp on the surface. Some sliminess on the rind can be dealt with and then ignored as long as the cheese has not become bitter or sharp. One of the world's great cooking cheeses as it rarely strings and a combination of Gruyère and Emmental makes the only true Swiss cheese fondue. Gruyère is quite the best cheese for topping gratins, flavouring pastry and sauces and for cheese soufflés, perhaps pointed with grated Sbrinz.

Raclette: the name literally means scraper. A semi-hard cheese made from raw or pasteurised milk that has a typically fruity flavour from a paste that is almost gold in colour and very buttery. Its name comes from its most popular embodiment, in a dish called *raclette*: the cut surface of a halved raclette cheese is exposed to an open fire or flame and as it melts is scraped on to a plate and eaten at once with potatoes boiled in their skins, gherkins and pickles. It is the *ne plus ultra* of skiing resorts, and not just in Switzerland.

Sbrinz: probably the country's most ancient cheese, and related to Italian *granas q.v.*, this extra hard cheese has for the last 400 years been made in the Lucerne Valley from the milk of its distinctive brown cows. Immersed in salt baths after pressing, the young sbrinz is allowed to sweat out fat and water in heated maturing rooms. Throughout maturation, the cheese is regularly wiped dry and over a period of at least eighteen months, it develops its aromatic, full flavour and becomes a very easily digestible cheese. In fact one old recipe recommends taking a small piece of Sbrinz daily to help with stomach disorders. Serve broken or shaved into thin slices. A favourite of mine is simply to slice it thinly and immerse in a little balsamic vinegar. Serve before the meal as an appetizer – it's irresistible. Try grating finely in sauces, on rice in soup – in fact, it never strings, which makes it very easy to use.

Tete de Moine: made in the Swiss Jura, this cheese has at least 800 years of tradition behind its tall cylindrical shapes and is made from milk drawn from spring through to autumn. Because it is uncooked but pressed, the body is soft and supple but what singles it out is the way the Swiss say it must be served to appreciate the cheese. It must not be sliced but shaved in a circular motion using a tool called a *girolle*. This creates thin shavings of Tete de Moine that are traditionally served as rosettes, that particularly release the spicy, aromatic flavour of the cheese. Served this way, I have always found it essential not to leave the rosettes too long before eating as they can quickly dry. Often eaten with pepper and ground cumin.

Tilsiter: used to be known in the UK as Royalp and is made in eastern Switzerland in the canton of Thurgau. It is enormously popular in Switzerland itself, a semi-hard cheese with a reddish-brown rind and a pale yellow paste that at four months develops a mild but creamy flavour. Those with red labels are made from unpasteurised milk, and the green labels mean the milk has been pasteurised.

Vacherin Fribourgeois: quite frequently confused with Vacherin Mont d'Or, which is a very different cheese and this is probably why the Swiss have increasingly dropped the Vacherin and tend now to call it simply Fribourgeois.

Yet another Swiss mountain cheese with a pedigree dating back to the 15th century, it is still made in the canton of Fribourg in small dairies. A semi-hard cheese with an ivory to yellow paste, it has a mild, delicate flavour and after three months it starts to develop a distinctive aroma. Those exported are washed at three months then covered with a yellowish brown coat. Good in mixed cheese fondue or in a pure Fondue Fribourgeois, and if you are offered it on a cheese board, do try it.

Vacherin Mont d'Or: unusual for being a winter cheese. Moulded in a strip of pine that gives a light resinous flavour, the cheese can be anything from 200g to 3kg in weight but all have top skins that crumple when ready to eat. It is exceptionally rich and gratifying, a true dessert cheese to crown a lunch or dinner, when it is correct to remove the upper crust and then to spoon out the body. If it is cut into wedges the paste of the remainder must be held back with a piece of wood or glass or it will flow away.

United Kingdom

There is probably more potential for exciting discoveries amidst British (and Irish) cheeses than anywhere in the world – at last count there are over 700 being made. Interest in British cheese has grown so much the iconic **Neal's Yard** cheese shop is no longer just in the yard but has a cavernous place at Borough Market SE1, where you'll be dwarfed by towering cheeses, encouraged to taste and amazed at the range of raw-milk cheeses now being made. By Appointment grocers **Partridges of London** has even commissioned a blue cheese of their own.

The UK has been particularly blessed with outstanding makers of goat and sheep milk cheeses, including wondrous blue varieties. These pale beside the fascination I have for the cheeses of Alham Wood, near Shepton Mallet in Devon. Frances Wood, granddaughter of a champion dairymaid, has imported buffalo from Transylvania, where they have been draught and food animals for a millennium. Their very white milk has a lower cholesterol rating than cows' milk but sacrifices no body because of this. Her range of fresh and pressed cheeses made with raw and pasteurised milks are genuinely innovative, offering a spectrum of flavours you recognize as milky but that have a piquant farmy edge, with none of the muskiness goat milk can have. The cheeses are based on the traditions of the Middle East and Eastern Europe, and so far mozzarella isn't in the range. But there is buffalo clotted cream, a traditional Eastern Mediterranean luxury. Phoenicians who sailed thence to trade for tin are thought to have introduced clotted cream and saffron to Cornwall, a culinary thread of history I find irresistible, and that we can now all pick up.

A thrilling place to find specialist cheeses is farmers' markets, where you often find the makers allowing you to put a face to your food, the way most of us could for all of history until industrialisation. Those buffalo milk cheese regularly appear in farmers' markets in London.

UK cheese winners

The Annual World of Cheese Awards in London judges cheeses from all around the world, which is how a **Société Baragnaudes Roquefort** won several blue cheese classes, a **Vallebona Gorgonzola** was best Italian, Wexford Creamery's **Spring Cheddar** was judged best Irish, best Welsh was a **Cambrian Mountain Welsh Brie**, and so on. Best American cheeses were a **Smoked Oregon Blue**, from the Rogue River Creamery and **Harvest Cheese**, an aged goat milk cheese from Hillman Farm. An **Isigny Sto Mère AOC** unpasteurised Camembert was judged Supreme Champion 2004.

British cheeses did well in classes that were virtually unknown to them 20 years ago – soft and hard goat and sheep milk cheeses particularly. But what everyone really wants to know is who makes the best of British, the best of the regional cheeses known for centuries. Here's what the judges thought in 2004. Remember they did not have all the cheeses made in Britain in front of them, and some of the dedicated artisans now making sensational farmhouse cheeses simply don't enter competitions. These names are presented so that if you find them, you will learn from their examples.

Caerphilly: The Cheese Co Malpas
Cheddar, best in show: Brue Valley Vintage Farmhouse
Cheddar, block made on a farm: Wyke Farms Mature
Cheddar, extra mature traditional, made after April 1st, 2003: Keen's Cheddar
Cheddar, mature traditional, made September/October 2003: Westcombe Dairy, unpasteurised
Cheddar, mature winter traditional: Ashley Chase estate, Ford Farm
Cheddar, vintage farmhouse, made before April 1st 2003: North Downs Dairy, Brue Valley
Cheshire, traditional: Wensleydale Dairy
Double Gloucester: A C C Dairy Farmers
Leicester, red: The Cheese Co
Shropshire blue: Cropwell Bishop Creamery
Stilton, blue: North Downs Dairy Co/Websters Dairy and Cropwell Bishop Creamery
Wensleydale, mature: Wensleydale Dairy

What follow are a few better-known or traditional cheeses you should find in delicatessens, cheese mongers and supermarkets. Eventually you should learn which maker of Cheddar or Caerphilly, for instance, you prefer and then buy it by name, as you would a beer or wine.

The PDO/DOP/AOC system is little recognized or used in the UK, and some of the cheeses with this status are hardly known and made by creameries, presumably because they have the time and the resources to apply. Most small or traditional cheese makers are too busy, and let the quality of their produce speak for them, magnificently.

Beenleigh Blue: a luscious blue, made with unpasteurised sheep milk by Robin Congdon and Sarie Cooper in Devon. Only made from late summer until January, as the sheep aren't milked when they have lambs at heel and Robin won't make cheese from frozen milk. Beenleigh matures for up to nine months, so count back to check how old it is when you buy, or ask the shopkeeper – he should be able to tell you. Its big flavour is very floral with a delicious light tang of salt and some acknowledged experts choose this as their favourite cheese, even replacing Stilton with it at Christmas. Harbourne Blue, from goat milk and Devon Blue, a Stilton style made only with unpasteurised cows' milk also come from these cheese makers.
Bonchester PDO: developed in 1980, this rich yellow soft cheese is made from unpasteurised Jersey cows' milk, the most difficult milk for cheese making because of its naturally higher fat

content. The PDO status guarantees it's made within a radius of 90km from the summit of Peel Fell in the Cheviot Hills.

Buxton Blue PDO: a little known cheese made in Hartington, Derbyshire, but it has applied for and got PDO status. A cylinder of russet-coloured blue vein cheese made with cows' milk, mainly from Derbyshire, Nottinghamshire and Staffordshire. Made by Nuttalls of Derbyshire, a subsidiary of Dairy Crest.

Caerphilly: a lightly pressed cheese made from pasteurised full cows' milk and matured for two or more weeks. White, granular texture, slightly crumbly; clean, sharp smell; direct, acidic, buttermilk flavour, and because the fresh cheese is dipped in a brine bath there should be a tang of salt on the crust. Made superbly by an increasing number of skilled artisans, but few are better than Todd Trethowen of Gordwydd Farm. White-grey mould is acceptable on such farm-house cheeses. Suitable ingredient, but an acquired taste in cooking. Creamery Caerphilly is sourer and turns quickly; excess moisture or yellowing is bad.

Cheddar, West Country Farmhouse PDO: England gave the world Cheddar but forgot to patent the unique cheddaring process or the name, and relinquished control over the standards of one of the best and best-known cheeses in the world. There are now fewer than 20 farmhouse Cheddar makers producing in the traditional way and only a handful of those use the traditional unpasteurised milk. And beware that word traditional on a label – it can mean only that the cheese is sold in the traditional tub shape, and could be factory made in much larger, plastic wrapped blocks.

Cheddar consumption in this country represents over 60 per cent of the total but most of this is immature, over-refrigerated, mediocrity much of which is 'matured' in plastic wrapping. I hate being so negative but there is a desperate need to save Cheddar – mainly from itself. If you have never done so, make the effort to buy a true West Country Cheddar that is at least ten months old and which was made on a farm in Somerset, Devon or Dorset. You will be astounded at its full complex flavour and join me in wondering how the other stuff can be allowed to masquerade under the same name; no sparkling wines but the genuine thing from a designated region can be called Champagne.

Cheddar is a hard-pressed cheese made from full milk, raw or pasteurised. There is a village called Cheddar and that gave its name to a particular process by which only farmhouse Cheddars are now made. Once the curd has formed and been drained, the curds are cut into blocks and piled on top of one another, and then the piles are restacked again and again, so each block has been on the top, on the bottom and everywhere else. This is cheddaring, and this particularly gentle way of draining whey from the curd over time, during which the curd's acidity is maturing, is what made true Cheddar unique, and is what adds so much to farmhouse-made Cheddars.

Creameries use another method of cheddaring, a process in which forced air whooshes curd particles to the top of a tower. They slowly lose moisture in the airflow, and once each is lightened to the correct state it's then tipped over and falls into what will become a cheese press. Sounds horrid, I know, and yet many of the prize-winning creamery Cheddars are possibly so good because of the process. You may disagree.

It pays to know where the cheese you're offered was made. Creamery-made cheese from the West Country offers a higher, sharper flavour than that made from the sweeter grass of Ireland, or from New Zealand. And it pays to know when. Cheddar cheeses noticeably reflect the seasons they are made: pasteurisation can't hide the effect of changing from grass to silage during winter, usually from about the start of November to the end of January or February, depending on location. So, the best Cheddars are made with rich milk made from sweet green grass from April to September. Whoever supplies your cheese monger has to know when each cheese is made, so your cheese monger should too.

Mild creamery-made cheeses are released after three to five months: mature should be over five months, up to nine and perhaps more.

Genuine cloth-bound barrels of farmhouse, hand-made Cheddars should be at least nine months old and are usually at a superb peak around 12 months. They have a smooth, yellowish, waxy texture, a full, sweet nose, and rich nutty flavour. The slight aftertaste bite increases with greater maturity – as does crumbliness of texture. Quicke's make their Cheddars with raw milk and animal rennet, and other names to look for are Keen's, Montgomery, Denhay, Chewton and Green. These days some are not released for two years, the so-called vintage or extra mature cheeses.

Creamery and foreign Cheddars often have bite but no deep flavour because the milk has been treated with a type of starter that develops quick acidity, to give the effect of maturity with none of the accompanying gains in flavour.

Traditionally, farmhouse cheeses were round and cloth-wrapped and you could tell creamery cheeses because they were oblong; today both sorts of establishment make both types. Cheddar, more than any other cheese, requires the buyer to beware.

Cheshire: a lightly pressed cheese made from full milk, invariably pasteurised, and which takes from six to eight weeks to mature. Crumbly, moister and less compact than Cheddar, and the best of it is still made in Cheshire, where the cows feed on grasslands that are noticeably salty.

Red: this is the best-known version, the salmon-pink one. It has a haunting mellow, sweet flavour with salty overtones and a light, clean smell. It is a very good cheese for cooking, and melts well on toast. A cloth-bound Cheshire from Hare's will be notably characteristic when only a few months old. But look also for Mrs Appleby's unpasteurised Cheshire, which develops for up to six months – an age when most Cheshires have fallen into inedible vulgarity.

White: this faster ripening variation, uncoloured, acidifies easily. Not much to recommend it, but sometimes used as substitute for feta, which doesn't say much.

Cornish Blue: created only in 2001, this gorgonzola-style cheese is made to be eaten when young and creamy. The cheeses are made entirely by hand at Knowle Farm on the edge of Bodmin Moor in Cornwall and after only a year on the market won Best New Cheese at the prestigious Nantwich Cheese Show in 2002. It comes in a variety of sizes from small rounds to cylinders for cutting.

Cornish Yarg: a relative newcomer, made from an ancient recipe found in 1970 that finishes the cheese with a wrapping of nettles. A simple direct mild cheese when young but which will develop distinct flavours of meadows and nettles in a cream-rich base if allowed to mature.

Derby: not very well known but a hard-pressed cows' milk cheese maturing in only four weeks. Flakier and moister than Cheddar, paler and more delicate in flavour, too. 'Lesser Cheddar' is an apt but sadly damning description of this subtle and overlooked cheese, which was the first English cheese to be made in a creamery, in 1870. **Sage Derby:** marbled, artificially coloured and flavoured with sage oil. Highly individual, rather perfumed flavour; best appreciated in rather small amounts. Interesting when lightly grated over tomato salad. The growing interest in good cheese means that sometimes you see sage cheese made the old way, with rolled sage; **Sage Lancashire** cheeses are the best I have tasted and such cheeses are made in New England, in Vermont particularly.

Dorset Blue PDO: based loosely on the ancient traditions of Blue Vinney, that is a blue cheese made from skimmed milk, something said to be known in Dorset since 1800BC. Irregular blue veining means a flavour that although piquant and peppery can vary from mild to strong.

Dovedale PDO: another soft blue-veined cheese, this time made by Nuttalls in Derbyshire, a company owned by Dairy Crest.

Dunlop: very much like Derby, this popular hard-pressed Scottish cheese is similar also to Cheddar and to Double Gloucester. It is paler, blander and moister. Naturally enough it is best with Scottish accompaniments, oatcakes in particular.

Exmoor Blue PDO: soft blue cheeses with a white mould surface, made only of Jersey milk by Willett Farm, Taunton in Somerset since 1990.

Gloucester, Double and Single: two relatively hard-pressed cheeses. The Double is commonly found and the Single is making a well-deserved comeback. The Double is orange rather than yellow, and has a smooth mellow flavour even when mature. It must never bite back in the mouth and has a particular affinity with fruit and salad. Double Gloucester claims two reasons for its name, first that it is bigger than the Single, and second, that it was always made from a mixture of the whole morning milk plus the cream of the evening's milking, thus making it a double cream cheese. Single Gloucester – also called Berkeley – is a faster maturing cheese of the same diameter but half the depth. Originally made from a blend of the skimmed evening milk plus whole morning milk. The Single Gloucester made by Gloucester Cheesemakers of Dymock has PDO status, guaranteeing it is made only with the milk from registered herds of Gloucester cattle.

Lancashire: a cheese that is ready to eat in two months or so, and well worth searching out in Lancashire. There are two distinct styles, essentially mild or mature, both the result of a unique farmhouse technique based on mixing fresh and matured curds over two or three days, sometimes even over five – something a factory would never be bothered to do. Both styles should be white, crumbly yet have a butter-soft texture. This mild but richly flavoured cheese is the one for cooking and melting, the proper cheese for rarebits. Mature

Lancashire has a wonderfully full flavour and developed sharpness, but must not leave any trace of bitterness on the tongue. Mrs Kirkham's Lancashire is made from raw milk, Sandhams make theirs with pasteurised milk and Carron Lodge is the maker who might take five days to get a mix of curds that's just right. Beacon Fell traditional Lancashire cheese has PDO status.

Leicester, Red: hard pressed and mature at six months, but is usually sold before this. Rich russet-red colour, granular looking but actually a moist, elastic texture that makes one of the best-ever melting cheeses. Clean, buttery flavour but not very much of it. Often marketed too young, as the flavour develops before the texture, so avoid dry, crumbly-looking cheeses. If you can find an example made by Quicke's in Devon, they are often aged six or more months, when a more focused personality develops.

Lincolnshire Poacher: created in the 1980s by Simon and Jeanette Jones, is the only cheese made from Lincolnshire milk, something not done before because the pastures weren't thought suitable. Yet it develops complex earthy flavours and a particularly creamy finish that has won major prizes. Amazing to tell, this raw milk cheese is made entirely by hand, except for cutting the curd.

Oxford Blue: a cheese with a great background story, just what's needed to keep dinner tables or customers amused. French aristocrat Baron Robert Pouget worked with a Derbyshire cheese maker to develop it in 1993, after Dons from the dining halls of Oxford told him they preferred soft and creamy blue cheeses. You'll probably have to visit the baron's stall in Oxford's covered market to buy some, and when you do you'll be rewarded, particularly if there's a 16-week-old example, described by Bob Farrand, founder of the UK Cheese Guild as 'extraordinarily creamy with a host of soft, spicy flavours, all in perfect harmony'.

Shropshire Blue: you might not have heard of it, yet in 1995 a Shropshire Blue from the Cropwell Bishop Creamery was judged Supreme Champion at the London International Cheese Competition. Although invented around 1970 it wasn't until 1990 when Ian Skailes began making it at Cropwell Bishop that it took off. They make the cheese with a creamy body that's a singing orange colour, and with tangy blue veining that's rarely as vigorous as a Stilton: the body and the blueing combine judiciously into a balanced, mellow whole that properly finishes with good acidity, but with little or no bite. Other creameries make it, but it's not the same.

Stilton, Blue PDO: none of this most famed cheese is now made with unpasteurised milk, but it once was and should be again. The slight risk associated with unpasteurised milk is wildly exaggerated, generally based on a misunderstanding of the listeria scare, which turns out to have been caused by cheese made with pasteurised milk, because the infection invariably happens after the cheese has been made.

There is a white Stilton sold, a crumbly, very white cheese with a strong nose but deceptively milder, slightly sour flavour. It's an ideal substitute for feta in Greek salads – but that's about all, and yet it also has PDO status.

Blue Stilton should have a soft buttery texture, and blue-green veins radiating from centre to crust. The wrinkled brown-grey skin should be dry, not slimy. Some brown discolouration close to the skin is acceptable, but anywhere else it is a sign of inferior milk or bad manufacturing. Neither flavour nor smell should be sharp or strong. Do not accept white and chalky (unfortunately not a rare commodity) or yellow and oily Stilton. One is too young, the other too old. Can, but should not, be used in cooking, and you should run like hell from anyone using the crust in a soup.

The best Stilton is three months old and made with the perfect grass of autumn – hence its popularity at Christmas time. But don't think all Stilton sold at Christmas has been made three months before: it freezes well and as this subterfuge is recognized only by the greatest of cheese experts . . .

Port is an accompaniment to Stilton, not an ingredient. To soak a perfect Stilton in an excellent port dilutes the flavour, texture and nuances of both. Putting a good port into an inferior Stilton is a waste of the drink's complexities and can do nothing to save the cheese. Putting cheap port into excellent Stilton should be a hanging offence. The idea, like fish knives, serving onion and egg with caviar or storing cheese in a cheese bell is Victorian pretension at its worst. If you like port with Stilton, and you should, introduce the two on your palate. And so to scooping.

A common defence of scooping from a cut Stilton is that you can thus start at the riper, bluer centre of the cheese and then work outwards to the crust as the cheese ripens. Stuff and nonsense. A Stilton is not riper in the centre; it is bluer because that is where the needles that originally added the blue mould spores have converged. One of the greatest joys of eating Stilton is to be given a wedge that includes all flavours, from the very bluest in the middle to the least blue close to the crust. What happens when you scoop from the centre is the cheese closer to the crust begins to decay as much as ripen: it picks up flavour, but it's not the sort you should be eating.

In any case, scooping increases the exposure of the cheese's body to air by an enormous amount, so hastening its death. If you must scoop and you don't finish it all, you must later spend much time assiduously pressing cling film into every crevice, crevasse and scoop-scar, to prevent air working its evil way.

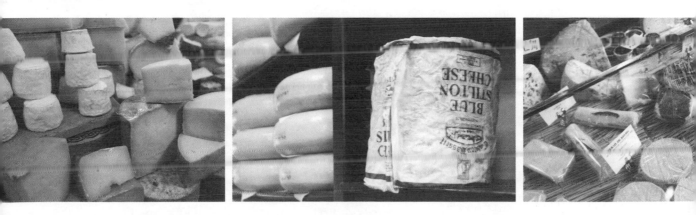

It's no good bleating about tradition. Yes, scoops were once served with the cheese; they were not for the cheese but for scooping up a portion of the thick wriggle of weevils that infested the skin and were considered part of its joy. One scoop or two, Madam? Sir?

Please don't make soup from Stilton. Hundreds of men and women spent a good deal of time protecting the cheese from heat so it would taste its best for you. You can't possibly know better.

As for making soup from its crust, I'd rather starve than be that budget conscious – or so culinarily unconscious.

Stilton is one of the few British foods protected by the PDO system, guaranteeing it is made only in Leicestershire, Nottinghamshire and Derbyshire, to strictly delineated standards. Colston Bassett is considered to have a bigger, more up-front flavour than the other most favoured Stiltons, from Cropwell Bishop, Long Clawson or Websters, the smallest of the Stilton makers.

Swaledale/ Swaledale ewe milk cheese PDO: made in Swaledale, North Yorkshire both the cow and the ewe milk cheese are full fat hard cheeses and can have a natural coat or be wax coated. Said to have been made in the area for centuries from a recipe still known only to a few. The curd is cut, stacked and cut again, a process rather like genuine cheddaring.

Teviotdale PDO: a yellow, salty and tangy cheese made from unpasteurised Jersey milk in the Borders between England and Scotland; to be precise it must be from within a 90m radius of the summit of Peel Fell in the Cheviot Hills. By the makers of Bonchester q.v.

Wensleydale: a lightly pressed cheese that has had a mixed history of late but which is now well on its way back to stardom, as a small number of farmhouse and traditional makers have found ways to distribute nationally. When properly made in Wensleydale, the cheese reflects the carefully protected high pastures of wild flowers and grasses unique to the area. Wensleydale simply cannot be made elsewhere, but it is.

White: a rapidly maturing cheese that has a definite character of its own, with a subtle, mellow, honey-like flavour that's one of the greatest rewards amongst the English territorial cheeses. Sourness and yellowness indicate excess age. It has no rival as an accompaniment to apple pie, a classic English combination of flavours well worth discovering. If you can ever find a 14-16 week Wensleydale in good condition, ideally a Hawes Wensleydale, you will rarely eat a more elegant or refined cheese.

Blue: though smoother, whiter, smaller and less veined, it is undeniably similar to Stilton, but has a grey, corrugated crust and when the honeyed body is in perfect harmony with the edgy blue veins, you have something quite distinct.   Hawes make it very well.

Others: there has been an extraordinary renaissance of small cheese-making and a tremendous return to goats' and ewes' milk in Britain and Ireland. Makers of classic farmhouse regional cheeses now tend to shy away from using unpasteurised milk, even though they are permitted to do so, in case of bacterial problems; yet some remain faithful and their products are worth seeking. But small cheese makers do it the old way. Some make new cheeses admired for their minimal saltiness, or use hops and nettle leaves mixing old and new techniques; others recreate old cheeses like soft **Cambridge**, pressed **Exmoor** or Welsh **Llanboidy**, made with the milk of rare Red Poll cattle. Jersey milk is the basis of Wales' **Llangloffen** and Scotland's most famous Brie-type, **Bonchester**.

The Specialist Cheesemakers Association has done a sterling job encouraging and maintaining standards of artisan cheese making throughout Britain, and thoroughly deserves every bit of your support.

* At the end of 2004 BBC 2 began showing Full on Food, perhaps the world's best-ever food show on television (No! I am not in it). Presenter Stefan Gates thought it time to rethink the classic English cheese board and in spite of loving West Country Cheddar and Stilton eventually chose these five personal favourites, all relatively new: **Oxford Blue** – see above; **St George**, a Camembert-style goat cheese from Suffolk that can also be grilled or fried like halloumi when young; an **Isle of Mull Cheddar** he thought lighter in texture but bolder in flavour than English examples; **Twineham Grange**, a cheese made close to Gatwick airport yet that Stef thinks better and sweeter than Parmesan; and, **Flower Marie**, a lightly pressed unpasteurised sheep milk cheese made near Lewes in Sussex that's his vote for best cheese in the world and that when baked or grilled puffs up into a light spongy texture.

United States

Cheese making in the USA is not only alive and well but flourishing in ways Europe hasn't dreamed about yet. From New England and from Wisconsin, particularly, large and small companies are making credible copies of European cheeses, creating new American cheeses and combining the two as well. At the American Cheese Society's 2004 Awards, the Best of Show was **Gran Canaria**, a robust Parmesan-style cheese aged three years in olive oil. It's made in Wisconsin by the Carr Valley Cheese Company, which also won prizes with **Cocoa Cardona**, a goat milk cheese rubbed with cocoa, with **Virgin Pine Native Sheep**, and with a **Cave-Aged Cheddar**.

Everywhere you'll find Camembert and Brie-type cheeses made to exacting traditional standards but also creatively rethought. Cheddar types can be found of great quality and you'll find plenty of these at East Village Cheese, NY, but they don't like giving samples to taste. Cutting edge cheese chatter is about Cheddar with five peppercorns, with horseradish, with kalamata olives, pesto, sage or rosemary, all good enough to win ACS awards. Using the Internet to drum up business, such companies even offer Cheddars aged up to seven years.

Spanish, Portuguese and Italian cheeses are commonly made close to or in such communities in big cities, but anything described as an 'import' or 'imported' remains a hypnotic lure in the USA.

Sheep, goat and cows' milks are often blended together as well as presented individually to make the entire spectrum of suitable cheeses, from hard-pressed to blue-vein. With over 3000 farmers' markets now in the USA, the lover of local cheese specialties need do no more than head to one, even in mid-New York.

USA has created a number of unique cheese styles. **Monterey Jack** is a Cheddar-type moulded informally to produce a robust, full cheese somewhere between a matured Cheddar and a Parmesan and thus good both to eat or to grate and use in cooking. The Cabot Creamery won the class in 2004: a second class for flavoured Monterey Jack cheeses was won by one with jalapeno peppers, closely followed by a garlic and chive version. The best I ever tasted was called **Dry Jack** and featured a rind coloured by cocoa, pepper and oil: when it appeared at a London cheese show it stopped everything. **Brick Muenster** is a brick-shaped washed-rindcheese but Brick is a brick-shaped semi-hard cheese from Wisconsin in which you can see the curd shapes and has a somewhat Cheddar flavour, with a gratifying pungent sweetness. **Colby** is a mild, sweet, pressed cheese that's very good to eat with fruit; **Limburger** is also from Wisconsin, and a classic washed rind cheese with a particularly invasive nose that's often lampooned in books and comics but remains a favourite, even with beer drinkers – **Leiderkranz** was a NY created variation but seems to have been swallowed up in corporate self-protection by one of the big cheese players.

As in Australia and New Zealand, goat and sheep milk have particular attraction for smallholder makers and big cheese makers alike, and plenty of thought is going into new ways to present the cheeses. Goat milk is aged in grape leaf, made Camembert style, marinated in oil with roasted garlic: Cabanon is a sheep milk cheese marinated with alcohol and maple leaves.

The Cheese Board

The classic cheese board goes for contrast. A savoury blue cheese (Stilton), a full-flavoured pressed cheese (Cheddar) and a creamy soft cheese (Brie) gives an ideal foundation. Within each of those flavour styles there is much opportunity for originality. The savoury cheese might be a goat cheese rather than a blue one, then the pressed cheese could be a lighter sweeter Wensleydale or Swiss Emmental, and the soft cheese made with unpasteurised milk. This is what might be called a vertical cheese board, offering a choice of flavours from top to bottom of the spectrum. But a horizontal board offers wonderful eating too, especially if it is to complement a wine you know well.

A horizontal board presents only cheese of similar style, either made by the same technique or from, say, goat or sheep milk. Such a board might offer both soft fresh and aged goat cheeses for an edgy, dry rose, a choice of flowery Swiss Gruyère and other surface ripened cheeses with a decent Meursault, English territorial cheeses with aristocratic Australian Cabernet Shiraz, or a trio of unusual French blue cheeses with a chilled sweet, late-picked Riesling from New Zealand.

Forget the decoration and garnish; throw away the straw mats and the vine leaves and all that: the only design feature to consider is that they will look better on dark plates, rather than on white plates, whatever chefs say. Fruit and nuts and celery and stuff? In my view these only accompany cheese when it is served directly after a main course and there is nothing else to follow. i.e. you are combining cheese and dessert. Otherwise, bread and crackers will do, ah yes, and butter too if that's what you like. Offering perfect cheese at optimum temperature needs no fol-de-rol.

Cheese Fondue

It's well worth giving you a proper recipe for Swiss fondue, if only to prove how sad anything else will be. But rather than dipping into the melted cheese and wine only with the traditional cubes of bread, offer guests lightly cooked green vegetables, boiled small potatoes, hard-boiled quail eggs or very small hen eggs, cherry tomatoes, baby corn cobs, cubes of grilled polenta, oil-soft sun-dried tomatoes – in fact anything that goes with this delicious mixture of cheeses and wine. With these more interesting offerings, the presentation looks great and there's a better chance of enjoying a refreshing and varied meal, rather than having a cheesy lump in your stomach.

Serves four
200g/7oz Swiss Emmental, coarsely grated
400g/14oz Swiss Gruyère, coarsely grated
1 clove garlic
300ml/½pint/1 cup dry white wine
1 tsp fresh lemon juice
1heaped tsp cornflour
small glass kirsch or other eau de vie
nutmeg
pepper
cubed bread, raw or blanched vegetables, sliced pears, apples, grapes

Mix the Emmental and Gruyère evenly. Rub a fondue dish or thick saucepan with the cut clove of garlic, and then add the wine. Heat until just simmering, and then add the lemon juice, which helps amalgamate the wine and cheese. Stir the cheese into the wine and, once this is melted and the mixture is creamy, mix the kirsch into the cornflour and quickly stir this in. Reduce the temperature and let cook a few minutes then season with freshly grated nutmeg and pepper – white pepper looks better than flecks of black pepper.

Put the completed fondue on the burner, reminding everyone that each time they dip they should give the fondue a stir, helping to keep it creamy right to the end.

There are all sorts of stories about what should happen to those whose food drops into the fondue. Generally if the accident happens to a woman she is expected to kiss a man at the table; a man making the same mistake is expected to buy more wine. What if it's a same sex fondue party? You'd hardly know where to turn.

Chocolate

Chocolate is sexy. It's sensual too, a temptress to excess,
yet able with one bite to soothe with careless effort.

The flavour has lots to do with this, and so does its chemistry, which stimulates the body's feelings of well-being – or better-being, anyway. But most of chocolate's thralldom depends on its unique oral effect. It's the only food in the world that melts at human-body temperature, hence the way it fills the mouth, coats the palate and releases divine flavours and aromas so soon after you have bitten; in seconds chocolate becomes at one with us. Thus chocolate is never challenging, is a staunch friend when in need, and gives a guaranteed good time whether you look your best or not.

Cocoa fat, called cocoa butter, is solid at 33C but molten at 34C and thus should melt in just a few seconds if held in the palm. Slower melting chocolate tells you it has low cocoa butter content or includes cocoa butter substitutes: in the United Kingdom five per cent may be added without being mentioned on the label.

On your tongue, this just-melted stage is when a 'bitter' chocolate – high cocoa solids, low sugar – is at its most naked. In those first full moments of melted flavour you will learn to detect the myriad flavours of well-made chocolate, discover nuances of finely balanced beans enhanced with genuine vanilla and a little sugar, will learn to identify berry fruits and almonds, sweet herbs and balsam, aromatic cedar or tobacco and to taste the tropical soils of the forest; all the intriguing flavours of chocolate.

While you are at it you might also detect over-roasting, inferior or artificial ingredients, super-sweetness and poor manufacturing, but what do you expect if you buy milk chocolate from a bargain bin at an outlet store?

Until I was 14 I had never tasted coffee, and I was 18 before I could be persuaded to try tea. Cocoa was the hot drink that fortified me through the rigours of cub camps, bible class socials and school examinations. It would not have if it had been like the first chocolate-based drink Europe enjoyed, which was often bitter, fatty, thick and scummy. Clearly, fashion was as much part of its popularity as pleasure, and the entire history of chocolate is equally redolent of the unexpected. It involves Columbus and Montezuma, a disgusted Pope, an Italian entrepreneur, Jewish exiles, a Dutch invention, crusading Quakers – and that's drinking chocolate, the only way it was known for its first centuries in the Old World.

Solid, eating chocolate in bars was an English invention that only emerged, with some nicety of timing, in the middle of Victoria's reign. Thence, their backbones further fortified by Mr Fry's novelty, Englishmen more readily went out to conquer; and still no mountaineer or explorer feels right unless there is a bar of chocolate about his or her person. But how many pause in mid-traverse to ponder the vital part cocoa beans played in the fertility and puberty rites of the Mayans? Or that Madame du Barry employed hot chocolate as an aphrodisiac? Or that Casanova found it more invigorating than champagne? Or that only English speakers say cocoa rather than the correct cacao? Apparently it was decided we couldn't pronounce the latter, so we didn't.

The cacao tree probably originated in the Amazon Basin, and was taken to the Yucatan by Mayans about 600 AD. Columbus carried cacao beans back to the Catholic kings, but they showed little interest. Later, when Montezuma, gorgeous in gold and shimmering queztalcoatl feathers, greeted Cortes he offered him a placatory drink of frothy, bitter chocolate, for he was thought to be the saviour promised to the Aztecs.

Cortes was to take rather than give life, yet throughout the slaughter and greed that followed, he recognised the restorative and energy-giving qualities (it contains caffeine) of the drink, and Spain monopolised the product for the next century.

Once Spanish grandees learned to mellow the drink with vanilla and sugar it became quite the thing. It seems to have been nuns who discovered it was infinitely better hot, and by 1569 hot chocolate had been brought to the attention of Pope Pius V. He didn't ban it during Lent, as he could not conceive anyone would ever care willingly to drink something he found disgusting.

Spain's monopoly was broken in 1606 by Antonio Carletti who managed to take the secrets of the fragrant drink back to Italy and by 1700 the famed coffee houses of Venice and Florence were equally acclaimed for their chocolate. The French were introduced to it by Jewish exiles from Spain. Switzerland, now Master Chocolatier to the world, learned of it in 1697, from Heinrich Fischer on his return from Brussels. 1657 seems to be its first mention in England, and by 1662 Henry Stubbs, a doctor returned from Jamaica, wrote a whole book about chocolate, *The Indian Nectar*.

London's coffee houses quickly learned to serve chocolate to those who could afford it, and Pepys used it to settle his stomach after the debauches that marked the coronation of Charles I. Yet it was not until 1828 that Conrad J. van Houten invented a press that extracted two-thirds of the fat from the chocolate, leaving a dry powder we would recognize as cocoa, thus making possible a simpler and more reliable form of chocolate drink. Only 20 years later Joseph Fry of Bristol discovered how to combine lesser amounts of that extracted fat – cocoa butter – with other parts of the cocoa bean plus sugar to make eating chocolate.

The new drink of cocoa was cheap enough to be useful to the poor and was seized upon vigorously by the temperance societies of the 19th century. Both the Cadburys and the Rowntrees were Quaker families and dedicated to the movement. They combined the manufacture and marketing of cocoa with a drive for social reform here and abroad and much of the profit they made went to practical, socially-responsible projects – they even organized boycotts in Europe as protest against the conditions of slaves in Portuguese Africa.

Although hot chocolate is enjoying a worldwide renaissance, it is to solid chocolate that most of the world looks for the voluptuous thrill of the cacao tree's products. Indeed, chocolate is perhaps one of the world's most enduring and universal treats; I have found it as much appreciated in sweets on remote Pacific Islands as in the lavish presentation boxes of hand-dipped confections without which many sophisticated urban celebrations would be incomplete. But what is it and how is it made?

Pictures of cacao trees always make me smile, and my first view of a real one, on St Lucia, actually made me laugh outright. They don't look real. The tree has large glossy leaves and white or pink blossoms that appear all year round and become ridged pods up to 25cm/ 10in long. These slowly turn from green to yellow through purples and reds to a russet brown – and that is the attraction. At any one time scarcely two of the pods are the same colour, and as they grow rather comically, direct from the trunk, it all combines to give the tree a perfectly ridiculous musical-comedy look.

Despite the tree's constant readiness, possibly why it was so worshipped in South America, it is harvested only twice a year. The pods are taken from the tree and split and the beans, or seeds, are left out on the ground for two to nine days to ferment, which diminishes bitterness and develops the fat content. This is where quality can begin to descend. The fermenting beans easily pick up the characteristics of the medium on which they sit. If they are fermented on aromatic wood they will absorb its virtues, but if fermented on asphalt or damp cardboard or sour soil these are the notes they carry forward. It is to control such subtleties that major manufacturers are investing in and dealing directly with more and more growers. Once fermented out, the beans are shipped to a factory, at home or abroad.

Processing continues with a roasting which dries the outer skin of the beans. This is removed together with the germ, leaving what are known as nibs. Once these have been ground into a paste with some application of heat, the cocoa butter can be removed under pressure, leaving a paste called chocolate liquor. This sets on cooling, and is the basic, unsweetened chocolate. The liquor might be further pressed, which results in cocoa powder. Or it can be blended with more cocoa butter, sugar and flavouring, including dried milk powder for milk chocolate, before the final process, conching. This is really a slow whipping that ensures even texture and a good gloss. Of course, every part of the process, from roasting to flavouring and beating, can be varied to produce different tastes and textures. Additions reduce the price but also the true savour.

Savouring chocolate

The first thing to check, of course, is the label. The higher the cacao/cocoa solid content, the richer the flavour and the less sugar will have been used, or should have been used. There is an element of incipient danger with the first bite into any new brand of chocolate bar, of never knowing if the bitterness is too vivid, if more sugar would have been welcome or less artificial vanilla would make a second bite worthwhile. Restraint with sugar costs a manufacturer money because weight for weight sugar is much cheaper than chocolate and the less there is the more the quality of the basic beans is revealed – that's why cheaper chocolates are always sweeter chocolates.

Vanilla is the most expensive addition to chocolate, followed by cocoa butter, generally four times costlier than cocoa solids.

The best chocolate will have only those ingredients and use real vanilla rather than vanillin for flavouring: vanillin and high sugar content are usually indicators of low-grade cocoa solids, depressing ways to reduce cost at the expense of quality. Sugar or milk products are the cheapest ingredients in chocolate and, as contents must be listed in constituent descending order of volume, you never want to see these preceding the cocoa solids count. Lecithin, a natural emulsifier, is widely used to enhance shelf life and is thus a sensible addition, even at the top end of the market. You will be surprised to find how many brands of self-annointed grandeur and expense contain it; appalled to discover how many include indefensible added 'flavours/flavors': a ferreting amongst the labelling of Israeli products sold at Harrods Hot Chocolate Bar will produce such a surprise.

The colour of high-quality chocolate should be deep, and any veering towards ruddiness rather than black is a sign of high quality. There should be a conspicuous gloss, almost a mirror finish. When you break or bite into it there must be a decisive crack and snap, revealing a texture like that of tree bark: the characteristic snap of quality chocolate is a major basis for judgement before tasting. The chocolate should also crack when you first chew it in the mouth, and then begin speedily to melt.

If you worry you might always over-indulge if there is chocolate in the house, here is some outstanding advice from John Tovey, who you will or should remember as the dazzling host and chef at Miller Howe Hotel in Cumberland for so long. He broke up into small pieces very good chocolate bars of high cocoa solid content and virtually no sugar. These individual portions were wrapped closely and then put into the deep freeze. Every day, when it was chocolate time he unwrapped a frozen portion and put it on his tongue. Of course it took time to get up to temperature and to melt fully, meaning he had extended the pleasure far longer than room temperature chocolate could ever provide, so he had more pleasure but ate less and felt very superior. Very clever.

The archetypical image of a spurned lover turning to chocolate is no idle fancy. For one of the properties chocolate has, like the chilli bean at the other end of the pleasure scale, is chemically to elicit feelings of joy and comfort in our brains, similar in fact to being in love. Must be why so few blokes seem to be chocoholics, although with this New Man thing, a chocolate obsession seems little removed from facials, waxings and hair replacement.

In Australasia, chocolate is often combined with orange to make a flavour they call jaffa. It is quite wonderful: try grated orange rind or an orange liqueur on (or in) some chocolate ice cream, or make a butter icing for a plain cake with orange juice and cocoa. To be shamelessly exotic, use orange flower water instead or as well as fresh orange. Fresh lime too makes an interesting but more demanding combination: I add lime oil q.v. to a rich chocolate cake mix, but only enough to suggest the flavour, and then make a butter icing with fresh lime zest.

Rose water mixes with chocolate to great libidinous advantage, and some combination of the two is the best way to prove how well both combine superbly with soft fruits – raspberries strawberries, currants, boysenberries, loganberries, and cherries, too. So pour a chocolate steamed pudding mixture over tumbled red berries flavoured with rose water, or bake chocolate cup cakes with a few whole berries in them and finish with a light rose water icing.

Most of the sweet spices have a natural affinity with chocolate, especially as additions to hot chocolate drinks or in icings for cakes and biscuits. Herbs are more dubious but I notice more and more successful combinations. Chocolate and mint is well known, so is ginger, both ground and freshly grated ginger root, and in Australia I found chocolate with lemon grass, with thyme and with tarragon, but thought only the first of these was worth it. La Maison du Chocolat of Paris, London etc. offers a tea flavoured ganache called Yoko and Garrigue, infused with the stalk and leaf of fennel and so an anise flavour; pretty damned good. Yet the best of the new flavours I encountered have been with exotic fruit and in New Zealand: the immensely fragrant feijoa and the acid-sweet tamarillo both make outstanding friendships with chocolate and do so on their own terms. I found kiwifruit ones not as successful but acknowledge I am in a minority.

As the taste for better chocolate grows, more and more small artisan makers offer chocolate or filled chocolates with a difference. The Cocoa Tree of Devon uses only organic, Fair-trade chocolate, but go a whole lot further to ensure they are true individualists: they collect elderflowers from hedgerow elder trees to make an elderflower fondant centre, grow blackcurrants in their own garden to make a blackcurrant fondant centre. You couldn't find greater dedication than that.

The prize for chocolate originality goes to Marie and Frans Havermans of The Natural Food Company in Belgium; most of their organic chocolates can be enjoyed by diabetics because they are sweetened with agave syrup rather than sugar. This is not just because the syrup that flows from a cut agave was a favourite with Aztecs, although that's good enough for me. Agave syrup is sweeter than sugar syrup, yet has fewer calories and a low glycaemic index. Imagine, chocolate, vanilla and agave, all once from the same region, reunited on your tongue.

Chocolatiers delight in making chocolate into other things, like the shells you will have seen: amongst the most beguiling are totally believable haricot, borlotti and flageolet beans from Rococo chocolate in London.

But who makes the best chocolate? The answer is thrilling; you will know only by eating as many as possible. As well as Valrhona, the Chocolate Society and La Maison du Chocolat you'll probably want to taste those of Michel Guizel. Many are developing a view that perhaps Amedei is

Chocolistas en Paris

Whatever else she might be, Paris is also queen city of chocolate shops, and some are the highest peaks of the art. There's even an invitation only *Club des Croquers de Chocolat*, just 150 makers, experts, writers and *chocolistas* who grade *chocolatiers* with up to five 'bars'. For more: www.croquerschocolat.com

There are pages of chocolatiers in Paris, even several devoted guide books to buy, but always check the shops are open before you set off. Here are a few recommended musts, from Jonathan Hayes of *The New York Times*.

Angelina: 226 rue de Rivoli, Arrondissement 1

For exceptional hot chocolate.

La Charlotte de l'Isle: 24 rue St-Louis en l'Isle, Arrondissement 4

Best hot chocolate in Paris, at least to the palate of Jonathan Hayes: he describes it as the 'absinthe of hot chocolate'.

Michel Chaudun: 149 rue de l'Université, Arrondissement 7

Less glamorously sited than many, and eccentrically filled with chocolate-related *objets* and wondrous chocolate models. Considered a little more artisanal than some, M. Caudun is thought the most successful at including pieces of cocoa bean into chocolate, currently top bite for the choc-chic.

Christian Constant: 37 rue d'Assas, Arrondissement 6

A cool boutique close to the Luxembourg Gardens featuring restrained ganaches with notes more associated with the scent trade, like ylang-ylang. Malabar Cardamom and Rose and Corinth Grape are musts, but there are huge servings of really thick fragrant hot chocolates; Bitter-Plus mercilessly needs sugar adding.

Pierre Herme: 72 rue Bonaparte, Arrondissement 6

Pierre Herme, perhaps the world's best patissier, presents new pastries in fashion run-way style and his chocolates are accepted as provoking, not least because he uses a lot of white chocolate – thought more the metier of the patissier than the chocolatier. He fills balls with caramelised apple or with a lemon marmalade and waywardly combines dark chocolate with kuzu, an extreme Japanese citrus you might vote too incompatible to be acquainted.

Jean-Paul Hevin: 231 rue St-Honoré, Arrondissement 1

Jean-Paul Hevin is a patissier who specialises in chocolates and pastries that include chocolate – your choice is helped by spot-lit glamour portraits of his newest creations. Pastry heaven is thought close with the Longchamp, which includes praline, hazelnut, meringue, chocolate and almonds. He's one of those with top five-bar rating.

La Maison du Chocolat: 8 boulevard de la Madeleine, Arrondissement 9

Start any Parisian choc-adventure with top-marked La Maison du Chocolat, for whom Baron Philippe de Rothschild has just collaborated on a red-wine chocolate. The mint bon-bons lay down new benchmarks of flavour accuracy. Five-bar rating, of course.

rather more than first amongst equals: it's an Italian company based in Pontevedra, Tuscany, and is owned and operated by a fantastically gifted brother and sister team, Alessio and Cecelia Tessieri.

Such a lot of chocolate to eat, and nothing to do with pleasure, merely the selfless pursuit of knowledge. And you still haven't been to the annual Salon du Chocolat in New York, Tokyo and Paris – 120,000 went to the last in Paris, for five days of tastings and celebrations, plus papers and lectures delivered by chocologues teetering in improbable heels on the didactic high-wire between pretentious and pompous.

Types of cacao bean

Traditionally there were two major types of cacao beans, the *forastero* and the *criollo*. Today these have been joined by a slowly increasing number of hybrids and crosses, the most important of which is the *trinitario*.

As with both coffee and tea, the precise flavour a bean gives is a combination of its essential characteristics, plus the effect of the climate where it is grown, whether harvested early or late and the method of fermentation and drying. To say nothing about the care with which any of these processes might be performed. And here and there ancient varieties or new hybrids will all be contributing to individuality, too.

Forastero: this represents 95 % of all the world's cacao trees, and is thus somewhat equivalent to robusta coffee. It is a high yielding tree and the beans give an immediate mouth flavour and sensation, which is generally rather coarse and undistinguished. Like poor quality coffee, it tends to be roasted very high to disguise the shortcomings. Thus any elegant forastero-based chocolate is evidence of very high-quality decisions and processing at every stage.

West African grown *forastero* beans tend be spicy and acidic, Indian Ocean beans are fruitier yet notably bitter. But the same bean grown in Ecuador gives a soft, floral and clear chocolate, with overtones of orange blossom.

Criollo: this is the aristocrat, appropriately compared to the chardonnay grape, which gives us champagne and Chablis in Europe. The *criollo* variety now grows particularly well around the Indian Ocean, giving beans with spicy, floral notes, welcome acidity and a long-lasting aftertaste, the *criollo*'s particular contribution to fine chocolate.

Trinitario: this is a remarkable cross between the previous two varieties. It rather combines the best of the *forastero* and the *criollo*, yielding a concentrated essence of the syrupy pleasures of dried fruit balanced by floral woodiness and good acidity, which together many think reminiscent of fresh tobacco. Most important, the *trinitario* bean gives a distinct lingering after taste, multiplying the most attractive skill of the *criollo* bean.

Porcellana: this is a unique, naturally porcelain-white bean, discovered in Venezuela, that's genetically pure *criollo*. The chocolate it makes is not white but the usual dark, red-brown, and it has a flavour of great intensity with decisive notes of roasted almonds and hints of sweet olive oil. The mouth feel is fresh and clean and lingers a very long time. Alessio and Cecella Tessieri of Amedei now have exclusive access and only produce around 20,000 bars each year. If you see it, buy it for you might never see it again.

Bean There, Tasted That

For centuries, no chocolate maker told you which beans they used but then the Valrhona Company of France erupted onto the scene by doing precisely that, selling chocolate by bean variety or origin or specified blend and with a choice of cocoa solid content.

When The Chocolate Society did a blind tasting of chocolates with over 50 per cent cocoa-solid content flavoured only with natural vanilla, Valrhona styles took the first three places. Their range includes Manjari, made with a single estate pure *criollo,* and Pur Caraibe, based on the *trinitario.* Now, single estate chocolates from gardens as far away as Papua-New Guinea, Surabaya, the Ivory Coast, Ghana, Venezuela and Madagascar are marketed by many of the greatest chocolate makers, giving chocalistas a constantly growing and more challenging hobby – comparative tastings of plantation against plantation within a country or area, or against others, of the same bean in estates around the world, or of different beans harvested in the same year. And then there is the Chuao bean.

From November 2000 to November 2007, the entire crop of this fabled chocolate has gone only to the Tuscan company Amedei; before that Valrhona bought it and you might still see its golden yellow packaging. Chuao has everything, arresting aromas including a clear meaty gaminess, extraordinary plum and red berry flavours and a legendary length, that lasts up to twenty minutes on my palate. Almost everything about Chuao is exceptional, so much so Cecelia Amedei, thought to be the only woman who creates the recipes and blends for a major chocolate company, discovered it takes 20 days for the flavours to develop their full expression each time she experiments to perfect the presentation of each year's crop.

If you fancy the idea of comparative chocolate tasting, a simple way to do this is with Amedei's I Cru: the box contains six tablets of each of six single cru chocolates, each made to produce the most immediate expression of the soil, sunlight and climate of a single plantation. You'll compare chocolates from Venezuela, Trinidad, Madagascar, Jamaica, Grenada and Ecuador, and each tablet comes with tasting notes on its wrapper. The language of chocolate tasting is pretty much the same as wine tasting; you'll be looking for individual fruits, for fragrance notes, for a nose that might be meaty or gamey, fruity or woody, and so on. Never be afraid of voicing your first impressions because they might be right; so far 400 aromas and 300 flavour compounds have been identified in chocolate.

You won't want to spit, the way a wine taster does. So take time, allow each chocolate really to disappear from the palate before trying the next. Lightly acidified water at room temperature is best for clearing the palate: iced water would solidify any remaining chocolate, and you'd taste it again when the palate was back to normal. The recommended room and chocolate temperature for ultimate enjoyment and credible comparisons is 18-20C, from 65 to 70F.

Otherwise, if you want merely to enjoy each mouthful of something chocolate with a refreshed palate, an elegant milkless tea with good acidity is recommended, a Darjeeling, or an Oolong perhaps. The oils in coffee stay on the palate and mix with chocolate to make a myriad of new flavours, fabulous for sheer pleasure, but not when you want fully to appreciate chocolate. So now let's talk about alcohol and chocolate.

Drinking with Chocolate

In my experience rather more alcoholic drinks make good combinations with chocolate than the experts say, particularly if you match weight with weight, or identify a particular flavour in the chocolate and pick that up with the wine. I think, for instance, the red-berry flavours of *trinitario*-based chocolates are great with Beaujolais and young fruity Burgundies, and a shiraz or Hermitage with pronounced fruit and black pepper is certainly worth combining with chocolate – but you do need to be drinking much more wine than you are eating chocolate, so the chocolate is picking up and running with wine flavours, rather than vice versa.

I've thought a chilled but gutsy tropical-fruit tasting gewürztraminer pretty good with milk chocolate mixed with toasted nuts. And there's more. But the simpler answer is that fortified wines are more commonly thought best: ports, amontillado or cream sherry and most particularly the venerable Pedro Ximinez, sweetest and most profound of all. Sarah Jayne-Staynes, author of *Chocolate: the Definitive Guide* (Grub Street) did taste tests and found the range of Madeira, from dry Sercial through Verdelho and Bual to super-sweet Malmsey, all had something to say, as did Hungary's magical Tokays.

Plenty of dessert wines stand up to the sweetness too, as long as they have enough accompanying acidity, often rather lacking in French Sauternes. Muscatels with big mouth body, like those of Rivesaltes or the lesser Beaumes de Venise are delicious with chocolate-fruit desserts in summer. To stimulate startled reactions, hunt out a bottle of Australia's little-known and very underrated Liqueur Muscatel: you'll have a good time, but run the risk of forgetting about the chocolate.

Spirits with lively aromatic notes like brandies and cognac, particularly Spanish and Greek ones which have added flavours, are good with chocolates and so is a fruit-based brandy or eau de vie: Poire William, calvados, framboise, fraises de bois, kirsch and so on. They are, after all, used in chocolates and that has always seemed to be a fair pointer to combining them in your mouth from separate sources. And if those work, then specialty *marc*, distilled from what is left after grapes are pressed deserve explorations: some are made just with the remnants of a single grape variety, gewürztraminer, for instance. Sugar should be part of the accompaniments.

Otherwise, enjoy chocolate with coffee, black rather than anything milky, remembering the two blend so well the points of nicety of each are likely to be ambushed, rather like a coach party drawing pistols on the highwayman.

Fair Trade

Like coffee growers, smallholders and families who grew cacao beans were long at the mercy of unscrupulous traders, who paid them as little as they could and then sold on for as much as they could. Now, decency has reared its kinder head, and not only are these smaller people being guaranteed a decent income, they're being helped to become more efficient and productive. Everyone wins of course, the growers have a higher standard of living and we get better and better chocolate. It is indeed through such caring attitudes that the number of companies offering single-estate chocolates of superb individuality are slowly growing. Given the choice, go for a chocolate maker whose income is at least shared with the pockets of others. Let good taste be your guide.

Chocolate Types

Baker's /baking chocolate: the former is a trade name in the United States and thus means little. But baking chocolate is the general term for chocolate substitutes, made from vegetable fats and chocolate flavourings, and thus should not really use the word chocolate at all. Be careful never to confuse this stuff with the next two.

Cacao/cocoa beans: whole cacao beans are being sold more and more by chocolatiers and we should all encourage more to do so. They have a raw and thrilling taste, not as far away from sophisticated chocolate products as you would think, but with undisguised feral, jungle notes that take the palate and mind to places they don't expect. A natural sweet spiciness is like a flashing neon light, telling you in no uncertain terms that cinnamon would enhance the flavour enormously. Rather than going to the trouble of making Mexican-style chocolate q.v. from them, I grate or scrape some coarsely to garnish and finish puddings, desserts, ice creams etc. When you do buy, check if they are raw or have been roasted and if not, get some advice. The high fat content means they are likely to rancidify, so keep them refrigerated or frozen. Probably the #1 snob ingredient to have in your cupboard.

Cooking chocolate: doesn't really mean anything for the term can be applied to any chocolate with which you decide to cook. In older cookery books, and to those with unsophisticated palates, cooking chocolate is likely to mean any bitter, high cocoa solid, low sugar chocolate, the sort that has now become so popular to eat. It is best not to use this term, for it denigrates and confuses. Unless you are in Australia, where cooking chocolate is still specified in recipes and branded thus in shops.

If you need a darker dark chocolate than you can buy or have, make a mixture of 20g/³⁄₄oz/3tbsp cocoa powder plus 15g/2oz unsalted butter for every 25g/1oz of dark chocolate in the recipe.

Couverture: a type of chocolate with a very high cocoa fat content, specially suited to professional and catering use because it melts and covers easily. It can vary in cocoa solid content, but it is generally good and high, and together with the high cocoa fat content can make couverture very expensive: often it's only available in big, professional sizes, too. All those vegetable fat chocolate-'flavour' products on the market attempt to do the same thing cheaply for the consumer market, but shouldn't. Couverture is often confused with the following:

Eating chocolate: all chocolate can be eaten, and this description is a hangover from the days when sweetened chocolate bars and elaborately filled chocolates were considered the thing, and plain, bitter chocolate was 'cooking' chocolate. Like cooking chocolate, it is a term that should be dropped.

Ganache: like so many good things, ganache is supposed to have been discovered by accident, and that's the sort of accident I'd own up to causing. Essentially chocolate is melted together with cream, in varying proportions according to its end use. More cream keeps it mellifluous on the tongue, less cream gives it more body, for use as a superior icing for instance, that will harden on the outside, stay luxuriant inside. It's used as a filling for meringues, cakes and biscuits, can be piped and spread, flavoured, stuffed with nuts, stuffed into prunes or figs; any left over ganache can be rolled into balls and called truffles, which they are.

Ganache may be flavoured with anything concentrated, from vanilla extract to any spirit or liqueur, crystallized fruit, toasted nut, alcohol-plumped vine fruit or even infusions of herbs and spices. See 151 for a seminal truffle recipe.

Gianduja: a very traditional, now classic, combination of hazelnuts and chocolate. Once made only with dark chocolate but now more commonly with milk chocolate. Check the sell by date carefully because hazelnuts easily get bored with perfection, and show this by going rancid after a few months.

Mexican chocolate: you are indeed more likely to find this in the local markets of Mexico than at home. There they make chocolate by rolling roasted cacao beans, which not only crushes them but also melts the fat. You have to use something nonporous, not wood or marble, for these soak up the fat. Into this thick liquid goes some or all of the sacred trinity of cinnamon, vanilla and sugar – and sometimes ground almonds, too – and then it is shaped or set. The result is rather like the pastilles of chocolate sold in Europe for centuries as the base of hot chocolate drinks, at once more acidic and richer because fattier, but with a greater spectrum of flavour than much marketed today.

Milk chocolate: chocolate to which has been added condensed milk, which thus means extra sugar, or dried milk, which has been caramelised and thus gives an unavoidable caramelized flavour that you love or hate. But this is mainly in the UK and USA. Milk chocolate made by European or South American companies seems cleaner and smoother even though it has less cocoa solids and less milk and thus more sugar. Milk chocolate is difficult to use successfully in cookery because its flavour is already diluted and sweetened, but this doesn't stop the serving of pallid, sticky, sickly and bland objects in cafes and sweet shops around the world.

Truffles: these most luxuriant ways of eating chocolate are the furthest away from the snap of quality chocolate, and are instead like biting into thick satin because they're all based on ganache q.v. Sometimes flavoured and sometimes 'plain' they might be rolled in cocoa or dipped in dark, milk or white chocolate in which case you have the exquisite pleasure of snapping your way through cracking good chocolate to get at the truffle.

White chocolate: some purists say white chocolate is not chocolate at all because it doesn't contain cocoa solids. It is however made from cocoa butter, plus sugar and milk, and has a similar texture. Whatever it should be called, it can be delicious and is increasingly popular. Be sure when using white chocolate in cooking that you buy one of good quality. Cheaper, mass market white chocolate gives very disappointing results.

Truffle Snuffling

It's got to the stage where truffles dug from the ground might be thought named after the chocolate truffle, for there are zillions more of the latter. If you do not always like your chocolate to snap and crackle before it pops onto your tongue, you should be snuffling out the very best chocolate truffles, or making your own to this recipe, from the redoubtable Sarah Jayne-Staynes, author of *Chocolate: the Definitive Guide*, and producer/creator of hundreds of thousands of superlative truffles.

Essentially, truffles are ganache q.v. with bite-sized attitude, and one of the few *haute-cuisine* pinnacles of chocolate-amateurs really can make at home.

225g/8oz (approx) high-cocoa solid chocolate or white chocolate*
300ml/½ pint double (heavy) cream
* white chocolate truffles need 25% extra cream

Break up the chocolate and put it into a big mixing bowl. Bring the cream to a rolling boil and pour it onto the chocolate. Stir until the two ingredients are very well mixed and then add any flavouring you choose. Rough brandy works better than cognac (you do know the difference, don't you? See below), brisk young Calvados better than a mature one, fruit eau de vies are better than fruit liqueurs. Toasted nuts of all kind can be incorporated into the mixture, as could chopped, dried or crystallized fruits. You'll make mocha by incorporating very strong coffee or, more creatively, finely chopped (not ground) coffee beans: with this and many other flavours, a soupçon of chilli, perhaps from a Tabasco sauce q.v., is a winner.

Leave to cool at a moderate room temperature, which will take up to 1½ hours.

For a soft, piping mixture, beat the cooled mixture until the beater just starts to leave a trail – beat it too much and it might separate. Pipe into stars, swirls etc and leave to set again, or use to sandwich sponges, meringues, biscuits, chilled poached pears, peaches, plums or nectarines. You can even make truffle sandwiches with brioche and sprinkle the ganache with toasted hazelnuts or crushed raspberries. Or fill tiny profiteroles and stick them to meringue bases with more ganache.

For the firmer mixture more suited to round truffles, use the mixture as it is.

When cooled, you dig in with a teaspoon and shape each harvest into a ball (nothing like real truffles, of course) using your palms and then roll them in superior cocoa, chopped nuts, crushed amaretti and the like.

If you also want snap, crackle and choc, dip your truffles into fine couverture chocolate, except this does not always give you the shiny look you'd expect from a shop.

This dull appearance is because, once melted, chocolate is unlikely to return to its crisp, tempered sheen, but by using the very highest chocolate solids product, ideally a couverture, you can often get away with this if you also heat it exceptionally slowly, over very little heat and for a very short time.

If you have the patience to do this, almost anything can be dipped in chocolate and stay shiny. You can dip preserved ginger or ginger biscuits, shortbread, brandy snaps and other biscuits (even out of packets if you enjoy cheating as much I do), dried fruits, strawberries, cherries, muscatel grapes, orange segments and, when no one is looking, your fingers.

NB: Cognac must be made only from grapes grown in the Cognac area of France, as must Armagnac be made from grapes grown in its designated geographical area. Brandy can be made from anything that will ferment, and can be made anywhere. Fermented and distilled turnips from Uzbekistan can properly be called brandy, which might explain a few headaches.

Cocoa Powder

The ultimate result of experiments to reduce the excessive and sometimes unpleasant amount of fat in cacao beans, which often made drinking chocolate unattractive.

Cocoa powder is about 20 % fat by weight, which is negligible in the amounts used. There are two types, straight-forward cocoa powder which has no further processing and is the most common in Britain, and 'dutch' or 'dutched' cocoa, favoured in the US and by the bakers of both.

In 1848 Conrad J. van Houten used an alkali to produce fat-reduced chocolate solids. Further processing gave him a dark powder with reduced acidity and a blander but more mellow flavour. In fact, the fats had saponified, that is turned into a sort of soap! Unsurprisingly the process quickly became known as 'dutching'.

'Dutched' cocoa is especially good for baking and for milk-based products or drinks as it more easily dissolves in milk and quickly blends with cake or biscuit mixes. Ordinary cocoa is harder to mix in but gives unquestionably richer flavours to baking, darker colour and bigger, broader flavour in drinks.

Chocolate makers in Britain usually use ordinary cocoa but some highly commercial snack products use the alternative, especially in the United States. As a drink, I find dutched cocoa a comforting, less aggressive choice from time to time, and thus usually keep both types around. In the United States dutched cocoa is commonly referred to as European-style cocoa.

Valrhona of France market an exceptional cocoa, that is easily mistaken for drinking chocolate.

Storage

Bar chocolate is quite forgiving at temperatures up to 20C//75F, and like wine it is more important to keep it at a constant temperature rather than somewhere the temperature fluctuates at all dramatically. Very fine chocolate, filled or ganache chocolates also manage up to the same temperature, but as they are also comfortable at any temperature above freezing, you'll get longer life and preserve the finer aromas of their added ingredients at a cooler rather than a warmer temperature. You bring cheese and wine up to a comfortable room temperature before serving them; do the same with chocolate and chocolates for maximum pleasure.

Cooking

Whether you choose ordinary cocoa powder or dutched cocoa for baking, the best tip I ever received was from Katie Stapleton of Denver, both one of the USA's great food personalities and a very dear and loyal friend. She said always to use cocoa powder rather than flour for dusting the baking tins or trays of chocolate cakes, biscuits, brownies and so on. It prevents unsightly white dusting or nasty combinations of unflavoured flour and butter on your baking, and adds extra chocolate depth, too. It's so obvious, and thus even kinder of Katie to pass it one.

If you feel a recipe is not going to have enough flavour, (don't you hate cakes that turn out purple and don't have the slightest taste of chocolate?) this is possibly because you have not been able to buy one of the fantastic high cocoa solid chocolates, in which case it is always best to add cocoa powder rather than more chocolate, for extra chocolate's fat and sugar may unbalance your recipe.

Chocolate is the perfect finisher of any rich, spicy game sauce. Try it the next time you make a casserole of hare, pigeon or venison and if these are not your usual fare, try it the next time you make a braise of beef or of oxtail. Just add a square of dark chocolate per person to the sauce, but taste as you go – it should only just be noticeable, and only if you know.

Chocolate or cocoa powder will transform the most ordinary chili con carne, and can go with impunity into every barbecue sauce already rich with tomato and capsicum and brown sugar. Use only a high cocoa solid chocolate, and nothing very sweet: absolutely no milk chocolate. You'll find men adore it and quickly adopt it as a personal speciality they have thought of all by themselves.

An amazing recipe I have demonstrated in many cities and countries is a chocolate and courgette/zucchini cake. It's a bit of a fiddle to start with, but the microwave makes it easier and the fudgy moistness more than repays this. You'll most easily find a recipe in older US books.Perhaps the most astonishing use of chocolate is to finish a sauce for fish, a traditional recipe from the north of Spain, where chocolate first arrived in Europe. I teach this recipe a lot for, although having but few ingredients, each must be handled perfectly. In particular the onion must be cooked the true traditional way, over low heat without browning for a long time, so the sulphuric and other nasty flavours are banished in favour of fructose and thus natural sweetness. Affinity is everything, and when it is perfect (it's actually very forgiving) this is one of the great revelatory recipes: it reveals more than any other how understanding affinities simplifies cookery but magnifies the eating. If you marry and then treat good ingredients respectfully, you will cook better and faster and with fewer ingredients; you might say this recipe represents everything for which this book stands.

Hot Chocolate

This is the fastest growing market for enjoying chocolate: hot chocolate or a mocha of chocolate and coffee are commonly available in espresso cafés all around the world. It began in cafés but has now moved into the mainstream and there are probably 50 or more flavours of drinking chocolate being sold; but I can't imagine why you'd want a flavoured hot chocolate when the labels tell you the hazelnut or strawberry or orange flavour is 'flavor/flavour' that is, the chocolate might be real but everything else about it is not.

The first dedicated Hot Chocolate Bar I found in London is tucked into a corner of Harrods, as though in disgrace. That's right and proper if the chocolate they use is the same as that sold in bars and snacks there, for yet again you'll have 'flavours/flavors' in the cup. The Chocolate Society's shop in Shepherd Market, Mayfair offers four types of true hot chocolate drinks, and when you are in Borough Market on Fridays and Saturdays The Cool Chile Company sells cinnamon-bright Mexican-style chocolate from a constantly whisked cauldron.

You can use any good plain chocolate to make a delicious hot drink without the fattiness, grittiness and flouriness our ancestors would recognise. There are some good chocolate powders too, and from very famous names but these are often very sweet, certainly too sweet for me. It's as though we are not big enough to be able to sweeten our own drinks.

Hot chocolate is traditionally served in small, narrow, straight-sided cups, which help conserve the heat by having a limited surface area. Increasing the amount of chocolate you use, adding more or less water or milk or incorporating some sort of liquid cream are all ways to create a chocolate drink of individuality from any of the following recipes. If you choose chocolate bars flavoured with natural ingredients you can make gorgeous flavoured hot chocolates.

The texture of chocolate should always be improved by whisking vigorously just before serving. In Mexico they use a special wooden whisk, the *molinillo*, but a wire whisk or an old fashioned rotary egg beater does as well.

Simple Hot Chocolate

Four to six servings, according to cup size
50g/2oz rich, dark chocolate or 3-4 tablespoons powdered chocolate per serving
8 tablespoons water
700ml/1¼pint/3 cups US/ cold milk
vanilla bean or 1 tsp vanilla extract
sugar to taste
cinnamon sticks
optional whipped cream at room temperature

Prepare the cups by filling them with very hot water and letting them stand like this while you make the chocolate. Gently melt the chocolate and water together, in a microwave or a double boiler. Don't use just a small amount of water or other liquid, as you risk the chocolate seizing. Put a vanilla bean into the cold milk and bring slowly to scalding temperature – just below boiling; remove the bean. If you don't have a bean handy, flavour the milk with vanilla extract. Sweeten the milk to taste but try not to use more than a teaspoon of sugar per serving. Pour the hot milk onto the melted chocolate, whisking as you do.

Empty and dry the cups and put a piece of cinnamon stick into each. Whisk the hot chocolate again until frothy and even, and then serve. Top each serve with a dab or more of whipped cream if you really must. Once made, the chocolate can also be served cold like the Aztecs did, or over ice cubes which they couldn't.

For a more authentic taste of older European times, use all water to make the chocolate. I'm sure I prefer it like this, and would bump up the amount of chocolate anyway.

Brazilian Mocha

Less rich than plain hot chocolate, but the coffee makes it more stimulating. Although from the steamy beaches and jungles of Brazil, this is quite the best pre- or après-ski drink, both invigorating and soothing. Cognac, rum or a fruit brandy (not liqueur) can be added judiciously, or sipped at the same time.

Four servings

35g/1½ oz rich, dark chocolate or 3-4 tablespoons powdered chocolate per serving
up to 2 tablespoons sugar
300ml/½ pint/1⅓ cups US/ boiling water
150ml/¼ pint/⅔ cup US/ hot milk or single/light cream
150ml/¼ pint/⅔ cup US/ hot double/light cream
450ml/¾ pint/2 cups US/ hot strong black coffee

Add the chocolate and some of the sugar to half the boiling water and stir until dissolved. Add the remaining water and bring everything back to a gentle simmer. Add the milk, creams and coffee, which should be very freshly made. Whisk well and then taste and adjust for sweetness. Vanilla extract and cinnamon can be added, and the very active can add whipped cream, with the promise they will soon exercise it off.

Spanish Drinking Chocolate

An egg yolk gives added comfort and richness to this style

Four servings

60g/2½ oz rich dark chocolate or 3-4 tablespoons powdered chocolate per serving
several pinches very freshly ground cinnamon
600ml/ 1 pint/2⅔ cups US/ milk
1 egg yolk

Melt the chocolate in the milk over gentle heat and then flavour with cinnamon and sugar if you like. Beat the egg yolk and then remove the saucepan from the heat and whisk the yoke into the chocolate mixture. Serve warm rather than hot.

Chocolate Fish

No, not the chocolate-covered marshmallow fish so beloved of New Zealanders, but something to surprise at lunch or dinner, a tradition from the Basques.

Serves four as a starter, two-three as a main
350g/³/₄ lb onions
120g/4oz/1 stick butter
1 tbsp plain flour
scant half glass fruity/off-sweet white wine
scant half glass water
25g/1oz extra dark/bitter chocolate
salt and pepper
12 or so button mushrooms
500g/1lb (approx) firm white fish, like cod, halibut, snapper, hapuku, grouper

Slice the onions as finely as possible. Choose a non-stick frying pan with a lid and then fry the onions in the butter over low heat until they have melted to become very soft and sweet but have not coloured: this can take 40 minutes and should be done with the pan covered for most of the time.

Stir in the flour and then the wine and water and let bubble for five minutes to cook out the flour flavour. Add the chocolate, chopped or grated, and when that is evenly stirred in, season with salt and pepper. Finely slice and then stir in the mushrooms and then put the fish on top of the sauce, in one piece or in serving sizes. Cover and simmer gently until the fish is just cooked through.

Serve the fish onto warm plates, and then stir up the sauce to even it out, adding a little wine or water if you see it's too thick. Serve the sauce around rather than over the fish, to enhance the contrast between the whiteness of the fish and the rich brown of the sauce.

Coffee

Forget all that stuff about you are what you eat. You are much more what you drink.

When you consider we are all essentially water held together in a greater or lesser state of appeal, it is amazing how little care we take with our liquid intake. Alcohol? Yes, of course, it is pleasurable, but actually dehydrates rather than quenches thirst. A bit of a blow that.

Water is commonly thought dicey, pricey or ignored altogether, and any way has become an absurd fashion accessory for those millions with UPNF syndrome, unresolved public nipple fixation syndrome, something kept private for millennia. Can you explain why men and women who spend thousands on clothes, shoes, makeup and hair now can't leave home without clutching a $2 plastic bottle with a teat on the end?

Soda waters and aerated drinks are largely for kids. That leaves us with coffee, tea, tisanes and hot chocolate or cocoa. Potentially, coffee, tea and tisanes offer more pleasure and reward than any aspect of the speciality food spectrum – all day and all night. But for too many, their experience will be slurps of tepid instant coffee or of water barely clouded by a double-dipped tea bag.

What a world of pleasurable discovery lies ahead, shadowed only by possible clashes with tea freaks and cappuccino clowns, those who need written introductions and complete genealogical and geographical backgrounds to individual leaf or bean before they buy. By the time they have chosen the blend, admired the equipment, explained the process and timed the extraction you've had to reach for a Diet Coke.

Somewhere between the two lies the norm. A world of genuine interest in good tea and coffee of all types and at all levels. Sure, enjoy your First-Flush Darjeeling, or Monsooned Malabar. But know how to get the best from a tea bag, and the best way to make instant coffee too. You owe it to who you are – to your watery body.

It is extraordinary to think the instant beverage millions drink has the same name as a drink once considered a gift from God, and which properly made smells and tastes as though mixed indeed by the Divine hand.

Coffee has been forbidden in Mecca by a governor who was later put to death, blessed by a pope, accused of making men unfruitful, banned by Frederick the Great, and written about by Bach in a temporal cantata. English coffee houses were temporarily closed by Charles II, but nonetheless changed the city of London forever.

Coffee, national drink of the Americas and of the Middle East, had its origins in north-east Africa. Tradition suggests it was first recognized in Ethiopia, by a shepherd who noticed a distinct sprightliness in his sheep – or was it goats – after they had eaten a certain red berry. Even he, the shepherd/goatherd Rhaldi, felt invigorated after trying some, and passed the knowledge on to local Sufi mystics. Deciding such pleasure could only be associated with the devil, the monks threw the berries onto the fire. The heavenly aroma that ensued convinced them of an opposite provenance; they raked out the remaining charred seeds, threw them into water... and so on.

The stimulus given by this new drink sharpened men's ability to worship God, and so Islamic clerics kept coffee secret for years. But no one keeps secrets from followers of Islam, who then adopted the drink with fervour, for it helped them through long and repeated religious services, too.

The first public coffee house opened in Mecca about 1511 and thence the habit of combining the stimulus of society with that of caffeine spread north via Constantinople into Europe. By 1645, anyone who was anyone, or hoped to be, had taken coffee with Signor Floriano in Venice, as noted for his prodigious propensity to gossip as for the excellence of the coffee he served on the Piazza di San Marco.

The first coffee houses in Paris were lavish and oriental, captivating bored society by having the drink served on bended knee by Turkish slaves, who would recommend most things to Parisians. In England, coffee houses became centres for democratic discussion, where for a penny a cup one could be assured of commerce and conversation. There was one in Oxford in 1650 and two years later London had its first, in Cornhill.

They were restless, exciting places where you could hear uncensored news, but they soon had their day. Although remaining a vital part of much European life, the coffee house in London disappeared; the few that survived altered out of all recognition into clubs or institutions. The Commercial Union, Baltic Exchange and Lloyds all have their roots in coffee houses.

Americans began by drinking tea, turning to coffee in protest at taxes on tea that went to England rather than to their benefit. Eventually they turned the East India Company's tea out of chests and into Boston harbour and drinking coffee became a demonstration of independent thinking. But was it just their colonial interests that have made the English so addicted to tea? In coffee's early heyday it was often flavoured with mustard, boiled unconscionably, mixed with oatmeal, ale, wine, butter or spices. I think the English prefer simpler food, and tea triumphed for centuries more.

It is coffee's turn but not for the first time in recent history. In the Fifties and early Sixties espresso bars rose and then fell. That was a chance to become a coffee nation again, but was refused perhaps because coffee bars were then part of youthful protest, a haunt of librarians with beards, of artists, and people who had been to Ibiza, of all places. It was hard to forget Tommy Steele was discovered in a Soho coffee bar.

But now all has been forgiven and every second site on the High Street with plumbing has an espresso machine. Just as well, for everyone is drinking it this time, from housewives trying to write novels about boy wizards to city types so terrified of red ink they wear black all the time. Coffee nationhood has taken root and vast fortunes are also being spent installing espresso machines at home.

None of this has dented the mystique of coffee making, and it is still much easier to ruin coffee than any other hot drink. Many who have persevered for years as makers of 'real' coffee have still to taste a good cupful. It is far easier to make tea, much easier to appreciate its differing blends and styles; or you can drink instant coffee, the worst of which at least has the merit of being simple to make and hot. The more I know about coffee the more I know getting value and flavour is never easy and cannot be cheap. Yet little else can be so rewarding if you succeed.

The path from coffee tree to you is no less fraught with danger, mystery and failure.

The coffee bean is the seed of an evergreen shrub with glossy green, lance-like leaves and a white flower with the heady scent of jasmine that grows in volcanic soil between the Tropics of Cancer and Capricorn; the best quality is produced over 1600m above sea level. The costs involved in coffee production become starkly obvious when you learn the very best trees only produce 3kg dried weight of coffee beans in a year: Brazilian bushes each produce only 500g of coffee a year.

Coffee's fruit are known as cherries, for this is what they resemble as they ripen from green to purple. A major complication is that everything from blossoms to green, ripe and over-ripe cherries may be on the same branch at the same time. Thus, harvesting should be done berry by berry as they ripen to the precise degree, for green or over-ripe berries add inferior flavour to the finished drink.

But, most modern foods are grown and processed with speed and economy in mind, and coffee is no exception. It is increasingly rare for it to be picked by hand or with any real care. Instead whole branches are pulled mechanically away with a mixture of beans in many states, the hope being that processing will separate the good from the bad.

Each cherry has a skin, a pulp, a tough parchment, a thin silver skin and the seeds or beans, in that order. Normally there are two seeds, facing each other with their flatter sides together, but sometimes only one bean will develop, and this rounder seed is sometimes separated out and sold as peaberry coffee. Theoretically it should be more flavourful. In fact such berries usually come from stunted or old trees and the liquor made from them is no different, but they look nice. Kenyan Peaberries are the exception and have a notably greater fragrance.

The pulp and skins can be removed from the beans in two ways – the wet or the dry. The wet method is far preferable but requires great amounts of water, not necessarily available where coffee is grown.

Once processed, green or unroasted coffee beans last well – indeed some, such as the Java, are said to improve for up to twenty years – but the flavour we appreciate so much comes only after the bean is roasted, which releases the oils and aromas present and adds others.

Washed coffee: a pulper removes most of the outside skin and flesh. Next the beans are fermented, softening the remaining mucilage, which may then be washed off. This fermentation must be most carefully timed for it affects both appearance and flavour.

Washed green coffee looks better than unwashed, but the process is no guarantee of higher quality. The special advantage of the washed coffee process is that under-ripe berries, which can give a distinct peanut flavour, float to the top and can be removed, radically improving the overall quality. Unfortunately over-ripe berries, known in the trade as 'stinkers' and which give a flavour rather like silage, will remain and can disastrously affect the flavour of the ultimate brew – well, it would to most Europeans, whereas many in the Middle East pursue and value this eccentric flavour. Some French fancy the flavour too, actually calling such coffee *le nectaire*, which is a bit of a worry when they are supposed to know so much about gastronomic pleasures.

The beans are now known as parchment beans, and a machine like a roller mill removes the parchment and silver skin. Washed beans are often given a polish in another machine, which makes both colour and quality more durable. The treatment undeniably gives finer looking coffee beans, but often the crop will be so big the available machinery cannot cope and the older, dry (unwashed) method will be used.

Unwashed coffee: the coffee cherries are dried in the sun until crisp. They need constant attention to dry evenly. Rain or dew means the cherries must be covered and as soon as the sun comes out they must be spread again or they will moulder.

Once the drying is thorough, often with mechanical help today, the pulp and parchment can easily be removed. The drawback of the dry method is there is no guarantee of consistency of colour or quality, and lesser beans and other debris are included in the final product – even after careful grading.

Coffee Varieties

Coffea arabica: is indisputably the finest coffee variety. Originally from Ethiopia, or somewhere close anyway, it will grow higher above sea level than other varieties and, like high-grown tea bushes, these slower growing beans produce greater amounts of integral sugar and a better, more refined flavour. The bean shape is an elongated oval and they are usually quite flat.

Coffea robusta: is native to Zaire but can grow more easily and prolifically over a wider geographical area than arabicas. It is far more disease resistant too. The faster-grown flavour is muddier and less refined than arabicas but when well-produced adds attractive and useful up front boldness to blends. It also contains up to two and a half times more caffeine than arabicas and, as it is also cheaper, is bound to be the dominant content of cheap bean mixtures. The special appeal of robusta in the past was its suitability to the instant coffee process but now that has been improved beyond conception, more and more arabica is being used in instants.

The green robusta bean is identifiable for being smaller, irregular, convex, and browner than arabicas, but not even experts guarantee to tell arabicas from robustas once they are roasted.

Coffea liberica: is a very bad third rate and can safely be ignored.

Savouring Coffee

Coffee as a drink is judged on its body, acidity and fragrance. Just as soil, climate and altitude will make the same grape give wildly different flavours, wine language is relevant to assessing coffee.

The range of effects is created by roasting, essentially caramelising the sugars present in the bean. Slow maturing, high-grown beans have bigger quantities of sugar and other aromatics and thus create richer and more complex flavours. It is a sin to highly roast the best beans and a blessing that the cheaper ones should be.

The *body* of coffee means its overall effect in the mouth; a full-bodied coffee fills the mouth with a velvety softness, stimulating taste buds over the entire palate to thus give a so-called 'long' finish, flavour and sensation which lingers in the mouth and down the back of the throat. Lesser coffees, robustas in particular, are flatter and less sensual and are usually 'short' or 'middle' finishers – that is they only affect taste buds in part of the palate, often boldly but just in the front, and do not do that for very long.

Acidity in coffee is what you would call dryness in wine, it is what makes the liquid feel clean in the mouth, giving satisfying balance to the initial sweetness. It is sensed more towards the edges of the tongue and must not be confused with bitterness, found in coffee which has been over-roasted or over-brewed. Bitterness is detected by an area across the back of the tongue, a last-chance warning before you swallow, because bitter foods are often poisonous foods.

Just as in wine, a good coffee will tell you much of what there is to say by its nose. Like wine, it should not be sniffed in namby-pamby whiffs but with a big, single breath, which is held so it can permeate and stimulate and inform.

Making Coffee

Not long ago Union Roasters of London invited me to a comparative coffee tasting, my first ever: these should be part of every school curriculum. Not only did we compare the flavour of coffee beans from many countries, we tasted the same coffee bean brewed three different ways. The difference is so startling I've had to throw away many views on which coffee tastes like what: I've discovered the way it is made has a far greater effect than any other part of the long process.

We compared the same coffee made by the filter method, made in an Italian stove-top coffee-maker and with coffee made in a plunger or cafetière.

The filter coffee was smooth, mild, elegant, nicely acidic and would have been enjoyed thoroughly for what it was, until we tasted the next. It was then I realized what I should always have known; in filtering solids from the brewing coffee, a paper filter also absorbs its oils, the source of coffee's most refined flavours and natural sweetness. Thus filter coffee is emasculated coffee, no matter how strong you make it. The oils and the fine particles suspended in coffee made other ways are very important contributors to the full flavour spectrum. Of course, I'm speaking here about paper filters, and I can't think machines with fine metal filters will do quite the same thing, except I have noticed oil deposited on them, and they will withhold some of the suspension.

Next came coffee made in the Italian stove-top contraption; the sort where you screw an empty top onto a bottom full of water, with finely ground coffee in a compartment between the two. Plenty of caution is needed, first not to tamp the coffee tightly – conversely a must for proper espresso – and not to have the heat too high. The trick of this technique is to understand water can be forced up through the coffee at a temperature below boiling, and this plus the small grind of the coffee assures maximum extraction with minimum damage. Ideally you should be watching and listening and as soon as you hear something is about to happen should take the pot off the heat or turn down the heat altogether. Because you get a more concentrated brew from this technique, you get a fuller body and a richer flavour that often comes with a degree more bitterness, sometimes because the water was too hot. With practice this coffee can be superb, but perhaps the technique is more suited to higher roast coffees, where some expectation of bitterness is part of your choice. Poured into a warm cup, this brew gave enormous flavour that invaded every crevice of the palate: even if there were no caffeine in the coffee you would have felt heartened for anything, except for guessing it was exactly the same coffee we had tasted made the filter way.

Finally, more of the same coffee was brewed in a cafetière or plunger, a simple seeming process but which is still highly dependent on an exact balance between the size of the ground coffee grains, the heat of the water and the length of time you brew. Union Roasters knew what they were doing, and this mild seeming method produced a racier coffee altogether, much fuller than the filtered version, and with much more body even than stove-top coffee, plus extra layers of flavour. You get all the oils and aromatics from the bean when you make coffee this way, and as a bonus you also get a fine suspension of coffee solids that add a zillion micro-flavours to the brew. But it too is easily ruined – by the use of boiling water, which almost immediately vaporizes or oxidizes the fragile aromatic oils.

Whatever we thought about each brew, every one agreed they would never have guessed we were drinking the same coffee.

The lessons to be learned were, filter coffee is for cissies, boiling water is for bullies, and that with care Italians had it right all along. We went home with lots to think about.

Unless you have a spectacularly priced espresso to call upon, the best plan is to make coffee like tea, so you don't even need a cafetière, but can use a jug.

Jug coffee: use coarse-ground coffee and put a level tablespoon or more of this per cup into a warmed jug. Pour in water that has boiled but been allowed to subside for 15 seconds or more, stir a couple of times and leave for three to five minutes. Strain as you serve. This has the very distinct advantage of letting you taste as it brews.

If jug coffee seems too strong or too bitter you have used grounds which are too fine, have brewed too long, or should change to a lighter roast or higher quality. If it is too light you have under-brewed, possibly because the grounds are too coarse, or should choose a darker roast. The medical view is that something in coffee made this way (not the caffeine) can cause cholesterol to rise, but you need to be drinking more than five big cups a day.

Plunger/ cafetière coffee: the same thing as jug coffee, but with gadgetry and for more money. You equally need to be sure of water at the correct temperature and that it is in contact with the grounds for the correct amount of time to extract what you have paid for. It is essential to encourage this by first lightly wetting the coffee and waiting 30 seconds or so for it to swell before pouring in the rest of the water, which again should be just under boiling point. Or you can add all the water and give an immediate plunge and withdraw, which helps even brewing. It's a little faster too, so a few taste tests are in order to get your timing correct. A coarse to medium grind is best.

Filter coffee: the coffee should be ground medium fine because water is in contact for a much shorter time. Wetting the coffee with just some of the water, to let it swell evenly before you add the rest of the water, is recommended practice. If you are unhappy with the results the observations about jug coffee are just as relevant.

Italian stove-top coffee: this is also called the stove-top espresso, and makes the best coffee domestically if you like a more concentrated brew. Because stove-top makers come in several sizes you can do it right every time, but you mustn't even consider making two cups of coffee in a machine designed to make four or six or more. Fine to medium-fine ground coffee.

Espresso coffee: espresso coffee was invented as a commercial process. The hissing machines not only filter the water but also deliver it at a precise pressure and temperature. Modern electronics make it easier for small domestic machines to get close to these, but I suspect espresso works best when left to the professionals. This is indeed another way of saying unless you spend unlawful heaps on a professional espresso machine to use at home, you are better off making it in a jug, yes, even that glass measuring jug. Except for the ristretto q.v. See special espresso panel.

Hot milk rather than cold certainly seems to add silkiness to coffee and warm cups keep coffee hotter longer. Raw sugars sound like a good idea for sweetening but their distinct flavour gets in the way of really good coffee, as will honey. If coffee is too bitter for you, drink a higher quality and get what you have paid for – natural sweetness and fragrance. Lemon or lime juice would counterbalance that bitterness in black coffee, rather than sugar, which can only balance acidity.

The continuing mystery for me is why people will wrap their palms around cups of coffee. Is the coffee somehow too heavy? Have they just come in from blizzards and decided actively to encourage chilblains? Or merely been watching too many TV advertisements? Mugs are worse.

Iced coffee can be made with leftover brewed coffee, but it should then be served without ice cubes or it is unlikely to be strong enough. Best brew a double strength batch, or make your own essence with lots of instant coffee and a little water, or to use a liquid coffee essence.

You may serve iced black coffee but most people seem to prefer it with some dairy addition. Mix it with chilled milk, cream or half-melted ice cream, in which case be creative, using, say, chocolate ice cream to make a mocha iced coffee... whipped cream would be a welcome topping and so I suppose you might as well add nuts, grated orange zest, crushed coffee beans.

Strong instant coffee seems peculiarly suited to being served iced: ideally make a very strong essence of instant coffee and very little water and then top up each glass with sparkling water or soda. Half sparkling water and half milk plus a scoop of ice cream gives a sparkling black coffee ice-cream soda, and if it's made with a robusta-based coffee, this will keep anyone awake. Very grown up if you ignore the children present and also add brandy or rum.

Choosing a Coffee

Knowing your way around coffee is a lifetime study, and much more exciting because of that. Just when you think you know it all, something changes. Some years ago frosts in Brazil destroyed their crops and world prices quadrupled: it seemed dreadful, but actually encouraged drinkers to look further afield and discover new coffee pleasures. The frost effect is unlikely to be repeated for Brazil has now moved much coffee production further north to areas where frost only happens on beer glasses.

Now there is world over-production by some 25 per cent, so prices and competition are getting greater which should mean your choice is better and better priced. Here are some broad outlines, which you will enjoy filling in with your own colours.

Africa

West Africa is the home of robusta coffee, East Africa is probably the origin of arabicas and produces some of the finest available in bulk, and most countries produce a quantity of both.
Western countries: West African coffee, largely from Angola, Cameroon and Zaire is virtually all robusta; strongly flavoured, reliable croppers but lacking character, subtlety or variety. You are most unlikely to find any sold by name.
Eastern countries/ Ethiopia: civil war has made these rare for many years but the market is moving again. At up to 2600m above sea level, the Highlands produce some of the world's highest grown coffees, exceptionally fragrant, almost perfumed and usually described as winey or gamey: at a comparative tasting offered journalists by Douwe Egbert in Utrecht, an Ethiopian Mocha Djimma was almost universally thought the best on offer, and there was sensational competition. Most Ethiopian coffee is unwashed and Harar Longberry is considered very superior, sweet and subtle rather than having the punch and acidity of a Kenyan. Look also for Limu and Sidamoo.
Kenya: almost universally good quality and the top ones are everything coffee should be. Kenya Peaberry really does offer small beans that have all the flavour and body normally packed into two beans. High-grown Kenyan coffee has superb natural sweetness and thus

can give a really full flavour when only lightly roasted; a medium (after dinner) roast develops extra acidity that balances the accompanying increase in flavour. Kenya has developed a system to remove over-ripe berries from washed coffee using ultra-violet light.

Tanzania: similar to Kenyan but perhaps a little thinner.

Uganda: outstanding arabicas, with all the quality of Kenyan coffees.

The Americas

Brazil: this country produces a quarter of the world's 60 million kg of coffee beans each year. It's an awful lot of coffee and a lot of it is awful. Unusually, Brazilian coffee trees have a main crop season from April to June, which means most beans are harvested then and subsequently hang around a while. A top Santos will have wonderful body, elegant acidity and excellent colour and flavour. Even more extraordinary is the rare true Santos Bourbon, an aristocratic traditional variety which few grow any more; when I last checked the entire crop of the major grower went to a single distributor in Britain.

Colombia: the world's second biggest producer, and the best is truly great coffee. Colombian beans actually produce more liquor per bean than anything from Brazil and have a full sweet flavour rarely marred by excess acidity. Its trees produce all year and thus continuously send fresh beans to the market. Of all coffee Colombian most deserves to be described as winey, for it typically fills the mouth with the velvety smoothness of a well-matured red wine. It is thus depressing to hear Colombian coffee sometimes described as bland, but that is probably because it is the favourite coffee of the United States.

Americans roast coffee much more lightly and brew it much weaker than Europeans, sometimes only a quarter the strength; they have been fooled into using fewer beans by the appearance of strength given by the fast and full colour of the high liquor production of Colombian coffees. If American coffee is not just pointless but also plain undrinkable to Europeans it was probably made in the unspeakable percolator or kept hot for longer than 30 minutes, which is almost as bad. Doing either deserves excommunication from coffee's rituals.

Colombians you might find and enjoy are Medellins, Excelso, Manizales, Armenicas, Libanos, Bogatoas and Buccaramangos – and doesn't the last one even sound great?

Costa Rica: the connoisseur's secret. Well-perfumed, mild and with quite a tangy acidity, rather like aristocratic clarets, delicious full sweetness supported on a firm elegant body gives an unusually balanced cup.

Ecuador: thin sharp coffee that appears anonymously but usefully in blends.

Guatemala: they have a rather heavy full body and good acidity, and high-grown Guatemalans are essentially mild and mellow with a particularly fragrant bouquet and aromatic flavour. Look specially for Coban and Antiquas.

Hawaii: stretching a geographical point, I know, but worth it. Kona coffee is grown on the volcanic soil of the Kona district of Hawaii, the Big Island. It is sweet and mellow but carries a unique extra flavour, best described as nutty. Even if it does not come from that precise district, all Hawaiian coffee is sold as Kona, except in Portugal where that is a fearfully rude word. I suppose it must be in Brazil too.

Mexico: mellow and mild coffees of excellent quality, but the coffee Mexicans drink themselves has often been roasted with a sugar coating that gives a strong caramel flavour at best, and which quickly slips into horrid bitterness.

Nicaragua: rich coffees with a complex array of flavour notes, sometimes of spice.

Peru: tangy and with well-bred body.

Venezuela: as elegant and delicious as Colombian coffees but more delicate and lighter and thus too easily misunderstood or dismissed. The most aromatic are the Meridas, described as peculiarly delicate and neither acid nor bitter. Caracas coffees are equally distinctive but lighter and popular in France and Spain.

Arabia

The Yemen is the home of what is thought to be the original Mocha, which can be so full-flavoured it is sometimes said to taste as though mixed with chocolate, an effect also described as gamey. Most Mocha sold is a blend if you look carefully. It is the proper high-roasted coffee/blend to be pulverized for making Turkish/Greek/ Arabic coffee. But beware: Mocha, or any other variety from this part of the world, may include over-ripe beans or stinkers, and then gamey becomes farmyard.

Caribbean

The phenomenal cost would persuade you Jamaican Blue Mountain is the world's best coffee. It is certainly rich, sweet and mellow but the cost is more properly a market-led reflection of the small quantity produced, and proof the quality-intoxicated Japanese pay almost anything to buy almost all of it each year. Like Mocha, any Blue Mountain coffee you might see at a reasonable price will be a blend and most of us will only guess at its accuracy.

Generally, all Caribbean coffees will have mellow, sweet and mild characteristics.

Cuban coffee growing is government controlled, and blended and graded to its particular specifications. The enterprising Monmouth Coffee Company sells Turquino and Serrano Cubans, both superior grades, 'dark, thick and strong' and specially suited to the stove-top coffee maker.

Cuban coffees can be just as good as Jamaican, and Haiti produces very top-shelf stuff. The Dominican Republic and Puerto Rico also produce respectable coffees.

India

Mysore is the one you are most likely to meet. It is mellow and quite light but to me can be muddy. It is commonly used in Mocha blends or blended with Mochas

Monsooned Malabar is recognizable in green form because the beans have turned yellow, if you follow me. When roasted they give a dark chocolate flavour with a bitterness, which in this case is attractive. The effect was originally the result of the humidity and time involved in sailing ship deliveries to Europe. Now the beans are monsooned by being exposed for some time during monsoon season temperatures and weather changes.

Indonesia

Java: rich, heavy and almost spiced, these are amongst the hallowed names of coffee. Old Colonial is the most common name these days for what used to be known as Old Java or Old Government Java, once guaranteed to have had a minimum ten years tropical storage. In fact the slightly musty flavour and dark brown colour was to a greater degree the effect of the slow humid shipping that also created Monsoon Malabars. Any you find are likely to be delicious, but younger and paler than they used to be.

Sumatra: when these are good they are now considered amongst the world's best. Like Javanese coffees they are notably heavy and full in the mouth, but syrupy and flavoury and thus refreshing and stimulating. Madheling and Lingtong are worth pursuing.

The Celebes: Bali and Timor produce pretty good coffee too, but Sulawesi produces one of the world's rarest coffees, Aged Sulawesi. Whereas Monsooned Malabar is exposed for only a few days, Aged Sulawesi matures in thatched barns in naturally high humidity for several years. Union Coffee Roasters in London sells this via their website, and describe it as having a very heavy body and velvety-soft mouth feel, 'vibrant, concentrated, hints of cedar and spice – outstanding to follow a sumptuous feast'. I found it like having a single, magnificent, live animal in my mouth.

Papua New Guinea

Coffee's home here is in the Highlands and these wildest ones of all now produce coffee quite as good as Kenya's, whence came the original stock. A constantly rising star, and a definite talking point at a sticky dinner party, which can acceptably go on to such related subjects as birds of paradise, uncontacted tribes, nose-piercing and penis sheaths.

Decaffeinated Coffee

Caffeine, the substance in coffee that gives you the lift, is also found in tea and chocolate. It upsets many a stomach when too strong and is universally blamed for many sleepless nights. Caffeine is an odourless, slightly bitter alkaline with the following improbable formula: $C8H10N42$ .The content in coffee can range from just over 0.5 per cent to about 2.8 per cent but the average is usually around 1.2 per cent, which means 0.1g per strong cup of coffee.

There are three basic decaffeinating methods, all applied to the green coffee bean. Liquid carbon dioxide, water, and organic solvent – ethylacetate or methylene chloride. Liquid carbon under pressure removes caffeine and then evaporates, leaving no residue. In the water method, the cycle begins when green beans are brewed in water, which is then drawn off: the caffeine is removed from this liquid which is used for the new brew and as it is then saturated with everything but caffeine, will only remove caffeine from the beans. The organic solvents that are specific to caffeine have been criticized of late, but as with most food scares, the facts barely warrant attention. They do indeed leave trace deposits, about one in a million; when coffee is subsequently brewed the traces are not measurable. You would need to drink oceans before any major effect might remotely be caused, by which time you would be dead through over-hydration.

Each method removes 97-98 per cent of the caffeine and there is a move to produce 'light' coffee with about 50 per cent of the usual caffeine levels.

Any criticism of taste changes detected in decaffeinated coffee is more accurately aimed at the quality of coffee used or the instant coffee process than decaffeinating itself. If caffeine is a real problem, remember robusta beans contain twice as much as arabica and that instant coffees are generally robusta based.

Instant Coffee

The range of instant coffees is fast approaching the complication of fresh coffee and the best instants are better than inferior real ones. This is because improved techniques mean more arabica beans are now used; on the other hand this will mean instant coffees are measurably less stimulating than before, because arabica beans have less than half the caffeine content of robusta.

First, the coffee must be brewed, usually by a carefully controlled percolating system for maximum extraction, and then the brew is concentrated; it is this prolonged exposure to heat as much as the quality of beans used which results in the difference between instant and fresh coffees.

The original technique then made a powder from the concentrated coffee by spraying that onto a hot drum. The heat involved lost even more of the valuable aromas and oils, so you always knew you weren't drinking the real thing, even though it was 100 per cent coffee.

Freeze-drying changed all that. Freshly brewed coffee is frozen then ground and when these are passed through a vacuum tunnel the solid water content is turned to water vapour which is exhausted without first having changed to a liquid. The particles are left dry and containing most of what the original coffee began with.

Instant espresso coffees are an innovation that has been particularly successful and they are very good for cooking, too.

You get the best flavour from instant coffee by using water which is under boiling point, and pouring it from rather an exaggerated height both helps guarantee that and aerates the brew, which always enhances flavour.

Coffee Additives

The best-known traditional additive to coffee is chicory, which is toasted and ground, and added for the sake of its bitterness and for economy. Understandable in times of war or famine, during which extraordinary foods have been used to eke out coffee, and chicory has always had its adherents and its enemies. Its popularity is slightly on the decline in the UK, where it has never had a really large following, but it is still popular in parts of France. You can also find Viennese coffee, which includes ground dried figs. The added flavour is fascinating, but I can't really see the point.

Spices are classic additions to coffee – cardamom, cloves or cinnamon being the most usual. The first two might be added in a pinch, ground, or as a whole spice or two put into the coffee pot. Cardamom is the most exotic and commonly found throughout the Middle East. A simple way to use cinnamon is to stir the coffee with a cinnamon stick until the desired flavour is reached. Otherwise sprinkle some ground cinnamon on top of whipped cream on each cup.

The mixtures of coffee and liquor are legion and very few alcohols are actually awful with hot coffee. It is certainly the most warming and stimulating drink imaginable when you are very cold or unhappy. But don't do it by half measures in small cups or you will not be able to use a practical amount of alcohol without making the coffee cold.

At dinner parties, tougher drink-drive laws mean it is not responsible to serve spirits or liqueurs in coffee, but when everyone is staying or walking use cups rather bigger than demi-tasse or hold back on the alcohol, so the coffee is not chilled by the alcohol – far better to enjoy coffee and liqueurs separately from their own vessels. But if you are doing something rugged outdoors, and if you use rougher eau de vie like Calvados, a mixture is obligatory and practical.

Irish coffee, which originated at Irishman's Wharf, San Francisco, is a good example of an ordinary thing becoming popular when generosity with alcohol is possible; is this coffee the only thing Irish about which no one has made a joke?

For some time now, it's been considered a bit of a wheeze to serve coffee made from beans impregnated with such flavourings as amaretto, raspberry, royal mint and almost everything else. Sure, with one stroke they remove the hassle of serving liqueurs and keep insobriety at bay, but is this any way to treat coffee, to treat yourself? You can be assured the beans so flavoured weren't much cop to start with – and anyway, how many of the additives are real?

Much better is the coffee bean enrobed in chocolate, a delicious snack and pretty useful for adding every type of stimuli to otherwise benign cakes, pudding and ice creams. They should not be shared with children, unless hyper-activity is your idea of fun.

Buying coffee

Much of the coffee we buy is blended – that is coffees from different countries or of different types from a country are mixed to obtain this sort of flavour, that sort of mellowness, another strength. The growing interest in coffee means many more enthusiasts are in the business, sometimes trading only a dozen specialty coffees, often unblended from a single estate: there will be one operating in your city, at least in your country you can find on the internet if not in the High Street.

The choice at the fingertips of the blender is extraordinary, as varied as the thousands of styles of wine, and within each country and type of bean there are also grades of quality.

Most blenders agree it is preferable to blend within the same or very similar grades and with some reference to how the beans are likely to be roasted. This latter point is of particular importance to those who like to buy and blend roasted beans.

The most important influences on the flavour of coffee are the two 'b's – the bean and the burn. The less roasting given to a bean, the more it must rely on its intrinsic 'bean' quality: the more a bean is roasted the less you taste the bean and the more you taste the roast or 'burn'. Many very fine roasters take the bean higher than thought appropriate some years ago, but do so to enhance the flavour of high-quality beans, rather than to add flavour to low-quality beans; in this latter case you are being suckered, because you taste burn more than bean.

Knowing this makes more sense of the next point – you should never mix together lightly roasted and highly roasted beans. It is no different from stretching high-vintage Chateau Lafitte with some of the Corsican plonk you rediscovered months after it had slipped behind your car's backseat. If you prefer the kind of flavour your blend of unmatched classes of coffee gives, tell that to a coffee roaster and they will find exactly the same flavour for you, from beans meant to be together. Whatever coffee style you prefer, there is a coffee or a professionally made blend that will give it to you without mixing high and low-roasted beans.

Expensive coffee blends should have a pleasingly regular appearance of size and colour. Blended or unblended, the best quality beans commonly retain a noticeable amount of silver skin in the seam down the middle of their flat side.

A mixture of arabica and robusta beans is generally spotted by the range of sizes seen, yet should not include broken or misshapen beans if the price is toward the high end, but you would be wise to expect more unevenness as you travel down the price range.

There was once an exceptionally large Brazilian bean from a single estate called the

Margogype and which commanded a premium. Today this is more likely to be large beans graded out of any type, and so the term is not a sign or promise of origin, quality or flavour, although many are high quality.

Expensive coffee beans in your shops should be even in shape and colour, and only lightly roasted. Never pay as much for a dark or Continental roast as for a medium or light roast unless you have chosen the green beans yourself and know what you are doing.

Roasted coffee beans are grossly swollen by internal gases created by the roasting, each a ticking bomb with an internal pressure of five to seven atmospheres. Roasted beans should not be put into a sealed container for at least 24 hours as there is seepage of the gas, which will blow plastic containers and find the weak points of every other type of container. This is why some coffee packs have one-way pressure valves, which meanly let off heavenly puffs of coffee-gas exactly when you don't have the time to appreciate it. Roasted beans revert to their original volume once processed, so a spoonful of beans gives half that volume once ground. Only when the coffee beans are broken, crushed or ground will the full aroma be released and investigating this is the best way to make quality judgements, at the same time seeing the colour of the coffee bean is even throughout – unevenness is not good for you will be getting only part value.

If you can, you should also smell the container from which the coffee beans came, checking for any hint of sourness or rancidity for these are quickly absorbed by beans.

The smell of a roasted coffee bean is tantalizing nasal shorthand for what might be possible; the promises can be broken easily. Once ground, its treasures can be plundered by how long you store it and how, by the way you make it, by the mineral content of the water used, the condition and heat of any milk or cream. But on the occasions when all is perfect, and you brew coffee that would interest the impotent dead, every battle on the way is forgotten and forgiven.

Espresso

Originally, this technique was invented to make coffee a cup at a time, to improve standards and to make life easier in cafés. It was first developed in 1822 by Louis Rabaut, a Frenchman, but it was Italians who perfected the technique and made it work faster, thus their term for the invention, espresso, not you will note, expresso. It took until 1902 for the Italian company Bezzera to patent the world's first successful commercial machine.

Essentially what happens is this; hot water builds up a head of steam in a tank and when a valve is opened beneath the water level, the steam pressure forces a measured amount of hot water out, through the compacted coffee.

Technically, the water temperature should be 93-96C, the pressure should be 9 bar and the finely ground, dark-roasted coffee should be a tightly packed wad of 6-7g, and the brewing or pour time from 20 – 25 seconds: with sophisticated modern technology these specifications alter, manufacturer to manufacturer.

Because the amount of liquid is small, and the coffee grounds retain much of its heat, espresso should always be made directly into warm cups; plenty believe the coffee is degraded in flavour if it hits something cool or cold. Even if this is untrue, an espresso or single black coffee will also have lost heat between the coffee grounds and the cup.

Arabica coffees are thought best for producing the correct honey-like dribble of flavour, but some robusta in the blend adds a brightness of acidity and extra effervescence to ensure a good *crema*, the lid of froth that should cover an espresso as a sign of quality coffee and a spotlessly clean machine. If ever you are uncertain which café of several you should patronise, look at the pipe through which milk is steamed: if this is shining and clean you are safe, if it is caked in old milk, perhaps even caramelised, take your patronage elsewhere.

The precise grind of coffee is very important and like cars, both commercial and domestic machines differ from one another, even when produced by the same factory on the same day. Getting exactly the right grind, the right amount, the right tamping pressure and so on can take a long time, but is very rewarding.

The home espresso machine was once a contradiction in terms, for who would want to install the correct water filters, pressure gauges et al just for good coffee at home? Modern electronics have brought the possibility closer than ever imagined, but unless you spend a great deal of money on a machine, you can never be sure you weren't better off making coffee in Mum's favourite jug, particularly if you live in an area with mineralised water: you can whisk up skimmed milk a dozen ways other than have it screaming in a jug.

Promptness of serving an espresso is also very important, although this would clearly be news to many cafes. This doesn't matter if you are drinking an espresso with milk in it, something done by millions of Australasians, who are suspected of not actually liking coffee, other than as a background flavour in hot milk. These drinkers of hot milk can be ill served if the milk is boiled, which changes its flavour, and if you are a foam and froth lover, note skimmed milk gives better results than full milk, because it is the protein of milk that froths, not the cream.

Choosing your espresso according to the machine that makes it is a game played only by few very picky people. You can join them and always win if you choose to drink from Italy's Elektra Q1-C, one of those espresso machines with wings on top of its brass dome. Built by hand, these have been equated to Lamborghinis and take for ever to make. One of the few you'll see in Britain is at Vergagno in Charing Cross Road, London W1. The company, which has been roasting coffee Italian style since 1882, was presented with their model in 2004 by the manufacturers, the first time their coveted award went outside Italy.

Here are some of the coffee styles the espresso machine can serve:

Caffe latte: should be an espresso shot with three times its volume of steam-heated, frothy milk, but little or no actual froth. The correct form is to be served both separately and then to pour them into the cup from opposite sides, but this is rare. Also called a Flat White and in Europe, Latin or South America would be drunk between meals.

Cappuccino: a cappuccino should be one third espresso, one third hot milk and one third foam. The idea of a large cup of hot froth, milk and coffee after a meal is anathema to most Europeans. Italians consider it only a breakfast drink, and wouldn't be seen dead drinking one after 10 am. Middle Europeans turn to it to accompany something sweet or savoury taken as a snack in the afternoon, but never with or after a meal. It is these afternoon snackers most likely to want it topped with a sprinkle of cinnamon, cocoa or grated chocolate. If you are not European, you should, of course, be true to yourself, but ordering a cappuccino with lunch or dinner appears very gauche when you are there.

Con panna: an espresso with a dab of whipped cream, also known as Vienna coffee.

Doppio/ double shot: two espresso measures in one cup, no stronger than an espresso, just twice the amount of it. It's an upsize.

Espresso: should be up to four tablespoons, about 60ml, of coffee. Sometimes also called a short black, if there is much more coffee than this, it is a Long Black. The European custom is to down such coffees in one or two gulps, usually while standing. Once the cup is picked up it won't be returned to the saucer until empty. Sipping is for cissies.

Flat White: see caffe latte.

Latte macchiato: a tumbler of foamed milk, about half filled, with a single espresso shot poured into it, so it 'marks' the milk with ever changing marbling: see macchiato.

Long black: an espresso in a bigger cup, with added hot water from a dedicated source: you should never see the extra water added by repeating the brew process through the coffee grounds; this is lazy and gives a nasty bitterness.

Macchiato: espresso marked with little more than a dash of hot milk – coffee with a dash: see latte macchiato.

Mocha: a mug of vaguely equal portions of espresso, unsweetened hot chocolate and frothed milk.

Ristretto: the ultimate pleasure for true coffee lovers. The water should pour through the coffee grounds for only half the time of an espresso, 10-15 seconds maximum, giving a couple of tablespoons or less of coffee. This early pour brings with it all the fragile oils, natural sugars and flavours, but none of the caffeine or bitter contents. The ristretto is why Italians can drink coffee all day, because each cup contains only infinitesimal amounts of caffeine, and as they use only Arabica there was little to begin. It is the huge flavour of coffee's aromatic oils, which coat the palate for an hour or more, which give the lift.

A ristretto displays the true worth of a coffee, it is the bean naked and can sometimes taste as though you have added spoons full of sugar, an attribute slaughtered by the flavours that come in the second half of the pour. It is an object lesson in perceived as opposed to received value if you ask for a ristretto in one of the world's biggest chains of coffee bars. Once past the hurdle of having to explain this absolutely basic coffee style to five out of six baristas you get something as bitter as cold revenge, something so awful I've had to go back and watch them make another. No, they made it right, the coffee is so second rate or over roasted it makes even a ristretto bitter. That's over-charging skill of immense *braggadocio*.

Short black: see espresso.

Romano: an espresso served with a curl of lemon peel or a thin slice of lemon, both of which will reduce bitterness.

Vienna coffee: see con panna.

Cooking

Strong coffee is used to marinate lamb in Sweden, but is more usually found in sweet dishes, iced desserts and baking. High-quality coffee is wasted and so strong instant coffee or liquid coffee essence is more commonly used. But if you are flavouring a custard, sorry crème anglaise, for a coffee trifle or pudding, a mousse, ice cream or icing, it might be more rewarding to use a coffee-based liqueur, Tia Maria or Kahlua; these are very good melted with chocolate to make mocha flavouring.

Rather more interesting is to use freshly crushed coffee beans. They must be very fresh so they make a real crunch or the curious texture is discomforting. Scatter them over anything coffee or chocolate flavoured, including cakes and biscuits, hot or cold puddings, ice creams and such. They are very good on sliced mango or peaches, particularly white or rarer red-fleshed ones.

Those beans flavoured with everything else under the sun offer broader horizons of affinity and use: use flavoured coffee beans with chocolate coating and there will be no limits to what you might do with them, or what the rewards might be. You might care, however, to give a thought to what these flavourings are, and why you are combining something as God-given as coffee with something rankly artificial.

Storing

The moment beans are roasted – light, medium or dark – the essential oils released, which give the flavour, begin to evaporate. Once the beans are ground, these evaporate even faster. Those that remain spitefully turn rancid. For value for money, coffee should be made from freshly roasted and freshly ground beans and the time between roasting and grinding should also be short.

Roasted coffee beans can be stored for up to two weeks at room temperature if they are kept relatively cool, but after that the loss of flavour will be noticeable. Ground coffee kept in an airtight tin will last no more than a week.

Very dark roasted coffee oxidizes very quickly and so bulk-produced varieties might be coated with vegetable oil, gum arabic or glucose after roasting. This encourages much longer life but adds alien flavours and effects.

There is much discussion about storing coffee in the refrigerator but I don't keep coffee long enough to know if this works to any noticeable degree; it is possibly more important that the coffee grounds are kept closely wrapped in foil. Very finely ground coffee, packed tight, lasts longer than coarsely ground coffee, through which air can pass more easily.

Coffee beans can be frozen but after a month the oils go temperamental. If you really have to store coffee for a long time, buy it in vacuum sealed bags or tins. Many shops now buy their bulk-roasted coffee for grinding like this, a great advantage to the customer, especially of the slower moving coffees.

Fair Trade Coffee

Happily this is not one of those apparent advantages that become debased by greed, distortion or treachery. Fair Trade coffee means the growers have been guaranteed a price for their coffee, provided it is of a certain quality. More importantly those who make the agreements actually help coffee farmers improve their land and thus increase both their crop and their family's standard of living. In my experience Fair Trade works, and by buying products with this imprimatur you are helping ensure the system works and that the big conglomerates will one day also face facts: coffee should be a daily comfort for those who grow it, not just for those who trade in it or drink it.

Some independent coffee traders have their own fair-trade equivalent, smaller ones may not even give their policy a name, but all will be proud of it and tell you clearly of their commitment on their web sites and in their brochures. They would be very foolish to risk telling lies.

Dairy Products

Milk must be the world's most important food, even though it is still largely ignored in China and other miscellaneous easterly places

It is fashionably railed against as being the source of much cholesterol-related disease but benefits it can bestow, particularly to the young, generally outweigh the disadvantages. Anyway, what would life be like without butter to melt on toast, without cream and whipped cream and ice cream? Very boring, that's what.

The modern Western reliance on products made from milk, or containing milk derivatives, is extraordinary and it makes it difficult to imagine that the entire American continent and all the great South Pacific had no knowledge of milk as a human food before the arrival of the Europeans. It is even more astonishing to remember that until a century ago milk was one of the most dangerous of all foods, contaminated with tuberculosis, adulterated with water and worse, dirty through lack of hygiene and a dearth of sealed containers – and usually sour. And that was just the stuff in the country.

The few people trying to improve soured milk and rancid cheese used such things as borax and formaldehyde. The herds and their maids were respectively dirty and slatternly, equally contributing to one another's painful demise. Yet it is these same maids who are so romantically sung and portrayed. The reason is quite simply a continuous publicity stunt of the first degree. The job had to be made to appear to be romantic, for no girl in her right senses would otherwise choose such back-breaking work at such unsociable hours. When Marie-Antoinette toiled for minutes in the rustic dairy farm she had built in the purlieus of Versailles, it was merely *pour encouragèz les autres*; the French queen had real dairymaids to do the real work.

Perhaps it was the dairymaids' requisite brawniness that gained them such universal admiration, but the flush of their cheeks was more likely to be tubercular than virginal. Milkmaids needed to be as strong as a bull, the sexual duties of which she might also have supervised, and needed a stomach quite as strong as the forearms that heaved pails of milk and wheels of cheese.

I've never been able to drink cows' milk and at times in my life have been forbidden all kinds of products even remotely associated with it, including tranquillizers, which like most drugs are sweetened with milk sugar, lactose. I often found it simpler to stick to a Jewish *pareve* (milk-free) diet and wish I had had the nerve to present my charge card at Selfridges Kosher Counter, to see the reaction to my surname.

Yet I look with pride at today's (other) huge milk-fed children – have you been to Japan recently – for it was an ancestor who prodded the whole operation into being, by first applying scientific methods to raise cattle exclusively for dairying.

John Christian of Cumberland was first cousin to Fletcher Christian of *Bounty* and head of the family. After his first wife died he married Isabella Curwen, last representative of one of England's ten oldest families. By combining the names, estates and fortunes of the Christians and Curwens with his extraordinary gift for advanced agricultural thinking, John Christian Curwen made himself into a one-man vanguard of experiment both on the farm and in mines. His achievements are many and include organizing the first agricultural shows. Early in the

19th century he noted the Cumberland town of Kendal had more milk carts and fewer child deaths than other parts of England. Deciding this was evidence milk was vital for health and growth, he consulted the few other people who had come to the same conclusions (notably in Scotland) and then set out to do something about it. By 1813 he had eschewed the traditional longhorn for shorthorn cattle and was getting an average daily milking yield of 10 quarts per animal – about 11.5 litres.

He achieved these unheard of results by unheard of methods: he planted grasses and clovers in his fields instead of letting nature take its course; he stall-fed his herds, making much use of oil cake, and thus established the country's first true dairying herd. And what did he do with these vast quantities of milk? He distributed them free to the poor of Workington, much to the amusement and derision of other landowners. It was the world's first organized free milk service and later John Christian Curwen introduced legislation into Westminster acknowledged to be the first step anywhere in the world towards the Welfare State.

This remarkable man and his achievements are almost unknown, perhaps because he twice refused a peerage.

It was the late1860s and 1870s before anyone else began seriously to establish specialized milking herds. Not only did they get on to a profitable band wagon, they also utilized the wagons of the new railway system, which allowed transportation of country milk to the towns for the first time. By 1900 the Great Western Railway alone carried 25 million gallons in one year, the produce of 50,000 cows. The unpasteurised, unchilled milk of the time would have soured and curdled terribly quickly as it was carted over the rutted roads of the time. Indeed, rail-transported milk still did as often as not, so country milk was not much better than that from the horrible town herds, which were tethered or wandered wherever there was room, and milked and fed and calved there, too.

In 1865 and '66 there were wide-spread epidemics of cattle plague that decimated the town herds to a state from which they never recovered.

Cooling and refrigeration were gradually introduced through the 1880s and 1890s. About the same time the first milk purity laws were passed and by 1900, with the invention of milking machines and the establishment of wholesale dairies, there was a distinct improvement in hygiene and a decline in milk-linked disease. But milk was still transported and sold in bulk, often by horse-drawn cart and did not begin to be pre-packed until the 1920s. Even at the end of the 1940s I would run barefoot down the front path to collect the billycan from under the letterbox after our milkman had filled it — this was in Auckland.

In the early Twenties the world began to recognise the benefit of pasteurisation, the process in which milk is heated to 71 C for 15 seconds and then cooled quickly. Since then the strictest safeguards have been rigidly enforced to protect us from contaminated milk or diseased animals, and our average consumption is about four times what it was a century ago.

Milk

The vitamins and minerals and proteins and so on of milk, and its abilities as a cure-all, are far too complicated for this book; in any case the structure changes according to the animal and its food, as well as the time of the year. It's more important to know how and when to use milk. For instance, hot boiled milk takes far longer to digest than cold milk, as all milk clots very quickly when it hits the stomach and hot milk clots even faster into an even harder curd and this can put a strain on a delicate stomach. Hot milk should be drunk as slowly as possible to allow the stomach to cope with it properly. Whole milk and skimmed milk take exactly the same time to digest, and the soured or fermented milks, including yoghurt, take the least time of all.

There is medical evidence to support the belief that warm milk helps you sleep. Apparently milk's calcium has a slight hypnotic effect on nerves, genuinely aiding a temporary relaxation of the body; anything else containing available calcium would be as effective. A word of advice to the elderly: a diet heavily balanced in favour of milk, acceptable to infants, who are thoughtfully born with a special store of iron, can lead to anaemia or at least an iron deficiency in an adult.

I once went to a lecture on food hygiene in a catering establishment and the bacteriologist speaking said that with all his knowledge of the horrors of food poisoning there was only one thing he would categorically not do, and that was to drink unpasteurised milk. He said many disease-free attested herds in the UK still contain animals with notifiable disease, including, in his opinion, tuberculosis, something rapidly on the increase again, worldwide.

If you are in the position of only having raw milk to drink, you should boil it, or failing that, leave it to ripen until it has a definite sourness; the gradual increase of lactic acid in souring milk acts as a germicide of sorts and makes it marginally safer. If undisturbed the acid-producing ripening process continues until the lactic acid level solidifies the milk protein, making sour curds. Although goats and sheep are tuberculosis-free, they can have other nasty diseases, but less commonly, so their unpasteurised milk is generally safer.

In the US plain milk is as difficult to find as sweet cream is in France. There is enormous emphasis on low fat (partly skimmed) milk and milks which are also fortified in some way, and although good to drink can do strange things to cooking Flavoured milks are very popular and easy to buy, and fermented kefir comes in an extraordinary range of natural flavours.

In Australasia, milk drinking is as much a religion as Vegemite and rugby. Milk bars, which are sort of like the UK's dairies but echo the soda shops of the United States in the 30s, 40s and 50s, still make fabulous milk shakes containing real ice cream – the flavour range is exceptional – and often use real fruit bases. The well-known Sanitarium shops, which are terribly old and well-established health food shops, also sell lots of healthy drinks and have a special meal-in-a-glass which includes milk, ice cream, wheat germ, lecithin and other goodies. Ice cream sundaes are still made and in many dairies you can have a takeaway fruit salad of tropical fruits put into a carton and topped with cream and ice cream – a fabulous lunch to enjoy in Sydney's Hyde Park on a hot day; there's more than enough flesh about, both rare and roasted, to balance the fruitarianism.

Soured, cultured and fermented milks

The fact a high acid content makes milk safer is behind the popularity of so-called fermented milk drinks, which are also easier to digest. Interestingly, they are found in both cold and hot countries – whereas I thought only the latter had need of preservative methods. Fermented milk drinks are made with the addition of a specialized culture of lactic-acid-producing bacillus; they give the milk a pleasant tang and thicken it slightly but do not let the process continue to form a curd unless left a very long time. In general these drinks are less sour than yoghurt and are also used as bases for summer soups and in cooking.

In Sweden you can buy all types of fermented milk and throughout the Middle East, including Israel, they are very popular, as they are in Middle Europe and the Balkans. In the UK their appearance is increasing, including *smetana*, which is of Balkan origin. You can make something similar by adding water and sugar to plain yoghurt, another common eastern Mediterranean and Eastern practice. Other fermented milk drinks include *leben* and *kumiss*.

Buttermilk: is possibly the best milk-derived but non-fermented drink and is what is left after you churn cream (milk fat) to make butter. If made from unripened cream it is quite sweet; ripened cream gives buttermilk with a slight sourness. To be sure you are getting the real thing, look for the word 'churned' somewhere on the label. Most buttermilk sold is actually:

Cultured buttermilk: has a bacterial culture added to it, a culture of bacteria similar to those that naturally curdle milk to make cheese but which are killed by pasteurization. Thus, cultured buttermilk ripens and thickens slightly, becoming slightly acidic as the lactose (milk sugar) is turned into lactic acid. If you want to use buttermilk in a cooking recipe it must either be cultured or made from unpasteurised ripened cream or it will not have the acidity necessary to interact with baking soda and so form a leavening gas. If you use sweet buttermilk in cooking you have to exchange the baking soda for twice as much baking powder or add a squirt of lemon juice.

Most buttermilk now sold is nothing of the kind, but is fermented skimmed milk. How can this be called buttermilk?

Kefir: best understood as being like a milk-based beer, kefir is first cousin to yoghurt, but different because this is milk fermented by the action of a quite different organism from that which digests lactose to form yoghurt. As well as working bacteria, there are yeasts and as they digest lactose alcohol and gas are created.

True kefir should be pleasantly sour, be thicker than milk, should refreshingly sting your tongue with its bubbles of carbon dioxide, have foam on top and be slightly alcoholic. In fact it can be as much as 5% alcohol, thus explaining its touted magical ways with hangovers – a hair of the dog really does work. It can be made at home if you get kefir grains, a unique combination of live bacteria and yeast which feeds on the milk, grows and can then be divided in the same way you'd treat a ginger beer or vinegar 'mother'.

Commercially produced kefir often has none of the expected attributes, and so will be flat and alcohol free. But this will still have the reputed health benefits, for unlike yoghurt bacteria which pass through the body doing whatever good they might, the live organisms in kefir stop-over and colonise your intestines. Once given a good home they are credited with being excellent housekeepers and your return comes not as cash but in increased health and longevity. Kefir generally has much lower residual lactose than yoghurt.

A slightly adapted kefir bacteria/yeast mixture will grow and perform in water into which dried fruits have been added, to make waterkefir.

Soured pasteurised milk: is not safer from germs than soured raw milk. Quite the reverse. All manner of bacteria make milk sour and thicken and most of those that settle and grow in pasteurised milk are downright dangerous. You should dissuade friends and children from drinking soured pasteurised milk.

Yoghurt

So many claims, so much claptrap. Yoghurt is simply pre-digested milk and when eaten its components are available to our system up to three times faster than would be the case with milk itself: it is this faster, easier digestion that was always its greatest claim, a simpler, cheaper and more available way of getting protein into the body. It doesn't matter what else you eat, without protein you can't grow and make muscles; with it you are healthier and stronger.

Curiously, yoghurt is not a natural product and so calling plain yoghurt 'natural' is sailing close to trade description acts. The pre-digestion is usually the work of two *bacilli*, *lactobacillus bulgaricus* and *streptococcus thermophilis* but neither is found in milk directly from any milking animal, and so must always be introduced, usually by adding some ready-cultured yoghurt to that milk. As the *bacilli* digest the milk to fuel their lives, they create acidity that thickens the milk and kills much intrinsic bacteria and, so, even if not pasteurised or boiled, the milk becomes safer and longer lasting. These qualities plus its protein has imbued yoghurt with seemingly magical health-giving properties. But in the west we gave it a reputation it did not deserve, we didn't need an alternative protein source but we did think the *bacilli* were the same as those in our digestive systems.

The theorists taught yoghurt would thus purify our bowels, making us healthier and less mortal. They reasoned this had to be fact because Bulgarians ate a lot of yoghurt and lived a long time. Quite apart from ignoring genetic contributions, yoghurt's proselytizers chose to ignore that Bulgarians also lived a basically healthier life on a more balanced diet than most in the west – but yoghurt alone was given the credit. An echo of this belief is still heard in claims that yoghurt will replace digestive flora lost by taking antibiotics. This simply is not so, for although yoghurt *bacilli* are similar to some in our guts, they are quite different and do not survive. Anyway, for many sick people eating milk products quickly and reliably makes them worse if their digestive system is upset, for milk is simply a ready supply of food upon which bad as well as good risk organisms thrive. Anyone who suggests milk will settle an upset stomach is living in the Dark Ages.

However, contemporary research shows that a much rarer yoghurt *bacillus, lactobacillus acidophilus* might have some part to play internally – even if it doesn't, it gives yoghurts a sweeter, smoother flavour that is very attractive, and as it is now widely available I should choose an *acidophilus* yoghurt over other types anyway.

Yoghurt is one of the world's oldest processed foods. Pharaohs and Israelites enjoyed it in Egypt, Greeks and Romans employed it medically and the Arab world has long respected it; a Damascene was extolling its virtues in a book written in 633. Even these are *un peu arriviste* as it is thousands of years older than that. Some go as far as saying it could have been accidentally discovered at the dawn of the Neolithic age, some 10,000 years BC; this is unlikely as domestication of animals didn't start until 4000-years later.

Persian invaders took yoghurt to India, where bare yogis mixed it with honey as part of their strict diets 2000 years ago. When the nomadic Bulgars of Asia settled in the Balkans in the 7th century, they too brought yoghurt and, like the Mongol hoards of Ghengis Khan, had used it as absolutely basic subsistence for they made it from the milk of the mares upon which they rode.

Yoghurt was probably first seen in Europe some time in the 16th century, but apart from pockets of fanaticism and monasteries it remained virtually unknown until the early part of the 20th century when Metchnikoff, leading light of the Pasteur Institute, succeeded in isolating the two bacilli responsible for turning milk into yoghurt. Now it was possible to make yoghurt commercially and save western man, or so it seemed. It wasn't until 1925, nine years after Metchnikoff's death, that a Spaniard called Carasso opened the first yoghurt factory, in Barcelona. This was the Danone company, still a major producer. It was many years before propaganda, sweetening and flavouring made yoghurt into the widely available and generally abused food it has become.

And now the burning question – is your yoghurt live or not? The answer is invariably yes, whatever the package says or does not say. But some are less live than others. The addition of growth inhibitors to lengthen shelf life make them distinctly untroubled, fighting for their own existence rather than winning bacterial battles on your behalf.

In the interest of high sales, long life and profit, this cheaper yoghurt is first extended by dilution with some liquid then emulsified and restored to something like its original viscosity with a chemical stabilizer, which works like gelatine. Natural yoghurt has a certain graininess but altered types are detectable by being jelly-like and smooth on the tongue. This treatment combined with low temperature storage means the further growth of the bacilli is inhibited, extending the yoghurt's life and emasculating the preservative quality of its acidic content. But even these yoghurts will eventually bubble and fizz and go over the top if left long enough. Higher quality yoghurts that have not been extended or stabilized artificially are likely to produce a thicker texture and a whey-like liquid, which can be stirred back gently. Vigorous stirring or beating causes yoghurt to thin considerably and in this state it is often used as a refreshing drink throughout the Middle East; in Turkey it is mixed with soda water, which is even nicer.

If you want really thick yoghurt, like that used in India or Greece, the simplest way is to hang yoghurt in muslin as though it were cheese curd and to let this drain.

Connections with good health mean yoghurt is often thought good for dieters, and it can be, provided you think clearly and read the labels.

The traveller in eastern Mediterranean countries will constantly be surprised where they find yoghurt. In Izmir I watched a chef make stuffed pasta, which was then cooked in broth, exactly the way you would ravioli or tortelloni. The hot pasta was drained into a serving dish and then dolloped with thick cold plain yoghurt over which was poured hot butter flavoured with paprika and chilli. It sounds and looks like the bland leading the bland, but turns out to be the most extraordinarily complementary and contrasted dish you will ever eat.

Scandaweigans bake layered fish and potatoes with yoghurt as a topping and yoghurt finishes many an American cheesecake. Strained yoghurt is essential to many Indian marinades – and if you can't be bothered cooking, few things are more refreshing or cooling than plain yoghurt diluted with soda water and a dash of rose water.

Fruit and flavoured yoghurts: may be made from any kind of milk, but are generally sweetened with sugar and thus offer far more calories than you imagined. Some of course are made from skimmed milk and some are artificially sweetened. But a fruity yoghurt that is genuinely lower in fat and also contains no sugar is hard to find.

Goat milk yoghurts: like sheep milk, goat milk cannot be separated – it is always full-fat. Bulgarian yoghurt was traditionally made with goats' milk, which gave rise to the widely held belief that only this is proper yoghurt. Although this is untrue, goats' milk yoghurt is thought especially delicious and is becoming more widely known. The greater availability of powdered or frozen goats' milk means making your own is easy.

Beware when serving it that some people simply cannot abide it anywhere near them.

Homemade yoghurts: anyone who makes yoghurt at home swears UHT or long-life milk gives the best and creamiest result, and that's possibly because it is homogenized. But you can use any milk, including that made from powder. In fact, to make thicker, richer yoghurts you can add milk powder to milk.

Low-fat yoghurts: will have been made from skimmed or part skimmed milk and can be usefully sweetened with artificial substances but not always. Look carefully at the label because many low-fat yoghurts contain more sugar than full-fat yoghurt, to compensate for the lesser mouth feel of the reduced fat content. It's one of the greatest and most arrogant tricks played on the public. Remember, any substance ending in –'ose' is a sugar.

Sheep milk yoghurts: the original Greek yoghurts were made with sheep milk, always high in calories as its fine fat globules cannot be separated from the milk, which is very rich anyway: so Greek yoghurt as in a strained sheep's milk yoghurt is a nightmare for dieters, absolute bliss for others. And sheep milk is never farmy, or musky.

Strained yoghurts: often called Greek-style yoghurts, for these were the types first marketed. By compacting the solids through straining off the whey the fat content is also concentrated and fat is calories.

Cooking

Unlike cream, yoghurt will infallibly curdle if added to hot liquid that is boiling hot or will subsequently boil. You should let the yoghurt come to room temperature then whisk it into the hot liquid just before serving. Otherwise you can stabilize plain yoghurt by heating gently and thickening with cornflour.

Condensed and evaporated milk

Invented for the easy transportation and storage of milk's goodness, all of these products have inbuilt problems of nutrition. But today's better methods of milk preservation have led to less dependence on condensed milks, especially in the poorer countries and they cause very few dietary problems now.

Condensed milk: diluted according to directions is easier to digest than ordinary milk but because condensed milk is always sweetened its basic imbalance, in favour of sugar and against fat, is inherently bad and it should never be used in the diet for extensive periods. Nevertheless, a couple of generations of the inhabitants of hot countries are hooked, and every beverage, including tea, is served with condensed milk, a habit I recently noticed sweet-toothed Englishmen quickly adopting in Bangkok. Usually the milk has been reduced by two thirds.

Evaporated milk: a term usually used for unsweetened condensed full milk whereas condensed milk usually indicates sweetened full milk or sweetened skimmed milk.

Milk powders

Milk powder is quite simply milk with most of its water content evaporated to produce solids with a moisture content of five per cent or less. It can be fine powder or freeze dried in granules and is made in quite a lot of different degrees of fat content, from full milk down to skimmed milk; all except the latter are homogenized before treatment.

There are two main ways of preparing this invaluable powder. The first spreads milk thinly on hot revolving rollers. The water evaporates leaving a film of solids that is then scraped off. This gives a powder that does not reconstitute readily and usually gives very lumpy results when mixed with water. The alternative method pumps milk as a fine spray into a chamber of hot air. As the water quickly evaporates the powder falls to the floor. This reconstitutes very easily and may therefore be considered preferable.

Whole milk powder contains all the nutrients of milk except vitamin C, thiamin and B12, which are affected by the heat of the process. Skimmed milk powder contains almost no fat and the other varieties of powder vary according to their original constituents. Provided the storage temperature is moderate-to-cool, milk powders keep a very long time. Those containing fat are liable to rancidity on exposure to air.

There is also available a range of dried milk powders that include non-dairy or vegetable fats, the advantage of which as far as I can tell is purely that of price. This mixture or total use of non-dairy fat is what gives us the 'whitener', a milk or cream substitute sprinkled into hot drinks in place of the real thing. Palm oil is the usual source of such fat, although manufacturers are not required to state the exact fat used.

Storing

Heat and light are the two worst enemies of milk, both of which destroy or affect flavour and vitamin content. So you must keep it cool and dark. If you don't have a refrigerator, keep it in a draught – the floor is always cooler than a table top. Cupboards should only be used if they are well ventilated.

The old-fashioned method of keeping milk cool works very well: you put the bottle or jug in a basin half filled with cold water and cover it with butter muslin saturated in cold water. You can also leave milk wrapped in a wet towel in a relatively warm place and it will become quite chilled – an interesting point to remember when on picnics.

Everything that comes into contact with milk should always be rinsed in cold water before going into hot; this avoids the formation of a film that is almost impossible to remove.

Pasteurized milk should keep in a refrigerator an average of six days.

Commercially frozen milk is pasteurised and homogenized and frozen extremely quickly by using a special brine solution. Domestically frozen milk can be problematical – it is better to freeze only cartons of homogenized milk.

Cream

Cream is the lighter but fatty portion of full milk and contains all the major components of milk but in a different balance. It is largely water but also contains most of the butterfat; in single/light cream this is up to 20 per cent of the volume but in double/heavy cream it is about 48 per cent and is then the biggest component.

Cream may be separated from milk in two ways. You can let full milk rest for 12 -24 hours during which time the cream will float to the top, and can then be skimmed off by hand. But you always include some of the milk and the composition of your cream is thus constantly varying. Mechanical separators first heat the full milk and then pipe it to a stainless steel bowl, fitted with conical plates, which revolves at about 6000 rpm. The heavier milk is thrown to the outer edges of the bowl whilst the cream flows towards the centre and each is collected through different outlet pipes. The skim milk is usually then heat-treated to clear it of bacteria and used for making milk products or for feeding to animals.

In America, cream is pretty much the same as the UK but with different names: our double is called heavy, our single is their light and coffee cream is Half and Half. But our whipping cream is not theirs. American whipping cream usually has the lowest possible fat content to comply with its definition – about 30 per cent – and gets its texture from added vegetable fats and oils that behave in the same way as cream.

Different types of cream are obtained not by subsequent dilution, as I once thought, but by different degrees of separation, so that single cream for instance has more of the original milk in it and double cream has less. To make single/light cream from double/heavy cream or to make double/heavy cream go further when you are whipping it, dilute with full or skimmed milk.

Most cream for sale is pasteurised to improve its keeping quality without affecting its flavour. You can buy untreated cream from accredited herds quite readily and if it is from Jersey cows it is altogether thicker, richer, yellower and tastier, and has a slight extra acidity which makes it a particularly good accompaniment to soft fruits, and chocolate cake.

It is not true, as I have seen put about in the United States, that French cream naturally has more lactic acid in it – it has been allowed to develop lactic acid, as any cream would do, and the French love this flavour best. To get fresh sweet cream in France you must ask for *crème fleurette* and if you get it you'll be lucky.

Bottled cream/long-keeping cream: this is now tending to disappear from the shops but a lot of old people like it for nostalgic reasons. It fits neatly in all respects between pasteurised cream and sterilized cream, both in keeping ability and flavour, and this applies to single, double or clotted cream, all of which are treated this way.

Clotted cream DOP: this is the richest and most heavenly cream of all and still mainly produced in Devon and Cornwall, where it has DOP status earned because the meadows are particularly rich in grasses that give elevated levels of carotene, that gives a naturally richer

yellow colour, and give measurably higher fat content to the milk of cows that browse on it. Cornish clotted cream will have a minimum fat content of 55 per cent and is traditionally made by putting full milk in shallow pans that are left until the cream has risen. Then you slowly heat this to a temperature of 82 C and allow it to cool overnight. In the morning the coagulated, lumpy cream can simply be skimmed off. Clotted cream is made in other places but rarely reaches the same height of flavour or develops the same contrasts of thick texture and crunchiness. The technique is thought to have been introduced by sea-faring Phoenicians, who came to trade for Cornish tin. Their country of Tyre is pretty much where Lebanon lies today and there you'll find they still make *ashtar* (among many spellings and names: *kaimak* is something else referred to as a clotted cream and in Greece, Cyprus particularly, you'll find *staka*, but although lumpy enough it's not a true clotted cream because it's made from sheep milk and its cream cannot be separated out).

Commercially, the same effect is obtained by scalding separated cream in shallow pans in specially built ovens and then transferring it into tins or bottles. I don't think it tastes as good, but this may be because it is subsequently sterilized.

A continuous controversy rages over the proper use of clotted cream in a traditional cream tea. Do you put your cream onto the scone and then add jam, (strawberry, raspberry or black currant only), or do you do it the other way round? Those who argue for the former say that as the cream is replacing butter it must go on first; but then you can't spread jam evenly over the cream and so you miss out the combination of flavours for most mouthfuls. Those who spread the jam first and then dollop on the cream are assured of the best possible tastes with every mouthful and that's the way I prefer it, perhaps because that way you can have butter on the scone as well.

When I asked the question on the Orient Express in England the enigmatic answer was that the jam did indeed go on first, except on Sundays.

Some authorities reckon the answer is geographical and that jam goes on first in Cornwall but cream goes on first in Devon, the only place that conceivably competes with Cornwall by having broadly similar pastures and the same technique. The differences between Cornish and Devon clotted cream, if any, are unlikely to be identified by most palates, and even then you'd have to think they'd sneaked a peek at the packaging. Right then, that's the end of my West Country holidays.

Crème fraîche: peculiarly French, but actually only a cultured soured cream. Because the cream might have 40 per cent fat content or more, almost that of double cream, it will be altogether richer, sweeter and creamier than sour/soured creams based on single cream. The gorgeously ivory-cream coloured crème fraîche d'Isigny from France actually has an Appellation d'Origine Controlee and is rather like eating smooth clotted cream with a touch of acidity. That slight bite is very similar to the flavour of unpasteurised cream which has been allowed to age a little and is thus a much more traditional flavour to enjoy with strawberries than ordinary whipped or clotted cream. Crème fraîche is particularly good for finishing or making savoury sauces and can be used anywhere you would a clotted cream. You won't ever have to substitute in Alsace, for there they have crème fraiche d'Alsace, IGP.

Double/Heavy cream: this has a minimum butterfat content of 48 per cent. It does everything, and can be diluted with milk to extend it. Reduced to half its volume by gentle simmering and then flavoured with herbs or a vegetable purée, double cream gives the simplest rich sauce of all. It does not curdle if boiled, unless you also include something very acidic. If you're combining with another liquid, always add the thicker to the thinner, or curd is what you'll get.

Extra-thick cream: double/heavy cream that has been homogenized in the same way as many fromage blancs, q.v. so it spoons from the carton as thickly as whipped cream.

Frozen cream: one of the best new products available. Double cream is frozen in single portions and sold in free-flow packs, so you never need go without cream or have to throw away any that has gone off. Thoroughly recommended.

Half cream: not widely available, this has a butterfat content of no less than 12 per cent. It's what is usually called coffee cream in Europe and Half and Half in America. Really a sort of super-rich homogenized milk, it is perhaps too rich for day-to-day drinking but excellent for cooking, for the higher fat content would help cakes and biscuits to keep longer.

Single/light cream: this must have 18 per cent butterfat and is used as a pouring cream. It can be whipped if you incorporate egg white into it. It is always homogenized to prevent separation of the cream and milk.

Soured/sour cream: this is single cream with a culture of bacteria added to it after homogenization and pasteurization. The culture forms acid as a by-product, giving the subsequent thickening and light acidic flavour. It keeps very well under refrigeration and is perfectly indispensable once you know about it. If you can't buy it you can appreciate the flavour and texture by reducing double cream over heat, cooling, and adding lemon juice; a better bet is to whip or sieve cottage cheese and then add a little milk or cream – cheaper too.

Sterilized cream: made exactly the same way as sterilized milk but packed in smaller containers. It usually has a butterfat content of about 23 per cent (between single and whipping cream) but can also be made from half cream (12 per cent). It is homogenized and the treatment gives it a unique flavour that does not compensate for its ability to keep virtually indefinitely until opened.

UHT or long life cream: treated exactly the same way as UHT milk to give a very long life with no refrigeration. It should mean that the individual portions of liquid used in trains, hotels and planes for your tea or coffee are milk or cream, for there is no wastage problem with UHT treated items. But if you look carefully, those little pyramids of liquid are nearly all totally artificial and nothing to do with the dairy.

Whipping cream: now more readily available since the price of milk and its derivatives began to climb. It has a minimum butterfat content of 35 per cent, which is the ideal for getting maximum whipped cream from your liquid cream. Because you have to whip it longer than double cream you incorporate more air, giving more ultimate bulk. Perhaps this is of interest to caterers, but I prefer the taste and texture of whipped double/heavy cream to such mouthfuls of air.

Cooking

To boil or not to boil cream is a very vexed question and there is a great deal of disagreement both within each country and between countries. Some of the hysteria is probably because cream is often added in association with egg to thicken and enrich – this will naturally curdle if heated too much but it is the egg doing it. Cream can be boiled and it can be simmered in sauces, and so can soured cream. There will be sauces or cooking liquids that have such high acidity that the cream will curdle when added but often curdling is a matter of bad technique, i.e. you must add potentially troublesome liquids in a certain way – you should always pour the thicker into the thinner (do it the other way and curdling is almost certain). If your sauce has a flour base, curdling is less likely.

Reduction of cream or a cream sauce is basic to fine food and when making a cream sauce I always reduce the double cream by a third or a half before adding it. The flavouring liquid is reduced even more drastically, if possible, for curdling seems more a problem when you have large amounts of liquid. You do not get globules of butterfat and any other fat that rises can be beaten in; indeed the beating in of butter is again basic to the proper finishing of sauces. English soured cream does not curdle in sauces in my experience, but perhaps I have been lucky for there are others who swear it always happens to them. I use soured cream more and more to finish wine-based sauces, partly because it is cheaper and partly because it gives extra dimension of flavour. You must never use cream which has turned sour, just as you must never drink pasteurised milk which has soured; neither is the result of the natural lactic souring of raw milk, but is the result of the sterile liquid being infected by whatever was passing. At best it will be bitter or unpleasant to eat and at worst be dangerous, especially to children and the elderly.

Storing

Pasteurized cream should keep in a refrigerator for an average of six days. Frozen single cream tends to separate, but double cream freezes very well giving best results if it is slightly sweetened. It should always be well stirred or whipped after defrosting.

Butter

Without mountains of glorious, glistening butter, there would have been no haute cuisine – and there would probably be fewer heart disease problems, too. But for me to attempt to live without butter because of possible future health problems would be the same as cutting off a leg in case I might stub a toe. I was brought up eating masses of butter with everything, and that's that. And the more I know about the suggested substitutes, the more I bless a world with butter in it.

Butter making is a specialized art, involving far more than churning cream for longer than required to make whipped cream. Even today there is no such thing as totally automated butter making. The great stainless steel churns which hold from 4500-6800 litres/1000-1,500 gallons of full cream all have windows through which watch expert butter makers, who must stop the churning at a precise moment or risk losing the whole batch.

Basically what happens is this: the rotation of a churn half-full of cream cracks the envelopes of non-fat solids that encase each of the fat globules of the cream. When this happens – it is called 'breaking' – the butterfat globules begin to coalesce into pieces about the size of a wheat grain and the other solids are dispersed into the liquid content of the cream, becoming buttermilk. This buttermilk is drawn off and the butter grains are washed with cold water to rinse out any remains of buttermilk, which would reduce the butter's quality and keeping ability. Once this has drained enough to reduce the liquid content to within legally enforced limits, salt may be added. This is a very delicate operation, requiring a balance between market tastes and marketing requirements; the former is purely nationalistic, the latter depends on how long the butter is to be stored or how far it is to travel. As might be expected, the more salt, the longer the butter will last.

The salted or unsalted grains are then churned a further 10-15 minutes, which is called 'working' and blends the grains into a solid mass. It is then packed into small packets or in large cartons for commercial use; in the latter process it is usually slightly compressed, which helps avoid problems of shortened life that can be caused by trapped pockets of air.

The wide variety of flavours offered by butters comes as a surprise to most people. These variations are achieved in three basic ways, starting with the characteristics of the cream used. This relies on the type of cow and the feed it is given. As these vary during the year, so will the resultant butter, but usually the changes are more likely to be in the balance of minerals contained, and flavour differences would be beyond the detection of most of us. Perhaps the most widely used method of flavour manipulation is treatment of the cream.

Provided there has been a preliminary 'holding' of the cream to ensure uniform hardness of the fat globules, you can make butter from sweet cream to which you have done nothing else. But if you leave it longer to ripen, the naturally occurring bacteria will multiply and their enzymic actions and side effects will increase the flavour, by raising the acid content in particular. Such a flavour enhancement or a flavour change can be aided by the addition of a cultured bacterial 'starter' as with the making of cheese.

The cream used to make most European butter is culture-treated, thus giving the distinctive and consistent but differing flavours of these countries' products. Confusingly they are sold as unsalted butters, as though they are merely cream converted into butter, but their flavour has been manipulated and they are more properly known as lactic butters.

Salt is the last and final way of affecting butter's flavour. The combination of basic dairying technique, treatment of the cream and salting gives an enormously wide potential of flavours.

Colouring is sometimes added also, but you shouldn't take it for granted that all brilliant butter has such additives. If the cream used is from Jersey or Guernsey cows it will naturally have a brighter glow.

There are three main types of butter generally found in the United Kingdom: salted, slightly salted and unsalted (lactic). Farmhouse butters can be any of these, and clarified butter or ghee can also be made from each of these.

Clarified butter: this may be bought or made at home: less easily available concentrated butter gives very much the same flavour.

The point is to make a butter-based fat or oil with no solid content for that is what makes butter burn. Clean butter fat – clarified butter – will cook smoke-free and safely at a far higher temperature than butter.

To make clarified butter melt a good quantity of salted or unsalted butter over very gentle heat and then let it simmer gently until those white particles of milk solids have stopped forming; only then has all the water gone and that might take as long as 45 minutes. Either scoop away or strain through muslin. It lasts as long as butter when kept refrigerated. Both clarified butter and its Indian equivalent ghee q.v., make cooking pancakes or eggs easier, and give better results when browning onions or spices because it won't burn before the job is done. Mixing either with a vegetable oil enables even higher frying temperatures without danger of smoking and burning.

Farmhouse butter: not the simple reliable down-home thing you would like it to be. UK farmhouse butters are usually from western counties, and are slightly less salty than most, which is one of the contributing factors to notoriously short life. In my experience it has a special predilection for rancidity, which may also be due to inefficient churning and washing or because it is often made close to cheese dairies and picks up foreign flavours. Either way, farmhouse butter should always be given a discreet sniff to ensure it is sweet and wholesome. You should also check for streakiness: this indicates the combination of different batches and possible problems with rancidity. Salted Welsh butter is possibly the saltiest regional butter of all, especially when cut from great blocks by farmers' wives in Swansea market.

Ghee: is the clarified butter basic to the cookery of the Indian continent, so if you don't fancy making your own, you'll get it easily from an Indian emporium.

High-fat butters: the explosion of farmers' markets has led many to think about what they can do with butter and the answer is to make them higher-fat, which makes them softer and richer. Their flavour contribution can be very notable in cookery, especially in pastry, but you have to compensate for the missing water, for removing water is how you get a high-fat butter; steam from butter's water content is very important to the lightening of pastry, particularly the layered types. Thus these are not that useful in pastry making but excellent in cake and biscuit cookery, although it is worth adding a touch more liquid than you might do normally.

Lactic butter. high acidity is quite as good at extending the life of cream and butter as salt, although for shorter periods. Whereas the Anglo-Saxon and US preference has largely been to salt butter, housewives in Europe preferred to age their cream more, so it would keep long enough to go to the market. The pasteurization that later became mandatory interfered with this process and so commercial manufacturers compensate by using pasteurised cream into which they add lactic starters. These develop unique flavour in the butter and are responsible for the various flavours in European butters – the differences have nothing to do with cattle breed or their feed. They are all sold as unsalted butters but are not sweet butter.

Salted butter: you can generally judge how much salt there is by ascertaining how far butter has had to travel; hence butter from New Zealand is likely to have a higher salt content than butter from, say, Wiltshire.

Slightly salted butter gives a blander flavour, which suits much continental cooking and many palates.

Soft butters: the answer to a major complaint about butter since the dawn of domestic refrigeration, these are made by reducing even further the water content of butter. Yet some manufacturers can't leave well alone and mix butter with oils to get the softer effect. To me it's a scandal in this day of greater health and diet awareness. What is simpler or more pure than cream churned into butter, what could be more natural? So why add vegetable oils or worse, hydrogenated fats made from vegetable oils. The mixture occurs nowhere in nature, so why should it occur on our tables. Other than for profit, of course. Surely not?

Sweet butter: made with unpasteurised cream or with cream that has not been subjected to the action of a lactic culture, even though it may have a salt content. It is exceptionally difficult to find in Britain but common-place in the United States. In cooking it gives a flavour of rich creaminess, rather like clotted cream, and this explains the vast superiority of the flavour of much American baking. The closest British bakers can get are the unpasteurised butters of France and I especially recommend beurre d'Isigny. Lightly salted Normandy butters also give outstanding flavour in pastry and baking but are much cheaper.

Unsalted butter: usually the most expensive and potentially the most trouble-some kind, for without the preservative advantage salt gives it is prone to all manner of afflictions. Again, a trained and perspicacious nose is a definite aid. More often than not unsalted also means a lactic butter, i.e. one that has had a bacterial culture added, that adds specific flavours.

Cooking

If you have problems with butter burning when you are frying or slowly cooking vegetables, the simplest technique is to lower the heat. Or you can add up to an equal quantity of oil, which allows you too use a much higher heat without the butter burning. Otherwise you have to buy or make clarified butter, which is quite a good thing to keep in your refrigerator. The correct time to cook in butter is when it has stopped chattering and falls silent.

Storing

All butter is affected not only by heat but also by light, so it should be kept both cool and dark.

DOP/AOC Butters

There are four French butters with DOP/AOC status. Butter is *beurre*.

Beurre Charente Poitou, beurre de Charentes, beurre des Deux-Sevres, and beurre d'Isigny: note this latter must be made from pasteurised cream, beurre d'Isigny made with raw cream does not have the same protected status.

Spain: butter is *mantequilla*.

Mantequilla de l'Alt Urgell and de la Cerdanya: from these two regions in the north-eastern provinces Lerida and Gerona, both in the central-eastern Catalan Pyrenees. These butters are said to reflect the pastures, and the hay and silage made from them, but flavouring cultures are also added to the pasteurised cream. Naturally yellow to bright yellow and guaranteed free of any chemicals including antibiotics, this butter is one of many found in Europe, including in France, that only came into being early in the 20th century, after phylloxera destroyed traditional vineyards.

Ice Cream

In the days when Saturday matinee movies were preceded by a stirring serial and Walt Disney cartoons, it used to cost sixpence to sit downstairs and ninepence to lord it in the superiority of the balcony. I used to be given ninepence, which meant an invidious choice. Did I sit upstairs and command considerable social envy? Or did I sit downstairs, enjoying the status of a twopenny ice cream, save a penny, and have two ice creams next week? The ice cream plan usually won. If I'd studied social history in my first ten years I could have saved myself the trouble of choosing, for ices have always had a greater social cachet than mere position.

The Romans and almost every other ruling power spent fortunes having snow and ice rushed over great distances so they could freeze food and so astound the hoi polloi. In England and America, lesser fortunes relied on the building of underground ice houses in which to store winter's ice, so providing them with the means to make cooling ices and sorbets, a special need in the humid summers of the southern states of North America.

It was the society-levelling Americans who popularised ice cream and it remains very much part of everyday life for millions and millions of children and adults. Huge containers of ice cream are stored in the family freezer, to be scooped into as a snack from breakfast to bedtime. But, like so many convenience foods now in the public domain, much of it has very little in common with the real thing, other than temperature. In fact, true dairy-based ice cream simply doesn't exist as far as most major producers are concerned: their product contains no cream and any milk is probably added in the form of powder. The fat, so essential to the texture and enjoyment of real ice cream, is nearly always from the oil palm, at least it is in the United Kingdom. Thus, if the EU continues on its legislative way, it will soon prohibit such products being called ice cream, which would be a very good thing. This isn't necessary in Australasia and in some of the stronger dairying states of the United States, where the real thing is protected as a birthright.

Ice cream in its simplest form was once just flavoured and frozen cream and even this probably didn't appear until the 18th century. Ices had been closer to what we would call sorbets; it's thought the Chinese invented these concoctions of fruit and that the Italians took up the idea and then introduced it to the rest of Europe. England's Charles I, who first fell for them in France, protected the recipe with a sentence of death for anyone who divulged it. You are quite right when you say bought ice cream isn't the same as Mum makes. That's because it is made from different ingredients by quite different techniques. At first these differences were invented to make commercial ice cream taste and look like the homemade thing, basically frozen creams or custards, but slowly its popularity generated the creation of absolutely new products, containing no cream, but priced so their pleasure was available to all.

Most of today's commercial ice creams are based on milk but, as that is icy when frozen, fats are added for taste and texture. The first process required by law is pasteurization to kill all possibly harmful bacteria. Next, to give the velvety mouth feel of frozen cream, the mix is homogenized, which reduces the size of the fat globules, keeping them suspended in the milk rather than rising to the top. The homogenized mixture is then frozen, and air is whisked in, which bulks and lightens the texture. The more air, the fluffier and easier it is to eat, and this 'stretching' of the ingredients means it can be sold more cheaply. Sugar, flavours, nuts and the like may be added at the start or the end of the process.

The commercial advantage of homogenizing is that the fats added to the milk may be of cheaper non-dairy or of vegetable origin. It will be no surprise that so-called standard ice creams also contain other ingredients to help emulsification, to slow down melting and so on, but all are approved to high government standards. Modern technology now means that by adding such emulsifying and stabilizing agents, even milk can be frozen to look and behave like ice cream, but in the United States this must be called Iced milk.

The days of only vanilla or chocolate ice creams and perhaps strawberry on a Saturday have gone thank goodness. The move mainly came from America, where ice cream is eaten by the gallon all year round. Dayville and Baskin-Robbins suddenly opened shops selling dozens of flavours with such fantastic names as Rocky Road, Blue Lagoon and Fudge Nut Cookies. The ice-cream parlours came and often went just as quickly but a taste for something bigger and better had begun. Super-premium ice cream has become a permanent High Street star. They are very high in dairy fat and use unusual, high-quality ingredients or should; a high price and challenging flavour is no guarantee you are eating something made from ingredients you would find in your kitchen.

Read the label. After that it is up to you, for the success of modern retailing is based on choice. And pleasure in eating comes from eating the widest variety of foods available. A totally confected construction of non-dairy fat and 'flavours/flavors', sugar and air does nobody any harm if eaten once in a while, and eaten knowledgeably.

The content not mentioned on ice cream packets is air, and it is not until you eat ice cream that you can tell how much has been whisked into it. In general the cheaper the ice cream and the larger the pack the more air is likely to have been included; the premium and luxury ice creams have progressively less air content and are generally packed in smaller containers, but as they are richer and more solid the amount of ice cream in them is likely to be just as satisfying as larger amounts of lighter products.

The classic homemade form nowadays is a flavoured egg custard made with milk or cream. The best I ever ate was made in an old-fashioned ice cream churn or dasher, in which the mixture is turned over and over again surrounded by salted ice. It takes a long time and a lot of patience but gives such a wonderful silken result. Other recipes give smooth results too and you can also buy small electrically operated machines which will churn ice cream in the freezer or the ice-box of your refrigerator. But, although rather satisfying to do, it may not be necessary. In the last several years there has been a distinct move back from artifice to the commercial making of true ice cream.

Dairy ice cream: when you see this on a label it guarantees the fats included are all dairy fats.

Emulsifiers: these are essentially a chemical way of achieving what homogenization does mechanically, mixing water and fats. But these emulsifiers are more certain to keep them mixed and thus the product may be treated a little more ruggedly.

Flavour/flavouring: if you find either word included in the name or description of the frozen product, it means precisely what it says, a flavouring has been used rather than the real thing, and that could also mean colouring too. Thus chocolate 'flavouring' means it is not the real thing; 'strawberries with strawberry flavour' means a mixture of strawberries and a flavouring to make them go further.

Milking Sheep

The growth of sheep dairying herds in Europe, the UK and USA is quite extraordinary. The greatest benefits to the consumer are new soft, hard and blue sheep milk cheeses and a greater interest in traditional ones, from Spain or Italy particularly. Said to be easier and more charming to keep than goats, sheep give a rich milk that never has the greasy, musky odours goat milk so easily shows.

Sheep, and goats to a lesser extent, were for centuries the greater mainstay of UK life, for cows' milk and its cheeses went to the big house, so we are experiencing a return to tradition rather than making new ones. It makes life so much more relaxing too; no more fretting when fresh sheep's milk cheese is required to entertain visitors from Uzbekistan, Azerbaijan or Armenia. You never know.

Ice cream: if the label only says this, the contents will be made from milk and other fats and the label must also say 'contains non-milk fat' or 'contains vegetable fat'.

Stabilizers: these act like sponges to soak up excess water. This achieves two things. First, ice crystals are prevented from forming when frozen product fluctuates in temperature and second, the product's ability to be whipped and thus to trap air is dramatically increased. This is no bad thing as long as you are not paying premium prices; premium products are unlikely to use stabilizers.

Sweeteners: sugar is essential to ice cream, especially for flavour but also for bulk and texture. Government regulations declare artificial sweeteners are not allowed in any standard or dairy ice cream; but the demand for lower calorie ice cream products means that sugar-reduced, calorie-reduced products are increasingly seen. Provided they are labelled as such, they may include fructose (fruit sugar) or alternative sweeteners.

Sorbets and sherberts: sorbets are water ices, basically a mixture of water, sugar and fruit juice or pulp plus other ingredients and frozen with the addition of air; without air they are the popular iced lolly. A sherbert has some dairy content, often milk or ice cream, and is always frozen with an air content. Those who believe they are saving on calories by ordering a sorbet rather than Ice cream will never get thin.

Ice Cream Types

Once you can understand what labels should mean and promise, you should be able to put any ice cream into one of the following categories, and then decide if you are being overcharged before you spend the money. Ice cream is the most classic case of the palate always being gratified with a smaller amount of something better-tasting and richer than with large amounts of low-flavour, fatty air.

Standard ice creams: the names you recognize, made to the basic standards and competitively priced. Always milk plus non-dairy or vegetable fat and containing the maximum amount of air permitted. Often sold in bulk packs. The type of fat should be clearly identifiable on the label, as should the flavourings, which are rarely real. Often sold as family packs, but I can't imagine why any parent who bothered to read the label would want their children to eat it.

Premium ice creams: can contain dairy or 'superior' non-dairy fats. Will contain less air, cost a little more and will generally be packed in 1 litre packs, maximum.

Super-premium or luxury: dairy ice creams exclusively, with high fat content and low air additions. More likely to be in smaller packs of 500g, 750g or individual portions. Egg and egg yolks sometimes also included.

FREE RANGE
GOOSE EGGS

Eggs

Eggs are magical. What else is as soothing when you need comfort as poached eggs on toast, what so spoiling as scrambled eggs made with cream and topped with smoked salmon? What else when boiled allows you to play with soldiers, yet what else is quite as sophisticated as the perfect soufflé?

Greater sensibility to how our food is produced means ever greater availability of eggs from poultry live and feed naturally. Do they taste better – or different? Most people think so, but few of them would comment if they didn't know there was social cachet to be gained from eating free-range eggs. No matter, because it's concern for the conditions of the laying birds that have most powered the changes.

Test eggs for freshness by putting them one by one into a bowl of water, the flatter an egg lies the fresher it is. It is all right but a bit old if it stands up, but once it starts to float low in the water, crack open to check it has not gone off. If it floats on top of the water, throw it away before it flies of its own accord.

Fresh eggs should display three distinct textures when broken: the yolk, supported by a thick cushion of white, itself surrounded by less viscous liquid. As the eggs get older the thick part of the white becomes more watery until there is only one texture of white and eventually the yolk also flattens out. These may still taste good, but don't look too good poached or fried – use them for baking.

Hens eggs: perhaps the prettiest eggs of all are from the araucana, a cross-breed from Chile. The very best looking are a gorgeous blue, and unusually the colour goes all through the shell. You will also find blue-green, green and olive brown araucana eggs. Araucana eggs tend to have larger yolks than other eggs but you can ignore scare stories about them having extra cholesterol – when they do it is not significant. The rumpless araucana and the cream leg bar chicken also lay green-blue eggs. If you simply must have speckled eggs, go for the gorgeous brown maran or welsummer eggsor for the speckledy which produce them all the time.

Poultry keeping is on the increase and because eggs are usually the comforting benefit, opposite is a guide to what colour eggs you can expect. It's from Broad Leys Publishing's web-site, where you'll also find all the information you need to be a poultry-keeper.

Duck eggs: rich and flavourful, these are popular with children because of their pretty green-blue shell. Let them be eaten, by all means, but never serve soft-boiled or lightly poached duck eggs from a farmyard or anywhere wild. Duck eggs have particularly thin shells, and because they are usually laid in wet and dirty places, they often contain much higher levels of bacteria than any others you are likely to eat and must be thoroughly cooked for safety. Yet even this is no longer an absolute in the UK, because duck eggs are being produced more carefully and now find themselves on the very best of menus, as beautifully soft-poached as can be.

 The ultimate use for duck eggs is for cake making, especially whisked sponges when their elevated colour and flavour make a treat into a masterpiece every time. They can be used in combination with hen eggs or alone. I remember sitting on a high stool in the kitchen as a child, whisking duck eggs for my mother; then she would make a sponge and win a prize at the local church. I can still smell the rich creaminess of those eggs now, and taste the sponge, but I'm still waiting for my name to appear on the prize certificate.

Eggshell Colour by Breed

Breed	Shell Colour	Breed	Shell Colour
Ancona	Cream/White	Fayoumi	Tinted/Cream
Andalusian	White	Friesian	White
Appenzeller	White	Frizzle	White/Tinted
Araucana	Blue-green	German Langshan	Tinted/Brown
Asil	White/Tinted	Hamburgh	White
Augsburger	White	Hebden Black	Mid to dark brown
Australorp	Tinted/Brown	Hisex Ranger	Brown
Barnevelder	Brown	Houdan	White
Black Rock	Brown	Hy-Line Brown	Brown
Booted Bantam	Tinted	Indian (Cornish) Game	Tinted/Brown
Bovans Nera	Brown	ISA Brown	Brown
Brabanter	White	Italiener	White
Brahma	Tinted/Brown	Ixworth	White/Tinted
Brakel	White	Japanese Bantam	Cream/White
Breda	Cream/White	Jersey Giant	Tinted/Brown
Bresse	White	Ko-Shamo Bantam	Tinted/Cream
Calder Ranger	Mid brown	Kraienkoppe	White
Campine	White	Lakenvelder	Tinted/White
Cochin	Tinted/Brown	Legbar	White/Cream
Cream Legbar	Blue-green/Olive	Leghorn	White
Creve Coeur	White	La Fleche	Tinted/White
Croad Lansghan	Brown	Lohmann Brown & L. Tradition	Brown
Derbyshire Redcap	White/Tinted	Malay	Tinted
Dominique	Brown	Maran	Dark speckled
Dorking	White/Tinted	Marsh Daisy	Tinted
Dutch Bantam	Tinted	Minorca	White
Faverolles	Tinted/Cream		

Breed	Shell Colour	Breed	Shell Colour
Modern Game	Tinted	Scots Grey	White/Tinted
Modern Langshan	Brown	Sebright	Cream/White
Nankin	Tinted	Shamo	Tinted/White
Nankin-Shamo	Tinted/Cream	Sicilian Buttercup	White
New Hampshire Red	Tinted/Brown	Silkie	White/Tinted
Norfolk Grey	Tinted	Spanish	White
North Holland Blue	Tinted/Brown	Speckledy	Dark speckled
Old English Game	Tinted	Sulmtaler	Cream/Tinted
Old English Pheasant Fowl	Tinted/White	Sultan	White
		Sumatra	White
Orloff	Tinted	Sussex	Tinted
Orpington	Brown/Tinted	Tuzo	Tinted
Pekin	Cream/White	Vorwerk	Cream/Tinted
Plymouth Rock	Tinted	Welbar	Brown
Poland	White	Welsummer	Dark speckled
Rhinelander	White	White Star	White
Rhode Island Red	Tinted/Brown	Wyandotte	Tinted/Brown
Rhodebar	Brown	Wybar	Tinted
Rosecomb	White/Cream	Yamato-Gunkei	Tinted/Cream
Rumpless Araucana	Blue-green	Yokohama	Tinted/White
Rumpless Game	Tinted	Transylvanian Naked Neck	Tinted/White
Scots Dumpy	White/Tinted		

Gulls' eggs: collected from the wild for a very short period each UK summer. These greeny-blue eggs, dappled with brown, are slightly more pointed than hen's eggs and up to 5cm/2in long. They taste very much like hens' eggs, with none of the fishy taste that many expect, but if anything are rather more mellow than the usual breakfast egg.

Although they look very pretty in their shells, I deplore the habit of serving gulls' eggs unshelled at buffets and cocktail parties. How do you peel an egg and balance a glass? Even if you manage, what do you do with the shell? Serve them shelled, slightly chilled, with bowls of mayonnaise, celery salt, sweet paprika and slices of brown bread. You can always display the shells around the dish or bowl or basket, to show the eggs are not from some frightful extruding machine. Far better is to be mean (they are not cheap) and serve them just to yourself hard or soft-boiled on a nest of mayonnaise with plenty of smoked salmon, and with a scatter of caviar if your ship has come in.

Quails' eggs: much the smallest of eggs regularly available quails' eggs are served the same way as gulls' eggs, but, being cheaper, they can be eaten more often. Fresh ones should be boiled for just one minute. Serve them as is, or include them in a special salad, or in mayonnaise with lobster, prawns or other shellfish. They look very nice served with cold asparagus mayonnaise, and are very special with hot asparagus and a sauce maltaise, hollandaise flavoured with blood orange juice. Leave just one or two with some shell on for a good effect. The Connaught Hotel serves them soft-boiled on pastry bateaux with a bed of much reduced mushroom purée, coated with hollandaise, and they or gulls' eggs on a nest of mayonnaise sauce are the perfect accompaniment to cold salmon, smoked salmon or gravad lax, especially if you chop plenty of fresh dill into the mayonnaise, and/or mix a portion of whipped cream in, too. You can buy them shelled in tins from China, and these are a very good standby, except if they have been on the shelf a long time their outer surface can seem crisp. Good to put into stews as an extender or just as a surprise.

But be bold. Fry them or poach them to tumble far more usefully and prettily through a salad or any sort of pasta dish or as a garnish on brioche toast; scramble them ditto if you like, perhaps with a few wild mushrooms, and then serve them with roasted quails.

Other eggs: some enterprising farm shops and specialty shops in the country will often offer other eggs, from an increasing variety of heritage breed hens or from other birds. You'll most commonly find the rich brown maran egg, a hen egg with a definite, elegant flavour that's captivating. I have also bought in London guinea fowl eggs, pheasant eggs and bantam eggs, these last from small varieties of poultry. Pullet eggs are attractively small and have been laid by hens about a year old. All these and others are good, interesting for their size rather than their flavour, although pheasant eggs seem to have something extra.

I've never eaten plovers' eggs, because now they may no longer be gathered, but they are supposed to be the best of the small eggs.

Cooking

The freshest eggs taste best for poaching, boiling, frying or coddling, but eggs for baking are

better for being several days old and this is an absolute if you want to whisk up the whites.

When baking, always bring eggs back to room temperature first. You will get more volume and lighter results; it is particularly important to have the whites at room temperature when making meringue.

Storing

Remember eggs are not designed as human food, but as the nursery and cradle of a future bird. The shells are porous and thus can collect flavours, smells and germs. If shells are dirty and wet but the eggs are very fresh, rinse them well and then eat these eggs quickly. Otherwise eggs with dirty shells should only be eaten if cooked through.

Kept cool and away from other strong smelling foods, eggs actually last much longer than is usually thought, but buy in small quantities.

Down-under Bacon and Egg Pie

Strictly speaking this isn't delicatessen food as all the ingredients can be bought from a supermarket. Yet, use dry-cured bacon and free-range eggs and pastry made with butter, and then a bacon and egg pie becomes very gourmet. You'll soon understand why no one in Australia or New Zealand could think of a day at the beach without one or two. Plenty of opportunity for you to make your own version too, by adding sun-dried tomatoes or bush tomatoes, or smoked paprika, or grilled red or green capsicum, chili-beans, slices of sweet-fried onion, chunks of boiled or fried potatoes (yummy), green peas, sweet corn kernels – anything that stands up to being eaten outdoors. Yet make it just with decent bacon and eggs and plenty of black pepper and you'll understand how real men and women might well turn from eating quiche.

Serves 6-8
350-400g/12-14oz all-butter puff pastry*
225g/8oz dry-cure streaky bacon, green rather than smoked
6 large eggs
black pepper, be generous

Line a shallow 20cm/8in pie dish with 175g/6oz of the pastry* this base can be a butter shortcrust, which gives a more interesting look and firmer bite to the pie, but the top is always better as puff pastry. Coarsely dice the bacon and fry until the fat starts to run. Spread the bacon evenly over the pastry and some of the interesting extras if you have them; never mind if you don't.

Working around the edge of the dish, break the eggs over the bacon, encouraging the whites to join together by gently tilting the dish. Best plan is to have five eggs around the edge and one in the middle. Try not to break the yolks and have an extra egg on hand just in case there is room for it. You might also fill such spaces with your chosen extras.

Pepper the egg yolks generously, cover with the remaining pastry, crimp the edges and decorate with any leftover bits and pieces. Glaze if you have yet another extra egg about.

Bake for 25 minutes in a pre-heated 200C/400F/Gas 6 oven, and then a further 15 minutes at 160 C/325 F/Gas 3. Serve warm or cold in slices and eat from the hand, no matter what it's been doing.

Fish and Seafood

Fish was once a mainstay. Every big house and most villages raised carp in ponds, the rivers were fished and salt cod or red herrings kept them going through the long hard winters.

Fresh fish was probably more easily available than it is in many areas today, at least it was during the summer when dirt roads were passable. There were laws to ensure such produce was edible: mackerel for instance which could be sold in the streets of London on a Sunday for their high fat content meant they never lasted overnight once landed. Other sorts of fresh fish were kept alive in huge tanks in the holds of fishing vessels as they waited to land the catch in the heart of London, at Billingsgate Market.

Salting and smoking as ways of preserving fish are increasingly unfashionable for dietary reasons, yet small producers are being rewarded for making them naturally again with smoke rather than smoke-flavoured paint. We want food to taste of itself, and if smoked we want to taste the smoke *and* the fish: these days smoking is not done to preserve but to complement. Our choice of fresh and preserved fish is different from what it has been, standards have never been better and, with frozen goodies as well, the fish lover has not had it so good for centuries.

Abalone

Meat from a number of univalve molluscs, sold frozen or in cans. The best kind is from Japan or the Shandong province of China. Can be eaten directly from the can, and if cooked again is best done quickly to avoid toughening. In New Zealand there is an equally admired equivalent, the *paua*; as well as curiously rich flesh that subtley tastes the way I imagine a pearl might, it has a specially irridescent shell that makes spectacular jewellery, often confused with butterfly wing. Much of the 'fresh' abalone you might eat in Japan and China will actually be frozen New Zealand *paua*, and some of that will have been imported by the black market in this very expensive commodity.

Anchovy

Once you've been introduced to anchovies you either love them to distraction or hate them with a passion engendered by no other finny thing I know. They belong to the herring family and although inferior to them when fresh are much superior when preserved. Basically, the anchovy should be thought of as a flavouring that's used to lift the salty notes of a dish, rather than as a major ingredient of a dish.

Native to the Mediterranean and the English Channel, the anchovy is nevertheless caught as far away as the Black Sea and Scandinavia. The best are said to come from the area between Nice and the Spanish province of Catalonia, as do many of the best recipes for their use; in Spanish they are *boquerones*, and France's *anchois de Collioure* have IGP status.

The simple method of salting and preserving whole anchovies originated with the Greeks and Romans, who also used them as the basis for their fermented fish sauce, *garum*. Like herrings, they are often preserved in fillets, flat or curled, which are considered easier for packing and selling these days. They are sold in many forms, whole or filleted, in salt or in brine, in oil or in vinegar, and only the older way of salting anchovies whole is difficult to buy these days. If you can buy dry salted anchovies they are thought superior but before use should be rinsed or soaked in water or milk.

The Russians preserve anchovies in a spiced vinegar, the Norwegians in a spiced brine. The Italian Rizzoli company of Parma do anchovies in a chillied oil, *alici en salsa piccante*, reckoned to be amongst the very best way of eating them.

In Freemantle, Western Australia, a new industry cans anchovies as Ozchovies, a beaut name if ever there was one, and Australian TV chef Iain Hewitson says they are good enough to eat.

You can sometimes buy fresh anchovies and they are easily distinguishable. A maximum of 10-12cm/4-5in long, they have an extraordinarily big mouth which stretches back almost as far as their gills. I have soused them and also served them freshly grilled, but they were not very good, not when compared to their preserved cousins.

Anchovy essence, which comes in all manner of mixtures and strengths, is perfectly magical, with the special ability to pull together flavours that aren't blending to make something new and wonderful, and not just because it is salty. Naturally good in fish dishes, it can be used to advantage if employed with discretion in many meat dishes, especially creamy sauced ones: you'll find many elegant Georgian dishes finished with cream, lemon juice, mace and a dash of anchovy essence. It can add intriguing life to rice dishes, to mayonnaise and, perhaps best of all, to vegetables. Broccoli or spinach take very well to a little anchovy essence mixed with butter.

Used secretly and in small amounts, anchovy essence or pounded salt anchovies make an intriguing savoury marinade for beef and lamb before roasting, but better not tell your guests even if they implore you for the secret – I once saw someone vomit at table on receipt of such information.

Serving

Anchovies packed in brine or oil are interchangeable; the former should be rinsed with water or milk and the latter are less highly flavoured. The most common uses for flat fillet or curls of anchovy are on pizza, or in salads such as Salade Niçoise, and for assertive canapés. The unexpected ability of anchovy fillets to dissolve into an unctuous paste when heated with olive oil, or merely to disappear into other liquids, is what makes them a standby of those who take to them. Merely stirring a couple into the oil or butter, or both, to go onto pasta opens new vistas of flavour. Naturally, you would add lots of sliced garlic from the start (chopped would be too mimsy here), and chunky fresh herbs. Parsley excels with anchovies, if you do not chop it too finely. To add life to tomato passata make the olive oil/anchovy paste and then boil it up with the passata until the anchovy essence is fully emulsified.

Along the edge of the Mediterranean and on some of her islands they make an extraordinary type of sauce-cum-dip, known as ancholade or some similar name. It's an anchovy paste, usually made from salted whole ones, parsley, oil and garlic, spread on oil-soaked bread and baked until brown, and so is a peasant version of the anchovy toast served as a savoury in London's men's clubs.

The Piedmontese of Italy make something called *bagna cauda*, which is used as a sauce for pasta, or as a hot dip for bread or raw vegetables, and which has always been regarded as completely indigestible unless you've been brought up to it from birth. You heat 75g/3oz each of butter and olive oil, and then add 75g/3oz of anchovies in pieces and 75g/3oz (that's right) of finely sliced garlic. Simmer for ten minutes then keep warm. In *Italian Food* Elizabeth David reckons it requires great quantities of coarse red wine and the constitution of an ox.

I think I prefer the French caper-olive-and-anchovy paste *tapenade*, or the civility of Patum Pepperium, the Gentleman's Relish, which is also anchovy-based and blissful when spread thinly on hot buttery toast with decent tea in front of a drawing-room fire. Having it spread for you is better.

Arbroath smokies PGI

Something superb; beheaded and gutted, salt-cured, hot-smoked haddock, weighing between 350g and 550g, and usually sold in matched pairs, the way they were smoked over beech or oak. They should be very moist and flaky, with their fish, salt and smoke flavours all mild and balanced. I love them eaten cold, but they can be reheated gently in hot water or milk, or flaked into a white sauce or made into excelling fish pies. Made only in Arbroath, an ancient fishing port of the shire of Angus, on Scotland's east coast. Finnan haddock are cold smoked and so must be cooked, and there is many a dreadful painted hussy promenading as the real thing.

Caviar

Those languid heroines of Russian sagas who existed on but a spoonful of caviar and a sip of champagne knew a thing or two. The hard roe of the female sturgeon has twice the nutriment of most meat and is equal to the finest pork flesh. But its powers of sustainment are not why caviar is so esteemed. It is worshipped both because of its scarcity and its superlative flavour.

The latter is often hotly debated, usually by those who have never tasted it, and with hissed platitudes about 'acquired taste' and 'just because it costs so much'. That's as may be, but I've adored it ever since I breakfasted upon a pot of beluga aboard a luxurious American cruise liner on January 1, 1961, my nineteenth birthday.

Genuine caviar comes only from the sturgeon, a fish once so common in Europe that its roe was used as bait. Caviar was eaten occasionally in Britain but did not become popular until the 19th century.

The sturgeon is one of the world's most ancient and fascinating creatures. There is a variety in every one of the earth's oceans, making it the most widespread species of fish. This is because, like the crocodile, it is an unchanged survivor from prehistoric times. For commercial purposes most caviar sturgeon are caught in the Caspian Sea, by the Russians and those who used to be Russians in the north and by the Iranians in the south, and all legal fishing is in government hands: some are caught in the Black Sea deltas of the Danube.

The biggest sturgeon, the beluga, can weigh anything up to 25cwt and as much as 158kg/354 lb of roe has been taken from a single fish; the usual haul is between 4-15kg/8-35lbs, depending on the species. Caviar can vary in colour from a yellow or brown to light grey and black, and varies tremendously in size. The colour and size has little bearing on flavour, for the most important factors are the time of year, age of the fish and method of preservation; the beluga for instance must be eighteen to twenty years old before its roe is considered suitable. It is generally considered that the earlier in the season and the lighter the salting, the better the flavour.

Although the fish and waters are exactly the same, Russian and Iranian caviar can be quite different. In Iran, on the southern shores, this is still an artisans' business, often family run and working on just one fish at a time. Thus they are better able to judge the amount of salt needed more keenly and to watch the process more carefully, giving a more consistent and, some would say, more elegant product, which will vary only to reflect the individuality of each sturgeon's age and eggs. The more commercialized operation on the northern shores of the Caspian, once Soviet Russia but now many things, must perforce work on averages and in greater bulk and thus will vary in sensitivity to differences of fish from fish. But I shouldn't worry, unless you have won the Pools and intend to eat caviar every day, such variations are unlikely to strike you.

Sturgeons are bled before gutting to avoid contamination of the roe, which is sieved several times to remove the connecting tissues of the eggs, and then lightly salted. All caviar so treated will be labelled *malassol*, which means little salt, and this is considered the greatest delicacy.

Virtually all the caviar exported to the West is eaten by people with their feet off the ground – no, not that! – by people in aircraft. And in spite of salting it has usually also been lightly pasteurised; the rare experience of eating unpasteurised and thus raw caviar was likened by *The Sunday Times* and *Vanity Fair* writer wit Adrian Gill as 'not only having the brass section, but the woodwind and strings, too'. On the other hand explorer Robin Hanbury Tenison lived on nothing but salmon and fresh caviar for weeks on end in the remote Kamchatka Peninsula but yearned for tea, toast and Radio 4.

As summer gets hotter caviar needs more salt to preserve it and 'hot season' caviar is packed in small wooden tubs and labelled 'fresh salted'; this is very rarely seen in Europe. End of season roe is inferior, and this is salted and pressed and then usually sold in tubes for relatively little. Pressed caviar – caviar jam some call it – makes pretty canapés and offers lots of decorative possibilities.

Types of caviar

Of all the types of sturgeon from which we get caviar the most productive is the monster beluga, the white sturgeon. It provides the largest eggs and many think the best, but beluga caviar is also the most fragile and does not keep well and is not generally thought the best flavoured. Beluga caviar is particularly admired in the United States.

The next most important source is the sevruga, which never exceeds 4m/l4ft in length and rarely gives more than about 4kg/8 lb of very small-grained roe. Many hold this fineness gives a better flavour than coarser-sized beluga, but this is a subjective argument that will never be solved.

The third important source and generally the cheapest is oscietre, which is spelled many ways, and which provides masses of eggs that vary from grey to black and are medium in size. Those lucky enough to eat plenty of caviar usually choose oscietre as the best flavoured and the most gratifying to eat, not just for flavour, but for the specially delicious pop of the eggs if you crush them between tongue and palate.

The oscietre produces so many sizes and colours of caviar it is not unknown for wicked packers to pass off larger eggs as much more expensive beluga. There is an infallible test.

If you crush a beluga egg on the ball of your thumb, or anywhere else for that matter, the resultant smear will be grey-black; oscietre will always leave a brown-yellow smear. And speaking of testing, the traditional test for freshness and flavour in caviar is to smear a small helping onto the ball of your thumb, nowhere else in this case, to sniff deeply and then to lick it off. The slightest whiff or taste of fishiness means something is wrong. You do not employ such technique if you have washed in something scented, or have not washed at all.

The fabled golden caviar is supposedly obtained three ways. In the days of the great Russian Empire, patriotic and hardy Cossacks would hack holes in the late winter/early spring ice, through which they would spear sturgeons. Their roe was very immature, golden yellow, and with a rich flavour that made the senses reel, so it is said.

A lesser golden caviar is sometimes sold these days; mature eggs from young oscietre. But I was once allowed to taste a few grains of a very golden caviar: the occasion was conducted with much secrecy and ceremony and I quickly inferred I was not to ask questions about its origins. The appearance was extraordinary, tiny translucent balls of sparkling gold, like sunlit dew, on a black horn spoon. No lemon juice, or bread, or anything, of course. The first impression was of lightly salted cream and then... of egg, good old hard-boiled egg yolk! Oh the disappointment. I hope this was the fabled golden caviar of the Shahs, which supposedly comes only from exceptionally rare albino oscietre sturgeon and was eaten only by those now-deposed potentates. No wonder they kept it a secret, for it was very much a Persian curate's egg.

The best place to compare each type and source of caviar, and thus to decide your preference, is a caviar bar and restaurant. They have long existed in Paris and open and close in London with diverting regularity. You can be sure those that have lasted serve what they say they serve and in optimal condition.

Caviar was once so commonly made in the United States that New York bars gave it away, expecting its saltiness would encourage a greater sale of beer. Pollution and world wars decreased both the fish and the knowledge. Today someone has done some urgin' and sturgeons are increasingly seen in the rivers of the north west States again. In Seattle you find sturgeon on menus and locally made caviar in bars and restaurants. They are different sturgeons from those found in the Caspian and Black Sea, but sturgeons nonetheless. There are even four caviar-producing sturgeon varieties in the Great Lakes.

The greatest encouragement for caviar lovers is the success of sturgeon farming, now getting well up to speed in California, France and Italy, Bulgaria – even in Uruguay; and in 2004 Bulgaria will export 250 tons of CITES-approved aquaculture caviar.

CITES is the Geneva-based United Nations' Convention on the International Trade in Endangered Species, and it falls to them to strike a balance between protecting sturgeons but allowing the profitable export of caviar.

The greatest problem they have, and that severely affects our caviar enjoyment, is the gross degree of piracy, and because so much of this illegal caviar is eaten domestically there is virtually no way it can be measured. Yet, without some idea of black market exports or the illegal side of the domestic market – thought to be many times the legal market – it is impossible to quantify a safe sustainable sturgeon catch, and thus to quantify export quotas.

The sturgeon is an endangered species all round the world and no country is now allowed to export caviar unless it has a CITES certificate, and none should import caviar without this imprimatur.

In November 2004 CITES published export quotas for that year for Azerbaijan, Bulgaria (aquaculture caviar), Iran, Kazakhstan (Ural river), Romania (including Danube Black Sea Basin) the Russian Federation, Serbia and Montenegro (Danube Black Sea basin) and Ukraine (Danube Black Sea basin) – a total allowed of 120.6 tons, down from 150 tons in 2003. No other country is allowed to export wild-caught caviar during 2004, because they have either not given the required information about their estimated total catch including that of the black market, or the information provided was not satisfactory.

So, there is currently no 2004 Keluga/ Mandarin caviar from the Amur river in China or Russia, and Canada isn't even allowed to export caviar from its Great Lakes sturgeons to the USA. Or vice versa one imagines.

You will come across tins labelled **Ketovia** or **Keta**. This is the hard roe of the dog salmon, common in both Canada and Russia. This 'lesser-caviar' is pink and large and much cheaper. But in candlelight and with overawed friends I have known it presented as the legendary golden caviar with total success.

American salmon caviar is almost certainly from the same or similar species of salmon. But the golden eggs are as big as tapioca and quite salty and fishy – would you eat fishy tapioca?

Considerably more delicious and attractive is small-grained, luminously golden **lojrom**, which Swedes make from the roe of the bleak. It is regularly touted as the new craze in this or that restaurant column but so far has valiantly resisted the dead hand of trendiness,

The Danes, bless them, have given us a black and red 'caviar-type' product at a most reasonable price and not too bad a flavour. Used to accompany smoked salmon or on canapés of thin, buttered toast, it is pretty and expensive looking. Once, desperate for a new idea for a dip for crudités, I mixed a pot of the black version with a little mayonnaise, lemon juice and cream cheese. It was an absolute sensation. Not for the flavour, but for the colour. It turned a bright blue and both children and adults ate it with mixed gusto, and horror. Blue food tends to do that.

These caviar substitutes are made from the roe of something called **lumpfish**, and have brought new meaning to the phrase 'like it or lump it'; you can like caviar but have to eat lumpfish roe.

Other roe than sturgeons' can be called caviar, that of the salmon most particularly. There are exceptionally viridescent **flying fish roe**, a favourite of the Japanese, but they have usually be mixed with violently hot wasabi, and have a determined crunch not a million miles away from having sand kicked in your face; well, not yours, of course, but my early, slimmer days were not fun on beaches.

And that's not all. Russia eats and exports an astonishing array of fish eggs, all of which they call caviar. There's **pike, pollock, herring, perch, carp, cod, hake, salmon caviar, zander, crucian** and **capelin caviar**. This latter caviar is particularly recommended, but that could be because there is so much of it. The capelin, better known as sparling in the UK, is a slim, olive-green fish that grows to about 25cm and is much the preferred food of North Atlantic cod; since the decline of cod it has increased dramatically. Capelin are generally not eaten, unless they are carrying roe, but sitting in the city it seems easier to unscrew a jar of capelin caviar than to wait for your fishmonger to offer pregnant fish.

The United States is highly successful with farmed sturgeon caviar, and also produces amazingly good roes from native fish. Tsar Nicoulai of San Francisco, was founded by Mats and Dafne Engstrom, who first spent years in remote parts of north-east China and Russia learning about sturgeon farming and caviar production. In San Francisco they raise **osetra** sturgeons and sell two types of their roe, a select tawny-brown to grey caviar with a medium to large bead and a smooth full flavour that's often described as creamy, and a brown-black osetra with medium sized eggs that is pretty much the same. Their Siberian osetra caviar is harvested from sturgeons from that part of the world but which are raised in Uruguay. As well, they offer roe from three native US fish. **Paddle fish** give a small grey bead, very like sevruga, and with a 'fresh sea-breeze finish' which I guess warns it is a little salty. **Hackleback** roe (they call it caviar) is jet black, with small eggs and another notably creamy taste. The roe of **whitefish**, native to the Great Lakes, is a gorgeous pale golden colour, with a mild flavour and clean pop to it – a caviar for those who don't think they like caviar. Tsar Nicoulai also flavour this – infusing it with truffle and vegetable juice to make Tiger's Eye caviar, as rich and brown as the semi-precious stone of the same name. Others are flavoured with fresh ginger, with beetroot and saffron, or with wasabi, and best of all these whitefish caviars cost only a few dollars per 25g/1oz. And of course there is bright orange **trout roe** with its medium pop and deep orange **salmon roe** with its big glabrous pop. If I lived in the

States here is where I would buy my sturgeon caviar, not just because it's an intriguing home product, but because it will be measurably fresher and in better condition and that means more delicious, which is the point, surely. Tsar Nicoulai plan to open a caviar café, which will further lift the pleasures of San Francisco and the Napa Valley.

There are seven varieties of sturgeon native to the US West Coast and since the 1980s Marine Harvest has been rearing the US white sturgeon, which can grow up to 800kgs in the wild; they harvest caviar when their female stock is 10 years old or more and now produce first-rate caviar.

Marks & Spencer UK seasonally sell French caviar, farmed on the Gironde river. Traditionally, French caviar was made from sturgeons native to this river but now it's made from farmed Baikal or Siberian sturgeons, the variety from the Amchur river which used to give us Keluga caviar; its delicious small-grained eggs are currently not included in the world's licensed annual harvest from wild sturgeons.

Serving

Sturgeon caviar has two natural enemies and hundreds of thousands of unnatural ones. The first two are air and metal. Caviar deteriorates rapidly when exposed to the air and the finer the caviar the faster the deterioration. It might last for an hour but if it has not been treated properly before opening it will oxidize and sour sooner – much sooner. You should open caviar to the air for no more than the moments it takes to transport it to the table. Those carved extravaganzas of ice into which you are invited to dip at buffets are a pretentious guarantee that the caviar they contain will be awful. Hours of exposure to hot, probably smoky air mean it will first oxidize and then freeze. Next, you should avoid touching it with metal; bone, horn, wood or semi-precious stones are best. On of the star exhibits at London's Victoria & Albert Museum's Fabergé exhibition was a caviar scoop carved from a single piece of amber. Its exquisite simplicity and delicacy was perfectly in harmony with its intended use.

Now for those hundreds of thousands of unnaturalenemies. These are the people who perpetuate the malpractices of our Victorian and Edwardian forebears who could not conceive of food being served simply. Their presentation of caviar with chopped eggs, pickles and, worst of all, raw onion, is sacrilege of the first degree. But it may not have been their fault. When caviar first became fashionable, transportation was slow and refrigeration non-existent. Or, as happened during the First World War, it had simply been stored badly and for well past its best. But serve it with onion to blind the nostrils to the smell, and egg to coat the palate so you can't taste the fishiness and *voila!* – you had your profit and your victims had their status symbols. Those who eat caviar so brutishly reinforce the opinion of others that they don't like the taste, but do like the conspicuous expense.

You cannot appreciate the flavour of caviar or much else with the harsh, acidic bite of raw onion in your mouth. Raw onion masks every other flavour even after it has been swallowed for it clings to the palate, and continues to flavour everything else you eat and drink for some time – that's why it is smelt on the breath for so long, something garlic doesn't do until the next day.

So, caviar should be lightly chilled in its container and then, just before serving, turned into a delicate dish of the finest, whitest porcelain and taken to the table over ice, with a scoop of something non-metallic per person. If you don't have implements of horn or lapis or malachite, then dip into the caviar with your blinis or toast. And make sure you finish every scrap.

Robert Carrier taught me to eat caviar on toast with thickly smeared unsalted Isigny butter, and, as usual, he was absolutely right. Soured cream is also an excellent accompaniment, and at Christmas time I like to begin the main meal with hot saffron-flavoured brioches, a bowl of chilled soured cream and as much oscietre as I can manage. The colour, temperature and texture contrasts forbid anything but festivity. Soured cream is the right thing to have on hand if you are being Russian and serving caviar with small blinis, pancakes of wheat flour or buckwheat. And lemon juice? Well, only if you use the absolute minimum, and even then...

All types of caviar are increasingly used in cooking. Jurg Munch at the Mandarin Oriental began it decades ago, serving fresh Chinese noodles with warm vodka and caviar grains. Now it is seen in French sauces; the best of those I ever had was served with sea bass, freshly smoked in the kitchens of the Michelin-starred Oak Room at London's Le Meridien Hotel, when David Chambers ran the kitchen.

If you have the will and the bank account to cook with caviar, ensure it is added at the very last second.

Storing

Official, CITES approved 2004 exported caviar will have an official sell-by date sometime in 2006. This means 2003 caviar will be past its best towards the end of 2005. There might be exceptions but there are few genuine bargains in legal caviar. Knock down prices on the Internet are likely to be soupy or fishy, both signs they are past their best: they might not harm you but they simply aren't worth the money. As with anything of quality it's not worth the risk – better 50g of something superb than 200g of fishy egg-soup or lumpy sand.

Optimum storage temperature for malassol caviar is -2 C/30F but this does not mean deep-freezing. A deep-freeze is fatal to caviar, reducing it to a sorry salty stew, but unopened tins and jars keep well for several weeks in a domestic refrigerator. As this is usually the way the biggest and smallest stores keep them it is always a bit risky to buy from anywhere that does not have a fast turnover – even then I could tell you a story or two! However you will usually find the bigger caviar agents will deal direct with you, but you pay retail rather than wholesale prices. Once you have your caviar it is important the container is turned upside down every day or so, to keep the oil evenly distributed. Anyone who does not know this and do this should not be allowed to sell caviar. If you are not prepared to go to that trouble, you had better gobble it up. I'll help.

Bullet Power

Blame Japan's Bullet Train. *Mentaiko* is a relatively new Japanese condiment, the roe of walleye pollack marinated in salt and chillies. From 1975 the train's expanding routes helped spread mentaiko's popularity throughout the country to the point where there is now *mentaiko* Yule Log at Christmas. When the roe sac is left whole *mentaiko* looks like a skinned rodent, but it can also be bought sliced or mixed down into a purée looking remarkably like taramasalata.

It was invented by a Japanese couple in Fukuoka, who had grown up in Korea and missed its myeon-granjeot, chilli-hot pickled cabbage (*kim chee*) mixed with cod roe. Originally the chilli-salt-fish product was intended to be eaten just with rice, but *mentaiko* has moved on to be found on pizza and pasta, on potato crisps, in instant noodles – there are even *mentaiko* restaurants, serving such specialties as sea eel with *mentaiko* mixed into a creamy sauce and mentaiko spring rolls. But *mentaiko* Yule Log? Still, it's good to know there is something new under the Imperial sun.

Clams

Baltimore is home to the famous Lexington Market. When I visited it didn't seem American at all, with its noise and untidiness and hundreds of small garish stalls selling everything edible and a few items that, although once falling into that category, were right over the top. It was nice to see Americans being unhygienic about food for a change.

Right at the back of the market was an oyster bar and as we were on Chesapeake Bay, which is famed for all manner of seafood, we had to make our way there. Far more than an oyster bar, it sold all manner of extraordinary fish, sea urchins, a variety of hard and soft shelled crabs plus some skinned animals that I'm sure were possums and others that I think were squirrels, and others...

Around a circular bar, men and women were slurping great raw oysters accompanied by special sauces and ice-cold beer. As well, they were eating clams, raw clams. I'd never heard of such a thing, and when I saw the size of them I still couldn't believe it. You had to cut each in two, at least I would have, but the experts here managed to slip the lot into their mouth, chew a couple of times and swallow slowly with bliss beaming on their faces.

Enquiries and many clam meals later proved that eating clams raw was indeed very common and uncommonly good. Not at all like the tiny things in Italian spaghetti or Japanese tins. In the British Isles you are only likely to be able to buy tinned clams or clam juice.

Canned clams or baby clams: these are essential in any store cupboard once you know them, and can be either Japanese or Spanish. There are far more in each can than you would imagine and almost any brand is good as long as they are in brine or a light soup of their own juices. They are cooked, of course, and can be used straight from the tin with the least preparation, just some lemon juice, perhaps some oil and garlic or a special mayonnaise. But they help all other seafood dishes too. Mix them with prawns to make the usual boring cocktail more interesting, or use them instead of prawns in fish sauces, stuffings and so on. Chop them roughly into batter and make fritters for lunch or serve as an extraordinary accompaniment to roast chicken or turkey, which were once regularly stuffed with oysters. Put them at the bottom of fish soufflés in lots of garlicky butter or stir them into pilaffs of saffron rice. Like all shellfish they toughen if cooked too long, so don't.

Clam juice: you constantly come across this in American cookbooks and occasionally on the shelves of better stores elsewhere. It is the liquor left after clams have been steamed open and is an outstanding stock for fish sauces or fishy flavouring. It makes a fish pie, and finishes a soup or can be the basis of one, cream or otherwise. It is also a rather interesting mixer with alcoholic drinks and is becoming so popular as an ingredient in Bloody Marys that you can now buy it ready mixed with tomato – it is called Clamato, wouldn't you believe?

Crab

America is a marvellous place for crab lovers to be. Either their crabs are more numerous or Americans like the meat more, but you can certainly buy and enjoy crab easily. One of the greatest American treats is soft-shelled crabs. If you see them on a menu, and ensure they have been cooked very simply indeed, order them. They are smallish, 10-15cm/4-6in crabs that have just shed one shell and are waiting for the next to grow. You eat all of them. I sat rigid with disbelief for quite some time in the august New York Yacht Club when told this, for the fact had not been vouchsafed until the creatures were placed in front of me. Once I was able physically to put a fork with a couple of claws and half a shell into my mouth, and that took some doing, I found the effort very worthwhile.

Further south, around Chesapeake Bay, you are very much in crab country and can hardly drive more than a few minutes without being exhorted by billboard and neon to try the 'only authentic' Baltimore or Maryland crab cake. Frankly, I found them all over-peppered and under-crabbed. That's until I was marched back to Lexington Market by Topher Russo and Father Anthony Parker and Gene Sartori and then introduced to Faidley's, which has been selling lump crabmeat cakes since 1886. These are big crab cakes, thick, peppery and solid with satiny crabmeat strands, not like anaemic stamens but as thick as, well, as infant fingers is the best I can come up with. You eat them hot in bread or in a white, brown or Kaiser roll: if you scale up to a platter you choose which roll or bread you want, and then two from fries, collard greens, macaroni salad, coleslaw, potato salad, pickled beetroot, cucumber salad or shredded carrot salad, all with noticeable sugar content. There's ketchup but that's for the fries, and tartare or cocktail sauce for the crab cakes. I can't think there are better or more generous crab cakes anywhere and there couldn't be a better way to enjoy them than standing at a bar with two much loved old friends and a new one.

If you like the idea of crab but don't live in Baltimore and can't face the expense elsewhere, use it as a flavouring rather than an ingredient. In a subtle cream or tomato sauce with some fine white fish fillets or even in a mayonnaise over a seafood salad, a little goes a long way. For the ultimate cheat, use it in a sauce over pieces of gently poached monkfish, which has the same texture and flavour as lobster. Make sure you have a dollop of brandy in the sauce, which is one of the most important ingredients of all in any fish sauce, hot or cold. It makes an extraordinary difference. Crab is excellent with avocado, pineapple, mango and other tropical fruit; a small amount added to a stir-fried mixture of vegetables or of vegetables and chicken will be a triumph. Otherwise it seems almost anything can be a flavouring for crab; in Singapore's restaurants their famed chilli crab relies on masses of tomato ketchup to be authentic.

The problem with buying much of the imported crabmeat on the delicatessen shelf is working out exactly what is inside the pack, frozen or canned.

Dressed crab: this usually means inferior brown meat from inside the shell plus other impertinences have been mixed with a small proportion of white meat, often into a khaki-coloured paste. Even where white and brown meat are both offered and kept apart in products sold as dressed crab, the proportion of white may be distressingly low in the interest of marketability. Buy warily, or do your own dressing.

Crabmeat: frozen or canned, this is usually better value for money as there is unlikely to be any adulteration. Indeed, you may be buying just white meat. Russian and Alaskan crabmeat is considered superlatively good and interchangeable as they come from the same geographical area. Any Russian crab from the Kamchatka Peninsula is sold under that name and this generally signifies the crab was processed within hours of being caught and the can will contain only the leg and claw meat of male crabs, plus natural juices. This is what the USA sells as Alaskan King Crab.

Eel

No one knows a lot about the private life of the eel, except that it lives in the sea and spawns in the rivers; where it lives precisely has never been discovered but it is thought the Sargasso Sea is one of the likeliest spots for European eels.

The Romans liked eel so much they used to farm it, but since then the UK seems slowly to have lost interest in eating it. True, there are still places jellied eel is available, but where are the shops that used to sell nothing else? Englishmen used to catch their own eels and send them to Dutchmen to smoke, who sent them back, expensively. Now with the continued growth of artisan smokehouses all through the British Isles they are prepared from Inverawe in Scotland to Dartmouth in Devon. In the 2004 Good Taste Awards a Norwegian took the only gold medal for smoked eel, which had been hot smoked.

Serving

You can find smoked eels in two forms. First is the whole thing, head, tail and fins included. This has usually been hot smoked: chunks are cut off and you take it home to skin it and serve it quite plainly. Otherwise you will find long, thin, cold-smoked fillets, which are often frozen. Cold-smoked eel is like raw but richer kipper, and is perhaps the least esteemed but one of the best tasting of all fish products, one that always leaves the mouth refreshed and the palate stimulated. Eel fillets go very well with other smoked fish as a starter, they particularly enjoy hot or cold scrambled eggs, and their shape is terrific for decorating such creations as a seafood mousse.

I have been served cold smoked eel with chilled melon and I'm still trying to make my mind up about it years later. Probably not an ideal match.

The Spanish like very baby eel, elvers, which they call *anguillas*. They are white and matchstick-like, and available in small cans. Being pre-cooked they are soft and delicate, with a nutty rather than fishy taste. Drain them gently and serve with a little oil, lemon juice and garlic. Or mix them with egg yolk and a splash of white wine, saké or dry sherry to make fritters, which is how I like them best.

In New Zealand, baby fish this infinitesimally small are what we call whitebait, and whitebait fritters are part of the standard diet. The crunch of the bones and stare of the eyes of the very much bigger European whitebait, which are the fry of herrings and sprats, have turned many a colonial's thoughts to home faster than snow and ice ever did.

When it comes to eels I have to skite, a good colonial word that means to show off or to brag. New Zealand's eels are the most hideous things imaginable and thus are not eaten much there other than by the Maori, who are delighted to have this delicacy to themselves. Or almost. Eel lovers increasingly agree hot-smoked New Zealand eel is possibly the best in the world and it can often be seen at Billingsgate Market, usually frozen. Thicker, fattier and more succulent than small European eels, it is wondrous cold but unctuous enough to survive grilling or other heat. It makes a sensational pâté, mashed and seasoned with lemon or lime juice and cognac, mixed with half its weight of melted but cooled unsalted butter and then folded with lightly whipped cream in the proportion of 300ml/½ pint per 500g/1 lb of eel: the lemon juice and cognac will firm up the cream and the butter set it. Use this as a spread with a choice of breads or biscuits. Fingers of toast or of dark rye bread spread with the pâté and topped with chopped smoked salmon and chopped capers convert the sturdiest disbelievers.

Herrings

Herrings are one of man's oldest foods from the sea; remains have been identified in prehistoric settlements in Denmark, France and Portugal. Native to the north Atlantic, herrings migrate in huge numbers from the polar seas to the English Channel and thereabouts, starting in March.

Each female herring lays some 50 million eggs a year, so it is little wonder shortages were rare until recently. They remain one of the cheapest fresh fish, yet are surprisingly unpopular in the British Isles, perhaps because of their past association with poverty.

Herring flesh is equal in nutrition to that of salmon, and a damned sight moister and more interesting much of the time. There is the problem of the bones, of course, but a little practice licks that. Start at the tail end and pull the flesh towards it, the way the bones point. Anyway, you can eat the bones, and they are very good for you.

Most of the herrings eaten in Scandinavia and Europe are preserved, usually by salting. Today the catch is deep-chilled at sea and mixed with coarse salt in great concrete vats on return. There is a great art to the salting: to be right, the salt should have combined with the liquid straight from the fish and fully dissolve to form a strong brine in ten days. This is your basic salted herring. It is distinctly inedible, but will last for ages.

Smoked herrings must also be salted to some degree, and depending on the exact cure, or the habits of an area, the fish will either be smoked close to the smoke source, which is called hot smoking and slightly cooks the flesh, or they will be smoked where they are not heated at all, and that is cold smoking.

Distinctions between types of salted and smoked herring are easily blurred, but I think the following list will explain most of what you are likely to come across.

British salted and smoked herrings
Essentially the most famous styles of processed herrings are all smoked to a greater or lesser degree.

Bloaters: in spite of today's excellent cold storage and chilled transport systems, these have virtually disappeared because they don't 'keep'.

Bloaters are whole herrings salted for a very short time, in brine rather than dry salt, and then only cold-smoked. The very best are supposed to have come from Yarmouth during October and November and were eaten almost as soon as they had come from the smokehouse. 'The epicure will eat them before he goes to bed rather than wait for breakfast,' said the Wine and Food Society in 1944, when you could still get them. They were grilled or lightly fried and a very few shops in Norfolk are said to make them still. Harrods sometimes have them, but for rather too long.

Buckling: these are lightly brined after having been beheaded and gutted, but they remain unsplit and any roe or milt is left in place. They are hot-smoked and so keep well. Increasingly more difficult to buy, they may be eaten cold or lightly grilled and make an excellent fish paste with just a little butter and perhaps cream, plus mustard. Bucklings were made in other countries; they were originally a German thing, but the similar sounding Dutch *bokking* is a cold-smoked entire fish, and must be cleaned before eating.

Kippers: relatively new on the scene, and probably introduced in Britain little more than a century ago. Kippering is a much older way of treating fish, salmon in particular, by splitting, brining and then smoking. What we called smoked salmon was once called kippered salmon. If either salmon or herring is cooked before smoking it may not be called kippered.

You only have to see one real kipper to be able to detect fakes; real ones have a glorious pale golden glow rather then a dark, treacle-like coating. Only the Isle of Man and a few places in Scotland still make proper kippers smoked over oak chips. Most you buy have been par-cooked by some method to prolong their supposed edibility, and the colour and flavour of the smoke will have been painted on, so they are not really kippers at all.

The only place I have seen a choice of all the properly prepared kippers available in Britain is at Borough Market in London, which operates on Friday and Saturday only. The best time for kippers from the Isle of Man is July and August.

Red herrings: you can rarely buy these nowadays, but they used to be the most important of standbys before refrigeration. Red herrings were highly salted and highly smoked and thus almost indestructible. If you find some, soak them for many hours in milk or water before grilling or poaching. A soft-poached egg, cooked without salt, is a perfect foil, as with so many smoked fish.

Continental and Scandinavian salted and smoked herrings

European processing styles are based on salt or vinegar rather than smoking.

Bismark: these are fresh herring fillets marinated in vinegar with onion, so are fairly rugged.

Fillets: in bulk or in jars, this is the way tons of herring are eaten. The fillets have usually been salted, then soaked and treated in a number of ways. Some go into a red wine sauce, some into a tomato sauce, some are in oil. There are dozens of varieties commercially available and hundreds more are made in the home. The Danish range, bought in jars, keep excellently in the refrigerator; use the fillets as part of an hors d'oeuvre, or slice them small for use in potato salads. They can be mashed into a paste with stewed, or chopped, raw apple and with egg yolk as a simple pâté. Most fillets are called *matjesfillet* (but they may not be, so see below).

Matjesherring: used very generally for all herring fillets or salted herrings but properly means a herring gathered in early summer when the roe is still developing. They may be treated two ways – either lightly brined with some sugar content or heavily brined in the usual way of salt herring. If you are buying them 'straight', i.e. direct from the brine, I think it likely *matjesfillets* have been lightly salted and only whole *matjesherrings* are heavily treated. In either case, soak them in water or milk to remove the salt you do not want. If preserved other than in brine, you will not need to soak them.

They may be eaten just like that, especially the fillets, or perhaps with onion – and in Holland green beans are usual. Or you can then make a marinade, warm or cold, and flavour them according to personal taste.

Rollmops: these are totally eviscerated fresh herrings, the two fillets joined together only by skin. No bone or fins should remain. The double fillets are rolled around pickled cucumber, sometimes with carrot and onion, and kept in an acidic-brine liquid, usually made with a white vinegar. It is easy to play with this idea at home, using spices and apple with cider vinegar for instance. Soured cream, dill and more pickled cucumbers are by far the best accompaniments. Oh, and ice-cold vodka or aquavit. It is said rollmops are a great cure for hangovers but I suspect the accompanying liquor is far more useful.

Salt herring: the basic preserved herring, which must be soaked for at least 24 hours before it can be used. Fillet this and serve it with soured cream, pickled beetroot and cucumber, onion rings, potatoes, hard-boiled eggs, gherkins and decent wholemeal or rye bread. Once soaked the whole or filleted herrings can be vinegar-pickled or put into any number of mustard, tomato, onion or sour cream sauces.

Stromming: this is a *sort* of herring, the Baltic herring, which is smaller and leaner than the Atlantic variety. It is less likely to be highly salted and once soaked is usually put into mild pickles, with mustard and dill sauces or in sour cream and dill – using small amounts of raw onion rather than vinegar to provide any acidity. The Swedes use an acid they call Attika, largely acetic acid and with a pleasant sweetness. All in all I think I prefer the serving style of the Baltic herring to the more fierce German and Dutch herring types.

If you are ever offered *surstromming*, think very carefully. These are Baltic herrings packed with only half the normal amount of salt, and then sealed in barrels that are left in the sun. Alan Davidson's *North Atlantic Seafood* says birds drop dead from the sky when the barrels are opened. It is acceptable to find canned *surstromming* bulging, a sign of proper fermentation. Barrels or cans should be opened in the open air, standing up wind, and with chopped red onion held close to your face, which allows you to get the fillets to your mouth before your nose realizes what is happening. Then quickly reach for water or beer or anything, so you can rinse out your mouth.

Mackerel

Although its cheapness means it is often ignored, the mackerel is quite one of the most fascinating – and delicious – fish there is. Even the reason for its name is bizarre. Mackerel is the English version of its French nickname, *maquereau*. *Maquereau* means 'pimp' or 'procurer', and the name was given because the female makes a point of escorting inexperienced female shad to ripe males; for this, American gourmets, Eartha Kitt and Noel Coward are grateful. When waiters bring shad roe to discerning diners, they bring what is supposedly the most delicious of all roes to table – only caviar excepted. When in the United States, and on the Atlantic coast during winter, it's certainly worth singing for. But, back to mackerel.

The mackerel has a furious temper when in schools, which it usually is, and so brave it attacks fish far larger than itself. Indeed, in Norway there is a story of a sailor being dragged underwater by mackerel while swimming and released ten minutes later bereft of most of his flesh. It is also a stupid fish, and frightfully easy to catch. It has the highest proportion of fatty matter of any fish and thus deteriorates very quickly.

Like so many fish, they spawn in August and September and fresh or smoked mackerel should be avoided then. In October they start putting on condition and by December are quite perfect. I tend not to rate tinned mackerel of any kind or provenance, especially the ghastly smoked mackerel pâtés, which are overburdened with *farinacea* (as, in my opinion, are most

English-produced seafood soups, but perhaps you have better luck). Many mackerel products come from abroad and are thus a slightly different and always inferior species, by common consent. The Spanish or horse mackerel is much bigger and more coarsely textured.

Naturally smoked English mackerel is a world of its own, and when good surpasses any smoked trout I have eaten. The boned, smoked mackerel fillets – flat and torpedo shaped – that are the staples of many a wine bar, are overcooked and then artificially coloured and smoke-flavoured, a process that often reduces the flesh to a gummy paste. But, when you find mackerel whole, with only the head and gut missing, their skins a pale, iridescent gold rather than lurid copper, well then you've found the real thing – almost certainly from Cornwall and quite superb. When buying them, avoid a slimy skin (which will actually be poisonous) and go for something firm but not rigid.

Interestingly, mackerel may be sexed at sight; those with wavy lines on their bodies are females, those with straight lines are male, and much tastier. Always good to know if there is a lull in conversation.

Serving

Smoked mackerel is best served quite simply and it is cheap enough to allow ventures into pâté making or mousses, which I don't normally hold with in something of this quality.

Whether serving a whole or a half smoked mackerel, you should take the spine out. This is simply achieved by first extending the slit in the gut right back to the tail. Then with the point of a sharp knife gently fold the top half of the fish back, having a pair of poultry scissors on hand to cut any intransigent bones. You can now lift out the whole backbone and it remains only to remove the finer ones that are still around the stomach cavity.

For basic serving I like them slightly chilled, served with lemon wedges and a good, creamy horseradish sauce, which is indispensable when presenting mackerel in any form.

Cubed beetroot, raw or pickled, also goes exceptionally well with smoked mackerel. For a stunning but simple buffet presentation, arrange boned halves of smoked mackerel like the spokes of a wheel, with the pointed tail ends in the middle. Pile cubed beetroot in the centre. Pipe horseradish cream down the centre of each mackerel half and sprinkle this with a little sweet paprika. Fill the space between each fish half with trimmed, thin lemon wedges and large sprigs of parsley. This is especially popular with men, who fall upon its hearty flavour with relief.

You can lightly grill smoked mackerel, which then need something quite sharp to accompany them. I would suggest spiced red cabbage and a purée of celeriac, into which you have stirred a lot of finely chopped parsley and garlic. Great on a boring winter's day for lunch or supper.

The most common use of smoked mackerel is for making a pâté, more a fish paste really, but whoever decided it should be combined with cream cheese? For years I made such a mixture for my delicatessen customers, and felt sick every time I did – a horrid idea with a nasty colour and, often, a disconcerting texture too. Eventually I found the alternative, canned kidney beans. Whizz together a couple of large, skinned and boned fillets with two or three small cooked beetroot. Then add 125g/4oz of drained cooked red kidney beans until you have a good rough look: pulse in a teaspoon of horseradish to taste, then spoon out and fold in a small carton of soured cream, or crème fraîche. Dribble on some olive oil when you serve it with lots of roughly torn parsley.

Smoked mackerel seem immune to experimenters so far, and the only variation found is fillets with lots of black pepper pressed into the surface and their engaging liveliness is highly recommended if you are going to eat outdoors.

Mussels

In New Zealand, mussels are huge, so huge that after de-bearding and de-tonguing they must be cut in half, at least. They have a certain rugged appeal, I remember, but cannot ever equal the sweeter delights of the smaller European mussels.

Now, somewhere between those types we have the Kiwi green-lipped mussel, recently, renamed the green-shelled mussel, for it is indeed the lip of the shell that has the green colour and someone got very worked up in the trade descriptions department. These mussels arrive in Europe cooked and still attached to shells that do indeed have jewel-like iridescence on their edges. They are farmed, processed and cooked within minutes of being harvested, and then deep-frozen. Some are smoked and specially good. You will see there are two colours, a rich buff cream and bright orange; these are not different varieties, but sexual difference. The pale ones are male and the orange are female. Sexual confusion has no place in that country. Increasingly available, green-shelled mussels are good just as they are in salad and seafood platters. If used in hot dishes they must only be warmed through as they are already cooked and will shrink and toughen if heated further.

Although available packed with flavours ranging from tomato to onion and pickles, or with vinegar, I find mussels canned only with brine and their own juices by far the best. They are usually from Scandinavia, Norway's Limford being perhaps the best source. They are exceptionally useful, not least of all because they have enough size and colour to make a contribution to the eye as well as the tongue.

Serving

Pasta salads seem particularly good receptacles for ready prepared mussels. Seafood sauces to put into pastry cases or to complement poached fish fillets are much more interesting with mussels than with prawns.

If you follow my instructions for cooking rice, add some saffron and use the juices from a tin or bottle to make up the cooking liquid. When the water level reduces to that of the rice, lay the mussels on top of the rice, then cover the saucepan and proceed as usual. They will be steamed to a succulent softness, any juices they lose being transferred to the rice. When it is ready, stir gently with a fork and you have a supper or lunch dish that is attractive, filling and satisfying.

Deep fried in a decent batter, heated in hot butter, garlic and parsley, tossed in a dressing with orange segments and foam-white mozzarella cheese or served in a hot white wine sauce on rice, mussels are worth your attention if they have so far escaped.

By far the best way to enjoy small fresh mussels is the *mouclade* of the south-west coast of France. Fresh mussels are piled on a plank on the sand with their mouths pointing downwards. Over them you build a huge pile of dry pine needles, and some time before you expect to be hungry set them alight. They burn furiously, to nothing, and in so doing cook the mussels just enough to open them. The ashes can then be swept away and the mussel then enjoyed, perhaps with a slight smokiness to complement their natural salt-sweetness.

Oysters

It would be possible to write an entire book on oysters, and I suppose someone has. It certainly sounds rather fun being an oyster. They all start life as males and from time to time equivocate and then become females, or is it the other way round? Anyway, they have no need to read modern novels to understand equivocation. In the UK oysters were once a staple of the grateful poor, as was salmon, and not so very long ago. Now like many simple local foods they have become rare and expensive and are likely to be served fancifully and badly.

The oysters of most European and American sources have been transplanted, cross-bred and artficially brought on to a degree that has eroded some of the ancient clear-cut distinctions of flavour. Most fishmongers who still sell oysters on the shell couldn't tell you what type they are. A far cry from France, where in the tiniest inland markets fish stalls offer a choice of eight or nine varieties for prices that seem far too low. The one really to go for there is the *verte de Marenne*, which is a bright, curious green – my hat goes off to the early human who was first brave enough to put one in his mouth.

The original European oyster, the native *ostrea edulis* is immediately recognisable for having a flat and only lightly ridged shell. This is rare, for it has been decimated more than once by disease. It was first replaced by the *portuguaise*, which isn't a true oyster but *gryphea angulata*, and, when that too succumbed to disease, by a Japanese variety, *crassostrea gigas*, often called a *creuse* by the French.

America has a wide variety of interesting oysters, some of them bordering on the monster-sized and sometimes offering quite different flavours just because you have driven around a headland to another beach. Coastal towns and cities make much of their local seafoods and you can usually get good advice and buy specifically to your taste or preferred method of eating or cooking. I was once driven to Petaluma in California to buy huge oysters, at least 15cm/6in long and surprisingly deep. When we got back to San Francisco, my host Fred Baumeister turned the oven onto maximum heat, poured me a drink and said he was off 'to find the other screwdriver'. When he came back the screwdrivers were set beside plates. The whole oysters were carefully arranged with their curved side down in a baking dish, so they supported one another. Then in to the seriously hot oven they went, just for the few minutes it took for the muscles clamping together the shells to be overcome. The screwdrivers were to help prise off the top shell to reveal the treasure inside. Barely warm in their briny juices, only slightly cooked here and there, the oysters had plumped their heat-insulted flesh so erotically they could be eaten only with silent introspection. They tasted like whipped cream through which an essence of salt-oyster had been magically threaded. I've treated screwdrivers more respectfully ever since.

In Australasia the choice of oysters is more limited but those who know rate the rock oyster of the eastern Australian coast as amongst the most succulent in the world. They have the added advantage of being equally suited to cooking. Even better to those who have had the experience is the Bluff oyster, dredged from the sea floors south of New Zealand. There's not much delicacy about the first burst of flavour, but then that goes on and on like an insistent *tsunami* determined to batter down your senses until you recognize the amazing ethereal qualities of the experience your palate is being bullied into accepting. They heat well too. The last meal I cooked before I left NZ in 1965 was done in a rush. So I bought half a fillet of beef, slashed and stuffed it with Bluff oysters, baked it in oceans of good butter and then served it with an apology. Fast food wasn't the thing then.

Smoked oysters, which usually come in tins from Japan and are eaten by old bachelors with as much relish as spinsters eat soft roes, are delicious. But they are often ruined by being served in the filthy cotton seed oil in which they are preserved. They should be fully drained and then sprinkled with the smallest amount of lemon juice. For special occasions I would take the trouble to pat them dry of oil with kitchen tissue and then present them in a nice, gentle lemon juice and oil mixture.

Smoked oysters may be treated with a little more abandon than the ones that come canned in brine or stock. Minced or chopped, they go a long way to flavour sauces for garnish or filling puff pastry cases. You can make the most of their flavour to replace bacon on skewers of seafood for your grill or barbecue.

Smoked or brined, canned oysters which have been well drained are very good plumped and warmed very gently in a lemon-sharp white sauce, to serve with poached fish or chicken. They also make an outstanding stuffing for beef and are a simpler way to recreate the cornmeal and oyster stuffing that is so good and American with turkey. They perfectly add the proper touch to authentic Lancashire hotpot (well, all right, they shouldn't really be smoked for that, but you know what I mean) and nicely finish a steak and kidney pie the old-fashioned way; best plan is to put them on top of the cooked meat mixture, so that their salt-savour is the first thing you smell when the crust is cut.

Pilchards

Often described either as a type of herring or a type of sardine, the pilchard is cleverly both.

A timid member of the herring family, it is actually an adult sardine, and thus by any measure good and fatty and delicious when fresh. They are a specialty of the Devon and Cornish coast between July and December but great care is needed when buying them, as they spoil extremely quickly. I'm not fond of tinned fish, a feeling particularly reinforced in the case of pilchards by seeing how many people buy them to feed to their pets.

A little known Cornish specialty is salted pilchards, and until the advent of farmer's markets they were in danger of disappearing. Up until 2005 there was one factory making them in Newlyn, and like its predecessors of the past few centuries they still exported barrels of whole salted pilchards drained under pressure of their oil, to Italy, where they are known as *salacche Inglese*. The company also makes and sells salt pilchard fillets in oil.

Serving

The most famous dish made with fresh pilchards is the variety of stargazey pies of the West of England, which can be several shapes and sizes, all noted for being baked with whole fish whose heads protrude from their pastry cases. This is done to incorporate the rich oil from the head in the finished pie, without covering the heads with pastry, which would make eating difficult. You'd be lucky to get stargazey pies of any kind these days, dead lucky if they included pilchards, whole or beheaded.

We are most likely to eat canned pilchards whole as part of an Italian mixed antipasto and should present them to doubters as grown-up sardines. The type in tomato sauce, mashed with a little vinegar or lemon juice and soft butter, or cream cheese if you must, can make a fish paste to go nicely on hot toast. Chopped capers, olives or anchovies, those enchanted saviours of anything else fishy, might all help.

Salted pilchards are apparently eaten just as they are but any amount of dressing with oils and vinegars will work additional wonders: in Italy the whole salted ones are eaten in salads.

Prawns and shrimps

Although different from one another, prawns and shrimps look alike enough to be called by one another's name. In the United Kingdom you are usually safe calling little ones shrimps and big ones prawns. In America they are all called shrimp, but the giant Pacific variety, a favourite ingredient of many American menus, are often called prawns for the saké of alliteration.

Canned: I am constantly astonished at how good canned prawns can be, and how cheap. Perhaps those from Malaysia can be a disappointment for they are often shrimps, tiny and floury. Usually, though, tins are packed full of moist plump, pink, crustacea, their shells removed. The initial outlay might seem high for such a small object, but the value for money is comparable with frozen prawns.

Frozen: there are several pitfalls and pieces of advice to heed when buying frozen prawns. Some types are free-flowing, that is, each prawn has a protective ice-glaze. This means you are paying for water rather than seafood, and in the case of some Indian prawns, the water is highly salted. I have ruined a very fine sauce for 100 people by adding these prawns frozen, liquid and all.

It is important to defrost frozen prawns very slowly, or you lose flavour, texture and moistness. The best way is to leave them in their bag in the refrigerator overnight. They will then be moist and plump and have retained most of their natural juices. If they are then to go into a hot sauce, first bring them to room temperature. Then they can be popped into the sauce just for the few minutes needed to cook them or heat them through. They do not need to be piping hot and the sauce should never be boiled.

You should carefully consider the size of prawn you want to use. Generally larger ones look better and they behave better if they are to be served hot. Prawns will inevitably shrink when cooked or when reheated. If cooked or heated for too long they will also toughen. Indeed, unless you are buying cooked prawns and they are to be used for stuffing something elegant, or pureed, or used as a garnish, bigger is always far better.

I do not understand the combination of avocado and prawns; both are bland and often even have the same texture. If you want something pink and green, then peel and cut some kiwi fruit into segments (not slices), soak those in Pernod for a while and serve your prawns on them with a mayonnaise flavoured with fresh lime juice and grated lime peel.

You can also extend prawns with cheaper seafood, especially mussels, as long as they have been canned in brine rather than vinegar. The two are especially good in pasta sauces, or in hot sauces to stuff vol-au-vents. Other flavours which go well with prawns are horseradish, tomato, garlic, basil, ground cumin and coriander, sweet or hot paprika and, of course, cucumber.

Potted shrimps: ones you buy commercially are very good and easily copied at home; they have simply been packed in butter flavoured with a little spice, mainly mace. But they should be served warm, with the butter in glistening pools. It makes me angry that famous fish restaurants, unable to make potted shrimps themselves, cannot read the labels on the ones they buy frozen and serve them ice-cold with limp toast made from plastic bread.

A Prawn Pâté

To make a truly excellent prawn pâté or spread, liquidize cooked prawns with half their weight of warm melted butter. Add white vermouth to taste. Let cool. Then whip some cream in the proportion of 300ml/½ pint to 250g/½lb of prawns. Gently fold the two together, keeping as much air in the mixture as possible. Add a little white pepper if you like. Fresh or dried dill is a most refreshing addition, and you might also like a squeeze or two of lemon juice or a touch of brandy. If you want to use less cream, substitute half the amount for curd cheese, cream cheese, or cottage cheese you have sieved.

Roe

It will come as a shock to many a spinster to learn her favourite supper of soft roes is the milt or sperm of male fish; but perhaps this explains their popularity. It's certainly a deliciously wicked thing to reveal as they are being enjoyed, and can quite spoil the most determined appetite, male or female. It is the hard roe that is the eggs of girl fish. Roe of both sorts are popular right round the world. In the Occident, the general agreement on flavour, excepting those mentioned in the caviar section is, in ascending order: mackerel, herring, and then shad and carp equal first. Most of the soft roe sold in fish shops or in cans is cod roe, but it can be herring, too.

Greeks are especially partial to the eggs of the grey mullet, and this is the proper basis for *taramasalata*. But try telling that to the shrill-accented debs in striped aprons behind a thousand deli counters. They'll dish out a pink paste by the hundred-weight and swear it's better than they had in Corfu or Kos or Katerini. It'll certainly be *different*, for although smoked cod's roe is a good substitute for that of mullet, this style of *taramasalata* is really only an emulsion of low-grade bread and oil with some little amount of roe and a great deal of colouring. When we made it properly (albeit with cod roe) at my delicatessen we sold it as fast as it could be made until the cod war put up the cost of the roe astronomically.

Much the most expensive of roe products is *botargo* (*botargue* in France), which is salted and pressed whole roe, again properly of grey mullet but sometimes of other fish. This is one of the oldest and simplest delicacies and, wouldn't you guess, inevitably one of the most expensive these days. It is found in many Mediterranean countries but belief in the disinfectant and protective qualities of the salting and drying process is ill-founded. When travelling companions of mine bought *botargo* from a street stall in Suez, we soon knew in which little room to find them the next few days. As *botargo* is eaten uncooked, perhaps with oil and lemon, you also eat whatever contamination it has collected. Most definitely a case of buying only the highest quality from the most reliable source.

Serving

Smoked roe, usually hard cod's roe, can be dipped in batter and fried, chilled and served sliced with light vinaigrette dressing, placed on toast and covered with a well-seasoned white sauce – but it really is rather too strong for most people's taste. It's better as an addition to a fish sauce or a garnish to something relatively bland of a fishy nature. There is one exception in my experience and that happened in New Zealand.

There you can buy the firm smoked roe of both snapper and blue cod; the latter when smoked was described by Andre Simon as being like Finnan Haddie gone to heaven. Served unpretentiously in thin delicate slices, accompanied by a perfect light vinaigrette and a garlic mayonnaise, it was worth getting off a jet to experience.

Salt Cod

Salt cod was the most important staple flesh of the medieval Catholic world, and continued so for much of the time after the introduction of Protestantism. During the long, universally observed Lent and the twice-weekly fish days, salt cod kept the wolf from the door. For the sake of Christian observance, millions of tons of cod have been pulled from the waters of the Atlantic and it was in search of bigger harvests that the first English colonies in the New World were established. In fact, so important was the catching and salting of cod to Massachusetts they incorporated one in the design of their Great Seal of the State.

As Catholicism gradually lost its grip on Europe, and the great explorers introduced new foods, salt fish became less and less important in Britain. Just as well, when you ponder the problems caused by latter day over-fishing and the struggles for territorial rights that led to the unpleasant cod wars.

Now, the past importance of salt cod to our ancestors is hard to believe, considering the difficulty of buying it in the United Kingdom. West Indian communities usually have shops displaying the dried, crusty sides hung from the ceiling. And one enterprising company is now pre-packaging smaller amounts and these are available at supermarkets where there is an ethnic demand. Good Portuguese, Spanish, Italian and Greek shops should also sell it. Sadly, like herrings, it is considered too cheap to be fashionable, yet it is commonly published as well worth the attention of any true gastronome. Maybe I am a false one, for I have never yet enjoyed it, not even when it was specially soaked and washed over three days for me; there remained a back taste I found nauseating, but perhaps it's the fault of the truculent trait of my palate that is revolted by goat cheese when others are smacking their lips.

There is a Norwegian salted cod called stockfish, which is especially popular in Germany, Belgium and Holland; you may treat it as if it were ordinary salt cod.
Ling: is the name given to the largest variety of cod, and as this is the type usually salted, salt cod was once known as ling a point to remember when using old cookery books.

Serving

Preparation of salt cod requires some forethought, as it should be soaked for a full 36 hours in several changes of water to hydrate and desalt it. Unless you also think it foul, a 24-hour treatment will probably suffice. When soaked, you drain off the last water, then put the fish in a saucepan with masses of cold water and bring the lot very slowly to the boil. It should now simmer, with the water barely moving, until the flesh flakes easily. It must never ever boil again, so if you have a large cooker like an Aga, even better results can be obtained if you simply leave the saucepan, once it has boiled, on the back where there will be just enough heat to give the desired results; that is what Icelanders recommend. If you haven't planned ahead you can put the dried salt cod in cold water, bring it slowly to the simmer, change the water and repeat the process several times. But it won't be as nice.

The classic English way of presenting salt cod is predictably boring, for it is simply boiled and served with a sauce of hard-boiled eggs. It is only when you start looking at the kitchens of Brazilians and Portuguese, the Spanish and Creoles that salt cod appears to be remotely exciting. In Provence they make a warm, fluffy paste of olive oil and potatoes and milk and salt cod called *brandade de morue* but even that can be foul: it's superb made with smoked fish instead.

Salmon

All salmon is not salmon, well not the same variety anyway. Atlantic salmon, farmed in the UK, Norway and Tasmania, is considered best, for its flesh is the most elegant of texture and flavour. In compensation four main varieties of Pacific salmon are thought to have a greater variety of use – nothing cans quite as well as the Canadian pink salmon.

The major change in salmon in the past two decades has been the extraordinary growth in farmed salmon in the shops, which in turn also means smoked salmon and more recently fashionable gravadlax are also cheaper and available to more people than they used to be. That is a good thing you might think, but others hate the very idea of farmed salmon and consider it irredeemably inferior. There are differences between them and wild salmon, that's for certain.

You can generally tell one from the other if the fish are whole, for wild salmon will have bigger, wider tail fins with a deeper curve of the fan, the result of having to fight to swim harder and further. If wild salmon are caught in an estuary or only a short distance up a river they will be superb eating, rich with fat and fully fleshed. They rarely feed in fresh water but live on stored fat and then their own protein, and so the further up a river they are caught the less good their condition, and the drier the flesh. Some few salmon are known to survive the breeding season and then to stay in fresh water, feeding again. They must be a rare treat. Otherwise, if a salmon has been caught early in the day, not instantly refrigerated and then battered in the back of a car, well, it's obvious they will not be as good as they might. For many, this is all they have ever known, out of condition fish that have been mishandled. Yet to them anything different is considered inferior.

Farmed salmon are harvested only in tip-top condition, immediately chilled and carefully shipped. They will invariably have a softer textured flesh than much wild salmon, but this is because they are fatter, in better condition: the argument is that fresh, farmed salmon is actually what salmon *should* be like.

The farmed salmon industry is fast learning the environmental effects of its activities on the remote waters they use. Some dreadful mistakes have been made, but monumental effort has made this a very important industry, bringing much needed jobs to otherwise barren areas. The farmed salmon's feed contains substances that replicate those in their natural foods that turn their flesh red; there have been scares about this, but they were exposed as wildly inaccurate. Some salmon farmers offer organic salmon to the market, fish fed only natural products and reared in a way that does not affect the environment too profoundly: others are farming in great cages miles off the coast, and this certainly prevents the build-up of excreta that has been such a problem in lochs and bays. Organic farming and sea cages might seem a solution, until you see organic salmon that is barely pink – what point is there in being organic if you're nothing like the real thing?

Now the world has been given it, farmed salmon cannot be taken away. Norway is a major producer and much of the smoked salmon in the UK is made from them, raised in deeper, more exposed fjords and coastlines than the UK. In NZ they farm Pacific salmon and some are having second thoughts, for complaints about the high-fat content are rumbling ever louder. It's dangerous to say as a native New Zealander, but I think they should have done what Australia did, and chosen the Atlantic salmon. Farmed in the cold waters of Tasmania, which are almost identical to those of NZ's South Island, Atlantic salmon produce a firmer and more elegantly fleshed fish altogether.

Canned: I clearly remember the first time I saw salmon in cans in shops. It was from Russia and it must have been in the early fifties when the Russians were, to us in New Zealand anyway, something terrifying and to be supplying us with luxuries was thought a bit much. Nonetheless it was with great relief that I found we were one of the first families to eat it, and it was wonderful. Later everyone was eating Russian salmon like mad and it seemed less appealing, even though it was only the finest red salmon being imported. Later still, the taste for tinned salmon rose to its pre-war level and cheaper pink salmon flooded the market. Shocked at its easy availability, I stopped eating both colours on the pretext I was sick of it and never touched it for almost 20 years, when I found a Robert Carrier recipe for an Easy Tinned Salmon Soufflé. I was prepared to laugh – you may still – but it turned out to be excellent. Of course, one had to add a little of this and a little of that, but it remains one of my most basic standbys, is the bringer of some of my greatest compliments, and has the appeal of being all the better for the use of cheaper pink salmon.

If you come across little white crystals in your canned salmon that look like glass, they

aren't. They are a harmless chemical called magnesium ammonium phosphate, which is the sort of thing that can occur naturally in man in the tartar film on teeth. You can check these crystals are not glass by squashing one between a fingernail and a hard surface. Glass would not crush. The substance is also known as struvite and dissolves in the digestive juices of the stomach with no harm to the ingestee.

Gravadlax/Gravlax: what a meteoric rise this product has had, essentially a sweet-cured salmon flavoured with dill. When I prepared it on BBC television in 1982 only travellers to Scandinavia and food freaks knew about it. Today it is in supermarkets, well almost for the commercialization of gravadlax has inevitably led to changes and some isn't the real thing at all.

The original product is whole sides of salmon smothered in salt and sugar and flavoured with crushed white peppercorns and masses of fresh dill. As the method was for preservation as much as anything, it was buried (the name means buried salmon) in the cold winter ground and the pressure of the soil contributed to the slow release of liquid and compression of the flesh. The released liquid would then dissolve the salt and sugar and then their flavours and preservative properties would be carried back into the flesh. If you made it domestically you would merely put a weight on top of the sandwiched sides. The flesh becomes firm and translucent and is generally recognizable on a buffet because it retains dill on its outer edges and is always cut in very short slices that are wider than deeper.

Although much that I taste from pre-packs is certainly edible, it is softer than that I would make, presumably because less salt, lighter pressure and higher moisture content has been allowed, in the interest of greater income and profitability.

One of the most interesting products recently released on the UK market is Romanov gravadlax salmon: this is cured like gravadlax with peppercorns and dill but with the addition of beetroot , which stains the flesh with a random marbling of striking magenta . Once cured it is lightly hot smoked with apple wood, which sets it up as a new base camp somewhere between the foothills of traditional gravadlax and smoked salmon. Even if there is confusion about what to call it, this new product delivers what it promises – you can taste the beetroot, and it looks wonderful. As you do, the manufacturers say it is made to a recipe wrested from the jewelled fist of a Romanoff Grand Duchess, or from some wretched retainer's death bed, or some thing. But it's not the only smoked gravadlax about; indeed a cold-smoked gravadlax from Norway, again, won the gold medal at the UK's 2004 Great Taste Awards.

If you like spending lots of money on yourself, then Balik, who have reinvented smoked salmon, make *sjomga*, cured with biologically grown dill and lightly smoked. Their unique cut and trimming method means there is no silver skin, so every slice is all salmon; like their smoked salmon they reckon it best if sliced vertically.

Experimenting is rife. There are versions of gravadlax guaranteed made with wild salmon, and of these the Irish ones are worth ferreting out. In Miami you'll meet a Cuba Libre version, cured with rum and Coca-Cola. That would certainly make one wild, Irish or not.

Make your own Gravadlax

To make your own, 50g or a few ounces each of coarse salt and of sugar, a good scatter of crushed peppercorns and a big bunch of dill will do nicely for two sides. Dried dill is very good and quite indistinguishable from fresh when it comes to it. Most of the mixture should be evenly spread on the naked flesh, which is then sandwiched head to tail. Sprinkle half the remainder on the base of a suitable container, add the fish and then the rest of the pickling mix. Cover with cling film and then a board or use another of the same flat-bottomed containers and then weight that: I reckon on two or three times the weight of the fish.

Leave at cool room temperature for 24 hours, turning the fish a couple of times and spooning the pickle that is being produced back between the sides. Then chill for two or three more days until all the pickle is dissolved and the fish is firm and evenly compressed. Scrape away most of the dill and pepper that is left, wrap tightly and keep chilled. It will keep well for a week or more.

Slice rather more thickly than for smoked salmon, and cut at a very steep angle right down to the skin to get the traditional shape, but should you wish to cut it like smoked salmon, nothing horrible will happen. Indeed this is easier to present. I twist the pieces slightly and form a ring on a flat plate with them. Into that I put some mixed salad leaves and a few shelled hard-boiled quail eggs. If the pickle is not too salty, a puddle of this is good, and then I sprinkle the lot with a little vodka; a pepper vodka or vodka in which you have macerated fresh green or dried black peppercorns and dill is particularly good.

Do not hesitate to substitute something else for the dill. Both mint and parsley are very successful, but not quite as wonderful as using rather a lot of finely sliced fresh ginger, an East-West marriage I expect would once have earned me titles and country estates in both hemispheres. As it is, I give it to you, and you should make as much from it as you can. Somehow the flesh is turned a brighter, more fascinating colour and together with the distinctly oriental flavour offers much opportunity for creative presentation. I usually stop at poached arcs of cucumber and a few quail eggs, but now I know about it I reckon I'd also offer a crinkly pile of benign pink, pickled ginger, the stuff you eat with sushi.

Gravadlax is eaten in Scandinavia with a sweet mustard sauce that I think is intrinsically disgusting and anyway, does nothing but harm. Dill cured salmon is best just by itself, with a little soured cream or with soured cream mixed with mild seed mustard.

Some recipes include cognac or vodka in the pickle but these cannot overcome the amount of salt and sugar and are thus wasted; if there were enough to defeat the salt and sugar they would turn the flesh opaque and change the flavour, neither of which would then be true gravadlax. Sometimes spruce sprigs have been included and this is very good.

Hot-smoked: increasingly popular, this is cooked salmon that has been smoked at the same time; in fact it is often sold as roasted smoked salmon. It is not pre-salted to any degree and thus it is thicker and flakier that cold-smoked salmon, more like the fresh fish would be. With care it can be heated and served warm – the microwave is by far the best way to do this without damaging the texture or drying it out, and you can even do this on the serving plate, which saves accidents ex-kitchen. Warm is definitely better than hot, because then the oil is running and whatever else you can throw accusingly at farmed salmon it's definitely true they are much fattier than a wild fish.

Serve a small amount as a first course with mustard, horseradish or a smart, sharp salad of ingredients not normally seen, like fiddleheads, or wild asparagus or the very best tiny rocket leaves, but include potatoes as a sop for the oil. Or flake into big pieces to serve instead of tuna with the same ingredients as a Salade Niçoise. Hot-smoked salmon makes a filling and gratifying main course when served with anything made from potatoes – a mash with a truffle oil, baby potatoes not cooked with mint but turned in fresh mint after cooking, a potato salad vivid with mustard and pickled vegetables. For the extreme end of comfort food, you should over-bake a large potato, that's to say for at least two hours so the skin is crackle-crisp for almost a centimetre deep, and then cut the potato in half lengthwise but not quite through the bottom skin. Loosely break up the hot-smoked salmon and put this into the chasm, and then top with soured cream and flat leaf parsley, and perhaps put some lemon or lime wedges on the plate. A decent dab of caviar doesn't hurt.

As with smoked salmon you'll find organic versions, and these are doing very well in competitions. There are some extraordinary variations out there too, and most are far better suited than when they appear on cold-smoked salmon or gravadlax. A few worth mentioning are lemon-smoked, coconut & lemongrass-smoked and Thai roast. There will inevitably be more.

Smoked salmon: rightly regarded as one of the world's greatest delicacies, but it's not the same as it was, and may not ever be again. The proper term is kippered salmon, as kippering is what is done to it: the salmon are beheaded and gutted, split, salted and then cold-smoked. The kippering process and name was only applied to herrings some time last century.

As with all old-established food processes there are many variations: some smokers will cook the salmon a little before smoking it, which is not true kippering. Some will hot-smoke it. Some will burn one type of woodchip and some will use others.

There are two traditional styles of curing and smoking, the Scotch (you are allowed to say that rather than Scottish if it is salmon or whisky) and the London. The London processing of salmon was long in the hands of European immigrants, usually Jewish. Because their market was on their doorsteps, they cured lightly and smoked lightly. Salmon from Scotland had to endure three or more days transportation by stage coach before it was sold, and for safety was thus salt-cured and smoked much more heavily, the Scotch cure.

Today, London curing can hardly be called traditional, because there are such strong laws about smoke emission; computer-controlled mechanical smokers do it without exhausting smoke into the air. Mechanics rule in Scottish establishments of size too. What with that, vacuum packing and modern transportation it means anyone can smoke to any style they like and the result will have many weeks' life. Add to this clever-dicks who salt the salmon far less, so the flesh retains more liquid and is therefore softer, and there you have an overview of the problem: smoked salmon made from a farmed fish that's flesh is softer than traditionally wild-caught salmon, flesh which is not salted enough and so has not firmed up further, and thus, squidgy, lightly salted flesh which is then barely smoked. Plenty of money has been saved and will be made, because the yield is better than it used to be. But, there's little to taste of the salmon or salt, and virtually no smoke flavour. Serve a blindfolded diner a thin slice of such 'smoked salmon' and they are hard put to identify what's in their mouth. Young people with their eyes open think that's the way smoked salmon is supposed to taste.

There are small smokehouses, in Scotland and Ireland particularly, that still smoke salmon and other foods by hand and eye, the old way, and you will find they universally favour a firmer flesh, and a more savoury smokiness. If you find one, encourage them, by buying.

The best Scotch smoked salmon is dark persimmon-red and firm in texture; when it is cut, it should be slightly transparent and waxy. The smaller fish, the grilse, have a more delicate flavour and need to be sliced slightly thickly. Only the larger and more mature adults have enough flavour in them to be sliced finely. But if you can find a wild Irish salmon that has been smoked you are much more likely to get excellent texture and flavour and a balanced smokiness that is present but dominant: you should share such a treasure with the young or soon smokeless pap will be accepted as the norm

I found something else, at Borough Market, of course. Applebee's wild salmon was line caught in the Baltic. It was barely pink but this was natural. The smoking was a joy to see, neither treacle-thick nor gruel thin, but a superb golden wash over the skin you knew had been put there by smoke and not by brush. When I sliced it, I stepped back thirty years to the first days of Mr Christian's, for the flesh barely moved under the knife; it had been salted enough to firm up the flesh. The taste, a truly noble balance of salt, salmon and smoke came with a texture that slightly answered back in the mouth and that needed nothing else. How I wish you could all experience this. How I wish the rest of the world's producers of squishy, bland 'smoked salmon' could be made to learn from it.

Canadian smoked salmon you will find to be redder, ruddier and coarser in colour, drier and coarser in texture, and denser, too. You might find it saltier, for it is expected to last longer, what with having to be transported either across Canada or across the Atlantic. The major difference is the variety of salmon. These are not Atlantic salmon but four varieties of Pacific salmon. Coho, pink, sockeye and king may all smoke well but the pink and coho are generally the ones you find. Think of it as smoked salmon, yes, but different smoked salmon. Really, there is nothing wrong with Canadian salmon other than being overcharged for it. And if you are catering for a lot of drunks, or family friends who haven't much knowledge of these things, it is a waste of money to serve the best wild Scotch or Irish smoked salmon.

A newer player in the field has completely rethought smoked salmon. With yet more references to secrets from the kitchens of the Tsars, publicly revealed only 25 years ago, Balik smoked salmon even looks different. Rather than a side of smoked salmon you buy just the heart of the fillet, a long, flattened 'D' shape trimmed from the fattest part of each side. The trimming also removes the silver skin, giving absolutely unblemished flesh that glows with imperial superiority. It is lightly smoked (in Switzerland, but in the tradition of the court of the Tsars, of course) and once complete and ready is not sliced the usual way but vertically in slices about 1cm/$\frac{1}{2}$ inch wide. It costs a great deal but when I lashed out a few Christmases ago and flew back to NZ with one, I wished I had bought two and then walked home. It tasted every bit as courtly and elegant as it looked, and it looked nothing like any smoked salmon anyone had ever seen before. Thus, enchanting the eye so completely before a mouthful had been enjoyed, it made us all feel we should have dressed up a bit more, perhaps even worn shoes. There is a version marinated in a porter beer, too.

To slice

Mechanization has also taken over one of the most satisfying things I have ever done, slicing smoked salmon to order. Now it comes pre-sliced which is some guarantee of freshness and quality I suppose, but it's hell to peel the slices apart and generally much more oily. Slicing smoked salmon is not difficult; only getting practice is and you'll never do anything more gratifying, even if only once a year for Thanksgiving or Christmas or Hannukah or Diwali.

When I was training others in Mr Christian's Delicatessen, in the days before you could so easily buy smoked salmon ready sliced, I found there are those who can and those who can't slice salmon, a gift easily discerned by watching those same people cut anything else. A man or woman who cuts a crooked slice of bread, or who always manages to crush bread while cutting it, does not understand knives. People like this think pressure is what cuts and will not let the knife edge do the work. Try it. Hold a knife lightly and instead of pushing the blade through, let the blade slip through the bread as you go back and forth with only the lightest pressure. You'll get a thin, even slice and, unless you can do this, you'll never be able to cut smoked salmon finely, although frankly I have never understood the appeal of thin slices. Thick slices are much more rewarding to eat.

If you are presented with an unboned side of smoked salmon, this is what you do. First, cut off the fins and remaining bones at the bigger, gill end of the side. Now put the salmon on the edge of a table or draining board, skin side down, and using a fingertip, ease back the skin around the edges. If you can, peel it back under the flesh a little. Now slice off that peeled-back skin, including the soft foundations of the fins, all the way along to the tail. Next you have to attack the fine bones imbedded in the flesh. Keeping a long, thin knife horizontal, take a thin slice off the highest part of the salmon, not much more than the smoked 'crust', starting at the gill end and working towards the tail. As you slice the smoked layer away you will, or should, expose the tops of the tiny white bones, which is what you are going to remove; if not, rub the back of the knife along the flesh from top to tail, using a little pressure, and the bone ends will pop up through the smoked crust.

The best tools are an eyebrow tweezer with pointed, ribbed ends or a pair of pliers that have a long thin nose. So as not to tear the flesh, don't pull each bone out by yanking up vertically. Instead, pull gently in the same direction the bones lie. Once these are out you can start slicing and there are two ways to do this.

Short slices: in this method, which is the easier of the two, you start slicing about one third of the way along and slice towards the tail. (I know Selfridges slice towards the other end, but they are the only people in the world who do.) The knife should be only very slightly angled and aimed so that you are cutting in towards the skin. Each time you take another slice you start a sliver further back and keep the angle the same and soon you will have a slice that starts at the top, goes through the flesh and ends up at the skin and is say 10cm/4in long: this is adjusted to be longer or shorter by keeping the knife more horizontal or more angled. As you continue this method you will have no wastage, because some of the darker flesh close to the skin will be cut and served with every slice.

Long slices: you start at the gill end and slice all the way along with a horizontal knife, trying to get slices that are as wide and long as possible. It is certainly very satisfactory to be able to slice a large salmon in thin tissues that could simply be laid one upon another to form the entire shape again. But this can only be contemplated privately or in catering when you know you can use all the fish. In a shop you tend to get left with the last layer of darker flesh, which, because you can see the skin through it, looks unappetizing. Indeed, if it has been waiting for a customer for some time, it will be dried and possibly rancid. If you want to serve and sell long slices, you need to charge rather more, to compensate for what will be left on the skin.

Presentation

Although it is the custom to serve smoked salmon with slices of lemon it really is too awful to spray it with such sharp liquid, for this immediately masks the delicate flavour that so many have laboured to create; if you are serving the worst of the modern stuff you will taste only lemon. Neither should smoked salmon be too cold, for this will also mask the flavour. To get the absolutely best flavour from smoked salmon take it from the refrigerator about half an hour before you wish to serve it, leaving it wrapped. Instead of allowing your guests to squirt lemon juice over it, rub each plate with a cut lemon wedge or a little grated peel, which is better. The perfume of the lemon juice or zest will soon penetrate the flesh with altogether more delicious results.

A disquieting but all together better idea is to sprinkle on neat gin or vodka, particularly if the latter is one of the flavoured types. You get just enough bite to contrast with the fish and the smooth texture of the alcohol is strangely complementary; many of the subsequent compliments will be equally weird.

I shouldn't have to say this, but the American custom of serving smoked salmon with raw onion is barbarity. It makes me seethe to see decent hotels and restaurants pandering to requests to serve it like this – perhaps they aren't such good establishments after all? Raw onion buries all the best flavour of the smoked salmon, indeed if you need onion it could be you don't even like smoked salmon. Except so far you haven't ever tasted it.

HRH The Prince of Wales is said to be happiest of all when comforted by a dish of scrambled eggs and smoked salmon, a man of regal taste indeed. For a really marvellous starter for an important meal, roll smoked salmon around cold, creamy scrambled eggs to make a stuffed horn, and sprinkle the overflowing egg with black caviar, real or otherwise. For hot scrambled eggs, you simply slice the salmon into fingers and throw it over the eggs as you are serving them or lay it on the toast on which the eggs are presented.

A very small amount of smoked salmon makes a wonderful addition to sauce for quite plain fish. It transforms cauliflower cheese, if there is not too much cheese in the sauce: better is to make a cheeseless wine and cream white sauce, and meanwhile to tuck buffalo mozzarella between cooked cauliflower florets, to strew these with smoked salmon strips, and then to pour on the sauce, sprinkle liberally with breadcrumbs mixed with lemon zest and chopped parsley and then bake until very lightly browned. You might be happier doing this with more robustly flavoured hot-smoked salmon.

Storing

Smoked salmon freezes and defrosts extremely well and provided it is allowed to do the latter slowly, can be as good as fresh, but, like all other frozen foods you only get out what you put in.

There are now a number of vacuum packs of smoked salmon on the market and they are an excellent way to transport and store salmon at ambient temperatures; however refrigeration will extend the life of such salmon even further. Be assiduous in protecting the plastic from puncturing and only accept those that are tightly bound to the fish by vacuum. If there is the slightest looseness anywhere in the packaging or, worse, ballooning, the vacuum has been broken and the fish may be harbouring and nourishing a great number of organisms that may be dangerous before you can smell them. Otherwise an unwrapped, uncut side of smoked salmon will keep for ages in a refrigerator if air is allowed to circulate; ideally it should be hung. Even a cold larder is cold enough to keep smoked salmon sides good for weeks. That was the point of the salt curing and the smoking.

Sardines

For a while you could almost forget sardines as a delicatessen product. I had calls from all round the world from people wanting me to get sardines in olive oil from Brittany. 'You know,' they would say, 'the ones you mature for a couple of years, turning them every few months.' There are very few traditional sardine canners left in Brittany, and for a long time the market taste moved. Thank goodness you can't fool all of the people all of the time. Although sardines do indeed come embalmed in countless horrors, they are increasingly available in olive oil and we must all buy as many as we can so they are not endangered again. The price range is tremendous, but all do improve with age and are the better for turning, which keeps the oil evenly distributed.

In fact, only refined olive oil is used, which is almost tasteless and even very superior canners in Portugal have told me that after six months in the can, sunflower oil gives virtually indistinguishable results and flavour.

There are three ways to test whether the sardines you have cherished have been worth the effort. When opened, none of the skin of the top ones should adhere to the lid; this means they were too fat and badly chosen or packed. When you scrape back a little of the skin you should see a wine-coloured layer, indicative of fattiness and flavour. Now turn back a fillet. If the flesh is white and creamy, the sardines were caught and processed quickly; if it is pink or red-tinged they were frozen before packing. The consensus is that it takes six months for sardines to mature in the can and they can improve for another six months. After that the packers say you should eat them up and replace them. Well, they would, wouldn't they?

Serving

Eat them direct from the can on hot toast, mash with a tiny amount of sherry vinegar to do the same thing, or grill one side of thick, fresh white bread and then turn it over and put sardines on the untoasted side. Put this back under the grill and bread will soak up the oil and juices and sizzle and brown with them. Simple but splendid. More so with a chilled fino.

Sprats

Not often seen, but when you find smoked sprats from Baltic countries, give them a try. They make a welcome change when arranging mixed seafood platters.

Sturgeon

Traditionally, the sturgeon is 'royal'. The first one taken in British waters each August to March season is given to the sovereign, and this was done in 1978 when one braved the polluted waters long enough to get caught. It's a shark-like migratory fish, living in the sea but going into fresh water to spawn. It's best known in the Caspian Sea and around North America, where it grows to well over 6m/20ft. It's much more interesting than that; it's one of the few species of fish found in every ocean and it's been that way for aeons, for like the crocodile and the tuatara, sturgeons are largely unchanged since prehistoric times.

The female's roe is caviar; its air bladder makes isinglass, an archaic type of gelatine that the Swiss Family Robinson used for windows.

The royal status of sturgeons is both ancient and universal. Throughout Imperial China commoners forbore to eat it, reserving it for the palate of the Celestial Emperor, who then cunningly used it to tempt other parts of his favourites. The Roman Emperor Severus had it served honoured with coronets and serenaded with musicians; Alexandre Dumas suggests doing this, too. It needs razzmatazz, for the firm flesh is difficult to prepare and present tastefully. Strangely, one is counselled to hang it for some days. Then it tastes like veal and is often cooked in exactly the same manner, served with the same sauces.

We less-than-royal mortals are more likely to see it smoked, but rarely. The flesh is still very firm but tends to crumble, so it benefits from being served with a little excellent oil. I've only eaten it at a London West End hotel where their prices gave the impression our small party alone was expected to reimburse the establishment for its new décor. The smoked sturgeon was insensitively inundated with too-sharp vinaigrette. Voluble displeasure brought new, untouched slithers. With the merest whisper of oil and zephyr of lemon zest it was quite delicious – but not quite as delicious as smoked salmon.

There is a case for using expensive smoked salmon to make exorbitant smoked sturgeon go further. Arranged in rosettes of alternating colour, the pair make a luxurious start to a meal. Fresh dill weed and a delicate cucumber mousse would be better and prettier than parsley with either or both.

Trout

The trout belongs to the same group of fish as salmon and the many types of trout divide broadly into two groups – plus one type that devilishly spans both. Basically, either trout migrate to and from the sea, or they don't.

The pretty rainbow trout confuses these categorizations by living in fresh water lakes but migrating up their incoming rivers to spawn. It is a native of California but has now been established with enormous success in New Zealand, Chile and Britain. The American brook trout is actually a char, as is their Dolly Varden trout. Brown trout are considered better sport, but are not as good to eat.

The smoked trout you buy in countries where they are taken in the wild and smoked naturally is superb. But I cannot help thinking the creatures we buy here, which are both farm-bred and then artificially coloured and smoke-flavoured, are pricey for the pleasure they give. Still, they are a basic component of many a menu and probably better than avocado and prawns. But you have to be very good at coping with tiny bones, and such difficulty can outweigh any pleasure the hard-won flesh might eventually give the victor.

Now there is something else of the same name in the shops; this is the flesh of farmed trout that have grown into comparative monsters and then been cured liked smoked salmon, kippered in fact. It looks the same and has very much the same texture and flavour as salmon, but there is a price advantage, and it's very easy to find and very good in New Zealand.

Flavouring of smoked trout is on the increase, so expect to find it smoked with garlic and dill or even, cold-smoked.

Serving

The small whole smoked trout you buy in the UK are hot-smoked and thus cooked through. You should always peel away the skin before presenting one, and it's churlish to serve less than one per person. A little lemon and freshly ground pepper is adequate accompaniment, perhaps soured cream too. The adventurous will enjoy grated raw beetroot or horseradish in the soured cream. If you have the time and skill you might like to take the trout off the bone and arrange it in strips with some of the more esoteric salad vegetables; I think raw fennel lightly dressed with oil and lemon excellent with trout. Flavoured mayonnaises go well too; perhaps present a choice of tomato, fresh herb and horseradish flavours. Alternatively, serve the trout plain but with thin soldiers of brown bread spread with a variety of flavoured butters, which are simply made and keep for ages.

Tuna

Now the world appreciates netting tuna kills mammalian dolphins and that most canners have agreed only to line-fish, this truly delicious fish is back on the menu. Like sardines, tuna is subjected to all manner of iniquity in cans, packed in totally unsuited mediums. Go for brine packed rather than a vegetable oil and then you will get the best advantage from drizzling with olive oil, or incorporating it into a salad with a decent dressing.

The rarest type of tuna is the albacore, which has very pale flesh and is sold in the United States as Chicken of the Sea. This is no hype, for the flesh is quite as useful, more finely textured than other varieties and very delicious indeed. Spanish packers often include it in their range too, in smaller packs. I'm always grateful to find it in a specialty food store; indeed it is one of the first things I look for when I am making comparative judgements.

Lomo of tuna is a thick air-dried fillet of tuna, enjoyed and served very much as a superior ham might be. Smoked tuna, increasingly seen, is made the same way as smoked salmon, so the flesh is firmed up by being drained of salt before the smoking, leaving it translucent and firm and particularly delicious.

Appetisers and Savouries

Anchovies are more usually used as a flavouring than as a main ingredient, but not so when it comes to appetisers or savouries at the end of a formal meal – then their piquancy is most fully appreciated. Here are some ideas.

To make anchovy butter, mix 15-25g/½-1oz butter with each pounded anchovy fillet. Only you will know how strong you like it.

Soak about 20 big Pruneaux d'Agen or Californian prunes in cold water overnight, dry them and carefully pit them by opening down one side. Then, pound the yolks of two hard-boiled eggs with 25g/1oz of butter and some anchovy paste or essence. Pass this through a sieve then pipe it into prunes, making a nice swirl, or just spoon and thumb it in while soft. Decorate with one anchovy fillet cut into thin strips. Spread the remaining stuffing on small pieces of toast and put a stuffed prune on each. Serve with good watercress.

Anchovy-stuffed mushrooms are a very simple and very good idea. Mix pounded anchovy fillets, anchovy paste or some essence with cream cheese, fromage frais or ricotta then beat in one egg to each 125g/4oz of cheese. Put this into peeled mushroom caps (they don't have to be too big) and bake in a dish until the cheese has started to set and the mushrooms are well heated through. If you can get your hands on some smoked salmon pieces, mix these into egg and soft cheese as above and then sharpen the flavour with anchovy. Very glamorous as long as you don't use too much anchovy and have the smoked salmon chopped very small, almost to a paste. This might be finished in pastry or on toast fingers.

Fruits, Vegetables and Nuts

These are the goodies that make eating so much fun.
And so they should, for we have had more practice with them
than anything else.

As hunters and gatherers the seasonal progression of wild fruits, vegetables and nuts kept us going between the feasts of meat; indeed without these we could never have gathered the strength to go hunting at all.

Modern transportation and genetic manipulation mean more and more produce is available fresh all year round but there remains a place for other types in every diet and every store cupboard. Canned or dried fruits and vegetables often offer flavours, textures and colours quite different from the original. And nuts are increasingly important as part of the vegetarian choice; luckily we no longer have to squirrel them away for a rainy day, but can enjoy them exactly when it suits us. If only to gather strength to shop for more.

Canned and Bottled Fruit

Canned foods have changed dramatically for the better. No longer useful just for inferior fruit salads or for quick meals for children, new techniques often using lower temperatures mean canned or bottled fruits are increasingly good to have in the store cupboard. These are extremely useful as a short cut to making traditional foods, say, ice creams or baked puddings. When you want a quick pie filling, look for tins that say 'solid pack'.

Apples: you might have to experiment, but the cans I have been using lately are superb, for not only is the apple unsweetened but the segments are nicely shaped and firm. As a blank canvas for you to paint flavours on you couldn't want better. And when the apple is dished up under pastry or a sponge, steaming hot, spiced and buttery, there will be few who could tell you took the easy route to the orchard. One of the best pies, with either a double or single crust, is apple segments mixed with fruit mincemeat and a little mixed spice, dotted with butter; just before you put on the top, zest a sweet orange directly on to the filling. Superb hot or warm and quite the best for eating outdoors, when cold.

Apricots: strangely, canned apricots often have far more flavour than fresh. Now I know why. Apricots, like pineapples, cannot ripen any more once picked, hence the lottery every time you bite into a fresh one. Canned ones are tree-ripened. With a little lemon juice, and perhaps some crushed macaroons or amaretti, which are flavoured with apricot kernels, they make an excellent pie or crumble filling and when puréed with orange zest make wondrous ice cream.

Bilberries: usually found in bottles from Poland and that sort of country, bilberries grow wild in Britain but are neglected. They are related to the blueberry, but smaller. Use them wherever you see a blueberry mentioned – with waffles, in batters, on ice cream, in ice cream, in soufflés, or as a sauce for soufflés. They may need dressing up with sweet spices, with a little liqueur or citrus juice, and also like a combination with vanilla. Or simply thicken the syrup with cornflour, return the fruit and bake between layers of pastry, with thick slices of apple and lots of cinnamon and nutmeg.

Cherries, black: such a bore to do yourself, and the higher quality canned ones, ready stoned, are just what you want for filling chocolate cakes, mixing with chestnut purée and whipped cream, or heating in red wine or brandy with bay and a little spice to serve with pork. Puréed, very slightly thickened with arrowroot or cornflour and then flavoured with black rum, they make a sensational chilled sauce for profiteroles.

Cherries, morello: red and less sweet than black cherries, morellos are thought better by some for inclusion in chocolate cake fillings. They are tastier in their sharp way, it is true, and are certainly much better for making pies. Drained of most syrup, added to white wine, heated with spices and slightly thickened with cornflour or arrowroot, they make an attractive sauce for pork, duck or chicken; sharpen with lemon juice at the last moment.

Cranberries: fresh or defrosted cranberries last for weeks and weeks in a refrigerator and thus make a remarkable treasure chest to plunder from time to time. They go directly into bread doughs, especially with nuts, stuff muffins and scones wonderfully, enliven any pâté or stuffing you can think of and can be popped into any number of sauces just before serving, and I've used them to add interest to apple pies and apple sauce.

Cranberry sauces made commercially are generally not bad but much sweeter than they need to be. To make your own, there are several simple rules. First, eschew water and use red or white wine together with some orange juice and a little very finely grated or sliced rind. Next, cook the cranberries only until they just begin to burst. Include some spice, preferably a cinnamon stick which can be removed, and most important of all, add sugar only after the berries have begun to open or you will toughen the skin. That will give you a sauce so much nicer than anything you can buy.

It is a mistake only to have cranberries with turkey. The homemade sauce is excellent with ham, with duck, with well-flavoured, garlicky sausages, and it is perfectly marvellous with hot or cold tongue.

But why do most cranberry sauces find themselves served cold? Pop yours into the microwave or into a bowl over boiling water and it will be very much more delicious. And don't stop there. Add green or roasted black peppercorns, a cinnamon stick, mace or lemon zest. Add black rum, vodka or whisky. Add fresh or dried mint to serve with duck or lamb. Add juniper berries or gin (at the very last minute) for hot tongue, goose or guinea fowl. Stir in grated orange zest, a little cardamom and cognac – for almost anything. There, I'm sure you have the idea.

A perfect gift at Christmas time is uncooked cranberry relish: whizz up fresh or defrosted cranberries with an equal weight of raw unpeeled apple, oranges and lemons which are washed and de-pipped but still with skins intact and a small amount of celery leaf. Leave overnight in a refrigerator, stir well and only then sweeten to taste, perhaps adding alcoholic spirit too. Then bottle and leave a week or so before use, still refrigerated. It will look pale but gets redder and softer as time progresses. I think it is best fairly rough, but you can make it as rugged or sleek as you like. It lasts up to a month or more, protected both by the sugar content and the very high vitamin C of the cranberries. Chopped toasted nuts, fresh pineapple, currants, or for really special friends, raspberries, may all be added.

Gooseberries: they will have lost their colour and much texture but a purée of canned gooseberries, strained, is the basis of a good, quick fool especially when given a lift with cinnamon and grated lemon or orange. I never purée fresh gooseberries for a fool, preferring simply to mash them slightly, which gives a far more fascinating result – every mouthful different and anyway, Jane Grigson believed the word 'fool' came from the French *fouler* which means to crush, rather than to purée. The blander canned ones, and the strange texture of their skins, make a less successful fool of this style than fresh, in my experience. The canned ones are too sweet to use as the base for fish sauces.

Greengages: occasionally seen from France. If they are very small they make an interesting accompaniment to cold hams and other summer meats: let them marinate in an elegant vinegar first so they seem slightly pickled. Or they make an excellent sweet purée for frozen or cream desserts. In French they are *reines-claudes*.

Kumquats: fragrant, citrus-related fruits, eaten skin and all. They make unexpected garnishes, or fruit salad contents, when used with great discretion; particularly good scattered over or through soft red fruits. Fesh ones make a great condiment; quarter lengthwise, de-seed and cook until tender in orange juice. Sweeten only then.

Lychees: generally as good canned as fresh, with almost the same texture – improved by being slightly chilled. If you liquidize a drained can of lychees, strain that, and then reduce the drained sugar syrup from the can over heat until you have just five or six dessertspoonfuls, mix these together and then flavour with a little rose water, you have the makings of a show-stopping sorbet. This is all the better for being re-beaten during freezing and then you should fold in a whipped egg white, which improves the texture. Drained of syrup and sharpened with lemon or lime juice, or soaked in vodka or dry sherry, lychees may be used as an ingredient of stir-fried Chinese dishes or served with roasted duck. But they are superb by themselves, helped perhaps by rose water, which has a remarkable affinity with lychees.

Mango: it is only worth buying mangos in tins if they are from India and are of the Alphonso variety – at least, that is so if you wish to use them as is. But for ice creams, fools, sauces and so on, other varieties, where the texture is less important, may be used. This most beguiling of all fruit makes the most bewitching of all drinks, which I call a Moghul Fizz – liquidize some mango, using lime or orange juice to get a light texture, whisk in a very small amount of clear honey. Put into a tall glass and top up with champagne or sparkling wine.

Paw paw: essentially the same thing as papaya. I don't think canned paw paw works. However it can add interest to a tropical sort of fruit salad but only when fresh passion fruit is also present; another wondrous affinity.

Pineapple: although a world away from fresh, some canned pineapple products are most worthwhile when treated with interest and care. I think the yellower, sweeter pineapples from Hawaii and from Malaysia are well worth paying extra for, if asked.

Crushed pineapple, a standby of cooking and eating in Australasia, should be a basic in any store cupboard. Drained (or otherwise) it can be used in cakes, in batters to make pancakes or fritters, or thickened with spices and butter to make sauces sweet or savoury. It can be set with gelatine in flans or on cheesecakes, or used in cheesecakes.

Plum Ice Cream Recipe

A can of Victoria plums is the basis for perhaps the most successful of hundreds of recipes I gave on BBCTV Breakfast Time, at least judged by the number of requests we had for it. You pour the contents of a 500g can of the plums into a sieve and save the syrup. Force the plums through the sieve using the back of a soup ladle. Now whisk a very well chilled small can of sweetened condensed milk for a few minutes and then add a small carton of double (heavy) cream and keep beating until it looks like lightly whipped cream. Fold in the plum purée and flavour with two or more tablespoons of lemon or orange juice. Cinnamon, ginger or cardamom make good additions. Freeze. The reserved syrup may be reduced over heat and served warm or cold, but will of course be fairly pulsating with calories The recipe works with 300ml/½ pint of any sweet fruit purée, and should you use canned apple sauce, cinnamon, some raisins and breadcrumbs fried in butter you will have an apple strudel ice cream to die for, by which I suppose I mean for which to die – you'll forget your grammar too when you taste it.

Pineapple has a special affinity with gin, and drained crushed pineapple mixed with gin makes a very special hot pancake filling; you could even flame gin over the top, too. Butter-fried pineapple rings or chunks make an unusual but popular addition to bacon and eggs but are more likely to be found with baked pork chops, roasted pork or chicken, spread with a little mustard for more interest; they are always popular when singed by the barbecue and added to outdoor hamburgers. This is better than good if you grind black pepper coarsely onto the pineapple, another unexpected but reliable flavour affinity that gives back more than you've put in.

When decorating cakes with pineapple pieces, it is also an idea to drain and marinate them in gin. It adds much flavour and contrasts better with the sweetness of the cake and icing.

Plums: pureed plums, of any colour, make good bases for fools, ice creams and sweet or savoury sauces. Spiked with a little red wine vinegar and mellowed with a little tomato purée, a lightly spiced plum sauce is tremendously good with any light meat, game or fowl. It's a sort of smooth, instant plum chutney. Add brown sugar if you like, and include a little ground clove.

At the other end of the meal, even canned plums blossom with a dash or two of mirabelle *eau de vie* and a slice of ice cream or custard sauce. Canned plums are good for pies and sponge puddings and crumbles, but remember they are already cooked so keep cooking times to an absolute minimum.

Soft fruits: most soft fruits do not react well to processing. I cannot understand why anyone would want to buy canned strawberries or raspberries, which have artificial colour and little resemblance in texture or flavour to the original fruit. Some of the darker berries like loganberries and boysenberries are better. I once slightly thickened the contents of a tin of loganberries and served them as a hot sauce to a hot chocolate souffle. There was rose water in one and black rum in the other, and they were superb. The best bets are frozen berries, individually or as a mixture, another absolute standby always in my freezer.

White peaches: expensive and seasonal, and apparently an appreciated Christmas present with the older generation. These are delicious and as few of us have ever eaten a really good one fresh, can be enjoyed just for what they are. I was once served a slice of white peach on a slice of freshly cooked foie gras but there wasn't enough of either really to taste properly; but it's something to which I'll return. Whizz up the white peaches into a thick syrup and top up with champagne or sparkling wine to approximate the famed Bellini cocktails of Harry's Bar in Venice – they use fresh ones and sparkling Muscat, like Asti Spumante.

Dried Fruits

Important sources of sweetening and of sugar during winter for our ancestors, dried fruits are a most ancient food. Today there is some chemical assistance likely to improve colour or keeping qualities, and often they are dried without the aid of the sun at all, but the basis remains unchanged – preserving fruit by reducing the moisture content thus allowing the natural sugars to act as a preservative.

Apples: one of the most useful of dried fruits as they retain their Vitamin C content. 500g/ 1lb of dried apple is the equivalent of 3-4kg/6-9lb of fresh fruit. They rehydrate nicely, often becoming rather fluffy and therefore good for purees. They are also a good stretcher of other fruits in pies, crumbles and so on. They can be rather rubbery when dried but chopped into smaller pieces make a worthwhile addition to muesli. Much better to look for a very modern idea, apples dehydrated by a technique that makes thin crisps that are a perfect snack food and excellent as something to crumble over breakfasts or desserts.

Apricots: always dried without their stones, whether whole or halves. 3kg/ 6lb of fresh fruit yields 500g/1lb of dried. I once found them drying under trees in Ibiza, directed thence by the wondrous scent on the air. They were tended by one of those black-swathed Mediterranean women. Now that site is a hotel or two. Apricots are more often dried in hot air after having been exposed to sulphur dioxide, which gives a brighter colour. My favourite dried fruit, it often tastes better like this than when fresh. The greatest of all snacks, pie fillings or breakfast fruit. Thin slices improve muesli more than anything else I can think of.

Bananas: these usually come from South America and are naturally sun-dried. 1kg/2lb of bananas makes 250g/½lb of dried ones. Golden brown, very sweet and chewy, they are an addictive snack, but can lead to a fairly determined loosening of the bowels.

They may be soaked in water overnight and eaten with lemon and orange juice plus brown sugar – again black rum would find itself most welcome. Chopped or sliced they make a fascinating addition to any cereal, hot or cold and can be chopped and used as any other dried fruit in breads, cakes and puddings.

You can also find long thin chips of crisp, dry banana, creamy coloured, and coated with honey. If you don't mind the extra sugar they are terrific at breakfast time.

Dates: Iraq alone grows 400 different types of date. They contain so much sugar that even the dried ones are sticky and moist, and they last for years after picking.

The Iraqi dates you most usually eat are the *Halawi* or the *Sayir*; from Tunisia or Morocco it is most likely the *Deglet Noor*, but it is not often you have a choice, so that may be useless information.

To many people dates are cloying and filling and so you should serve them in small amounts. They really are most enjoyed when offered as a sweetmeat after a meal, or as a very high energy booster snack when doing something exhausting like climbing a mountain or sailing. I don't much like dates that are filled with marzipan or cream cheese, but lots of people think they look nice. The only occasion I have used them in cooking was to recreate a Moroccan recipe that was also current here as a Lenten dish in medieval and later times.

You take a nice big baking fish and clean it thoroughly. Then cook some rice until it is just done and drain it well. When it is good and dry, mix in some ground almonds, cinnamon and a touch of sugar. Stuff some dates with this mixture, and close each with a smear of butter. Put the dates and as much extra rice as will fit into the cavity of the fish and sew it up or hold together with toothpicks – sewing really is better this time.

Put the fish in a baking dish with a little water, smear it with butter, and sprinkle with more cinnamon and bake under foil. You can sprinkle onion over the fish and lay it on a bed of onion, which will make a more savoury liquid for basting and for pouring over the finished dish. It is very good. Interestingly, this sticky-sugary type of date is not that upon which desert nomads can live with the addition only of milk. That type of date, starchy, crunchy and with little flavour, is called a bread date.

Figs: I don't wish to pry, but if you think you have private problems, spare a thought for the fig. Figs have their flowers inside their fruit, and the palaver that they and certain wasps have to go through to get fertilized makes each fig a miracle of sexual perseverance.

The Smyrna or Turkish fig is one of the most popular varieties for drying, originally named for the town through which most were exported from Turkey, now called Izmir. They are best known for their assistance to the constipated and useful as a snack but little used in cooking except in baking.

Peaches: generally the least common fruit in mixed packets. If they are soaked only in water they can seem floury, so I always use orange juice and that is a great success. They are especially good when subsequently grilled, which caramellises them here and there. I sprinkle them with rose water and orange flower water whilst still hot and serve them with a decent vanilla ice cream or let them cool and put them onto meringues with a little cream.

Pears: there are two places I've especially enjoyed these. In Alsace they turn up constantly in savoury dishes of meat and game, and I often put them under chicken or game birds while roasting, so they swell with the cooking juices.

Prunes: these are dried plums and now the Californians have taken to producing them, have changed out of all recognition. Rather than those hard, small things of yesteryear we have jumbo prunes and soft prunes and ready-soaked prunes and goodness knows what else.

If you must eat them for breakfast, then add a little orange juice or spice to the water you use for cooking, and serve them very cold.

The very finest prunes of all are the French Pruneaux d'Agen and it seems a pity to muck about with them, but people do. Carlsbad plums are actually prunes and, like the best of dried fruits, meant to be eaten at the end of the meal. They are available in wooden boxes but are so expensive they must be eaten instead of a meal. Poles provide us with something even better and even cheaper. They are called plums in chocolate and are stoned small plums (which is to say prunes), filled with a delicious soft toffee and coated with chocolate and decoratively wrapped. They make stunning gifts because everyone expects them to have cost far more than they do.

A purée of cooked prune makes excellent sorbets and ice creams; you can flavour it further with orange or a little praline, add egg in the usual custard-making proportion and then bake it as is or in a pastry flan case.

Prunes are common in stuffings, but you will probably prefer them as an accompaniment when treated this way, something I found in *The Guardian* over thirty years ago. Take some prunes and cover them with red wine; add cinnamon, mace, a clove or two, a sliver of orange peel and, most important, quite a few bay leaves. Let this cook for a long while, gently, until the prunes are plump and the flavours have blended. Complete the flavour by adding brown sugar or redcurrant jelly if you think sweetness would be an improvement. Remove the prunes and strain the spices from the sauce. Serve hot or cold with game, ham, tongue, duck or goose.

Sweet Ginger

Preserved or stem ginger in syrup is one of the great mysteries of Christmas. Everyone seems to be given it, but almost no one knows what to do with it, other than to slice it onto ice cream. In fact there are many uses. Preserved ginger in slices, or chopped, together with a little of the syrup, is delicious on melon and far better than the silly idea of using powdery ground ginger. It is equally good with fresh or poached pears and can be used for baking in a host of ways, with apples and pears, with peaches, with soft fruits in pies, sponges or crumbles. It is also very good with chocolate sponges; in fact if you put pears and ginger at the bottom of a chocolate sponge mixture you will turn out a memorable pear, chocolate and ginger upside down pudding; this looks better when baked in a ring mould.

Fine slices are a nice addition to any fruit salad, and can be added to homemade ice cream, sliced or chopped, especially when also flavoured with honey. The syrup itself is equally useful for some dribbling onto hot fruit, pancakes or cakes as a moisturizer, or it may be used to mix an icing sugar.

Preserved ginger can rarely be used in savoury cooking, but might be included where there is already a mixture of sweet and sour in the sauce, or where the meat is very fatty, say game, ham, duck orwith goose. But fresh green ginger would probably be better.

See sushi ginger page.

Vine fruits: it is thought the Egyptians discovered they could dry grapes in the sun, and what a good thing that turned out to be. Dried vine fruits have eight times more invert sugar than other types of fruit: as invert sugar is predigested sucrose, ordinary white sugar, the body is able to use it very quickly, hence the usefulness of such fruit as snacks when you are labouring or

Fruit Vinegar Pickled Fruit

A few small bottles of spiced summer fruits, kept chilled in the refrigerator, take little time to make and are an excellent adjunct to meals both simple and super. Although I've specified fruit vinegars in the recipes, wine vinegar would give equally interesting results and cider vinegar is particularly good in this sort of thing. It is important to leave on the skins as they impart colour to the preserving liquid.

500g/1lb firm peaches, plums or pears
1 cinnamon stick
8 dstsp white sugar
2 dstsp pickling spice
300ml/½ pint raspberry or strawberry vinegar

The fruit should be only just ripe and nicely firm. Rinse them under running water. Dry and then cut into four, six or eight segments, according to how big each is. Put the other ingredients into a pan and bring to the boil very slowly, to extract maximum flavour. Cover and simmer gently for 10 minutes. At this stage you can strain out the spices if you like, but I usually leave them in.

Add the fruit segments and simmer for 5-8 minutes, according to firmness. Spoon the fruit into a sterilised screwtop jar, and then pour over the liquid. Store in the refrigerator for at least three days before eating. I have kept them in perfect condition for four weeks – they may have lasted much longer but by then they were eaten up. Serve them solo as a fascinating pickle or slice and add to salads or to mayonnaise.

Options: if you want the fruit to last longer, cook them for only three minutes, which keeps them firmer, of course. You will need to wait three weeks before eating them but they will stay firm for some months longer in the refrigerator. Vodka, brandy or peach brandy added to the cool pickle would also prolong the fruit's potential life, but adds so much extra pleasure they may be eaten even sooner.

having an adventure.

Generally, 500g/ 1lb of dried vine fruits began as 2kg/ 4lb of fresh.

The types you most come across are:

Currants: not dried black currants but a special type of seedless black grape. Originally they were from Corinth in Greece, and you can see them in old cook books as 'raisins from Corinth'. Today Australia is a major grower and supplier.

Raisins: these are dried red grapes of several types, sometimes seedless. The biggest and sweetest are muscatels, which can be found without seeds if you look hard enough. Muscatel raisins that have been dried on the stem are a marvellous thing at the end of a meal, and amazingly good with strong, opinionated cheeses. Stem-dried muscatels are slowly disappearing, so should be snapped up when seen; this is most often around Christmas time, when they ache to be eaten with perfect Stilton.

Sultanas: are made from dried white grapes. They were a specialty of Smyrna, now Izmir, in Turkey and are still sometimes called Smyrna raisins. Sweeter and more aromatic than raisins proper, I find them the most delicious of all in cooking. When you want a guarantee of a rich, mellow flavour add rather more sultanas than raisins in mixed fruit cakes and desserts, especially the British-style steamed puddings made for Christmas.

Glacé Fruits

France is the best-known manufacturer of luxurious sugar-preserved fruits and Apt in the Vaucluse region is one of the oldest centres of this skill. The most popular lines are apricots and mandarins, mainly because they best survive with some flavour intact. Pears, greengages, figs, melons, pineapples and cherry are quite common. Chestnuts (*marrons glacés*), ginger and kumquats are rarer and more expensive. The fruit must be picked before it is fully ripe or it will be too fragile to withstand the processing, which is still barely mechanized.

Once sorted and graded the fruit is generally stored in underground tanks filled with brine. When required the fruit is rinsed, stalked and pitted and then subjected to a process called osmosis, in which all the natural fruit sugars are replaced by sucrose through being soaked in increasingly stronger sugar solutions. Some fruit is then further coated with a sugar solution and lightly baked, which slowly clouds and flakes as the fruit becomes pensionable. A light deposit of sulphur on such fruit helps prevent clouding for longer than expected, and acts as a further preservative.

Moist, succulent and screamingly sweet, glacé fruits are the ultimate luxurious snack. But I like to linger rather longer than the few mouthfuls that demolish, say, a glacé apricot. So I slice them to use as an exquisite topping for fresh fruits – apricots or mandarins on strawberries, *marrons* on raspberries. Of course they are perfectly wonderful with ice creams or with cream, whipped and frozen together. Indeed you can make yourself wickedly ill simply by mixing sliced glacé fruits into mascarpone and not even bothering to freeze it. A hint of rose water adds the ultimate touch of degeneracy and thus is urged.

Apricot Sheets

In Middle Eastern, Turkish, Greek and Cypriot shops you can buy thin sheets of *armadine*. This is dried apricot purée, and being made from Middle Eastern varieties has a much bigger flavour than Western dried apricots; it is sharper too, sometimes because citric acid has been added. You can simply rehydrate *armadine* over low heat in a little water or wine, melting it into a purée, watching it carefully, and then serve it chilled with cream and almonds as a smooth apricot cream. I've also added eggs, black rum, sugar and vanilla to the apricot purée, poached the mixture in ramekins, and then served them very cold on an almond-studded pastry with thin cream flavoured with more rum and vanilla.

Chopped into small pieces *armadine* can be stirred into ice cream or sorbet mixtures: imagine a small mint sorbet flecked with piquant apricot as a refresher during a long Christmas meal. Not only would it be something grateful, its origins in the Eastern Mediterranean would make it relevant, too. *Armadine* adds rare flavour and colour to stuffings for baked apples or to an apple pie, is terrific in or with chocolate cakes, brownies and other baking, yes, including real scones.

Armadine is equally useful and delicious used in savoury cooking and ambrosial combined with fresh or dried mint – another superb example of profound affinity meaning 1 + 1 = 3 or more. In stuffings or to add colour and zest to a pilaff, I simply snip it into small pieces. Its sharp fruitiness is very good in rice or couscous-based stuffings for meat or for vegetables. But it's best of all mixed into pork-based stuffings for lamb, chicken or for turkey, that include sweet spices as well as mint; combining apricot and mint is as basic to the cookery of the Eastern Mediterranean as sage and onion in the West.

Nonetheless, expectation is often greatly more than the delivery of such pleasure. The combination of being picked greener rather than riper, of being soaked and otherwise processed, can mean each fruit is little more than sugar in a clever shape and with negligible flavour reference to the original. If you are not sure, go for the apricots, which seem to come out of the process better than most.

Also very good are small halved Williams pears. Excellent and fun as they are, they become spectactular when put into clear spirit, vodka or gin for some months, so the sugar sweetens the spirit and the pears flavour it too. The alcohol makes a delicious flavouring or digestif, and the pears, now relieved of most of their sugar are alcoholic and sharper and altogether more a good thing. Serve them with globs of clotted cream, with or in chocolate ice cream, or baked in a custard of ground almonds and cream and a dusting of cinnamon.

And then there are Elvas plums, the unchallenged queen of processed fruits, and Portugal's

Pennsylvania Dutch Pears

These are intended for use as a pickle with cold meats and poultry and cheese, but because this is a sweet pickle they are excellent to serve with cheese as a dessert. The quantity will depend on the size of the pears you choose. Smaller is better, but go only for evenly sized fruits, so they all cook at the same rate.

1⅓kg/3lb white, golden or demerara sugar
1 tbsp whole cloves
425ml/¾ pint cider vinegar
3 cinnamon sticks
300ml/½ pint water
about 3kg/6lb firm, ripe pears

Combine the sugar, vinegar, and water. The cloves and cinnamon sticks – which should be broken into pieces – may either be added as is or put into a firmly-tied muslin bag. Simmer all together for 30 minutes from the time the syrup comes to the boil. Taste carefully and then add more cinnamon if your sticks were not as strong as you thought – don't be bashful about bumping up to a sky-high flavour because the flavour is going to be very diluted when the pears are added.

While the syrup is simmering, peel the pears but leave on the stems and do not core them. Brush them with a little water and lemon juice to keep them white if you are using white sugar, otherwise a little discoloration can be overlooked. What they don't see…
Put the pears into the syrup and cook gently until tender but still firm. Spoon the pears carefully into sterilized containers and then cover but do not seal. Boil the syrup fairly rapidly for 30 minutes, pour carefully over the fruit, poke an extra clove or piece of cinnamon in between the pears if you like and then seal. I would leave these a couple of weeks before eating them.

Options: I think fresh bay leaves help knit the flavours together, and thick slices of fresh ginger root would be a delightful addition to this fairly simply flavoured recipe; indeed, one day I intend to use masses of ginger as the only flavouring. Although not authentic as far as Pennsylvanians or the Dutch go, crushed cardamom pods add a wonderful fragrance and I also intend to use fewer cloves and then to incorporate saffron one day.

finest food product, yes, even better than those egg tarts. They're not plums at all, but seraphically elegant whole greengages, a gorgeous sepulchral green-gold, a luscious texture, and a profound perfumed flavour that's underpinned rather than overburdened by the sugar; and then the most aristocratic small stone. Save up. Try not to share.

Another Old Chestnut?

Marrons glacés are made only from the marron chestnut, which does not split into two in its shell but remains a squat single dome shape. Are these yet more triumphs of technique and texture over taste? Are they really worth the great expense? I'm inclined to think not, even after adding a decent cognac to the syrup and letting that be absorbed. It's just as good a thing to hunt out bottles of broken *marrons glacés*, which are very much cheaper. They too can be flavoured with alcohol and used to sprinkle onto cakes, stirred into ice cream mixtures and such. Upper class stores throughout the world sometimes offer *marrons glacés* singly: I urge you to try one and make up your own mind. Sweetened purées of chestnut, with or without plenty of vanilla are another world, cheaper and more rewarding.

Canned and Bottled Vegetables

You are missing out if you think canned or bottled vegetables have largely had their day. Some are simply better when bought this way; others can only be bought this way.

Asparagus: although cooked to a softness we would never entertain in fresh asparagus, the canned green ones, perhaps because of their specific variety, are addictive. Rolled in thin, buttered white or brown bread, canned asparagus spears are as basic to Australasian entertaining as lamingtons and pavlovas. Asparagus rolls seem to be creeping into the repertoire of caterers in Britain, too, and are scoffed up with unseemly greed. They are even better if you butter the outside of the bread too and brown and crisp them in the oven before serving. In this case prosciutto or pancetta could be rolled in with the asparagus.

If you make a sieved purée of green asparagus, this can be folded into mayonnaise to serve with cold fish or poultry, or you can stir it into a bechamel to make a sauce or soufflé base.

White asparagus, blanched in earth banks to keep the sun away from their thrusting stems, are not very much to the British taste anyway, and even less appealing when they are canned. But there are those who cleave to European tastes no matter what, and serve them with smoked or unsmoked ham, often baked in a cheese sauce.

Very thin asparagus is called sprue, and in London's markets might also be 'sparrers' grass' or just 'sparrers'.

The curious ingredient in all asparagus that can give urine an extraordinary smell is one of nature's fastest acting compounds: some people boast of results in minutes. Yet not everyone's body creates the effect and strangest of all to tell, only some of us are wired up to smell it, whether we create it or not. Such information will do nothing to enhance your culinary life, but can spice up awkward moments in pub chatter.

Artichokes: artichoke hearts, *coeurs d'artichauts*, are an excellent addition to any cold hors d'oeuvres, and I like to slice them in half to add to hot or cold pasta dishes or potato salads. By themselves they should be served with a good olive oil vinaigrette, in which they have soaked for some time.

Artichoke bottoms, *fonds d'artichauts*, the little caps of solid, nutty tasting artichoke flesh with no attached leaves, taste just as good from a tin as fresh – well, almost, as long as they have been canned in brine rather than something acidic. Labels can be consciously opaque about this. Artichoke bottoms make good additions to mixed buffets. They may be sliced and dressed as a rather high class salad themselves, perhaps with a few cold peas, orange segments, some olives and a few anchovy fillets. Or they can be served sliced in to salads, ideally of the chunky, tomato, hard-boiled egg, green bean sort. At grander dinners, they are best warmed and filled with a vegetable purée. Green pea is most traditional but anything with the bite of lemon or garlic will work, celeriac or Brussels sprouts with nutmeg, carrot with allspice or thyme, and so on.

Bamboo shoots: sold in cans in chunks or large slices. Ivory-coloured. If the smell seems rather rich, rinse them in cold water or blanch. Mainly used as a squeaky/crunchy contrast of texture in oriental dishes but there is a definite deep woodiness of flavour that is useful in occidental salads, too. Keeps a long time refrigerated in water.

Boretanne: very small, flattish specialty onions from Italy, with a pale yellow flesh and natural sweetness. Like *lampascioni q.v.* they are a sort of civilised pickled onion and are often found grilled and then stored in balsamic vinegar, making them a smart sweet-sour addition to antipasti.

Celery hearts: these are indistinguishable from braised fresh celery. Sprinkled with lemon juice, a little chicken or beef stock and some butter, they reheat wonderfully. They are also good reheated with lemon juice and garlic and served with a dressing of walnut oil and toasted walnuts, with thinly sliced sun-dried tomato for exceptional flavour affinities.

Golden needles: Asian ingredient expert Jenny Yee says these are dried day lilies, something eaten fresh whenever fashion so dictates, especially in the United States. The dried ones are soaked and then stuffed and have a flavour she describes as somewhat like courgette/zucchini flowers.

Hearts of palm: also called millionaire's asparagus. Each heart is the central young stem of a special palm tree, which dies when this heart is removed, hence the expense. They are found and enjoyed in many parts of the tropical world and the best are usually from Brazil. The ivory-coloured, embryonic leaves have a delicious and unusual sweetness enveloped in woody, earthy flavours, and a texture that can squeak as you eat. Basically served chilled with vinaigrette or mayonnaise as though white asparagus, and often with prawns, or lobster, which appreciate the sweetness. Better if you bump up the tropicality; so flavour either type of dressing with lime, and here's also a definite place for angostura bitters, with restraint. The hearts can be woody and fibrous and rather unpleasant, so if you are serving them for a special dinner it is wise to check each piece individually, and to have a spare tin on hand. They don't seem to take to being served warm or to being further cooked.

As a substitute for white asparagus, palm hearts easily earn their keep through novelty value, and provide additional glamour to smoked salmon, to gulls' or quails' eggs, or with smoked fish including smoked salmon. By themselves with a barely warm sauce or mayonnaise *maltaise,* that is flavoured with the juice of blood oranges, and finished with lime zest, they set up the best of dinners. One of the few times I have used toasted cashew nuts is to chop them over hearts of palm in a light tomato mayonnaise.

Lampascioni: commonly sold as wild onions, these are actually the bulbs of a type of wild hyacinth that flourishes in Puglia. They look and taste rather like shallots, and have usually been chargrilled before preserving in olive oil. Don't tell an Italian I said this, but they are best thought of as a pickled onion with airs and graces, so are good to accompany cold meats and salami or the sort of cheese that has a definite mind of its own.

Lotus root: recognized easily as the slices with the holes in them. Crisp, crunchy and slightly sweet; for mixing into oriental stews or into your own for discreet sensation. Oxtail would be a first choice to add them to, just towards the end so their flavour is not diluted. Most are usually bought canned. When I explored China's Treaty Ports for a BBC TV series, we called in at a specialist health hotel, where meals are prescribed rather than ordered. I wasn't consulted and so was intrigued to find they served me with sliced lotus root; I supposed it had something to do with exotic torpor, lotus eating and so on. Not so. It wasn't lotus root at all, but sliced and poached bull's penis. I was particularly pleased not to understand the translator's explanation.

Mushrooms: don't bother with canned mushrooms, whatever ubiquitous home economists/nutritionists say. And ignore hideously expensive bottled ones too, which are just as unsatisfying. Look instead to dried wild mushrooms, later in this chapter.

Peas: apart from mushy, or processed peas, which are a world unto themselves, canned peas have been cancelled out by the frozen variety. *Petits pois a la francaise,* cooked with baby onions and shreds of lettuce, retain a devoted following. I suspect this is based on nostalgia rather than inherent quality, because when cooked very fresh, microwaved ideally, the combination is delightful, clean, sweet and pretty to look at, too.

Potatoes: because they are generally small and waxy, canned potatoes are very good for making salads that do not fall to pieces. Always heat them slightly before dousing with a vinaigrette and garlic, even if you are later to mix them with mayonnaise, then dress the potatoes only with soured cream and dill, or with a mixture that's half yoghurt and half mayonnaise. You might colour either of these lightly with tomato purée, add brightness to that with horseradish sauce and black pepper, juice squeezed from fresh ginger in a garlic press, and then add arcs of poached cucumber and plenty of chunky prawns, for a potato salad smart enough for a main course.

Pulses: these can very well and are a blessing to have in the store cupboard. Beans can become first course salads or main courses or added to soups and stews – chickpeas are particularly good in soups. The Spanish Navarrico range does very good beans, and by far the tastiest are their *gigantes*, huge, creamy beans with a big, distinctly spiced flavour that's very gratifying and that go with anything with residual sweetness, from salmon to orange segments. Whizz up any canned or bottled bean with olive oil, lemon juice and/or feta and you have a delicious dip: also add chilli compound to red beans, add parsley or coriander and garlic to chickpeas, toasted walnuts and sun-dried tomato to cannellini – you really can't go wrong.

Red peppers: or capsicums or bell peppers, depending on where you live – are canned and bottled in many Mediterranean and Middle European countries. The most useful are those preserved in oil or brine, but if you liked pickled goodies there are plenty, perhaps most, preserved in vinegar or something else acetic. They have generally been char-roasted and skinned before processing and so are both sweet and convenient. Cut into strips they finish a salad far better than the raw ones, can be added to scrambled eggs, puréed for stuffings, added to pasta, added to almost every sandwich, toasted, grilled, wrapped, rolled or made with sliced white. There's barely a salad bathed in olive oil they couldn't improve, and the same goes for pilaffs, and, even risotto. Quite one of the best things to have in your store cupboard, and they last ages in a refrigerator once opened.

Simply drain oil or brine-packed ones well, dress with garlic and good olive oil plus a splash of lemon juice or vinegar for a simple but robust accompaniment to plain grilled lamb chops, chicken or pork dishes. Good mixed with slices of artichoke bottoms, too, with capers, with excellent mozzarella, perhaps anchovies.

The *piquillo* pepper is unique to just one region of Spain and has developed an individual style, sweet and rich with only a hint of heat. Those of Lodosa have DOC status. They are still baked and lightly smoked, peeled and packed by hand in only their own juice, and are worth every bit of their keen market price: you buy them packed whole, which you could stuff, or in irregular strips, that are cheaper and much more versatile. A slab of *piquillo* pepper, with a hot, split, sweet chorizo, a handful of biting rocket and generous *arbequina* olive oil on a split and chargrilled bread roll is one of the many reasons to go to London's Borough Market on Friday or Saturday. The roasted *Pimiento asado del Bierzo* IGP is also processed entirely by hand and comes canned or bottled only in its own juices plus a little salt, olive oil, citric acid or lemon juice. The *Pimiento Riojano* IGP you find in cans or bottles will be a mixture of red, green and striped ones, the characteristic *entreverado*: only citric acid can be added to the natural juices of these hand processed, direct-flame roasted peppers.

From France come *piments d'esplette* AOC, with somewhat the same characteristics, but from the French Basque region.

Sott'olio: the catch-all for a wide variety of vegetables cooked and preserved in oil, or under oil as the name suggests. All are great for forking directly out of the jar and onto a plate, into a sandwich, wrap or roll, onto pasta or pizza.

Sweet corn: whole kernel or cream-style, these taste just about as good as you would make.

Tomatillos: fundamental to Mexican and South American cookery, these look like small green tomatoes, but the flavour is much fruitier and more intense, very much like physallis or cape gooseberries: if you can grow tomatoes you can grow tomatillos, too. You are bound to like the subtle, fascinating difference they add, even if only combined with tomatoes in olive-oil rich sauces.

Tomatoes: good food is barely possible without tins of plum tomatoes processed in their juices. And now there is far more than mere whole tomatoes. We have chopped tomatoes, chopped tomatoes with any number and style of flavourings and we have *passata* or cream of tomatoes, which is pretty much any of the above put through a sieve. Each type of canned tomato is interchangeable, depending on whether you want texture or not – and how long you intend to cook. Whole tomatoes generally do best in long cooking, so they reduce and concentrate, and thus are a perfect medium in which to cook other food, from strongly flavoured vegetables to meat and poultry. Break the tomatoes roughly as you add them, which will keep good home-made texture in the finished dish. If you don't cook in such a medium, a severely reduced version is an excellent way to sauce such as cauliflowers, parsnips, artichokes, pumpkin, zucchini, potatoes or green beans. Good as it is, because you have included olive oil as you boiled it down, and a simple rustic thing to do without any squashing or sieving, so maximum texture remains. You might choose sometimes to be additionally rugged with the late addition of pre-cooked bacon, pancetta, ham or salami pieces, chopped garlic and torn basil leaves; it's a great way to top bean or root vegetable soups. Additionally dotted with thin, short sticks of Parmesan or sticky cubes of blue cheese, this is one of the best things you can hurriedly put onto pasta. When very reduced and so enhanced, a spoonful will transform a soup or freshen up any dish of long cooked red, white or black kidney or other such beans.

Chopped tomatoes are even more a cook's dream. If you strain off a little of their thick juice, you can use these to finish a sauce or as part of a last minute sauce for pasta without any long cooking. The terrific texture and colour added into an otherwise ordinary stew, or on baked fish, say, means there is a sporting chance someone will think you have been chopping all day, and neatly, too. Even when cooked longer and reduced to even thicker textures, chopped tomatoes keep texture. They are very good for cooking things to look rustic, green beans, cannellini from a can, and so on.

Passata or cream of tomatoes is basically what we'd get if we strained whole or chopped tomatoes. It is not like thinned down tomato purée or paste, for these often have a slightly caramel taste. Yet even though it seems thick and concentrated, it too cooks down even more, to give faster results for a Bolognese ragu for instance. If you cannot get a passata, squash a can of whole plum tomatoes, including their juice, and cook in an open pan until very reduced, liquidize and then strain, using the back of a soup ladle to squeeze maximum yield though the sieve. Only then flavour with olive oil, perhaps a few drops of vinegar or red wine, anchovy fillets rather than salt, and some herbs. If you use fresh mint which is particularly good, basil or thyme, they will have scented the mixture in five minutes and may then be strained out. If you boil down the sauce rapidly, the oil or butter you have added will be emulsified and give enough flavour and body to make anyone think you had started from scratch.

If you are determined to have a detectable onion flavour in any of these canned-tomato sauces, stir-in snipped chives just before serving, or, if I am at table, offer them separately.

Sun-dried Tomatoes

Many people are confused about the explosive popularity of sun-dried tomatoes over the past decade. I'm not surprised. Every time I have been part of a tasting panel there has been universally expressed horror at the low standard and extraordinary range of flavours – from burned caramel to vinegar. Excepting individual preferences, my recommendation is to avoid those which come hydrated in oil or any other liquid (they are hardly dried any more) and to buy dried ones with the greatest care, tasting first and avoiding anything with detached skins, browning or broken shapes.

The idea is simple. Tomatoes are fruits. Fruits can be dried – for use later. So, sun-dry tomatoes. The Neapolitan cook who taught me about such things almost 30 years ago said her job as a child was to cut the tomatoes, lay them in the sun and bring them in every night. We luckier but sun-starved types can dry tomatoes overnight in a slow oven or in domestic dehydrators, which are very good indeed because the drying technique is less important than the tomatoes you choose; the sun doesn't add a flavour other drying techniques cannot. I expect there are exceptions, but the only commercial ones which taste anything like tomatoes are from California: they are tomato-red, smell sweet, and are soft enough to cut and eat as they are, a texture somewhere between ready-to-eat dried fruit and old-fashioned hard ones, and even with your eyes closed you know it is a concentrated tomato when you put it in your mouth.

Sun-dried tomatoes can be used just as they are, sliced or chopped. If they are to have no further processing, in a sandwich perhaps, they should be smaller, and if they are to be baked with fish or stuffed under the skin of a chicken or put into a stew, they can be in bigger pieces as they will absorb moisture and be easier to eat. Otherwise you rehydrate them with a quick microwave burst and added water, or let them wallow overnight in water or in olive oil, with or without crushed garlic, torn bay leaves, crushed coriander seed and ground black pepper and lemon; orange or lime zest are good additions too. The leftover oil is a terrific dressing for salads or those sandwiches, or can be heated and poured onto cooked and crushed potatoes.

In fact, how you use sun-dried tomatoes is as legion as the uses of fresh tomatoes. They may be sliced and tossed onto almost anything, from potato salads to green ones, used in omelettes, pasta dressings, risottos, pilaffs. In all these they will give wonderful chewy explosions of flavour. If they are cooked in sauces, stews, stuffings and the like they will expand and become softer, adding their flavour and some degree of colour. They are very interesting in tomato sauces, where they add fascinating levels and variations of the same basic flavour. I add them when I am reheating a ratatouille, for instance.

I like also to put sun-dried tomatoes into cognac, vodka or black rum for a few hours: the flavoured alcohols make the most perfect salad dressings, which I use with no added oil. Let the tomatoes and alcohol dally longer and both improve immeasurably, giving one an ideal last minute addition to sauces, or a flavouring to sprinkle on grilled or simply cooked fish, meats and poultry.

Every year I make a flavoured eau de vie for Christmas, ideally with a flavourless spirit bought from a French supermarket for remarkably little money. Last year's version was smokey with sun-dried tomatoes, bright and clean with fresh lime zest and piquant with fresh peppercorns I had bought earlier in the year and frozen until I wanted them. It took about four weeks for the flavours and colour fully to develop and then I strained out the peppercorns or they would have added too much bite, the mistake of another year. It made the perfect welcoming shot for those who drink such things, but I tended to use it more as a dressing for foods such as smoked salmon or game pâtés, when it gave great lift to festivities without alarming those who thought they might not drink that night.

Green Wrappers

Banana leaf: a common wrapping for food while cooking. It is not expected to add flavour, yet long cooking will encourage a leafy, tea like flavour to be passed to the food. Very useful for barbecuing and grilling fish, which might otherwise burn or stick or both: even if the leaf chars it takes a long time actually to burn away. Folded and pinned with water-soaked wooden cocktail sticks, banana leafs work very well in the microwave, to wrap fish coated in a curry sauce perhaps. Or as a simple fascinating seal on ramekins in which something sweet or savoury is being cooked or warmed. For instance, line ramekins with banana leaf and then fill them with an exotic egg custard made with coconut milk and *mali* or *pandan* q.v. flavouring.. The top can be pinned or stapled together. Once steamed or poached in a tray of hot water, and then allowed to cool, each leaf-wrapped custard can be taken from the ramekin and served, with chilled tropical fruits. The leaf is usually very lightly oiled before use, and the older it is the less flexible it will be. Banana leaf is never eaten.

Lotus leaf: the lotus leaf of Asia and the Orient gives a subtle extra flavour when used as a wrapper especially to rice, pork and poultry. More likely to be used for steaming than boiling, and thus flavour exchange will be minimalised. Usually bought dried, the leaves should be soaked in warm water before use. If you grow your own, dip fresh leaves into very hot water, both to wilt and to rid them of unwanted animal matter. They are never eaten.

Vine leaf: vacuum-packed, bottled or canned, these will have been lightly cooked and stored in brine. They are ready for use after a good rinse, and add a slight honey-like flavour to any food with which they are in contact for some time. Unlike the previous two, these leaves are eaten, but require fairly long cooking if this is your plan. As a wrapping for fish, for roasts or for baked pâtés they may be allowed to add their flavour without being eaten. Fresh vine leaves from any type of grape may be used after quickly blanching in boiling water.

Although usually used for savoury food, vine leaves were used in a very old English dish of pears baked very slowly between layers of leaves to give a golden colour and their honey flavour to the fruit. I made this just once when entertaining two A-list NZ foodies to lunch in London. It was meant to be a fascinating, luscious end to a meal that had already gone wrong – the black olive flan, we agreed, was one-dimensional. Sadly I had not soaked or blanched the canned vine leaves long enough – I thought I had – and the remaining salt overruled every other flavour. Both tragedies reminded me to heed the advice I so easily give to others: be sure you are tasting what is there, rather than what you would like to be there, and to do this, get out of the kitchen for at least half an hour before doing final tasting, to give your senses time to dial back to zero. The palate and the nose get tired, and go to sleep or tell lies when you smell the same thing all the time.

Dried Mushrooms

The dried wild mushroom is an absolute must in my kitchen, used for everything from saving a mundane soup or stew to being served in homemade brioches or darkly to flavour a Venetian risotto that is perfectly *all'onde*.

It is sad they are so expensive when Britain fair groans with wild mushroom varieties that are neither eaten fresh nor dried. You don't even have to go down to the woods today. Wander onto a lawn looking for a fairy ring, and when you have checked no-one else cares, collect and dry these mushrooms: they develop a remarkably strong flavour and wonderful aroma akin to the cep or porcini, the best flavoured of dried mushrooms.

Cep, cepe (Fr), porcini (It), steinpilz (G): The most important of all, this has the botanical name *boletus edulis*, something important to remember as you will find. When fresh the cep can be bland and slimy, even after baking has concentrated its flavour; but when dried it has a wondrous velvety golden brown colour and a robust earthy-sweet flavour that is unmistakable. The best qualities are usually sold in dried slices taken through the cap and stem, but chopped segments or broken pieces are very much cheaper, especially in French and Corsican markets, and somehow seem to give a stronger flavour too. Check both carefully for too much damage by bugs, either before or after drying. If you pay the price you must be able to enjoy the way they look as well as their flavours.

Either way dried ceps must be rinsed quickly in cold water in a coarse sieve or colander to get rid of the inevitable grit. The liquid in which they then rehydrate is invaluable and should always be incorporated into something; if the mushrooms are to flavour a stew for instance, rehydrate them in that, just chuck them straight in. Otherwise cover with liquid and put over a low heat, which does it faster and gives the stock greater colour than steeping in cold liquid. The microwave is fastest of all. I particularly like to use an amontillado or oloroso sherry or a dry Sercial Madeira, but something alcoholic is always better than mere water.

When you use them in a stuffing for, say, chicken or roast beef, you might like to mix the ceps in dry so they are hydrated by the cooking juices. The same would go for vegetarian dishes, such as stuffed peppers or courgettes. If you want to give rice or barley pilaffs a lift, add dried ceps when you start to cook.

For really yummy sauces that are relatively instant compared to making béchamels and reductions and the like, rehydrate ceps in double cream. If you take 20 or so minutes while other ingredients are cooking, the cream will have reduced to the perfect consistency of a nicely made béchamel; finish with cognac. If you do not care for quite so much cream, rehydrate in sherry, white wine or vermouth, and when the mushrooms are soft and the liquor has reduced, add double cream and continue heating until the texture is to your taste.

The combination of potato, cep and cream is almost too good to eat, but here is something to do if you insist: rehydrate ceps in Madeira, remove them and reduce the wine to a syrup. Layer the mushrooms and reduced Madeira with sliced potato, pour over some thick cream, bake slowly, and then dare anyone not to eat it all. It makes cooking potatoes with truffles seem more insane than ever.

More and more you find mixtures of dried wild mushrooms being sold, and their cheaper price makes them quite irresistible, once. Most are opportunistic mixtures of mushrooms that were once wild, but are less than tame in flavour. The biggest con is so called porcini or cep mixtures. Look again, look to see where *boletus edulis* comes in the order of ingredients, remembering they must by law be in descending order of their presence. You will find other types of boletus, but none of these has anything like the flavour of boletus edulis. You'd get more flavour by using less of the real thing.

A relatively new way to do this, to me anyway, is porcini powder. This makes it easy to stir the flavour into rice or pasta or to any sauce. I had my greatest success with it when I baked a whole fillet of beef for breathing-guru Dinah Morrison. I lightly oiled the fillet, and then patted the porcini powder onto that. I left it for an hour while it came back to room temperature and then baked it quickly in the middle of the oven, resting on a wire shelf above a drip pan. It was served in thick pink slices at room temperature some hours later, and I don't think a single person could help exclaiming when they took their first bite.

I've not had the money or the mates to be able to repeat this, but use porcini powder to flavour pasta that has first been allowed its proper time to steam dry on the outside. Magic mushrooms they certainly seem.

Morels, morilles (FT): these are the pointy wrinkled ones, alarmingly like any image you might have conjured of the exposed brain of an alien. They are rather expensive but repay that with huge flavour, which is definitely mushroom but also of meat and of bacon, particularly. Their appearance, flavour and cost mean they are usually used as garnish or to finish a sauce, which is fair enough. They take longer to rehydrate than ceps but the use of cream, wine or sherry rather than water is well recommended. Fletcher Christian's grandmother's 17th and 18th century cookbook from Netherhall in Cumbria, combines morels with sweetbreads and bacon cubes to stuff a boned chicken, served in luscious pastel-coloured slices with a sauce of cream, wine, lemon, mace and a dash of anchovy. Why did he go to sea?

The rest: *chanterelles* and *girolles* and the very black *trompettes des morts* (we call them Horns of Plenty rather than Trumpets of Death) all look good but have virtually no taste when dried, so I shouldn't bother, except for presentation. The very distinct exception is the fairy ring mushroom, that dries to give a really rich flavour almost as strong as ceps, but you should discard the thin stems as they rarely become tender again.

Poland irregularly sends dried mushrooms to Britain, often in traditional strings or garlands, which are cheaper than the French or German, without being cheap. They are usually ceps but not always, so give them a good sniff, hoping to find a rich, almost wine-like scent, honeyed at first but finishing with a dusky earthiness. If you do, they will be the real thing.

Asian Mushrooms

Golden needle/enokitake: often cream rather than golden, but always a long, slim stem and a tiny cap. Usually sold in clumps they are delicious when raw and so make one of the easiest and prettiest of garnishes you expect also to eat. Otherwise the Japanese use them in clear soups, added at the last minute.

Honeycomb: a fungus rather than a mushroom, and equally known as honeycomb, white-ear or snow-ear fungus. It's usually sold dried and needs to be reconstituted by soaking in warm water with or without the inclusion of some rice wine. Before use, the tough central core is removed and the remainder chopped or sliced. It's one of those Asian ingredients eaten as much for its gelatinous texture as anything else, yet there is a mild honey scent and taste, but only if eaten raw or very lightly cooked. The frilliness remains when its cooked, so it's added at the last minute for visual as well as textural interest.

Moer/cloud ears: a specialty from Szechuan province. A crinkly and thin tree fungus, which should be soaked for 30 minutes before cooking. Any hard core should be removed. Sold in dry chips and adds a curious chewy crunch to stir-fried dishes and stuffings; the sort of ingredient that confirms you are not eating a fry up at the local caff.

Oyster mushroom/pleurotte: this is the fan-shaped one sold as a wild mushroom when it is neither: it's cultivated and it's a fungus. The French name, *pleurotte*, is a clue; these weep copiously when heated and so should be cooked very quickly indeed. They can be eaten raw, which gives you a better return for your money, and are available in other pastel colours – pink or yellow or blue.

Shiitake: the very best oriental mushroom and a much bigger flavour when dried than fresh. They look like ordinary mushrooms except for the speckles or geometric shapes which so prettily pattern their caps. The colour varies from a black to a speckled brown or grey. And it is said the medium sizes have the best flavours. The very best grade is a 'flower mushroom', with star-marks on the cap and will be fearfully expensive. All must be soaked in warm water for up to 30 minutes before cooking, so that they will resume their normal size and shape and become soft again. The stems will always be tough, and are always discarded, although you could use them and the soaking water to make stock. They don't need to be cooked but can be braised. Otherwise slice or chop them into stir-fries, into stuffings or to throw into sauces.

Straw: small yellow mushrooms with pointed black caps, sold in cans. Use within a week, as their delicate taste is lost soon after exposure to air.

Wood-ear and cloud-ear fungus: eaten for their texture and unruly frilled appearance, as they have negligible flavour. Most often encountered in stir-fries or where there is a mixture of other mushrooms. Usually bought dried, they are soaked in warm water until softened.

'Other Mushrooms'

A fascinating stall in Portobello Road Market, one of the highpoints of Saturday in London, is The Camden Mushroom Company. They sell only 'magic' mushrooms including grow kits, with varieties from as far afield as Mexico, Colombia, Ecuador and Hawaii. They carefully insist the array of 'fantastic fungi for your amusement' is provided solely for the sake of research and natural curiosity. They do not condone the use of their wares for illegal activities. Heaven forbid.

The company is also socially responsible at Camden Lock and Covent Garden Markets, 7 days to 7pm but MH Government seems to be moving to put a stop to their services.

Truffles

When an author as august as Colette describes a fungus as the 'most capricious and most revered of black princesses' you can be certain it is rather more than a mushroom. She was writing about the black truffle, the black diamond of cookery, and one of the rarest of all the world's exotic treats.

Truffles have been popular and acknowledged as special for thousands of years and like all rare things have been credited with aphrodisiac powers, particularly by Francis I of France, but I suspect this was rather a matter of expecting more for so much money than passing gastronomic gratification.

The flavour of black truffles is found in nothing else – indeed it isn't found in truffles most of the time. The delicacy is fugitive, easily overpowered and expected to perform tasks of which it is incapable. It is more a perfumer or catalyst than a flavouring and the true flavour is only passed on to other foods by standing together or cooking together very gently for a longish time.

The real black truffle is **tuber melanosporum**. It is unmistakable when cut for it is indeed very black; there are many other truffles but only this type is so black and deserves anything like its reputation. The greatly lesser **tuber aestivum** or summer truffle is always rather marbled when cut, and a definite brown rather than black; this has virtually no flavour and is the object of some very opportunistic marketing – see **Truffle Kerfuffle** panel.

Although widely known as coming from Périgord, the true black truffle grows in an area ranging from there to Italy, including parts of Spain, Provence, Piedmont and Tuscany. Lesser types grow in other parts of France as far north as Alsace, but they aren't the same. In France, the usual way of finding them is with trained pigs that apparently get sexually excited by the pheromones of black truffles, or by dogs, preferred by many because they are less likely to eat them. But in Provence peasants were too poor to keep dogs or pigs just to find truffles and so they hunted with long sticks, indeed they still do. You walk towards the sun, tapping a long stick ahead of you. If you tap the ground over a truffle, a colony of midges will be disturbed, and as they fly furiously about in impotent rage, their tiny wings reflect the light. You have a truffle.

If you follow the truffle through history, and people do, you would find its abundance has fluctuated wildly but regularly. There are those alive who remember it was nothing to return home with many kilos of truffles each when they were young, and who were told by their grandparents that this was nothing compared to the harvests of their youth; for one person now to find a kilo in total throughout an entire season is thought fortunate. It was this bounty that made their flavour so appreciated in the 19th and early 20th centuries: there were enough of them!

It is idiotic to follow recipes that purport to recreate, say, the truffled turkey of the last century, but with just one or two truffles. Then, they used several pounds of fresh truffles to stuff a turkey, and buried that in soil for several days to allow the truffles to perfume the flesh. What possible effect can a single, ready-cooked truffle popped under the skin before roasting have?

Black truffle is best enjoyed with other fragile flavours, ideally something fatty, such as foie gras or creamy scrambled eggs, but both must have been in contact with the raw truffle for some time. Although a standby of buffets, banquets and ballrooms, the practice of decorating with slivers of cold truffle is nonsensical and wasteful – the truffle has not been brought to full flavour and the food cannot possibly be perfumed by it. Serving truffle sliced onto something else is about as gratifying to the palate as licking a clean fork. Far better to use slices of black olive, first blanched to desalt them. An extraordinary number of people will believe it is truffle if you tell them so, everyone will if you don't.

Truffles are gathered between the end of November and mid-March or so. They are probably at their best in January, thus the rush to use truffles for Christmas cooking is generally pointless if you are using fresh ones, for they are most unlikely to have reached full maturity; and as preserved ones will not have anywhere near the flavour of fresh ones, the exercise is doomed anyway. I have decided only to use truffles if and when I can get them fresh or frozen, the latter a technique I first heard about from elderly gatherers in Provence, who remembered the time it was nothing to come back from a morning's foraging with a kilo or so each.

Black truffles are most commonly found under oak trees in 'burnt' areas, so-called because no other vegetation can or will grow there.

But if they grow under oak trees, are there no English truffles? Well, there is an English truffle, the Bath or Red truffle, but it has largely been lost to us by the creeping of our towns and cities into our fields and by a dearth of those who have the knowledge to train animals to find them. I once had an elderly Lithuanian gentleman working for me who said regularly, 'Oh I know where to find truffles all over England'. Initial excitement gave way to inertia on my part, a dampening of disbelief. Imagine my face when he returned months later with a small paper bag full! There were black ones and white ones – and one extraordinary fragrant one the like of which I've never come across before or since. I knew rather less about truffles than I do now and probably ruined some of them in my experiments – but... truffles to *experiment* with. My friend told me he knew where to go because he had actually sown the spores all over England, having brought them from Europe after the war. I've not seen him for years now, but somewhere in England there are treasures as valuable as any Graeco-Roman silver hoards.

Others are trying to do this trick professionally and stories abound of success in Spain, but the only time I was treated to their produce was a grotesque pose of a do at The Savoy, where the kitchen had been instructed to do just about everything you should not do with truffles. None was a true black truffle and there had been no attempt to allow their wizardry to permeate and enliven the other ingredients.

On the other hand, science has progressed immeasurably, and truffle farms, *truffières*, are being planted everywhere, not least in New Zealand, where there are several, including the largest in the Southern Hemisphere. In Gisborne, on the North Island, there's been a *truffière* for a decade or more and not only does it regularly publish harvest successes, these have had them analysed and proven to be the real thing.

With so few truffles about, you need to get maximum value, and canned or bottled ones really are not the way if you are choosing them for flavour rather than public display. If you can find someone who has sterilized rather than cooked a truffle in a small jar at home, this might have lost much liquid but kept rather a lot of flavour – but they may not sell it to you. It is best to pay extra money to buy a frozen raw truffle, to let it defrost very slowly in light olive oil, to which it will add some savour, and then to use it as many ways as you can. Seal it up with some eggs for a few days so it perfumes them or store it in rice, which is the way to transport a fresh one if you become its owner.

You can eat black truffles raw, one way to get a little flavour from the early ones; in Provence I was told they were grated over salads on Christmas Day, 'but only because they were the first, we did not cook with them yet'.

Whatever you plan eventually to cook with your truffle, it must be allowed at least a day in contact with the other ingredients, in a cool and moist place. Otherwise, really to know truffle flavour you must bake one whole, the way Colette and Alice B Toklas and others recommend. Each must be absolutely sealed. This might first be in very thin air-dried ham, in turn in a crepe and then pastry: or if you had several they might be braised in wine or Madeira in a small sealed cocotte. It is less attractive but more efficient to use cooking foil which will then neither a lender nor borrower of flavour be. However you cook them, whole truffles should only be revealed in front of the diner so the accumulated scent can be gathered in a single huge sniff. Don't serve them on a white napkin, for you are as likely to smell the bleach that made it so pristine.

The curious flavour remains fugitive even when you have a complete mouthful, but there is a definite sense of very superior bacon gone to heaven. If you are about when there are fresh black truffles to spare, bake one in a fine bread dough, will you, and let me know. I have always imagined that would be wonderful. The black truffles of Provence have been amongst the very best I have ever tasted, but they were barely out of the ground, and only lightly preserved anyway.

Black truffles are sold fresh, canned or bottled. After the laborious brushing and peeling and sorting, which can only be done by hand, truffles stay fresh for just three to four days and will be sold in the chilly winter markets of French villages whole or in pieces. Otherwise the truffles are preserved in one of two ways: they are either cooked before canning or bottling which gives some control over weight loss, or they are slightly salted and sterilized after packing which keeps all the flavour and bulk but converts 25 per cent of the weight into liquid. If you have a fresh truffle and wish to keep it, poach it in Madeira and leave it in this liquid, itself a wondrous addition to sauces.

Frankly, though, I am disillusioned. I've never been knocked out by the flavour of a black truffle, even when it has been left for days to perfume a sirloin of beef. In fact the flavour that seems best is that of the Madeira in which a truffle has been poached. Twice I've been served a whole, baked truffle but neither was such a thrill as, say, a slice of pan-fried foie gras or a few spoonfuls of caviar. I'll walk a long way to eat freshly grated white truffle, but the black ones? I don't think any of us will ever understand the fuss until we have a kilo or so of raw ones to play with. Each.

Tuber magnatum is the white Piedmontese or Alba truffle. It is very much more expensive than the black truffle, anything up to and over £2000 a kilo, and has a penetrating smell and overwhelming flavour, redolent of every possible perversity and prohibition and impossible to describe because it is like nothing else: all you might do is relate what it makes you think about, and then, like me, you will probably keep that to yourself.

White truffle is never cooked but grated or very thinly sliced indeed over risotto, over pasta or onto hot brioche, a specialty of the pavements of Florence. It is even more difficult to cultivate than black truffles and such an idea can effectively be dismissed altogether. Such Italian enthusiasts as Antonio Carluccio imports them for use in his Neal Street Restaurant, and he once brought over a kilo to my BBC television studio, with a security guard too. A very high profile Labour MP refused to stay on our famed red sofa, nauseated he said by the smell and sickened by the thought of so much money being spent on luxuries. But he stayed when offered one.

Although associated so publicly with Alba in Italy, white truffles are also found in the Savoy, particularly around Chambery. They too may be frozen and defrosted most successfully and repay better than black truffles the ploy of storing them amidst eggs or rice or both, provided everything is very cool or refrigerated. There is a month long Truffle Market and Truffle Fair each year in Alba, ending with the charity auctioning of a handful of superb examples early in

Truffle Kerfuffle

I'm sorry to say truffles remain the basis of a very public swindle, and many people are spending good money for little reason and for no flavour in return. You may have noticed truffles and truffle products are increasingly available, even in supermarkets. You have to be an expert to realise the beautifully packaged contents are neither the fabled black, nor the fragrant white truffle, but *tuber aestivum*, the almost tasteless summer truffle. It says so on the label, of course, but who knows there are different types of truffle, and that only a couple have sought-after flavour? The disappointment being peddled is cruel.

When cut, *tuber aestivum* is rather a good-looking brown, with hair-like veins of white. Good looking, yes, but the flavour is less than negligible to begin with and processing defeats even that. Summer truffles have no culinary merit other than their rarity. They are no different from the bland sand truffles of Egypt or those of Nepal, which are thrown into pots by the handful when there is not enough meat.

The purpose of this cynical marketing exercise is clearly only to make money from perceptions of rarity and luxury, but with no principle.

One company markets pastes and spreads of this or that truffle, which should be a good idea, extending the flavours, making them cheaper and thus more accessible. But look at the list of ingredients. Would you choose to put vinegar, amongst other extraordinary things, onto or with a truffle? And a white truffle at that? Of course not, and neither should they.

Truffle flavoured oils q.v. may well be made with 'nature identical' flavouring rather than the real thing, but at least they taste of what the label says.

November. One year, just one white truffle with the extraordinarily rare weight of 500g sold for $US30,000 to a Las Vegas restaurateur: but the bidder in London put it into a safe and then left the country without passing on the key, so it perished and was buried with ceremony, accompanied by very gritted teeth. As I write there is serious talk about it being exhumed and returned for burial whence it came.

Yet such pleasure is still not reserved only for the super-rich. They are a wild food and can be found by many who know the trick. In Auckland Rafaella and Paulo del Monte, who run the local branch of the Slow Food Movement, both have their mothers from Italy to stay during the northern winter. One of their gifts is rice amidst which a white truffle sits for months. Rafaella made the last of the rice into a sort of risotto, and then fried it quite thinly and slowly in butter. In spite of the usually forbidden cooking, the flavour of the white truffle was sensational, undoubtedly the best truffle dish of any colour I have ever eaten. It was then I knew; white truffle oil is terrific but the real thing more so. As in life, once you've had the real thing, you may not go back.

White truffles might be able to help you there too, for they have long been granted aphrodisiacal properties, and even been called 'testicles of the earth'. The man who began the white truffle fair in Alba used to send one to famous people around the world. Marilyn Monroe wrote back to him, saying: 'I have never tasted anything more tasteful and exciting. Thank you so much for the pleasure that you procured me. Your faithful and affectionate, Marilyn.' Procured?

La Fontana, a long established restaurant chic-to-chic with Viscount Linley's emporium in London's Pimlico, specialises in truffles, and from them I learned dishes with tomato don't work with white truffles. They offer a dedicated menu of dishes to marry with white truffles, lovely light things with lots of eggs and Fontina cheese. You can have these with or without the shaved white truffles, and they tell you how much extra this costs, so there are no surprises greater than the beguiling flavour. I'd let La Fontana truffle with my flavours anytime.

Sea Vegetables

Although very much associated with Japanese food or unwanted reminders of unusual experiences with Welsh laverbread, sea vegetables/seaweeds are slowly demanding more and more attention, particularly from vegetarians, but also from anyone with a true interest in eating broadly. At food shows over the past years any stand featuring them has always been one of the busiest.

Except for laver, all seaweeds come dried and will rehydrate in cold water in five minutes, after which they may be boiled to be served hot or cold, although I should be very certain of your guests' tastes before you dare either! Small amounts boiled up in water make very good stocks for cooking fish.

Agar-agar: this is seaweed, and a vegetarian substitute for animal gelatin. Instructions are usually printed on the packet, which you are most likely to find in health stores. Generally you use about a tablespoon to 300ml/$\frac{1}{2}$ pint of boiling water. You'll need this when setting a dessert with fresh pineapple or kiwi fruit, as these contain an enzyme which prevents gelatine setting.

In China agar agar comes as strips of processed seaweed that look like cellophane. After being soaked in water it looks and behaves like transparent rubber, and with various flavourings is usually served cold, which multiplies the comedic effect; but apparently it's not a joke.

Autumn dulse: this comes with a dark red colour and very full shellfish/seaweed flavour. Once soaked, dredge with seasoned flour and deep fry, to make frivolous but arrestingly flavoured snacks or garnishes.

Dabberlocks/wakame: very accessible and unseaweed-like flavour, rather like combining green nuts and young peas. It's olive green, good in chicken stews and soups

Dulse: greenish red coloured and a definite marine/shellfish flavour, but less so than autumn dulse.

Fingerware/finger kombu: olive green with a meaty, beefy flavour that is nonetheless uncompromisingly marine. Rather limited in use by itself but good mixed into salads and other vegetable mixtures, or in stuffings. Interesting to boil it for 20 minutes and then to grill it to crispness as a garnish for fish dishes.

Grockle/ herb kombu: looks like a fleshy vine leaf and is much the same olive colour as cooked ones. It has a slight astringency behind a chestnut-marine flavour. Fry in egg batter as tempura or deep fry in seasoned flour

Kombu/konbu: dark green or brown sheets of the giant kelp which shows high quality if it has a sheen, a powdery surface and is thick. It should be wiped rather than rinsed. This is the seaweed one cooks in water very briefly with dried bonito flakes, *katsuobushi*, to make *dashi*, the basic Japanese stock.

Laver/ sloke/purple nori: can be red or black depending how it is cooked. Has an iodine-like back taste which is easily balanced by good vinegar or orange juice, but rarely is, which is why I find it difficult to countenance the favour in which Welsh laverbread is held. It is sold ready prepared after cooking for hours, and may also be bought in cans.

Nori: essential to sushi. This is dried Japanese laver, and is usually slightly toasted before use; it may simply be crushed and sprinkled as a condiment. Can also be bought ready-toasted.

Sugarwart/sugar kombu/girdle tang: a delicate looking and tasting seaweed, not unlike a salt-sea version of spring greens. You can do almost anything with it. Once rehydrated it makes a jolly good wrapping for fish that is to be baked or steamed.

Nuts

Nuts are fruits with a hard or leathery casing around an edible kernel. But not everything commonly referred to as a nut is one: for instance, peanuts are technically legumes, brazil and cashew nuts are seeds, and tiger nuts are tubers. Nuts to all that you might say, but you'd be overlooking a very important source of protein, fats, minerals and vitamins, which is why vegetarians are so keen on them.

In Europe the fruit of the oak, the acorn, was part of earliest man's diet. Pliny called the oak 'the tree which first produced food for mortal man'. Remains of acorns have been found around the Upper Great Lakes in settlements dating from at least 2000 BC and the early Yosemite Indians made a porridge with them. Almonds and pistachios are referred to in the Bible and right up until the end of the 18th century almonds and walnuts were blanched, pulverized and soaked in water to provide a staple milk.

As well as being edible in their own right, nuts are very important commercially: the oil from hazelnuts is widely used in cosmetics and soap making, almond oil is used for moisturizing creams, and a rather nasty component of the whole cashew nut is used making plastics.

There's hardly a country in the world that does not have an indigenous edible nut, but here in the West we seem to have settled for rather a short list.

Almonds: probably the world's most popular nut and grown commercially in Spain, Italy, France, Portugal, Morocco and the Canary Islands. The United States is now largely supplied by the fast-expanding Californian industry.

The pretty almond tree, with its ornamental blossom, needs soil rich to a depth of 3.6m/12ft and with very good drainage. It starts to bear useful fruit in its third or fourth year and increases its yield annually for 12-20 years. Harvesting must start as soon as the outer hulls are fully split open; if they are left too long the nuts stick tightly to the shell and are known as 'sticktights', a dread thing if you are an almond farmer. Usually the nuts are dislodged from the trees with long thin poles but in California the pole has a padded mallet-like head and this collection method is called chubbing. Immediately after hulling the nuts are put in the sun to dry – if this is delayed the shells darken in colour. They're left to dry for two days to three weeks depending on the weather. This is one nut where you need to know something about types:

Flaked almonds: one of the most useful of all ingredients in a kitchen. They are expensive but you need very few to add flavour and interest to an extraordinary variety of food. They should usually be toasted but for use in cream sauces can be left their natural colour, although a quick flash in a microwave will firm up their texture without changing the flavour.

Toasted or fried in a little oil, microwaved or dry-fried in a non-stick pan, they finish off salads superbly and are excellent in sauces with rich fish and seafood, as their crispness complements the solidity of such flesh. Wonderful with potatoes, peas, beans and squashes. Creamy tomato sauces, white wine sauces and richer pasta sauces containing cream are all much the better for the addition of a few toasted flaked almonds.

Toasted flaked almonds convert ice cream into something far more interesting too, and make a simple two- or three-fruit salad into a specialty of the house. An easy way to smarten up a simple cold pie or mousse is to whip cream, flavour it with orange flower water and then fold in toasted almond flakes. Almost good enough to serve by itself – perhaps with a mountain of baby meringues. My newest use for them is incorporated into meringues: add some untoasted flakes to the mixture and cook a little longer than usual. The almond will toast and flavour the meringues, which are all the better for being flavoured with such liqueurs as Mandarine Napoleon or Creme de Cacao.

Ground almonds: another invaluable standby and I'm sorry soaring prices don't let me use them as lavishly as once was possible. They add wonderful richness and moistness to fruit cakes, make superb custards and tarts, transport stuffings into heaven, enrich sauces, and generally lift the ordinary into the extraordinary. I prefer to grind my own, for ground almonds can be very soapy and it's hard to know whether this is because of intrinsically low quality or staleness; it's not worth the risk. When well-flavoured seedless white grapes, muscatels ideally, are in season, make a generous layer of grapes in a rich blind-baked pastry shell and then fill this with a mixture of 125g/4oz of ground almonds, two eggs, about 300ml/½ pint of double/heavy cream and sugar to taste. Bake in a gentle oven until set and lightly browned and then serve warm or cool.

Slivered and nibbed: these fancier shapes, one long and thin, the other short and sort of fat, are mainly recommended for special decoration or where you want to add some texture – in a nut stuffing, for instance. In most cases flaked almonds would be as good, and probably cheaper.

Whole blanched or unblanched halves: used mainly for cake decorating when they are all the better for being lightly toasted or roasted all through, and in some Chinese dishes, notably with deep-fried seaweed. If you are going to use them in cakes they really should be roasted first, otherwise they will soften during cooking and their flavour will also be diluted. The best way to roast is in a microwave, which guarantees they are cooked through and not just browned on the outside. If you want to finish a sauce with whole or halved blanched almonds then they should be added only a few minutes before serving, again to conserve crispness.

Bitter: although very important in many dishes where just one or two round-out an almond flavour, these are very harmful if eaten in quantity. They contain the deadly poisonous prussic acid, 'given away' in detective stories by its lingering smell of bitter almonds. Very hard to come by I find, but an excellent adjunct if you use almonds a lot in cooking; they work like lemons, orange or other fruit, bringing out all the essential flavour of the sweet almond yet without intruding. You can get something of the same flavour, without the intensity, by using cherry or apricot kernels.

Californian: a new type grown only in California with advanced techniques and irrigated orchards. Used mainly by confectioners.

Californian nonpareil: the principal variety grown in California, it is of medium width but quite flat.

Jordan: mainly grown in Malaga and Alicante and sometimes called the finger almond as their long, slender shape resembles the little finger. Jordan almonds are the sweet dessert kind and extensively used in cooking. Graded according to size, large Jordans are sold retail, and the small ones go to confectioners who need a long variety for making sugared almonds. These are the ones with which the eyes of oriental beauties are compared.

Valencia: grown in Spain and Portugal, these are the flatter, heart-shaped nuts, with a rougher, tougher skin and less sweet flavour. Sold mainly for cooking, they are usually blanched and skinned and used widely for cake decoration, especially for Dundee cakes.

Argan: used for oil – see page 452.

Brazil: the brazil nut does indeed come from Brazil, but you might not know it's a seed and not a nut. Each is one of the 8-24 seeds arranged like segments of an orange inside a globular fruit 5-10cm/2-4in in diameter.

Other names by which it is known include butternut, cream nut, castanea and paranut. The nut's rich flavour indicates a very high fat content and it also contains protein, iron and thiamine, one of the vitamins necessary to prevent you going nutty.

They are the only major nut which cannot be cultivated but must be collected from the tropical forest, produced by wild trees which grow up to 35m/115ft, and are thus altogether as resolutely and immutably organic as it is possible to be. The harvesting season is between January and June, which is how they get to us so nicely in time for Christmas. They are not much used in cooking, for no other reason than the expense I expect. They are very good with chocolate, a not unexpected thing when you consider their common birthright.

Cashew: native to Central and South America, the cashew was taken to East Africa and India in the 15th and 16th centuries and now grows abundantly along their coastlines, so much so India serves them as a curry.

Related to the American poison ivy and the poison sumac, the tree and its fruit must be treated with great care. The nut – which isn't a nut but a seed – looks very odd on the tree, rather disturbingly like a worm eating its way into or out of the base of a soft, fleshy apple. The flesh of the cashew apple is used to make jams and jellies and drinks, a roadside stall staple throughout much of Central and South America.

After the whole nuts are detached from the apples they are left to dry in the sun. The edible seed is enclosed in two shells between which there is a brown oil that blisters human skin; this oil can be collected and used as a lubricant, an insecticide, and in the production of plastics.

The traditional method of extraction begins with the burning of the nuts amongst logs. This causes the tough outer shell to crack but the burning of the oil releases intensely injurious fumes. Modern methods get over this by roasting in enclosed cylinders. Either way, the inner shells still have to be broken open, usually by hand, and the kernels heated again to remove the remaining skin. I wonder who first bothered to cope with all this fuss and danger – they must have been very hungry.

Left raw, cashew nuts have definite vegetal flavour and the pallid, wrinkled look of anaemic distress. Ah, but when roasted they seem to plump up with good heart and offer a full flavour that's uniquely appealing, with or without salt.

The Chinese use toasted cashew nuts in combination with chicken and pork, at least those living in London do. I use them in stuffings for pork and chicken and they are my favourite snack. The Indian curry uses raw cashew, but I think roasted ones are much nicer to eat, and tastier, too. Otherwise I don't know of much specialized use for them in food, but I reckon the time is coming when I should experiment with tarts and flans, scones and with biscuits for cheese, perhaps with equally sweet oatmeal.

Chestnuts: chestnuts roasting by an open fire are an essential component of any vision of Olde England – and of Tin Pan Alley. What the songs don't tell you is that pieces of red-hot, chestnut shell burst in all directions, burning you and your carpet. If you wish to sin by the fire with Elinor Glyn on a bearskin – or to err with some other kind of her – there are ways to protect yourself and eat your chestnuts. You buy a small but very long-handled pan enclosed by a lid with holes in it and roast chestnuts in this, thus ensuring the safer pursuit of other traditional fireside activities. The combination of fireside and chestnuts has also been used to tell amatory fortunes. Dorothy Hartley tells us in her seminal *Food in England*: 'It was a fortune-telling trick to name the row of chestnuts set along the top bar of the hot grate, and the first name to pop was to be the first lover to pop the question. If he jumped into your lap, you had him; if he popped into the fire and was burnt up... well, you didn't!'

Chestnuts are different and interesting for many reasons. They are the only nut we treat as a vegetable and, as they contain the least amount of oil and most starch of any nut, are the most digestible and the only ones we can turn into a useful flour. Personally I find the shelling and peeling of fresh chestnuts a bore and for most recipes the canned or dried kind are perfectly adequate and now these have been superceded by wondrous cooked, vacuum-packed ones; you just snip and use. I wouldn't begin to try to make the wonderful French vanilla-flavoured chestnut purée, the discovery of which converts any cook into a better cook of biscuits, pastries, cakes and puddings. Buy it whenever you see it.

If you do want to prepare your own chestnuts, you would once have pierced the flat ends, put them into boiling water for five minutes or so and when cool enough to handle then removed the shell and skin very easily. Today it is easier to pierce them and then to put them into a microwave cooker, with just a little water. But, everyone has their favourite method and if yours isn't the same as mine I won't argue. An important thing to remember is chestnuts don't have a great deal of flavour, and that without care even this can be diluted.

There are several varieties of chestnuts, which mainly differ by having one or more nuts inside the shell. Only when there is a single floury nut in the shell can it be called a marron, and the best of these are held to come from the Ardeche, a beautiful French region of lakes, rivers, pine and chestnut tree clad hills. It was once a centre of the French silk trade, but when there was a slump in 1882, a certain Clement Faugier set up a chestnut-processing plant in a town called Privas. Faugier is now the most famous marron producing firm of all, and still run by descendants of its founder: that's the name to look for on the cans of vanilla-chestnut purée. Chestnuts can be bought in a wide variety of states, all of them worth your investigation.

Chestnut flour: mainly found in Italian stores and almost exclusively used in Italian kitchens. When mixed with water it makes a non-elastic dough (there being no gluten content) and this is made into fritters, porridges of various kinds mixed with cream, milk, water or oil and an extraordinary yeast-leavened cake flavoured with aniseed. It is also used for a chestnut-type polenta.

Dried (dehydrated): expensive but an excellent standby in the larder of any imaginative cook, so buy plenty when they are in the shops at Christmas. Provided they are stored in a cool place, dried chestnuts keep for at least 18 months. All you have to do is soak them in warm water until they can be bitten through or cut with a knife; but you can be more inventive than that.

I simmer the dried chestnuts gently in red or white wine spiced with cinnamon, nutmeg, a little orange peel and bay leaf and these can be served as is. Or I'll cook them with red wine, a little garlic and some small pieces of fatty bacon, for chestnuts take to fat and smoky flavours like anything. Either way, reduce the liquid until it just covers the chestnuts. These reconstituted and reflavoured chestnuts are then ready for roughly chopping into stuffings and sauces, to add to Brussels sprouts (a classic combination), or to serve by themselves with roasted meats and poultry. Another wonderful idea is to drain them after reconstituting then turn them in a hot caramel of butter and lightly browned sugar – very gala, very simple.

You can also reconstitute them plainly to mash with sugar and spices and vanilla as the basis for sweets and puddings, but it's hard to make one as good as that you buy. If you want to use whole chestnuts or chestnut halves in any dish, I think the reconstituted dried ones have more bacon/smoke flavour than those in tins (in fact I'm sure of it). As dried chestnuts are invariably from Italy it may have something to do with the variety used.

Dried chestnuts make excellent additions and stretchers to casseroles. In this case I often don't reconstitute them first but put them into the cooking liquid in the dried state. This way they make their contribution to the overall flavour and benefit in turn from all the flavoured fats and liquor; if you use ready-constituted chestnuts they would be more likely to give their flavour out and take nothing back and thus should added only long enough for them to heat through.

Chestnuts are especially good foils to the richer winter stews that include pieces of fat bacon, and are wonderful with pigeons and pork dishes of all kinds.

Purée, plain: not something you might use a lot of, but its concentrated flavour and delicious rich colour is useful. Mixed with breadcrumbs, chopped celery green, some brandy and a little onion or garlic it makes a simple moist stuffing for veal or poultry, although this is better baked separately, or made into small balls and cooked around the meat. Or the purée can be added to a pancake mixture to make chestnut fritters to go with all manner of vegetarian, poultry or meat dishes: the best version also includes some buckwheat flour and is served thick and hot with pork sausages for breakfasts and brunches.

It's common to accompany duck with chestnut purée in some form; you might simply mix in some cream, salt and pepper, beat in one egg to each 150ml/5fl oz of purée, and gently bake this beneath the roast for 40 minutes or until it has a crisp brown crust. This would then be a superior chestnut polenta. You might also consider mixing in some whole, uncooked cranberries before baking.

Purée, vanilla: perhaps one of the most delicious things you can buy in a can. No, not perhaps –

definitely! It's too rich and sweet for most people to eat as it is, so what you do is this: fold it gently with equal quantities of whipped cream, and then add a tot of brandy or sherry for good measure. Simplicity itself, and yet truly heavenly.

Here are just a few of the ways I have used this mixture. It can be crammed into freshly made profiteroles, perhaps with a black cherry in each that has been soaked in black rum for a while; stick the profiteroles together in a pyramid shape with light caramel. For a wedding at which 60 guests in formal dress sat down in candle light to a ten-course dinner, I had to make a pudding that would also serve as the wedding cake. So I sandwiched one chocolate and one vanilla meringue together with this chestnut cream mixture, thus achieving a very pretty three-tone colour graduation. These were then built into a mountain some 90cm/3ft high and, having alternated the way they were presented, the mountain appeared to be made in stripes of white and brown. It created a sensation when brought in but nothing compared to that caused when served up, for each plate was also sauced with a mix of pureed black cherries and black rum, thickened and glossed with arrowroot. The bride said it was worth getting married for: the groom had his mouth full.

Chocolate goes well with chestnuts and with the chestnut and cream mixture; next time you want to make a spectacular cake, bake a couple of chocolate sandwiches (use Betty Crocker mixes for something really rich and fail-safe), join them with a thick layer of the mixture then mix icing sugar with more of it for a firmer icing. You might sprinkle orange or coffee liqueur onto a layer of the cake; you could also add a layer of fresh mandarin sections, or more black cherries, a combination that is also fool-proof. If you make the mixture taste more of cream than chestnuts, you can serve it with almost any fruit, but it's fantastic with strawberries and raspberries.

I'm not going to give you all my best ideas but here's a last one worth remembering: make some millefeuille squares from puff pastry, split and rebake to crisp right through. When cool, spread thickly with the chestnut and cream mixture then arrange unsweetened strawberry halves that you have flavoured with a little orange juice, orange flower water or orange liqueur: if you use too much the fruit's skin will go mushy. Cover these with the top layer of the millefeuille, then if you have the time and inclination, glaze each with some lightly coloured caramel which you should allow to run willy nilly over the edges.

Vacuum-packed: unquestionably one of the best ideas ever from the French. Just right for crumbling into stuffings, for bulking up stews and casseroles, tipping through Brussels sprouts, pumpkins and squashes: excellent to give unexpected texture and flavour in a vegetarian lasagne too.

Coconut: the coconut has been admired for countless generations, and relied upon for far more than just food and romantic backdrops. Some of our earliest civilizations, certainly those in the Indus Valley, ate them, and the Chinese have included them in their diet for almost as long and are thought to have been the first to use coconut meat and milk in confectionery.

The tree is probably native to India, the coasts of south-east Asia, South America and the Caribbean and could have got to the South Seas in several ways. The coconut is an extraordinarily hardy traveller and can survive in salt water for a long time, and then will happily take root on hitting land. Or the people who became Polynesians may simply have taken some along when they left parts of south-east Asia and settled on islands throughout the South Pacific; or later invaders from South America could have carried them to these islands, as suggested by the great Kon-Tiki expedition. Those in the Bahamas were planted in the famous pink sands after Columbus had found them further south.

Every part of the coconut palm is useful and the Sanskrit word for it means 'tree which furnishes all the necessities of life'. The leaves are used for walls, thatching and packaging; the trunk is used for building; the hair covering the mature nut makes coir matting; the oil from the meat appears in cosmetics, soap and suntan oils; the meat itself is food, either fresh or dried (copra); the water is used as a refreshing drink, milk is used for cooking; the shell is an eating or drinking bowl, or, for centuries, a top-people's travel souvenir. If you wanted to keep up with the Marco Polos in 14th century Venice you had to have a silver-mounted *noce di coco* in your palazzo. Even in the late 19th century polished coconut shells were still being mounted in silver and sent home by the adventuring scions of European families.

But there's always something new, even with such an ancient food. Clever – or lazy – men in Thailand now have trained monkeys to shin up the palms and carefully choose nuts of the preferred degree of ripeness and then to pick them, which saves their owners either (a) doing it themselves or (b) paying someone else. The state of ripeness of the nut is rather important, for although it will drop to the ground all by itself when nice and ripe, the coconut water contained in the younger, green coconuts is more plentiful and more delicious.

When I stayed in a beach hut on an otherwise deserted 20-mile strip of burning white sand on the Gulf of Siam, I was impressed to find our host had thoughtfully imported lads to shin up the trees to gather fresh coconuts each morning, so we could drink that cool and refreshing liquid. What he had overlooked was to tell us that coconut water has a decided laxative effect – something we found ourselves learning *a posteriori*.

The name coconut is based on old Portuguese and Spanish words which mean 'grinning face', a reminder of the appearance of one end of the nuts, on which there are three darker spots looking like eyes and a mouth. Dr Johnson referred to it as the cocoanut, which was an accident, but it took a long time for the spelling to revert to its original.

The coco de mer is a double coconut of enormous size found only on two islands of the Seychelles; polished specimens have become the new tourist status symbol and their undoubted resemblance to oiled and suntanned buttocks or voluptuous female thighs ensure the neighbours notice them.

If you don't fancy coping with whole coconuts, the meat and milk can be bought in two basic forms:

Desiccated or flaked coconut: particularly popular in Australasia, where desiccated coconut is put into or onto more sweet and savoury dishes than even Dame Edna Everage could deride. Lamington cakes are squares of sponge coated with chocolate syrup and coconut and are as essential at a Down Under christening as the vicar or, these days, the celebrant. Coconut bumblebees, coconut ice and coconut-sprinkled fruit salads and curries will be as lifeblood to the newly named child. Actually, it is very good in all these foods, especially in curries with which it can also be served as a condiment.

Coconut cream and coconut milk can be made from desiccated coconut by covering, say, 150-200g/6-7oz with boiling water and leaving it to cool. Then put the coconut into a sieve or some muslin, and mash or squeeze it to extract the creamy-white liquid. If you leave it thick it is 'cream', or you can dilute this with water to make 'milk'. The liquid inside a coconut is not coconut milk but coconut water, and although widely drunk is rarely used in cooking.

Cream of coconut: although you can sometimes buy coconut milk canned it has usually been adulterated and sweetened. Better to buy a solid block of cream of coconut, which lasts for ages, is pure, and can simply be reconstituted by dissolving an amount in hot or boiling water. The thicker it is the richer, obviously, and as both thick cream or thin milk it can be used like the dairy product. Thick coconut cream separates and 'oils' if heated to boiling point and this is done deliberately in West Indian, Malaysian and some Thai cooking.

Thick coconut cream spread on top of a grilled pork chop or roasted chicken gives an interesting and instant lift to otherwise ordinary food. Even such basics as vanilla ice cream, sliced oranges or grilled bananas are magically transformed; and used with care in association with finer fruits like strawberries or the wonderful mango, thick, chilled coconut cream makes child's play of creating new desserts during hot summer months. I always keep a block of coconut cream in the refrigerator.

You don't always have to eat it, coconut milk is terrific in long summery drinks with rum and fruit juices – a hot evening, a barbecue, some friends, some coconut cream, assorted fruits and alcohols and you'll have a memorable party – or, if you are really lucky, a party that no one remembers!

I like to finish a spicy, gingery curry sauce by leaving solid coconut cream to melt in the liquid, and it can add new dimensions of flavour to the most unexpected vegetables – I think you'll like sliced aubergine baked gently in coconut milk spiked with a few rings of green chilli peppers. Rice cooked in coconut milk or cream is a revelation, and so is coconut cream as a dressing for crunchily cooked green beans, or on lettuce, both favourites of my Pitcairn Island relatives.

Gingko nuts: mildly flavoured and with a rather strange starchy-rubbery texture, these small buff-coloured productions of the gingko tree are used as garnish or ingredients in all types of Chinese dish. Best bought canned in brine.

Hazelnuts: hazelnuts are cobnuts are Kent cobs are filberts; the differences are technical and determined by the relative length of the nut to the husk, cobs usually being rounder and filberts somewhat longer. In the United States all types are called filberts, a name originally given because they ripen on or about St Philbert's Day, August 22nd. In Europe, filbert usually denotes a hazelnut that has been cultivated.

The 15 species of shrub and tree from which this small and important nut come range in height from 2.7-36m/9-120ft and belong to the birch family. They need deep well-drained soil with plenty of sun, and thus Turkey, Italy and Spain are the chief producers. The finest nuts are said to come from trees best described as Eurasian – the European and the giant hazelnut. Hybrids of these with the American and Beaked Filbert are also excellent producers. Constantinople nuts is a trade name for Turkish hazelnuts, and those from Spain are known as Barcelona nuts. In New Zealand they call them monkey nuts.

From a culinary point of view hazelnuts are essential to a great part of the finest traditions of European cake making and confectionery, when they are usually used in ground form. Although there is some argument as to whether one should use hazelnuts, almonds or both to make praline, I think the purely hazelnut variety infinitely better.

Hazelnuts taste much better when lightly toasted, or, if you have the patience, slowly roasted until golden all the way through: microwaving is a faster and better way to do this. Lightly toasted and carelessly crushed hazelnuts are good to sprinkle over fruit dishes, in cereals, muesli, yoghurt, cream and with green vegetables. They are specially good with the aristocratic mangetout, or with broccoli, particularly if bathed with some garlic-ridden butter.

Toasted hazelnuts, whole or chopped, crushed or ground are quite one of the best additions to stuffings and dressings and make a fascinating addition to meat gravies and game sauces. I recently stuffed boned trout with a mixture of grated celeriac, chopped hazelnuts and garlic, baked them in a hot oven and served them with a dollop of chilled soured cream – perfectly simple and quite memorable. So too are strawberries served with whipped cream stiffened with ground or chopped hazelnuts.

Macadamia: a relatively new arrival on the international scene and still little known in Europe, macadamia nuts are something of a cult food in America, particularly in Hawaii where macadamia shops are as shiny and well-staffed as gas stations used to be. There they've done more things with macadamia nuts than you can – or would want to – imagine. Every kind of chocolate shape, every kind of jam, jelly and marmalade, every kind of cake, biscuit, cookie and character includes the macadamia.

The extraordinary thing about this is the tree upon which it grows is Australian, a native of Queensland and New South Wales. The shucked nut looks something like a pale, fat hazelnut and has a curious, fatty, waxy texture and a somewhat fugitive taste that can barely be described as 'nutty', perhaps slightly buttery. The ones I've been sold as cocktail snacks were all helped with a little coconut milk oil, so perhaps there's not all that much unaided flavour. Why the fuss?

Well, good marketing strategy excepted, they have a most valid claim to the world's very serious attention for they have an exceptionally high protein content and are being studied as a new and simple alternative protein source in remote tropical areas. If you manage to get some you will probably find them so expensive you won't dare eat them. Best plan is to pop into a macadamia shop on Waikiki Beach and taste one or two of their confections offered as free samples.

And the name? It is associated with the man who pioneered the use of a tar mixture on our roads; the nut was one of Mr Macadam's later interests.

Hemp seeds: hemp seed and hemp oil are used more and more in foods in the US – you can even find hemp milk, ice bread, butters, cheese and beer. The seeds have a good high amino acid count, almost as high as soy beans but come with the blessing of being less 'windy'. Their taste is in the range of the sunflower/pumpkin seed, and when toasted it becomes more delicious and, well, nuttier. One of the few things that can work as a substitute for pine nuts.

Peanuts: peanuts, which are not nuts at all but legumes, are also called groundnuts, earth nuts, monkey nuts... and goolers. Yes, that's right, monkey nuts and goolers. Perhaps it's to avoid such names that peanuts hide underground: if it's not this, then the dying flower burrows down in the soil to protect her offspring. At harvest time the entire plants, except for the deepest roots, are pulled up and left to wither in the sun for a day. Then they are built into large stacks around a stake with the pods towards the centre to protect them from the weather. In 4-6 weeks they are ready to be used to make all manner of goodies – peanut oil, peanut butter, salted peanuts, spiced or dry-roasted peanuts, or the peanut sauces that make Indonesian foods so original and full of flavour.

Traces of peanuts have been found in ancient Peruvian mummy graves and from their native South America they have now spread to India, Indonesia, China, West Africa and the United States.

Peanuts are very much better for you than their usage as monkey food would suggest. Pound for pound, they have more protein, minerals and vitamins than beef liver, more food energy (calories) than sugar and more fat than double cream.

A superb snack treat is freshly marketed peanuts that have just been boiled; before this is done the flavour is rather feral. The skin is very soft and peels away easily and the flavour of the warm peanuts is immensely comforting. I've only ever seen and bought these in the fruit and vegetable section of Paddy's Market in Sydney.

Pecan: native to North America where they were widely used by Native Americans, who called it pecan, a word describing all nuts with shells so hard they need to be cracked with a stone. As well as eating its meat, the Indians ground it into a milky liquid for use in gruels and maize cakes, a combination that would be very good. It is now grown in a belt stretching from New Mexico to the Carolinas, and as far north as Illinois; South Africa, Australia and New Zealand also cultivate some.

The pecan is claimed to have the highest fat content of any vegetable food, with a calorific content similar to that of butter. The trees grow anything up to 48m/160ft high with a span of up to 21m/70ft and so harvesting is mainly by variations of beating branches or shaking the trees. Shelling is difficult, and a labyrinth of conveyors, blowers, reels, fans, graders, pickers, dyers and packers can take up to three days ultimately to separate the kernel from the shell and sort it into uniform grades; this complicated processing is the reason for its relative expense. Although most pecan trees are wild and grow on the banks of rivers and creeks, there is also a cultivated variety made possible by the experiment with grafting successfully carried out by a Louisiana slave in 1850. The cultivated tree produces a nut with a thinner shell and thus gives a better yield for being less tiresome to process.

Whole pecans are recognizable by their red, grey-brown, shiny appearance, something like an acorn without its cap. They can be infuriatingly difficult to crack – using a hammer often disintegrates the shell and the nut, or forces splinters of one inextricably into the other. The best way is to hold two nuts in one palm and then to squeeze; one of them should crack right round the middle and the two halves can be extricated. Well, that's what should happen.

Pecan halves and pieces are good in sweet pies, vegetable purées or dessert pastries that include spices, they are often said to be interchangeable with walnuts, but in my opinion the substitution could only be made for reasons of economy. The pecan has a far richer and more elegant flavour, without the acidic bite walnut so often has, perhaps because it is going stale. If you ever want to bribe me, give me pecan pie: I'll do anything – before, during and after.

Pepitas: these are raw, green pumpkin seeds, either toasted as nibbles or used in some versions of mole sauces q.v.

Pine nuts/pine kernels: these delicious morsels really are from pine trees, usually the stone pine, but other pines can sometimes be the source. They are the quintessence of one of the world's most beguiling cuisines, the epitome of luxurious ingredients made accessible, an inescapable essential for the food of the eastern Mediterranean, and North Africa, as well as Turkey and Greece.

The small, moon-coloured nuts, slim and elongated, are rich and oily and taste of the merest startle of a whisper of pine resin, and are perfectly addictive once you begin to eat them. More so once toasted: generally they are browned lightly before being used, either in a little oil or in a dry non-stick pan, but the microwave is more reliable and does not need the addition of oil or butter, and noticeably concentrates the flavour.

Pine nuts are an important ingredient in the famed basil pesto of Genoa, pounded with fresh basil, garlic, oil and Parmesan into a famously fragrant sauce for pasta, tomatoes, roasted vegetables and fish – for almost anything good you eat in summer.

To convert any rice dish, even plain rice, into something Levantine, toasted pine nuts with or without currants and chopped pistachios are all you need, scattered on at the last moment. Added to a saffron-scented pilaff they are even better.

Once sweetened, I find pine kernels make a delicious and unexpected garnish for simple puddings like ice creams and lemon mousses; they go very well with fresh, lightly flavoured cream cheese, too. The most spectacular way to sweeten them is first to brown a little butter (carefully) then to add sugar and to let that caramelize before you add the nuts. The sugar and butter will coat the nuts with a crunchy toffee; I first did this to top poached whole satsumas, served in their syrup with rose water flavoured cream cheese.

You are likely to see two sizes of pine nuts: the bigger ones, fatter and proportionally shorter, will be from China.

Pistachios: this is the most maddening nut of all – once you eat one you have to eat another, then just one more... until your fingernails ache and bleed from opening the shells, you cry out for liquid because of the salt, and your surroundings are littered with raped shells. But what bliss!

I've not been able to discover why pistachios are nearly always sold still in their shells, slightly cracked open and salted. Perhaps they keep better that way, as good a reason as any. They can also be bought shelled and unsalted, which is what you use for cooking.

This green nut, rich and decorative too through its wine-red skin, is grown from Afghanistan to the Mediterranean and in the United States, where it is particularly popular as a flavour in ice cream. The pistachio is expensive and has always been so, for there are records of complaints about its prohibitive cost from Ancient Rome. Of the more accessible places, Aegina in Greece's Saronic Gulf produces the most wonderful, and no visit to this island can be considered unless you are prepared to gorge yourself. Strangely it is the only place in Greece they grow.

Pistachios are invaluable for decorating, chopped finely over sweet or savoury food, hot or cold. Pistachios are essential, chopped roughly, in good Middle Eastern pilaffs that also include saffron and toasted pine nuts. Finely chopped pistachios are part of the fillings for baklava q.v., those siren-like Greek, Turkish and Arabic pastries and are also excellent in poultry stuffings. But Europe and the USA have never really taken this nut to their heart – or stomach – and it appears only rarely in specialized cakes or ice creams, usually in association with a muddy green colouring, which has nothing to do with its natural state of affairs. In fact most pistachio flavouring is achieved by artificial means and tastes more like almonds, which is a terrible let down. I always send pistachio ice cream back if it tastes of almonds – especially if it is expensive and served in a restaurant with airs.

To get the really bright green colour that looks so good, boil the nuts for 30 seconds in water and then peel away the skin; if the nuts do not brighten, too bad, for they are not of the best quality and you'll shop more carefully next time.

Pumpkin seeds: at least as addictive as salted pistachios and quite as messy. You have to break the outer shell to get at the green-black inner meats. A way of life in Turkey and many near and Middle Eastern countries, and endemic in Mexico and South America, where they have probably been discarding the husks for thousands of years – this continent is whence pumpkins and squash came to the Old World. Not used in cooking, but see pepitas.

Tiger nuts: these are the least nut-like nut of all, for they are actually tubers. Looking like a cross between shrivelled peanuts and extruded, dried dog food, they are perhaps better known under their Spanish name = chufas or alchulas, those from Valencia has DOP status.

Mainly eaten as a snack they have an extraordinary chewy texture and flavour, not unlike coconut crossed with brazil nut. They were very popular in Britain before the last war but disappeared with the corner shops. One supplier who is reintroducing them told me he has had letters from old people telling them how much they appreciate seeing them again: their new popularity might have something to do with package holidays.

In southern Spain you drink rather than eat them, in a very popular beverage called horchata. This is made by soaking the nuts overnight (start them in hot water) then putting them all into the liquidizer with the water. Drain well and reserve the milk, and then put the residue back into the liquidizer again with a little more water. Drain and save again, and then put the residue into muslin once more, tighten that and squeeze out the remaining milk. It is a really refreshing drink served chilled and if you've ever wondered what people do in a Spanish *horchateria*, now you know. *Horchata* can also be heated very slowly indeed in a double boiler and it will eventually thicken to make custard.

Tiger nuts are rarely used in cooking, but when soaked, apparently go well in apple pie.

Walnuts: walnuts have been with us a long time and have been eaten just as long. The Greeks used them lavishly, and still do in sweetmeats and pastries. The Romans spread walnut trees wherever they marched. Some can be seen preserved in the volcanic ash at the Temple of Isis in Pompeii and legionnaires may have introduced them to the British Isles.

The black and the butternut walnuts grow in the eastern states of North America; the English or Persian walnut is common throughout Europe, the Middle East and China and has been introduced to the United States. The nut of the English variety is the only one commonly picked green and dried or ripened off the tree.

The walnut is a particularly versatile nut, found successfully in sweet and savoury dishes throughout the world. It has an astonishing affinity with tomatoes and the Caucasian combination of tomato and walnut sauce is sensational. Perhaps the simplest 'gourmet' dish of all is a bowl of sliced ripe tomatoes invested with slightly chilled walnut oil, a dusting of salt and plenty of roughly torn flat-leaf parsley – and even those last two can be forgone without diluting the pleasures. I also like toasted walnuts crushed together with green peppercorns and a drip or two of cognac in butter, and for this to then be slid under the skin of a pheasant before roasting.

Walnuts were once crushed and soaked to make milk but the almond variety is the only flavouring of this kind now made. Vegetarians like walnuts and use them extensively, usually eating them in combination with cracked cereals to form their vegetarian steaks.

The best advice when buying walnut halves is that light is right – the lighter the colour the higher the grade. If you are being asked to pay exceptionally high prices, the nuts should not only be pale, there should be no surface chipping and no smaller or broken pieces present, both of which are signs of a lesser grade. Remember when you are making cakes or pies with walnuts, that if they brown they often become very bitter.

Walnuts have more recently become a commercial crop in New Zealand and I have learned something astonishing. Fresh walnuts are creamy, rich, fascinating and don't have a background sharpness or bitterness: those that do are rancid or well on the way to that state, but this is the way most of us eat walnuts most of the time. From now on I am only going to buy or eat walnuts I know have come from close by.

Pickled walnuts are increasingly hard to buy, and like so many traditional English foods they seem to be disappearing because commercial manufacture is uncommercial. Some are made, but it is usually easier to buy them bottled from America; however, these are sweet pickled which is not to the English taste.

Game and Poultry

A somewhat misused term, game. Properly used it meant animals or birds that had to be hunted and killed before you could eat them.

You might still do this to grouse, partridge and pheasant, even to venison if you are rich enough – or poor enough to live in suitably remote areas. But generally a happy combination of greed and sense means most such birds and animals are now farmed, yet remain as game in the vocabulary.

The most important thing for serious cooks and eaters to remember is that farmed game will almost always be blander in flavour, not necessarily a bad thing, but it does mean that old-fashioned, strongly flavoured marinades are neither needed nor, necessary. This is particularly true when cooking venison.

The best use of game in the delicatessen and specialty food store is probably in pâtés and pies, especially Britain's famed raised pies. Or so the theory goes. I regularly find there is more presence of the pheasant or partridge or pigeon on the label than on the palate, and thus the premium we have paid has been obtained by false pretence. There's a good recipe later in this chapter and more about getting maximum flavour from game in the chapter Pies, Pâtés and Terrines.

As the taste grows for more interesting food, I expect the traditional country side flavours of the past will come more and more to the fore: pigeon and Barbary duck, rabbit and hare are regularly featured in national supermarkets and they are bound to work their way into more and more produce. It is as well you know what they should taste like before you are persuaded otherwise. And then you can work on liking wild boar, or ostrich.

Barbary duck and magret

This comparatively huge duck gives thick and long breast meat portions which are positively steak-like: indeed before the word magret came into fashion they would be seen on French menus as *steak de canard*. Duck breast meat is increasingly found available as an independent purchase and makes a terrific change from steak for those who like red meat. Generally the cooking instructions are grotesquely wrong – suggesting 40 minutes cooking for something that requires ten at the most. The best way is to score the fat in a deep criss-cross and then to cook at very high heat in a non-stick pan, fat side down for 4-6 minutes depending on how well cooked you like duck. Then pour away the fat, turn the meat and cook the same amount of time or less if you like very pink meat. If you eat this now it will be tougher than boots, new or old. They must, absolutely must, rest for another ten minutes, during which they tenderize and the colour evens, but they won't get cold, I promise you. They may also be grilled/broiled for about the same overall time.

But are these breasts magrets? Not if you wish to be accurate. A true magret is properly only the very lean breast of a Muscovy duck or of a relative that has been force fed to make *foie gras de canard*. Magret is derived from *maigre*, meaning slim or lean, because when Muscovies are force fed all their fat production goes into their livers and there is little under the skin and none in the flesh. This doesn't happen with Barbary duck breasts, but the name seems to be sticking,

Bison/buffalo

Don't blame Kevin Costner. America had rediscovered its great native mammal some time before he took sides with native Americans. Both in the United States and in Canada the animal is being successfully farmed for the gourmet. It tastes like beef but behaves like venison: it has very little fat and thus overcooks and toughens very easily. When it is good it is exceptionally good. So too is the much rarer and smaller musk ox of the Northern Territories, also being marketed now the species is on the increase. But so far the Inuit language names they use for it prove even more off-putting than calling it musk ox.

Chickens

At last, someone has listened and chicken is getting decidedly better to eat. To be fair much criticism was unfairly based; chickens did not taste fishy because they were fed with fishmeal, for this is expensive and would have put the price up. Like so many criticized foods, there has been and is enormous scope for improvement in standards and flavour, but minor shortcomings in basically decent produce were exacerbated by dreadful cooking advice on labels and packets from the very people who should know better. It is these 'recipe developers' rather than the producers who should have been shot: recipes that suggest you rub a microwaved chicken with gravy browning or worse – what is wrong with a nicely steamed chicken, that should be pale to be interesting?

The great appeal of chicken to the supermarket shopper is its cheapness compared to other meat, and for that it must be welcomed. Yet the birds who produce this meat are not really chickens, but have been bred to do things as far away from nature as possible, that is they put on as much flesh in six weeks as their ancestors might put on in ten to 12 months. They are puffed up monstrosities.

Today we have an increasingly excellent choice of more poultry available, including corn-fed, free range and a few less well-known varieties, and in Britain there are imports from France, too. For many people, chicken is once again becoming a special treat, for they only eat it when they can afford to buy one of these more natural ones. The rewards are manifold; not only does almost everyone exclaim with pleasure on their first mouthful, but stock made from the bones of a genuine free-range chicken is a revelation to the young, a nostalgic leap backwards for those of us who grew up watching grandfathers wring the neck of backyard chickens that had scratched free on the lawn, and dined only on grain and household scraps.

Petits Poussins/baby chickens: are increasingly heavily marketed. They look good, especially at picnics or when you are eating with your hands. But because they are so young they offer precious little flavour and so you should resist any temptation to be too clever with herbs and spices, or they will be all that you taste. In some parts of the world these are called spatchcocks, but that is properly the name for any bird that has been split down the back and laid flat: spatchcocking is an excellent way to cook and to serve poussins.

Needless to say the EU has issued very clear directives on what may be called what, based partly on stocking rates and partly on what the birds are fed. For AOC status birds from France, look for Chapon de Bresse, Volaille de Bresse, Poularde (pullet) de Bresse and Dinde de Bress. Only slightly less grand are the IGP status Volailles de Bourgogne, de Bretagne, de Challans, de Cholet, de Gascogne and de Janze.

Foie gras

Means fat liver, and that's what it is, the extra fatty livers of geese or if it is *foie gras de canard* of the Muscovy duck or of a new variety the Mulard, a sterile cross between a Muscovy and a Peking duck. The discomforting fact is this supreme delicacy is obtained by force-feeding the birds to such a degree the livers bloat with fat, for this is where it collects rather than under the skin: force-fed ducks are otherwise surprisingly lean – (see Magret). The process is seen by many as exceptionally cruel; others reckon both geese and ducks are so contrary and bad tempered you couldn't get them to do anything they do not want. You must make up your own mind.

Until the late 20th century foie gras came almost exclusively from geese, although there are mentions of fattened livers from capons, amongst other birds. Since then duck foie gras (*foie gras de canard*), has become very much more common. It most usually comes from the south west of France, notably Gascony, where the sudden leap of availability is put down to the simple ploy of shading the ducks during summer, keeping them happier and healthier. *Foie gras de canard* is cheaper than that from geese and many think it much better value, for it is less likely to explode into pools of melted fat thus further frustrating the gourmet, who must already make do with just 15 per cent of the foie gras produced – the remainder is unsuited to use whole and must be made into mousses and other commercial products. Some think goose foie gras is more finely flavoured and it probably is, but I belong to the ranks that think the flavour of foie gras de canard is more complicated and thus more gratifying. EU regulations state a fattened duck liver should weigh at least 250g and most are between 600g and 700g: geese livers should be at least 400g and thus up to 1.5 kg or so.

Fattened livers are nothing new, for the Ancient Greeks and Romans adored them and Ancient Egyptians seemed to have force fed their geese with figs. I've read the idea was based on the Ancient Egyptians' observation of geese fattening themselves before they migrated, and the experience of finding these birds alarmingly better tasting. So, they kept the geese and force fed them: grossly fattened livers were first the unexpected by-product and then rapidly became the target.

It was probably the Romans who brought the idea to France. Foie gras of both kinds are generally associated with Périgord but they are also a specialty of the Landes, Gascony and Alsace. Interestingly, its presence throughout Europe is usually associated with traditional centres of Jewry (they wanted the fat for cooking) and of ancient poverty: poor areas couldn't afford salt to preserve food for winter and thus fattened geese so they could use the fat as a winter preservative. Geese convert what food there is into flesh and fat more efficiently than almost any other animal and so the bloated liver was again pretty much a bonus rather than the goal.

Until the Second World War foie gras was produced widely all along the Danube, mainly by Middle Europe's Jewish centres; Hungary and Czechoslovakia used to export their livers to France and have started to do so again. Poland is producing them again and, continuing the Jewish connection, Israel has become a major exporter.

In Canada and the USA Mulard ducklings are available, sold as specifically suited for foie gras production. A particularly successful US producer is Hudson Valley Foie Gras in upper New York State, but that's only since 1989. In California Sonoma Foie Gras is made only with the original Muscovy duck, saying it has a more delicate cell structure and thus a more buttery texture and more intense flavour: additionally the livers have fewer sinews and veins and thus provide a higher yield, even when grilling or sautéing.

Foie gras/ foie gras d'oie/foie gras de canard, fresh: these are available in most European countries, including Britain, vacuum packed. They can be simply sliced and seared quickly in a very hot non-stick pan, less than a minute a side at the most. If everything is right a little of it will caramelise but it is not important it should brown. The technique is a racy balance between changing the texture of the liver and running the risk of melting it. There is nothing else without a pulse that has quite the same effect on the tongue: unctuous, smooth, slippery, satiny, delicate are not enough individually or combined. *Vanity Fair's* *Food Snob Dictionary* calls it 'a velvety ooze'. I've enjoyed slices on sweetcorn fritters, and on nothing but an expensive plate, but most memorably the venerable Poule au Pot in London's Pimlico, served two slices on toasted brioche pointed with pan juices deglazed with balsamic vinegar and with a glass of Monbazillac on the side. No wonder they've been in business over 30 years.

The flavour is as unique as the texture, for as the foie gras coats the palate and then slowly dissolves, layer after layer of infinite variation are revealed. Smaller gobbets of hot foie gras are used as garnishes for much simpler food, like potatoes, or black pudding (superb), often with game birds. These also make excellent additions to salads, but should come with a warning: suddenly finding a warm explosion of fat amidst the crunch of green leaves is remarkably like eating slugs.

The most extraordinary foie-gras moment in my life was the night I met uber-food-writer A. A. Gill. He was teaching a bray of doe-eyed debs to cook in his kitchen above High Street Kensington and I was writing for *The Sunday Telegraph* and so expected only to hover. Something was baking in hay from his own meadows, intricate boning to make something simple was in progress, when a friend arrived with a fresh foie gras. Adrian, for that is his name, turned and asked me what we should do with it? My nonplussment was severe enough to encourage one of the girls: 'a soufflé', she asked?

Met with puzzled silence she said, honestly she did: 'I once had dinner with three princes in New York and they cooked me a foie gras soufflé'.

Two of the three princes we telephoned weren't at home, and the Russian one confirmed the occasion but remembered nothing of their combined technique. I made something and everyone was very polite, but now I ache for a foie gras to come through the door, because now I know how to do it, I think.

André Daguin in Gascony served me raw foie gras, having merely salted it overnight and yet he seems not to be in horrid cahoots with the local undertaker. I survived. It's nice, but I found it required rather more mental effort than I expect to give food.

However you eat freshly cooked fresh foie gras, you will always need to rest afterwards, so both mind and palate can fully absorb and then remember the experience. The next best way to understand what all the fuss is about is *mi-cuit* or semi-cooked foie gras.

Duck foie gras with IGP status comes from Chalosee, Gascogne, Gers, Landes, Périgord and Quercy.

Semi-cooked or semi preserved foie gras/ mi-cuit: these are sometimes seen as *terrine de foie gras/ foie gras de canard* because the livers have been oven baked in a terrine. This is considered the finest way of preserving fat livers and although quite different in texture from freshly cooked foie gras, offers celestial flavour and texture unique in their own ways.

After being deveined, the liver lobes are cooked gently at a low temperature with little extra seasoning in a tightly closed container. That of Alsace will have been lightly kneaded and slightly spiced, whereas that from the south west of France will have been layered pretty much the way the lobes came, with just a little cognac or armagnac.

The juices that come out during cooking are soaked back into the liver. Some of the bright yellow fat will have escaped but that must be expected and then celebrated, for it has yet another different flavour and texture. With a low temperature and the sealed atmosphere nothing is lost, but more important nothing new has been gained. You need also a very loud timer, for if baked a moment too long the slight melt of fat becomes a major breakout, and you are left with quite nice liver in quite nice yellow fat, neither of which tastes as great as it might.

Provided the seal is not broken, and the liver has been cooked right through, and it is kept between 0°C and 5°C, it may last six to eight months, but remember it is not fully sterilized. Not normally available commercially and so the whole pieces you see in small glass preserving jars with the lid held by a wire hinge might look right, but have been cooked at a much higher temperature. It must say *mi-cuit* on the label.

A terrine of foie gras is not cooked in the usual sense you understand: instead the fleshy parts of the liver are set by heat that's gentle enough to do this without reducing the fat content to a puddle. In my experience, unless you are eating privately in areas of foie-gras production, the only place casually to enjoy *mi-cuit* foie gras is in restaurants in production areas. Little is as awe inspiring as watching your serving being moulded or scooped from a terrine that holds a kilo or more of nothing but gently cooked foie gras. The restaurants that take this trouble know ceremony is important to appetite and play discreetly to the importance of the occasion. In Alsace, anyway, they also understand the rituals of hospitality; after the briefest hesitation, the waiter always adds a little more than you thought you would get. This always tastes sweeter.

Mi-cuit foie gras is traditionally served at room temperature and with lightly toasted slices of bread or brioche and an excellent chilled sweet wine. Because both fruit and residual sugars are needed, Sauternes is a classic choice and so are the two unusual sweeter champagnes, champagne *sec* or *riche*. The luminous muscats of Rivesaltes or Beaume de Venise are commonly the more florid choice in the south west of France and any botryitised dessert wine from Australia or New Zealand makes a terrific show. Old menus from Gascony show foie gras was traditionally served at the end of a meal, making this style of wine more understandable: a Verdelho Madeira or the rare Palo Cortado sherry would be my other choices. I comfortably serve foie gras as a first course with a chilled sweet or fortified wine, for I find the huge flavours of both set up the palate for anything that follows. You don't need much else.

Now I am old enough to have eaten enough foie gras to have an opinion, this and flash-fried foie gras are the only cooked foie gras that taste like the real thing. The higher temperatures used in other processes change the flavour, moving it closer to chicken liver pâté. Sometimes, much of the luscious texture of foie gras is retained, but without the full fabled realms of traditional flavour, why bother? Even when offered a whole lobe of nothing but foie gras cooked at a high temperature, as anything in a can or jar must be, you might be better thrilled with chicken liver pâté.

Indeed, it's worth remembering chicken liver pâté when tasting foie gras: that way you will know if you are being fobbed off, promised the real thing on a menu but served with something from a can. It's happened to me twice, in the most august of London restaurants.

Pâté de foie gras/ fois gras de canard: there should be absolute clarity between *terrine de foie gras d'oie/ foie gras de canard* and *pâté de foie gras*.

Terrines are lightly cooked solid liver, as above, and never referred to as a pâté. Neither is any foie gras in cans a true pâté de foie gras. Cans contain foie gras in greater or lesser union with pork and other ingredients, the mousses and so forth to which unsuitable livers go, and so seem like pâtés, but the term means something very different, very precise.

Pâté de foie gras – actually foie gras with a pâté – was created in the late 18th century by Jean-Pierre Clause for the table of le Maréchal de Contudes, governor of Alsace, who sent some to Louis XVI. One M. Doyen is supposed to have perfected it, adding truffles. It is properly whole foie gras wrapped in a farce or forcemeat of pork (actually the pâté) and then baked in pastry or, occasionally in brioche. Unless made with exceptional skill the pork farce will overwhelm the flavour of the foie gras; thus unless you buy from a traiteur or restaurateur who comes highly recommended you are better off going for nothing but foie gras *mi-cuit*.

Canned foie gras products: the labelling on cans containing foie gras is complicated. When French products are made with goose liver, they need only say foie gras; if they are made from duck they say foie gras de canard. Once you have tasted the real thing you will find these quite a different product and not always easy to tell from pastes of lesser livers. They commonly have speckles touted as truffles, and indeed these may be, but I have yet to taste the effect on anything but the pocket.

Presented foie gras: a fancy way of saying canned whole foie gras. Fully sterilized in the usual way of canning. It is important the preserved liver is allowed to mature after processing – it needs six to eight months at least, but even so . . .

Natural/ au naturel: this indicates the content of the tin will be foie gras in one or several pieces. The label should tell you if a marinade or seasoning has been used.

Block, lingot, tombeau, massif, terrine, roll or **pâté:** any of these used as an adjective describing foie gras means a minimum of 75 per cent foie gras with pork, veal or poultry meat added.

Purée, mousse or cream: these adjectives indicate a minimum of 75 per cent foie gras, plus pork, veal, or poultry plus eggs, milk, wheat or cornflour up to a maximum of three per cent.

Mousse – foie d'oie: the trick is to notice it is foie d'oie not foie gras. It is ordinary goose liver and the mousse need only contain 50 per cent of it. The purées and mousses are mainly used as spreads on toast, but are often used in scoops or slices as garnish and should be very cold.

Goose

Dark meat, but not much of it, is the usual thought on goose. It's true, but the long shape of a gorgeously golden goose has something particularly festive about it, as does the smell of the sweet fat that puddles profusely during the cooking. No need to cook this bird on its side as the amount of fat keeps the flesh basted without any help from anyone. For special glamour, stir a couple of egg yolks into a saffron solution – a few tablespoons of boiling water poured over saffron strands and left for 20 minutes. Paint the mixture on to the goose's skin and return for the last 10 to 20 minutes of cooking, to make a genuine golden goose, the way medieval cooks would do. The old name for such gilding is endoring.

The most special thing about goose is how difficult it is to get one. Geese breed only once, in spring, and the offspring are considered best to eat in late autumn. This makes them good for Christmas in the northern hemisphere, but only just, and far too old and fat for a southern hemisphere Christmas. But they freeze particularly well, which helps. Apple sauce is a classic accompaniment, as is spiced red cabbage. When buying you have to allow at least 500g per serving.

Grouse

Few wild things are as rewarding as the red grouse. It is one of the game birds you can bounce directly into the oven the moment it drops from the sky, for it is always fabulously tender and sweet. Let it hang until whiffy and it becomes something different but equally worth your attention.

Best cooked dead plain in my view, and served with earthy celeriac purée, parsnip chips and watercress rather than the fatty palaver of game chips, bland bread sauce, bacon and such, all of which so coat the palate you have precious little chance of tasting all for which you have so heavily paid. As there is no fat under the skin, grouse may be peeled, skin feathers and all, rather than plucked.

At higher flavour levels grouse is the very best of ingredients for pies and pâtés, but not if you follow the 'traditional' method of expecting only the roasted flesh of a bird to flavour layers of fatty farce.

Cold grouse is perhaps the best breakfast I have eaten, in turn the only possible reason for subjecting myself to cooking for 14 in a remote Scottish farmhouse in August.

Guinea fowl: the oven-ready guinea fowl looks rather like a sick chicken with a pigeon chest. They have less fat than chickens and thus require more careful cooking or they will be dry. The taste is like, well, like chicken, but with subtle overtones of smokiness and farminess. A nice change if only for the sake of new table talk. It's particularly good with something sharp and fruity, like apples or quinces or spiced plums.

Hare

Dark, red and delicious, the hare is always wild. Like rabbit, the saddle will be tender and everywhere else a bit of a gamble. Best cooked on the bone so the meat does not shrink and an excellent ingredient in game pies and stews. Spices help a lot, and so does a little dark chocolate to finish the sauce – either that or blood – its own not yours – as in the classic *Lièvre à la royale*.

Kangaroo

Not everyone in Australia chucks a bit of 'roo' onto the barbecue. Indeed you can't even buy it in many states. But in South Australia kangaroo meat has been officially sanctioned for some time and there are dedicated kangaroo butchers. You'll find one of these in Adelaide's amazing Central Market. There are roasting, braising, grilling and stewing cuts and the stall is constantly busy. As a visitor to Australia you are most likely to find only the better cuts offered in restaurants, quite often with Native Australian herbs or spices: Adelaide's famed Red Ochre restaurant served it with wild greens, quandongs q.v. and small hotcakes mixed with Cooper's Special Ale: Cooper's ales and beers are brewed in Adelaide city and widely accepted as 'the wine of beers and the beer of wine-makers'. Expect grilled or roasted cuts of kangaroo to be served medium to rare, to taste like good steak, with perhaps passing references to the sweetness and fine texture of venison.

Mallard

The biggest of the wild ducks, and possessor of a dark flesh with a wonderfully fine and refined flavour that is duckier than duck. The habit of singeing the down which sits under the feathers can taint the flesh flavour, particularly when the plucking is inadequate and then the bases of the feathers are also burned and carry the flavour into the flesh. Because they have so little fat, it is as practical simply to peel off the skin without plucking. If you shoot or buy mallard from estuaries there is the chance of a fishy flavour, but I have never experienced this in 40 years of being a mallard fan. They say cooking with a potato in the cavity helps.

Mallard have precious little fat and particularly benefit from being cooked on their breasts.

Rest them well before serving with sharp, fruity accompaniments rather than a sweet orange sauce. Other ducks, like teal and widgeon are treated and served the same way, but cooked relatively quicker, of course.

Ostrich

Yes, you may well gasp. The ostrich farms you see all around the world have more than the sale of feathers in their mission statements. They want to sell you ostrich steaks, and roasts and braises and more.

Gamey turkey, pallid venison – just two of the descriptions I have heard, but much of that is just nervous chatter.

Once you get over the flesh being red, rather than the pale colour of poultry, this is something very special. The flesh is butchered as individual muscles for more reliable cooking, but there are so many this comes close to being counter productive. The finest fillet-cuts can be roasted as though venison or as a beef fillet, something equally fatless and about the same thickness. Allow to rest for at least 20 minutes before thinking about carving. I have seen this served to tables that universally commented on the tenderness, loved the flavour, complimented the chef and asked for more, without suspecting they were eating ostrich. It's that good.

In Australia they now farm emu to the same culinary end; apparently the flavour is very similar and some airlines flying to Australia include it on their business class menus for passengers who want to worry about cholesterol levels at 30,000 ft – like most game meats it has exceptionally low levels and is thus considered healthier.

Partridge

Perhaps my favourite game bird, just right for one person's treat, and a half bird makes a delicious first course, hot or cold. Partridge flesh is whiter, finer, sweeter and altogether more elegant than its competitors, and thus deserves to be cooked very plainly, with only a little butter rubbed into the skin before roasting. Should you wish to extend the pleasure of a partridge, pot the pureed or finely chopped roasted flesh with unsalted butter, ground almonds and mace and then serve with lightly chilled muscatel grapes. Or with pears if it is Christmas, I suppose.

There are French red-legged and English grey-legged partridges but I don't care to identify the small differences if one of them is one my plate. Farmers' markets in Britain are a great source of partridge for very much less than charged in shops and department stores.

Pheasant

Most pheasant sold are a combination of farmed and wild; they have been bred in captivity and then released to fatten naturally before being hunted. At least this is so in Britain. In the United States where almost no truly wild game may be offered commercially, fully farmed pheasant seems to have less flavour than a battery chicken. This might also be because they have not been hung for any length of time. There are both wild and farmed pheasant in Australia and

New Zealand, and the farmed ones available are frozen before despatch, which does not alarm me as much as defrosting them to find they are as tasteless as their packaging, because they have been frozen as soon as they were dead.

Pheasant needs to be hung. It is naturally a dry-fleshed bird and decomposition (let's not mince words) tenderizes it, so making it edible. There is a concomitant increase of flavour, which beyond a certain point becomes very much a matter of personal taste. Those who insist on hanging birds by their legs until they drop to the ground are increasingly rare, a sign the world is becoming more sophisticated. Once you understand the game smell is what converts to sensational sweetness when cooked, you will want to find the perfect balance. For me this means pretty high smelling legs, but a breast that is still fresh seeming. Too much gaminess means you do not taste the pheasant meat, and this seems pointless.

If you are presented with pheasant, hang them somewhere airy, with their guts in place and still in their feathers. When they are ready don't bother plucking but peel away the skin, feathers and all. I know it sounds radical but think – there is no fat under the skin so it offers little protection or flavouring when the bird is cooking.

The smaller hen pheasant is sweeter than the cock bird, and whoever reckons you can feed four people off a single bird is a rotten host. Innuendo about what size male pheasant a customer might prefer has been the mainstay of many a licensed game dealer for centuries.

Two pheasants might serve six people. Leave off the nonsense of bacon or pancetta on the breast, because they both hijack the natural flavours. Instead, use a little butter and cook the birds only on their sides or breasts and leave them to rest well in this position after roasting; those are the better ways to ensure moistness.

Pigeon

Now corn-fed farmed pigeon are competing with the more rugged and darker fleshed wild birds, the pigeon is fast climbing the culinary ladder: the scourge of Trafalgar Square sits comfortably with truffled cabbage and foie gras at banquets on Park Lane.

There are a few tricks worth knowing about pigeon. If you think it smart to remove the breasts before pan-frying, think again. They will shrink so alarmingly your thoughts will only be to leave by the back door or to change the menu. It is always best to roast or grill pigeon as whole birds and then to butcher them when they have rested (on their breasts) until lukewarm, when they will taste better anyway.

Even if you are more inclined to braise than roast, know that most pigeons are ruined by cooks waiting for the legs to cook and thus over-cooking the breast. Judge cooking time only on the breast and whilst that is resting, remove the legs and sauté them to finish; or remove them first and stew them in the liquid over which you braise the resultant heart-shaped breast and rib cage. For casseroles, cut the back bone out of whole birds and then cook as halves with wing and leg attached.

The pigeons eaten so lustily in Egypt and Morocco and in most places between are pale-fleshed sweet and small. Their breasts are the greatest ornament of the pinnacle of Moroccan cookery, the *b'stilla* or *pastilla*. They are layered with eggs, spices, sugar, flower waters, herbs and almonds between thin sheets of pastry, like filo but made entirely differently. Little in European, American or Australasian cookery prepares you for the assault on your senses. Once you taste a *b'stilla*, ideally in Morocco, your palate's expectations are never the same again, although a good *chachouka* q.v. could sneak it higher.

Possum/Opussum

In some parts of Australia these are a protected species, in New Zealand they are vermin, responsible for major degradation of the country's unique native wilderness. Eating them is just another way to reduce the numbers or, at least, to get something back for the huge cost of controlling them. Compared to the big beefy flavour of kangaroo, possum meat is thought more refined, more like veal.

Quail

These small birds have more flesh on their deep breasts than you expect. They are sweet and juicy and have a flavour rather like the dark meat of chicken. Considering quail hens lay an egg a day, and that quails' eggs are commonplace, it seems surprising they are so expensive. There are those who bone them and stuff quails. It's a jolly good wheeze and excellent to eat, but unless you are a boning boffin, life really is too short.

For special occasions, roasted quails are a terrific first course, when one per person is quite enough; they are commonly served with peeled grapes, which I used to call Quails Beulah, but so few have now seen the incomparable Mae West haughtily ordering her maid about: Beulah, peel me a grape.

For a main course, two or even three quails would be the norm. The simplest way to cope with the cooking is to spatchcock, a term often thought to mean a small chicken or pigeon, but actually meaning the following technique: split each bird through the back, open flat, and then apply pressure to the front until the wishbone breaks, which makes them really flat. Push bamboo skewers through them leg to leg, to keep them prone, after which they are simply grilled or barbecued. For roasting whole, vine leaves make an excellent wrapping, the way I ate my first quails so very long ago in Trastevere, Rome. It's true about never forgetting your first time.

Rabbit

If you buy this ready prepared it will probably be frozen and invariably be from China. Not that tasty, but invaluable for bulking out game pies and stews and such. Wild rabbits make excellent if scant eating, but you cannot cook the meaty legs and tender saddle meat the same way or for the same time; braise the legs and grill the saddle, having marinaded both, is my answer.

Snails/Escargot

Snails are available three ways, in cans or frozen or live. The canned ones sometimes also come presented with empty shells. The very best live in vineyards, and so the best places to eat them are wine-growing regions. It was in Bordeaux I was first presented with snails with no shells and no garlic. They were served simply with very good melted, unsalted butter, lots of coarsely chopped parsley and a grind of *quatre-epices*. This way I had to taste the snail and, although there wasn't much snail flavour, there was enough that was enjoyable to make me doubt the habit of garlic butter.

If you think carefully, it is not the snails you enjoy but the butter, usually with far too much garlic, so the bother of stuffing snails back into their shells, then pulling them out again with special and expensive instruments seems a bit silly. If you must have garlic butter, make it less of a bully, and then serve the snails with parsley on beds of pastry or in tiny vol-au-vents.

Other people serve them other ways and the most interesting alternative is in a red wine sauce flavoured with anise – either the seed or some suitable alcohol and fennel seed can also be used: I found both ideas in a Sicilian restaurant in Soho, London.

There are constant scandals about the true origins of snails you are offered in France, and how they are treated. If you have the French, you should ask if they are the genuine thing, *les vrais*, and if they have been caught locally. To get good answers you need either very expensive or very simple restaurants: one will be able to afford the best, the other will have gathered and fattened them themselves. Snails are being bred for the table in England once more, in the Mendips, as they were by the Romans, but they seem rather small.

In case you were wondering, snails have little food value. Neither it seems did the plan to make a fortune from marketing snails' eggs, which flared, briefly flickered and then turned to ash some years ago. They had a fleeting flavour of almond, but that disappeared faster than a live snail on firecracker night.

The best way I ever served snails is mixed with a buttery sauce of ceps and morels, (dried ones, rehydrated in wine), with masses of flat leaf parsley, between high, crisp shapes of puff pastry. No shells.

Venison

It is a mystery to me why farmed venison is not on everyone's table every week. It is thought by many to be the world's healthiest red meat, very high in protein, low in saturated fats and very delicious indeed. The Bambi factor is partly to blame, I know. So is the lack of a united marketing front internationally by producers, which keeps the prices high. And then there is the stupidity of chefs and, sad to say, the cooking recommendations of some producers who continuously misunderstand the place of marinades.

Wild venison often needed to soak in strongly flavoured marinades for two good reasons. First, it may have been tough, an enzymatic reaction within the flesh triggered by trauma if hunted; the acid in the marinade counteracted that and tenderized the meat. Second and almost more important was the big, often rank and tainted flavour of the flesh, sometimes a reflection of what natural fodder had been eaten, and which had to be diluted, masked, or both.

Farmed venison is neither endemically tough nor highly nor unsuitably flavoured.

The flavour to expect of decent cuts of farmed venison is that of fine fillet steak, delicate, subtly sweet beef-like. The flesh is somehow silken in texture too, helping create the privileged sense of elegance and superiority. Light marinades of superior subtle wines, sweet fruit juices and citrus zests, herbs and spices are a good thing, only if they add supportive new dimensions rather than mask what is there. Harsh rough wine, large amounts of acidic raw onions, too much garlic, citrus juice, vinegars and the like have no place in marinades for farmed venison.

Venison may be hung for added flavour, indeed some hanging is essential, and those who are interested in buying venison to turn into other products would be best advised to choose meat that has developed deeper flavour than that which might be simply roasted and served.

Venison sausages can be a very good buy, but only if they are made the old way and use the 'umbles', the internal organs; venison liver is considered one of the best types possible and should you see anything that says it includes this cut, and think the manufacturers likely to have used enough to taste, it would be well worth exploration. Unfortunately most venison sausages are completely without individuality: made from tough, flavourless meat mixed with pork and goodness knows what else, the enjoyment is cerebral rather than actual. I think most people love the idea of wild food, but many hope they can't taste it. Venison burgers and sausages to the rescue.

Smoking has become a popular way to finish venison, especially in pre-packs, but for my taste it is usually wildly overdone.

Wallaby

Another marsupial you might be offered in Australia or New Zealand and another credited with having delicate flesh, with being the veal of the marsupial world, where kangaroo is the beef. I just can't bring myself to do it.

Wild Boar

One of the newest of traditional products to return to our table. It became extinct in Britain about three centuries ago, but had been a regular on the table. The wild boar is immediately identifiable for its extraordinary narrow body tapering behind a big, brutish head and neck (which carries most of its fat), black hairiness and spindly legs, all a help to skittering through bush and brush I suppose. They are slow growers but their flight or fight genes produce red protein flesh rather than the pallid white protein of domesticated pigs. The meat is tender if cooked properly but will always appear more textured and grainy than domestic pork.

Most farm producers in Britain claim not to interfere in their natural growth with hormones and the like, and although some animals are also claimed to feed absolutely naturally, others will be offered supplements.

In reality, the perceived pleasure of eating wild boar can, like venison sausages, be rather cerebral. In the first place it should not taste like ordinary pork, and if it does it means you are eating a cross-bred animal: the in-built possibilities for disappointment are thus enormous. Neither should there be the strong or gamey flavour found in wild venison; indeed even producers find it difficult to describe what we should expect – a veal-like flavour between rabbit and hare was thought to be accurate. To add to the confusion, it is not just the boar that is eaten, but both sexes, usually killed at about 12 months.

Products on offer, apart from such cuts as haunches and saddles, include wild boar sausages, dry-cured hams and bacon and smoked shoulder. I have also tasted pâtés and pies and everything else you would expect. In many cases the marinade overpowered the taste of the flesh and thus one could be forgiven for wondering why the fuss. But I'm sure this will all work out and I welcome the pioneers and thank them for reintroducing the wild boar to our table.

Cooking your Birds

For anyone with experience of it, spit-roasting is the only way to cook birds. As the birds constantly turn in front of a bright fire, their juices stay inside because the constant rotation defeats gravity; only basting juices become true drippings, collected in a pan on the floor. These are what were once thickened with almonds if you were rich, with bread if you were poor. It was only when closed ovens became the norm in households that we began cooking birds flat on their backs and then put the bread inside them, both of which contribute to dry birds or those not cooked enough, so that dangerous salmonella remains on their bones.

To get as close as possible to the effects of spit-roasting, all birds should be cooked on their breast or on their sides, in which case they should be turned from time to time. Any stuffing inside the bird should be minimal and based on ingredients that will create steam – apples, oranges, onions if you must. Butter or pork-based forcemeat may be pushed between the skin and breast of bigger birds, which may then be spared cooking on their breasts, as the fat will drip through the flesh and keep it moist and flavoursome. Forcemeat or stuffing which contains bread should never be put inside a bird, for it absorbs the juices which should remain in the flesh; instead it must be rolled into balls and cooked around the bird, where it will absorb fats and cooking juices that have been exuded. Interestingly the United States, which we do not always credit with much cooking style, generally follows this practice, calling their forcemeat balls dressings.

True roasting is to cook in front of a fire, and cooking in a closed oven is baking. It's just that roast haunch of venison or roast sirloin of beef sounds better than baked venison or baked beef. We used to roast meat in front of coals well into the 20th century, even when coal ranges became refined enough to have temperature gauges on oven doors. Once gas and electric cookers came on the market the technique died away. After so many centuries of roasting it's no wonder the word sticks around.

Unless you are spit-roasting basting is pointless. It does not give moister flesh, for how do the juices get through the skin? If juices could get through birds' skins, farmyard coops would be decimated in a downpour.

Basting takes time, continuously reduces the oven temperature and thus affects cooking time calculations, and contrary to what you might think, it has absolutely no effect on the end eating result. If you are spit roasting, the internal juices stay where they are because of the constant turning – neither seeping out where the skin is broken nor dripping into the cavity: spit-roasted birds were basted only because it made them browner.

More important than basting is to rest birds before they are carved. Ideally the bird should rest on its breast, so juices seep into the flesh rather than into the body cavity. If the bird is so big its weight would put the breast out of shape; either take the weight in a gentlemanly way by putting uncooked potatoes under its wings, or rest it on alternate sides.

A chicken should rest at least 15 minutes, a turkey at least 30 minutes; such small birds as grouse, petits poussins, partridge or pigeons and the like are best cooked entirely on their breast with only a brief upright flash for browning, if that is important to you, and then rested on their breast for another five to ten minutes. Please, please do not cover cooked birds in foil 'to keep them warm'. It's a horrid and unthinking modern habit with no authentic provenance and less contemporary reason. The foil traps steam which risks toughening the flesh in the same way a grilled or fried steak will toughen if you add liquid. By also retaining heat unnaturally, the foil covering can continue the cooking and thus overcook what it is supposed to be saving. Successful oven baking is a gradual concentration of the flesh juices and this must continue when the bird is not in the oven.

If it is not cut, any bird will remain piping hot for a very long time in even a moderately warm kitchen, just as it did for all those zillions of centuries before aluminium foil was forced onto us. Early carving, slow or inexpert carving and cold plates do far more to chill roasted birds than resting uncovered ever will: hot plates and a sauce or gravy quickly restore what might be lost during serving, and it will be juicier and more tender. As is ever the case with good basic foods, less mucking about always gives more pleasure.

If you are not a good carver, but expected to perform, say at Christmas time, the secret is to remove the wishbone before you cook the bird. That way you can carve in long easy slices or remove the entire side of breast meat and carve that like a loaf of bread.

Game Seasons

There are two reasons for game seasons. The most important one is to leave birds and animals alone when they are breeding or have very young to care for. The second is said to be for health reasons, protecting the public from being sold food that was putrefying because it had travelled long distances in high heat. That second reason can now be discounted and there are serious moves to have many hunting, shooting and fishing seasons extended. In the meantime here are the seasons for Britain: you'll find most of Europe with similar game, adopts similar dates.

The least regarded, most broken rule is that no distinction is currently made between fresh and frozen game, neither of which is supposed to be sold more than ten days after the open season is finished. Pigeons enjoy no closed season, perhaps because they are not classed as birds but as vermin.

Game Bird Seasons

Black game: August 20th to December 10th; in Somerset, Devon and the New Forest September 1st to December 1st

Grouse: August 12th to December 10th

Partridge: September 1st to February 1st

Pheasant: October 1st to February 1st

Ptarmigan: August 12th to December 10th

Wild duck, including mallard, teal and widgeon: September 1st to February 20th but thought best from October to December.

Wild Venison Seasons

England and Wales

Red and sika stags: August 1st to April 30th, hinds November 1st to February 28th

Fallow: as red and sika

Roe: bucks October 31st to April 1st; does November 1st to April 30th

Scotland

Sika: stags July 1st to October 20th, hinds October 21st to February 15th

Red/sika hybrids: as sika

Roe: bucks April 1st to October 20th; does October 21st to March 21st

Fallow: bucks August 21st to April 30th; does October 31st to February 15th

Red: as sika.

Grains

Grains are simply the seeds of various types of grass, yet they are largely responsible for man's long climb from primitivo carnivoro to his modern peak of dietetic sophistication.

The switch from meat to grain as a primary food signals the change from semi-independent hunting or foraging on a nomadic basis to a settled community existence. Grains need continuous care; the newly formed groups who gave it, received in return new comfort and security plus a staple that could be stored for use in winter, when there was suddenly free time to explore emerging skills we would recognise as arts and crafts.

Meat remained an important part of the diet, of course, but hunting slowly became less crucial to survival and developed into more of a recreation; in any case the mutually dependent and defended groups were also learning to domesticate the animals on which they liked to feast. While man ate grain, the cattle and other animals ate the straw that remained after harvesting. A balance had been struck that became the basis for civilization.

The new reliance on grains began about 10,000 years ago, and subsequently Babylon, Egypt, Greece and the Roman Empire were founded on the cultivation of wheat, barley, rye and oats; in the Far East it was millet and rice, in the Americas, maize. The villages, towns, cities and empires that everywhere arose through the decision to cultivate grain stimulated the cooperation that eventually shot men and their machines from the plains to the moon and planets.

The leaders of those ancient civilizations had learned by observation or intuition what we know scientifically – that grains supply most of our nutritional needs. Even now, five-eighths of our teeth are shaped for grinding and crushing, as opposed to the tearing and shredding teeth required by natural meat-eaters. Our saliva contains the specific enzyme needed to begin the perfect digestion of grains and our relatively long intestines are adapted to derive maximum food value from such a diet.

One of the greatest advantages of eating grains is that their high proportion of starch is only slowly broken down into energy-giving sugars, providing a steady and sustaining flow of stimulation. The bran (outer husk) of whole grains is equally vital, contributing vitamins and minerals to the supply of necessary roughage, which keeps the digestive system healthy and active. Thus grain is potentially our chief giver of health and energy. Except, relying on grains alone is dangerous and will lead to ill health through dietary deficiency.

No grain, with the possible exception of the wheat variety *petit epautre* q.v. has the complete spectrum of protein needed for human health, usually eaten in milk, cheese, eggs, fish and meat. Vegetarians who won't eat milk, cheese or eggs must eat grains with beans, pulses and a fair smattering of mushrooms, a combination that magically replaces meat. Otherwise they must turn to soy products for the soy bean does provide the full nutrition of meat, the only member of the plant kingdom accepted widely as doing so. See The Vegetarian Option.

With minor variations, all grains are constructed in the same way, but taking wheat as the example, the outer part, a fibrous container, comprises six layers of skin. This is the bran, only recently recognized as being a mineral-rich food as well as an invaluable source of roughage. The innermost bran skin, the aleurone layer, contains important additional protein and fat.

The endosperm makes up more than four-fifths of the wheat grain and its protein content of 25-33 per cent is similar to that of dried milk or meat. It is mainly starch, which goes to make white flour when sifted from the bran and germ. In its natural state wheat endosperm, ground or milled into flour, is a creamy colour. With ageing it slowly turns white. It is in pursuit of ever-more, ever-whiter endosperm ever faster, that man has made his most remarkable advances in grain breeding; but it is in the treatment of such endosperm with bleaches and other chemical 'improvers' that some people consider excessive and even dangerous measures have been taken.

The germ is the embryo of the plant. As it must sustain the early growth of the grain, it can be likened to the yolk of an egg. The germ also contains significant quantities of essential vitamin E.

Whole grains supply significantly more nutrition than crushed grains or whole grain flours. For once a grain has been crushed or ground, the vitamin-rich oils in the germ begin to oxidize and lose food value, eventually becoming rancid and sometimes dangerous. Many commercial products made of grain are degerminated precisely to avoid oxidization, giving long, trouble free shelf life at the expense of nutrition.

It is worth soaking many kinds of grains before use, especially wheat and rye. The prime reason is not to shorten cooking time but to improve flavour and usefulness to the body. Soaking in water begins the germination (malting) process, activating a digestive enzyme similar to that in our mouths. This process converts starches into sugars – maltose particularly – making the grain sweeter and tastier and promoting fuller and more efficient assimilation. Once cooked, some grains continue to sweeten and improve in flavour, the result of a broadly similar process.

There can be a serious digestive problem with the gluten found in wheat flour, which is what expands to contain bubbles of gas in bread doughs. Coeliac disease is an inability to digest the gliadin in gluten. This malabsorption problem is of relatively recent recognition, but now there are many books on the subject including those that tell you how to cook without gluten. Gluten-free wheat flour is more easily available and gluten-free foods are even sold in supermarkets.

If we don't explore and enjoy the wide world of grains we miss some of the world's greatest dining experiences, both ancient and new. Jenni Muir's prize-winning *A Cook's Guide to Grains* collects grain recipes from great and small chefs – and from her own cutting edge kitchen; it's heartily recommended, and I thank her for opening my eyes to more than I dreamed possible. You'll run to the kitchen.

Milling: the purpose of milling is to break open a grain to expose the endosperm and then to grind this to flour. Once a liquid is added the interaction with the starch and other components allows you to make a dough, batter or porridge. Man's first attempts at milling crushed the grain rather than shearing or grinding it, giving a very coarse meal contaminated with grit, stones and other foreign matter. After the laborious task of cracking the grain open by pounding one stone upon another, the meal was mixed with water and cooked in the sun. You had to eat the results hot, for once cold they would be as hard as the boulders on which they had been baked.

As refinements were slowly made to the process of the friction of two stones upon each other, crushing became grinding. The domestic hand mills, or querns, still in common use throughout the world, have always been tiresome and slow to use, whether employing a circular or up-and-down motion, and made a centralized grinding service impossible. It took enough time and energy to grind your own grain, let alone somebody else's. In Europe, the advent of the windmill changed that dramatically.

Considering wind had long since been harnessed to propel boats and ships, it is strange the water wheel preceded the windmill by over 1,000 years. Water mills originated with the ancient Greeks and were introduced to Europe by the Romans. But historians cannot agree as to who invented the windmill, or where; they are first mentioned only in 10th and 11th century manuscripts from Persia and soon afterwards were known in Europe. It is possible they developed independently, but either way, wind and water-powered mills gave local people an extraordinary new social freedom; freedom to grow either more grain than they needed and sell it for profit or to buy it and to grow and grind none at all.

Centralised wheat milling meant the miller quickly became all-powerful as he bought, sold and, most importantly, stored grain. Mills freed other men from the toil of absolute self-sufficiency and the centre of any thriving community had to be a miller and his mill. Without them progress was impossible: without them there simply wasn't the time to progress. So it continued right up to the late19th century. Then men perfected both the heavy-cropping Turkey Red strain of wheat and the first-ever, consistent compressed baker's yeast. Next, the roller mill was introduced to the UK from Hungary and that allowed milling on a scale undreamt of before.

Once the first roller mill started operating in Glasgow in 1872, the water and windmills that for so long had threaded British society together were soon out of business, and country life unravelled further and faster.

Stone-grinding: grinding grain in a central mill needed two huge, circular stones of a special granite, each weighing well over one tonne; the bottom one was stationary and the top one revolved. Both were corrugated or grooved in such a way the grain is sheared and the top stone may be raised or lowered to control the fineness of the grinding. The culmination of the movement and the corrugation of the wheels enables grain fed through a hopper at the eye of the upper stone to work itself gradually out to the edge, where it escapes through apertures which are the ends of the grooves in the bottom stone.

Stone grinding can only produce 100 per cent whole grain flours. The great advantage of wheat flour milled by stone is that heat and pressure generated during the operation distribute the vital wheat germ and its vitamin E through the endosperm in such a way that they cannot subsequently be separated. This makes the flour markedly more nutritious, but the same ingredient also inhibits dough rising, and makes the flour more liable to become stale.

To get white flour from stone-ground wholemeal flour you must sift – or bolt – away the bran. It takes time and time has always cost money – thus the rarity and expense of white flour in the past, when only the rich and the clergy could afford it as a matter of course. It would not be considered as white by most people today, as there were always some tiny pieces of bran left. Even after being sifted of its bran to leave a high proportion of endosperm only, this stone-ground white flour would have been more nutritious than today's roller-milled version, for it was in full possession of its share of the vital wheat germ and wheat germ oil.

Roller mills: roller milling makes flour by gradually breaking down the grain in a series of processes, rather than the single operation of the stone method. First, fluted steel rollers gently crack open the grain. The endosperm is immediately separated and goes off to closer and closer set rollers, which reduce it to flour; meanwhile, the bran and wheat germ go their separate ways to similar processes. White flour made this way clearly cannot have an iota of the vitamin or mineral content of the germ or bran. In the United Kingdom legislation ensures that some of these are replaced; the replacement vitamins are usually synthetic, but not known to be less good for that.

In many countries, roller-milled flour has further indecencies perpetrated upon it in the interests of commerce and at the expense of nutrition; the worst of these is considered to be bleaching, which is specially common in the United Kingdom and United States. Freshly milled wheat flour is normally a comforting pale cream colour, and will gradually whiten if left for six to nine months during which other natural changes occur that improve its performance in baking. White, very white, flour is what the public has come to demand but having hundreds of thousands of tons of flour sitting about waiting to whiten is not an idea that appeals to big business.

In France, where food is second only to God in importance, they have managed to keep what might be called a healthy respect for the cream-coloured flour and no tampering is allowed. But elsewhere flour is artificially bleached with a variety of highly technical, complex additives. There is no hard evidence to show there is any cumulative harm in these additives but the reverse has by no means been proven either. Increased consumer interest in commercial manufacturing processes has recently lead to the wider availability of both stone-ground wholemeal and white flour and of unbleached white flour.

Grain Types

Amaranth

Of the many questionable acts by the Catholic church in South and Latin America, banning amaranth as a food not only interfered grossly with an established society's rituals, but also nearly starved them. We all might have been better off too, for the tiny sand-like seeds of amaranth have twice as much calcium as milk, three times more fibre than wheat, has a couple of elusive amino acids and because amaranth is so digestible it is an excellent source of nourishment for the sick, oh and the leaves, raw or cooked, are a better source of iron than spinach. Jenni Muir's amazing research turned up the fact that in ancient civilizations from California down to Peru amaranth was mixed with honey and human blood, a recycling of sacrificial by-products, and then shaped into figurines and eaten. Conveniently forgetting they were presumed to be eating the actual blood and flesh of their deity every time they took Communion, the appalled Christian Conquistadores banned amaranth in any form. It wasn't until the 20th century that the Catholic church admitted defeat and allowed amaranth to be used openly again, as long as it was for Christian ritual – the seeds were even incorporated into rosaries.

With dozens of varieties able to adapt to every kind of climate from hot and severe to wet lowlands, there's an amaranth for everyone. One of the best to eat is grown ornamentally in the UK as Prince's Feather, and much-cherished Love Lies Bleeding is also an edible amaranth.

Amaranth has a pleasing warm but mild flavour but can go sticky easily. The seeds can be ground for use as additives to breads, biscuits and cakes, and when popped can be made into sweets and snacks, even into a breakfast cereal.

Amaranth's importance nutritionally means we should all actively be introducing it into our diets, but shouldn't be surprised if savvy vegetarians have got there first.

Barley

Although it was among the earliest grains eaten and cultivated by man, barley is rarely eaten nowadays until, perhaps, the first, crisp, golden-leaved days of autumn put us in mind of the pleasures of steaming, barley-thick meat soups and pottages. Yet it is much more important than this. Without barley we would not have our fine Scotch whiskies and there would be no Guinness. There would be no malted drinks, no malt flour and no malt extract, all of which are used to a greater extent than can be imagined. And half the world's barley crop feeds livestock, making us dependent on it second hand, at least.

Hardy and widely grown, barley has little changed over the centuries; it's much the same grain that was popular with both the nobles and the workers of Pharaonic Egypt some 7000 years ago, was a staple in China over 4000 years ago, and was used in the training diets of shapely Greek athletes. In Europe it was extremely important as a major bread grain right up to the end of the 18th century: it grew where fickle wheat would not, and this was vital when most people were too poor to eat any food that had to be transported or bought.

Today, barley remains a staple in much of Eastern Europe and in parts of Africa. And yet, nothing is static. Watch out for black barley q.v.

Barley couscous: a very traditional Moroccan ingredient, served mainly within the family – wheat couscous is reserved for visitors. The pearly-grey colour and delicious sweetness of barley couscous make it a great and simple hit: I've had greatest success serving it with roasted game birds, mixed with fresh mint and parsley with roasted lamb, mixed with dried apricots, cardamom, coriander and orange zest with pork. It's very good with grilled vegetables, a throaty olive oil and a fresh white cheese.

Even less common is green barley couscous, made from grains that have plumped but not ripened; it is *marmez* in the north east and *zembou* in the rest of Morocco. It's actually browner than basic barley couscous and has a rather forward and grainy flavour that is much like fine burghul. And that set me thinking. Are either of these really couscous, a type of pasta? I don't think so. The barley grains are cooked by steaming and then dried and crushed, the same process as cracked wheat or burghul, and it is prepared for eating simply by adding hot water and waiting.

This shows the simplest and most artisanal products (barley burghul) can misrepresent themselves (as barley couscous) simply because of poor translations on labels; equally this can be conscious opportunistic subterfuge by sharp marketeers. You find such practice everywhere, from the smartest food boutiques to the simplest farmers' market. Sad, isn't it?

Barley meal and barley flour: are difficult but not impossible to find. Terms are confused and transposed but generally the coarser meal is made from pot barley and finer flour from pearl barley. Country dwellers of determination could apply to their local animal foodstuffs dealer and sift the coarse ground barley meal they will find there. The best use for barley flour or meal in bread making is as the basis for a sourdough starter, otherwise simply substitute anywhere from 20-50% for your normal flour or flours, to add a sweet and wholesome flavour, remembering the more you use the flatter the bread will be. A simple barley flour bannock or soda bread mixes two cups of barley or bere q.v. flour with one of strong, (high gluten) white wheat flour and two teaspoons of baking powder and combines these into a stiff dough with milk or buttermilk: divide into 4-6 pieces and cook on a griddle. Lashings of butter please, even if Enid Blyton and the Famous Five aren't invited.

Barley sugar: twisted and golden, this boiled sweet is increasingly hard to find and probably isn't the real thing anyway. It was so called because barley water was once used in its manufacture and you would be hard-pressed to find companies prepared to go to such bother nowadays. Basically it was a superior boiled sweet, and saffron once gave the lovely golden colour, as well as a subtle extra flavour.

Barley water: to make this old-fashioned treat, put 50g/2oz pearl barley into 600ml/1 pint of cold water. Bring to the boil, simmer 15 minutes, drain, then replace the drained liquid with 900ml/1½ pints boiling water. Simmer until reduced by half. Strain. Sweeten or dilute according to taste, and add extra flavour with the traditional lemon, orange or lime juice.

Bere flour/meal: an ancient, slow-maturing variety of barley grown in Scotland, the Orkneys and wherever traditionalist Scots have settled, like Canada. Bere grains are uniquely kiln-dried, which adds notable flavour before being stone-ground. George Argo of the Orkneys, hoping to save the grain from extinction, is developing new biscuits and breads based on bere. Once you taste bere, you won't want to go back.

Black barley: grown mainly in Arizona and California and developed from an Ethiopian variety, this is considered by Jenny Muir as 'one of the nicest grains you'll ever eat, its smart coloured coat adding an earthy flavour . . .' Others say it differs from ordinary barley the same way wild rice differs from white rice. Not widely available outside the USA, but it should be.

Flaked barley: lightly rolled grains, usually of pot barley. This is my favourite for breakfast porridge, soothing, chewy and satisfying. Make it with milk rather than water and sweeten with a natural brown sugar.

Pearl barley: is the most common form of barley grain, and is invaluable for thickening soups and stews as it has a natural affinity for fatty liquids, both in performance and flavour. It is the barley grain, husked, steamed and then polished to give the characteristic rounded shiny appearance. The dark line down one side is a remnant of the husk.

Pot barley: also called Scotch barley, has only the indigestible part of the husk removed, so it is extra nutty and nutritious. It is more commonly available in health or wholefood shops.

Cooking

Barley is always improved by being soaked overnight. And if you like a roasted flavour, first stir your barley in a hot pan with a little vegetable oil until it colours. Do this also to barley flakes. When cooking barley use three parts liquid to one of grain. I like to use good chicken stock or, failing that, try to put something fatty like a chunk of bacon into the saucepan. Pot barley will take about 45 minutes to cook, pearl barley considerably less.

The flakes can be added to muesli as well as being used to make porridge.

Being almost gluten-free, barley flour, meal or flakes, makes heavy, moist bread, not at all to the modern palate. Its lumpeness dictated a round, flat form, perfect for use as the absorbent bread platters, or trenchers, that were so economical and filling in primitive and remote cottages where every drop of gravy counted.

I think barley's most underrated use is as a fascinating and unusual alternative to rice in pilaffs, something I first came across in the gorgeous dining room of Katie Stapleton in Denver, Colorado. Made with either roasted or unroasted barley, such a pilaff is naturally wonderful with fat-rich lamb, mutton and chicken casseroles. Many restaurants offer barley as a risotto but no matter how esoteric the stock and accompaniments every one I have seen is a pilaff, because there is no sauce holding the grains together. Very soft, over-cooked barley does not a risotto make.

Barley excels with game birds. I like to pack cooked, roasted barley into individual moulds (ramekins will do) and turn them onto the plates just before serving. Then, dribble over all those mixed bird-and-bacon juices. Rich, I know, but so much of the best flavour is lost when you pour away the fat from a pan in which, say, a pheasant has been roasting.

Individual quails, pan-roasted with fresh tarragon sprigs and then flamed in brandy, should be perched in hollowed nests of barley pilaff, both for effect and for scrumptiousness. To add fun, you might secrete a few peeled grapes at the bottom of each nest to imitate quails' eggs: the inclusion of real ones, softly boiled and then shelled, would be a coup. But grisly.

Storing

There are no problems in storing barley provided it is protected from heat, light and damp. Common sense, really.

Buckwheat

Cooked and eaten as a cereal grain, buckwheat comes from an herbaceous plant related to dock, sorrel and rhubarb. Its pretty pink flower is a great favourite with those devoted to the natural floral arrangement. Native to Manchuria and Siberia buckwheat thrives in a harsh climate and so has been a staple in northern Europe, Asia and Russia for centuries, and there are signs of it being grown in Japan up to 5000 years BC.

Buckwheat and pre-roasted buckwheat are often called kasha but this is incorrect. Kasha is the collective name commonly used in eastern Europe and western Russia for almost any grain-based dish, whether porridge-like or dry and puffed up in the manner of a pilaff; it just happens that such kashas are usually made with buckwheat. A buckwheat pilaff excels wherever there is fatty meat or gravies or stock, sometimes ruggedly with boiled brisket, other times elegant with a poached chicken and vegetables.

Buckwheat has also been an important food in Japan for a very long time and the recent Western interest in the Zen-based macrobiotic diet has introduced some to its oriental usages; for instance, there is a Japanese buckwheat noodle called soba. See Pasta & Noodles.

Buckwheat was also popular in Western Europe right up until the end of the last century. Now we eat only ten per cent of what we did a century ago and it is really only popular in northern France and Belgium, where it is known as black wheat *blé noir* or saracen wheat *sarrasin* as it is thought to have been brought to this part of Europe by Crusaders returning from fighting the Saracen in the eastern Mediterranean: it was certainly traded through their conquered countries by the Moors, but they rarely ate it.

The Dutch introduced buckwheat to the American continent, when they founded Nieuw Amsterdam in the 17th century, and it survived the name change to New York to remain very much in favour with other European immigrants. The popular American habit of eating buckwheat cakes (pancakes) with syrup for breakfast is not original – this is exactly what you would have found in the breakfast rooms of better off gentlemen at the English court of Queen Elizabeth I.

Buckwheat cakes with hot maple syrup were, as a boy, as magical and romantic to me as Roy Rogers, Lois Lane and Lassie were to other kids. Somehow I just knew they would be terrific. I had to wait until I was 17 before I finally tasted the combination, on an American cruise ship, SS *Mariposa*, in Auckland harbour. Until that moment I had been the ship's agent's office boy. From then on I was their slave. Although I've had many and varied American breakfasts since, and even enjoyed some of their more extraordinary combinations (would you believe blueberry muffins with ice cream and bacon) I always return to where I began. I like about five smallish buckwheat pancakes, preferably leavened with yeast, hot maple syrup and butter, two fried eggs with runny centres sunny-side up, and some strips of really crisp, hickory-smoked bacon, Once, in Washington D.C, I ate this for breakfast, lunch and dinner; I could happily have gone to meet my Maker.

Buckwheat grains: the small, whole grains are triangular-shaped and reminiscent of the beechnut: Germans and Dutch call buckwheat 'beech wheat'. The whole grain is used in Russia and Eastern Europe in as many guises and disguises as their politics. Buckwheat can also be bought coarsely ground usually as buckwheat groats, when it is cooked in exactly the same way but with more speed. Both forms are available roasted or unroasted. Although the first is undoubtedly tastier when freshly produced, buckwheat deepens in flavour as it ages and becomes pungent and unpleasant. For the sake of gentler flavour best buy unroasted whole buckwheat or groats, looking for the palest ones, which will be the freshest and most fragrant. Roast when needed by stirring over heat in a non-stick pan with a little vegetable oil, or in a microwave without. Buckwheat is not usually soaked before using but there is no reason why it should not be.

Buckwheat groats: between whole grains and flour, so cracked buckwheat really, a state that makes for faster cooking. Roasted groats that are then soaked to soften them make interesting additions to crisp biscuits or to cakes; more finely ground groats, not quite a flour, can be used similarly. You only need a few spoonfuls in basic pancake or bread dough to enjoy its warm, haunting flavour.

Buckwheat flour: speckled buckwheat flour gives a remarkable flavour to batters and bread doughs and complements such equally assertive flavours as game: a paler coloured flour, a fresher flour, will give more elegant results. Buckwheat flour has no gluten content, so it must always be mixed with wheat flour in yeast baking.

In Brittany, buckwheat flour is the dominant ingredient of the famed *galette*, a huge, thin, savoury-filled pancake that is the staple of the peasants there – *and* of the cognoscenti of chic creperies in Paris, London and, umm, Brighton. Sometimes the flour is sifted and mixed with plain flour, which avoids the pink-grey colour that buckwheat pancakes have and make an altogether more elegant thing.

The Russian yeast-raised *blini*, made to accompany caviar, are perhaps the noblest buckwheat pancake of all. The English with typical eccentricity don't eat much buckwheat but hand it to gamekeepers, who feed it to pheasants, with excellent results all round.

Cooking

There is one basic way of cooking roasted or unroasted buckwheat. You sealrthe outside of whole or of coarsely ground buckwheat groats in a little hot oil or butter, and then cover it with water or stock in the proportion of three-to-one. Replace the lid of the saucepan and cook gently until the liquid is absorbed. Made softer and moister by the addition of milk or more water, it can be eaten with milk or cream and sugar. Or you can fry sliced onions, garlic and bacon in the pan first and then use a wild mushroom or other flavoured stock to make a sort of pilaff. All these dishes can be called *kasha*.

Storing

As with all grains, you should buy only in quantities that will last no more than a week or two, unless you have perfect cool and dry storage. Once you introduce warmth you induce the reproduction of creepy crawlies, especially with organic produce, which has no protection.

Corn

In modern English corn means maize, but it was once used as a collective noun for all bread-making grains, including wheat, and such usage may sometimes still be heard in unsophisticated areas. In this book it means the grain native to the Americas and source of corn flour, corn meal, polenta and popcorn.

Corn has been cultivated so long, perhaps for more than 7000 years, it cannot reproduce itself, but needs humans actively to gather and plant its seeds. This grain was the basis of the extraordinary civilizations of the Mayas, Incas, Aztecs and other almost unknown peoples of Central and South America. Smaller tribal societies of North America also relied upon it and in all parts of the continent it was worshipped. Corn came to Europe only with the successors of Christopher Columbus, the Spanish Conquistadors. It spread round the world like wildfire, and was known in China as early as 1550.

Of all grains, corn is the least nutritious and most lacking in essential proteins. Yet all the civilisations of the American continent knew to grow and eat beans with their corn, to ensure nutrition equivalent to meat, eggs or milk. Corn is also one of the greediest food plants too, exhausting soils in just one season. Classically these first inhabitants planted each corn seed over a fish or other animal flesh as dedicated manure, and then beans were planted, which would later use the tall corn stalks as growing support; and what was grown together, was eaten together. We'll never know how long, where or when this profound affinity was discovered; but we do know what happens when such traditional wisdom is ignored.

When corn was taken to Africa in exchange for slaves the beans did not go too. Many of Africa's ills are still exacerbated by the very food that was supposed to prevent them: pellagra and kwashkior are both deficiency diseases encouraged by relying on corn as a staple and also being too poor to add essential complementary beans, lentils and vegetables. See: *chakalaka*.

Although we usually see only yellow corn, it can also be red, purple, orange, white or blue. Blue corn flour, muffins, chips, crisps and the like have recently enjoyed a spell of fashion, although it has always been the staple of many of the native American tribes of the southwest United States. If the fashion lasts you will doubtless enjoy the extra depth of slightly smoky flavour; but the inky-chalky colour is always a surprise.

Baby corn: specially bred miniature corn cobs eaten whole in oriental and Asian dishes.

Corn flour: see flour corn.

Corn meal: see polenta.

Dent corn/feed corn: a corn variety that develops a dent in its top as it dries and that is most commonly fed to animals in the USA and throughout the world. It fattens stock cheaper and faster than other grains but also creates more fat, and as for flavour, well, do cattle naturally eat grain or grass? Poultry is different and corn is only a variation on their normal diet. Both dent and flint corn are cooked in Latin and South America with an alkali – seashells, wood ash or limestone – which releases the hull and changes the grain's chemical composition so its niacin and protein content are more easily available. Called *posole* these treated grains give us masa harina the flour used in tortillas, tamales and their many relations.

Flint corn: another variety used for making posole and masa harina in Mexico and her geographical neighbours, but also used in Europe to make polenta. It is called flint corn because the small grains are particularly hard and difficult to grind, but the labour is rewarded with a big rich flavour. See polenta.

Flour corn: a soft sweet variety used for making elegant cornflour or somewhat coarser corn meal, similar to polenta but mainly used for fast, non-yeasted breads.

Cornflour: gluten-free, light and sweet and quite the best for custards, blancmanges or baked puddings. Substituting cornflour for some of your soft white flour when baking cakes gives excellent lighter results. Mix one part of cornflour to three of wheat flour and keep it aside as a special baking mix: the advantage only works if you are then leavening with baking powder, as the mixture works in reverse for yeast leavening, making a sweeter but heavier loaf.

The most important use of cornflour is the lump-free thickening of sauces.

Although when first added it makes any liquid cloudy, cooking gives a nice clear, glossy sauce; thus it is much used in Chinese cooking, usually as the very last stage. Instructions for use are always given on the packet. The white colour of cornflour is artificially induced. Its disadvantage is that cornflour sauces will eventually begin to thin if cooked for too long.

Cornflour can always be used instead of arrowroot and gives results almost undetectably different, as in *kissel* a luscious thickened concoction of berries and juices introduced by Swedish Mrs McKee to the nursery of Prince Charles et al.

Cornmeal: like other gluten-free meals this makes a delicious addition to wheat bread but should be used sparingly as it tends to produce a crumbly, cake-like texture. This is why American breads made largely or only of cornmeal are usually eaten by the spoonful straight from the shallow pan in which they are baked, hence their most common name, spoon breads. The flour and meal may be found called maize flour and maize meal and are commonly so in the US. Cornmeal made from flint corn is the one used for polenta, q.v.

Grits: yellow grits are made from whole grain, coarsely ground dried corn (usually dent); white grits made from the hulled grain are hominy or hominy grits. Like hominy, leftover grits are often incorporated into the rest of the day's baking and cooking.

Hominy: is whole dried dent corn without its yellow hull and was the chief food of the enslaved African-American. It was boiled or baked in water until the white grains were very soft and swollen and then served as a mush or porridge. Eaten with gravy and meat or with milk and sugar, or just with salt and butter, it is still a great favourite throughout the southern United States. Cooked hominy can be incorporated into muffins and cakes or fried in lard.

Masa harina: see dent corn.

Mealie-mealie: is finely cut corn grain with most of the vital bran and germ removed and is an important staple food in Africa. It is cooked into a rather noisome porridge that has the advantage of being warming but there is little else to say for it, considering its importance, unless eaters can afford to complement it with beans, pulses and vegetables. See: *chakalaka*.

Polenta: although the terms are interchangeable, polenta is not a type of corn meal, but a specific dish made from bright yellow flint corn; it is so common in northern Italy the chief ingredient has been given the name of the dish. Essentially polenta is thick corn porridge, usually flavoured with Parmesan cheese and butter or olive oil. It is very time consuming to make the classic way and splutters vengefully, landing the hottest and most blistering blobs all over your person – which is why it is traditionally stirred with a very long-handled wooden paddle. But that effort is now behind us. Instant, which means pre-cooked, polenta is available, ready to eat in five minutes or so, but it will still spit mercilessly.

Traditional and instant polenta both cook terrifically well in the microwave, removing at a stroke even the least dangerous splatters.

Polenta is traditionally served three ways but all use it thick and solid. It may be served as a thick mush, or left to go cold and then sliced and fried or grilled, or baked with savoury ingredients which add flavour – small birds roasted in polenta is a great favourite of the Veneto.

Although sniffed at by traditionalists, serving soft creamy polenta, perhaps instead of potatoes, can be triumphant, single-handedly justifying your new microwave. In New York I was served lamb with a very soft, almost silken, polenta mush flavoured with melting chunks of dolcelatte cheese. Soft polenta can also be grilled/broiled as the base for everything from fish to roasted vegetables, and can be layered with many of the same good ingredients, covered with cheese sauce and baked again. Thin polenta mush is an excellent medium in which briefly to cook finely sliced vegetables, finished with chunks of mozzarella and tiny cubes of a blue cheese and/or Parmesan, and then dribbled with a jolly good olive oil: it's one of those mushy, mucky one dish meals that can be so gratifying and is even better for being flashed under the grill/broiler.

The trouble is polenta dishes relentlessly rely on lashings of fat or oil in one way or another and so are tremendously high in calories. As an alternative I found a very light flavouring of fresh rosemary leaves stirred into a warm polenta mush with chopped black olives plus a touch of good olive oil when served is terrific: if allowed to cool and then baked brown under a grill the flavour intensifies. Sun-dried tomatoes, basil, pesto and almost everything else from the modern kitchen's lexicon of husky Mediterranean flavours can be served in, on or under polenta in some form or another. We have not yet heard the last of it.

Popcorn: the kernels of this strain of corn have a skin under greater tension than the other varieties, hence its propensity to explode dramatically when heated.

Homemade popcorn can be served in hundreds of interesting ways, though this form of corn gives even less nutrition than others. Still, it's fun to run up a batch of garlic-and-herb-butter popcorn to serve with some roasted chicken and then to watch your guests' amazed faces. They usually can't decide if it is their first course or their pudding, and if it is either, what the hell is it doing on the plate now?

So-called Indian corn and Indian popping corn is close to being the original strain of corn grain and easily recognizable by its high proportion of bright red kernels. Although undoubtedly prettier, it is less good for popping than the newer, all-gold strains.

Posole: see dent corn.

Sweet corn: known as corn on the cob in its natural state. Distinct, soft and succulent varieties,

Popping Corn

If your popcorn doesn't have instructions, you cover the bottom of a saucepan with a thin layer of oil (butter burns too easily for this job) and a layer of popcorn. Cover and shake gently over a high flame until you hear one grain pop. Remove from the flame and continue shaking for another minute then put back onto the flame. Shake more vigorously until the popping stops then quickly turn the popcorn into a bowl and add the flavouring you've chosen; for plain salted popcorn simply add butter and salt. Microwave popcorn packs are less fun but more reliable.

Here are some other flavouring ideas: _

- put 1 tbsp peanut butter (crunchy is best) in a pan with 2 tbsp butter. Melt together, add salt and mix with the popcorn.
- melt 3 heaped tbsp butter, then add 3 crushed cloves of garlic, chopped parsley and salt.
- melt 2-3 tbsp butter and add several good squeezes of lemon juice and then a good pinch of dried parsley, sage, rosemary and thyme. You could call this Scarborough Fair popcorn and serve it to your folk-singing friends.
- to 2 tbsp melted butter add 1 tsp coriander, 1 of cumin and 1 of turmeric. Toss together and add salt to taste. You could also add lemon juice and garlic to this – or you could cheat and simply reach for the tin of curry powder.
- for dessert popcorn, melt 50g/2oz butter with 125g/4oz sugar and grate in the rind of 1 orange and half a lemon. Cook until it starts to caramelize. Add the juice of 2 oranges and a lemon. Stir to make a thick, smooth sauce. Add the popcorn and toss until covered. Serve with ice cream or thick cream. A sprinkle of cinnamon would do only good.

and eaten as a vegetable rather than as a grain. After picking, traditional varieties degenerate in goodness and sweetness with breathtaking rapidity; native North Americans taught you should walk to a cornfield and run back to the pot. Once you have eaten newly plucked, freshly cooked sweet corn, you may find difficulty in enjoying cobs you have bought frozen, or tinned, or shrink-wrapped in a supermarket, not just because most have lost sweetness and savour, but because some new varieties have been bred to be so lubriciously sweet as to be confrontational. The longer you cooked older varieties, the tougher they got, and the less you cook new varieties, the better they taste. Whether barbecueing, roasting, baking, grilling, broiling, boiling, steaming or microwaving, cob corn tastes much better if you first pull back the leaves, remove the wine-coloured silks, and then smooth back the long green leaves. The intact leaves give added protection to the corn grains when you cook on, over or under direct heat.

Sweet corn, fresh and tinned, is very popular in Australia, New Zealand and America. The kernels stripped from the cob are often used in salads, especially when combined with green or red peppers or made into fritters, which are excellent with poultry and *de rigueur* with proper fried Chicken Maryland. Creamed sweet corn is also used in batters but more usually served as a hot vegetable, and is very good with pork. In Australasia you might be offered it on toast for breakfast; in Europe, though, sweet corn is largely unknown as human food and confused with maize grain. When I, fresh from New Zealand, asked for some corn in a restaurant in Torremolinos, I was told with mixed horror and pity for my background that, in Spain, corn was for animals. Something similar happened to me at a high-class grocer in Hampton Court when I asked for pumpkin to roast with my Sunday beef. The reply was: 'In this country, sir, pumpkin goes in beef, not with it.' Forty years later pumpkin is now super-chic in the greatest restaurants; will corn enjoy the same sweet success?

Storing

Corn should, like any other grain, be treated with special care, for whole cornmeal still contains the fragile germ. You might be able to buy corn products that have been 'stabilized'. Achieved at the expense of a few of its nutrients, this stabilization prevents the germ oil going rancid and is higher in nutrition than products that have been degerminated.

Millet.

For much of the world millet's *raison d'etre* is to feed caged birds. But for almost a third of the world it is their staple grain – from northern Manchuria to the Sahara and especially in north China, India, Pakistan and North Africa. It is the third most important grain in the world after rice and wheat and is a generic term for a variety of small-seeded grains. Sorghum wheat and Kaffir corn are other established varieties, the first being used a lot in America, where sorghum syrup is sold as a substitute for cane sugar syrup. In South Africa sorghum is malted and ground into maltabella, a profoundly comforting porridge with a chocolate-like flavour.

The millet we best know in Europe is yellow millet, which has many tiny, spherical kernels on each head. Japan, China and much of Russia use the whole grain like rice. African millet is ground to a meal and cooked into a sort of porridge. It must always be very freshly ground because it goes rancid very quickly indeed.

All millet has the unique property amongst grains of being alkaline rather than acid, and its blandness makes it an excellent foil for strong flavours and spices, as the pilaff base for stews, curries and so on. It is blessed with another distinct advantage to poorer nations – it hydrates astonishingly, so 500g/1lb of kernels will easily feed eight people when cooked.

Whole millet grains mix well with oats for an interesting porridge and in English cooking you are most likely to find it used for a baked pudding like semolina. References to it can be found in the oldest cook books; I found one in the manuscript recipe book of my great-great-great-great-

great-great-grandmother, a Senhouse of Netherhall in Cumberland and grandmother of Fletcher Christian, leader of the *Bounty* mutiny; she baked millet with honey, sultanas and dried apricots.

Millet flakes: are quite common and make simple additions either to porridges or to muesli where their alkalinity is an advantage.

Millet flour: is fairly rare but is gluten-free and used by itself can make only a flat bread; one such is *tef*, made into *injera*, the national plate-like loaf of Ethiopia. You can use millet flour as a thickening agent in soups and stews, but I prefer the whole grains to do this for less trouble and more interest. The flour is easily made at home if you have a strong liquidizer.

Puffed millet: something to consider for breakfast.

Cooking

Millet should first be browned slightly in a very little vegetable oil in a saucepan, and then you'll find its light basic flavour compares admirably with better-known grains. In the meantime, put the kettle on and then pour the boiling water onto the pan-roasted millet in the proportion of four to one. If you have it, a stock or vegetable water would be even better for making a savoury dish. For a wetter, softer result add a higher proportion of liquid, but this is entirely a matter of personal taste. It will take about 20 minutes over a medium heat for the grains to absorb the stock or water. Toss lightly with a fork then season with salt and a few herbs – even something as simple as fresh parsley, mint and garlic chopped together.

Perhaps, the best way of cooking millet is in the same liquid and at the same time as your vegetables or meat, to create a main dish or substantial pilaff. This way you keep all the goodness of all the ingredients. And nothing could be simpler, cheaper or better for you. It's no surprise that most such recipes come from Russian peasant cooking but a real surprise there is how well pumpkin goes with millet, a natural affinity that transcends usual pumpkin experiences.

If you must have meat with a meal, accompany a millet pilaff made with vegetables and stock with a few slices of bacon, or with some garlic-laden boiled Polish sausage – perhaps a couple of *mazurska* or some thick slices of *zywieska*.

Plainly cooked millet can be sweetened with sugar or honey and mixed with fresh or cooked fruit and chopped nuts for a light delicious pudding, hot or cold. Yoghurt is a good foil for this, but if you are using sharp-tasting fruit then pile on the cream or soured cream instead.

Storing

Whole millet is reputed to store for up to 20 years without fear of insect infestation. But millet flour goes off very quickly.

Oats

Oats probably originated somewhere in the east and slowly worked their way westwards as a weed. Their hardiness and very high and sustaining fat content appealed to the hardworking, bone-chilled inhabitants of northern regions, and thus it is the Scots we must thank for nurturing them in the UK.

Like rye or barley bread, heavy oat bread was made where wheat would not grow; but even when bigger crops and better transport made wheat flour more widely available there were many who preferred the way heavy oat porridges and breads lay longer in your stomach, warming and strengthening as you toiled in icy mines, fields and highlands.

Oats are bought as whole grains, rough cut groats, fine or medium oatmeal, or as flakes. **Grains** are best for porridges, **groats** are best for thickening stews or broths and for oatcakes. **Medium oatmeal** is the one for mixing with other flours to make scones, bannocks and such; **fine oatmeal** is best for pancakes, for flouring grilled herrings or making a thin, gruel-type porridge.

Quick-cook grains and **flakes** have been partly pre-cooked; in the process of husking, oats are steamed, and an extension of this process followed by kiln-drying gives you this time-saving version with only little loss of dietary value. **Jumbo oat flakes** are rolled whole flakes; all others have been cut into smaller pieces. Oatmeals that are 'steel cut' are considered superior nutritionally as they have not been subjected to any heat during processing.

Oat bran: While a fibre-rich diet is good for you, not all fibre is the same and so a little discernment is required when choosing bran as a 'cure' for your health problems. Wheat bran speeds up the passage of food through the digestive tract and primarily consists of insoluble fibre. Oat bran contains a large portion of soluble fibre and this is capable of lowering cholesterol levels. Oat bran also provides protein, energy-giving carbohydrate, and the B vitamin thiamin as well as maintaining normal glucose levels in the blood of diabetics. Making oat bran part of your daily diet can help lower both total cholesterol and the harmful LDL cholesterol while not depleting your stores of the protective HDL cholesterol. The easiest way to consume it is as part of your breakfast cereal and you might also incorporate it in muffins, breads, cakes, biscuits etc.

Cooking

When cooking whole or flaked oats for breakfast there is no doubt they are better if allowed to simmer gently overnight. But with the cost of today's fuel this is sadly impractical other than for very special occasions, or unless you have an economical Aga or similar stove. Best alternative is to soak your oats overnight and then cook as long as is practical in the morning. For a change, roast your oat grains or flakes first. This can be done over low heat in a pan with some oil or in a tray in the oven. They should only just turn colour, and because they contain oil the microwave also does this with nothing else added.

Another way to make porridge (often called just oatmeal in the USA) overnight is to bring it to the boil with five times its volume of water and then leave it overnight before cooking again, for twenty minutes in the morning. There is a simpler faster way.

The high fat content of oats mean they cook very quickly in a microwave cooker. There are instructions on most packets these days: you'll find what took 20 minutes or more can take just a couple of minutes. Add up to twice the volume of water, milk or a mixture, go and have your shower, and your porridge will be ready for you – remember microwaves are obedient cookers and safely switch off when they are told. Very easy to cook individually as people arrive for breakfast and if you cook the porridge in a deep bowl from which it can be eaten there is no sticky pot to scrub. If the oats have been soaked overnight they will be even faster and even tastier.

Scots may well blanch at the thought but the inclusion of such dried fruits as apricots or peaches adds a great deal of interest and further nutrition to porridge. Sliced, properly ripened bananas are particularly good, too – yes, with hot porridge and dark brown sugar! And now you've gone this far be bold with your oatmeal porridges and mix in the same ingredients as go into your muesli – all sorts of other grain flakes, sunflower seeds, dried apple, coconut, chopped nuts, soaked whole grains. Then top it with molasses or treacle, with a choice of unrefined sugars and, of course, plenty of salt. The only food that goes with muesli but that I don't like with porridge is yoghurt. You may think otherwise.

In fancy baking for special occasions, oat flakes have long been used as a sweet addition to scone and cake doughs. To take regular advantage of their rich food value, you might sprinkle flakes over bread dough before baking, sprinkle meal into the greased baking tins or knead some soaked oats into the dough. Other traditional uses include oat flakes in poultry stuffings or dressings and in sausages. White pudding – the sausage – should include a measure of oatmeal, and Cumbrian oyster sausages famously rely upon it; and where Manx , Scots and Scandinavians use oatmeal to flour the humble herring, the English feed it to fatten their aristocratic native oyster.

Incidentally, if you always include citrus juice or vitamin C in any meal in which you eat oats, you will get far more of that important iron content into your blood.

Storing

Keep your oats calm by keeping them cool, dark and dry and don't go wild and buy in large quantities.

Rice

As well as being its most important grain, rice has the distinction of being the single most important food source in the world. It supports the cultures of China, Japan, India, southwest Asia and much of the Middle East. Its origins are in the Far East, and one ancient Sanskrit word for it means 'sustainer of the human race'.

The beauty of whole grain or brown rice is its ideal but not complete balance of essential nutrients – carbohydrate, protein, oil, vitamins and minerals – in a soft, digestible bran which allows it to be cooked and eaten as whole kernels, with only the husk removed.

Mainly grown on submerged land, the viridescent paddy field, there are as many varieties of rice as there are climates to which they have adapted. Although expected by travellers in Asia, the shocking, violent green of young rice shoots is a surprise when encountered outside Valencia in Spain, in northern Italy or southern France. Louisiana, the Carolinas, Arkansas and

California grow great quantities of rice of extremely high quality, and so does Australia. Once it was grown in England, but as an increasing population caused the draining of marshy areas, the rice fields became more suited to pasture or other grain crops.

Rice makes it easy for the layman to identify and enjoy a variety of styles, thereby ringing dietary changes with ease. The basic choice is between brown and white, short or long grain.

Brown (whole) rice is whole rice, with only the outer husk removed. Once the bran has also been removed by milling, you have white rice, which is usually polished with a mixture of glucose and talcum. When such naked rice became fashionable amongst the Eastern rich, as white bread did in the West, the masses clamoured for it. Eventually they got it. And ghastly endemic diseases followed, including beri beri and pellagra, caused by deficiencies of thiamin (vitamin B1) and nicotinic acid respectively. Even in brown rice thiamin is fugitive, being quickly leached out into cooking water; up to 30 per cent can be lost even when using the technique which absorbs all the cooking liquid.

Slowly the lesson is being learned and whole rice is replacing white rice as a staple food in those countries where rice is often the only food available.

Today, in the West, many brown and white rices are available, each with a flavour and cooking performance peculiar to itself. Even brown rice, too easily associated with the drearier side of vegetarianism, now offers a remarkable range of imports, from the elegant, pale, true long grain of Surinam to a choice of shapes and flavours from California.

Yet even when we familiarly use varieties from all round the world there are still specialist rices to discover and enjoy. From China, the imperial green rice once reserved for the emperor and which keeps its colour when cooked, is waiting development and international marketing. Black Forbidden rice has already left its oriental home and is being developed in Italy. The success of Camargue red rice, developed over the past few decades, has now encouraged an Italian variety. Mix them up and you have confetti rice, an original way to get noticed at weddings.

Arborio rice: is the most widely available rice for a risotto, something too often confused with pilaffs – see Risotto rices. It's stubby and releases starch into the cooking liquid, something you normally avoid, and so contributes to the sensuous rich sauce that should bind a great risotto. Like all risotto rices it has a dead white eye you can see, and that when cooked must retain a slight bite.

Basmati rice: one of the world's great rices, from the Himalayan foothills. It has an elegant, some would say dainty, long grain and an unmistakably appealing fragrance that fills a house with sweet expectation. Its inherent sweetness is the perfect foil and balance to spiced foods and also makes it an excellent choice for stuffings and rice salads. All kinds of Indian dishes seem better with basmati, especially the rice-based ones, like birianis. Brown basmati is commonly available, but the bran somehow seems to mask the very flavour one has chosen this rice to appreciate. The addition of bay leaf to the cooking water, especially for rice salads, underpins the flavour of the basmati beautifully. If you cook by the absorption method, basmati rice needs only an equal volume of liquid; the brown version needs two times.

Black Italian: a new Italian cross by Gli Aironi, this time of the Forbidden or Emperor black rice from China with an Italian variety. Called Venere Nero or Black Venus rice it is still seen mainly in Italy's top restaurants and black rice flour is being made into biscuits, pasta and gnocchi. The same company has also produced a new whole-grain red rice, *rosso integrale*.

Brown rices: all rices can be brown rices, for they are merely rice that has been dehusked, leaving behind the layers of nutritious, fibrous bran. It is altogether a healthier food, with more protein and vital ingredients than white rice, as you would expect, but in spite of its nutty, sweeter flavour it is bland to many and also requires both longer cooking and more chewing. If you always cook it in stock, or add soy sauce to the cooking liquid, you'll find it more acceptable to more palates.

Brown rices should always be cooked by the absorption method so none of the vitamins and minerals are lost and you generally need two to three times their volume of liquid, to allow for the inevitable evaporation. Although the basis of macrobiotic and many vegetarian diets, any belief in brown rice as a complete food is seriously misguided: to be so it must be eaten in balance with pulses and legumes or as an accompaniment to vegetarian full-protein sources such as eggs, milk, cheese and soy-based produce.

Calasparra rice DOP: the proper rice for a paella Valenciana, this remarkable DOP-protected grain grows on Spain's east coast around and south of Valenciana. It has the greedy ability to absorb three or four times its volume of liquid and thus yields far more food for your money. When it is cooked in the highly flavoured liquids of a paella Valencia the concentrated savour of the result is unbelievably delicious, without the rice going starchy, soggy or soft. The best paella, like bouillabaisse, is a Sunday lunch dish cooked only by men, but this time it is a large flat pan of saffron-infused rice with seafood, chicken and vegetables. Men properly cook both iconic Spanish dishes over a wood fire, so the dish absorbs some smoke. Without calasparra rice there could not have been Valencian-style paella but it's tremendously useful anywhere you want rice packed with flavour and robust enough to stand up for itself, perhaps in *pollo con arroz*.

Incidentally a paella is not just the Valencian fiesta in a pan; anything cooked in the wide, shallow, flat-bottomed *paelleria* is properly a paella, anything, so arguments about what is or is not acceptable in a paella are fatuous.

Camargue rice: a wondrous brick-red sport discovered by chance amongst traditional Camargue white rice and now an important crop the world has taken to its culinary heart. It's whole-grain rice that takes as long to cook as 'brown' rice and so has a big flavour and keeps good texture. It should come with AOC or DOP status clearly shown on its packaging: the white one has IGP status.

Carolina rice: once a specific but now rather a generic for American long grain rice, very much a New World version of Patna rice. Can be used for sweet as well as savoury dishes but it brings distinction to neither.

Converted/far-boiled rice: it sounds a lesser rice but is quite the reverse. It has been part-cooked before being husked and milled. This forces thiamin and nicotinic acid into the grain so that even though it looks white it is closer nutritionally to brown rice, at least where it matters so vitally, satisfying both society and sense.

Cristallo rice: is par-boiled arborio rice.

Fragrant rice: the rice type with a wonderful fragrance so particularly popular in China and Thailand, and thus also called jasmine rice. There are many grades and varieties, and sometimes it is sold by the vintage and particular district, and discussed and assessed as deeply as Bordeaux and Burgundies. If you ever have the chance, spend time browsing in a rice store in China, observing the care with which it is bought, the amazing choices, the pride with which the higher grades are sold – and bought. You will never again think of rice as merely a valueless starch for filling the stomach.

For me one of the world's most entrancing experiences is to be walking through the food and restaurant streets of Hong Kong or the Chinatowns of other cities when rice is being cooked for lunch. Everywhere you see people tilting their noses for a better sniff, confirmed all is well in the world, at least until after lunch.

The best flavour comes from cooking jasmine rice by the absorption method, but note the proportion of liquid to rice should either be equal or 1½ times at the most and that this rice cooks up to one third faster than other types. Remember it is supposed to stick together a little, or it could not be eaten with chopsticks.

Glutinous/sticky rices: these are types of rice that go slightly jelly-like when cooked and thus cling stickily. They contain no gluten, so glutinous is rather a misnomer, but merely have a very high starch content. The savoury ones are specially liked in Asian countries because the stickiness means they are easier to eat with chop sticks. Sweeter ones are much used in puddings and cakes of great variety, often fluorescently coloured and flavoured with coconut or jasmine and wrapped in banana leaves. One of the highlights of the Thai culinary year is eating sharp and nutty slices of green mangoes with cold mounds of sweet sticky rice.

Sticky rices are sometimes called sweet rices and they are a little sweeter. The unpolished or brown version is very dark, almost black, rather like wild rice and is used a lot for desserts. The most usual preparation method is to part cook them in boiling water and to complete the process over steam: sushi rice is also from this family.

Jasmine rice: see fragrant rice.

Louisiana rice: an undistinguished long grain rice grown in the States that's essential to the gumbo, a Southern dish of soup served over a tightly packed mound of rice. Louisiana rice is also cooked in rich brown stock to make Dirty Rice and with mixed meats and vegetables in the one-pot jambalaya. Cooked Louisiana rice is mixed with peppers, onions and celery and the flesh of the famed local crustacea to make crawfish pies.

Paella rice: see calasparra DOP.

Patna rice: a generic term for basic long grain Asian white rice. It is pretty much all-purpose and well behaved, except it will not make wet risottos. Increasingly less used as a phrase in favour of the all-encompassing 'long grain'.

Pecan rice: a variety of rice from the United States that claims to taste of pecans. It is certainly a little different, and delicious, but I have yet to be reminded of pecans.

Pilaffs: often confused with risottos, but they should not be. A pilaff is a pilaf is a pulao, pilau and a plov; all are what you might call dry rice dishes in which the rice grains are cleanly separate, even if cooked in a stock. A pilaf etc might be flavoured with spices, and will usually but not always contain other ingredients and the rice is always a long-grained variety. India's birianis, in which rice is cooked in the liquid of stews to make a one-pot dish, or which is layered with a cooked dish and then reheated, are in the same general culinary vein, and so are both Spanish *pollo con arroz* and paella. Fried rice with leftovers might conceivably be called a pilaff, but banish the least thought of it being a risotto.

Popcorn rice: a local name for the sweet and appealing new flavoured varieties of rice being developed in the southern states of the United States, especially in Louisiana.

Pudding rice: a nice comfy term for white short grain rice used for slowly cooked rice puddings. It swells and joins up and feels wonderful to eat but never goes sticky if cooked slowly enough. Although traditionally done in the oven, the same result can be achieved slightly faster on the hob. If you take your time, pudding rice cooked in skimmed milk and sweetened with a sugar substitute tastes just like the real thing but has almost none of the calories. Such famous culinary rice dishes as *Rice a l'Imperatrice* are usually made with long grain rice, first blanched in water then cooked in milk. Middle Eastern rice puddings are always cooked over heat, and once a creamy rich consistency is reached commonly further flavoured with rose water, saffron and cardamom: specially good served chilled, strewn with pistachios or pomegranate seeds and with a very superior dessert wine.

Red rice: see Camargue rice and *rosso integrale*.

Rice flakes: like other grain flakes, these are the result of a steaming and rolling process; they can be made either from whole or white rice and used for a faster cooking porridge, for baking and for muesli.

Rice flour: may be used in bread and cake making but gives a dry, rather flat product. It is better combined with wheat and cornflour mixtures in this context. Otherwise it can be used to thicken and set interesting milk and fruit puddings and delicacies, the like of which fragile Victorian women just managed to absorb.

Risotto rices: medium to short grain rices known generically in Italy as *superfino*. They are all rather fat and chunky with a hard white core you can see: this stays firm when cooked properly, whilst the rest of the grain leaks starch into the liquid to make a velvety sauce that is the sign of a proper risotto. Arborio q.v. is the best known risotto superfino but **carnaroli** and others are now found more easily as risotto becomes more and more popular... **semifino** rices look the same but do not perform quite as well and are best for drier dishes or as an accompaniment – **vialone** and **nano** are the ones most often encountered in Britain. Vialone is the only one of these rices protected by a DOP.

Sticky rices: see glutinous rice.

Sushi rice *sushi-meshi:* a short grain rice variety that is slightly glutinous when cooked, so it holds together.

Valencia: another generic for a number of varieties of medium grain rice grown on Spain's east coast and which are particularly absorbent. The one to buy when you are on holiday in Benidorm, where you will find some of the best restaurants and food supermarkets in Europe, is Calasparra DOP, q.v. I wonder which came first to this area, the paella or this kind of rice?

Wild rice: the immensely beautiful, deep mahogany to black seeds of an aquatic grass and not related to rice at all. But who cares? Wild rice is less romantic and much more common than it used to be, for it is no longer truly wild. Wild rice has been tamed. It is farmed in northern California, amongst other states. Just recently Poland harvested its first crop – they will sell it as Indian rice and it should or better be relatively cheaper.

Persevere and the original can still be found, beaten by hand directly into the canoes of a few privileged Native American tribes in northern US states, Minnesota particularly. Truly wild rice looks unruly, it will be different colours, different lengths – and hence offer greater striations of flavour and texture than the sleek, even farmed grains.

So now neither wild nor a rice, but whatever its source, it has a profound nutty flavour and can take about the same time to cook as brown rice, depending on size and quality; the finest quality of farmed wild rice will be the darkest, longest, most lustrous and evenly graded grains. The grains are cooked when butterflied, that is the skin has split, the grain has slightly burst and opened out from its central seam. Native Americans used to do this by adding a succession of hot stones to rice and water, and modern Americans often cook it by bringing it to the boil and letting it cool several times, which does give wonderful flavour and results if you have the time – several hours. Otherwise the absorption method will do and you can expect it to take 30 to 40 minutes.

Unfortunately, chefs who cook with their eyes rather than their palate often serve wild rice undercooked, because you see more of the attractive brown skin I suppose. It is then starchy and chewy and if really raw will be sharp enough to puncture tongues, gums and throat: I saw this happen to two people at my table at a well-regarded restaurant in London's Kensington Church Street. But as the eponymous restaurateur-chef-hostess was intent on retrieving a cork from an expensive Burgundy (ours!) with a pencil at the time, she not only failed to notice the distress just feet away from her, but subsequently refused to believe it happened.

Wild rice is frequently extended by being mixed with white rice, which should always be cooked separately because it cooks so much faster. It can be cooked with brown rice or red rice in the same water, but these should be added ten minutes after the wild rice has come to a simmer. Wild rice in commercial mixtures of rice will have been scarified, scratched so the water can more easily penetrate and cook the grains, shortening the time considerably. Yet some mixtures will never work, like one I bought just for the joke of it that combined wild rice with basmati rice, the rice that takes the longest and the rice that takes the shortest time to cook. I keep the package on view as a *memento mori* of what happens when people go into the food business who know little more than how to eat, if that.

Nutritionally, wild rice has a higher protein content than true rices and an excellent range of vitamins. But it does not have the equivalent of the complete protein spectrum of meat or soy beans, and to say so is dangerous.

Even in the United States it can be prohibitively expensive to serve a pilaff or stuffing exclusively of wild rice. But used to flavour a rice-based stuffing it is a memorable experience, especially with poultry or game. As the flavour is so strong and pervasive you can mix it with up to two or three times the amount of white or brown rice and it will still be fully appreciated. A sprinkling in a salad of cold chicken mixed with a flavoured mayonnaise is terrific and I once incorporated some into thickly whipped cream with which I decorated a cucumber mould to be served with poached salmon. Another time I topped wild rice and cubes of cooked pumpkin with quickly cooked chanterelles and morilles and arranged this salad in a scooped-out pumpkin. This rich, earthy-tasting mixture was dressed with olive oil and lime juice and the glistening browns against the bright orange receptacle were a wonderful sight, made even better by a ring of poached cucumber crescents, almost transparent and fluorescent. I also remember served to me in Medford, Mass. a sensational combination of hot wild rice with roughly cut fresh nectarines and toasted pecans, designed to eat with a roasted ham.

It is better to serve wild rice in such combinations than on its own, whatever your finances; besides it's tiresome to eat solo as it requires major mastication.

Cooking

I *refuse* to listen to one more person telling me how they cook rice. Everyone thinks they know best. In case you don't, read on. The size and shape of rice grains usually tells you how they will cook and how best to use them.

Long grains give the separate, fluffy grains enjoyed as an accompaniment, in stuffings and in pilaffs and birianis, where the rice is cooked with other ingredients.

Medium grains are nearly always used for dishes where the starch in the grains is expected to lend a creamy richness to a sauce made from its own cooking liquids, as in the true risotto.

Short grain rices are particularly suited to the long slow cooking of milk puddings and in Southeast Asia and in Japan the starchier varieties are vital to many specialties, including sushi.

Rice is easy to keep hot if covered with foil and kept in an oven with a few dabs of butter. But it's better to do it over steam, which is the way to get those really light and fluffy grains that are so maddeningly delicious in good eastern restaurants, especially if they have used basmati rice. If in spite of all precautions you end up with sticky rice unintentionally, a 15-minute steam should save the day if you have the time. Simply put the rice in a strainer or colander over a saucepan of boiling water, cover with a cloth and a lid and keep over gentle heat. Once you see the grains start to separate – after, say, ten minutes – you can fork it over gently.

Leftover rice, brown or white, makes an excellent addition to yeast-leavened baking. If it has also been allowed to sour slightly, by being kept at room temperature for a day or so, it is remarkably good in the heavier 'health' breads favoured by followers of grain and vegetable-based diets.

Absorption method: this retains maximum flavour and nutrition in every type of rice, recommendation enough to make this the preferred method. First, gently saute the rice in butter or oil until it is opaque but not browned. My experience is that this is the best way to neutralize any stray starch, talcum, glucose or whatever else might cause stickiness. I *never* wash rice unless it has been bought in a foreign market and might contain stones and other unrelated debris; it's just one more thing to put people off cooking. Then I add some sort of liquid in the correct proportion according to the type of rice, using the same cup or plastic bag or measuring jug, plus salt and sometimes a bay leaf or two. This is brought to the boil and simmered at a steady pace with no lid on the pan until the water is level with the rice and a few bubbling holes can be seen. A folded tea towel, clean and dry, is put over the pan and the lid clamped very firmly on.

If cooking with electricity I then turn the heat off and put the pan on the edge of the element; if gas, I put it on the lowest possible heat, and this is where a heat diffuser is useful. Either way, the rice is left for seven minutes exactly and is then ready. That's it. You may find your saucepan is thicker or your burners are hotter and have to adjust the final timing. Otherwise it is simple, unfussy and easy to do at the last moment, avoiding the horror of soaking, washing, rinsing and reheating, all of which reduces or loses altogether what vitamin content there might be. My way conserves the maximum possible of everything for the minimal fuss.

To cook brown rice I use exactly the same method, and it can take up to 45 minutes. But, white or brown, *you must never, ever, stir rice when it is cooking* for this more than anything else will make the grains sticky. The sole exception to this rule is risotto, when you must stir, whisk even.

Electric rice cookers do it all very well, and as I don't know a single Asian or Chinese household without one, why should you be different? Specially designed microwave rice cookers are utterly reliable and give amazing results for the least possible bother.

Coconut rice: the cooking of Indonesia, Thailand and all South-east Asia is full of fascinating ideas for using rice. One of the simplest you'll come across is coconut rice, made simply by cooking long grain rice in coconut milk. Fabulous. It can also be flavoured with the addition of a curry leaf and some lemon grass, both of which are available at oriental food shops. But a good squeeze of lemon or lime juice is equally rewarding. It may also be coloured and further flavoured with some yellow turmeric powder. Either way it is very good with curries and other spiced dishes, or simply with cooked chicken.

Pudding rice cooked in coconut milk and sugar is an idea I found on Pitcairn Island. It became a firm but sticky favourite of all my 1980 expedition, especially when served with a little hot orange, lime or lemon juice. To be more exotic use palm sugar rather than cane or beet sugar; a sprinkle of black rum is wonderful too.

Fried rice: the leftover standby of many provincial Chinese takeaways but which rises to greater heights in Indonesia: there it's called Nasi Goreng and should be accompanied by or include strips of beef, chillies, prawns and soy sauce, topped with soft-fried eggs, or sliced omelettes: this dish is served particularly well in the Indonesian restaurants of Amsterdam. In Thailand fried rice would include pork and the inevitable chopped green coriander leaf.

There's no great secret to making fried rice. If you have the time, it's useful to let the cooked rice dry somewhat before it is fried, left uncovered in the refrigerator overnight, or spread on a baking tray. Then, you simply fry cooked rice in hot oil until nice and brown, then stir in all manner of bits and pieces, especially crunchy and colourful goodies like shrimps, bits of bacon, cubes of ham or flakes of fish, sliced up omelette, green or red pepper, herbs, garlic, green ginger, chillies, apple, pineapple, leftover vegetables etc.

When the rice and everything else is well heated through, dish onto a platter and serve accompanied by soy sauce, and an Asian hot sauce or Worcestershire sauce.

All fried rices are strangely improved by the inclusion of cucumber cubes, sticks or slices. But don't ask me why.

Iranian method: if you can be bothered, the Iranian method is fun. Use about one quarter less water than normal then, when the rice has absorbed all the water and is still a little hard, transfer it to another saucepan in which there are a few spoonfuls of water plus 25-50g/1-2oz of melted butter. Put more butter over the top, cover with a cloth and lid as above and let steam over low heat for 15-20 minutes. The rice will then be cooked and separate but have a crisp golden coating on the bottom. They call this *dig* and it is a great honour to be served it.

Microwave method: one of the world's greatest inventions is the special microwave rice cooker, a sort of plastic bucket with a lid. It's quite superb, foolproof unless you enter the wrong timing, in which case they can burn, melt and cause untold nastiness: this happened to me in the kitchen of the QVC Shopping Channel in London over ten years ago and has still not been forgotten, judging by the smirks and the pointed fingers. They come with all the instructions. Otherwise you can microwave rice in any container that is both microwave safe and deep enough to cope with the inevitable bubbling boil up – a deep Pyrex bowl or a large measuring jug for one or two servings work admirably.

Savoury rice: this is what supermarkets and small-town restaurants would call a *pilaff, pilau* or *plov.* There are so many recipes in so many books I won't bore you with any more. For hot or cold buffets I always colour rice with saffron or turmeric and mix it at the last moment with chopped pistachios and some pine kernels that have been gently browned in the microwave with no additional butter or oil. Both these nuts are expensive but a few go a long way and make a considerable and luxurious difference. You could serve rice the Middle Eastern way simply by preparing your favourite stew of meat or poultry and then adding rice for the last half hour of cooking, which will then absorb the liquid. That's all there is to it really.

Risotto Rituals

A risotto can only be made with a particular kind of rice, one that creates a thick unctuous sauce based on its own starch, and is cooked over heat: a pilaff must have separate grains and can as easily be cooked in an oven as over heat for its distinction is the grains must be separated.

The risotto belongs to northern Italy, around Venice particularly, where it has its roots in the ancient addition of rice to soups; the balance is now reversed and a risotto is rice to which stock, a sort of soup, is added. To be absolutely correct, the rice must first be turned in rather a lot of butter until it whitens, rather the way a fish eye does when cooked – onion is not needed here if the stock used is well flavoured, but it seems endemic. Boiling stock or broth is then gradually added and the mixture is supposed to be whisked all the time it is cooking, so the liquid, the butter and the starch of the rice form a voluptuous emulsified sauce.

That is the received testament. When I have looked closely and questioned carefully those who cleave to this as the only technique, I universally found men and women who love the ritual of standing over the risotto rather more than they believe it's necessary to get results.

Outstanding risotti are made every day of the year by renegade cooks who whisk only when they add extra stock: but even they are likely to shudder to learn the microwave makes equally notable risotto, with perhaps only two whisks, although with little saving of time. When I mentioned this in passing in New Zealand's multi-award-winning *Cuisine* magazine, the intrigue was so great they had to publish the recipe in a later edition– you'll find it on page 335.

A true risotto is always finished by having a mixture of butter and Parmesan cheese whisked in finally, to polish and thicken the emulsion. Venetians call this *mantecari* a fascinating word based on the Arabic for butter just as is *mantequilla*, Spanish for butter. Without a final emulsification and sharpening with butter and Parmesan a risotto doesn't fully live. I know you aren't supposed to put Parmesan cheese onto seafood pasta, but I usually include it in this final nuancing of a seafood risotto and it's only been notably better.

The rice of a cooked risotto should retain a bite in the middle but this should not be brittle or starchy: think of *al dente* pasta. For many Venetians, the dish should be almost too wet to eat with a fork: it should be *all'onda* or wavelike. Because this is Italy, others like it to stand its ground, but it must still be the smooth sauce that binds the rice grains, and not just stickiness or starchiness of the rice – that's a pilaff.

Risotto must be eaten the moment it reaches perfection and so is properly only a first course, or a main course with nothing to precede it. One of the few times it is served as an accompaniment is a saffron or risotto Milanese with *ossi bucchi*, correctly a dish made with the sweetness of pale young veal shins but that is too often butchered and made with the coarse, dark soup-meat of much older animals. The difference is astonishing.

In general, the simpler the better: a wild mushroom risotto incorporating the strained soaking liquid from dried porcini, fresh sweet peas to make *risi e bisi*, squid ink to make a black risotto scattered with other seafood, finely chopped fresh vegetables and herbs to make a risotto *primavera*, chunks of blue cheese, toasted walnuts and sage leaves to make someone sit up and take notice.

It is painful at the time, but I try hard always to have leftover risotto. Gently fried in butter or olive oil, until it is a thick fritter that's crisp outside and melting inside, it is perhaps better than the original.

Pace Gordon Ramsay and the infamous pomegranate risotto he so comprehensively rubbished on television, there is a slow move to sweet risotti, cooked in sweetened and flavoured milk, or in vanilla and spice-flavoured sugar syrups; some have fruit beaten in and then more stirred in to serve, others are served cold as a variation on rice pudding, or layered with fresh fruit and whipped cream as parfaits or pies. Pitted and lightly crushed fresh cherries folded with rich cream into a sweet risotto studded with roasted almonds is a show-stopper. And if a sweet saffron risotto is united with the nobility of rose water and ground cardamom, there is nothing but pomegranate seeds and pistachio nuts to finish it. If Gordon comes around, tell him it is your 'take' on rice pudding; there is little difference.

The classic risotto Milanese is made with a rich chicken stock and then flavoured and coloured only with saffron, which should have been soaked in boiling water for at least 20 minutes before being used.

Quinoa

One of man's oldest cultivated grains and fittingly called the Mother Grain by the Incas and by the many civilizations who preceded them over thousands of years in the long thin lands between the Andes and the South Pacific. Like amaranth, quinoa has a protein balance very close to meat and soy beans making it particularly important nutritionally: it is not actually a cereal grain but a herb seed and related to spinach.

The small seeds always need rinsing before use or the cooking water goes soapy, even if suppliers say it won't. The grains always retain a slight bitterness that is mollified by serving with something acidic, and keep a little crunch, from their equatorial bands, that cutely uncurl during cooking. Quinoa looks and tastes rather like millet with a kick of sesame to most people and has no real competition on that score. Of the many things that recommend it to your attention, the best is that quinoa cooks in about ten minutes. True fast food, but from our ancient past. *Plus ca change* . . .

Quinoa makes excellent sprouts but best of all for jaded and driven culinistas, it comes in the widest range of colours imaginable, perhaps the widest. As well as the creamy-yellow one most likely to be found, they come, like jelly beans, in green, pink, orange, purple, red and, just as well, in black.

You have my permission to scoff at the knee-jerk instruction in every magazine and newspaper to say keen-wah when you encounter quinoa: imagine how ridiculous it would sound if we pronounced every foreign word in our language the way it's said to be said in its original country? There's nothing wrong with saying kwin oh a.

The Microwave Risotto

You do not need to start the rice with onion if you have a good enough stock; if you do use onion chop it very finely indeed, so it dissolves into the sauce rather than intruding noisomely.

The following serves two or three as a main course, four or more as a first course. Whether your cup is 300ml or less, or whether you use a mug doesn't matter, as long as you use the same for the rice and the stock. Note, no salt is used, as the reduced stock plus the Parmesan usually provide enough.

1 large cup arborio or vialone rice
2 generous tablespoons butter
2½ -3 large cups good stock
75g/3 oz Parmesan cheese, freshly grated
extra 1 or 2 tablespoons butter

Heat the stock to boiling in a measuring jug in the microwave, remove and then cover. Put the rice into a 2-litre microwave safe glass bowl and top with the butter. Cook on High for two or more minutes, stirring once, until the rice is buttered and turning opaque but is not browning.

Pour on half the stock and then cook on High for five minutes. Remove the bowl and whisk its contents well. Pour in half the remaining stock, and then cook on High until that is almost absorbed, about three minutes. Whisk well and then repeat with half the remaining stock and then test. The rice should retain a little resistance in each grain, but if not cook on further but only in increments of a minute.

Now only your judgement and personal preference can help you. Remembering you will emulsify any excess liquid with cheese and butter, judge if there is too little. If so, add more, whisking as you go and aiming for a thick glossiness of the binding sauce. Stir in the butter and the Parmesan and whisk again until the texture of the sauce is rich and unctuous: you can, of course, add more stock if you think it's all too thick for you.

Vegetables and other delicate ingredients, should be cooked separately and added towards the end so they are not broken up by the final whiskings.

Although generally served warm rather than very hot, you can give your risotto a burst in the microwave, but not so much you cook it on. Serve on hot plates.

Plain risotto made with a special stock, like partridge or Barbary duck stock, is always admired but a few additions are usually appreciated; halved white grapes to one, segments of blood orange to the other, and rugged, barely torn leaves of flat leaf parsley. Adding small fresh or frozen peas gives the classic *risi et bisi*, always much better than you can imagine. Or reconstitute 15g or more dried porcini, ceps or fairy ring mushrooms and then add the strained liquid to the stock; stir in the mushrooms with plenty of flat leaf parsley just before serving. A mint or basil risotto is extraordinarily good as the base for any kind of fish, seafood or poultry. Infuse a good handful of mint or basil leaves in the hot stock, and then remove when the flavour is good and strong: complete the risotto by stirring in 15-20 fresh leaves or by swirling through a good basil or mint pesto. Add flakes of cooked chicken breast, fish or seafood that has been cooked separately just before serving; flakes of hot-smoked salmon are very good.

Rye

A very important bread-making grain in Scandinavia and the former USSR, rye can be cultivated in conditions where other grains fail. Once it used to be sown with wheat as a matter of course, so that if the wheat failed there would still be something to harvest. The mixture of wheat and rye that was thus the usual crop was known as maslin and used as it came with little regard to the proportions of each grain; but as this added interest to an otherwise repetitive diet, the inconsistency was probably welcomed. For some genetic reason, wheat and rye never crossed with one another; this has now been achieved by science and the new grain is called triticale.

Bread making is by far the most important use of rye but a loaf made with 100 per cent rye flour is dense, dark, nutty and dry, for there is not enough gluten in rye to allow a high absorption of moisture or a good rise. Thus rye is always mixed to a greater or lesser degree with wheat flour. When rye predominates the dark so-called black bread is often further coloured and flavoured. Caraway seeds are the most common additives but others are molasses and caramel; and one American recipe I saw advocated instant coffee powder.

When white flour predominates the result is a light, creamy bread with an agreeable denseness. It's commonly accepted in Eastern Europe and Russia that dark or light rye bread is better if made by the sourdough technique, something that also contributes to the texture and deepens the sweet flavour. With or without caraway seeds a light rye bread is the only bread for hot salt-beef or Reuben sandwiches.

 Pumpernickel breads are usually based on rye and other whole grains but the name is loosely applied to a range of breads.

In many rural areas a dry loaf is actually preferred for its long keeping qualities and ability to sop up gravies, and far more of Europe makes such rye-inclusive loaves than I first thought. I best remember sawing chunks off a huge, low, round rye loaf of this type at Hautfort, near Perigord, though it had been bought at a village some distance away. The surprise of finding such a loaf there was somewhat diminished, overwhelmed perhaps, by eating it in the huge kitchen of a chateau, magnificently restored by Australians Barbara and Max Freeman. The simple bread was served with home-cooked foie gras, local truffles, omelettes stuffed with scorzonera flowers and a wine called Pécharmant, 'charming fart'. Not, I imagine, such a bread's usual milieu. Nor mine.

In the past, rye straw was invaluable for thatching, packing and brickmaking, but for all its positive uses, rye was also a potential killer as it is subject to attack by a fungus called ergot. This extraordinary mould is responsible for a disease of the human nervous system called Saint Anthony's Fire, which was specially prevalent during the Middle Ages in northern Europe, but huge epidemics caused by infected rye bread were common before and after this. The last small epidemic in England was in Manchester in 1927, but in France it was seen as late as 1951 in the aptly named village, Pont-Saint-Esprit.

Rye flakes: good in mixed grain porridges or in muesli. For general use I think they are best when used in or on bread doughs, after soaking and cooking.

Rye flour: quite easy to obtain and only useful for bread making. Most countries like a mixture of rye and wheat, say 15 per cent rye to 85 per cent wheat for a light-coloured and tasty loaf, and other than making such a flour mixture you might use rye flour exclusively for your sourdough starter and then use wheat flour for the rest of the dough. I don't know of any other major use of rye flour, other than for the unleavened Scandinavian crisp breads.

Cooking

It is unrewarding to serve cooked whole rye by itself but it makes a worthwhile contribution when added to other grains or as a bulker in casseroles. Treat it like wheat berries, by soaking overnight and then cooking for about 12 hours. Even so you might have to cook the grains on more, in a soup or casserole, to get them really tender.

Storing

Keep all rye products cool, dry and dark and they will store well. Ideally, buy only as much as you can use in a relatively short time. Buying in bulk has distinct disadvantages, especially in summer when the hotter weather encourages the reproduction of all manner of grain pests.

Spelt

See below under Wheat.

Triticale

Until quite recently, although wheat and rye almost always grew together, they never crossbred. This was finally achieved scientifically in Sweden in the 1930s, when the resultant cross was called triticale, a combination of the Latin names of both grains. Work on further development continues in Mexico City and Manitoba.

The main advantages of this artificially inseminated grain are nutritional, for it seems triticale can always be relied upon to give a higher yield of protein, amino acid balance and general food value than any wheat strain under the same conditions. Triticale has a gluten content higher than rye but lower than wheat. It is also somewhat fragile, so treat triticale lightly and never knead its bread dough other than with feather-light fingers. Otherwise you can use triticale like other whole grains to add interest and nutrition to pilaffs, porridges, mueslis, breads and biscuits.

Wheat

Over 90 per cent of the flour consumed in Western Europe, the United States and the countries of the old Commonwealth is made from wheat. It is without doubt the western world's most important grain, and always has been.

Archeological evidence shows wheat has been cultivated since about 7,000 BC, which suggests its use for a much longer period. It is a grass of the *Triticum* family, the true origins of which have never been determined. Recent research has come closer to breeding it back to its very early forms, which will be used to strengthen or create new strains.

For nearly 9,000 years man cultivated wheat in exactly the same way, introducing new varieties rarely, and usually by chance. But it was never cheap or plentiful enough to be a universal food; neither would it grow in northerly climates. In the empire of Ancient Rome or Greece only the rich could afford flour so laboriously refined it was white and so made white-ish bread, and well into the 19th century bread made only of wheat, especially whiter bolted wheat, was still a status symbol in Europe and America. Then the wheat variety known as Turkey Red was introduced into North America. It began to produce such mammoth crops, so easily, that the wheat farmers of the world all wanted part of this bounty. So did the public, keen to establish their improved social position by eating only wheat bread and forgetting the barley, oat and rye breads of their forefathers. Soon Russia and Australia, too, had developed heavy-cropping wheat strains that were specially suited to bread making, the high-protein so-called strong wheats. In just a few years the world's wheat growers had to change every agricultural, cropping and manufacturing technique so they could cope with the size of the crop and the demand.

The world's wheat is still being developed, sometimes by giving us back varieties that have almost disappeared but which have distinct health benefits.

Burgul or bulghur: known commonly and incorrectly as cracked wheat but is quite different from that. It's actually a processed food, probably the world's oldest. Berries of local wheat in Middle Eastern countries are cooked to a mush that is spread out to dry, sometimes having first been strained. When crisp and dry it is broken down into varied textures. To use it you simply pour twice the quantity of boiling water over it and eat it plain or flavoured when the liquid has been absorbed; butter or olive oil improve it immeasurably. It is a delicious alternative to rice, especially wonderful in stuffings, and used throughout the Middle East in highly individual and often exciting ways. Simplest is tabbouleh, the salad made with cracked wheat and masses of very finely chopped parsley, fresh coriander and onion: the most esoteric use to our taste is probably kibbeh, which is a wheat and raw lamb construction of great popularity.

Couscous: the national dish of much of northwest Africa is not a grain as so many think. Instead it is a curious sort of pasta, made from two types of flour. On one hand, literally, you have the small hard grains of semolina, the hardest part to grind of wheat. In the other you have fine white flour that is lightly hydrated so it is sticky enough to hold tight to the semolina pieces. Laboriously the connection has to be made, semolina piece by semolina piece rolled in the fingers, so each is enrobed in a film of flour paste. There then comes long laborious steaming rather than boiling and this will eventually be finished over spectacular stews and sauces, redolent of ginger, cumin and coriander and saffron, glistening with fats and butters, burgeoning with exotic vegetables and meats.

Two things you should know. First couscous tastes exactly the same whatever you steam it over, including plain water, as steam cannot carry flavour with it; steaming couscous over stews in a two-tiered *couscousière* is simply a matter of using one heat source rather than two.

Secondly, without the stews and sauces couscous would be pretty boring, particularly considering the effort and care to make it. But look at the label.

More and more couscous has now been pre-cooked and all you need do is to add liquid, as with burghul, so you might as well choose it. If you want it faster and want it hot, it will swell and steam to perfection in a microwave in minutes, seconds if you start with hot water or stock.

Couscous is said to be made with many other grains, but I'm sure they are more properly variations on bulgur/burghul, not that this is any easier to spell. – see barley couscous. But there is another type of couscous:

Mougrabieh is as big as pearls, up to 6mm/¼ inch in diameter, and sometimes quite as hard to swallow. I find it commonly in Australia and New Zealand, less so in the UK. Some call it Israeli couscous, but that's only because it's made and exported by that country. It's actually Lebanese and we should call it only Lebanese couscous or *mougrabieh*.

It's made from finely ground semolina flour, rolled into balls with a little water. Traditionally *mougrabieh* is steamed over a stew, like Moroccan couscous, but it can be cooked other ways. It can be bought ready toasted and that's a clue to one of the best cooking methods: put it untoasted into a shallow pan with plenty of butter and take time to brown it, maybe twenty minutes or more if it's for four servings. Then add stock and or gravy, ideally from something with which you will cook it and gently simmer it, gradually adding more liquid until the *mougrabieh* is soft and tender.

You could also cook it just like the pasta it is, provided you toss it into a great deal of boiling water or stock. The less cooking space you give it, the more likely it is to stick,

I feel sure you could reverse the cooking, that is to cook it in water or stock and then to brown it in butter, perhaps with such a gorgeous Middle Eastern spice mixture as *baharat*, q.v. and then lots of roughly torn flat leaf parsley; what a pasta pilaff that would be. Simply cooked and nakedly served pearly white, as once happened to me in Melbourne, it looks too much like raw tapioca, and might as well have been. It's a pasta for heavens' sake, it screams for garlic, yells for the sweet bounty of oven concentrated tomatoes and salty olives and capers, demands the assault of anchovies and spices and herbs and old, hard, grating cheeses – all of them, ideally. You could just chuck some into an explodingly delicious oxtail, chicken, duck or beef stew before you serve it, as small, chic dumplings.

If you put *mougrabieh* into soup, children either play with it or refuse to eat it.

Emmer: see Farro.

Epautre, petit: the grain world's equivalent of the soy bean, for it is the only one with the complete spectrum of eight protein/amino acids. 100g will give the average human with a day's supply of protein. This amazing old wheat variety, *triticum monococcum*, is vigorously being restored to popularity in Provence, where it has been known for millennia. There is no explanation for its falling from favour once the Romans arrived, unless it was the age-old belief something new was necessarily better. Keep an eye out for the growing number of products made with petit épautre, including beer. Bet that's specially good for you. Spelt q.v. is *le grand épautre*.

Farro: as *emmer* or *einkorn* this old variety of wheat went nowhere. As farro it is taken up by smart restaurants, and offers an unusual eating profile, for although it looks like a whole grain it is actually semi-husked and so is lighter and more elegant to eat than its looks suggest. *Farro della Garfagnanai*, (*triticum dicoccum*) has been grown without interruption in districts around Lucca in Italy, and is thought to be the wheat carried by Roman legionnaires. Its IGP status means it is still guaranteed cultivated without synthetic help, and is then stored without the use of pesticides.

Farro is easily confused with spelt but there are differences: farro must be soaked but spelt can be cooked directly: farro keeps texture but spelt eventually cooks to a mush.

Freekeh: a hoary Middle Eastern staple made from green wheat stems that are bundled together, dried a little and then burned, a technique probably discovered by accident and in which the moist green grains don't catch alight but are left with a delicious smokiness from the burned husks, which are then easily rubbed away. Cooked like rice, freekeh is particularly high in protein and has four times the fibre of brown rice, but its low starch content means it's nutty rather than starchy to eat and is particularly gratifying; you need half the amount you'd need of rice to feel as well fed.

The traditional way of burning the green wheat on the ground inevitably meant it came with stones and grit, and freekah could take longer to sort out than to cook and eat, hence its low profile. Then up came Tony Lufti of South Australia who has invented new ways of harvesting and preparing freekeh, so much so Adelaide has adapted it as its keynote ingredient, selling (comparatively) prodigious amounts in salads, or added to wheat flour bread, as flour or as whole or cracked grains. Traditionally freekeh was also made with barley.

Kamut brand wheat: developed by a Montana organic farmer who's also a plant and agricultural scientist, this wheat has a grain twice as big as normal varieties and protein and gluten content in higher than usual proportions. There is growing belief seven out of ten people who have wheat malabsorption problems can tolerate Kamut wheat in a suitably varied diet.

Kibbled and cracked wheat: are generally considered the same thing in the United Kingdom, but there is a difference, and the latter is also very much confused with burgul or bulghur. A kibbler is a machine that pricks the whole grains, splitting them into small pieces; cracked wheat is crushed under light pressure. In both cases the object is to split the grain to enable faster cooking, at the same time as preserving the nutritional values of the whole grain. Either can be used like whole grains and I like them soaked, cooked and then sprinkled over or incorporated into bread doughs. This makes a good basis for stuffings, too, far more interesting than boring, pulped-up plastic breadcrumbs.

Semolina: is probably one of the most widely known but least used wheat products, loved or hated depending on the standard of puddings at your school. It is often, but not always, made from durum wheat and is the boltings of flour – that is to say the hard unground pieces of wheat endosperm that do not pass through the sifter. At least that would have been the case before the roller mill. Now, semolina is just as likely to be coarsely rolled strong/hard wheat. The old semolina pudding, slow baked in milk to make a gritty sort of custard can be made fabulous, with orange flower water, with spices, and by having cream folded in before serving – but why?

Spelt: the undisputed leader of born-again wheat grains, spelt was once the staple grain grown throughout Europe. Although of the same genus as common wheat, spelt has a different genetic structure providing more protein per grain, a greater concentration of minerals and vitamins, and a propensity for adding unique flavours to breads that do not crumble when sliced.

Modern farming, commonly at odds with good food, changed the ancient dependence on spelt wheat. For although the close husk of spelt gives it superior protection against pest and disease, it is difficult to thresh mechanically and thus the winning appeal of modern varieties with looser husks: organic farmers are more impressed with spelt's disease resistant qualities which guarantee a decent harvest, and they don't mind the extra work in husking.

There is also a view that the protein in spelt does not cause as many problems to those who are gluten-intolerant, and may indeed allow those sufferers to eat wheat produce, provided they introduce it into their diets slowly. Spelt is being grown again in Britain and, should it or spelt bread be offered, it will be well worth your interest See: farro.

Trahana: What? No, not another East European car but a rustic wheat-based food from northern Greece that looks like a crumble ready-mix. It is a dried and broken paste of flour, goat milk and eggs. You cook it in water to make a creamy yet textured porridge. Made thin it is served as a soup into which feta cheese, herbs and olive oil are added. Made more thickly it can be used as a rude polenta, either as such or a medium in which to cook vegetables.

There is a sweet version too and between them they offer something new to explore that is traditional rather than sparkling fresh from a laboratory. Like burghul and instant couscous, trahana is a wheat product that even the inexperienced cook can conquer.

Wheat flakes: are the result of steamed and softened berries being gently rolled under pressure. They are best used to make a delicious wheat porridge or as a major component of cold grain breakfasts – the ubiquitous muesli. As with all flaked grains, I also like to use them to change the daily flavour of mixed-grain winter porridges, for no matter how good a flavour is, I cannot abide eating or drinking the same thing day after day.

Wheat flours: it is thought that there are now over 30,000 varieties of wheat, each with its own local advantages. Today's crop is estimated to be in excess of 300 million tonnes annually, broadly made up of just two types, the strong and soft wheats.

The grain of **strong wheat** has a relatively higher proportion (13-14 per cent) of gluten-producing protein, essential for bread dough. When water is added to strong wheat flour, the protein hydrates to form a continuous web of gluten throughout the mixture. The elastic gluten is expanded by any yeast-produced gas and, being strong enough to trap that gas, causes the mixture to rise in millions of little bubbles. The risen mixture can support both itself and the addition of whole grains, fruits and so on but if allowed to rise too long the gluten is stretched to fragility and the loaf will collapse. The grain of strong wheat is frequently red and always long. It flourishes in hot summers and snowy winters, but cannot abide humidity.

Soft wheat grows in more temperate climates and is lower in protein (7-10 per cent) than strong wheat and thus will not give a good rise when leavened with yeast. But it is higher in starch, which contributes to the light foamy texture desirable in cake and scone making, when chemicals are used to give the rise. Soft flours also absorb less moisture, so baked goods also with a low-fat content will quickly become stale. French bread, especially the well-known long shapes, are made with soft flour but this makes only a minor contribution to the special flavour and fast staling of these loaves. A long slow rising gives their characteristic holes and flavour, and the special crisp crust comes from being baked in commercial ovens with controlled bursts of steam: they were never produced domestically and cannot be.

You cannot reproduce the flavour of an authentic French loaf in the United Kingdom without proper French soft flour, as enthusiasts will have discovered; but if you use soft, unbleached white flour, let the dough rise very slowly and then eat the bread almost immediately, you will get close.

Most commercial plain white flour is a mixture of soft and hard wheat blended to produce an average taste and average performance, hence the description 'all-purpose' seen on some packets.

There is one other major strain of wheat – the **durum** – which, as its name implies, is the hardest and strongest of all. Its special use is in the making of pasta of all kinds and it is suitable for semolina, too.

Wheat germ and wheat bran: are usually used as additives to bread doughs or sprinkled over other foods. Take great care in the buying and storing of the former; indeed, only buy it if its packaging and provenance are impeccable, or it will be rancid.

Wholemeal and wheatmeal: these terms are synonymous and indicate a flour made from the whole grain, with nothing added or taken away. ·

Much confusion has been caused by the term wheat meal, which is *not* a 100 per cent wheat grain flour, much as manufacturers would like to have you believe this. It is what is called an extraction flour and is often also sold as 'farmhouse flour'. The term wheat meal has now been phased out in the United Kingdom and, indeed, may not be used. Farmhouse or equivalent flours are 85 or 81 per cent flour which simply means that 15 or 19 per cent of the original grain has been sifted out, giving you a flour that is subsequently lighter in colour than wholemeal, gives lighter results in baking and can be kneaded in bread making.

Remember, if you are making bread with 100 per cent wholemeal flour the dough should not be kneaded, as this increases the deleterious effect of bran on the gluten.

Cooking

Perhaps because wheat is so universal and ancient it is sold in more forms than most grains. Whole wheat grains, known as wheat berries, are not commonly used domestically, but when soaked overnight and then cooked in water for an hour or two, can make a mild and nutty contribution to bread dough, to soups, stews and to mixtures of cooked pulses or rice.

If during the final minutes of cooking you let the water boil almost away and then replace it with milk and let that thicken up you get a delicious and especially chewy type of porridge that is specially enjoyable with the darker sugars, or with palm sugar. Freshly harvested wheat cooked like this becomes furmenty or fruminty, which if you believe Thomas Hardy, was often laced with rum and other liquors and could then lead to the sale of spouse and offspring. With suitable precautions against such loss, frumenty is a time-honoured accompaniment to venison. The jelly-like results of letting it sit and cool is an unusual refreshing summer treat.

Gluten

Gluten malabsorption makes life desperately uncomfortable for coeliac disease sufferers. Yet in China they extract this protein from wheat and cook and eat it with relish.

They make a dough of strong, bread-making flour with water, salt and baking soda, and leave it to stand until the gluten has swollen and the dough is lighter and more pliable. The lump is then washed and washed again to rinse away the starch, leaving them with a smaller lump of gluten. This is shaped in many ways and offered for sale at the same shops and stalls that sell tofu; but it is easy to tell the difference. Tofu is always a pleasing creamy white, and gluten a depressing, grubby grey. The particular use of gluten is in long cooked stewy things, for whereas even fried firm soy curd will eventually dissolve, gluten keeps its texture, if that's what you want.

The Vegetarian Option

The only people who could possibly think vegetarian diets less meritorious than meat diets are those who produce meat. The vegetarian diet is absolutely sustaining and healthy. But only if you do it properly.

If you don't know the rules a vegetable, pulse and grain diet can lead to hideous complications, particularly in children and teenagers – eating only rice or pasta and lots of vegetables is not a healthy diet but an unhealthy pathway to ill health and possible permanent damage.

To live healthily as a vegetarian you must eat a protein source with the complete amino acid spectrum found in milk, eggs, cheese and in the flesh of meat, game birds and animals, poultry or fish. Only four earth-grown foods have anything like the complete protein spectrum of animal flesh, and only one of these is certain. If you are vegetarian and do not know this, you are increasingly malnourished, day after day, week after week. Milk, and cheese and eggs are complete proteins that replace meat, but quickly become boring. A diet based on low fat and skimmed milk produce cannot be said to make getting out of bed worthwhile, and if eating is not enjoyable, life is not worthwhile.

The only fully acknowledged complete vegetarian protein source is the soy bean. When I went to Nanking with Sam Twining on a trip to look at tea gardens we first met our first young soy beans, fresh and green and tasty, so utterly delicious and unexpected we swept aside the potions and oils and dressings offered on the table and gobbled them up quite plain, although the occasional wistful sigh recognized quite how far we were from any possibility of gobbling the beans with butter.

As a mature bean the soy bean is curiously bland and curiously textured and thus almost no one eats it. Instead the Orient converts it to tofu, a white curd made from soy bean milk. It is basically flavourless and requires a high boredom threshold or considerable cookery knowledge and skill to be enjoyed on a regular basis. This is why orientals tend to use it as part of their protein spectrum rather than as a total alternative. Anyway, switching to soy products is not simple.

Of all beans, soy creates the greatest intestinal gas problems and many would-be converts quickly avoid it for they find themselves bloated and uncomfortable or relieved and embarrassed. Thus vegetarians turn to grains and pulses, if only for variety. These also provide welcome texture, a spectrum of vitamins and minerals, vital fibre and are generally fat and cholesterol-free.

Otherwise only the rare *petit epautre* wheat appears to be a complete vegetarian protein, with the almost complete but less-known amaranth and quinoa close behind, followed up by expensive wild rice. Either difficulty of obtaining or expense means they are not easily adapted for everyday use: anyway the easier, cheaper grains lack the vital amino acids, lysine and tryptophan; and all beans except soy beans lack methionine. Yet nature is a great and good provider, because when you eat grains and pulses together the spectrum is completed, the combination is as powerful as eating meat, fish, cheese, eggs or milk.

The blueprint for grain and pulse founded vegetarian health is simple to tell, simple to remember. You should aim for 60% pulses or beans to 30% grains, making up the other 10% with mushrooms for their vital but otherwise elusive vitamin B12, plus salad or vegetables. The most direct way to remember this is to picture baked beans on wholemeal toast, an almost perfect substitute for animal protein. The basic Indian equivalent is a lentil-based dhal served over rice or with a wholewheat-flour chapatti.

Ideally the combination should be in the same meal, although opinions are more flexible these days, with the view that you should aim to eat your mix over the day. It is also a good idea to ensure you eat or drink something with Vitamin C, often added to bought food and drink as ascorbic acid, a natural preservative, and that helps release iron, often harder for the body to get from vegetables than from meat: consciously or not the world's habit of drinking orange juice with a breakfast that invariably includes grains in some form is an important guarantee the iron in the cereals will be released for use.

Wind problems won't just blow away because you don't eat soy products. Grains and such pulses as beans and lentils can create equal problems. The answer is to introduce them into your diet slowly and not to make an overnight change unless ordered to do so by a doctor. So serve beans or lentils as a side dish rather than a main dish for a week and gradually increase the amounts and the proportions over a month. You'll find the bowel will meekly have adjusted and you can be a happy vegetarian without it going, or blowing, against the grain. If you continue to have problems it is worth having your digestive tract checked out.

Thus with little trouble and in no time at all it is possible to be a healthy vegetarian, almost thoughtlessly getting the high-variety, high-fibre, low-fat, low-sugar ideal of modern diet. Milk, cheese or eggs each day, or some soy product, or grains and pulses mean you are both safe and well.

Teenage boys and girls should never be allowed to become vegetarian without supervision and advice. To eat less of anything, at a time when they need more of most, is a recipe for true disaster than can have long-lasting effects. Without proper diet puberty can be arrested, and it is common for girls to stop menstruating or not to menstruate at all, the supplement treatment for which is said to be particularly horrid. Once teenagers have gone through puberty and have fully grown and matured sexually, they have every right to become informed vegetarians, vegetarians who eat a broad variety of balanced foods.

And yet . . . there is hardly a vegetarian cookery book that rehearses these facts. Might they cynically be exploiting a confused market, and casually be putting at risk the health of thousands of teenage boys and girls; surely not?

Herbs, Spices and Flavourings

Herbs are always leaves and usually green, and everything else is brown and a spice, which includes seeds, fruits, flowers, pods, buds, bark, stalks and roots.

There are many books to give fascinating lore about herbs, but knowing garlic supposedly sprung from where the Devil once trod has never made a better cook. I'm sticking to culinary information, well, mainly.

Two specially interesting things have happened to herbs and spices since I first wrote this book. The first is the number of companies finding and marketing authentic herb and spice mixtures from all around the world, making it simple for us to visit Saudi Arabia for lunch and West Africa for dinner. The other is the growing interest and market availability of indigenous herbs and spices that might have been used for centuries in their native country but are only just being offered to the rest of us.

Both these categories of herbs and spices are now dealt with in their own section.

But first some general tips.

Storing

The one golden rule for dried herbs and spices is to buy as few as possible and store for as short a time as you can. Although convenient, the storage of herbs and spices close to a cooker is rather silly, as the heat will hasten their deterioration. Light destroys them too, so although it is very pretty and homely, it's no good thing to hang sprays of herbs in a warm kitchen. Find somewhere cooler and darker and they will be longer lasting, better tasting and more rewarding. For ground spices and for particularly aromatic whole spices, like cardamom, a plastic box in the refrigerator is by far the best idea.

Special uses

Both herbs and spices can be used to make a remarkable number of interesting drinks, hot and cold. The rule is that leaves and flowers are usually infused in boiling water and roots, barks, stalks and so on are usually boiled for a few minutes. The former should always be brewed in a cup with a saucer over the top or in a pottery teapot; the saucer or lid keep in the essential fumes and keep the drink hotter.

If you don't like the look of leaves in your cooking, and many people don't, then brew some strong liquor from your herbs and use that instead, or macerate them in distilled spirits or vodka and use this in moderation.

Herb vinegars are another wonderful way to utilize fresh bunches of summer herbs and details of how to make a variety of these useful condiments are given on page 551. Once you've made them you'll find them perfectly invaluable.

Flavours, Flavours and Flavourings

Commercially, most herb flavours are obtained from essential oils. These are proclaimed as the true flavour of the herbs, pure and unadulterated. And that is the trouble. Being unadulterated with the vegetable matter and minute trace fragrances, the oils don't reflect the true spectrum that all good tastes have but imitate only the loudest: it's like letting a bully dictate what we eat –

and for bully you can of course substitute commercial interests. It is simpler for commercial interest to add a small amount of oil than to cope with fresh or dried herbs and spices, and so once again the customer loses out, has to make do with second best.

Ajowan: tiny, power-packed seeds tasting like a combination of thyme and black pepper. Use with discretion if you are new to them and just as they are: they are too small really to need grinding. Just the thing to add to savoury baking, like cheese biscuits, or to thread through bread dough but they could be very lightly crushed first to ensure you get their full virtue. Very useful as an unexpected sprinkle anywhere a clean acidity is welcome – on every type of grain, starch or vegetable, but most arresting when scattered on or rubbed into something made of fish or seafood. If you have used fresh thyme in a dish ajowan seeds also offer a bright way to refresh the flavour when serving; I have used them most successfully to finish coq au vin. Remember, fresh seeds are very powerful so don't go overboard, which is where to throw ajowan seeds that have no lift or tang. Speaking of which, ajowan is another of those ingredients that deflate flatulence and colic, and these seeds are also credited with adding to a 'husband's enjoyment in middle years'.

Allspice: one of my favourite devices for giving a boost to all manner of food, allspice is the dried, unripe berry of a myrtle-related tree discovered in the New World by Christopher Columbus. Its hot spicy smell and taste are similar to a mixture of the sweet spices of the Old World – cloves, cinnamon and nutmeg. And thus its name, a single spice that tastes the same as a combine of the others.

Allspice is not commonly encountered in Middle Eastern cooking, where they have the originals to enjoy, but Turkey uses it a lot with great success, especially in meat stuffings that might also contain fresh parsley and coriander.

If your mixed spice is too sweet or has lost its flavour, add freshly pounded allspice berries. Freshly pounded or ground allspice goes well in rice stuffings for poultry and lamb and is essential in pork or veal-based pâtés, with sweet root vegetables like carrots and parsnips; fruit pies and sauces, pickles and curries can also benefit. The whole berries are nice in pot pourris and ground allspice can be used for pomander-rolling mixtures.

In old books allspice is often called Jamaica pepper or pimento or pimiento pepper, but it must not be confused with pimiento, which is the vegetable we call capsicum or red/green/whatever pepper.

Amchur: another way of adding acidity to curries, and thus an alternative to lemon or lime juice, or tamarind. It's simply dried green mango, sold as slices or ground, and is sometimes sold as green mango powder. It also has a tenderizing effect, so it's a good thing to include in marinade for the often cheaper cuts of meat suggested for barbecues. Dried slices, rather than powder, are used in fruit chutneys, adding a refreshing contrast.

Angelica: a member of the parsley family, the lovely angelica bush was once a mainstay of herb and flower gardens; its handsome foliage can grow as high as 1.8m/6ft and you can make it into a perennial if you keep its flower spikes cut.

Every part of the plant has been used, and the celery-flavoured leaves are still popular as the base for a tisane or herbal tea, sometimes in conjunction with a little juniper berry. The root may also be boiled for tea, and root or seed oil flavours both liqueurs and wines.

The best-known use for angelica is in the form of candied stalk and leaf stem for cake decoration. If you have an angelica plant or know where there is one try making your own glacé angelica; masses of them grow wild, usually close to rivers where there are rich, moist, shady conditions.

Cut the selected stalks and stems into lengths of 10-12.5cm/4-5 in, place them in a glass or crockery dish and pour over a boiling solution in the proportion of 600ml/1pt water to 100g/4oz salt. Cover, leave for 24 hours, drain, peel and wash in cold water. Boil syrup of 900ml/l _ pt water with 700g/1½lb sugar for ten minutes, add the angelica and simmer for 20 minutes, then remove and drain on a wire rack for four days. Reserve all syrup. After the four days of draining, put the angelica back into the reserved syrup, boil for 20 minutes, and then allow the angelica to cool in the syrup. Drain for another four days, sprinkle well with caster sugar and store in airtight containers.

Anise/Aniseed: once used to pay taxes and a supposed bringer of good luck when included in wedding cakes. The plant is an annual which grows about 60cm/2ft high overall, a native of Asia Minor and probably one of the oldest known aromatic seeds. It has a sweet, liquorice-like taste with a broad spectrum of uses, from marinades to fruit salads, cakes and pickles, and is very good with cabbage dishes hot or cold, or scattered on bread dough.

The tea, made by steeping the seeds in boiling water, is a good digestive after a large meal; but then so is aniseed liqueur – *anisette*. The Dutch candy anise seeds, as *muisjes*.

Anise is the flavouring of all the pastis drinks and these are a simple way to flavour fish dishes and many dried fruits. A discovery of mine is sliced kiwi fruit marinated for a brief time in Pernod and then served with prawns and a lime-flavoured mayonnaise.

Barberries: some varieties were used by Native Americans as food stuffs, but in the Old World it's only Iranians who eat them. In many ways they are like cranberries, tart but fruity, and so are like fresh red currants too; yet barberries can be eaten without sweetening. They come as dried dark red berries and rehydrate quickly. The most common place to find them in Iranian food is topping a saffron pilaff or *plov*, when they will have been fried in butter, with or without a little sugar and sometimes with extra saffron too. Related in flavour to sumac, of course. The Iranian word for barberries is *zereshk* or *zershk*, and that's enough for me to want to use them very day.

Basil: the very essence of summer. Once fresh basil starts arriving in markets, the pungent warm smell seems to attract people from miles away, and it's sold in hours. Actually a native of India and Persia, basil nowadays is particularly associated with Italian cooking, but is also important in south-east Asia, Thailand in particular. Yet its name is Greek, and means king.

Basil's peak of culinary achievement is its simplest use – freshly chopped on slightly chilled slices of rich, red, knobbly tomatoes; it is an insult to something so regal, to say nothing of your palate, to combine basil with those woolly orange bullets. Use fresh basil with any tomato dish, hot or cold, including pizza and spaghetti sauces.

Although some people wouldn't add herbs to ratatouille, I think a combination of basil and sweet marjoram gives a quintessential element of hot Mediterranean summers to this glorious vegetable mixture. The different but still peppery sting of dried basil is surprisingly good with parsnips.

All basil grows well in a sunny window but should always be grown under cover if you have only one or two plants – once they discover basil birds become besotted with it and can devour a large specimen in days.

Bush basil has a smaller habit and leaves, and is rather more like marjoram in flavour. It seems easier to grow if the summer is not hot enough to encourage the full-sized plant.

Holy basil is a darker, smaller leaved variety much used in Thai cookery. It has a slightly more focussed flavour and is the one chosen there to cook with meat: European sweet basil can be substituted but doesn't have the same oomph.

Creative cooks should look beyond the initial anise-like flavour of basil and think about its citric notes, and the peppery ones. Once, at a press reception for tourism representatives from Seattle, I served brioches with basil leaves and oysters. The brioches were warm and split. The oysters were dipped into a hot but not boiling, buttery Chardonnay just long enough to scare them into submission, and then put onto a fresh basil leaf in the brioche. The wine gave the fruity butteriness oysters like so much, the basil gave the citric and pepper balances: so there was no pepper or salt offered. Triumphant? I should say so, and everyone left talking rather more about the new dimensions they had discovered in basil, rather than Seattle. This didn't give me a single sleepless night.

Bay leaf: I think bay is indispensable in any red meat dish or the sauce that goes with one; it is the boards of a stage upon which every other flavour performs better. Knowing cooks use two or more times the number normally specified in recipes. But don't forget bay leaf has a remarkable flavour of its own and this is very much underused in our kitchens.

There are unsuspected heavens of aromatic taste and pleasure just by stuffing lots of fresh bay leaves under the crackling when you roast pork, or under the breast skin of a chicken. Prunes, simmered with bay leaves, red wine, spices and a little brown sugar become the most unctuous accompaniment to poultry, pork and game dishes; simmer until there is just enough liquid left to cover the fruit, then remove the leaves and whole spices.

When you add a wine or stock to a roasting dish, also add some torn bay leaf to pull together the gravy flavours.

As the prime ingredient of a bouquet garni, bay also lends its flavour to many of the great sauces, particularly white ones, and I like always to use bay when I am cooking fish; it is essential in all but the most recherché marinades.

The most interesting way to appreciate the individual perfume of the bay leaf is to use it to flavour rice; use two big dry leaves or four fresh ones, torn roughly, to 225g/8oz or 1 cup of uncooked rice. Served with plain or spiced food it adds a truly individual aromatic/spicy touch but too strong a flavour can be cloying. Basmati rice flavoured with bay leaf is by far the best way to start a rice salad.

There is a rare golden-leaved bay; it's more ornamental to have about the place and its flavour is more fragrant and elegant, too. The only place I know to buy a tree is the Duke of Cornwall's nursery.

Bay-flavoured custard is an old favourite with baked apple, and very elegant when chilled; get the depth of flavour by simmering several leaves in the milk, removing them and proceeding in the normal way. Not long ago I bought a book called *Freud on Food*, written in the 70s by the remarkably witty English food writer and food guru, now Sir Clement Freud. Apart from the alarming number of canned foods considered necessary to make 'gourmet' foods then, he puts bay leaf into the cream being heated to make crème brûlée, and what a welcome, cleaner and more complicated flavour that would be.

Bay rum, beloved of 'gentlemen's hairdressers' is made of bay oil, plus essences of orange and clove, plus black Jamaican rum.

Powdered bay is very useful in pâté mixtures and in spaghetti sauces, but generally the leaves are more reliable. When using them fresh, check the underside for nasties, as my tree regularly plays host to all manner of them.

Bergamot: also known in 'olde worlde' gardens as Bee Balm, because its scarlet flowers are very popular with honeybees. The crushed leaves give off a citrus-like fragrance that has unmistakable overtones of the exotic, and the flowers are very good to eat in salads. The leaves can be brewed into a tea of sorts and it was this with which American patriots comforted themselves after the Boston Tea Party deprived them of tea from China.

Oil of bergamot, which flavours Earl Grey tea, has nothing to do with this plant. It comes from a variety of eastern bitter orange and is so named only because its perfume is like that of true bergamot. The kumquat liqueur you will know from holidays in Corfu has somewhat the same flavour as bergamots, even though it is only distantly related. Some of the best bergamot oil comes from Italy's Reggio Calabria, in fact it's so good it is protected by a DOP registration.

Borage: the cucumber-like flavour tells you what to do with it; sprinkle it over salads, use it in sandwiches, layer it in gelatin moulds, put a sprig in long, cold summer drinks – especially in Pimms. A salad of borage and fresh strawberry halves is extraordinary and as good as it is unusual – very. But if you do not chop or slice the leaves very thinly, you will be distressed by the hairiness of the leaves; better to use only the vivid blue flowers.

Camomile: recently I came across a recipe from an American woman chef using camomile in a custard sauce. It took me a while to come around to it, but with judicious sweetening and a little orange zest it seems rather good, if startling. Otherwise, camomile is one of the most commonly used bases for a tisane. The yellow liquid obtained by steeping or boiling the dried or fresh flowers is a natural tranquillizer and used extensively as such in Spain, Italy and Greece. It is also very soothing to upset stomachs and can help relieve diarrhoea. Blondes use it to rinse their hair, to which it adds golden highlights.

One of its oldest uses is as a strewing or treading herb, grown in the cracks of paving stones to release pleasant smells as you saunter through herb and other gardens. It has the distinction of being a fighter; the more you tread on it the faster it grows and it has thus become the emblem of humility. Vast stretches of the garden party lawns at Buckingham Palace are camomile.

If you have space for a lawn but not for lawnmowers, plant chamomile and you'll soon have ground cover you can drink.

Caraway seeds: you love or you hate these, the tiny grey sickles of sharp aniseed flavour that populate seed cakes, and some rye breads. They can be rather interesting if they are used in moderation on hot vegetable dishes and cold salads; a few sprinkled on buttery carrots are very nice and they seem to suit coleslaw and beetroot salad very well.

Caraway has a certain affinity with apples, both raw and cooked. The nicest combination for a baked apple pie is to grate half an orange over roughly sliced raw apple and then add brown sugar, butter, nutmeg and few, very few, caraway seeds. A casserole of liver and sliced apple cooked in cider is all the better for a sprinkle of caraway, too.

The popular Kümmel liqueur relies on these seeds for its flavour and digestive qualities. You can make your own thus: steep two tablespoons caraway seeds and 250g/8oz caster sugar in 450ml/16fl oz of brandy for at least one week, shaking vigorously each day. Strain and use. I think this even more interesting if you use gin or vodka and add thin slivers of orange peel. Perhaps most interesting of all is that Kümmel is the drink of golfers in the UK, well, at some of the spiffier clubs anyway. I met a man over dinner who had been given so many as prizes, or in friendship, he was anxious to give one away to anyone at the table who showed interest; it has to be Wolfschmidt brand. He's the only golfer I've ever met who didn't dream of a hole in one.

Cardamom: quite one of the most aromatic and pungent spices of all and native of south India and Sri Lanka. It has a distinct whiff of eucalyptus and camphor behind an otherwise concentrated sweet fragrance. It is not as tropical as you might think, but grows in shady forests some way above sea level, and so cardamom is an interesting and easy plant to cultivate, perhaps even indoors. Its big leaves look luscious, and, even if you never get seeds, the leaves can be chewed for pleasure or to sweeten the breath, or sliced finely into sweet or savoury foods.

Cardamom is one of the most important flavourings of Indian and Middle Eastern sweets and is also used in drinks. A sprinkling of ground cardamom over hot coffee, morning noon or night, or a few bruised pods in the coffee pot, is often the cause of more comment than the most complicated and original dish.

If you like your curries fragrant rather than hot, add crushed cardamom pods to your garam masala or curry mixture. The most sensual combination with cardamom is saffron and rose water in warm rice puddings: cook rice in milk slowly on the top of the cooker, and only sweeten and flavour once the rice is very soft and an unctuous sauce has formed. The same combination of cardamom, rose water and saffron is also mixed into thick yoghurt along the coast of the

Maghreb, and then served chilled.

The most common way to use cardamom is to bruise the pod, slightly cracking open the fibrous casing and only lightly splitting the long, rippled seeds, so the pod still contains them. Otherwise you must remove the seeds and crush them very well indeed; if you do not reduce them to a powder your dish will look distressingly as though a loose rodent has passed through.

The Vikings introduced it to Scandinavia, where it remains the saviour of their commonly bland food. Cardamom is the spice that often gives elusive appeal to good Danish pastries, and can also go into meatballs, marinades, curries and fruit dishes. Crushed cardamom cooked with the syrup you make for a fruit salad, and then strained out, adds a sensationally exotic lift.

You'll find three if not four types on offer, two of which are actually related but offer different flavour options:

Green cardamom: the basic and most elegantly flavoured.

White cardamom: these are bleached by sun or other processes, and are not as good as the green ones.

Brown/Black cardamom: a bigger seed pod with the same sort of flavour but more of it. Not inferior to green cardamom but different and Ian Hemphill says its unique, woody and smokey flavours are invaluable aids to Indian foods that should be cooked in a tandoori oven. True cardamom of this kind is native to the Himalayas, but there is a variety grown in China: it has even bigger pods, up to 3.5cm, and is less smoky and more medicinal seeming than the Indian one. The message is not to use one as a substitute for the other, but to use both where they are best and most authentically suited.

Ground cardamom: although available is not recommended. Cardamom is so expensive you should get every last bit of goodness by crushing your own whole seeds and anyway, it loses its strength quickly. A coffee grinder will do the crushing for you. Absorb the oil left behind by then grinding rice and mixing the result into your store of rice. Otherwise a mortar and pestle do nicely, and a wodge of bread or ground rice will collect up the oil bound to be left behind.

But there's more. I recently found cardamom extract at an Indian warehouse in Auckland. It has the consistency of light oil and the label confirms it is pure and natural and the flavour certainly bears this out. The bottle I bought was surprisingly inexpensive but very strong and superb for adding entrancing flavour, for when you want to be beguiling, unfathomable, mysterious. I've whipped it into butter to flavour phyllo pastry, used it with rose water, of course, in a rose-tea ice cream, stirred some into a spiced chai cake mixture, sprinkled it judiciously into a tropical fruit salad, tossed buttered rice with a little and rubbed some into a young leg of lamb and let that sit around for a few hours. And of course, it can be dripped into after dinner coffee if you think you can be lean. You'll think of other ways, like adding a thread to pomegranate molasses as a dipping sauce for lamb kebabs from the barbecue. Or to add to the pan juices of a duck you have roasted, with pomegranate molasses, crushed mint leaf and a little fresh orange zest. And fresh pomegranate seeds, of course.

Cassia: the bark of the cassia tree is sold as 'Chinese' or 'bastard' cinnamon and can be used as a substitute for the real thing, but it is stronger and coarser. The use of cassia precludes that of true cinnamon, and I am indebted to the late Tom Stobart for learning that in a chemist shop, cassia is another name for senna pods.

Cassia buds are sweeter and tangier, like cinnamon and cloves combined, and especially good with cherries; you may well see them specified in recipes for Hungarian cherry soup.

Even when preserved in salt and sugar, its tiny yellow flowers have a wonderful fragrance, presumably because cassia is a member of the jasmine family. Traditionally used for scenting teas and wines and otherwise for sweet dishes, but I remember them best when creatively used in the sauce for a duck dish at the 1993 Hong Kong Food Festival.

Cayenne: a hot red pepper of sorts, indispensable to cookery and cookbooks in the early 20th century and until the 70s or 80s, commonly used to finish egg, cheese or fish dishes. In such restrained quantity it gave no more than an elegant jostle to the palate: another lesson from the past we have failed to respect. Generally it was a mixture of chillies, sometimes with paprika, to give a uniform and trustworthy flavour and colour. More often than not it was sprinkled over food just for its colour, and so although quite hot it rarely menaced the fine food or wine that it accompanied. See Chilli/chille

Celery seed and salt: the seed, when ground in a pepper grinder, can be used as a condiment and is good with fish, soups, tomato, potato salad, eggs, cheese and vegetarian nut dishes. It can add an interesting lift to a marinade if you heat the liquid slightly to stimulate the extrusion of fragrant oils from the seed. But never include the whole seed in food: the flavour is really rather coarse and you are better off with chopped celery greens or the more subtle flavour of dill weed, even though not quite the same.

Celery salt is a mixture of salt and ground celery seed, much beloved of vegetarians and drinkers of the Bloody Mary. It is common to use too much and this is why many delicate vegetarian dishes all taste the same, but it is nonetheless a very handy helpmate when bland dishes need resuscitation.

Chervil: this looks like a fragile parsley, but tastes of aristocratic drawing rooms, and of *parterres*, rather than of something from a bucket at the back door. The great leaps up the social scale are largely from its discreet flavour of anise, a more finely spun thread of the finer notes of French tarragon. Sometimes called French or (in America) gourmet's parsley.

Used instead of parsley, chervil transforms the mundane into something to be taken seriously: crushed belle de Fontenay potatoes with a little cream and chervil as a bed for seared scallops comes to mind, thanks to the inspired food of Jean-Christophe Novelli in London. Eggs in all kinds of way but fried, and all salads, are improved immeasurably when diners find chervil has been included. Vegetables love chervil and it makes an astonishing difference to what you thought you knew about vegetable soups, even if only sprinkled on as garnish. As tarragon has an affinity for chicken so use it there too, hot or cold.

Butter sauces for firm white-fleshed fish or for lobsters are both very good places to find chervil, too. It is an important component in *fines herbes*.

If you enjoy startling your friends with innovation, but don't care to spend money or time on them, add chervil rather than parsley to something simple, and you'll seem to be in league with wizards.

Chilli/chillies and chili/chilies etc etc: every man, with or without dogs, has their version of what is chili and what is chilli, or chile or chille. My research on the spot in places where such ingredients are grown or used has taken many years, and together with my conversations with Elisabeth Lambert Ortiz, one of the greatest writers on South American food, seems to solve the argument very simply.

An 'i' or an 'e' on the end of the world doesn't matter. Otherwise, chilli with two 'l's is the basic ingredient whether fresh, dried or ground, easily remembered because it is likely to be as hot as hell, which also has two 'l's. Thus chili with just the one 'l' is any dish that includes chilli or the mixed spice with which you make one.

Chilli powder would be one of the ingredients in a made-up dish called a chili: it would be just ground chilli. But chili powder should always be a mixed spice, based on cumin seed. When you want to make a chili, you must use the mixed spice.

The world equivocates and does this a dozen ways, so check the label.

The extraordinary battle by chillies to take over the world and banish flavour in favour of hot vulgarity is almost lost, particularly as more and more people believe 'spicy' means hot, when it should mean spiced. It's not that I don't like chillies, I do, but I don't like them being over used or used to the exclusion of other tastes in a dish. That's a waste of time and effort and money.

Here's how they work. Although some chillies have very good flavour, particularly the dried ones, it is the heat for which they are usually included in cookery. But heat is neither flavour nor culinary ingredient; it is mouth trauma. You are burning your tongue: once you go beyond a certain point, which differs from person to person, the brain recognizes the trauma and releases endorphins, natural opiates. They do little to dull the pain of the injury, but make you feel great. It is this euphoria that comes truly addictive and is the saviour of many poor people around the world.

If you look carefully, chilli is indeed the refuge of the poor, used most lavishly where there is little else to eat. A bowl of rice with scraps of vegetables does little to make the belly or body feel good. Add the heat of the chilli and at least you get some pleasure, some buzz from eating.

Most people, perhaps everyone, reading this book, will have no need to rely on natural drug-induced euphoria to get pleasure from food and eating, they will have enough and enough variety available to them all year round.

Like all drugs, the more chillies you eat, the more you must eat to get the euphoria. In the meantime you are scarring your tongue more and more deeply and so taste less and less of what accompanies the chillies.

Most travellers who first visit, say, Thailand or Nepal, return believing that to be true to their experience and to continue eating authentically, they must burn and sweat, because that is the sort of food they were served there. Not so. There they were eating a chilli content measured for those who have eaten it all their life and who have become increasingly immune. If you were to have very little chilli indeed, you would more accurately approximate what the locals taste. Never mock someone who asks for little or no chilli, for not only are they respecting their palate, they are the ones eating most authentically.

As a final argument for caution with chillies, look at Thai food, which is divided in two styles, one called Royal Thai. In the West we have our food and we also have *haute cuisine*, but the recipes, ingredients and techniques in each have little to do with one another. In Thailand, the recipes and techniques of the two styles are almost the same, except the further up the social and income scale you go and the closer you are to the lush market gardens of Bangkok and the south, the less chilli is used and the more ingredients are allowed to speak for themselves: Royal Thai uses virtually no chilli, instead relying on higher cost or more sophisticated ingredients. Whereas the home cook in Thailand might use chicken in a certain dish and a certain amount of chilli, Royal Thai food might choose prawns and use no chillies in the same dish.

Next time you want to eat really hot food think about this. Are you really an under-privileged peasant with little choice of what you eat, and who gets no pleasure from that anyway? Are you really so disadvantaged you must injure your tongue to get pleasure at the table? No, I thought not.

Listen to the advice of rock star Joe Perry, of Aerosmith. In *Bon Appetit* magazine he said: 'I found a lot . . . bury the flavour of everything else. A really strong habanero flattens your taste buds. It's like listening to really loud music all the time. You don't hear any of the nuance anymore.'

The most important thing to know about all chillies is what to do with the seeds and the membranes, sometimes called placentas, which hold the seeds to the inside of the skins. Contrary to widely held opinions, the seeds in fresh chilli peppers hold only about 3% of the capsaicin oil, which is the heated ingredient in chillies, but the membranes contain a great deal more. If you remove the membranes (and thus the seeds) from fresh chillies, the fire is reduced considerably: Mexicans think this emasculates the chillies and call them capons.

In dried chillies, the capsaicin has spread more evenly throughout all the flesh: the seeds have none and have no flavour either, so removing them becomes almost pointless and anyway is a great fiddle. For lesser heat just choose a milder chilli. You might still shake out what seeds you can and develop a relationship with the texture of those you can't.

When fresh, it is generally true the smaller the chilli the hotter it will be. As a double check, look at the colour of the inner membranes, the placentas, where the seeds adhere. If there is an orange-yellow stain, this is an indication of elevated heat.

The comparative heat of chillies changes and so do chilli names between fresh and dry. So two lists follow, one of comparative heats when fresh and one dried. These tables are very rough, for fruit on the same plant can vary in intensity, and fruits of the same variety will be hotter or milder depending on the soil, climate and time of the year they are harvested.

Classically, chillies were measured on the Scoville chart but this has been simplified into The Official Chilli /Chille Pepper Heat Scale of 0-10; you'll find both here. Some chillies are mentioned twice but under a different name. The hottest recorded so far was a habanero with a Scoville reading of 577,000 units! Here's the comparison of fresh chillies.

Rating	Varieties	Scoville units
10	Habanero, Scotch Bonnet	100 – 300,000
9	Bahamian, African Birdseye Santaka, Chiltepin, Aji	50 – 100,000
8	Thai (prik khee noo), kwangsi, Piri piri, Piquin, Cayenne, Tabasco	30 – 50,000
7	de Arbol, Habanero Hot Sauce	15 – 30,000
6	Serrano, Hot Yellow Wax	
5	Tabasco Sauce, Jalapeno, Mirasol, Amarillo	2,500 – 5,000
4	Large thick Cayenne, Louisiana Hot Sauce	1500 – 2500
	Cascabel, Sandia	
3	Hot Yellow Wax, Ancho, Pasilla, Espanola	1 – 1500
2	Old Bay seasoning, Big Jim	500 – 1000
1	Cherry, pickled pepperoncini, Hungarian hot paprika	100 – 500
0	Sweet Banana, Bell, Capsicum, Sweet Peppers	0 – 100

Now, here's a list of commonly available dried chillies in ascending order of their heat quotient, simplified into a scale of one to ten. Note how some chillies change their name when dried.

Choricero: 0. A sweet mild chilli, that's wrinkly and a gorgeous rich brown colour. Can be stuffed whole, or used in sauces, soups and stews.

Ancho (dried poblano): 3. Usually big enough to stuff, it has a full sweet flavour with mild heat. Good in general use, as above, but is very partial to being served with chocolate, a nudge for creative cooks to start experimenting with sauces, cakes, cookies, ice creams and the like.

Guajillo: 3. Although a mahogany colour the guajillo (little gourd) brings a bright tannic flavour, not unlike green tea. Very good with tomato and anything else that would make a chili, a pizza or a pasta sauce.

Mulato: 3. Deep herbal flavours that combine well with root vegetables and mushrooms, in sauces perhaps, or cut into strips and tossed with the cooked vegetables.

New Mexico Red: 3. A tangy sweetness that's very good with tomatoes and garlic and very good in chilis or soups.

Cascabel: 4. There's a nutty woody flavour accompanying the increased heat of the brown cascabel (little rattle), and that combines well with lime, lemon or orange in sauces for meat, fish or all kinds of pumpkin and squash.

Pasilla: 4. Herb and dried fruit flavours and a brown-black colour explain the pasilla name, which means little raisin. Can be snipped into rings for garnish and is specially good with seafood and lamb. One of the traditional ingredients of mole q.v. sauces

Chipotle (smoked jalapeno): 6. Now it's getting truly hot and chipotle heat lingers on the palate. Smoky, nutty and with some bitterness but very useful to add flavour depth and width to anything wet – soups, sauces, stews salsas, etc. Chipotle need to be stewed whole in water until very tender. Pull off the top so any internal water can escape and then use in stews and casseroles.

De arbol: 8. Hotter still, in fact close to searing but still with a discernibly clear clean flavour. Because they're red and quite small they're perhaps the ones to store in oil or vinegar to give teeth to either or both.

Piquin: 8. Another definite sear here, but with a nut and corn flavour. Also small so can be used as the de arbol, or simply to add heat.

Habanero: 10. Intensely, threateningly, fiercely hot, as hot as you can get. These orange-brown chillies still pack a good fruity flavour, and so are good with tropical fruits, tomatoes and the like, raw in salsas or cooked in sauces. But why? Once you are kitted up in long rubber gloves and protective goggles to stop you touching your eyes or being damaged by the acrid fumes given off by the soaking water, you drain them and use them as is or lightly crushed in cooking. It is usual and advisable to remove them once they have added heat and flavour to your dish, for very few people actually want to eat them. Those who do need counselling.

Generally dried chillies are reconstituted in a warm liquid (milk, water, beer, wine) weighted down to keep them submerged and then they are pureed. The purée is a more controllable way slowly to add chilli without the risk of overdoing it. But you can cut them into strips, mince or stuff them and also use them whole or crushed. What you can do with each variety depends on the thickness of their flesh. So:

Thin-fleshed smooth-skinned chillies: de arbol (8), piquin (8). Can be soaked or used dried and may be scrunched, crushed or used as they are, so you can remove them from cooking when a desired height of heat and flavour has been reached. These can also be toasted for richer flavour.

Medium-fleshed, smooth-skinned chillies: New Mexico reds (3), guajillo (3), cascabels (4). All these are the better for being pureed and sieved, thus getting rid of the tough skin. Then they get added to sauces, soups, stews and gravies. Mayonnaise or butters are good too.

Thick-fleshed, wrinkly, thin-skinned chillies: ancho (3) mulatto (3) pasilla (4) choricero (0). After soaking and puréeing these do not need to be sieved and so the purée can be used as above. All can be cut into strips before being soaked: they can then be used in batters, breads, stir-fries, sauces, pasta and so on. Dried chillies can be toasted for extra flavour, but it is a risky business because the fumes damage your eyes in the blink of a lid, and you also run the risk of going too far, burning them, which makes even worse smoke, and turns them bitter.

And here seems the ideal place to tell you what to do for those who have burned themselves with chilli.

The worst things to gulp are water, beer or wine, which spread the burning oil about, often straight down to burn the intestines, which makes everything worse tomorrow, or sooner. Rice (of course), sugar or banana will soak up the oil and dairy products like milk or the yoghurt that might be on the table quickly also absorb it. So do butter or ice cream.

You see why those who use chilli a lot in their ethnic dishes rarely drink when they eat hot food? You shouldn't either, but eat rice in equal proportion to what else goes in your mouth, mouthful by mouthful, not one of one and then of the other. Imagine your fork or spoon is a hand: to get any food at all you would have first to gather up rice and then go for the curry or any other sort of stewed dish, ending up with roughly equal amounts of both. That's what should be on your fork or spoon. Any soup on the table should be sipped discreetly throughout the meal and never gulped before the meal.

Much of the information on dried chillies came via the great generosity of spirit of **www.coolchile.co.uk**, who do all the above and more by mail order.

Finally a word of added caution. When handling chillies, fresh or dried, it really is worth the effort to put on rubber gloves. Quickly rinsing under running water doesn't get rid of chilli oil at all, and you risk burning any thing you touch for quite some time. I finally learned this to my exquisite embarrassment when I ran quickly to the lavatory after preparing chillies, rinsed quickly, and then went directly into the studio and live on air on QVC. The fire in my pants was so extreme I had to admit what was wrong to several million viewers on live television. Rubber gloves, or soap and hot water.

See also: Chilli powder: Tabasco; chilli sauces, chilli oils and paste, sambal oelek, harissa.

Chives: although billed as the mildest member of the onion family, I still doubt the place of raw onion flavour of any kind in serious or subtle cooking. If you disagree, you'll find yourself using it chopped over chicken soups, on sour cream garnishes, in omelettes and cheese dishes.

Chives work very well as a relatively subtle onion flavour in a fish stock, or cooked into soup for a few minutes, or in a poultry stuffing. Too often they are used in or on dishes without thought, and certainly without mentioning them on a menu when they might actually be the most savoury ingredient on the plate. Scrambled eggs with smoked salmon is quite a different thing from scrambled eggs, smoked salmon and chives, and you should be told they are included when ordering. For me, chives are the other acid rain.

Cinnamon: the spice for which the New World was discovered. Introduced to Europe between the 11th and 13th centuries from the eastern Mediterranean by returning Crusaders, it soon became one of the most popular spices in the West. Demand was so high ruling families knew if they could find an alternative way to the East Indies they would be rich and secure: eventually Spain's greed was greatest and so its queen backed the Italian Christopher Columbus and his universally ridiculed plan to sail westwards towards the Spice Islands; as if you could, on a flat world.

Cinnamon is the inner bark of a fragrant type of laurel. Cinnamon sticks are rolls of this soft bark and make wonderful swizzle sticks for coffee or hot wine, for hot chocolate and, surprisingly, for hot tea, a combination that is soothing and delicious. Sticks are important ingredients in curries but should be removed before serving.

Ground cinnamon is multifarious in its usefulness. We occidentals frequently use it with fruit and with cakes and pastries; try cinnamon sprinkled on thick, chilled slices of a blood or navel orange – strikingly simple and unbelievably good. The Arabs are rather more voluptuous with it. They sprinkle it over poultry, with rose or orange flower water.

Egg dishes, sweet or savoury, also go well with this warm, comforting flavour as is seen in the American breakfast combination of cinnamon coffee cake with eggs and bacon. Rice stuffings for lamb or whole fish benefit from the addition of cinnamon, especially if some ground almonds and a little, very little, sugar is also included.

The best cinnamon is thought to come from Sri Lanka, and high quality cinnamon should always be yellowish rather than reddish brown and slightly pliable. A good tree can go on producing for almost two centuries. See Cassia.

Cloves: two thousand five hundred years ago, Chinese courtiers were obliged to have cloves in their mouths when addressing their Emperor, to sweeten their breath. Our name comes from the French *clou* meaning nail, for these unopened buds of an evergreen tree from the Moluccas look like shrivelled nails and seem as hard. They are grown commercially in the West Indies and on the islands of Madagascar and Zanzibar or the Malagasy and Mozambique Republics, as they're now mundanely called.

I regularly reach for ground or whole cloves when I'm cooking pork, rubbing some into roasts or incorporating either form in casseroles and pâtés, where I think them most important. With fruit, marinades, spiced biscuits, rich fruitcakes and mulled drinks cloves always work better in combination with such sweeter spices as cinnamon. I also think orange has a special affinity with cloves, so in hot cross buns, Christmas puddings and Christmas cakes, I always add extra ground cloves to the mixed spice and incorporate grated fresh orange peel. Cloves and lemon is rapidly medicinal.

The classic pomander for scenting cupboards and keeping moths away is an orange entirely impregnated with whole cloves that's then allowed to desiccate slowly.

Once ground, cloves lose flavour very quickly, so for important cooking throw out the old and start with well-sealed new.

Coriander seeds and leaves: the orangey bite of freshly ground coriander seed is something

I'd like to see used more. I mix equal quantities of coriander seed, black and white peppercorns for a taste better than either one or both those peppers. In fact I now keep one grinder full of that mixture and one filled just with coriander as it makes an unobtrusive but satisfying flavour change to a huge variety of foods, sweet and savoury. It can be used in rather greater quantities than most spices.

I use it with apple in pies and with anything that is remotely citrus-like or that is known to be good with citrus; it is good on a salad dressed with lemon juice rather than vinegar.

Pork goes very well indeed with ground coriander seeds, and this spice is a favourite of mine when making interesting marinades. Coriander is very nice in breads and biscuits or in custards and is commonly used in sausages in Europe. Peas, carrots, lentils and pumpkin are other vegetables that go well with it.

Coriander is a prime requisite in curry powders and if you decide the commercial one you have bought is rather boring or just plain horrid, you can improve it by adding a generous amount, or a mixture of coriander and cumin powder in the proportion of two to one. A sterling tip, that one; sometimes you might even reverse the proportions.

Coriander leaves look like flat parsley but are something else entirely, and have a bitter-sweet and haunting flavour endemic – some would say epidemic – in countries as diverse as Thailand, Mexico, Spain, Greece and Cyprus. It is used as a basic flavour or an almost inescapable garnish in the first two countries where life can be very difficult if you don't like it. I must say I didn't mind it when balanced by, say, a lemony coconut milk that bathed a large steamed fish, but it is aggressive enough to become boring when served too often. I know one man who banned its use in his Bangkok kitchen and immediately lost his entire staff.

It was once used extensively in Britain but I expect the story of the Latin name for it got about: apparently Romans called it the bed-bug plant, for the smell of the leaf is that of crushed bed bugs.

Fresh coriander is sold with its roots attached, more often than not, one way to tell it from flat leaf parsley. Although the stems can be rather tasteless, the roots are a power house of flavour, yet only Thailand makes use of them regularly. They are scraped free of skin and threads and then pounded with garlic and black pepper as the basic flavouring Trinity in Thailand. I do the same but poach the garlic first and also add coriander leaf and whiz it all together: it is then a powerfully fragrant pomade to use as a marinade, to fold into mayonnaise or other sauces or, best of all, to spread over fresh white dough instead of tomato as the base of a Thai-style pizza, topped with sliced lemon grass, tiger prawns, coconut cream, basil leaves and so on. Yes, you can even add a few sliced chillies, but I prefer to give people a choice and have a bottle of Tabasco q.v. handy

Cream of tartar/tartaric acid: made from powdered dried grapes, it is a basic ingredient of baking powder. The combination of baking soda and tartaric acid together with liquid and heat is what causes the manufacture of gas and the subsequent rising of cake mixtures. If you only have baking soda, you must use something acidic in the mix, such as sour milk or milk and lemon juice.

Cream of tartar is also used in making sweets.

Cubeb pepper: not easily found, these are native to Indonesia and look like comic book bombs – each peppercorn has a tail. They are as pungent as a good black peppercorn, but the scent and flavour also go off into the realms of camphor and pine forest. Best used with other peppers or in spice mixtures, such as *ras el hanout* q.v., and particularly good in pâtés and sausages, where they either complement or can substitute for the allspice you would properly use. Because it is very comfortable with fattiness, it can be very useful in cheese dishes, even sprinkled into a cheese topping. Sometimes called Java pepper because it is still freely used in Indonesian cookery, where you find it as *tabe djawa*.

Cumin seed: together with coriander seed, the basis of curry mixtures, and one of the most important spices throughout the tropical belt of the world, New and Old alike. Most of ours comes from Malta and Italy.

Cumin works very well with tomatoes in sauces and goes surprisingly well with seafoods: prawns bathed in a pink sauce of tomato and cumin are wonderful. The Moroccans combine cumin, sweet paprika and tomato, which is magical. It is also found on yoghurt and bean dishes. Its special tang goes very well with the bite of chickpeas, cooked whole or made into a purée.

See coriander section for advice on how to zip up a boring curry powder mixture.

Cumin and coriander make a good flavouring for rice salads, and I think that whereas coriander and clove work extra well when orange is present, cumin reacts well with lemon – and this marriage should always be arranged when possible.

Toasted cumin seeds are invaluable to have about. Toss them gently in a non-stick pan until they smoke lightly; it is very like burning old rope or the sort of smell which came from fat, hand rolled cigarettes in the Sixties. It's more controllable if you do this in the microwave, arranging the seeds in a circle around the edge of a plate and mixing and reshaping them every minute or so until done, lightly or deeply. You can crush these, of course, but the slightly crunchy sickles of bright flavour are perfect strewing material, on salads, sandwiches, fish, poultry and meat.

Curry leaves: leaves that smell and taste of curry, funnily enough. Available both fresh and dried. Fresh leaves are lightly fried at the start of cooking. Dry ones are added once the cooking liquid is in. Arguments rage over whether or not bay leaves may be substituted, and I think the consensus is not.

Dandelion: one of the great wild foods if you can get the leaves before they get too old and bitter – and from somewhere dogs don't parade. Ideally, find dandelion in your own backyard and put a garden pot over a young plant to blanch it. Add just a few raw leaves to a salad, or blanch green ones quickly in boiling water, drain and flavour with salt, pepper and good olive oil to serve warm or cold. The French *pissenlit* salad wilts dandelion leaves with hot bacon fat in which garlic and croûtons have been fried.

Dill seed and weed: the famous foundation of Scandinavian cookery, but also found in Turkey and Greece, whence it actually originates. The seed, lightly crushed, is sharper and more pungent than dill weed, and can be used in rice dishes and breads, with fish and with cucumber. It is used as a condiment in Russia.

The feathery fronds of dill are absolutely wonderful to use, quite different from anything in the basic repertoire of flavours. When dried and sold as dill tips it has almost the same flavour as when fresh.

Dill is superb with fish of all kinds, and on anything to do with cucumber, yoghurt, vegetables and, surprisingly, with meat. The Turks make delicious stuffed courgettes and aubergines, filled with dill-flavoured mincemeat and cooked in a sauce of tomato and butter.

Dill is basic to *gravad lax*, the Swedish dish of lightly salt-pickled salmon, and the Swedes also cook their crayfish feasts with festoons of the weed. It goes well as an unexpected flavouring with spinach and feta in Greece's *spanokoppita*, their superb filo pastry spinach pie.

An unexpected affinity is with black pepper, in almost everything, but particularly if you macerate the two in vodka for some time.

Epazote: a Mexican variation on the universally popular citrus-like flavour, but with distinctive notes of its own. The raggy-edged epazote leaf seem to fall between parsley and coriander and yet can be too strong and unpleasant by itself and so is rarely used fresh, although it can be an interesting minor player in salsas that mix tropical fruit with tomato, avocado and a little chilli. It is an essential flavouring in such cooked dishes as mole q.v., and in Mexican black bean stews but that might have something to do with alleged flatulence-beating properties. Can be happily used with cheese, fish and pork. If you buy it dried make sure you are getting leaves because the stems are also sold, and used to brew up a medicinal tea.

Fennel: in New Zealand I was constantly chastised as a child for chewing the stalk of both fresh and dried wild fennel. No one knew in Auckland that the fabulous fresh fish hauled out of the harbour would have been even better if cooked with fennel stalks burning under it or fennel fronds in it. I had to get myself to the Mediterranean to find this out.

Similar in taste to the liquorice-like anise and dill seeds, and somewhat interchangeable, fennel seeds are specially useful in cooking oily fish such as mackerel as they help cut the richness, and they are good in the butters which go with snails. I think the frond and fresh stalks should be used lavishly: red mullet and other oily fish should be stuffed full and if you have a barbecue, the dried stalks should be put onto the charcoal to smoke and smoulder just before the fish is done. You can put the sticks to burn under the mesh of a grill tray, if you do not have a barbecue.

Root fennel, F. *vulgare dulce* is a different animal and quite one of the world's most delicious vegetables; its name in Italian is *finocchio*, which is also a vulgar name for flaunting homosexuals, presumably because both are highly scented. It used to be very finely sliced and served at the end of a meal, something I find remarkably refreshing on a hot summer night, or in a hot dining room.

Fenugreek seeds: the name translates as 'greek hay' because Ancient Greeks used it to sweeten hay. The bitter-sweet taste is used in the curries of southern India and Sri Lanka

and over-used in many commercial powders, giving a characteristic damp, stale smell.
(See Curry Powder.) The flavour becomes more generally appealing if it is first dry roasted or microwaved. Very little, ground and sprinkled over vegetables, can be rather appealing. In Greece fenugreek seeds are eaten raw or boiled with honey. The seeds are also recommended for sprouting and make a good ingredient in or on breads, as they do in Egypt and Ethiopia.

File: in Creole cooking sassafras leaves are ground and made into *file*, a strange green powder that has a thickening effect on hot liquids, but which must be used with great care or the results can be most unpleasant and stringy. It is the most important ingredient, of course, in file gumbos, one of the staple rice dish of Creole food. If you don't have some you can replace it with a little corn flour, which will do the thickening but won't add the strange flavour that seems a cross between eucalyptus and marijuana. The ideal gourmet gift from New Orleans.

Galangal, kha, laos root: a highly aromatic root, with distinct overtones of camphor and that looks like a thinner, paler, pinker version of ginger root. Galangal has a crisp, much less fibrous texture than ginger, so is sliced rather than chopped or squeezed. Must be used with moderation, even though the flavour lessens when heat is applied. To tell them apart in a market, a ginger root looks like a foot, and galangal looks like a hand and is often tinged with a delicious rose colour.

It is specially important in Thai cooking, pounded into pastes with other basic flavourings My instinct was always to combine it with fresh ginger, but my Thai mentors said you never mixed the two, and anyway, ginger is very rarely used in Thai cooking at all. Galangal is one of the important flavours that make good Tom Yam Goong soup, the sour-hot-citric soup you should sip throughout a Thai meal rather than before it. Kai Tom Kha gives the flavour of galangal a solo starring role, in a soup with chicken and coconut, and this can be supremely elegant.

Galangal is indeed galingale, which so often appears in the sumptuous ingredient lists of mediaval cookery, but it was then used dried and ground.

Garlic: like the onion, garlic was supposedly one the chief nourishers of the thousands of men – probably volunteers for a sort of national service, rather than slaves – who built the pyramids and was the common food of Roman labourer and legionary. From a pariah state in the 50s and 60s, when only foreigners and people who ate by candlelight in bistros knew about it, garlic seems now as common as onions. It can be used with more foods than you could imagine.

All meats do better with garlic and all birds should be rubbed over with a cut clove whatever else you are going to do with them: duck `a l'orange is far better when the crisp skin yields the scent and flavour of garlic.

It is a peculiarly European warning to beware of browning garlic or it will have bitter flavour; sometimes this is true, sometimes it's not, and other times it just doesn't matter. Thai cooks regularly brown sliced garlic to use as a last minute garnish or tempering, scattered on just before serving, and very good it is. Be bold, brown your garlic. I think the trick is to do it over low heat so the natural sugars caramellise, rather than turn to cinders.

Bitterness is a common problem with the fashion for roasting garlic. This is done by slicing the top off a whole bulb and slowly roasting it, often in a bed of coarse salt, not that that does anything but stop it keeling over. Otherwise unpeeled cloves of garlic are slowly roasted until browned through, but I cannot think of a time I thought these good, although they might all have been overcooked and should have been taken from the oven when still cream-coloured. I think you should blanch the scalped heads two or even three times, before roasting them. When I want to serve browned garlic cloves, I first poach them with their skin on and they are always sweet.

The poached flesh goes the most wonderful old-ivory colour and develops an unctuousness close to mayonnaise; they may be tossed in olive oil and lightly grilled to give the skins a little cosmetic colouring and then used in warm salads, or as a condiment – you squash out the flesh and mix it into other foods and sauces as you go.

Otherwise you simply throw whole unpeeled garlic cloves into the liquid of stews and casseroles as they cook and serve a few to everyone, so they enjoy their cream of garlic as and when they like.

The simplest use of garlic is to flavour butter, melted or otherwise. I also usually add lemon juice and chopped parsley and this is wonderful with hot cobs of sweet corn, as a dip for artichoke, with fresh asparagus and with broad beans. Hot vinaigrette sauce with garlic and parsley is a specially good idea with simple salads of hot or cold pulses, potatoes or mixed vegetables. If you make your garlic butter too strong, melt and cook it a little and that will reduce the harshness. Once you get the idea there's no limit to what you can do... I use garlic with a free hand on and with fresh salmon, particularly when I want to serve red wine.

If you are saddled with someone who says they loathe garlic, use it anyway and simply say it is 'a secret ingredient from Turkey (or Brazil)...' It's astonishing how many people do not recognize garlic when it is used with subtlety and appears in profound incognito.

Wild garlic, which brightens up many corners of woods, is perfectly usable – the green tops sliced finely make an interesting addition to salads, and the young bulbs are fascinating used the same way or lightly cooked to serve with gentle foods, like white fish.

In the first years of this 21st century, garlic of all sizes and ages including very young garlic shoots and bulbs, has become a hot ingredient in New York City, because the state has become a major grower. Indeed you don't have to go to Gilroy California to eat garlic to perplexity at the annual garlic festival each summer: there is also one in New York State late every September, the Hudson Valley Garlic Festival in Saugerties, 100 miles up the Hudson river. Garlic croissants, chocolate-garlic milk shakes, garlic-vodka stingers, and raspberry-tobacco-garlic ice cream are the very least of it.

Credited with amazing medical powers, garlic seems to be accepted as good for the blood and strengthening to the throat, so is beloved by opera singers.

A garlic devilment you might encounter is a fascination with growing rare and unusual varieties of garlic – there are exchange websites, of course, with amazing claims for hundreds of red, white, purple, violet, small and large types. Most of this is imagination, for science has decreed there are only six varieties of garlic: these are rocambole, porcelain, Asiatic, purple stripe, marble-purple stripe and artichoke. As with grapes or tea or coffee, perceived differences are a result of the growing medium. The answer is indeed in the soil.

Dried minced garlic /garlic powder: these never quite work in my opinion, usually giving an unwelcome bitterness.

Garlic salt: useful for final hints of flavour but you must remember it is largely salt – you'd be amazed at the number of people who don't. Make your own, if you like, by mixing three or four parts salt to one of garlic powder and use it to flavour mashed potatoes, gravies or seasoned flour. Frankly you are better off without – use freshly grated nutmeg or black pepper or horseradish, instead.

Smoked garlic: once you had to sail from Dover to Boulogne for this, but now oak-smoked garlic is more commonly found, and very useful it is indeed. Try it anywhere you would expect the flavour of smoked bacon – in stews of beans or pulses – but be unexpected too. I like it poached whole, squeezed from its husks and then whisked in to mashed potatoes or in salad dressings.

Ginger: grown all round the world, ginger is very different dried from when it is fresh. Indeed, whereas many herbs are used both dry and fresh, it is rare for spices to be so used.

Fresh ginger is far more worth exploring than dried and ground ginger, except in the tagines and other stews of Moroccan food where dried ginger is essential.

Peeled and sliced thinly, the intoxicating mix of pungency and perfume is fabulous with stewed rhubarb, wonderful with beef, excellent with chicken and almost indispensable with fish of all kinds, particularly when poached. Always use a little more than you think for the pungency soon cooks out.

I chop fresh ginger root and squeeze it through a garlic press and often use this juice to refresh the flavour of any sauce just prior to serving. This green juice can also be put on the table for people to use as they wish, as a dip for something oriental or fishy. The garlic press trick will also extract useful juice when ginger is too fibrous to use in slices or to chop. Use this tasty sap to flavour a chocolate ice cream, a chocolate custard or mousse, or in a butter cream to paste together a sponge you will top with cream and strawberries.

Ginger root keeps very well in the bottom of the refrigerator, although it might dehydrate a little. I've read you can bury it in moist earth and keep it for ages by watering occasionally, but surely it might grow and ginger is usually hideously invasive. If you live somewhere it is too cold to grow, plant it and dig it up when you want some, and replace the unused piece afterwards. Keeping it in a plastic bag in the bottom of the refrigerator seems a deal easier.

Ideally, use fresh ginger root wherever you have used dried or ground ginger before and you'll discover a world of subtlety that makes the simplest and most familiar dishes different again. It is very good with many vegetables, especially green beans. If you have made some nice stock, cook it for five minutes with matchsticks of ginger plus four or five other contrasted vegetables – cucumber, green pepper, celery, carrot, radish and so on and you'll have an elegant oriental soup.

To put an authentic oriental flavour into Chinese, Thai or other dishes add chopped green ginger and garlic in equal quantities, a few minutes before serving.

Although specially associated with eastern food, whence it originated, the best ginger comes from Jamaica, although the industry in Queensland would argue that.

Thinly sliced young ginger, lightly pickled in Chinese white vinegar with a touch of sugar, is used as a condiment and as you would any other pickle. Far better by many leagues is:
Pink sushi ginger: this has a light subtle sweet-sharp flavour and crisp texture that together are invaluable once discovered: it keeps forever in the refrigerator and I feel bereft without it. I think of it as pickles for aristocratic palates: pickled onions and piccalilli and so on are always served with robust foods but this would hold its place with caviar. If carrots with grated green ginger are good, they go up many steps when served with strips of pink sushi ginger strewn about their persons.

Sushi ginger is heavenly served with fish of all kinds, even the most expensive smoked salmon and I stir some into any sort of seafood risotto just before serving – it is fugitive when heated. It's terrific in salads, fantastically good to enliven even such simple sandwiches as ham and just as good with poached fruit. It doesn't take much to realize how good it would be with an apple pie, except the baking would over power it: I chopped some up to serve in the cream to go with an apple pie, adding just enough sugar to further temper the acidity but not enough to disguise it. 'Yummy pink stuff' said great-nephew Daniel, aged four.
Dried ginger root and ground ginger have more fire but less fragrance, and I do not use dried ginger very much as it often seems to add a dimension that is medicinal rather than culinary. But of course it is *de rigueur* in cake making and then I like it enormously. Gingerbread can be many things – from a rich treacley dark cake to the thin, almost crisp, Grasmere gingerbread still made only in the village of that name in the Lake District, and one of the world's least known treats.
Preserved ginger, the one in syrup, is dealt with in more detail elsewhere and can be used in ways that its sweetness would seem to belie. Elizabeth David recommends its use in white dough to make ginger tea breads, and it certainly goes well with ice cream of several flavours – vanilla, chocolate and coffee for example. The syrup in which it is preserved is very useful and far more elegant an accompaniment to chilled melon than the awful eye-watering dust of sugar and ground ginger usually served.
Crystallised ginger is pieces of ginger impregnated with sugar and with a light dusting of sugar on the outside. It's very good for chopping into baking from cakes and shortbread to banana cakes, just perfect for adding to ice creams, trifles, grown-up jellies, fruit salads or for the cream that accompanies them. Chopped very finely, it's an intriguing addition to sweet and sour sauces, or for gravy for chicken, duck, goose, salmon or lamb.
Golden needles: these are dried day lily flowers *hemerocallis fulva*, and definitely not dried tiger lilies as is often said. The flavour is haunting, almost unique, with definite brown overtones of earth and musk; it is most often found in northern China's *mushu*, a dish of chopped pork

with fresh coriander, chopped peanuts and sugar served in a pancake. The other dried ingredient included is usually cloud-ear mushrooms.

The dried flowers should be soaked for 30 minutes, after which you cut off any tough end pieces. They are then tied into knots or cut into bite-sized fragments and added to the dish or to any sauce.

Grains of Paradise: also known as Melegueta pepper, these are often called for in older recipes but I've never seen it in shops. They have a fairly strong sharp flavour, with the eucalypt/camphor tones of cardamom, and the best equivalent or substitute is a good quantity of cardamom or black pepper or a judicious mixture of both, but its sting is more like that of the Szechuan or Australian mountain pepper for it numbs as well as bites. If you know anyone or any place associated with voodoo you might be able to put your hands on this spice, for it is integral to such charms and love potions. Otherwise they can be chewed to sweeten the breath and are used to flavour Swedish Akavit.

Juniper berries: their ancient reputation as an appetite stimulant is probably what made the English and Dutch flavour raw spirits with the juniper berry, thus giving us gin in its many guises. The unique flavour of juniper – half resinous, half scent – is very important in marinades, especially for game or when you want to add a gamey quality to anything. Pig's liver, usually too strong to eat by itself, becomes very good indeed if soaked overnight in milk and then in a marinade of white wine with crushed juniper berries with which it is baked whole.

The berries can help make rabbit taste like hare and lamb like mutton, although I'd rather have the flavour of both untampered with. Better to use the berry to complement, but not vanquish, the natural flavours of venison and other game animals.

The juniper-based flavour of gin is not used a lot in cooking, possibly because it is fairly fragile. But if it is strengthened with crushed juniper berries you get some delicious results.

Gin and pineapple have an astonishing affinity that is very appealing when hot. A layer of thinly sliced fresh pineapple doused in gin should sit for several hours, and then be cooked beneath a soufflé flavoured strongly with Galliano. To call it smashing is only to describe the effect; the flavour is wonderful. But simply serving fresh pineapple slices with a slug of gin on them is just as mystifyingly wonderful – I know nothing else so magically different in flavour from how it began.

Krachai: a rarely used Thai ingredient, this wild or white ginger has a fascinating flavour, rather citric at first but perfumed enough to be confused with galangal. The only time you are assured of tasting it is in kapi balls, an essential part of *Khao Chae*, the extraordinary dish of iced jasmine rice that forms the basis of a banquet of Royal Thai food

Kokum: little known outside southwest India, kokum is sometimes known as fish tamarind, which gives you some idea how use it: basically you soak it and then use the refreshingly acidic liquid rather than the kokum itself, as if lime or lemon juice. It has particularly good cooling qualities and kokum sherbet is grateful relief to locals during the long stultifying days of summer. The colour of the dried, halved fruit is purplish, so looks a bit like shrivelled plums; the darker the colour the higher the grade. Grain queen Jenni Muir told me that when she was down that way the aromatic pink liquid was topped up with gin (she thinks) to make the best cocktail she's tasted before or since.

Lemon grass: although particularly associated with Thai food, this fragrant citric grass is also used in Sri Lankan, Mauritian and many other tropical cuisines. Its fragrance is closer to lemon balm than lemon and there is thus a hint of sweetness. It really only works when fresh, although dried versions are available. The best flavour is in the fleshier bulb end, and precisely how much and which part you use depends on the dish.

When used fresh, perhaps to finish stir-fried prawns or to flavour a western-style salad, the bulb end only is crushed and very thinly sliced, but even so it can be woody. In long-cooked dishes, the whole stem is more likely to be bashed flat and used whole, and then removed before serving; but thinly sliced fresh lemon grass will be added for the last few minutes to freshen the flavour. Thai cooks usually combine lemon grass with other citric flavours, including lemon zest and lemon juice, lime juice and kaffir lime leaf q.v. In Sri Lanka it is likely to appear in their sensational white curries, based on coconut milk and cream and gentle spices.

Lemon grass is a natural companion to fish of course, but its extraordinary new popularity in the West means its full range of affinities is still being discovered. Essentially it does anything and goes anywhere lemon or lime might. It is terrific on tomato salads and a welcome change from the inevitable basil. In Sydney you can buy an exceptional lemon grass chocolate. It makes a terrific flavoured custard: I'm sorry, should that be *creme anglaise?* But you have to be bold. I ordered a lemon grass creme brulee at Groucho's, London's media-clique club, and it must only have been shown a lemon-grass bulb, one still in Thailand I suspect.

The flavour-challenged chef had clearly never enjoyed the Mauritian habit of stuffing lots of bruised lemon grass into a tea pot with boiling water and then drinking its bristling full flavour.

Lemon grass grows in warm windows and gardens, but supermarkets also sell it. You may freeze excess stocks, but it loses its crunch and is then best used for cooking rather than salads. Store slightly damp whole lemon grass in a sealed plastic bag or tall screw top jar in the refrigerator and it lasts weeks.

Just to get it right for Thai and other cookery – you use big pieces for stock and for cooking, and then fish them out and refresh the flavour with finely sliced bulb end.

Lemon balm: regarded as a weed by many for it is even more prolific than pet rabbits. But that's a good thing, for then you can use it in greater quantities. Like so many herbs, its very smell and flavour dictate its use. Use it instead of, or in tandem with, lemon; in stuffings for poultry or fish, finely sliced in salads (very good) and to add a tang of taste and colour to fruit salads. It is one of the greatest bath fragrancers. Strew great bunches in your bath while it is running and you'll be rewarded with a heavenly smell that would normally cost an astronomical price. It makes delicious tea, too, but separately.

Lemon verbena/verveine: Often macerated in eau de vie as a digestive with kick.

Lime leaves/Kaffir: the fleshy, dark green, shiny leaf of a knobbly variety of lime used almost exclusively in Thai cookery, but with a great deal to offer to others. It lends a full, rich citric flavour with overtones of sweet brilliantine and thus must not be overdone. It is especially good when used in conjunction with lemon grass. Each leaf is an unusual double, somewhat like a figure of eight; Thai recipes mean the whole, double-lobed thing when they specify a 'leaf'.

There are distinct ways of using kaffir lime leaf. If you are using it to flavour a stock or a stew, they should be torn into big pieces, a visual reminder to diners the fragments are not meant to be eaten. Then when all is ready, you fish them out, and replace them with very finely sliced leaves, which freshen the flavour dramatically and can be eaten.

The flavour reward used in this way or as an ingredient in cold food is in direct proportion to how thinly the leaf is sliced, presumably because this releases more of the oils. Scissors are better than knives for the slicing.

Kaffir lime leaf has a spectacular affinity with lamb. Stuff rolled leaves under the skin, the way you would rosemary, roast the ordinary way. It is one of the most delicious things you can imagine and even better when cold. What picnic sandwiches it makes, but remove the leaves as you slice. And then resolve to do something similar to chicken or turkey or duck, particularly. Young leaves, shredded or chopped, are excellent on such as tomato salads and can be whizzed up into all kinds of sauces, pesto alternatives and the like; in all such cases, remove the central spine and ignore older leaves which will be coarse.

Pounce on any kaffir limes you see. They are the same sort of size as other limes but very, very wrinkled. There is next to no juice, so don't expect this. But there is the most transporting zest imaginable, and just using this freshly grated directly over something, so the almost invisible oils are caught, can be enough to convince guests you have been cooking all night and day. It keeps its flavour very well when cooked: one of the very best things I ever helped create, with my mate Chris Beech in Sydney, was meatballs, flavoured very lightly indeed with a Thai red curry and quite a bit of grated kaffir lime zest, directly from the tree on his high balcony overlooking Sydney harbour. They took ages to eat, for the flavours were so fantastic we just had to stop to convince ourselves anything could be so delicious.

Be bold; don't let the fusioclasts stop the proper pursuit of new flavours. Use kaffir lime where you would have used ordinary lime or lemon or orange. A crème brûlée scented with lime leaf and served with tropical fruits perhaps, or in a chocolate sauce for ice cream, or in a ganache for chocolate cake or grown-up fairy cakes; and think about macerating them for the milk for a bread and butter pudding, a baking powder loaf made with kaffir lime zest rather than orange, or dare I say it, madeleines, too. Think skate wing with kaffir lime rather than orange zest in the scorched butter, a rabbit pie served with grated zest – or kaffir lime butter on lobster or scampi or turbot or snapper or . . . you get the idea. This is not fusion cooking but deliciously taking advantage of what is around. Just wait until you taste lemon myrtle, another new citric flavour to you, this time from the Australian wilderness.

Kaffir lime leaf is regularly available in Thai shops, and freezes very well, so buy a bag when you see it. The trees need only a temperate climate to flourish, and so make a good addition to any orangerie or sunny terrace, as long as they can come inside when frosts threaten. The little effort is vastly repaid if you raise fruits as well as the leaves.

Liquorice/licorice root: a natural sweetener that contains no sugar, it can be used to stir drinks or made into a sweetening brew by boiling in water. Chewing this instead of sweets is said to have helped many give up smoking, but it's also said to be an infallible aphrodisiac, especially for women. Liquorice – or licorice – strap or pastilles are another old-fashioned sort of thing enjoying a revival. Liquorice hardly disappeared from Denmark or from the Netherlands, where it's called *drop*, but beware if you buy it there for they like theirs salted. Liquorice ice cream has been appearing in restaurants for a few decades now, but has always seemed bizarre. The solution, suggested by great-niece Natalia, was to chop liquorice allsorts into a simpler flavoured ice cream, and this works exceptionally well – with coffee ice cream, with chocolate, vanilla and with raspberry ripple. There will be others – I haven't put them into New Zealand's iconic hokey-pokey (baking soda 'honeycomb') ice cream, but I will.

Locust beans: see Carob.

Long pepper: whole ones look like small catkins and like cartwheels when cut across. The better ones are from Java, well, native to it anyway, and have an extraordinarily evocative aroma and taste; peppery-hot yes, stingingly so, but to me also supremely sensual, for there are clear notes of frankincense and iris, perhaps even of Parma violets, so, suggestive of the stew of harems rather than the cope and mitre. Javanese long peppers can be up to 2.54cm/1 inch long: Indian long pepper is shorter and not quite as stirring of the senses.

Lovage: looking like huge celery and having something of the flavour, all parts of the lovage plant can be used. Mainly it is added to soups and stews. In the West Country they make a cordial with it, which, mixed with brandy, is said to be the best soother of upset stomachs there is. You can make your own simply by steeping the root in brandy. It's supposed to be very good in baths, too, the leaf I presume.

Mace: the outer covering of the nutmeg kernel and altogether more elegant. Mace is essential in fruit cookery and in pork pâtés, in chocolate dishes and with vegetables. Use it as an alternative to nutmeg, or as a way to add individuality to any spice mixture. It is extra good in a crumble topping over rhubarb or apple. Some say it has a special affinity with the cherry, and a dusting is good with hot shellfish sauces. Mace, whether whole blades or ground, should be a very pale yellow-ochre – the paler the better. In Malayasia they candy them.

Marjoram: closely related to oregano, sweet or knotted marjoram can be used in exactly the same way, with grills, tomatoes, poultry and fish. The flavour is reminiscent of thyme, but warmer, slightly spicy and definitely sweet. Although it can play an important part in flavouring strong vegetable dishes such as ratatouille, I don't think it works with red meats like beef or game. Instead, I use it when making smoked mackerel pâté, where it seems to complement the flavours perfectly, possibly helped by the inclusion of tomato purée. It is quite fugitive and should only be added to hot dishes shortly before serving.

Wild marjoram is usually the much stronger pot marjoram, and when this is grown in dry sunny places it becomes oregano.

The Greek *rigani* is also wild marjoram, and by far the most pungent and delicious of the bunches. This is the one for pizza.

Mint: the large family of flavoured mints provides a simple and accessible way to start experimenting with herbs and herb teas. Any decent plant nursery will have a variety of them, most of which can be used for culinary purposes.

Spearmint is mellow and usually has a green stalk. Peppermint, thought to be a hybrid, has a definite extra fizzle on the tongue, has a reddish stalk (the darker the better) and is the proper one to use to make a good mint tea. Either can be used in cooking.

The leaf of these two mints tends easily to overpower a salad, I find, so only add them at the very last minute and in whole leaves because cutting or chopping gives bitterness.

Other mint flavours include eau de cologne, pineapple, lemon, orange, apple and champagne. These smaller, whole leaves are perfect for salads, for decorating or perfuming cakes and fruit dishes – (see Geraniums). Eau de cologne mint is pungent and needs to be used with great discretion but is wonderful in summer salads and drinks.

I loathe 'traditional' mint sauce, even though it is interesting as one of the few survivors of medieval sauces; the idea of dousing sweet lamb meat in sugar and vinegar is appalling, and certainly not traditional, well, not for long anyway. Lamb was always served with jellies or sauces made from the berries that grew on the same hills it did. In fact it was rarely eaten; mutton was the thing and the forequarter considered infinitely better than the hind leg. But, once New Zealand began to send Britain cheap frozen lamb, budgets and good sense persuaded a national change of taste. At the same time the growth of the cities meant it was more likely you had a patch of mint at the door than a rowan tree. Thus convenience rather than culinary sense meant the acidic mint sauce, which perfectly complemented the strong meat of mutton, was thoughtlessly served with the sweet flesh of lamb. Horrid.

But stuff lamb with sprigs of mint, roast it on a bed of mint, and serve it with a spoonful of the juices you have pressed from that bed, and you have something quite superlative. This works sensationally with chicken too, and cold minted chicken is the most marvellous picnic food.

Dried mint, which tastes virtually the same as fresh mint when heated, works rather well in grain based stuffings; it makes a tantalizing, original contribution when added to Eastern combinations that also include currants, dried fruits and nuts. Both dried and fresh mint reduce in flavour alarmingly if heated for any length of time, so always use at least twice what you first thought of when cooking with them.

Mint teas, the subsistence drink of millions of Arabs in tea shops, are also beloved of the French, the Italians, the Greeks, the Austrians – they must be the most popular of all tisanes – and can be made in many ways. The Moroccans make it by plunging stalks of peppermint into a pot of brewed gunpowder green tea, and very nice it is too; in Egypt they simply brew up with fresh bunches of leaves. But in all cases they sweeten it rather too dramatically for my taste. Like them, you can use whole bunches, leaves or chopped leaves on their own, or you can combine mint with any other black or green tea. You can use them fresh or dried. It is always refreshing and enormously soothing.

Mint is used in cold drinks, too – in the famed mint julep of the southern United States, or in a powerful Pimms, which is doubly good and dangerous if made with champagne rather than lemonade.

Pennyroyal, a member of the mint family, has extra dimensions of flavour that I recommend. It also grows wild, even more of a recommendation.

Mustard: there are three types of mustard seed – white, brown and black – all from plants of the cabbage family. Combinations of ground seeds (flours) or mixtures of the coarsely crushed seeds together with a variety of liquids are what give the broad palette of mustard flavours.

Although introduced to Western Europe by the Romans 2,000 years ago and thought of as basic to English cookery, it is actually used very little other than on our plates and for devilling. I think the introduction of the rather sweeter American mustard that coincided with the invasion of the hamburger has done more to create interest in mustard in the United Kingdom than the tiers of gaudily packaged prepared mustards that come from everywhere and contain everything.

Mustard flavour only develops when the crushed or ground seed is in contact with water; both salt and vinegar inhibit the development of flavour, as will very hot water. Mustard powder, even when used to flavour, say, a cheese sauce, should first be mixed with water and left for ten minutes.

It is also important to remember the hotness and flavour of mustard disappears with time and cooking; thus should you want the heat rather than the flavour of mustard, you should add to sauces or casseroles just before serving, or use a great deal. If you use too much you simply cook longer, if you can. Your reward is a remarkably fragrant flavour that is savoury and fascinating and far more profound than expected. Seeded mustards are commonly added to finish a sauce for rabbits, but are also marvellous in sauces for leeks, in cauliflower cheese, to flavour baked salmon or other fish, or in a sauce to go with them . Mixed generously with yoghurt it is a great marinade for chicken or pork, and this can be used as a barbecue dip, too, perhaps with a squeeze of garlic.

Having a germicidal action, mustard is used as a preservative, which explains its use in piccalilli. The seeds, or lightly crushed seeds, keep their virtue relatively longer than does the powder. When you see it called for at the start of a recipe for mayonnaise, it is not there as a flavouring, but because it is a wizard at keeping emulsions together, and you don't need even to taste it.

As well as the types of mustard listed below, there is a mustard oil, more easily available in Indian shops. Very hot, it is a good way to get a controllable heat plus interesting base flavour into curries if you use it instead of a blander oil.

English mustard: sold as a powder or ready prepared and usually made of brown and white mustard seeds, with the addition of wheat flour if it is for the United Kingdom market. The English mustard sold in the United States is hotter than in England, because it is pure ground mustard seed. Mix with cold water and leave to stand for five to ten minutes, which allows the pungency to develop. Personally I think this is quite horrid and the use disguises any flavour the food may have. But if you then mix it with milk, cream or a mixture, the flavour is mellower and more of a complement. Those who insist on ruining their food and their palate might mix mustard with malt or wine vinegar and even add horseradish, which is what they do to Tewkesbury mustard.

Prepared English mustard is not quite as strong as the freshly made kind.

French mustard: a broad term this, covering many mustards which in general are far less strong than the English type, mainly through being mixed with other aromatics, thus lessening the proportion of heat to flavour. Dijon mustards are mixed with grape juice only, whereas the Bordeaux usually have herbs added. Either is excellent for spreading on steaks or other meats before grilling or roasting, and give a touch of interest when mixed into a good mayonnaise. Currently popular to the point of swamping the market are French mustards made with whole or crushed grains, the red-wax-topped Moutarde de Meaux being first and best known. Although I've seen some people in print say they are not much use for cooking, I think they are most useful for they add visual interest as well as flavour. Use them liberally in stuffings particularly for salmon or trout (the heat cooks out, remember) or in vegetable purees.

German mustard: this is usually mild and sweet, often with an important herb content. Austrian mustard is tarragon flavoured, at least the one I buy is.

American mustard: sweetened with sugar and made only with the milder white mustard seed, this is made into a creamier consistency than we are used to, thus it can be spread with a nonchalance that would strip your mouth if it were the English type. It's the only mustard to eat with hamburgers or frankfurters, and an interesting base for sauces. It can contain a lot more additives than other mustards, which are largely unnecessary in view of mustard's own preservative abilities. Making your own mustard is easy with a pestle and mortar: try and get a variety of mustard seeds and grind some into powder, some into pieces. Honey goes very well in mustard mixtures, but isn't a good idea if you are going to coat meat or fish for grilling, as it will caramelize and burn.

Nam pla: See Fish Sauce.

Nigella: no, not Ms Lawson spreading herself about a bit; a southern Indian seed with a good range of flavour in each tiny black seed. Dry roasting or microwaving brings out more of their nutty, slight pepperiness. Generally used as a sprinkle, over rice, say, or vegetables particularly potatoes. Mark of Marco's café in Auckland cooks stupendous food of North African origin and every day makes loaves of white bread flavoured with nigella seeds to go with his Algerian, Moroccan and Tunisian specialties. Original and different without being challenging, just what you want to start conversation around a table.

Nutmeg: must be used sparingly and should always be grated from a whole nutmeg for it loses its flavour and develops a soapy, thin taste when ground and left. It is extraordinarily flexible, equally at home in sweet and savoury dishes. There are very few cheese dishes, for instance, that do not benefit from the addition of nutmeg (although perhaps those which include tomato, like pizza, are better without it). Fondues, soufflés, sauces, rarebits, cheesecakes, salads and sandwiches all benefit.

Nutmeg is a prime ingredient of mixed spice and is thus important to cake, biscuit, or pastry cooking, particularly in association with apples. Hot green vegetables are good with nutmeg, specially green beans and spinach. It is very good with many meats and excellent in pâté; fine-textured sausages like frankfurters and Bologna invariably include some.

You can buy nutmeg graters, but it's just as simple to run a kernel up and down the finer side of a grater or to scrape with a knife. Once upon a time the gentry used to carry their own nutmeg and a pocket-sized silver grater partly to flavour hot chocolate and partly for swank. Because they were so common they were little valued and few were preserved: now they are among the rarest small pieces of silver.

The evergreen nutmeg tree looks like the pear and is distinctly sexed; only the female produces fruit, which looks like a small yellow plum. Beneath the flesh lies a hard case surrounded by a membrane, which dries and becomes mace; inside the case is the softer, fragrant nutmeg.

Oregano: when cooking Greek or Mexican style, it is worth making the effort to get their particular variety of this herb, for they are definitely stronger and more aromatic than what's usually sold. Much better for pizza, too. The most pungent oregano is said to be Sonoran oregano, harvested by hand from the islands and coast of the Gulf of California, by the endangered Seri Indians. It's credited with so many antioxidant properties it is touted as better than Vitamin E at holding off signs and symptoms of ageing.   See Marjoram.

Paprika: there is more ignorance or confusion about this spice than any other. Although there are dozens of flavours of paprika, they all come from two basic varieties of the same plant, one hot and the other sweet, both of which you would recognize as varieties of capsicum or red pepper *capsicum annum*, and which has developed unique characteristics wherever it grows.

A recipe that includes paprika as an ingredient but that does not say whether it should be hot or sweet is no recipe at all. In fact, in most countries where it is indigenous to the cooking a single choice is unlikely, as most houses actually mix the two to get a taste to their own liking. The combination I like most is three parts of sweet paprika to two parts of hot.

In Hungary or Spain you can buy both hot and sweet paprika but elsewhere where even the spice distributors seem not to know there are two types, you will generally find so-called Spanish paprika is only marginally sweeter than so-called Hungarian paprika, which might be slightly hot.

Sweetness or hotness come essentially from the choice of pepper but further sweetness is sometimes added with sugar, which is why some sweet paprikas tend to caramelise easily. The very finest sweet paprika comes from Spain with DOP status: **Pimenton de Murcia,** ground from the *bola* variety, originally developed at La Nora. Fresh Nora peppers are one of the secrets of great and authentic paella.

If you wish to add a little heat to paprika at home, judiciously mix in cayenne pepper, or straight chilli powder.

Don't be alarmed at the amount of paprika called for in some recipes, you do use a lot – 20-30ml/3-4 tsp for 900-1200mls/1½-2 pints of liquid is nothing. I usually only put in half the specified amount when starting to cook and add the rest ten minutes before serving, and this gives more vivid flavours.

Paprika of both types is excellent with tomato-based sauces and in Morocco is used in conjunction with cumin powder, an unexpected but excellent combination. In Sri Lanka they use it to keep up the red colour reading in a curry based on red chilli peppers, but where fewer than usual have been used, to lessen the heat.

Just to show how easy it is to be wrong about the cuisine of other countries, here is an official definition of the basic types of Hungarian food flavoured with paprika. Note beef in a rich tomato sauce finished with soured cream, which we all know and love as goulash, doesn't exist. What's more, paprika only became popular in Hungary a century ago.

Goulash or Gulyas: more a soup than a stew, made with beef or veal, onion and chunks of potato and sometimes with small pieces of pasta too. No soured cream.

Paprikas: this is the proper name for dishes made with paprika and finished with soured cream or sweet cream. A paprikas is always made with white meats – fish, fowl, veal and lamb. Red meats and fatty birds like duck and goose are never traditionally used for these dishes.

Porkolt: a meat stew braised rather than boiled, with masses of finely chopped onions that become a thick sauce.

Tokany: fewer onions and only a little paprika, finished with mushrooms and soured cream.

Smoked paprika is the newest paprika kid on the block. It's not really new but seems to have been discovered as a 'next big thing'. The best – or most popular – seems to come from Spain, where the still-artisan production is only a century or so old. There are sweet, hot and bittersweet versions, all made by additions to the basic ground paprika. The smoke does pick up and run with some of paprika's inherent flavours, but it also emphasizes its bitter compounds, which is why not everyone likes it.

If you find you have added too much paprika, smoked or otherwise, and the dish is too bitter, the solution is to add acid of some kind and not the sweetness you might first turn towards; instead choose a touch of dry sherry or balsamic vinegar, lemon, lime or orange juice, pomegranate molasses or, even, tamarind. Soured cream also aids this amelioration, and this is why it traditionally accompanies many but not all paprika-flavoured recipes.

Parsley: the only things you may not already know about parsley are: (a) the best flavour is in the stalk so use that for flavouring stocks, soups and so on, and (b) chewing parsley neutralizes the odour of onion or garlic on the breath.

Don't ever use dried parsley; it nearly always has a hay-like quality, the antithesis of its appeal when fresh.

Flat leafed parsley, also known as French parsley or *petroushka*, looks much better than curly parsley and offers a more flamboyant flavour spectrum; but its leaf looks similar to coriander leaf. Most markets differentiate by leaving the root on coriander bunches, but cutting it off parsley.

Parsley is so under used, sprinkled on as a mindless knee-jerk 'for colour' when the cooking is finished, the way others might sprinkle on chives, but at least parsley adds flavour to food rather than noisily stamping it out. Thinking of parsley as an ingredient adds terrific zest to your table with negligible effort or cost. Chop up masses and swirl it into a mash – of anything. Pluck leaves from the stalk and toss them through a salad, even if only of tomatoes. Save leaves for garnish or mash or gravy, but ensure a supporting cast of flavours by roughly chopping the stalks to use as a base for anything you're roasting. Crush the juices from them before straining them out.

And use parsley in sandwiches and wraps and rolls. Little is as refreshing as the clean, green taste of parsley with otherwise dodgy cheese or ham: yet it can be the height of elegance with salmon, masterly in hot or cold pasta dishes.

Find a recipe for Burgundian ham, good chunks of good ham set willy-nilly in a firm, off-dry, white-wine jelly with masses of parsley: now we are braver about rethinking tradition, you might prefer a light and fruity red Beaujolais or pinot noir, but don't stint on the parsley. You have, of course, steeped the stalks in the portion of the wine you had to heat to melt the gelatine. Glorious.

Peppercorns: possibly the most important spice in the world, certainly the most widespread in use. Native to India and the Far East, peppercorns were the basis of the earliest trade between East and West, and at one time all manner of public debts, dowries and rents could be paid in them – hence the origin of the peppercorn rent.

All colours of peppercorns, black, white, and green, come from the same climbing vine, and the variations are due to the manner and timing of harvesting.

Black peppercorns: aromatic, sharp tasting, and beloved of food writers who demand freshly ground black pepper with everything. These are the whole peppercorns picked when slightly under-ripe and dried and sold in their entirety. Black pepper is indeed very good but it is dangerous in the hands of those frightful people who *will* screw it all over everything before so much as even asking if the food in front of them is seasoned.

When used in cooking it is better not to add it too early for it goes bitter but no-one seems to mind as we are all so used to this. The pungent oil with all the flavour is called piperine and starts to oxidise after about five minutes of cooking, so add whole or coarsely ground pepper to anything hot no more than three minutes before serving and the flavour is then amazing, zingy and fresh and complicated. Such a good trick, and another of those that make people think you have been cooking for days.

Try it and see.

Of all the uses for black peppercorns, I best like them ground onto thick slices of slightly chilled red Moroccan or beefsteak tomatoes. Ground black pepper is also very good on strawberries; it takes some nerve to try this one but I recommend it. However, peppercorns don't finish there, there are different varieties with different talents to bring to your table.

Brazilian: these are very hot with piperine and aromatic. A good, robust, all-purpose pepper.

Indian: a hot pepper with rather less aroma and character. Thus useful in cooking for heat, but not as gratifying to use fresh on food.

Sarawak: the mildest, sweetest and most fragrant and by far the most rewarding to use freshly ground on vegetables and salads, and for tossing into sauces just before serving, which really dramatizes the flavour.

White peppercorns: these are the whole peppercorns left to ripen fully on the vine and then soaked to remove the outer husk. The creamy corns underneath are hotter than black pepper but do not have its extra perfume and full flavour. The main use for white peppercorns is in fine stocks (but black ones taste better I think) and for flavouring sauces that would look nasty with black pepper pieces floating about. Thus you would use white peppercorns in béchamel sauce, in scrambled eggs, cream soups, quiche mixtures and so on – you can always put some black pepper on afterwards.

A combination of white and black peppercorns is rather interesting to have in a peppermill, and sometimes I add coriander seeds to this mixture. In France small allspice berries are often added to white and black pepper, and that is very good indeed.

For some reason white pepper has always been more popular than black on the English table and it's only since long frocks, sandals and scrubbed pine have come back from continental holidays the latter has become popular. I can only imagine the simpler, hotter flavour was previously preferred because it was less scented, less foreign tasting.

Green peppercorns: these made a strong impact on the fine food market for ten to twenty years but are seen less and less. Mainly from Madagascar, they are exactly what they say they are, under-ripe peppercorns, and really most delicious. Being quite soft they crush into butters or marinades; the colour is useful and the flavour has mild heat and a truly wonderful aroma that is quite unique. Be very careful to buy green peppercorns packed only in brine; those packed in vinegar lack elegance and usefulness.

The brine from green peppercorns is a useful flavouring agent itself, just right for adding a dash to a stock or sauce, particularly for fish.

To keep green peppercorns once you have used some, turn the remainder out of the tin into a screw top jar and just cover them with medium strength brine solution. They will last for months in the refrigerator and that brine will soon take on their flavour. It may go black, but the peppercorns will be fine once rinsed; make more brine and recover them. It is simpler to use vodka, of course, and a sip of the vodka is a remarkably stimulating thing when you're out of cookery ideas.

Steak au poivre made with green rather than black peppercorns is delightful: I'm tempted to think this is the proper way to do this overdone and often palate-searing dish. Green peppercorns go very well with fatty meats and thus complement well a duck or goose.

Dried green peppercorns need to be ground or crushed and don't have the subtle overtones or flavour of the tinned ones.

Red or pink peppercorns: let the colour warn you – these can be dangerous. Pink peppercorns, which quickly became the *ne plus ultra* of nouvelle cuisine in the United States, never caught on in the United Kingdom, and just as well. Still, when I first tried them, I found the flavour perfectly wonderful, something truly new, and my excited broadcast in the early days of London's LBC Radio is still remembered for having hundreds of people scouring the shops in vain.

Although suspicious of why I could not determine their exact provenance I decided to use them in a tight-security dinner for five very highly placed politicians. Their main course was roasted wild duck with grilled figs and pink peppercorns and it went down very well. Just two days later I discovered the ghastly truth: those pink peppercorns were not peppercorns at all but the processed berries of a pesky plant known as Florida Holly, a relation of poison ivy. They would, I was told, cause nausea, giddiness and fainting, and could also stimulate the eruption of excruciatingly large and painful haemorrhoids. Many years later, I still do not dare ask for, or tell, the secrets – political, medical or physical – of that dinner party. Why, I may have wiped out a whole generation of our future leaders, so to speak.

After many relaunchings, pink peppercorns are something quite different these days, they are usually the berries of the *schinus*, that most fragrant and beautiful of weeping trees, and commonly called a pepper tree because of the pungent oil expressed when you crush leaves, something I still remember doing on my way home from my very first day at Owairaka primary school. See: cubeb pepper and long pepper, also.

Poppy seeds: you'll have to take my word for it, unless you are quite mad, and have unlimited time: there are over 900,00 tiny, blue-black poppy seeds to the 1lb/450g weight. The mild, nutty flavour is very rich when mixed with such other ingredients as eggs, almonds and sugar as fillings for middle European or Russian cakes and breads. I find the seeds often have a strange bitter taste that stays on the tongue for ages, but this is not supposed to happen if you first roast poppy seeds in a moderate oven for five to eight minutes until a light golden brown.

Roasted poppy seeds are quite nice when incorporated in salad dressings or in dips. They can be added to rice or included in cream sauces for noodles or other pastas.

Commonly they are sprinkled, unroasted, over unbaked bread, bread rolls and savoury biscuits, in which case they are usually first mixed with salt or sprinkled with strong brine to add extra flavour. There is a white poppy seed, which is used in Indian cooking.

Originally from Asia, poppy seeds, *papaver rhoeas* are now widely grown in Europe, especially Holland. Those who are weak of will should not worry about possible addiction; opium and morphine come from the different *papaver somniferous*

In my experience they are always best when orange zest or glacé orange is also incorporated. There is a curious Polish dish for Christmas, made of cold pasta shapes with roasted poppy seeds and glacé orange and so good you wish for a month of Christmas Days.

Rosemary: the thin spiky leaves of an attractive bush, rosemary has a camphorous, piney, smoky flavour, particularly liked in Italy but often hated elsewhere. Some food writers – Elizabeth David, I think – don't like rosemary and some cooks worry about the spikes 'getting' everywhere. I like it very much when fresh and used with great discretion: I dislike it very much when it is dried.

The warm, smoky but nicely sharp flavour of fresh rosemary is quite unlike anything else and makes an incomparable contribution to good eating. I like to plunge a whole branch of the fresh stuff into a tomato sauce for 10-15 minutes; this is more than enough for its perfume to be transferred, and then I yank the branch out leaving only a few potentially offensive bits. If I'd used a dried twig it would leave a mess of spikes behind.

Rosemary twigs are extraordinarily good for perfuming barbecued or spit-roasted food; this was dramatically demonstrated to me when I arrived in a thunderstorm at a converted medieval nunnery in the South of France to ask if I could stay for an unspecified time with two people I had never met. One was a morose Swedish writer, the other a Frenchman, and both were caretaking the magnificent house during the winter. They were as pleased to see me as I them, for life was lonely.

They decided on an indoor barbecue and that night we dined on spit-roasted breast of lamb cooked over masses of rosemary. Conversation was tricky as none of us spoke each other's language to a noticeable extent, and there was the complication of a large and unpredictably incontinent pet ape of some sort, who shared the banquet and the room and got most of the attention.

The most common uses for rosemary are with all cuts of lamb, with chicken, shrimp and prawns, in bread, in sauces that contain tomato, and in conjunction with lemon or orange to finish simple butter or grilling sauces. A small sprig of fresh rosemary is excellent when brewed with Indian tea – very good for relieving tension headaches.

Rosemary is for remembrance and where it grows it is said to show the woman rules the house. I think it should be grown far more as hedges, when it makes something dense, aromatic and useful. Hedges of rosemary surround many holy places in the Moslem world, but it's rarely used by them in the kitchen.

Rue: this bitter aromatic herb is not very fashionable in the kitchen nowadays, but if you come across some it should be used with great moderation with the lighter-flavoured red meats and poultry and perhaps with potatoes. The only time I've actually enjoyed it is in combination with *grappa*, the fiery Italian equivalent of *marc*, which in turn is a fairly rough spirit distilled from what's left after wine has been pressed – skins, pips and pulp. The Sardinians put a long stem of rue into each bottle of their *grappa*, for rue is thought to be a digestive aid. *Grappa con rutta* turns a pale green and has a most appealing extra perfume and flavour.

A man, whom I was assured was a *bandito*, walked into a bar in Alghero and ordered dynamite, with Italian vowels of course, and was poured a huge glass of *grappa con rutta*. After I had expressed a liking for this drink, the same man agreed to send me some made illicitly by him in the mountains. Its arrival was accompanied by checking of windows and doors, two cars full of very big men, and a number of hissed sentences that I presumed promised death either through revealing my source or drinking too much at one time. Apparently the punishments for boot-legging are as severe as for kidnapping, which turned out to be their other interest in life. You have to be careful with whom you drink in Sardinia.

Safflower: this flower can give the same colour as saffron and thus is substituted for it but it doesn't have the same subtle flavour. It was used by native Americans to colour breads and porridges, by Japanese courtiers to dye their lips, and is used in Mexican food. It is also known as American, Mexican or fake saffron. Safflower is more important as a source of a low cholesterol cooking oil.

Saffron: delicate and very expensive, for saffron comes only from the stigma of an autumn-flowering crocus. They must be picked by hand and it can take between 370 and 470 hours of work to produce 1kg of dried threads.

Saffron has been used since time immemorial. Phoenicians used it to colour the crescent-shaped cakes eaten for Ashtoreth, goddess of fertility. Her rites and name have become our Easter and our hot cross buns are directly traceable to these earlier Phoenician offerings. Saffron goes particularly well in yeasted doughs, and saffron cakes and scones and breads are specialties as far apart as Sweden and the West Country, Russia and Spain, Italy and Armenia.

With fish saffron is superlative; both bouillabaisse and the Spanish rice dish paella are impossible without it. The Milanese use it to flavour the moist risotto named after the city and which they serve with *ossi bucci*, which should incidentally be made with delicate pale veal rather than slabs of dark, soup-meat shin: the delicacy of veal shin is why the dish is made with white rather than red wine.

Saffron is available powdered and in stigmas. Some say the powder is often made of ingredients other than true saffron. If so I don't think it matters for I've not been able to tell the difference and I think the desecration to be largely imagined. The powder can be stirred in to a dish when it is cooking, but you must prepare stigmas to get the best value.

There is a school suggesting you should lightly toast or dry the stigmas but none of the suppliers I spoke to think it a good idea, as this has usually been done during its preparation for marketing, anyway. Instead they recommend pouring on hot but not boiling water and leaving this for 20 minutes; you do miss out if you stint on the time. The stigmas can be strained out but I find people like to discover them. With or without them, pour all the liquid into rice at the start of cooking and it will not just colour the rice but penetrate it. This also happens if you cook quite slender slices or barrels of a waxy potato in saffron water, and then leave them to cool in the water – saffron potatoes create sensations and are perhaps even better cold in a salad.

Next time you make a white wine and cream sauce for seafood stir in one or two sachets of powdered saffron, or make a brew of stigma and then stir in. The warm, slightly sweet, slightly bitter flavour and the wonderful colour transform something quite ordinary into a treat. You need so little to make such a large difference I really can't think of it as expensive. If you think your sauces wouldn't stand saffron – for instance because it would change the colour incorrectly – there are other ways to use it. I often mix it into an egg yolk and use this as the glaze on pastry coffins or vol au vents in which seafood is going to be served. You get a glorious golden glaze and a tantalizing flavour, and it's good to do this to a Christmas goose or chicken.

Saffron also gives an intriguing lift to rich tomato-based sauces – try it with tomato-casseroled lamb, perhaps also adding a mixture of hot and sweet paprikas.

The eastern Mediterranean and Middle East treat saffron with great respect and use it for their most refined sweetmeats and desserts, most often combined with rose water and cardamom. A slow-cooked rice pudding so flavoured, ladled into ramekins and served lukewarm or lightly chilled is always a sensation. Sprinkle lightly toasted and chopped pistachio or almonds over the top, perhaps a whisper of cinnamon. If you are flavour-curious, a few grains of mastic in the rice, and a switch from rose water to orange flower water, will reward you with Paradise. I think so, anyway. The same flavours can also flavour thick yoghurt.

There are good and bad saffrons and the difference is plain to see; yet I have only recently discovered how to judge it. When you look at whole saffron stigmas it's clear there is a darker top and a paler yellow or white base. All the colouring and flavour are in the dark part, so buying saffron that includes the culinarily useless lower part included means a lesser result and should also mean a lower price.

The highest quality saffrons are Iranian *sargol* and Spanish *coupe*, both names indicating the lesser bottom parts have been cut away: these are also known as cut saffron of course. Their undiluted colour is mystical, a dark vibrant, red black you've seen nowhere else: the scent also tells you of its superiority – it doesn't do to try to think what it reminds you of, what perfumes you detect, as though yet another confused TV wine buff-babbler. Saffron is redolent uniquely of saffron, and that is description enough. This husky, bewitching scent is the top note of Dark Rose, an entrancing fragrance from Czech and Speake in London's Jermyn Street. Two sorts of rose notes follow the saffron, equating the most exotic use of saffron in Middle Eastern desserts. It is at once a culinary and an olfactory triumph, the most edible and most noble fragrance I've ever found.

Pushal saffron is from La Mancha, Spain and is never cut, meaning it gives less colour and flavour than *coupe*, but it's nevertheless a good high quality. Below this are many inferior grades, detectable by a gradual dilution of saffron's stigma-top colour. You'll note when most big international names sell you whole saffron filaments in glass jars, they always wrap it in an orange-red film thus preventing you from properly judging the quality; the greater amount of white and yellow filament you'd see without that coloured paper tell you at once the product is inferior.

If you are offered saffron in bulk that seems too cheap to be real, it is not saffron but safflower and fairly useless: I learned this lesson from a market in Old Jerusalem.

Among the most interesting uses of saffron I've tasted recently were a saffron-cream milk chocolate truffle, and a cardamom-saffron white chocolate truffle. Whatever else you do, don't let excitement run away with your tongue so much you call saffron stigma either stigmata or smegma. I heard both when I was behind the shop counter.

Sage: the time-honoured flavouring in the true blue British sausage, but you'd be hard pushed to find many that do actually contain it. Pork and veal together with goose, tomatoes and cheese, are the best foods with which to combine sage. Fresh sage tucked under the crackling of pork works very well and the classic veal dish is *saltimbocca*, in which thin slices of veal sandwich ham and fresh sage leaves.

Sage and onion stuffing is traditional for poultry but I can't think why the commercial variety is so popular – possibly because so few people have tasted the fresh leaves? Most dried sage tastes distinctly like the smell of a musty damp room that's been lightly disinfected, and that is not what the fresh herb does.

The worst perfidy thrust upon sage is the use of its name in association with Sage Derby cheese, that stuff with the green marbling; they use sage oil and colouring. I can't think why people bother to eat it. Especially now there is a Sage Lancashire and a Sage Cheshire on the market in which rolled sage leaves are incorporated. No colour, no oil and a perfectly delicious way to convert someone to the pleasures of sage, as I had to be.

Excellent natural sage cheeses were once a specialty in the US and the artisan cheese movement should see this happening again: definitely something to look for and to buy.

The affinity of sage with tomatoes is why some people suggest you crumble a sage-flavoured cheese over a tomato salad. It's very good.

Samphire: not really a herb or flavouring, but I don't want to put it under pickles, and here's why. Samphire – *salicorne* in French – is crisp, brilliantly green, long cylinders joined together to make a low many-branched bush you find in salt flats. It looks like a miniature desert succulent. You can eat it just as it is, and each segment bursts in the mouth with pointed brininess that's mellowed with a grassy sweetness. Served with fish or seafood it's a sensation, but I often put it into the microwave just long enough to warm it and turn it an even brighter green and hand that around with drinks. The French and some parts of England pickle samphire, which destroys its colour and flavour, replacing its natural zing with nasty vinegar. Samphire is one of the few genuinely wild treasures left to us, and should be eaten as close as possible to that natural condition.

Sansho: a sort of pepper widely used in Japan, with sharp citric flavour that leaves a pleasant tingle.

Sarsparilla: it's not a very nice flavour all by itself, but the root of the sarsparilla, a sort of climbing shrub, is the basis of a tonic and a root beer Temperance bars and workshops thought vital to their cause. Once flavoured with liquorice and ginger it's still a little startling but very easy to like, if only because it makes you feel virtuous. The best sarsparilla root always came from Jamaica and in Britain it's enjoying something of a come back as a cordial diluted with sparkling water, a drink that used to be known as 'sass & soda' but which isn't the origin of 'sassy' but it could be because the origin of that is a West African tree bark that . . . no, this is far too complicated. In the USA sarsparilla is likely also to contain wintergreen, as a preservative, and to me that makes it more medicinal than worthy.

Sassafrass: one of the very first exports from the United States to Europe, the bark of the aromatic sassafras tree can be made into a warming drink. It was once a flavouring for sarsparilla q.v., but sassafras is a recognized carcinogen and although legally able to be used, you need a licence and so most makers of root beer don't bother.

Creole cooking grinds sassafras leaves to make file powder q.v.

Savory: often confused with thyme. Summer savory has a slightly more peppery taste and the leaves are longer. It is particularly good with beans and often grown between rows of broad beans for it repels the black fly which normally attacks the latter. What grows together gets eaten together and the French are very fond of savory with broad beans; I think you should try it too, otherwise use it where you would thyme.

It is generally used much more in Europe than elsewhere and there is a good but expensive *michèvre* (half-cow, half-goat milk cheese) coated with savory, which is called *sarriette* in French. Winter savory is inferior.

Sesame: extremely versatile and used in the Near, Middle and Far East for aeons, the sesame seed has only recently become popular in the west, mainly due to increased travel and the growing influence of Eastern diets.

Raw, the seeds have high nutritional value and a sweet nutty flavour and can be made into a milk, but are generally used as a sprinkler over breads, in casseroles, sauces, pie crusts, puddings, and so on. When browned lightly in butter they are excellent on almost every type of vegetable or on plain noodles. Sesame seed bars make terrific snacks as long as you have good teeth.

We are probably more familiar with sesame in halvah and as tahini. Halvah is a Turkish/Greek/Israeli confection made of ground sesame seeds, honey and flavouring. It can have all manner of other ingredients including dry milk powder and dried fruit. The Poles make excellent halvah, for some reason, and their chocolate-flavoured one is particularly good.

Tahini is sesame butter, ground sesame seed with nothing added or subtracted; it can be used just as you would peanut butter and is also used to flavour salad dressings when thinned with a little oil and lime or lemon juice, or to flavour dishes like hummus, a paste of chickpeas. Vegans can use it as a substitute for butter in pastries and bread, for it makes one of the best oils of all for cooking. Marco Polo was one of the first to extol its virtues in the West, but he probably didn't know it was so good for those on low-cholesterol diets.

If you wish to cut down your salt intake, *gomashio* may be the answer. It is Japanese, but not so strange it can't appear on your more ordinary table. Toast sesame seeds, mix with salt in the proportion of five-to-one, crush or grind and keep in an airtight container. I like it sprinkled over food rather than in it.

If you are offered a tahini that is rather darker than you expect, this may be because it has a lower oil content; some Greek storekeepers say that a proportion of commercial tahini is made from what's left over after the seeds have been lightly toasted and crushed to extract the oil. I can only surmise there are several ways to make it, and you buy and use the type you like best. **Sorrel and wild sorrel:** if you were a horse and called a sorrel, you would be a bright reddish chestnut colour. If you were a plant you would be green, and bear acidic leaves that are steps to rare gastronomic heights. You would also be as rare as hen's teeth in stores, even though you grow wild everywhere.

Sorrel looks a little like dock or anaemic spinach; the cultivated leaves grow quite big but the wild is sometimes not much bigger than a man's thumb. Some shops sell it fresh but I earnestly recommend you grow it for it goes floppy and dull with great speed. Although used raw in salads for a lemon-citrus contrast, it is mainly a superb flavouring for sauces; I don't like the sorrel soup touted as basic because it is mainly a white sauce, and universally khaki.

To make a sorrel sauce you first melt the destalked leaves over gentle heat in lots of butter. They shrink prodigiously; a couple of handfuls of small leaves end up as a puddle on the bottom of a saucepan. Try not to brown them. Now sprinkle over a little flour and some more butter and cook gently for a few minutes, which gives you a strongly flavoured roux. Add liquid that suits your dish to make the sauce. You can use white wine or milk or cream, but be careful about curdling. Stock is good, especially vegetable water, for although the sorrel is strong it can end up just being acidic and having its flavour overshadowed by strong sauce ingredients.

Now, how do you use your sorrel sauce? Well, it's outstanding with fish, especially eel, salmon and sea trout. It is excellent with sweetbreads, giving a wonderful contrast of sweet and sour and is very good with eggs and with young green vegetables. I like to make this sauce and then put it into the choke-free centre of baby or teenage artichokes, so you dip into it with the cooked leaves. Provided it is not too strong, sorrel sauce also makes a nice change on asparagus spears, too.

One point: it isn't worth simply chopping sorrel and putting that into a white sauce or hollandaise; unless it is reduced and concentrated as above the flavour isn't strong enough. Unless you have enough to add by the armful.

Star anise: an important base note in much of Chinese pork and poultry cookery, this warm liquorice flavour easily overpowers and becomes sickly. Best used in combination with other flavours, as it is in five-spice powder q.v. Ground star anise can seem to be full flavoured, but it's likely only to be what's left of its original aromas. Sometimes it's just as easy to break off one or two of the points of a single star to get enough flavour, sometimes you need only put star anise into a finished dish, as with the *chachouka* of squid rings I ate at Marco's Café in Auckland. This North African specialty has many guises, but this was not like anything I'd heard of or eaten.

A soup bowl was filled with a gorgeous, soft magenta-pink liquid that apparently came from capsicums and something else I wasn't told. My guess was some of the colour came from hibiscus, used to make drinks in North Africa. The amazing initial flavour was clear and citric but softly so, beguiling and many layered and I couldn't place it; it was based on masses of fresh and dried mint plus bay leaves, all strained out and replaced with a little dried mint. The final flavourings were rose water and star anise, added at the last moment, the lot all so balanced they combined to make something entirely original yet you could taste individual ingredients if you concentrated.

I have never eaten anything so slowly, as each mouthful filled me with wonderment and pleasure, with awe, as I identified the flavours and combinations again and again. I had never before been so entranced by food. The white soft tender squid rings were as sensual as the liquid. Since then I've recommended others go to Marco's and all have the same stunned reaction if they order his *chachouka*. Imagine, after living over 30 years away, I had to go home to Auckland to have perhaps the greatest taste experience of my life.

It didn't take much to work out that the teeny-tiny amount of savour added at the last minute addition by whole star anise would be sadly missed if removed. This is food balanced as finely as Earth on its orbit – one wrong move and there'd be disaster.

Sumac: usually seen as a red powder, actually dried and ground berries. Sumac has a wonderful fruity flavour with delicious acidity. A staple in Iran it is used throughout the eastern Mediterranean and Middle East as an all-purpose seasoning on almost everything: I like it with lamb and duck, but I love it as an important part of *za'atar/ zahtar q.v.*

A small bowl of sumac on your table will quickly become something you don't like to be without, and next time you reach to scrape lemon zest into anything, use sumac instead.

Szechuan peppercorns/fagara/brown peppercorns: nothing to do with peppercorns, but the berries of Prickly Ash. They have a pungent, slightly anise smell and are always bought whole and then roasted and crushed before use – only the petal-like husks have flavour. They have a strange but not unique effect in the mouth, for they numb rather than burn – Australia's mountain pepper and New Zealand's *horopito* have somewhat the same curious effect.

To roast them toss lightly in a dry non-stick pan until smoking slightly, or do the same in a

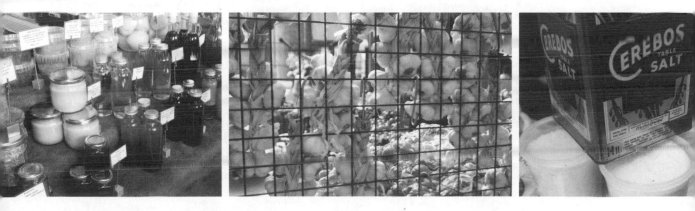

doughnut shape on a flat plate in the microwave; when cool crush roughly. Some will strain out the kernels but this is a little fanatic. A common seasoning used as a dip for deep-fried food or anything else which needs a little zip of flavour is mixed roasted Szechuan peppercorns and salt: mix one teaspoon of the peppercorns with three tablespoons coarse salt and dry-fry over low heat until the peppercorns are lightly smoking and the salt is lightly browned. Cool, crush and keep in an airtight bottle. This can also be done in a microwave.

Less common but terribly useful for adding imprecise fascination to bland dishes, is to steep roasted Szechuan peppercorns in vegetable oil; a few teaspoons to 300mls/½ pint is about right and the process is considerably speeded if you add the oil to the pan after the peppercorns are roasted and apply gentle heat for another 10-15 minutes; it's either a frying medium or a discreet condiment.

Tansy: an old-fashioned sort of herb that has the peculiar ability to make rhubarb taste sweet, perhaps because the bitter-sweet of the herb cancels out the high acidity of the rhubarb. It's traditionally been added to sweet omelettes and puddings, sometimes with apples, and often these were called tansy puddings. Because it keeps flies away tansy was rubbed over meat before it was cooked, and planted by door ways to repel ants. It's also a reliable preserver of corpses. How do we manage without it these days?

Tarragon: a necessity in every herb garden and kitchen, basic to French cooking, and to anyone who cares about fine flavours. It is warm and aromatic but must have both bite and an air of liquorice. There are two sorts, the Russian and the French, but grow and use only the French for the Russian will add a flavour not much more useful than fresh lawn clippings. I can't understand why garden centres sell it at all.

Tarragon's great affinity is with all dairy products and with eggs, hence its appearance in classic sauces, and so I always try to get some into savoury soufflés. It is extraordinarily good with melted butter over virtually every vegetable but does have a special relationship with courgettes/zucchini. This also applies to chicken, and chicken roasted only with butter, a little lemon and fresh or dried tarragon is really hard to beat. When you cook chicken, courgettes and tarragon in the same dish and then finish it with cream, the result is... well, try it for yourself.

A lesser-known affinity is that of tarragon with lamb, another recommendation; so is lobster baked with tarragon.

Tarragon is essential to sweet, mixed herbs and wonderful in a herb mayonnaise for serving with cold fish, especially salmon, when the bite of the tarragon is a good foil for the smoothness of the flesh. Tarragon vinegar is one of the finest of all the flavoured vinegars and adds instant elegance to almost anything. Vinegar is often overlooked as a finisher for casseroles and sauces, but shouldn't be.

Tarragon is better for being grown with lots of sun, but its flavour is very changeable, being affected by the slightest variation in soil and climate. No two plants taste the same so always test the strength on your tongue when using tarragon. And remember, don't even think about using Russian tarragon.

Thyme, lemon thyme and wild thyme: a favourite herb of such long standing the ancient Greeks used it with incense to purify their temples. For quite as long, thyme has been a favourite of bees, and thyme honey from Mount Hymettus is regarded as the best in the world – by the Greeks anyway.

There are many different thymes, most of which are useful in cooking. Basic and wild thyme are related in flavour, with the wilder being the headier. Lemon thyme is more citrus than plain thyme and its fresh flavour gives a clue to one of thyme's greatest affinities – lemon. One of my earliest cookery successes was Egyptian Chicken, from a Robert Carrier book: crushed garlic, lemon zest and juice, olive oil, butter and masses of thyme sprigs, all in great abandon, are used to marinate chicken pieces, which are then cooked in a hot oven. It's still a favourite. Some rarer thymes have the flavour of caraway and should be used with great discretion.

Thyme loves tomatoes and tomato sauces, goes well in savoury sausages and stuffings and indeed is fairly basic in my opinion. Dried thyme imported from the Mediterranean may be very much stronger than fresh but weaker stuff from a damp English garden. You have to be careful. White flesh, rabbit, veal and poultry go well with the slightly sweet-sharp flavour and it is good with garlic. Nearly all vegetables like thyme, but carrots are its best and prettiest companions.

Thyme is one of the original strewing and paving herbs, for it doesn't mind a bit if you stand on it, so releasing its fresh pungency. When HRH the Prince of Wales suggested a long walkway of irregular flagstones planted with every possible type of thyme in his Highgrove garden, there were titterings in the potting sheds. Once the gardening fraternity saw it and walked on it, they swiftly adopted the mixed-thyme path as their best-ever idea.

Turmeric: the brilliant yellow colour and pungent flavour of turmeric are basic to piccalilli and curry but well worth exploring in their own right. Related to the ginger, it is the plant's ginger-like roots, called fingers, that are used and sometimes found fresh. They are quite thin and small, rather like psychedelic babies' fingers because when fresh they are far more orange than you expect. The flavour is mellow, perhaps peppery but has exotic layers of fascinating earthiness. If you use too much the flavour goes flabby and can taste like wet cardboard, not a good thing to discover after serving.

Essentially the inexperienced cook should use turmeric as a colouring rather than a flavouring – on or in rice dishes, in stews, fish dishes and in kedgeree; mixed with a little butter and garlic it can make an interesting enlivener of vegetables.

Sometimes turmeric is suggested as a saffron substitute but there is absolutely no similarity in flavour at all. I discard and spit on any book that reckons to substitute turmeric for saffron, and so should you.

Verbena: see lemon verbena.

Vietnamese mint: another relatively new kid on the Western world's block with a nice heart-shaped leaf and fresh flavour that mixes well with other exotic herbs. It's not a member of the mint family and although there is some mint flavour, it actually tastes more like basil in party mood, warm but zingy, sharp and acidic but still aromatic, and contributing a definite numbness to the tongue towards the end. It contributes greatly to such 'wet' foods as soups and *laksa*, can go into any green salad, but is greatest for the refreshing lift it adds to Vietnamese rice-pancake wraps.

Zedoary: the name alone should recommend this to curious and creative cooks but it's also called wild turmeric and with its bright orange flesh you can see why. It is, anyway, related to turmeric and ginger; its camphorous notes make it a bit more like galangal than either, but it's warmer and has a useful acidic finish and a fragrance rather like ripe mangoes. Zedoary is one of the spices Mark Steen of Seasoned Explorers calls sultry, such a good word. The light bitterness it can leave on the palate means it is not used as often as ginger or galangal these days, but it's still very useful if you like to blend your own spices, as it adds a lot of interest to curry mixtures, especially the milder ones you might use for seafood and lamb. There are two sorts sold, the round and the long.

If you are injured in the sort of tropical rain forest where this grows, or in an Indian kitchen where it is used fresh, zedoary has antiseptic qualities and can be made into a paste and put directly on to the wound. While waiting for the healing, zedoary taken internally aids digestion and absorbs flatulence and colic.

Zereshk/zershk: see Barberry.

Herb and Spice Mixtures

The advent of buying and selling on the Internet has been greatly to the advantage of creative cooks, for the range of spices, herbs and mixtures available is far greater than in any shop. Indeed, supermarkets sell fewer choices than they once did, which runs counter to the view that cookery is a major interest, for certainly modern media makes what is eaten in other counties familiar and stimulating to us. Here are some mixtures to make life more interesting in your armchair kitchen.

Achiote: these sauces and marinades for barbecues in Mexico mix powdered annatto q.v. with herbs and chillies and mix this with citrus juice or vinegar. The Yucatan take on achiote is a paste with more ingredients than the barbecue mixture and which you mix with orange juice, and then use for roasting, baking or barbecuing.

Advieh: this Iranian mixture of cinnamon, cardamom and cumin with rose petals is boiled with rice.

Bahar: a Kuwaiti mixture, that's spiced and peppery but has neither cumin nor coriander, and offers heat only from black pepper and ginger. Very much a flavour familiar to this part of the world for centuries and another reminder heat can, and once always did, come with sensual flavour.

Baharat: quite new in the West, to me anyway, this Seraphim-bright spice mixture is from the Gulf States and is also used in Iraqi cooking. Like curries, it is based on the dual marvels of cumin and coriander: it then gets colour and body with sweet paprika, heat with fragrance from black peppercorns (the old pre-chilli way), a sweet lift with cassia bark, added edge and aroma with cardamom and nutmeg and then, the clincher which lifts it out of the ordinary; it's pulled together with ground cloves. Ian Hemphill, he of *Spice Notes*, the best book yet on the subject, is a man capable of nailing a spice description in a few words yet says this about his Baharat mixture:

". . . beautifully balanced spice, with a woody bouquet, aromatic bay-rum notes, mellifluous cinnamon/cassia sweetness, deep pungency and an apple-like fruitiness. Its flavour is round and full bodied, sweet and astringent yet with a satisfying and appetite-stimulating pepper bite . . . "

I think he's liking it.

In many ways baharat is like a primer for *ras el hanout*, your starter for one, a rugged country cousin but from an equally noble family who has something good to pass on. It's just fantastic with lamb or mutton. Lyn Hall, who has taught and shared her unique kitchen experiences with so many London and UK food writers, rubs baharat into a leg or shoulder of lamb, puts that in a roasting bag in a low-to-medium oven for three hours or so, and gets quite as many compliments as for her classic French cooking.

Baharat is very good on roasted or other vegetables, lovely in root vegetable mashes, and great with beef roasts and stews, too, making a sophisticated, chilli-free, sort of curry I suppose and is a real hit in steak or steak and kidney pies.

There's even a place for baharat in pasties, made the real way, only with flaked beef, potatoes and swede; you could put the baharat into the filling or into the pastry. Please don't call them Cornish pasties.

Berbere: another mixture now seen more commonly, it is from Ethiopia and can be searingly hot, but is better when it is not. Its base is roasted and coarsely ground cumin, coriander, fenugreek and allspice berries, heated up with ground ginger, cloves and nutmeg plus small and thus very hot chillies. It can also be made into a paste when it is mixed with cooked onion and mild paprika. Use this as you would a curry mixture.

Bouquet garni: the fresh version of mixed herbs and much more acceptable. The bouquet should be one or two fresh or dried bay leaves with thyme sprigs and parsley stalks only: other herbs can be added of course. Using two bay leaves as outer covers makes the pack easier to tie together; when you do this leave plenty of string or cotton free, so you can tie this to the pot's handle and thus retrieve the bouquet garni easily. I see no reason to use mixed dried herbs as an alternative and this includes the 'tea-bags' of bouquet garni.

But here's a thought, or at least something to think about. When have you ever looked at a mixture to which you're adding a bouquet garni and thought about the proportions? Is one bouquet garni really enough? Do you dare cook without the bouquet to prove it makes no difference? Is the bouquet garni just another knee jerk, the way so many food writers finish a recipe with ' serve with crusty bread, freshly ground black pepper and a salad'?

Although you want the herb flavours to blend into the background, one bouquet garni is rarely enough when you are going to simmer for more than an hour. There are several solutions. First use more or bigger to begin, but also fish out the old one and put in a new one about ten minutes before serving, to brighten the flavours that have gone flabby through long cooking.

Chermoula

Claudia Roden kindly shared this recipe soon after I came back after making my first . television series out of Britain in 1982. This revelatory voyage around the Eastern Mediterranean taught me that here – and further east – are the origins of many foods, dishes and flavours we now consider quintessentially British. One day I reckon chermoula might join the ranks. The sauce can be used as a marinade – particularly for fish – as an excellent barbecue sauce or as a dip for roasted vegetables, cold chicken, hard-boiled eggs and, well, almost anything. Need I add you can vary this however you like, but please don't add brown onions, red onions, white onions, spring onions, scallions, shallots or chives.

1 large bunch flat leaf parsley
1 large bunch fresh coriander
6 garlic cloves
1 tablespoon ground cumin
1 tablespoon ground coriander
1 tablespoon sweet paprika
pinch cayenne or ground red chillies
150 ml/$\frac{1}{4}$ pint/$\frac{1}{2}$ cup lemon or lime juice, or of wine vinegar
150 ml/$\frac{1}{4}$ pint/$\frac{1}{2}$ cup hearty, extra virgin olive oil

Finely chop the parsley and coriander, using all the stalks plus the scraped roots of the coriander if they have been included. Finely chop the garlic and then mix everything together and let them sit for an hour or more at room temperature before using or storing in an air-tight container: it remains fresh and vibrant for many days in a refrigerator. After marinating, say, fish or chicken, bake, roast or barbecue with more of the sauce and then serve with even more as a delicious fresh sauce. Skate wing is specially good with chermoula.

That's such a good trick.

Chermoula: a rugged purée of herbs and spice that's very big on fresh coriander. Although Moroccan it has been taken to Israel and become a great standby. Some recipes use raw onion, but I think it intrudes and acidity comes better from fresh lemon or lime juice when serving. Chermoula makes an original dip for hot breads and to serve with kebabs and can be used, with or without mayonnaise as a terrific binding for a potato salad or a chunky chicken salad to which is added avocado or tropical fruits, say pineapple or mango.

Chili powder, seasoning or compound: confusion about this is why so much chili con carne is only chilli con carne and thoroughly disgusting – undercooked, sour, watery onions and grey mince have been sprinkled with chilli rather than chili, nothing but a bit of heat and no flavour.

Chili powder or compound is a mixture of ground chilli pepper plus spices and herbs, the most important of which are cumin and oregano. Without cumin you cannot have real chili or chili con carne or chili con anything.

When you buy chili to flavour foods check to see it is a mixture, or insist on tasting it. There are some packers who call a powder or compound by the simpler and incorrect name of just 'chili' or, worse, 'chilli'; and there are scoundrels who simply grind hot chilli and call it chili powder, which it is not. The heat range is huge too, anywhere from very mild to very hot, and can only be judged by experience. If you find some chili mixtures are not hot enough for you, that's the time to call on your trusty bottle of one of Tabasco's sauces, for now they offer a choice of heats and flavours.

To add even greater appeal to dishes cooked with true chili powder or compound or seasoning, the judicious stirring in of cocoa powder or a very few melted squares of very dark chocolate works a treat. This gives the faintest of culinary glimpses into the myriad flavours of mole q.v., complicated sauces of spices and chocolate evolved from the cuisine of the Aztecs by those who conquered them.

Once I came back from a long overseas trip to find my pet bird had fallen permanently off his perch. Naturally distressed I changed the subject and asked what would be for lunch: chili con canary.

Curry: see also masala: the word curry is almost certainly based on a Tamil word *kari*, which means a spiced liquid. If you look, the essential ingredients are cumin, coriander, with chilli and turmeric: the first two for flavour, the third for heat and the last for flavour and colour, but turmeric doesn't have to feature at all. From then on it's up to you and the sort of flavour you like best: ginger, cinnamon, cloves, cardamom can also be included.

Few curries are thickened with flour, for lots of thin liquid is more refreshing in a hot climate and will be used like soup throughout a meal. For thicker liquids you simply boil down the curry while cooking without a lid. Otherwise you might start your curry with an onion paste perhaps with peppers/capsicums and or tomatoes. It's a technique worth noting:

Fry a lot of chopped onion gently in oil, at least 150g/6oz per person, until it becomes a mush.

To get the flavour going right from the beginning you might use mustard oil. Add chopped peppers/capsicums, green rather than red. You must cook the mixture long enough so there is no excess moisture left and it doesn't matter if you let the onions caramelise a bit. You can expect the process to take half an hour or more. Only then do you stir in a curry powder or curry paste and cook on until the spices have released their heady perfumes, at least five minutes. Because there is no liquid left, you can also brown the meat in this mixture and once that is done, add water, stock or canned chopped tomatoes slowly and the mixture will gradually thicken. For richer and darker flavour and colour, brown the meat in a separate pan before adding it to the onions.

You should always heat curry powder before use; it is almost pointless to add curry powder straight from a jar or packet to a stew or casserole in the hope of converting it to a half-decent curry. Even a quick burst on a saucer in a microwave will make a difference; and if the smell you get isn't fragrant and appealing, this is a timely message telling you your spices have had it.

You don't need to be told it's far better if you roast and pound and mix your own spice mixtures from whole spices. Those who do not will probably get better results from using pastes rather than commercially produced powders but both are infinitely more useful if they are regarded only as a starting point, and you add individuality with your favourite spices.

Anyway, these days, it is as common for city dwellers throughout India and other easterly nations to buy ready-made spice mixes from markets as it is for us to use them: the difference is they will buy small amounts and use them only as a starting point.

Virtually every spice mixture for curries in countries east of Greece will begin with some mixture of coriander and cumin. Coriander is sweet and lightly orange-flavoured: cumin is more peppery and sharp with a lemon undertone. Between the two you can create thousands of flavours, not only by varying the proportions one to the other, but by using the spices roasted, raw or a mixture of both, by crushing roughly or grinding them. Thus either coriander of cumin can be added in a number of ways and textures to any curry power to change its basic appeal or to freshen up what is there.

From then on the choice is from every possible spice and every possible balance of each. The best results come from using those with most fragrance and going easy on the chilli which has little flavour anyway: if you want more heat it's more controllable if you use Tabasco. Fenugreek adds a certain something but is over-used in many commercial mixtures and is responsible for that ghastly sour smell that hangs around cheap Indian restaurants. Discreet fragrance might come from zedoary, grains of paradise, kaffir lime leaves or curry leaves or . . . well, see above.

Fresh ginger root is an excellent way to add a little heat with added flavour, and so are black pepper, cubeb pepper and/or long pepper.

For a clean acidic note, that both balances the sweetness of some spices and any bitterness, lemon juice, dried or fresh whole limes or the sharp juice obtained by soaking tamarind in water are used. Some curries use water as their main liquid, some like lots of tomatoes and other use coconut milk and coconut cream. You are unlikely ever to want to add more fenugreek or turmeric. Don't forget asafoetida, which adds a good onion-like savoury note without using onions.

Dukkah: from nothing to indispensable in just a few years, dukkah is the epitome of culinary magic in a single container, for as many ways you can think of using it, another hundred will tumble in behind them. The idea is simple; a mixture of two or three nuts and sesame seeds, all lightly toasted and then crushed with cumin or coriander, salt and pepper. It's easy to make your own flavour by under or over roasting, or by swapping the usual hazelnuts, pistachios or almonds for other nuts or other balances. There are dozens of versions on the market to give you inspiration. The classic use for dukkah is as a dip with olive oil and good Turkish or other flat bread. Dip into the oil, dip into the dukkah and there's a surprisingly filling snack. But dukkah hit European and American kitchens running, and is used far more interestingly. As a finishing sprinkle it helps everything from salads to roast potatoes; in mashes or vegetable purees it should be added at the last minute. It is particularly good on almost any pasta dish, warming up the basic flavours with the toasted nuts and then adding bright notes with the spices.

I prefer to use it *after* grilling chicken, lamb or fish, to ensure it isn't over toasted or burned, and it makes fascinating flavours with tropical fruits, particularly banana and fresh, chilled mango: it's just as good with stewed fruits or mixed dried fruit salad, in stuffings for baked apple, sprinkled on sliced oranges. It's miraculous in any salsa you might construct.

When you are using dukkah with savoury foods, you might want to add extra sharpness with sumac: with sweet foods, you might like to sprinkle on a little cinnamon or cardamom too.

Australia and New Zealand have adopted and adapted dukkah almost demonically, with brilliant new versions. Prize for most original name goes to the mixture of nuts and Australian native herbs and spices: bush okkah. For the uninitiated I.e. the rest of the world, okkah is Aussie slang for the quintessential Aussie bloke, a charmer but not very interested in art galleries.

Fines herbes: in contrast to the mixture of herbs in a bouquet garni, which should be robust, fines herbes should be a combination of three or more sweet delicate herbs, such as parsley, tarragon and chervil, and, if you really really must, chives. They go very well with eggs. The mixture sold as mixed herbs, and used to excess by those who know not how to cook, is much more rugged, often contains sage and is better consigned to the back of the cupboard or, in extremis, to assist an ailing stuffing or sausage mixture.

Five-spice/Five-fragrance powder: a powerful mixed spice with a predominantly anise and cinnamon flavour but which may be any combination of star anise, cinnamon, cassia, fennel seeds, cloves, liquorice, nutmeg, Szechuan peppercorns and ginger. You can make your own mixture, from as many as you like, for inspite of the name many Chinese mixtures contain six or seven, but the flavour of the first two must predominate. Especially used in marinades, and I like it in poultry and pork stuffings, or rubbed well into their scored skin before roasting.

Gomashio: sea salt and sesame seeds together make the basic Japanese flavouring, used on most ingredients.

Harissa: this Tunisian mixture has a reputation for being super-hot, as indeed, it is. Based on dried chillies with paprika, cumin, coriander and unusually, caraway: freshly made it should include mint leaves and this is a clue as to how you can freshen up the versions usually bought in tubes. Most often used as a condiment rather than as a flavouring or cooking ingredient, but when *diluted* it's very useful in a chicken stew, for poaching whole fish, even cooked with or stirred into rice.

Herbes de Provence: just because these mixed herbs have a French accent doesn't mean they are any better than ordinary mixed herbs. The variation in content is astonishing, and often nothing to do with Provence at all, particularly if bought in Provence. Thyme, savory, parsley, bay and perhaps rosemary are expected. Lavender flowers are commonly included but thought

Curry Favours

As exotically spiced food becomes more and more popular all around the world, there are as many companies and families marketing superb authentic mixes as there are those who sell dross. Some of the worst mixtures come from the biggest household names, whose ideas of what goes with what, and how many pointless extra chemicals they can add, puts them well to the fore for fantasy-writing awards.

The basic retail rule applies – look at the label and if the contents contain something you or an ethnic cook wouldn't have in the kitchen, put it back. The producers of some of these 'aids' to cookery completely misuse or misunderstand traditional words and meanings – from curry names to their ingredients, and even wickedly use spicy to mean chilli-hot, when it shouldn't; this seems a battle lost.

Here is a guide to some of the curry mixtures you might see, all of which quite properly offer a range within each definition.

Indian Curries

Bhuna: a mild mixture of up to 20 spices for meat or chicken.

Biryani: actually a style of serving rather than a recognized spice mixture, by layering rice with cooked or cooking meats; but a biryani spice mixture should be no more than medium hot and very fragrant, often with some whole spices included. Biryanis are often very elaborate and expensive and served decorated with real silver or gold foil.

Delhi: should mean mild spicing.

Dopiaza: from northern India, it should be a tomato and onion base with a clearly recognisable preponderance of cumin.

Jahlfrezi: a succulent Kashmiri style based on sweet peppers/capsicums and coconuts

Kabuli: from Afghanistan way, medium spiced with cracked black peppers rather than chillies and with almonds.

Karai: medium hot mixture starting with the classic cumin/coriander base, and adding fennel seeds and tomatoes.

Korma: the real meaning is braised dishes, but the word is commonly used for any sauce, which is lightly spiced and creamy, often because it is finished with coconut. This makes it very popular.

Madras: one of the hottest and so it matters little what else is included.

Makhani: medium spiced and buttery, with fennel seeds dominating.

Moglai: must be very aromatic and as it should contain expensive saffron it should also be mild to medium in heat: can be finished richly with butter and cream and almonds.

Pasanda: generally favours the fragrant spices plus the richness of almonds – very good with lamb.

Rogan: tomato and cumin-based sauce commonly used for lamb: thus rogan josh.

Tikka: medium spice and heat, largely flavoured with turmeric and ginger.

Vindaloo: the hottest of all, so western-style eating is pointless. Very hot curries, all of them in fact, should be eaten in very small amounts per mouthful and always accompanied by at least the same amount of rice. Put another way each mouthful should always be half rice and half curry and with very hot curries you can have more rice and less curry. Believe me you and your digestion will have a much nicer time. For ways to ameliorate and pacify a chilli-fired tongue, see Chilli.

Sri Lankan Curries

Curries here are identified by their colour, and although they should in theory be quite different, cooks can make each of them anything from mild to super-hot. Take nothing for granted but double-check a curry you order is going to be the way you want.

White curry: very mild and liquid, doubling as soup: coriander, fenugreek, turmeric, curry leaves, fresh green chilli plus coconut milk and coconut cream

Red curry: a very high content of both fresh and dried red chillies can make these very hot indeed. Some cooks incorporate mild red paprika, to keep the colour but very much reduce the chilli content.

Black curry: the most common Sri Lankan curry, and so called because all the spices are pre-roasted to a dark rich brown, browner than you expect.

Pepper curry: an intriguing survivor of the times before chilli came calling, these fascinatingly rely on plenty of black pepper for flavour, fragrance and telling heat.

Thai Curries

The colour of Thai curries has no bearing on their heat. Although you expect the fresher green chillies used in a green curry to be milder than the dried red ones, the result depends on how many are used. Thai curries always start with a paste pounded in a mortar and pestle and usually contain kapi/shrimp paste. Remember also there is nothing like a classic recipe in Thai cookery – innovation and novelty are encouraged within very fluid boundaries.

If you haven't much time, and need to use bought curry pastes, don't worry for most Thais seem to buy theirs from markets. Look carefully at the ingredient list of something you have bought, to see what you might add or beef up: there's usually something missing and sometimes just fresh lemon grass and kaffir lime leaf can work wonders.

Green curry: green chillies, shallots, garlic coriander root, lemon grass, kaffir lime zest, peppercorns, coriander seeds, cumin seeds and kapi/shrimp paste.

Jungle curry: Kaeng Paa: usually yellow and meant to be made only with ingredients a traveller could find in the jungle, so largely vegetarian and never with coconut cream or milk, which would have to have been carried from the coast.

Musselman/Muslim: the only Thai curry using the sort of spice we'd use for an Indian curry – cinnamon, cloves and cardamom. But it's still based on a red curry paste and finished with coconut milk and cream.

Red curry: as above but with dried red rather than fresh green chillies, galangal, cinnamon, turmeric and perhaps a little star anise.

Tom Yum: the base of the famous hot-sour prawn soup, Tom Yum Goong. Read the label and then add what's missing, particularly such fresh ingredients as lemon grass or kaffir lime leaf.

Thai Curry Pastes

These two recipes were collected for my BBC TV series Glynn Christian Tastes Royal Thailand. Because there is no such thing as a classic recipe in Thai cookery, feel free to add, subtract or multiply.

Green Curry Paste

This recipe from the glamorous Oriental Hotel in Bangkok is intended to be quite hot, so remove the seeds and membranes and reduce the chillies if this is what you'd prefer. It's what I do. It makes about 12 tablespoons of paste and will keep a very long time in the refrigerator if very well sealed. Thai shallots are quite small and violet coloured. Ordinary lime zest can replace the kaffir lime zest. Fresh ginger is not a good substitute for galangal and anyway is rarely used in Thai cookery.

12 small green chillies, chopped
2 Thai shallots, chopped
4 garlic cloves, chopped
4cm (1½ in) fresh galangal, chopped
1 tbsp chopped coriander root or whole plant
6 tbsp chopped lemon grass stalks
1 tsp chopped kaffir lime zest
1 tsp coriander seeds, roasted and then ground
1 tsp cumin seeds, roasted and then ground
2 tsp kapi (shrimp paste)
6 tbsp vegetable oil

Pound together or process the chillies, shallots, garlic, galangal, coriander and lemon grass. Add the lime zest, peppercorns, coriander and cumin seeds plus the kapi and continue until you have a smooth paste. If you are using a food processor it is very worthwhile pounding the processed paste as this breaks down the ingredients in a way a processor cannot. Then gradually work in the oil until you have a homogenous paste. Store in a screw-top glass jar.

Red Curry Paste

The Thai House is a traditionally built Thai dwelling on a klong outside Bangkok, where you can stay while learning to cook. Theirs is a particularly fragrant red curry paste, and so tasty I have made and used it with very little chilli indeed. It makes about 15 tablespoons of paste. Don't use fresh ginger if you can't get galangal. Note that it is not diluted with oil and so you should use rather less than of the green curry paste.

12 dried red chillies
3 tbsp chopped Thai shallots
4 tbsp chopped garlic
1 tbsp chopped fresh galangal
2 tbsp chopped fresh lemon grass
2 tbsp chopped kaffir lime zest
1 tbsp chopped coriander root or plant
2 tsp white peppercorns
1 tsp cumin seeds, roasted and then ground
1 tbsp coriander seeds, roasted and then ground
2 tbsp kapi (shrimp paste)
2 tsp salt
2 points of star anise

Soak the chillies in warm water until soft, drain and then seed them – this doesn't reduce the heat much so reduce the number of chillies if you want to turn down the heat. Then pound or process everything together and store in a well-sealed jar in the refrigerator.

by some not to be authentic and only to be there to counteract the low quality of other ingredients: this could be true because the rule with lavender is to use only the English types for culinary purposes. Can you imagine Provençals importing foreign lavender for a mixture touted as reflecting the scent of their sun-bleached summer countryside?

In *Spice Notes*, Ian Hemphill gives a recipe including tarragon and celery seeds, which both seem very un-Provençal to me, but would at least be far nicer to eat than most *herbes de Provençe*. The one unusual ingredient I would add is dried orange peel, used down that way a great lot in stews and as part of the base for a bouillabaisse.

Next time you buy this mixture take time to read the ingredients – I'd bet money you'll be more inclined to put it back than to use it to remind you of Provence.

Khemeli-suneli: something very unusual, not just because it is from Georgia, the country, but also because it combines herbs and spices to give an elegant, multi-faceted and elevated flavour to anything to do with vegetables, including soups but can be used as a marinade or rub for roasting meats and birds. The secret is the mixing of dill, mint, savory, fenugreek leaves and marigold petals with coriander, cloves and cinnamon.

Masala: the word simply means mixture, so all curry powder mixes are masalas but some mixtures, like chat masala and garam masala are always sold like that, rather than as curries.

Otherwise if you see, say a Benghali masala or a Kalahari masala this is just another way to say Bengali curry mix, Kalahari curry mix and so on.

Chat masala: I am used to seeing this as just five or six spices but was given a tub of an Indian one with 15 ingredients by Robin and Manav Garawal, who hospitably welcome travelers at Opou Country House, close to Gisborne, chardonnay capital of New Zealand, and possibly of the world. *Chat masala* is meant specially for fruits and vegetables, both raw and cooked and can be cooked with or sprinkled on. It adds a delicious lift to salads of all kinds, even to cold roasted vegetables. There should be very little heat indeed, ideally none.

Chat/chaat is an Indian word for potatoes, which gives a clue where *chat masala* often shines most brightly, but who can explain why small potatoes are called chats in so many parts of Australia?

Garam masala: this should not contain chilli and is not properly added in classic Indian cookery until just before or just after a dish is ready. To be correct it is a tempering spice mixture, for tempering is the right term to use when refreshing or adding flavours right at the end of cooking. Garam masala should be very fragrant and lift and refresh many of the spices used at the beginning of the cooking.

Mixed herbs: the biggest step anyone can make towards being a good cook is to throw away the mixed herbs and never use them again. Ever. It's not that some mixtures are bad, but all tend to be put to the back of the cupboard and used well past their life span, which heightens the flabby, mouldy, dank taste. Anyway, there seems no agreement about what should be there.

My career in food, much longer than anyone predicted, only really began when I controversially stopped using onion, stopped using mixed herbs, and instead concentrated on getting more focused flavours from fewer ingredients. Move on from the broad strokes of mixed herbs, cook with one herb and get to know that, and only when you know a number really well, then perhaps add another and another based on cooking recipes from food writers you trust.

Mixed spice: although generally a mixture of cinnamon, nutmeg and cloves or allspice, a really decent mixed spice can include far more than that, so don't be afraid of experimenting by adding others to get a really good spicy taste rather than just the usual sweet and aromatic notes. Dill and fennel seeds give liquorice flavour, which is good in conjunction with lifted clove notes. Coriander and cumin both give warmth and can be added together or individually for a sense of orange or lemon. Ginger adds bite as well as flavour, but so could grains of paradise, Melegueta pepper. Cassia serves to heighten the cinnamon taste. Fenugreek can also be used, and Elizabeth David added black pepper to her spice mixture and if she said it's all right it must be, but I'd try hard to ensure I used Sarawak peppercorns, undoubtedly the most fragrant, perhaps with some cubeb pepper too. Finally, mace adds unmatched and too often overlooked elegance, and cardamom an unmistakable touch of the exotic but it can easily overpower, so be careful.

Mixed spice bought in a shop should be used quickly and the remainder thrown out soon afterwards, unless you manage to buy resealable packs, like those of Seasoned Pioneers, that are lightproof and that you keep away from heat.

Mojo de ajo: translated as a bath of garlic, it's more like garlic in a bath. Whole garlic cloves are simmered to softness in oil together with lime and chipotle chillies. Squash the well-bathed garlic with some of the oil for prawns, fish, and mushrooms or as a bread dip and spread. One enthusiastic young chef at London's Friday and Saturday Borough Market, strews the oil over baked beans on toast: 'it's making me famous down there'.

Mole sauces: these most fabled mixtures from South America were created by Spanish nuns, it is said, who combined the intricate Old World spice blends of medieval and Moorish Spain with the challenging ingredients they found in the New World, particularly chocolate and chillies. A mole (*mol-ay*) is profound, thick and packs both flavour and heat. Genuine mole recipes can take days, getting richer and darker as they do; and the one dish you should always try if offered is turkey with a mole sauce for it is considered the pinnacle of such cookery.

Mole sauce mixes and mole sauce kit sets are offered, containing a mixture of chilli types, cocoa or chocolate, many spices, sesame seeds, almonds, raisins and more. Sometimes a mole will be identified by the chilli that dominates its recipe, as Mole Poblano, and this gives some clue as to how hot or aromatic it will be before you buy – see page 358 for heat comparisons of chillies. There are lighter coloured green moles, made with *pepitas*, raw, green pumpkin seeds. Do it yourself mole makers should look in *The Book of Latin American Cooking* (Grub Street) by Elisabeth Lambert Ortiz for authentic background and recipes.

Pickling spice: this mixture of spices, with a few herbs like bay thrown in, has more uses than for pickling onions. I use it to flavour vinegar for my red cabbage, and to flavour wine or cider when sousing mackerel, sprats or sardines. There is no agreed recipe for pickling spice, but a quality blend would have mustard seed as its main component and fragrance and interest can be added with most of the following: coriander seeds, peppercorns, ginger root, allspice, dill seed, chillies, fenugreek, whole cloves, mace and cut bay leaves.

Sousing is a good way to do fish, especially the sardine and mackerel; long slow cooking with pickling spices and a light or diluted vinegar allows the vinegar to dissolve the bones which in turn act with the liquid to form a jelly.

Poudre de Colombo: I can't resist the name of this Caribbean curry mixture that has no chilli in it, and thus offers clear citric notes over warm spices. Very good with fish, and I'd use it to make a difference to the mayonnaise or vinaigrette dressing of a potato salad or a mixture of roasted vegetables.

Quatre-épices: a backbone of French domestic and commercial kitchens, and used a great deal in charcuterie, it's a mixture of: white pepper, ground ginger, nutmeg and cloves. Quatre-epices is available commercially but it's easy to mix the ingredients yourself and keep them in an opaque pepper grinder – the mix might well taste different every time you use it, no bad thing. Quatre-épices, like all ground spices, should only be made in small quantities, kept dry, cool and airtight and used quickly. There is a sweet version used for ginger breads and the like, where the white pepper is replaced by allspice, often disguised by being called pimento.

Ras el hanout: once you couldn't find this most majestic of mixed spices unless you went to Morocco, a favourite food country of mine ever since I first went exploring the markets and restaurants in 1975: in cities like Fez you still eat the same extraordinary specialties they ate in Britain centuries ago, like shad stuffed with dates stuffed with cinnamon-almond rice. Even in Moroccan cities with the very highest levels of cuisine, you must grind *ras el hanout* yourself, indeed considering the expense you would want to, to be certain of what went in to it.

Ras el hanout is the very Valhalla of mixed spice, the blissful, ultimate prize for all the conquering, looting and lusting by Muslim nomad, soldier and proselytiser, a culinary lexicon and souvenir of all the countries they once overran physically or intellectually. It is at once floral and sweet-spiced, sharp but immensely refined, arresting and disarming, sensual but never vulgar, raw, rough or challenging. To call *ras el hanout* heavenly encourages reminders of Sydney Smith's imagery, of dining on foie gras to the sound of trumpets, but that reeks too much of the Infidel. Think instead of palm-belted oases, of scanty veils and the scent of orange-blossom, of smoke from musky, rose-scented oils drifting over fountains dribbling cooled wine, and golden bowls of fresh almonds and dates, as firm-fleshed fingers massage closer and closer to. . . whoops, sorry, but you do get the picture, do you? *Ras el hanout* is not ordinary.

The name means 'top of the shop' for that is where the spice-soukh's merchants will keep its expensive ingredients, far from robbing hands. Many of the contents are strange to us and its claim to be aphrodisiac is based on the inclusion of something I thought apocryphal – Spanish fly or cantharides. Oh, and hashish, but its effects are so unpredictable for that sort of thing, person to person, I've given up on it. It sends some to sleep almost immediately, while others . . . but I digress. Again. That's *ras el hanout* for you.

You can now more easily buy *ras el hanout* ready ground, but then you might not get the best quality and certainly won't have the best fun. This comes only with watching an expert put together the whole ingredients, weighing this, counting that, wrapping each one separately: a good *ras el hanout* customer is honoured and treasured, deserves time to be spent on him. The average number of ingredients is said to be 27, and unless there are at least 20 it's stretching it a bridge too far to call the mixture *ras el hanout*. And yet, ultimately none of the ingredients is overwhelmed, all are available to the palate, so much so you use far less than expected and still get a satin-smooth hit of hedonistic reward.

In the version I took back to London from Fez in screws of Arabic-scripted newspaper, there were six different peppers – Guinea pepper, long pepper, black pepper, grey cubeb pepper, Melegueta pepper (grains of paradise) and monks' pepper, which comes from Morocco. Fragrance was given by cardamom, mace, galingale, nutmeg, allspice, cinnamon, turmeric, cloves, ginger, lavender flowers, rose buds, cassia buds and fennel seeds. Orrisroot, *cyparaceae*, ash berries, bella donna and quite a few untranslatable things were also included. Then to top it all, the metallic glint of whole cantharides, counted more carefully and tellingly. I don't think this mixture included hashish.

When you get them home and begin to grind and mix, the perfume is intoxicating, and although meant to be used in winter dishes to heat the blood, hands, feet and other bits, I find it does very nicely all through the year. So far the libidinous effects of Spanish fly, although monitored sensitively, have remained undetectable. Either that or my smiling guests aren't letting on.

Commercially, *ras el hanout* is becoming a victim of sloppy wordsmiths. It has become enmeshed in the awful belief exotic spice mixtures should be hot to be authentic, in part because the world has been allowed to confuse spicy with hot – to me spice should mean just that, spiced. Where hamburgers and fast food are concerned spicy means hot and so all savoury spicy flavours are expected to carry chilli heat, too. Now, I know every family and every spice merchant in Morocco has their own recipe and flavour of *ras el hanout*, but I believe heat should come only from the flavoursome peppers and ginger, rather than from chillies, which would anyway be a late comer to this classic, from South America remember: Ian Hemphill uses a half teaspoon of cayenne in a mixture of 21 ingredients that makes up to about 12 tablespoons (see the recipe in his book *Spice Notes*) and that's more than enough for me. It is so self-defeating to pay for such voluptuous fragrance and then to ambush it with heat and they certainly didn't use chillies in any of the stalls I visited in Fez, Meknes, Marrakech, Rabat or Casablanca.

I think *ras el hanout* is best stirred into cooked couscous or rice, ideally with plenty of butter. It's specially good with green vegetables, with carrots, or celeriac root and on roasted beetroot. Anything eggy reacts gratifyingly, as indeed does anything creamy or creamy of appearance and texture – so chicken and duck and turkey for sure.

This is an aristocrat of the most noble breeding, so don't for heaven's sake treat it as a rub and then blacken the spices on a barbecue or grill or roast them into a cinder. Think about its fluctuating striations of flavour and scent, those subtly changing flavours – the amount it cost!

Fry pieces of chicken or squid to a golden brown first and then add the *ras el hanout*, so it is not scorched or blackened. It's a great surprise in frying batters for fish and seafood, especially squid rings.

I once sprinkled some over very hot poached plums, served with grilled peaches, rather as you might do with less complicated chat masala or garam masala, another mixture that should have no more than a whisper of chilli, if any at all. My latest triumph with *ras el hanout* was to whisk some into the eggs for a simple potato fritatta.

Sabzi ghormeh: an excellent mixture of dried or fresh mint, parsley, chives and coriander with lime and perhaps some fenugreek, used in Iran in their many stews, or with rice.

Sambal oelek: a south-east Asian paste of chilli and aromatics, not unlike harissa, and a source of chilli ferocity for those who don't fancy the flavour of what they've cooked.

Shichimi: a very interesting Japanese mixed spice with a fascinating flavour if it is not made too hot. It should include sesame and poppy seeds, tangerine peel and a number of untranslatables, plus chilli. Noodle dishes are commonly served with this on the side but it is also used in stews.

Tagine spices: with the huge interest in Moroccan cookery these days, tagine has become a common word in kitchens. A tagine is so-called because it is cooked in a vessel of the same name: the lid is a tall cone designed to drip condensation evenly back onto the food and keep it moist. But not too moist. Moroccan foods rely on thickening sauces by a slow reduction and concentration of their liquids and slow emulsification with the butter and oil used at the start of cooking; another clue to authenticity in tagine recipes will be ground ginger, something that gives Moroccan food a unique footprint on the palate. Did I just put my foot in your mouth?

Most tagine recipes come with a list of spices but here and there specialty tagine mixtures are available. The best come from Fatema Hal, a Moroccan woman restaurateur in Paris, who has cooked at the Mansouria since 1984. She offers all manner of mixed spices for Moroccan cookery, even a mixture for *b'stilla* the ethereal pie of pigeon, egg, cinnamon and paper-like pastry. If you haven't eaten Moroccan food you trust to be authentic, Fatema Hal has a website and sells her mixtures and her book on couscous and on Moroccan foods.

La kama is a tagine mix you might find elsewhere and in classic Moroccan style incorporates rather a lot of ground ginger, this time with pepper, cinnamon, nutmeg and turmeric.

Tsire: an African flavouring based on peanuts with spices and chilli used on meats and vegetables. Plenty of red chilli with salt, mace and allspice make a difference to the common cumin, coriander and others of the usual suspects.

Za'atar, zahtar: I first met this most delicious of seasonings in the streets of Jerusalem, where although Arabic, it is especially popular baked onto flat breads, or spread onto bread with olive oil when it is toasted.

The ingredients are simple, toasted sesame seeds, ground thyme and sumac q.v., but the big flavours and acidity of the latter two have an extraordinary affinity with one another and with the sesame seeds and the palate reward is far greater than you might expect.

Once you have some in your cupboard you'll find it increasingly easy to reach for, in fact wherever you could use dukkah, or perhaps sumac alone, *za'atar* does equally well but with fewer crunchy nuts and a crisper flavour.

Truly fabulous on grilled or oven-roasted tomatoes and in any tomato sauce including pasta sauces, yes and even on pizza. It's also a treat on scrambled or fried eggs especially with ham or pork sausages, and in or on omelettes, when brunches or light suppers allow a bit more flavour on a plate than breakfast might welcome. Plainly roasted chicken legs can do with a coating before going into the oven, and so can a roasting chicken but don't use it as a rub and then scorch or burn the ingredients in a pan or under a searing grill.

As neither the Arabs nor the Jews of Israel might have worked this one out, I'll have to tell you za'atar is extra good with pork: rub it into the skin or lift what will be the crackling and spread plenty between that and the flesh before roasting. This will once and for all prove how much better thyme is with pork than sage can ever be. Pâté makers could do no better than to bake their creations with a topping of *za'atar*. I've not done it yet, but *za'atar* must be fabulous in bread dough.

Zanzibar curry powder: a particularly good mixture for vegetable curries and for roasting vegetables that includes brown sugar and roasted spices including fennel seed and fenugreek.

Flavours, Flavourings and the Like

Anardana: dried pomegranate seeds that, like fresh ones, are syrupy, crunchy and wonderfully sweet-sour. They can be added dry to curries, pulse and vegetable dishes, used in pickles and chutneys. Once soaked they develop a lighter texture and like this can be strewn over almost anything, as their delightful texture and sweet-sour balance seem to enhance everything. I specially like them with grilled fish.

Angostura bitters: originally a fever cure, these get their bitterness from the inclusion of quinine, but are said also to incorporate tropical spices, citrus and some rum. Of course, most of us know them only for the pink they give to pink gin, or the way they jazz up a cocktail, but they can be far more useful than this, if used with great discretion.

The most fascinating assistance bitters give is to fruit salads, especially where there is a good proportion of fresh orange. Add it to the sugar syrup early on.

Angostura bitters are good with creamy things and I have found them useful for finishing sauces for fish, for chicken and for pork. They are fascinating and always get conversation going around a table.

Annatto: small red seeds ground to give colour to rice and marinades in Mexico and there abouts with a small, musky flavour. In the rest of the world, the dried fleshy outer covering of the seeds is used to colour cheese, cheese rinds and, sometimes, butter and because it is so diluted there is no discernible flavour left. It should be the red colouring on Chinese barbecued pork. If you heat seeds in a little oil, you will always have a red colouring agent on hand to brighten up roasted meats and birds and such.

Asafoetida: strictly neither herb nor spice, but a gum from a variety of giant fennel with a perfectly horrid and persistent smell, rather like rotting garlic. It is considered the most blessed of flavourings amongst Brahmin and Jain Indians, who eat neither garlic nor onions, for it adds savouriness without either of these. For the many millions of people who can't or won't eat raw or undercooked onion, asafoetida is a godsend, and Indian cookbooks that dismiss onions and garlic as intimates of the Devil are revered. Well, they are by me. Quite why I think onions ruin more food than they ever help is another book.

Asafoetida's savouriness adds real interest to vegetarian dishes that might otherwise taste only of undercooked onion and over-aged mixed herbs and it also gives a gentle lift to fish dishes, where onion or garlic would be too coarse. But there's more. Asafoetida is a great defeater of intestinal wind, and that alone recommends it for inclusion in any and everything that includes lentils and beans. You probably have to go to an Indian shop to buy it.

If it is a yellow powder this means it has been diluted with flour and turmeric, a reminder to use it scantly. If it is a brown powder it will smell quite a lot for it is just ground brown gum.

The real thing, the gum, comes as red-brown lumps of different shapes and sizes. The degree of aroma is in direct proportion to its freshness, for its volatile oil escapes easily and its essence fades. Only buy it if you can seal it away hermetically, at least double wrapped, or you wake to find the entire house smells like yesterday's garlic. The powder is much the better way

Capillaire: this rather extraordinary flavour is that of the maidenhair fern, and was very popular towards the end of the 19th century but almost unknown now: Dorothy Hartley in *Food in England* says maidenhair itself was used to garnish sweet dishes in the same manner parsley is used on savoury ones. Only one maker, from France, still offers it as a cordial: such *capillaire* syrup was mainly used to flavour drinks, and was thought to be a tonic – the sort of thing to take 'on rising in the morning'.

The black ribs of the fern when boiled with sugar make a thick aromatic syrup, which was usually improved with orange flower water and saffron.

To make your own, stew 50g/2oz freshly gathered maidenhair fern in water for several hours, strain and boil the liquid with sugar in the usual proportion of 450g/ 1lb to 600ml/1 pint. When thick, add a good spoonful or more of orange flower water and cork or bottle tightly. Miss Hartley suggests the following uses: put a dozen cherries, pounded till their kernels are cracked, into a large glass with crushed ice and a wine glass of *capillaire*, and top up with iced plain water; soda might be nicer. You will probably never want to make or drink *capillaire*, but when you come across it in a book you will now know what it is.

Carob: made from the abundant locust bean, carob is used as a substitute for chocolate by those who want such a flavour but none of its accompanying fat, calories or caffeine. The seeds are held in a sweet pulp, and this makes one of the syrups thought to be meant by the phrase 'land of milk and honey'. Carob molasses, which you'll find in Lebanese or Syrian shops, can be used much like any other pour-over syrup as a sweetening in cookery.

Once dried the pod can be chewed, like a fruit leather. Otherwise, the pod of the locust bean is cooked and then roasted and ground. The roasting caramelizes the natural sugars present and gives a cocoa-like reddish brown colour. The flavour is definitely like chocolate, but with fudgey, caramel overtones that make it not the same thing at all, unless you like milk chocolate: because it is naturally sweet it cannot be used as a substitute for dark or bitter chocolate.

Mainly available in health food stores, carob can be used in cooking as though it were a sort of sweetened cocoa. To replace chocolate, use a couple of dessertspoons per chocolate square. If you stop thinking of it as a chocolate substitute, carob then becomes a very interesting ingredient in its own right.

Chrysanthemum: you'll come across these petals in a most regal Japanese soup; I recommend you try it for they give a spicy fragrant flavour. One or two flowers infused also make a delicious tea, hot or cold; they can also be added to your usual tea.

Citric acid/sour salt: a pinch of citric acid gives as much acidity as the juice from half a small lemon, or from a lime, and gives a cleaner, fresher flavour than concentrated juices, which have been ameliorated by processing, of course. Its long been a favourite trick in northern and eastern European countries, where citrus fruit is or was rare, and is very good with that style of cookery – beetroot borscht, cheese cakes and the like. It's not expensive, so buy some when you see it and you'll have a reliable standby.

Citrus oils: I feel naked without bottles of pure cold-processed lime, lemon and orange, tangerine and grapefruit oils from Boyajian of New York. They are pure, they are exact and both magical when something isn't working, and the tools to make magic otherwise. And no wonder, when it takes around 220 oranges, 300 lemons or 400 limes to produce just 150ml/5 fl oz of oil. You really need these in your refrigerator, where their life is unlimited, even if it is only to add a whiff to gin or vodka. Boyajian do other equally wonderful spice and fruit natural flavouring oils. But start with the lime.

For instance, when pasta is drained and has been allowed to steam dry for a few minutes, as it should, I then toss it in a mixture of olive oil and lime oil. The dried pasta surface sucks it up and voila! Lime-flavoured pasta, extraordinarily good with anything tomatoy and enthralling as the basis for a cold pasta salad with prawns or roasted vegetables – or just about anything.

Something different in a chocolate cake or in brownies? I add lime oil in the proportions they suggest and voila! Again. And if I forget then I mix some in to the icing. You can buy big bottles but they are expensive and unless you are a professional chef or baker you always use more of one flavour than another: there is a pack of small bottles of each of the three citrus oils. I use lime more than lemon or orange, but you might use others.

Clover blossoms, red: dried or fresh, the honey-like flavour of these flowers makes a delicious tea and can be employed to make sensational but delicate creams and ice creams.

Cream of tartar/tartaric acid: not a flavouring, of course, but something important to understand. It's made from powdered dried grapes, and is a basic ingredient of baking powder.

The combination of baking soda and tartaric acid together with liquid and heat is what causes the manufacture of gas and the subsequent rising of cake mixtures. If you only have baking soda, you must use something acidic in the mix, such as sour milk or milk and lemon juice. Cream of tartar is also used in making sweets.

Coconut milk and cream: See entry also in Fruits, Nuts and Vegetables, page 281. The liquid that comes from a coconut is coconut water and used as a refreshing drink but rarely in cooking. Grating fresh coconut, adding hot water, steeping and then squeezing make coconut milk and coconut cream. If you use a little water you get a thick rich cream, if you use a lot you get a thinner milk.

Recipes for the use of coconut milk and cream can confuse, for coconut cream is available in different forms. The most useful, but not available in all countries, is the cake of concentrated coconut cream that can be grated and mixed with water in whatever proportion you like – to make something as thick as whipped cows' cream or as thin as coconut milk.

Otherwise you buy coconut cream or milk in liquid form, sometimes frozen. But if you can get only coconut milk you make coconut cream by reducing the milk by boiling. In the many Thai curries that use coconut milk as the basic cooking medium, a cook will begin by boiling down a quantity of coconut milk. When rich and thick, most of it is ladled off, and what is left in the wok is used when frying up the red or green curry paste. The portion set aside is used as a dressing for the final dish.

Coconut milk can be used wherever you would use ordinary milk. On Pitcairn Island, as on many Pacific islands, it is used for making rice puddings, and less usually as a dressing for salads and for green beans. It will transform any kind of baking when substituted and ditto any stewed dish. Of course, when cooked at a high temperature for a long time it will separate and create puddles of oil. In most south-east Asian cuisines this is considered a good thing, an indication the meat is now tender or the sauce is the right texture and flavour – or both.

Pouring boiling water onto desiccated coconut will make you a decent coconut milk or cream if you're caught short but want to bake or cook.

Elderberries: like elderflowers, these usually find themselves made into wine. Provided you use a recipe that incorporates spices like nutmeg and cloves, you will, after several years of patience, be rewarded with a wine that in my experience has all the elegance and nobility of a fine Burgundy. I know that sounds unlikely.

I've never eaten elderberry jam, but believe it to be very good. What I have done is combine elderberries with apple in a pie and that was very successful.

Elderflowers: the honey-scented, muscatel-flavoured elderflower is making the most sensational comeback, in the UK anyway. Largely unknown as a flavour even to those who had a tree in the back garden, it has been discovered by very big food and drink manufacturers: their most successful combination is elderflower and apple juice, but wouldn't you know it, the biggest manufacturer's supermarket-shelf product has so little you can't detect it. Proves once again, you can't eat or drink labels. At the other end of the scale, The Cocoa Tree makes chocolates with elderflower fondant centres, from blossoms they've gathered from hedgerows.

Traditionally elderflowers were used to make delicious muscatel-like sparkling wine. It improves dramatically with keeping and then serves as a dessert wine accompanying puddings, but is even better as a flavouring agent for other drinks: I can hardly think of anything better than fragrant strawberries served only with a few spoonsful of concentrated elderflower cordial over them.

Recipes for elderflower champagne are terribly easy to make, you basically bung some yeast-laden heads into sweetened water, tighten the cap and wait a wee while. It's very entertaining but the result is more a child's drink – very sweet, only slightly fizzy, and filled with clouds of dead yeast. But, if you have the bottles and have the tree or access to them . . . . Curiously although seeming such a country thing to do, elderflowers grow happily in city surroundings and even in Central London it's amazing the harvest you can make from other people's trees during a short walk.

More classically, elderflower is cooked with gooseberries, but gooseberries ripen just as the flowers fade and you can miss out. When cooking gooseberries for a fool, one or two heads of rinsed elderflower will be enough to add the required flavour. Gooseberry and elderflower jam or jelly is particularly recommended.

Cream perfumed by soaking elderflower in it overnight is a lovely surprise with all sorts of summer fruits, strawberries and raspberries included. One of the most successful hints I gave on BBC TV Breakfast Time was to stuff a head or two of elderflowers into a bottle of medium dry or Germanic white wine overnight. By morning you have a Muscat wine to drink chilled as an inimitable aperitif. Judi Dench, well before damehood, was just one who told me how much they enjoyed it.

Elderflowers apparently pick up lead easily so should not be gathered beside busy roads. Each flat head should be smelt as it is picked for some have a distinct catty smell that, like all bad things, dominate the rest no matter how much or little you have. It's a very ancient thing to mix the florets into a cheesecake mixture or to stir them into a pancake batter.

Fish sauce: think of this as liquid salt with added flavour and you'll find it more acceptable. **Nam pla** is the Thai version and **Nuoc mam** is fish sauce from Vietnam, and both are salty seasoning made by fermenting whole small fish in salt, the same way Romans made their indispensable *garum*. Worcestershire sauce is made rather the same way, if that helps a bit more. It is the essential salt/savouriness of south-east Asia, and like shrimp paste, is something you soon learn to miss when eating from another type of kitchen. If ever you are offered the chance to tour the open pits where the fish and salt ferment, plead poverty, insanity or anything to avoid it. The hotter the day, the greater should be your pleading.

Food colouring: generally, if you can do without food colouring, I think you should. The exceptions are two – occasionally for children's food and always for absolute disasters. I suspect many people rely on colouring to cover overcooking, especially where cucumber-based food is concerned. Most colourings are very artificial and contain ingredients about which the long-term effects on the human system are totally unknown. Every year a different yellow or green, or red or blue is suspected and this is enough reason not to use colouring for children's food and drink on a *regular* basis. For fun, and from time to time, should be the rule. In fact if you look you can now find natural food colourings, green, red and yellow particularly.

At medieval banquets even quite ordinary food had to be brightly coloured. Sandalwood made food red; saffron made it yellow and spinach made it green. It was gilded with egg and gold leaf, silvered with silver and most spectacular it must have been. For very special occasions I think such presentation is worthwhile and a few years ago I experimented to find out how one could recreate coloured pastry without having to find sandalwood and so on. It was easy.

After you put the pastry top on your pie, you simply paint it with undiluted food colouring of which there is now a vast range. Once the colouring has dried, cover it with the usual egg glaze, let that dry and then bake away. Lighter colours are fugitive so if you are using light greens and yellows glaze only for the last few minutes of baking: the same advice goes if the pie will bake for more than 30 minutes, glaze for just the last ten minutes.

 The simplest stripes look good; try diagonal stripes of bright green and saffron yellow on, say, a chicken, lettuce and cucumber pie.

Artists can really go to town. For a wedding reception in a grand country house I cooked a ten-course banquet for 60 people in evening dress, them not me. The *pieces de resistances* were hot game pies delivered to each table of six, gilded and decorated and painted. One of the guests was a fairly well known artist from Paris, so she came to the kitchen and made each pie crust into her own brand of picture. A sensation. Another time I made a fresh peach and rose geranium pie for Glyndebourne. I decorated the top, over-decorated some might say, with roses, leaves and vines of pastry and painted them carefully, leaving the crust its natural colour and only glazing the flowers and foliage. Others on the Glyndebourne lawn came to take photographs and it is still mentioned with awe, perhaps, I like to think, because it also tasted so good.

 It is far more fun for a child to have their name or portrait on a cake than to be presented with blue, yellow and green striped parfaits. A damn sight less trouble, too.

One of the most commonly used colourings is caramel or gravy browning, but good cooking technique should make this unnecessary. Use minimal flour and make sure your meat is very well browned before adding liquid. If you need browning, then cook white sugar until it turns golden brown and then dilute it with a little water to keep the mixture concentrated: keep that bottled until you need it. Commercial gravy browning is the result of an extraordinary process that incorporates ammonia and some authorities recommend it should not be used as human food.
Geranium leaves: scented geraniums usually have rather small leaves and these have many uses in the kitchen for someone who likes exotic but traditional effects without fuss.

There is one geranium with very big leaves, and that is my favourite, the genuine rose geranium. The true rose geranium is easily recognized because it has leaves at least the size of an average hand and grows up to two metres tall. It grows as easily as you blink from any old bit of it stuck into any old bit of ground, and in the right place can even make a scented hedge. It should be encouraged to spread over the pathway so passersby brush the leaves, and this releases the scent even on quite chilly days. On sunny days the heady, spicy scent travels and concentrates in your garden where you least expect it.

The rose aroma of the leaves has dozens of uses. An old English way is to flavour plain or chocolate sponges by putting two or three overlapping leaves on the base of the baking pan before you add the cake mixture. A little rose water in the icing completes this transformation of a basic cake into something very special. Otherwise slice up four or five or more lusciously scented leaves you have picked early in the morning for maximum intensity, and then slide these into a bottle of inexpensive vodka; I'm speaking relatively about expense, of course. In a few weeks you will have something very special to drink as very cold shots or to sweeten and serve as a chilled *digestif*. It's a thrilling way to flavour the cream for summer fruits, too.

Other geraniums have almost the same scent but smaller leaves and these are more convenient for making rose geranium sugar: slightly tear some leaves to help release the oils and then mix with caster sugar in a screw-top jar. After a week you'll have a scented sugar that is good on soft fruit or in baking, and far more interesting than vanilla sugar. The little orange-scented leaves of the Prince of Orange geranium are good for this, and so is a combination of them with rose geranium leaves.

I like to chop a few rose geranium leaves into soft fruit salads just before serving, and after pressing leaves onto the side of pats of cream cheese that's left overnight, the result is a wonderful accompaniment to raspberries. In the same way the leaves can be macerated in cream and then strained out, to use as is or for making a very sexy panna cotta. Orange-, lemon-mint-, nutmeg-, apple- and coconut-scented geranium can be used too.

Tunisia makes **rose geranium water**, subtler and a mite more complicated than the usual rose water.

Gum arabic: this natural, edible gum has virtually no scent or flavour but is used as a fixative and binding agent in scented foods and beads. If you are sybaritic enough to want scents wherever you go, mix one part (a tablespoon, perhaps) of powdered gum arabic to three parts rose water, or almond oil, vanilla extract or something equally aromatic. Mix until a thick paste forms, and then use your palms to roll small beads that are then left to harden overnight. They can be threaded and worn close to the skin or carried in a warm pocket, whence they will dispense their headiness.

A few drops of your favourite commercial scent can also be added and it's worth experimenting with powdered spice mixtures.

To crystallize flower petals, mix one part gum arabic with three parts rose water, brush them all over with this solution, sprinkle with caster sugar, and dry on a rack in a dry, warm place.

Honeysuckle flowers: the woodbine's heady perfume can be captured and used to flavour creams and syrups, including ice cream. Dried honeysuckle can usually be bought in Chinese food shops.

Horseradish: this habitué of English railway cuttings is used more as a condiment than a flavouring but start to experiment and you'll be impressed. It is called a horseradish because the root can grow as long as 30cm/12 in, very big compared to an ordinary radish, and horse is commonly used to indicate excess size, as in horse mushrooms, horse mackerel and so on.

The distinctive super-pungent, tear-jerking aroma and taste-heat only happen when the root is grated or scraped, for this breaks down the cells allowing two components to form a volatile oil, the same oil as in black mustard seeds.

When freshly grated, the taste is severe, the fumes alone making your eyes water and nose run. Thus I'm not too fond of it in its common guise – freshly grated and mixed with vinegar or a little milk to accompany roast beef – as it seems to overwhelm the meat's flavour. I recommend you look out for packets of imported horseradish from Germany or Sweden. They may be mixed with milk or cream and make a far nicer sauce. The best way to use prepared horseradish cold is to fold a little into whipped cream and then leave it for some hours for the flavours to mix. This is rather good with fish, especially smoked fish like eel or mackerel. Or, you simply buy a tube of *pepparots visp*, which is a preparation of horseradish and cream the Swedes use to smear on thin slices of reindeer meat. Next time you serve cold meats, make a very gentle horseradish and cream sauce and just see how good it is.

Once you get used to using horseradish cream with discretion try it in seafood sauces, hot or cold; in the former some of the heat will cook out, making it more delicate and hard to discern. I first ate horseradish with fish at the Red Fox Inn in Middlesburg VA, said to be the first 'pub' on the United States east coast. If not for the iced water, the huge portions and low prices, the low ceilings and panelling might have created an atmosphere just like an English inn. But I wouldn't have been served split Pacific prawns with horseradish cream sauce in the Thames Valley, I bet.

If prepared with a very light hand, horseradish and cream sauce can be served very successfully with grilled lobster or salmon. And if not on the salmon then stir both horseradish cream and cream into crushed potatoes, with garlic too, and a few scrapes of nutmeg: that goes with almost everything but is best with grilled steak or roast beef. *Cuisine brute.*

An easily available Polish condiment mixes horseradish with beetroot, as *krajne* or something similar: however it is said or spelt nothing is much better with smoked trout, salmon or smoked mackerel, or indeed with any smoked or salty meat.

Irish moss: also known as carrageen, this seaweed-based product is very good for you, and is used to set liquids in the same way as agar-agar.

Jasmine essence/extract: called *mali* in Thailand, where it is used to perfume sweet syrups and custards. You should do the same. Add it to thick coconut cream and serve that instead of dairy cream with tropical fruits or, wondrously, with strawberries. But it can be used in anything milky or creamy, in ice creams, cakes, icings and biscuits. Wonderful stuff. It is sold in Thai shops, where you might also look for essence of *pandan,* q.v.

Kapi: see shrimp paste.

Katsuobushi: shaved flakes of dried bonito (tuna), a basic of Japanese cooking, used with kombu seaweed to flavour dashi, the basic stock. Although sold in flakes, these lose flavour very quickly: keep them well sealed and buy only as much as you expect to use quickly. Can be tear jerkingly expensive.

Katsuo dashi: liquid bonito extract – a simpler way to make dashi, used by itself or with kombu dashi, which is liquid kelp extract.

Lavender: I used to use lavender quite as much as rosemary, but now use both much less and turn to lavender more easily than rosemary; lavender has an extra, musky perfume that is quite addictive. The spikes and leaves can replace rosemary in almost any recipe, especially with fish and veal. Lavender and carrot soup is very special, and you can use the flowers or the leaves. Lightly, lightly is the rule and perhaps one of the best ways to use lavender is to incorporate it in your favourite sweet herb mix; it comes as a surprise to many, including Provençals, to find it included in *herbes de Provençe*. Some of those most surprised are suppliers of traditional mixtures. They say the lavender has been added to disguise the poor quality of the other ingredients and I still don't know which side to take. But the answer could be geographical.

Before you dash outside to gather lavender blooms, beware. The only lavenders you should use in kitchens are English lavenders: rather than confuse you with Latin names, English lavenders do not have that butterfly thing on top – those are French lavenders and not suitable for the kitchen, as they are far too bitter.

In fact it's not the lavender you should be eating anyway, but the lavender oil. I've now visited countless lavender farms with cafes, and in every one was surrounded by people guzzling lavender scones. To me they were inedible, for lavender flowers had been mixed in, so every few bites your tongue was nastily assailed by a bomb of bitterness. Properly to use lavender in cooking you should macerate the flowers in warm water or milk and then strain them out, or you should store the flowers in caster sugar, allowing it to absorb the essential oil. You can do the same with tea as long as the tea leaves are smaller than the lavender, so you can strain them out.

Otherwise you gently simmer masses of lavender flowers in water until you have a rather concentrated lavender essence. Don't use this for cooking, but dilute it and use it to spray your linen when ironing.

Looking for decent English lavender for culinary purposes is great fun for only very few varieties are powerful enough: the dusky-dark darling Hidcote is very good, but best of all is a very old variety, 'Dilly-dilly', yes, and I thought the song was just a nonsense, too.

Laksa: in the past decade this has been taken up and pushed to stellar heights by lovers of Asian and Chinese fast foods in Australasia, in Sydney particularly. Laksa is a spicy, hot nourishing main course soup from Singapore, packed with any of a hundred ingredients and noodles and with a sauce that is thickish rather than thin. A runny curry with stuff in it, seems the best of the many identifications I have heard. Sauce and spice mixtures designed for laksa are appearing on the market with great speed.

Limes, dried: a basic of Iranian food, cooked in meat dishes to give another experience on the wide spectrum of the world of citrus. The flavour is like lime, higher, thinner and sharper lime, with a fragile woody note, and they blossom into richer flavours once in the same saucepan as anything buttery or sweet. I've used them with all manner of vegetables; most notably a couple of dried limes cooked with pumpkin, apple and potato made a very superior soup indeed.

Maidenhair: See *Capillaire.*

Mahlab: these are cherry-stone kernels and can be bitter or sweet. Available more commonly in Greek stores and probably Turkish and Middle Eastern ones, too, they give a great density of almond/cherry flavour, and are a basic of Turkish Delight. Russians use *mahlab* when making cherry kissel, and the Greeks use it to flavour their large Easter loaves – *Tsourekia.*

Mali: See Jasmine Essence.

Marigold: not commonly used now, but the dried petals are recommended as an interesting alternative to saffron for colouring stews and casseroles, soups, breads and buns. The slight flavour can be rather exciting with poultry dishes and the fresh petals make an excellent addition to mixed salads.

Marigold flowers should be dried fast rather than slow – do it in a low to middling oven. To use them either grind the dried petals and use the powder, or brew a few petals in hot milk or water and use that.

If you are a butter or cheese maker, marigold was the original colouring before annatto began to be imported. It can still add life to cream or cottage cheeses.

Mastic gum/gum mastic: a gum, and so mastic has all the resinous overtones you would expect from the natural gum of a tree; the precise tree is the lentisk, a type of Pistacia. The flavour is fascinating when used in moderation, but is bitter and unpleasantly haunting when over used – a little is amazing in rice pudding and it is also good in cakes and sweet breads. Mastic marries very well with rose water or orange flower water, and so with all their sweet-spiced friends, when it adds a hint of resinous mystery. No it doesn't, said one friend: 'it adds a taste of frankincense and myrrh'. That's not unlikely as they are both gums too; perhaps I used too much?

Although related to the flavours of ouzo and retsina wine, mastic is a different substance from the ones used in those. The Greek island of Chios makes a rather special liqueur called *mastica*, flavoured with the gum from their variety of lentisk, unique to the island; the Turks use mastic to flavour their fire water – *raki.*

If Greeks come bearing gifts of gum mastic, always accept because it can be hard to find. If you find the Greek has delicious breath, he or she may well have been using mastic as chewing gum.

Mirin: a sweetened Japanese rice wine that is rarely used for drinking, and perhaps that's just as well. Instead it adds flavour, especially to marinades and grilled dishes and thus can be combined with soy and other sauces; Chinese rice wines, like Shao-Hsing are equivalents, but these are also used for drinking. There are processed and flavoured varieties, generically known as *ajimirin*

Monosodium glutamate (MSG): don't stop reading! MSG is potentially one of the most important and useful ingredients in your kitchen, particularly if you have a heart problem. Like salt, MSG does not alter the flavour of food but stimulates the flavour buds of your tongue so they can taste what is in the mouth. Unlike salt it has no flavour of its own. Those who say they can taste MSG are quite wrong, but they may well be able to detect the effects of over-use of the substance, for then the taste buds will be stimulated to such a frenzy of sensitivity they will taste aspects of food, even of their saliva, never encountered before; if salt stimulated such a reaction all you would taste is the salt, and probably be sick, too.

So, you can forget posturing about MSG allergy: funny how it seems to have been replaced by other 'allergies' today. Provided it is used properly MSG is perfectly safe, even for babies according to the United States FDA, one of the world's toughest food safety agencies. There will be a few who have unfortunate reactions but this is particularly rare and orange juice is more likely to be the culprit. The problem is that we in the West misuse it.

A large amount of MSG on an empty stomach upsets in some way almost 50 per cent of the world population, including the Chinese. When we order Chinese soup as a first course we put ourselves right in line for a problem, for these are likely to have the highest amount of MSG on the menu, to make weak stock taste stronger. Yet, eat the soup in the middle of the meal, or sip it during the meal and those who might well have had some reaction will have none. That's how the Chinese eat their soups, slowly and throughout a meal, rather than first and into an empty stomach. If they ate their soups like this, at least half of them would have problems, too. Of course, bad chefs do over-use MSG, and that is to be deplored. But would you want to ban chips because sometimes they are served too soggy or oily and made you feel sick? Of course not, you would only eat them when they were cooked properly.

Of the many surprises about MSG, one of the biggest is that our own body manufactures glutamates, and it is contained naturally in many popular savoury foods, tomatoes and roasted meats in particular. Indeed it may be their very presence that makes them so enjoyable and differs us from animals. There is a serious school of thought positing that appreciation of the specific glutamate flavour of roasted meats was one of the first steps from ape to man.

The particular savour given by glutamates is called *jian* by the Chinese and this may be added to the five basic flavours of all cookery – sweet, sour, bitter, hot and salty. *Jiang* is a seventh, translated as fragrant or aromatic flavours, especially the effects of wine and spirits, garlic, spring onions and spices.

MSG is very widely used in processed foods as a flavour enhancer because of its ability to make the tongue taste more flavour when less is actually there.

One of its greatest contributions is to anyone with a lazy tongue or with heart problems. Each of us has a tongue that works at a different pace, hence it is arrogance of the highest plane to tell another how much or how little salt they should have on their food; it's an absolute that saltiness can only be subjective.

Those unfortunates with lazy taste buds require more salt to get flavour of any kind, and often end up using so much that salt is all they taste, but at least something is happening in their mouths. Take the salt away, perhaps on the recommendation of a doctor, and they get so little gratification from eating they are bound to slip from their diet. The secret is judicious amounts of MSG. It has far less sodium than salt and is, anyway, used in far smaller amounts; by helping the subject to mouth gratification they will be likely to stay on their diet.

A broad rule is to use a quarter to half the amount of MSG you would of salt: for those who merely want to cut down a little, a mixture of MSG and salt works wonders.

Even for those with no health problems, MSG can be a boon. If you have created something you know tastes terrific, but is fairly light on flavour, you don't add salt. Sprinkle in small amounts of MSG, and that will greatly enhance what you have created. But remember, that is only in your opinion. To some it will be over-flavoured, to others it will still require seasoning to make their tongue work. But at least the MSG will help prevent your food tasting only of salt.

Manufactured monosodium glutamate is made from dried fermented wheat gluten and/or soy bean protein often enriched with powdered dried shrimp or seaweed, and available named just as MSG or under a variety of brand names.

Nam pla: See Fish Sauce.

Orange flower water: a standby of my kitchen, as it was in every British kitchen until well into the 20th century. For some inexplicable reason, perhaps the increasing victory of mediocrity, perhaps the trauma of the First World War, both this and rose water suddenly fell from favour after a reign that lasted from the days of the Crusaders, who first brought them to Europe.

Distilled from the flowers of the Seville or bitter orange, the liquid can have a brilliantine scent, which can be off-putting and is a warning it should be used with discretion. Once it is sprinkled over food this scent softens and becomes as fragrant as moonlit nights in orange groves, and quite as sensual too.

Arabian and eastern Mediterranean kitchens use it lavishly on every conceivable type of meat dish, in breads, pastries, cakes – and you. In Morocco, for instance, it is frightfully good form for a host to have his guests sprinkled with orange flower water by servants after dinner. If it happens to you and you're also drinking good wine, quickly clap one hand over your glass.

Sometimes orange flower water is called orange blossom water and sometimes bitter orange water, but they are all the same. Equally you will find something called citrus flower water: this usually comes from somewhere Greek, where I suspect lemon blossoms are also included, rather heightening the brilliantine effect, but not badly. In Egypt or Morocco the water seems softer and richer and I recommend travellers get some, or ask friends to bring some back. Wherever you are, read the label and check – it can be made with an imitative chemical and this must not be encouraged.

Orange flower water combined with almonds, pistachios, rose water and honey is what gives such flavour to the range of Arabic pastries collectively known as baklava q.v. In eastern Mediterranean countries, it is diluted and served as 'white tea'. This is said to be a soporific, especially for young children.

Orange flower water is also good with anything creamy, from cream itself to such creaminess as rice puddings, panna cotta, egg custards, crème caramel and, yes crème brulee: indeed in the days before vanilla was common, my great great great great great great grandmother Mary Senhouse (Fletcher Christian's granny) wrote in the mss cookbook of Netherhall, such puddings weren't worth making if you did not have orange flower water. Interestingly she put caramel under the baked custard as well as on top of it.

Peaches or strawberries with orange flower water are extraordinary: the best way to enjoy this is to sprinkle the cut or sliced fruit with caster sugar and then to sprinkle on the orange flower water. Leave the combination at room temperature for a couple of hours or in a refrigerator overnight, turning from time time as the syrup develops. Adjust for sweetness or voluptuousness just before serving.

It will be more difficult to convert you to sprinkling orange flower water over lamb stews, over chickens and over roast kid, but once you've tried it… look for recipes that include this and just see how long you can resist running into the kitchen.

Once you have been hooked, move on to rose water: you are just as likely to make these discoveries in reverse; rose first. When you have both in your cupboard you are master/mistress of a thousand new flavours, all by varying the amount of one to the other. Other than with strawberries I can think of nowhere I don't mix rose and orange, to blend a different exotic flavour each time. Together or separate they offer the most effective way to stun or impress.

The only way to go wrong is to use too much orange flower water – but who is to say how much is too much? Pretend something excessive is your norm and others will follow. The entire fashion world relies on this principle; why shouldn't you?

Orgeat: rarely seen nowadays but once a standby at balls and for summer teas, this a base for cordials and syrups based on barley water flavoured further with almond milk and orange-flower water.

Palm sugar/jaggery: a wonderful rich-tasting sugar made by boiling down and slightly caramelising the natural sap of a number of palms, these days including coconut palms. When mixed with desiccated coconut and sweet spices, it makes a sensational filling for small thin crepes, the way they do in Sri Lanka, for 'small eats' served with tea in the afternoon.

The culinary point of palm sugar is its complexity. It gives special flavour wherever you might otherwise have chosen dark sugar or molasses, and it adds greater depth of flavour and gratification than the single dimension of white sugar: substitute palm sugar in anything from a poaching syrup to a chocolate sauce, in pumpkin pie or on grilled fruits, in whipped cream, custards – even your latte or cappuccino – and you are more than rewarded.

Left alone the sweet palm sap ferments to make an alcohol of such poisonous effect you need only one hangover to understand the appeal of temperance.

Palm sugar keeps forever, but is best sealed and refrigerated, for it can attract moisture, and then become a syrup and seep any and everywhere. Equally it can go absolutely steel-hard, in which case cover it with a damp tea towel and leave it overnight, or put the lump in a saucepan with a sprinkle of water and heat it gently, stirring in a little more water from time to time until you have a thick paste.

Pandan/pandanus: another heady, perfumed flavouring, which is as suggestive, seductive and outright sexy as its other name, screw pine. Look in Thai books for uses, or use sparingly in cream or whipped cream for luscious fruit desserts, for which it also makes an outstanding ice cream.

Pomegranate molasses: fresh pomegranate juice is a refreshing balance of sweet and acid, a natural sweet-sour sauce you would probably use much more if it did not stain so fearfully. Pomegranate molasses is simply the same juice boiled down so it is thicker, sweeter, more acidic and luscious. Strangely, the molasses don't like extended heat much, and go brown if baked or boiled. So, best to use it as a finishing sauce. Baked or grilled fish love the stuff and together make something seemingly exotic for little effort – a few olives, some buttered couscous and Abdul is your uncle. Chicken and pork are other great friends of pomegranate.

A good idea is to combine molasses and fresh pomegranate seeds for entrancing spectra of flavours, colour and texture. At the simplest, add both to a salad dressing. But don't forget sweet treats too. Pomegranate molasses are very good with hot apple pie, indeed with all baked pies or roasted fruits. And you can never go wrong with scattering pomegranate seeds over anything.

Pomegranate syrup, which you see less often, is the same thing but thicker and thus sweeter.

Red currants: the most classic of accompaniments to lamb and game birds, particularly used in sauces and gravies. Bar-le-Duc in France makes the most perfect of jellies and preserves, with pitted currants, but these once rare berries seem now so broadly available the huge price of these preserves is much less justified. Rather than bothering to make a jelly, just lay a perfect bunch on each plate. There is much enjoyment to be had from each explosion as you crush them one by one in your mouth. For times when dinner parties lag, you might ask if anyone knows the answer to 'Can anyone remember the funny word used for taking red currants off the bunch by running the stalk between fork tines?' You should pretend not to remember either, until the last possible second; it's strig.

Rose water/eau de rose: this brings the entrancing glory of the rose to your table. Classically distilled from the most fragrant red Damask roses, it was hardly possible to cook throughout the Middle East and Europe right up to the death of Queen Victoria unless you used this. Now almost forgotten in Europe, it is still vital in the Arab world, sprinkled into everything and over you.

Do, I beg you, go out and get a bottle and start experimenting. It is wonderful with milk-poached pudding grains, especially barley and rice, goes surprisingly well with poultry, and is amazing with things chocolate and fruity. If you bake a chocolate cake with several rose geranium leaves underneath it, and then mix a chocolate icing with plenty of rose water you've made something out of this world. Or flavour a particularly rich chocolate soufflé with rose water, serve it while very runny in the middle, after only 20 minutes baking, and with a little hot soft fruit purée – loganberries would be very good. Soak dried fruit overnight and then serve them with chopped pistachios and lavish sprinklings of rose water and orange flower water – this is almost embarrassingly sensual, regardless it seems if served hot or cold, in the morning, afternoon or evening.

Rose water goes very well with cream cheese or cream and, as with orange flower water you can make much of ordinary puddings by using simple combinations. I once made a wedding cake out of profiteroles stuffed alternatively with orange and rose-flavoured creams, and held together with the lightest caramel. Pouring cream was chilled and also flavoured with rose water and the whole concoction was finished with a scattering of rose petals. The scents were bewitching and the flavours tantalizingly difficult to identify.

Rose water-flavoured cream or syrup goes especially well with raspberries and fresh peaches.

Florentine curd pudding is an old English curd cheese, egg and spinach custard tart with the addition of currants, spice and rose water and a 'talking point' end to a meal – well, when did you ever have rose-flavoured spinach for pudding?

Whenever using roses for culinary purposes you first cut off the lower, white part of the petal, which would be bitter. Red damask roses were traditionally best but there are now so many strong-scented varieties that rules are pointless. If it smells, eat it. A few rose petals in a salad look and taste good, rose jam is great with a traditional cream tea, and pink petals are wonderful on summer pudding.

Another way to enjoy the flavour of roses is with Rose Pouchong tea q.v., and in authentic Turkish Delight; rose-flavoured vinegar is excellent too.

After all that I suppose I should tell you what the stuff tastes like. It tastes like it smells, very rosy but surprisingly spicy and slightly smoky. There is no rule about how much you use, sometimes I like to use very little and other times find I can get away with making the flavour very strong indeed – for instance to flavour a syrup for sliced oranges or with raspberries. In fact, until you have eaten raspberries with rose water you have never tasted their full prospect: it is almost the ultimate cookery goal, that of making one plus one equal four or more yet still remain true to themselves.

I repeat, get out and buy some, and give yourself the pleasure not only of recreating the food of our forefathers, but also of inventing new ideas with the broader range of ingredients at our disposal today

Rowan: the bitter, bright, scarlet-orange berries of the rowan or mountain ash are associated with the countryside but like elderflowers and elder berries also grow smack in the middle of villages, towns and cities. Gather them up and follow the usual recipes for making jellies and your reward is a gorgeously red jelly that retains acidity, has a hint of bitterness and a light, distinctive flavour. This was once a favourite with lamb but I like it with almost any roasted meat or bird – but perhaps that's because I so enjoy telling people what it is and that I made it myself after foraging fearlessly in Chelsea, and in Notting Hill Gate.

Salt: neither herb nor spice and if used properly it shouldn't be tasted, so it's not really a flavouring. Yet salt, the vernacular for sodium chloride, is what encourages us to taste at all. It's also an essential part of our body chemistry but its role can be misunderstood, and so may be used to our detriment.

Salt can be addictive, at least the flavour can be, and too high an intake is thought to be dangerous to the heart. To understand this, you have to know how it works.

Salt does not alter or improve the flavour of food one iota, other than to add its own or, in the case of salt-preserving, to hinder or help the development of flavour-giving bacteria.

What salt does is to stimulate the taste buds of the tongue to discern what flavour is inherently present, and the more salt present, the greater the stimulus and the greater the flavour reward. But – the more salt you use, the more you taste the flavour of the salt rather than of the food.

It does not necessarily follow that someone who uses more salt than you has a saltier flavour in his mouth; they may have slow or dull taste buds and thus need a higher degree of stimulation to experience the *same* taste as you.

If there is but one truism in the food world it is that you cannot, *absolutely* cannot, tell someone else how much salt they need.

Chefs who refuse still to put salt on tables are in the wrong business, are cooking for their palates, rather than the palates of the bums on seats that pay for him or her to prance about. You cannot tell someone else how much salt they need to experience the same flavours you do.

The risk of a high salt intake because you have slow taste buds, and that these often need massive stimulation before they taste anything, is that eventually the salt taste becomes paramount, and that is bad for you and boring for the cook. Like sugar, salt is present naturally in a great deal of the food we eat, especially that which is processed, and it is worth taking a really hard look at the amount added and the amount really needed. Are you really tasting the food or are you tasting salt?

A proven way to reduce at least some salt intake is only to microwave vegetables, covered but ideally with no added water. This way the natural salts and flavourings can't be leached out, but are actually concentrated and many people find this increased harvest of flavour needs less or no salt. Much better nutrition than leaving all the goodness in the water you've used for boiling or steaming, which unless done the oriental way on plates and in bamboo is no better nutritionally than boiling.

There is a difference between the many salts you can buy, a matter of how they are made, whence they come, and with what traces of other chemicals each is mixed. After water, salt is possibly the most currently fashionable accessory: there are those who carry a personal favourite even to restaurants.

It is true a pink salt from an Hawaiian island or from South Australia's Murray river, a blinding but yielding *fleur du sel* from France and sun-dried one from the Dalmatian coast can all taste different, but the differences are all additives, some naturally there, some not. What's more, although detectable if you dab some on your tongue the likelihood of detecting differences when salt is diluted by cooking water or chewed in with food are about the same as you becoming Pope tomorrow.

The only possible advantage there might be in taking your own salt to a restaurant is to be sprinkling salt flakes or chunky salt grains, for those will have a different textural effect in your mouth. You usually eat far more salt than is good for if you do this.

So, save your money. Use ordinary tubs of kitchen salt for salting food when it is cooking and save your more expensive Maldon salt for the table: and if you live in a country like NZ where iodine is rare in the native soils, meaning goitre can be a real health threat, use only iodised salt in the cooking water: nothing will taste different but the traces will do you a whole lot of good.

Play with salt colours and textures when the time comes to salt food at table. But as we should all be eating less of it, do you need to do this at all? Here are some of your choices:

Rock salt: this is mined in ready-formed crystals, and is the deposit of a long-gone dried sea or other waterway. It is invariably mixed with a great number of other tastes, some of which you may not like, so it is an idea to taste rock salt before you buy. It can be even better than the more common...

Sea salt: evaporated from the sea and thus bound to include a number of other trace elements and chemicals. Yet it is perfectly safe and free from anything nasty.

The broad spectrum of ingredients that complement the sodium chloride is what recommends sea salt to the health experts. I simply prefer its flavour. It is not that simple, of course. Slaves to salt go to extraordinary lengths to find *fleur de sel*, the first and finest flakes, which have been whipped by the wind onto the shore or the edge of the saltpans. They say different weather conditions, tides and temperatures will all produce different flavours and so they might on your tongue, but there is rarely enough concentration to taste these once mixed with food.

Bay salt/kosher salt: is a cruder form of sea salt, often rather greyish, as it is less likely to have been purified in any way. It will be flavourful and is commonly the salt used for preserving and brining. If you wish to dry-salt fish or meat, the large crystals of this type of salt gives better results.

Common or kitchen salt: this is made by extracting salt from the earth by dissolving it in water, pumping this brine out, and evaporating the liquid.

There are various forms, and this is what used to be made into solid blocks. Vacuum salt, that is salt that has been extracted and purified in a vacuum, is 99.9 per cent sodium chloride, but this is usually then turned into

Iodised salt: salt to which iodine salts have been added as a necessary dietary supplement in some countries as defence against goitre. It has a definite taste of its own, but this disappears when diluted by cooking.

Flavoured salts: sometimes called seasoned salts, these are traditional for flavouring meats but were usually made at home with preferred mixtures of cloves and nutmeg, peppers, and some of the sharper, sweeter herbs. Garlic salt is increasingly popular but beware when you buy it – check the label and you might find it also contains monosodium glutamate and other ingredients. Fresh garlic tastes better.

Celery salt is beloved of vegetarians and can be very delicious if used with infinite restraint. Quite simply, it is salt pounded with celery seed. Hickory-flavoured salt is a favourite in the United States. You can try pounding any fresh or dried herb with salt, and they keep for a long time. Kelp salt, mixed with seaweed is a new New Zealand product, and so is Karengo salt, this time mixed with seaweed that's the same as Welsh laver bread and Japanese nori.

Smoked salt: I first talked about this 20 or more years ago and now it is suddenly appearing all around the world. I'm not sure if you can tell the difference between apple wood-smoked salt or manuka-smoked salt because it will inevitably be so diluted by whatever you are eating, but it's a great marketing ploy. Whatever the wood the salt needs to be highly smoked or it is pointless.

Although a fine preservative, salt behaves rather strangely when deep frozen. Whereas salted butter keeps far longer than unsalted butter in a refrigerator, frozen salted butter lasts safely only a month, and unsalted butter can be stored three times as long. The salt content is why dishes containing bacon cannot be frozen for very long periods. Strange, isn't it.

Table salt: the purity is interfered with by the addition of starch or other chemicals to promote free running. The combination of such essential purity and bland additives makes its flavour pretty boring but this is not bad thing if it makes other ingredients sparkle more.

Sansho: the most common Japanese condiment, used rather the way we use pepper, which they don't use, and related to the Szechuan peppercorn. It is only available ground, and only used by the Japanese.

Sapa: See *vin cotto*

Sarsaparilla: the root of a plant indigenous to tropical America from Mexico to Peru, sarsaparilla is used to flavour a drink with so-called tonic properties. Certainly sarsaparilla tastes as though it should be good for you, rather like combined winter green and chewing gum if early teenage memories serve me well. Then it enjoyed a brief vogue as a soft drink variety, but the emergence of Elvis Presley shortly afterwards quickly returned us to Coca-Cola, which is flavoured by berries from the cola plant and once also included extracts from the coca plant, source of cocaine; its instant success was hardly surprising. If you want to try sarsaparilla, look in Jamaican communities. The best root comes from there and they still drink it as though it were life's blood.

Like sassafras q.v., sarsaparilla is one of several root beers that were once all you could buy at Temperance bars. They have recently been rediscovered, together with dandelion and burdock, and are certainly increasingly available all over Britain. Traditional pie and mash shops in London's East End often sell sarsaparilla to drink with their wares.

Shao-hsing wine: a yellow wine made from rice that tastes like minor sherry and is always drunk slightly warm, even when of the highest possible quality. It is usually barely drinkable and so the same rule applies as with all wine: cook only with something you would drink with pleasure, but not so good its finesse will be ruined by heat. All grades are used extensively in Chinese cookery, sometimes first to intoxicate live prawns – that really is getting the flavour through the flesh. A specially good use is as a final sprinkle on to Chinese greens:

knowledgeable western chefs will sprinkle a sweet wine into many fish sauces and dishes – dry white wine is actually the last thing fish needs.

Drunken Chicken is one of the best summer dishes of all: poach or microwave at medium heat, skinned chicken breasts. Let them cool a little and then tear lengthwise into generous strips, about the width of a little finger. While still warm, cover with a decent (it is possible) Shao-hsing wine and chill very well for at least 12 hours and then serve very cold. Forbid it to children, teenagers and the very old, for nothing has diminished the alcohol content.

Shrimp, dried: the great divider, and one of the principal flavouring agents of south-east Asia. Like all dried fish they have a penetrating cheesy smell that nauseates many, although in mitigation they never taste as bad as they smell. Generally used as a base flavouring, they must be soaked in water for 30 minutes before using, but may also be soaked overnight; sherry or rice wine makes them less noxious. Dried shrimps are often pounded and are the basis for shrimp paste/kapi, the noisome but necessary flavouring paste of Thai cookery.

Shrimp paste: kapi is the Thai version of an extraordinary ingredient endemic to south-east Asian cookery. Invasive and nauseating to many, this paste of fermented and dried shrimps nevertheless becomes addictive very quickly. The paler the colour, the higher the quality and the more freshly it is likely to have been made. some versions can be very purple when just made, because of the dye in the black eyes of a particular variety of shrimp used.

Sometimes shrimp paste needs to be roasted before use, and this should always been done in a wrapping of banana leaf or aluminium foil. Put the air extractor onto maximum and toast under a slow grill until inspection shows it is evenly dark in colour. Use oven gloves or tongs if you don't have the asbestos fingers of a seasoned cook.

Stevia: a native South American, stevia is related to asters and chrysanthemums and yet is a powerful natural sweetener. In its natural state stevia is between four and eight times sweeter than sugar by volume; that is a teaspoon of stevia will give the sweetness of four to eight teaspoons of sugar – and with no calories. You can use the dried leaves or, in some countries, buy a refined syrup or white powder. There's a hint of bitterness if you use the dried leaves, but that has been excised in the syrup and white powder.

Many western countries are still going through processes to approve its use commercially, but the plant can be bought easily. In Japan even such mega companies as Coca-Cola and Sunkist use stevia widely. It could be the next next big thing.

Tabasco: this is what I tend to use when I want to add heat to food– it's simpler, cheaper and so very much more controllable than chillies. More important to the generous cook, who realizes through gritted teeth some guests like more heat than others, it is the perfect way to cook richly flavoured food without heat, but to allow others to add it to their plate. Better look the other way while one person massacres your food, than to be facing a table full of guests pretending they are not in pain.

If ever you are close to New Orleans, it's worth adding in a visit to McIlhenny's factory on Avery Island. They use a specific Tabasco pepper, store them for some years in concentrated distilled vinegar to develop flavour, have alligators on the front lawn and a super Tabasco shop selling excellent cookery books, kitchen implements for Mexican cooking, and a frightfully smart range of specially designed Tabasco ties.

Once you have Tabasco in the kitchen you can add a little heat to almost anything, as the idea appeals. To cheese scones, for instance, to a chocolate cake or chocolate icing, to brighten up a chili to which you have added too much cocoa or chocolate, into poached, stewed or grilled stone fruit, Moroccan tagines, stir-fries, chocolate truffles, whatever.

The best thing I ever did was to add Tabasco to a punchy Mocha-Rocky-Road ice cream. You didn't know it was there until the ice cream had slid down your throat, and then a pleasant minor warmth of Tabasco seemed to clear the palate for the next spoonful.

There is now green Tabasco, too, made from the much milder jalapeno pepper, plus a Habanero Tabasco that is hotter, very much so! and since 2003 a Chipotle Tabasco, a medium heat with the definite flavour of smoked jalapenos, great for adding mystic flavour to barbecue marinades, even to salad dressings. If you look, you should also find hot and mild pepper jellies marketed by this iconic brand.

Tamarind: essentially an Asian and oriental way to add the acidity for which we would perhaps use lemon juice. Dried tamarind should be soaked in very hot water and then strained, and only the liquid is used. You can reduce it over heat if this amount would disturb the texture of the dish. A walnut-sized lump in 300ml/$\frac{1}{2}$ pt of hot water for 20 minutes is about right. Excellent in all curries, otherwise throw in a halved or quartered whole lemon or lime. Well worth experimenting with, say, to flavour a sauce for fish rather than using lemon, to sharpen a tomato sauce for pasta, in a vegetable soup or as part of an oriental-style salad dressing, with soy sauce and chopped toasted cashew nuts, yes, and a few chives if you must.

Tangerine peel: a common but sometimes very expensive Chinese flavouring ingredient; its expense means it is often never used in enough quantity to taste, but only as a menu come-on. Although you can buy it, you may as well make your own, by drying in a slow oven or by following the instructions that came with your microwave. The slightly bitter pith is usually scraped off first: you can use roughly cut pieces but fine slivers are better.

Actually I use any orange-related citrus. Definitely go for what we call a mandarin, which has the added appeal of being almost pithless beneath the skin. The thicker rind of sharper Seville or bitter oranges give a better ultimate result than, say, sweet navel types, but even these make a good addition to your mix anyway. I de-pith, finely slice and dry citrus peel whenever I think of it, which is more often if I am eating really aromatic citrus, like minneolas, or using limes, another good addition.

Grapefruit could be used but should be stored separately, for some modern drugs affect their ingesters badly if grapefruit or its juice is eaten.

Keep the dry peel in glass in the dark. It will slowly turn to black, but this is an advantage, as provided it is kept dry, it will improve in flavour for several years, at least.

The dried and aged peel is commonly used as flavouring but discarded before serving but I have never had complaints when I have left it in. It is a particularly good ingredient if you are making a sauce tending to fattiness or sweetness, say an oxtail stew or boiled tongue. Provençals use fresh orange peel in most of their stews, so I add the dried version to all stewed or braised or boiled meat dishes, usually as background fascinator rather than a forward flavour: it is quite proper for orange peel to be found in a true bouillabaisse, too.

If dried peel is chopped finely it makes a fragrant final addition to a stir-fry, especially of vegetables. If you plan this, soften the chopped peel in a rice wine or sherry first. Can also be used to flavour sugar.

Iranian shops are a trusty ethnic destination to buy ready-dried orange peel, for Iran uses it a lot – while you are there pick up an Iranian cookbook; be prepared to faint with pleasure.

Tonka beans/Tonquin beans: a flavour that hovers on the edge of being 'discovered' every few years. The dried bean looks like a small leathery thumb, and has a heavy, sensuous aroma of woodruff, that's also so like vanilla it has long been used to extend vanilla or as a substitute, even in tobacco. The problem is that coumarin, the major flavouring ingredient, is suspected of being poisonous and carcinogenic: the solution is it can be used in very small quantities. In case you live somewhere tropical and have a tree in the jungle over the back fence, coumarin is extracted by soaking the beans in rum for 24 hours or so. L'Artisan du Chocolat in London is currently considering introducing tonka bean into its edgy flavour spectrum: Pierre Marcolini includes it already, of course.

Vanilla: this ultimate of sensuality is the flavour of the sun-cured seed pod of a climbing orchid native to Mexico but now grown throughout tropical areas, including India, Indonesia, Tahiti and Madagascar.

So widely used is it these days, vanilla is barely regarded as a flavour; how often do people say 'plain' when they mean vanilla custard or ice cream? Vanilla's basic uses are to flavour milk, cream, sauces or sugar syrups for hot and cold fruit or desserts, but it is increasingly used successfully in savoury dishes, particularly with fish and seafood, where its unique rich but discreet sweetness is a generally unsuspected advantage. Even *Larousse Gastronomique* recommends vanilla as an ingredient in fish soups.

Otherwise vanilla has the most serene of unshakeable relationships with chocolate, originally from the same broad geographical area.

Vanilla is one of the most labour-intensive of food products. Even in its native Mexico, vanilla is always pollinated by hand and must be picked by hand. In an ideal year the long green seed pods are left on the vine until they have turned golden, a technique that enhances flavour. Then they are sun-dried over a number of months, first to prevent them sprouting and then to encourage the extraordinary transition from green bean to dark leathery repositories of entrancing perfume and taste, each only about 20% of their original size. There is nothing in its green seed pod to give any clue to its ultimate flavour. Do you like me ever wonder who was the first ancient Mexican to link the scent of a sun-dried vanilla pod to culinary use, and then to chocolate? There must have been someone who was first.

Vanilla beans develop characteristics according to where they grow and to how carefully they are processed.

From Mexico you should expect a full rounded vanilla flavour with hints of coffee and cinnamon and it is specially suited to calming the acidity of tomato in any sort of sauce, including chilis. The US company Nielsen-Massey buys a big portion of the limited Mexican crop and so is the most reliable source if you want these nuances.

The next best and better-known vanilla is Bourbon vanilla from Madagascar (where most of the organic vanilla available comes from), so-called because French interests introduced it into the area, first to what we now know Réunion and the Comoros Islands but then called the Bourbon Islands: this is easier to source too, as Madagascar grows around 60% of the world's supply, even though still recovering from devastating cyclone destruction of a third of its vines in 2000. Bourbon vanilla has lots of perfumed body without the spicy notes of Mexican, and is preferred by many pâtissiers, not least because the supply is usually more reliable but also because it seems to work best with ice cream and creams and such. Pieces of Madagascan vanilla are best for pot-pourri and other room fragrancers.

Indonesian vanilla is another spicy one, and a blend of Madagascan Bourbon and Indonesian vanilla is recommended for baking: a good tip is always to cream the vanilla extract into the butter or other fat, as the globules protect the vanilla and give a better, bigger ultimate flavour.

Tahitian vanilla is now believed to have evolved into a distinct variety, no longer *vanilla planifolia* but *vanilla tahitensis*. It has fatter, sweeter pods and is strongly perfumed and fruity with less natural vanillin but more heliotropin, hence its common comparison with cherry – heliotrope plants are known as the cherry pie plant, because its pretty flowers can smell just like that. Knowing this it will be no surprise Tahitian vanilla is particularly good at supporting other fruit flavours, including in sauces and frozen desserts. Tahitian vanilla is also the one largely targeted by the fragrance industry.

When I wore vanilla-based after-shave to visit an elderly relation stricken with a brain tumour and otherwise confused by the world, I barely walked into the room before she said: we must be having ice cream for lunch. A powerful reminder of the emotive directness of smell, which goes directly to the most primitive part of our brains, even though we are no longer hunters and gatherers.

Vanilla beans are graded according to size and appearance, and smooth ribbed appearances and good lengths usually get a higher price. Other vanilla products include a paste just of vanilla seeds, and vanilla powder, both specially useful to the catering trade.

Some sources are better than others in producing a thin gloss of tiny white crystals on the beans called *givre*, which is French for hoar frost, and which is a sign of elevated quality.

If stored in a closed (not airtight) jar, vanilla beans improve with keeping, and if they dry out are easily plumped by soaking, even in water. A more classic ploy is to make your beans pay for their keep by flavouring something else. So store them with caster sugar to make vanilla sugar: as you use it, put more sugar in, shake it all about and soon it will be back to strength. Use the flavoured sugar wherever you want a sweet vanilla flavour, to sprinkle on fairy cakes, to bake cakes especially cheesecakes, in cocktails, on poached or grilled fruit and about one thousand other things. You shouldn't eat the bean itself, so I don't agree with those who suggest you grind it to mix with sugar. But the sticky seeds scraped into custards, creams and sauces, are the greatest way I know to advertise silently your pleasure in doing things the proper way.

Vanilla sugar is very good in coffee and surprisingly so in tea: in fact vanilla tea is outstandingly good, luxurious and calming in flavour, but only if it is real tea with pieces of vanilla bean chopped up in it rather than added 'flavouring'. Fauchon Paris makes a very superior version, and when you are in Mauritius you can buy packets only marginally less good, but very much cheaper, all over the place. A strong brew of genuine vanilla tea is the most fascinating flavour for ice cream: see page 543 for a recipe.

For an unsweetened vanilla flavouring, make your own vanilla extract by pushing beans into a screw-top jar and topping that up with a spirit. I usually use black rum, which adds its distinctive notes, but vodka, white rum, brandy or flavourless spirit all do and the concoction goes on with full virtue for many years. I still use beans I bought in Mauritius 12 years ago, although their long life might have something to do with the cognac in which they are stored and because the smell is so wonderful I rarely use the beans or the extract.

For maximum Christmas cheer, I make another special brew in cheap brandy or dark rum and use this to make brandy or rum butter (hard sauce) for Christmas mince pies and for the custard that more properly accompanies the pudding.

The vanilla beans flavouring sugar or alcohol can be used for flavouring other food the usual ways, either in pieces, or a big piece or, as chefs love to do, by scraping out the inner seeds and using those. If you use a piece or pieces to flavour milk or to make a syrup, say for iced teas in summer, don't throw it away, rinse and dry it and it will be good for use a dozen or more times.

There are many substitutes for vanilla so when you buy liquid vanilla flavouring, ensure it says vanilla extract or pure vanilla extract – vanilla *essence* is artificial. Vanilla extract should be kept cool and dark. Vanillin is a white powder used to give a vanilla flavour to vanilla essence and thus to over 90% of foods sold as tasting of vanilla. It has the same chemical formula of the ingredient that makes vanilla beans smell, but it is only half the story, for real vanilla comes with countless other trace fragrances and flavours. If it means anything to you vanillin is C811803.

Verjuice: this is a tough one to talk about, because verjuice is made by a number of people in Australia and New Zealand I admire enormously. But is it the real thing, does it taste like it did in the Middle Ages, and can you use it the same way?

Essentially verjuice (green juice, *vert jus*, verjus) is an acidifier, an alternative to lemon juice or vinegar or perhaps tamarind. You know how sharp these can be, and verjuice was considered an alternative.

In Britain, verjuice was made from the juice of unripe grapes or from crab apples. In the bad old days there were many years in Britain when an entire vintage was made into verjuice because the grapes did not ripen. You have to ask yourself why Britain stopped using verjuice, because the weather hasn't changed that much. I reckon the simple answer is the distinct down turn in grape growing in Britain for so many centuries, first after the Romans left and then after the Dissolution of the Monasteries by Henry VIII. These meant a reliance on vinegars and imported lemons because they were easier to source. Verjuice was, after all, a default crop, made only when grapes never ripened. It was never made when the grapes ripened enough to make more useful and more profitable wine: verjuice was not something you planted vines to make. It seems to me that as a default product it shouldn't cost much either.

It is said verjuice was used in Europe only in the Middle Ages, which seems odd to me considering the extensive vineyards the Romans planted. But verjuice could well have been yet another idea brought back from the eastern Mediterranean with Crusaders between the 11th and 13th century. Nevertheless, once it was common, and then it wasn't for a very long time, and now it is being made again, in Australasia, in Britain, in Spain and in the USA, and highly laudable that is.

The trouble is verjuice made from today's grapes can never be the same as it was over half a millennium ago, because grapes are very different. Grapes have been bred to behave in all sorts of once-*verboten* climates – in Britain again, for a start. They are not only better-behaved grapes but have been bred to be very much better flavoured, too. At the point they are still green but plumped and ready to ripen (you wouldn't get enough juice if you harvested earlier) the juice is sharpish, but nothing like the rude, unruly flavours of old grapes; certainly you can't compare this unripe juice to vinegar, for it is greenish, rather than outright acidic, mellow rather than not.

At first, all the modern verjuices I tasted were from Australia and New Zealand where grapes grow like mad and have been bred to behave. These modern verjuices are honeyed and velvety, delicious enough to drink, but they are in no way an ingredient you could use by the tablespoonful as an acidifier, for they don't have the spine. This is easily seen with a check of recipes in which modern verjuice is used. Invariably, large amounts are used as a cooking medium, and then lemon juice is added and sometimes sugar too. So, the very virtue of verjuice is negated; adding lemon juice not only defeats the acidity of the verjuice, but disguises its other appeal, its honey-sweet flavour. You don't add lemon juice to beef up the acidity in vinegar. And then what is left of the subtle honey flavour is sweetened; all very curious ways to treat something supposed to be and to work like vinegar. And of course, it gets very expensive to use verjuice in great quantities. Spending money on an acidifier with a honey flavour, neither of which you can identify in the final dish, seems to be cooking for castles in the air.

Frankly you get the same effects by using less wine, and wine doesn't mind being acidified or sweetened because you have chosen it for its flavour not its background acidity. For small amounts of acidity with big flavour I think nothing is better than excellent sherry vinegar; indeed it is very instructive to sip a teaspoonful of verjuice and of sherry vinegar for the sake of comparison.

Perhaps modern verjuice is just too aristocratic to be used the same way as the original? In my experience it must be used only with very few other ingredients or it is drowned before its first breath out of the bottle. But it's not useless, indeed it is just terrific for poaching fruit, when it needs no additions to its own honeyed, lightly acidic finish, and gives a flavour wine could not. If you want a more apparent sweetness, add a vanilla bean to the verjuice, otherwise don't reduce its acidity with sugar but serve additional sweetness separately, as cream or ice cream. As a poaching medium for apples, pears, nectarines and peaches modern verjuice works superbly, maintaining its individuality even while combining with the fruit flavour: you can also reduce verjuice over heat until quite syrupy and then pour this over grilled fruit, or mix it into whipped cream. It is outstanding as a poaching medium for fish, which always likes both acidity and sweetness. But note that in all these cases modern verjuice has been used in quantity and with nothing else: true verjuice was used in small quantities to help balance sloppy flavours, just as vinegar does.

The best way to use modern verjuice economically is as a de-glazer, in salad dressings with an aromatic nut oil and little or no vinegar, or simply to splash on to grilled fish or chicken.

And then I tried a modern British verjuice, made by the Carr-Taylors from grapes that had been planted in hope, but which simply couldn't cope with the British weather, and never reliably ripened. One of the varieties was a chardonnay, a very cheeky choice never really expected to triumph.

By *default* the Carr-Taylors investigated verjuice and after experimenting made theirs with some alcoholic content: this helps preserve the product, of course, and also makes it easier to store.

Like me, David Carr-Taylor doesn't believe verjuice was first used in Britain during the Middle Ages. We agree it is something the Romans would also have known and used: they simply weren't the sort to stamp their sandals when grapes wouldn't ripen and to then leave green crops on the vine. His verjuice is lighter and sharper than the colonial ones, and with the alcoholic content tastes a little like a diluted sherry or somewhat oxidized light wine. It's called a *vert-jus* vinegar and might well be useable the way I think verjuice should, but the modern chardonnay grape still makes it better mannered than I expect. There was one more type I needed to try, I needed to buy verjuice from countries that never stopped making it. Iranian shops usually have it, sometimes calling it just grape juice, and as they also sell the juice of unripened grapes you must be careful.

To be certain you are getting the real thing look for a label I treasure, found in an Iranian shop at the Olympia end of High Street Kensington. 'Unripped grape juice' it says, and explains on the little back label by calling it 'sour grape juice'. It doesn't rip your tongue apart with acidity, but it has a damn good go at it, and has an equally unrefined flavour, leaving a very long-lasting, cleansed, acidic feel throughout the mouth and very little fruity or honey taste; you can certainly taste its relationship with vinegar. It is also cloudy, and the suspended matter gives the same added-flavour differences you find between filtered coffee and plunger coffee see pages x x

Filtered coffee is refined coffee, dumbed down because the paper filter absorbs its aromatic oils giving a lighter, less-challenging flavour: plunger coffee has a much greater body and presence in the mouth both because it keeps all the oils and because it's a suspension of fine solid particles, only some of which settle as sediment, all of which are adding thousands of micro-flavours. Australasian and UK verjuice is filtered: the old styles I found are not.

For those of you finding other verjuice made in the USA, Spain and elsewhere, I think you have two judging criteria. One, does it taste good, and if it does you should welcome it: two, decide if it is almost as sharp as vinegar or is it mellow, and then to use it accordingly. Perhaps these newer verjuices should be qualified, sold as 'Mellow Verjuice'. There'd be no argument with that and chefs might then respect the flavour in the bottle, and put the lemon and sugar back where they came from. Sorry friends, but one taste of an old-style verjuice, and you'd know at once; these new verjuices are just too well bred to do most of the jobs for which they are touted. They do others excellently.

Vin cotto/mosto cotto/sapa: must or grape juice that has not fermented, but has been cooked. In the southern Italian province of Lecce, the grapes chosen are the tasty Negro Amaro and Malavasia Nera. First left to wither on the vines for about a month so a degree of raisin flavour develops, they are then pressed. Boiling reduces that juice by half and the result is aged in oak barrels. You're right, this is balsamic vinegar but made with different grapes and not aged long enough to develop enough acidity to be called a vinegar.

Although old, traditional products, *vin cottos* have only come on to the international market in a big way since the turn of the century, and very useful they are, for the end product is very sweet and very complex, yet has a clean acidic finish.

Sapa is the same thing from the Marche, on the east coast, opposite Tuscany: there they recommend it is eaten with poached quince, which seems too much of two good things, and they also eat it with polenta, something I intend to try. Honestly.

If you give credence to Italian claims for these products you will believe they can be used in any dish in any amount, and all the while be healing you of flood, famine and pestilence. And do the same for your dog. Well, they might, but like modern verjuice this is an ingredient that gets too easily lost in clever or complicated recipes and which is best used fairly straight, as a dressing rather than an ingredient.

Sweet vegetables, like parsnips or turnips or carrots become perfectly heavenly, with a dribble of these syrupy delights. They are indeed interesting with grilled meat or almost any kind of fish. But the best I've tasted was when spooned over something plain and creamy – like a chilled petit Suisse. Some *vin cotto* are flavoured, with figs, with raspberry etc and, again, are very delicious by themselves, as a treat by the teaspoon. I use them as a variant on the fruit, so chilled poached figs served with fig *vin cotto*, or a raspberry ice with a raspberry *vin cotto*: I suppose you could mix and match, say serving a raspberry *vin cotto* over a fig panna cotta or ice cream. Rather than stirring an orange or mandarin-flavoured *vin cotto* into a gravy or sauce for duck, spoon it directly onto the carved meat.

For a much simpler thing than creme brulee, simply bake the custards and chill them well and then dibble a toothpick or slender kebab stick here and there and pour on enough *vin cotto* to dribble into the holes and then some more to make a skinny puddle on top. Not creme brulee, but creme puddlee.

Fruit fools benefit from *vin cotto* ladled upon them. A thin slice of very, very rich chocolate cake, slightly chilled, might well make your week if served with whipped cream and icy cold fig or orange or raspberry – or any – *vin cotto*. A slice of aged cheddar, or a soft blue cheese, eaten with a few drops sprinkled on to them, could out do the wonder.

They all make wonderful dips for thin biscotti or such other Italian biscuits, or indeed, for warm madeleines if you think your memory bank could handle such assault. And if you want your pleasures colder, pour *vin cotto* or a sapa into a tall glass and then fill up with champagne or a top sparkling wine, invariably from New Zealand these days.

It's easy to make *vin cotto*. Find a couple of bunches of very highly flavoured grapes, ideally something with a definite muscatel note. Put them into a bowl, stem and all and squash the grapes with a fork or something. Pour cold water on this, cover and leave 24 hours. Press the grapes again, and then remove. Strain the liquid through a fine sieve and then put it over a gentle heat until it's reduced to a nice syrup. Put into a bottle, and kept cool and dark it will last months.

Wasabi: one of those Japanese ingredients particularly associated with their most sophisticated dining, but which does not stand up to close scrutiny this side of the globe

Wasabi is a very hot green oriental form of horseradish, either grated fresh or dried and mixed with water to form a paste. Although indeed more aromatic than ordinary horseradish, it gets right up your nose and then scours your sinuses and then does it again; it is very hot indeed, yet served almost exclusively with sushi, or sashimi, exceptionally delicate raw fish, which is considered best when almost flavourless. If sushi is soaked in soy sauce into which a little wasabi has been whisked it may as well be a wodge of white bread dabbed with fish paste, for all else you will taste. But that's the Japanese way.

To me, wasabi seems the Japanese equivalent of serving raw onions and cooked eggs with caviare, an ancient way to conceal all possible shortcomings of age and condition in food too expensive to throw away. In the modern world of fresher, safer ingredients wasabi is just not needed with sashimi and sushi except in the most minimal amounts: the freshness and texture of ocean-fresh fish needs no such thuggery to hide what they offer, indeed they need help to open up their fragile flavours.

In any case, read the label. Most 'wasabi' is anything but the real thing, and artificially coloured too: you'll find it more likely to be a fluorescent paste of horseradish powder, mustard, and blue and yellow colourings, a part of the ingredient list usually printed on the crimped edge of individual servings and so particularly inaccessible. Once deciphered these are not what I would want to put on cooked fish, let alone raw.

The real wasabi has many defenders who think its flavour far more complex than horseradish, so if you do come across it give it a try and make up your own mind – but take teeny-tiny baby steps or you won't get your nasal passages back for ages.

As an alternative to chillies, to mix with other rugged flavours in occidental foods, genuine wasabi is worth exploring but not, perhaps, as deeply as the wasabi panna cotta and wasabi soft cheeses I have encountered. See special panel: Sushi and Sashimi, page 521.

Australasia's Indigenous Ingredients

Native or indigenous ingredients are causing a buzz in Australasia. Perhaps stung by unfair criticism of their robust new style of cookery that often combines Asian and occidental flavours and ingredients, chefs in Australia and NZ are taking serious interest in the flavours offered by their native lands, and taking advice from the indigenous peoples, the Aborigine in Australia and the Maori in New Zealand.

Some of these ingredients offer a brand new flavour experience, others are simply a new take on flavours we know already. Either way, they are not difficult to use and well repay the effort. Frankly, I am astonished every level of the international culinary world isn't fighting to use them. The opportunity is no different from being a medieval cook in Europe, confronted for the first time with cinnamon or nutmeg or black pepper. There's a real chance for many to make a mark by making these new flavours as familiar as the old.

Outside Australasia you might more easily find these products sold in sauces, jams and the like, and these make a very good introduction both to the flavours and to the intensity level at which they should or should not be used.

Some of these ingredients are now being grown commercially, many are still harvested from the wild, but you should find all native foods in Australasia are sourced through Aboriginal- or Maori-owned companies or with local agreements.

Australia

Bush tomatoes/akudjurra: a fruit of Australia's Central Desert they have a gutsy, full tomato-ish flavour heightened by definite raisin notes and a clean acid finish; an alternative name is desert raisin. The raisin effect is encouraged by allowing these small fruits to sun-dry on the bushes and Aborigine women then collect these manually. The flavour can be considered a wilder cousin of sun-dried tomatoes, and thus can be used in all the same ways – on pizza, in pasta sauces or stews.

When the bush tomato is ground it is known and is sold as *akudjurra* and this is easier to use in baking, where the warm flavour is very pleasing: bread and pizza doughs and scones are simple ways to enjoy it. It mixes well for rubs etc. with most other indigenous flavours. Bush tomato chutney gives amazing new life to robust cheeses, and to anything barbecued, particularly kangaroo and other game meats and birds.

Davidson's plums: damson-sized and flavoured but too acidic to be eaten raw by most people. Yet cook them with sugar, or make a jelly from them, and the wondrous flavour is one of the best of all indigenous ingredients. The commercially made chutneys with Davidson's plums will astonish you and create much talk around the barbecue.

Illawarra plums: the dark red berry of the brown pine, a semi-tropical tree found from New South Wales north to Queensland. Curiously, it grows its seed on the outside of the fruit. About the size of a grape they have a rich plum flavour but with the common resinous overtones of many indigenous ingredients, which can be ameliorated with cooking: lemon juice holds the colour and keeps the resin flavours at bay. Used in compotes and sweet sauces for cheesecakes and other desserts, but also as or in sauces for meat. Very popular in wild food restaurants.

Kakadu plums: looking like a miniature quince these yellow fibrous fruits have a vitamin C content 600 times that of a fresh orange, and are found in Western Australia from Katherine to the Kimberley. They make a terrific sweet jelly that adds an evocative new note to cream teas.

Lemon aspen berries: another intense lemon flavour that's not acidic but does come with the common wild-food flavour profile of honey and eucalyptus: found in rain forest from Sydney right up to the Far North.

Lemon myrtle: perhaps the Australian rain forest's greatest gift, and certainly the easiest to use. The leaves taste of lemon with a touch of lemon grass, but then move into a clean, clear citrus flavour all their own, perhaps with elusive hints of kaffir lime and eucalyptus. The flavour heightens when it is dried, but none of the finer notes is lost.

To create a minor sensation, simply use lemon myrtle anywhere you would use lemon, from fish sauces to ice creams and custards. A word of caution: if cooked too long at a high temperature the lemon flavour disappears, leaving only resinous and bitter flavours. Commonly found commercially in biscuits, shortbreads etc, both in stores and in Australia's excellent farmers' markets. A New Zealand-made white chocolate truffle flavoured with Australia's lemon myrtle won a bronze medal in Britain's Great Taste Awards 2004. How's that for fusion? Outstanding.

Lilli pilli/riberry: a number of these trees have edible berries, but the most stunning is the clove lilli pilli, which offers a concentrated spice flavour with top notes of clove. Excellent when used judiciously for both sweet and savoury concoctions including jams, baking and meat cookery.

Mountain pepper leaves: a new way to get the flavour and heat of pepper but with more dramatic aromas, and a definite tongue numbing effect too. Native to Tasmania, the leaves have such perfume and flavour they can be cut finely when fresh, or crushed when dried, and added to salad dressing, into a herb mixture for egg dishes, for barbecue spices and marinades. But

beware, they are intense, and you should use only half the amount you would of ordinary black pepper.

Mountain pepper berries: bigger than black peppercorns and with the same flavour profile as mountain pepper leaves, but the berries have both more heat and more of the palate numbing sensation, so start by using only a tenth the amount of black pepper you would use. I tasted a mountain pepper alcohol made in Tasmania that seared and deadened my tongue and made my eyes bulge but was first to wake me up and tell me Australian native ingredients are a new world, with something important and fresh to say for themselves, or in this case, to yell.

Muntries: sometimes called a native cranberry and can be used much the same way but they have a bigger, better flavour of apple.

Native mint: curiously refreshing, the leaves look nothing like mint but have the characteristic slight resinous undertone of many native ingredients, and of black peppercorn. Good, in fact, extra good to give lamb a fascinating move sideways and excellent combined with lemon myrtle and mountain pepper. It loves anything to do with garlic.

Quandong: one of the best-known and best-loved Australian native ingredients, yet less commercially marketed than many. I have always found it at a couple of stalls in Adelaide's overwhelming Central Market, which should be on every foodie's must-visit list, perhaps during the stupendously successful biannual Tasting Australia fiesta, which attracts top food writers from countries all around the world in October time every two years.

Quandong is quintessentially Outback produce and most common in arid areas of South Australia. European settlers used quandong from early days, and made it into jams, chutneys and, best of all, double crusted pies.

Usually bought dried, what you eat reconstituted looks like the peel of a small citrus, and is a rich red-orange colour.

I best liked it when I baked a good handful with apple in a pie topped with lemon-myrtle fragranced meringue. But it must be terrific in salsas with poultry or fish and in chutneys for spreading on decent hams and salamis and the like. Also known as the bush peach, native peach and desert peach.

Paperbark: not used to flavour food, but to wrap or carry it. Dampened, it makes a superb way to roll up or fold up anything being cooked in the oven or on the barbecue, fish particularly, for although the paperbark might burn and might suffuse the food with a mild smoke flavour the food is unlikely to dry out or burn. If you cook in parcels of paperbark, serve them whole at table, so every diner gets the full whoosh of aroma when the bark is cut.

Riberry: See Lilli pilli.

Rosella/wild Rosella: the fruit or calyx of a climbing vine related to the native hibiscus, rosella gives a magnificent magenta-red colour and a comforting flavour that shuffles between rhubarb and red berries. Excellent as a jam, it's also a terrific basis for chutney that's just right for turkey instead of cranberries, and, because of the sweetness, with scallops, mussels and prawns.

Warrigal greens: can be used as a spinach substitute, as it was by Captain Cook in 1770 or as a substitute for Asian greens. Only the youngest leaves and buds should be used and cooked for at least three minutes to reduce the oxalate content. The same plant as NZ spinach.

Wattle seed: don't try making this at home. Only some wattle (acacia) varieties from west of the Great Divide are suitable – the rest are poisonous. The seeds are lightly toasted and give up a flavour reminiscent of coffee and roasted hazelnuts. It can be used for both sweet and savoury. Wattle seed biscuits are commonplace, as are wattle seed ice creams, meringues and pavlovas; they bring a zing to anything with chocolate, like tiramisu. Also use them in stuffings and sauces for poultry, mixed with other indigenous flavours for fatty fish such as eel or salmon.

Wild limes: about the size of a hazelnut and with an intense, distinct lime flavour, perhaps with a touch of grapefruit too, just waiting to be used creatively. They make an excellent pickle with Indian spices to eat with cheese, beef, and seafood – almost anything where a citric note is welcomed. Recommended for the innovative.

New Zealand

Horopito: a perpetually fascinating herb-that-tastes-like-a-spice, obtained from the dried leaves of the eponymous native tree. Its flavour profile is huge, rushing in the mouth from pepper to garlic to celery and many other places before, during and afterwards. It has heat and a degree of numbing effect too; all in all, something very special. However I'm sad to say it is not always marketed with much respect or understanding. The flavours are fugitive and most disappear when heated, so the horopito rubs, barbecue mixes and horopito pastas are a dead loss. Instead, use horopito as a final seasoning on warm pasta or green vegetables or roasted chicken or scrambled eggs and then it's a definite winner. Horopito also has a number of medicinal uses you can read about on the web.

Kawakawa: also known as native or bush basil, and there is a degree of that flavour, as part of the spectrum of nice pepperiness; it's related to kava, but the leaves makes a tea that doesn't have its narcotic effect.

Piko piko: neither flavouring, herb nor spice, these are the exquisite curled emerging fronds of some of New Zealand's unique species of tree ferns. They are a vibrant green and look like the scroll of an over-embellished cello, but are not much bigger than a big thumbnail. The flavour is vegetal but provoking, a bit like asparagus that's gone bush. They are also marketed with stem or stalk, making them even more musical

The Maori name for the shape these make is *koru*, symbolic of new life, of rebirth: it's commonly used as a motif in Maori carvings and by Air New Zealand. Used as a garnish or feature in salads or vegetable mixtures piko piko must rate as one of the world's most beautiful ingredients.

In other parts of the world young fronds are also taken from brackens and low growing ferns and, of course, called fiddleheads. They are a particular treat in and around Boston, Mass. And if you are in the least bit important in Canada, they are considered the number one treat; Her Majesty the Queen always gets them there, usually with salmon and wild rice.

Defusing Fusion Confusion

From being the only game in town, fusion food is now publicly mocked, most loudly by those who first espoused it.

The clever expression was thought up to give culinary unison to chefs who take advantage of the myriad new ingredients global markets make available, and who combine them in previously impossible ways. The new combinations stimulate new thought, sometimes beguile and often baffle but they equally gratify a public forever clamouring for something new.

The fusion can be simple, Italian pancetta rather than ham with your eggs, and a chilli sauce rather than tomato sauce. More usually it mixes Asian or oriental flavours with those of the west. Sometimes it worked – vodka and caviar on Chinese noodles – sometimes it was horrible. But the horrible ones shouldn't have made fusion food into a joke: we all eat fusion food every day.

If we really threw up hands at fusing different worlds of flavour and ingredients, we would never eat the New World produce once fused with those of Europe, like potatoes and tomatoes, capsicums or vanilla, allspice and beans, or turkeys or Jerusalem artichokes or sweet corn or chocolate and many more. Neither would Europe earlier have adopted flavours and ingredients from the Middle East and from further afield, from the Spice Islands – like oranges and peppercorns and mint, like buckwheat, sugar or lemons, rose water or the sweet attractions of cinnamon, cloves, nutmeg, mace and cardamom. They too were once welcomed and fused with what was there.

All food today is fusion food and anyone who pours scorn on chefs who want to explore something new are in the wrong business, have no sense of the long, long, continuing staircase of culinary innovation on which they are permitted to stand fleetingly, but somehow wish to abandon by rehearsing such silliness as calling fusion food confusion food.

Let's not forget when tea first came to the UK is was boiled and served with a butter sauce. It must have seemed a very bad idea until someone told them how it worked best. So let chefs and cooks and writers make mistakes as they fuse Laotian with Lebanese, or Portuguese with Tahitian, for who knows what they might discover?

Once, apple pie with cinnamon had to be invented by fusing local and imported, new flavours. Singaporese fused the potato into their Nonya cooking, so why shouldn't we use Australian native ingredients in French food, or lemon grass in egg custards?

The only confusion about the acceptability of fusion food is in the minds of those who can't cope with the new, those who confuse the passing frisson of a glib phrase with their own relevance.

Oils

An edible oil is an edible fat that is liquid at normal temperatures. Although earliest man in northern Europe relied on animals for fat, the rest of the ancient world looked equally to vegetable oils.

The type varied according to locality. In Mesopotamia sesame seed oil was used and records survive of the 'best quality' being bought for Nebuchadnezzar's palace. In Anatolia it was almond oil; in the Americas oil from the peanut, maize and sunflower; in China and south-east Asia they used soy and coconuts as oil sources. Before the introduction of the olive, you would have used radish seed oil in Egypt, walnut and poppy seed oil in Greece. Poppies of a different type were used in northern Europe, as well as oil from flax and the cameline.

Not all these oils were used exclusively for cooking, nor are they now. Pliny gives an explanatory quote, which I vote the most tantalizing of any. He said: 'There are two liquids especially agreeable to the human body, wine inside and oil outside'. And I shouldn't think he was speaking of salads al fresco...

Together with wine and wheat, olive oil is considered one of the three commodities that encouraged and made possible the early civilizations of the Mediterranean. The Egyptians used olive oil as a lubricant for moving heavy building materials. Homer mentions it as an aid to weaving and it has been used to make soap since the days of ancient Rome, where it also powered lamps. In Minoan Crete, olive oil was considered part of the king's treasure and an important commodity for earning foreign exchange.

Oils were also used as protective agents on ships' hulls and in painting. Modern emulsion paints, which are now water soluble, are descendants of tempera, an emulsion in water of oil and pigments stabilized with vegetable gums or egg yolks.

Oil's uses pharmacologically are manifold, and far more sophisticated than the purgative spoonful of castor oil. This perhaps is the time to simplify the vexed question of saturated and unsaturated fats and all that.

Animal fats have a high level of so-called saturated fats. These are solid at normal temperature and are believed to increase blood cholesterol, leading to hardening of the arteries and heart problems. Medically it is well established that most excess cholesterol in our system has been manufactured by our body rather than being a by-product of what we eat. Nonetheless it is a good idea to be aware of what sort of oils and fats we eat, and to keep the balance in favour of the unsaturated and mono-unsaturated oils, some of which actually help decrease cholesterol levels.

Vegetable oils mainly contain polyunsaturated fats, which are always liquid unless specially treated. They also contain linoleic acid, which when eaten with food helps lower the cholesterol level and aids the burning up of carbohydrate, preventing its conversion into fat. The major uses of vegetable oils are for cooking, and as the basis of margarine; they also go into cooking fats, salad dressings and ice cream, and there is the problem.

To convert liquid oils into solid fats they must be hydrogenated, and on the way this creates trans-fatty acids. Increasingly, evidence seems to show trans-fatty acids can cause cancer and, although part of spreads sold with cholesterol-reducing benefits, the cancerous potential seems far to outweigh the cholesterol-lowering advantage. It's up to you to read the label and make up your own mind. All fats and oils have the same calorie count.

So why bother to eat chemical creations when we have butter and we have olive oil, both of which are naturally better tasting too. Some newer spreads make a point of telling you they do not contain hydrogenated oils and 'virtually no trans-fatty acids'. Good on them. Yet if your body makes most of your cholesterol I still think you are better off eating natural butter and natural oils.

Over the last decades we have all heard the message about olive oil and, thank you very much, we agree. Olive oil does taste terrific and does do us good and we are all using it like mad. Except some people are insane, quite missing the point of virginity and ignoring the qualities of other oils.

A cook who understands oil has at least three olive oils in the cupboard: a very superior extra virgin olive oil to use as a dressing and that will never be heated; a lesser extra virgin olive oil or a virgin olive oil for cooking and frying, but which is also good enough to be a dressing, and a third, blander oil for frying or for mayonnaise bases. This third oil could be a 'light' olive oil or one of the vegetable oils.

To these basics I would add walnut or hazelnut oil, for a delicious change, and sesame oil for finishing Asian and oriental dishes.

Those who buy the very best extra virgin olive oil and use it for all their culinary chores are either pretentious, which is sadly common, or have been misled by ill-informed writing, which is depressingly common. Heating fine extra virgin olive oils destroys the finest flavours and aromas, the very graces that cost you so much.

Olive Oil

The silver-gnarled olive tree – its leaves a symbol of peace, its fruits of resurrection and renewal, its oil used at baptisms and coronations – thrives only on a narrow border of sea-lapped land. It can't grow at heights, won't grow very far inland, but where it is suited it is utterly reliable, which is why early civilization could trust it. Nothing short of dynamite can guarantee an olive tree's death. Snow, fire and brigandry merely destroy it above the ground. They live an average of 600 years, but many are reputed to be thousands of years old.

Today's huge interest and use of olive oil is possible because commercial processes make more olive oil than ever before, extracting it where it was not once possible and making so much more of higher quality than before. Much of this extra bounty is extra virgin oil, and where once you never threatened its superiority with heat, it can be cheap enough to be used as an everyday oil. Now, it's ok to have a battery only of extra virgin oils, some supermarket names for cooking with, estate oils as a dressing for cold or hot foods.

In case you have not kept up, olive oil is considered an important component in the modern, varied style of diet, based loosely on the Mediterranean paradigm of eating more vegetable-based foods than meat based foods, more olive oil than butter and cream and bacon fat. It tastes wonderful too, an ingredient to choose and use as a flavouring rather than as mere emollient in salads or as a medium for frying.

Being extra virgin is no guarantee an oil has been extracted traditionally, that is, first crushed into a paste and then pressed between fibre mats. These days mechanical methods prevail, first to chop the olives and then using hydraulic presses and centrifugal force so every skerrick of decent oil is extracted in a single process, which goes some way to explain the sudden increase of extra virginity on the shelf.

Virginity and extra virginity are states largely evaluated by the acid content of otherwise unprocessed oil.

It is an absolute fact that there are few rules guaranteeing the origination of olive oils. There is a huge international trade: the south of France has always been a net importer from North Africa, only some of which makes its famous soaps, and Italy cannot exist without oils from Spain. This it not a criticism, for consistency of flavour and style within a commercial label is important, just as it is with wine. If you find a cheap olive oil that you like, and that has no famous name or label, you are far more likely to be paying for what is in the bottle than what is on it. And it might not have been produced in the area in which it was bottled. Who cares if you like it?

Like olives themselves, the flavour spectra of olive oils are contrary and complicated. There are hundreds of varieties, each of which gives different oils in different soils, and from year to year. The south of France still has countless small olive oil presses and it was there I first realized that each day's pressing can taste different, sometimes because of the varieties pressed that day, other times because of the humidity or temperature. Most countries have strict rules about how long olives might wait before they are pressed: too long or too warm and the flavour changes as the acidity rises alarmingly.

If you speak a local language and can be at a small olive press when others are not, it is an educative treat beyond compare to be able to taste the storage tanks that hold individual pressings, first comparing these and then those from a previous year, probably bottled by then. It quickly makes nonsense of any belief there is such a thing as very particular flavours produced in an area; if there is consistency it is almost always due to blending, as with champagne.

Although I concentrate here on the four major producing countries you will know, olive oil is produced in dozens of countries, including every one with Mediterranean shores. Australia produces small amounts of outstandingly good oil, oils from New Zealand are winning major international prizes, and the trees thrive in Argentina, Mexico and in California, so nothing should surprise you when you read the label.

Broadly speaking olives – and thus olive oils – are sweet and gentle in France, get stronger in Spain and become increasingly robust as you move eastwards across the Mediterranean, or southwards in a Mediterranean country. Thus an extra virgin oil from southern Spain or Provence may seem positively honeyed and vinous compared to the same quality from certain regions of Italy which can be distinctly biting and peppery or from Greece which will be altogether thicker and throatier, except this will depend on whereabouts in Italy or Greece. And the year of course: now I see some better suppliers put the harvest months on the label of their finer products, a really useful tool if you are an olive oil freak.

Today, the popularity of olive oil is such we can spend large sums on small bottles from single estates, and like great vintage wines some are sensational, some eccentric beyond belief. Tuscany was a pioneer in 'boutique' oils, making much of its tradition of Michelangelo-designed palaces and great and ancient titled family names on outlandish-shaped bottles. And yet... to my palate, Tuscan oils can be so peppery you would think they had been sitting about with fresh chillies, and that bite camouflages any delicacy of its own and transforms into brutishness any delicate food upon which it falls. Not for me, not at those prices. And anyway, the sums do not always add up. How does the supposedly artisan production of a single small estate become a year-round best-seller in a national supermarket chain?

Olive oil must beware it is not lubricating its own dead-end, as did own-label champagnes, which first created a new market and then betrayed it with ever less good product.

Time, taste and budget are all necessary partners to finding the olive oil you most like. What follows is a mixture of personal experience, the advice of respected specialist oil importers, and of Anne Dolamore's *Essential Olive Oil Companion* and *Buyer's Guide to Olive Oil*. I specially like those books because her palate seems to be exactly the same as mine. You will find a complete list of DOP olive oils too, always a fine starting point when you are visiting a country or shopping for quality. Yet do not fear to disagree, for exchange of opinion is the most piquant flavouring of food.

Australia

It didn't take long for Australia's olive trees to be discovered by the Italians and Greeks who flooded to Australia after the Second World War. A few were in groves, but most had been planted and forgotten as shade trees by earlier settlers. For decades, individuals would gather olives from trees more properly described as feral, and make oil just for their families: if Aussies with a British heritage knew what they were doing they'd laugh, mocking Mediterraneans for being 'greasy' and eating food 'swimming in oil', while they had the grease of roasted mutton running down their chins and a cold beer in one fist. As with NZ, the success of a wine culture has changed everything, and in Australia's couth cities and towns there's now hardly a single hunk of meat goes into mouths without olive oil associated somehow.

In some areas, such as the Fleurieu peninsula close to Adelaide, feral olives are collected for olive oil production every year, and these oils are particularly well worth seeking out as are those oils made from Koroneiki olives.

Australia makes enough quality olive oil to be able to export; one brand you might find is NJoi, illustrating a typical flip Australian attitude that is most apparent when the quality is most good.

France

The provinces with a Mediterranean coastline produce olive oil, and as with all horticulture down there, little of it is mechanized or produced by large cooperatives. Instead thousands of small olive mills press local produce and make truly individual oils of finesse and delicacy.

In broad terms the expression *Huile de Provence* is generally a guarantee of decent standards. In Provence, Nyons is the great olive centre, relying heavily for eating and for oil olives on the invaluable *tanche*, a small black olive introduced by the Romans; it adds terrific sweetness and fruit to oils. In the village of Mirabel the Farnoux family produces Le Vieux Moulin oil only from these olives.

Because France produces relatively small amounts of her own olive oil you don't easily find it available. But if you are travelling in the south an olive oil tasting and buying expedition is great fun. There are five olive mills just north of Marseilles on either side of the A7; here local varieties *aglandaus* and *saurines* make very individual oils. Head also for Mausannes-les-Alpilles, Mouries, Beaume-de-Venise, and the famed Les Barronnies, also at Nyons. The oils of La Lucques in Languedoc are considered quite the equal of Provencal oil, if not better, which will give you something to argue.

The admirable French AOC system, now married to the EEC's DOP status guarantees the origin and standards of four olive oils and four olives.

Extra virgin olive oils:
Huile d'olive d'Aix-en-Provence
Huile d'olive de Haute-Provence
Huile d'olive de la Valee des Baux-de-Provence
Huile d'olive de Nyons

Jordan
The Hashemite Kingdom of Jordan is the world's 10th largest producer of olive oil, and some very superior olive oils are now being exported. Terra Rossa is one brand to look for, its name reflective of the iron-rich soil in which their ancient olive trees grow. As well as extra virgin olive oil, Terra Rossa markets a sinolea oil, made by an ancient method quite different from others. Once the olives are crushed they are not pressed: instead knives (now of stainless steel) dip in an out and the oil that clings is allowed to drip off for collection. Because sinolea oil is picked up and no pressure is used the method is thought by many to be superior even to Spain's 'flower of the oil'q.v. which is allowed to run freely under the weight only of the olives.

New Zealand
The combination of a Mediterranean climate and an 'I can do that' attitude means New Zealand produces sensational olive oils, but has only done so for the last 20 or so years. Olive trees were introduced by very early 19th century settlers, but were largely ignored or harvested for table olives by a very few 'foreigners'. Olive oil production was ignored until the country's palate was lit up by its equally late but stupendous embracing of superior wine production. Now most of the country grows olives and in some places has discovered varieties flourishing in NZ long enough to have adapted and become distinct. Many of the groves are still very young and most,

but not all, are associated with a wine growing area.

Waiheke Island, for instance, sits in the middle of Auckland harbour, and produces red wines considered amongst the world's best: here enough olive oil is produced to warrant the formation of a sales collective. In Marlborough, one of the country's greatest wine-producing areas, Seresin olive oils are produced, so superior they won an international olive oil tasting in the USA. Hawkes Bay, Bay of Plenty, Northland, Otago . . . all these and more produce olive oil of outstanding quality but with little universality of flavour or style. It's probably true to say most growers have opted for the richer, grassier and spicier style of Tuscan olives, yet there are plenty of exceptions, as there should be. Olive oils from NZ are expensive, even when at home, suggesting perhaps a misplaced view they will recoup their long investments in just a few harvests. I think not. You are unlikely to find a range of them if you live elsewhere. But like their wines, they are clear, direct, utterly faithful to the olives, and highly recommended.

Portugal

I very much like what I have tasted of these rather uncommon oils, which often have a fresh taste of apples, a much better way to balance unctuousness than pepperiness. The oil of Conservas Rainha Santa from Estremoz is available in Britain and I find it wonderfully supple, clear and gratifying in the mouth. A definite destination for serious olive oil researchers. But these are all examples of new style oils; Portugal's traditional preference is for meaty, big oils made from over-ripe olives, which I find rather too challenging unless you like salt cod too.

Spain

Two surprises for most people here. Spain is the world's largest olive oil producer and exporter (especially to Italy it should be noted) and was also the first to declare officially guaranteed areas of origin and production standards for olive oils, their DO or *Denominacion de Origen* system, now what the EC calls DOP.

To my taste, many Spanish oils have it just right, elegant and individual without being assertive or show-offs, the way one hopes those at one's table will behave. The queen of Spain's oil producing olives is the *arbequina*, believed introduced from Mallorca, and now grown particularly elegantly in north-east Spain, Catalonia and thereabouts.

Many areas in Spain make two oils from the same fields. Early oils are greener and lighter for being made before the olives have turned colour and mellowed. The remainder are picked and pressed each day as they turn to yellow and purple and then black, which makes a noticeably yellower and softening oil as the year progresses.

'Flower of the oil' is a specialty, most associated with the Nunez de Prado brand. Once the olives have been broken up, they are allowed to sit with no pressure other than their own weight – the same way grape juice runs freely to make Hungary's Tokay wines. This process takes up to 11kg of olives to make one litre of oil, more than twice what it takes when pressure is applied. The result is yellow and unfiltered, and yet it is not more expensive than other extra virgin Spanish oils. A talking point that more than answers back in the mouth.

Spain has more protected olive oils than any other country: this is the 2004 list:

Extra Virgin Olive Oils, all DOP*

*Mallorca: made from *Mallorcan/empeltre, arbequina* (native to Mallorca) and *picual*, with a maximum acidity of 0.8%. Two types predominate; one is almond-like with minimal pepperiness or bitterness, and the other notably sweet, but with little or no fruity, apple or almond flavours. Yellow to greeny-yellow.

*Monterubbio: from the east of Badajoz province and with a maximum acidity of 0.5%. *Corezuelo* and *picual* olives predominate. A greenish-yellow colour, with a romantic fruity taste, a little almond like and with a slight bitter sting to finish.

*Terra Alta: made in the southwest of Catalonia with maximum acidity of 0.5%. Mainly *empeltre* with some *arbequina*. Always shades of yellow and a good fruity flavour, with some sweetness developing during the season, with reminders of almonds and green nuts.

*Baixe Ebre-Montasia: from several areas in the province of Tarragona, the southernmost part of Catalonia, with maximum acidity of 0 .8%. Three local varieties used are the *morruda* or *morrut, sevillenca* and *farga*. A green to bright yellow oil that is notably tasty and aromatic, with sweetness sometimes detectable as the season ends.

*Bajo Aragon: made west of Aragon in an area straddling Zaragoza and Teruel and with a maximum of 1% acidity. Yellow to gold colour from the *empeltre, arbequina* and *royal* varieties. Fruity flavours at the start of the season with no bitterness, and that tend to sweetness and a light pepperiness as the olives ripen.

*Baeno: produced in the south east of Cordoba and with two grades: Type A has a maximum acidity of 0.4%, an intense fruity aroma and flavour with a hint of bitter almonds to finish. Type B can have an acidity of 1% and will have a sweeter, more mature olive flavour. The colour is always rather greenish-yellow but varies.

*Les Garrigues: made west of Barcelona in the province of Llieda this oil has a maximum acidity of 0.5%. The arbequina olive dominates. Oil made from earlier harvests is greenish, full bodied and offers a light bitter almond finish. Later harvests produce a yellow oil of less viscosity and a mellow sweet flavour.

*Montes de Granada: from the mountains north east of Granada a lively green to greeny yellow. *Picual* olives dominate, and the characteristic fruity/bitter, fresh olive taste is softened by four localised varieties: *escarabajuelo, negrillo de Izxnalloz, holiblanca* and *gordal de Granada*.

*Montes de Toledo: made around the city of Toledo and in adjoining areas of Cuidad Real, with a maximum acidity of 0.7%. The *cornicabra* olive produces an intense golden yellow to green oil depending on the time of season, with a notably full mouth feel, plenty of balanced aroma and flavour, and a slightly bitter finish.

*Poniente de Granada: made in the west of the province of Granada, these are light, nicely balanced oils with nutty/vegetal flavours and slight pepperiness and bitterness. Yellow-green to gold.

*Priego de Cordoba: produced in the south east of Cordoba, bordering the provinces of Jaen and Granada, with a maximum acidity of 1%: *picudo*, *hojiblanco* and *picual* olives.

*Sierra de Cadiz: seven municipalities in the north east of Cadiz province and two in Sevilla province make oil that reaches a maximum acidity of 0.6%. The olives used are all varieties of the *Sevilla lechin*, giving medium to intense aroma and flavour with hints of something feral plus pepperiness and bitterness, but all nicely balanced, of course.

*Sierra de Cazorla: a maximum acidity of 0.7% from *picual* and *royal* olives, grown in the south east of Jaen province. Early oils are dark green, later ones a golden yellow but both have a very full fruity flavour, reminiscent some think of apple, almond and fig, with a slight bitterness to finish.

*Sierra de Segura: from the north east of Jaen province, and made with *picual*, *verdalam*, *royal* and *de Jaen* fruits to a maximum 1% acidity. A very ancient oil of great quality.

*Sierra Magina: the production area is a natural park in the central south of Jaen. Here the olives grown are the *picual* and the *manzanillo de Jaen*, which give a maximum acidity of 0.5%. During the harvesting season the colour will vary from deep green to golden yellow, but the oils are universally fruity and with a slight degree of bitterness.

*Siurana: *arbequina*, *royal* and *murrut* olives are grown in the prescribed districts of the province of Tarragona to produce oil with maximum 0.5% acidity. Early harvesting gives a greenish oil that is full bodied and has a distinctive bitter almond flavour: later harvesting gives a yellow oil that is lighter in feeling, delicately balanced and with little or no bitterness.

Italy

This is where I start to get into trouble. Of course I have enjoyed truly wonderful oils throughout the country, but there is an awful lot of hype. Lucca oil? Yes, jolly nice, luscious even, but most of it is merely bottled in Lucca rather than produced there. Tuscan? Yes, it is wonderful to enjoy single estate oils from houses designed by Michelangelo and more ancient titles on a label than an entire issue of *Hello!* But the *frantoio* and *moraiolo* olives sometimes give such an exaggerated chilli-type pepperiness I find it difficult to enjoy either the oils or the foods onto which they might be poured. Tuscan cooking is remarkably straightforward and unseasoned; even so I suspect a lesser oil and freshly ground black pepper would be kinder and more fragrant. And they are terribly unpensive oils, too.

Laudemio is a consortium of Tuscany's greatest and oldest producers, who market individually under this label to exceptionally high and rigidly controlled standards: the shape of the bottle and Laudemio trademark are universal but the name of the producer will change. That of the Marchese de Frescobaldi has been softened a little with *leccino* olives and I have also enjoyed that of Marchese Antinori: the independently marketed Ornellaia of Marchese Ludovico Antinori, produced on a maritime estate not affected by the infamous frosts, is deliciously full and unpeppery.

Much Tuscan oil is made by the same estates which make Chianti Classico and the tall, green, square bottles of Badia a Coltibuono are a prime example; *very* robust and a balanced amount of the expected peppery aftertaste.

Umbria, next door to Tuscany, uses the same olives to produce oils that are notably more elegant and well balanced: they are often grown in association with the grapes for Orvieto wines.

Liguria, very much the upper armpit of Tuscany, geographically speaking, specializes in the *taggiasca* olive. The oils can be arresting sweet and thus doubly delicious but beware their freshness suddenly can disintegrate in only 6 months, very much one to enjoy in situ.

The Molise region of Central Italy makes tremendously rich oils with a clean grassiness. The estate of Prince Colonna uses a blend of four olives: the *ascolera tenera* is a green eating olive which adds delicate fruitiness; the black eater *leccino* adds sweetness, the *coratino* (actually from Apulia) keeps its rich fruitiness for a long time and the *nocellara Etnea* from eastern Sicily gives a deep greeny-gold colour and a distinct perfume.

Apulia in the south is the country's largest producer, mainly from the *coratina*; when pressed, even Italians from other areas will probably agree most of the time that this is Italy's best, with a full olive flavour that is balanced and has a clean aftertaste but no pepperiness.

Ravida oils from Sicily's southern coast are highly rated, light but flavoury oils and made from thrèe varieties: the *cerasuola* olive is picked when changing from green to violet and gives a hearty full oil; the *biancolilla* offers a silky texture and light green tint; *nocellara del belice* have a distinct olive taste and are used green for oil and ripe for eating.

There are many excellent commercial extra virgin oils marketed by Italian companies, which have all the appeal and none of the eccentricity of estate oils. This may be because they come from Spain.

Naturally Italy protects its best with a DOP rating. Here's the current DOP list, but note I haven't been slacking and leaving out information you might want – unfortunately the authorities don't supply the same information for every oil.

Alto Crotonese: an extra virgin made from the *carolea* olive that varies from light green to bright yellow depending on season but is always fruity and light. Made in designated municipalities in the province of Crotone.

Aprutino Pescarese: a fruity oil with a pronounced aroma and taste. With a maximum acidity of 0.6% it's made anywhere in the province of Pescara.

Brisighella: using only the *nostrana di Brisighella* olive this is a big oil that's fruity but bitter and peppery, and with a clear notes of grass and vegetables. Produced in the provinces of Ravenna and Forli.

Bruzio: a fruity greeny-yellow olive oil of up to 0.8% acidity. Individual areas are permitted to attach their locality, so you'll find *Bruzio Fascia Prepollinica, Bruzio Valle Crati, Bruzio Commine Joniche Presilane* and *Bruzio Sibaratide*. All are in the south of the province of Cosenza and bordered by the Apennines and the Ionian Sea.

Canino: a very individual oil with a clear nose and flavour of fresh but ripe olives and a defined character that comes with a little pepperiness and sharpness and has a maximum acidity of 0.5%. It can be made exclusively from any of five olive varieties or from any mixture, so expect a variety of flavours even in the same year if from different groves. The olives grown are the local *caninese* plus *leccino, pendolino, maurino* and *frontoio* and must be grown within the province of Viterbo.

Chianti Classico: at least 80% of the olives used must be *frantoio, correglio, moraiolo* or *leccino*. This oil shows a definite green with golden highlights and has an attractive olivey nose and the expected peppery/lemony flavour. Grown in specified districts around Siena and Florence, the same as for Chianti Classico wines.

Cilento: a maximum acidity of 0.7% with a greeny-yellow colour and a warm fruity nose: fruity flavour too with a little pepper and citric lift. From 62 districts in the south of the province of Salerno, in the National Park of Cilento.

Collina di Brindisi: deliciously sweet when freshly made, this oil is considered of particularly good quality. Made in the north of the province of Brindisi with at least 70% *ogliarola* plus *celinna, nardo, coratina, frontoio, leccino* and *picholine*. Maximum acidity is 0.8% and it's greeny-yellow.

Colline di Romagna: it must contain 60% *correggiolo* plus up to 40% *leccino*; growers are allowed also to use *pendolino, moraiolo* and *rossina* but are restricted to these varieties not comprising more than 10% of their groves. 0.5% acidity maximum, colour that varies from green to gold and a notable olive nose and flavour with just a little citric and pepper touch. From parts of the Rimini and Forli-Cesena provinces.

Colline Salernitane: produced in 82 districts from the Amalfi coast to the Cilento, another DOP olive oil region. It's another notably sweet olive oil when very fresh, has a maximum acidity of 0.7% and a good fruity taste with very light citric and peppery notes. Olive varieties are *rotondella, carpellese, frantoio* and *leccino*.

Colline Teatine: a comforting olive oil made only from the *gentile de Chieti* olive, which gives a warm fruity nose and flavour. Can be made in a number of areas in the province of Chiete and so may be found as **Colline Teatine Frentano** and **Colline Teatine Vastese**. 0.6% acidity.

Dauno: a complicated DOP rating here as five varieties of olive might be used, each giving a particularly interesting and diverse flavour. All have a maximum acidity of 0.6%. *Basso Tavoliere* oils are 70% *coratina gargano* to produce oil with an intensely herby, fruity nose, dense texture and a flavour that balances citric and pepperiness to give a final artichoke taste. *Gargano* oils are 70% *ogliorola garganica* giving a pronounced olive nose and a fragrant flavour reminiscent of almonds. **Alto Tavoliere** oils must be 80% *peranzana*, which gives intense herbal and floral notes and an excellent balance. *Sub Appenino* oil is 70% *ogliorola* plus *coratina* and *rotondella* for a fruity nose and sweet flavour. They grow and are made in districts in the province of Foggia.

Garda: a single name for three distinct areas which grow different olives and mix and match them seemingly at will but always to give an oil that's 0.6% maximum acidity and with a fruity nose and definite almond-like flavour underpinned with citric spiciness.

Garda Bresciano: at least 55% *casaliva*, *frantoio* or *leccino* mixed or separately and produced in Brescia; **Garda Orientale** is at least 50% *casaliva* or *drizzar* but may also be made with *lezzo*, *favarol*, *rossanel*, *razza*, *fort*, *morcai*, *trepp* or *pendolino olives*, again mixed or separately; **Garda Trentino** is made with at least 80% *casaliva*, *frantoio*, *pendolino* or *leccino* olives, mixed or separately.

Laghi Lombardi: two types here and the possibility of oil that's big and peppery or big and citric and with a maximum acidity of 0.55%. **Laghi Lombardi Sebino** should have no less than 40% *leccino* plus *frantoio*, *casaliva*, *pendolino* or *sbreso*, either mixed or individually and is from Brescia and Bergamo. **Laghi Lombardi Lario** should have at least 80% *leccino* plus *frantoio* or *casaliva* and is produced in the provinces of Como and Lecco.

Lamentia: with a maximum acidity of 0.5% this is an oil with a good fruitiness, both on the nose and on the palate. Grown in Piana di Lamezia and districts in the province of Catanzaro.

Molise: usually with an elevated fruity nose and palate with light underlying pepperiness and bitterness. Pressed from the *aurina*, *gentile di Larino*, *Colletorto nero*, *leccino*, *paesane blanca*, *sperone de Gallo*, *olivastro* and *rosciola* varieties of olive in a few areas of the Molise region.

Monte Etna: produced in the areas surrounding the Sicilian volcano, including the municipalities of Catania and Messina; you should find a yellow-gold oil with fleeting green tints, a very light fruity smell and good olive flavour with a touch of pepper and a little bitterness.

Monti Iblei: fruity oil with maximum acidity of 0.65% made in eight areas within Syracuse, Ragusa and Catania, each with its own mix of olives. The most important olive varieties are the *tonda Iblea*, *cetrala*, *prunara*, *abbunara* and the *tuna*.

Penisola Sorrentina: produced in the province of Naples with a maximum acidity of 0.8% this oil has an attractive olive fruit nose and a definite olive flavour with pepper and citric notes.

Pretuziano delle Colline Teramane: a big name for an oil with a rather restrained fruitiness plus a touch of the pepper and citric undertones common with the area and the olives grown: 75% of the total must be *leccino*, *frantoio* and *dritta* olives, with the rest of permitted local varieties that give individuality. Made in a 25-35km wide belt of the hilly province of Teramo, running from the sea inland in the Abruzzi region.

Riviera Ligure: made throughout Liguria using only the *taggiasca* olive, which gives a medium to light, green-gold oil with accentuated sweetness – maximum acidity of 0.8%.

Sabina: this golden oil is noted for a particularly velvety mouth feel and aromatic sweetness, although expect early season oils to have a little sharpness. Made with a maximum acidity of 0.7% from the *carboncella*, *leccino*, *raja*, *frantoio*, *moraiolo*, *olivastrone*, *salviana*, *olivago* and *rasciola* olives. Grown to the east of the Tiber in districts to the north east of Rome and the south east of Rieti.

Terra di Bari: as you would expect, pressed in the province of Bari and with a maximum acidity of 0.6%. Oil with a light citric pepperiness and an unusual aftertaste reminiscent of herbs and nuts. Three areas of production: **Castel del Monte, Bitonto, Murgia deli Trulli/ delle Grotte.**

Terra d'Otranto: made with maximum acidity of 0.8% in an area extending from the Ionic to the Adriatic and including Lecce and parts of the provinces of Taranto and Brindisi. The colour varies from greenish to yellowish, leafy notes accompany the fruity nose, and the flavour has only light pepperiness and citric tang.

Terre di Siena: a rather special recipe this one, for the olives used must be only two of the *frantoio, correggiolo, moriaolo* or *leccino*, each for at least 10% and mixed together to form at least 85% of the whole: the other 15% can be other varieties. Made in the province of Siena, the oils have a green-golden colour, which can change with age. Maximum acidity of 0.5% and light citric and peppery nuances to the flavour.

Toscano: not yet a full DOP rating but heading there from its current IGP status. Made throughout Tuscany, the oil has a very fruity flavour and nose, with aromas that can remind you of artichokes and ripe fruit. Maximum acidity of 0.6%.

Umbria: oil with a fresh leafy note on the nose and a fruity taste that also presents pepper and citrus. Made throughout Umbria with a maximum acidity of 0.65%.

Val di Mazara: made in the province of Palermo in Sicily plus a few districts in the province of Trapano. A fruity nose and flavour with only light citric and pepper notes.

Valli Trapanesi: an elegant delicious oil with maximum 0.5% acidity and made with the *nocellara del Belice* and *cerasuola* olives. Green with gold highlights, the oil offers herby scents to those of fruity olives, and has a good olive flavour that balances light citrus and pepper notes with a good aftertaste of sweet almonds. Largely made in the Two Valleys, la Valle del Belice and la Valle di Erice in the province of Trapani.

Veneto: grown and pressed in the provinces of Verona, Padova, Vicenza and Treviso under several denominations. Veneto Valpolicella is made from the *grignano* and *favarol*; Veneto Euganei e Berici is made mainly from the *leccino* and *rasara*, Veneto del Grappa is made mainly from *frantoio* and *leccino*. Veneto oils have a maximum acidity of 0.6%, tend towards greenness and have a medium intensity of fruitiness on the nose; the flavour is also fruity with an appealing light citric edge.

Greece

No one can accuse these oils of delicacy. But the generally robust, straight-forward flavour can be neat and clean behind a full, flavoury body — and they have probably been making them longer than most, too. The two main areas of production are the Peloponnese, which includes Kalamata, and the island of Crete, where olive trees cover more than half the cultivated land.

You will find organic oils made in remote areas, and Cretan oil pressed from a particularly small variety of olives with negligible acid content. Many experts rate the best of Cretan oils as amongst the most delicious and balanced of all olive oils. Kalamata oils are outstanding, but not what you might think. They are not made from the exceptional *kalamata* olive but produced in the Kalamata area from the major Greek oil olive, the *koroneiki*, but then so are most mainland oils, whatever they are called.

Cooking

The single great culinary immutable of extra virgin olive oils used to be that none should be used for cooking, ever. Heat destroys the very complexity you have paid to enjoy, but now there is so much extra virgin oil around the prohibition stands only for estate-bottled oils of high expense and great nuance. Once cooking is complete nothing is quite so engaging as a spoonful of extra virgin olive oil poured over food as a condiment, in vegetable soups, thick or thin, on simply cooked vegetables, on grilled fish, on fowl or decent bits of an animal, in a small bowl for dunking bread, or a salad, of course. Long-baked potatoes drizzled with olive oil, a minor squeeze of garlic and plenty of parsley are almost too good to eat, as are floury potatoes mashed or crushed only with olive oil – but don't stop there. Rich butternut squash mashed with olive oil and brightened with sweet paprika made a Michelin-star chef sit up at my table; that's rather Moroccan. For a flavour from further down the Mediterranean, cook sliced white turnips with a tiny amount of chopped onion and garlic over olive oil, butter and orange juice until the liquids are reduced to a thick emulsified syrup; finish with fresh dates, parsley and cinnamon.

For new-fangled Mediterranean British cooking and to placate those who don't take to olive oil's flavour, buy lesser extra virgin olive oils, or olive oils, or choose one of the excellent cheaper mixtures of olive and vegetable oil, sometimes labelled as green oil. These lesser oils are marvellous to flavour by storing with sprigs of rosemary and thyme, crushed garlic cloves, coriander seeds and pepper; a month in a warm but not too light place is usually enough and I find it good to remove the flavouring and replace with just a small amount of fresh, which adds an edge to the flavour. Use these flavoured oils to marinate a leg of lamb or, say, cod steaks before grilling, to make a potato salad or to fry eggs. With chilli and oregano you concoct wonderful oil for sprinkling on pizza, both before and after cooking.

I don't hold with the school that olive oil should be used only for Mediterranean dishes; eggs and chips fried in olive oil are fabulous, British salads of beetroot or cucumber a revelation, and frozen peas dressed with oil rather than butter worth eating by themselves. But when you use olive oil you must want its flavour to make a recognizable and tasty contribution and not because it is 'healthy'. The silly home economist who sent me recipes for curries for four people, and who thought using two tablespoons of extra virgin olive oil in them a good idea, should be stripped of her undoubtedly neat aprons and boiled alive in butter and oil.

Storing

Virgin olive oils easily deteriorate through oxidation after exposure to light and air. Thus cans and green glass are better than clear glass and storage should be in a cool, dark larder or the refrigerator, except in the latter oils will cloud and thicken unpleasantly and there is always the risk of picking up off flavours. The neck and pouring mouth should be kept clean as drops will acidify. Oil left exposed to air should never be poured back into the bottle.

Types of Olive Oil

The classification of olive oils is vexing for the beginner, as it is based on a combination of objective scientific principles and a rather more subjective assessment of organoleptic characteristics. Organoleptic is a word French and Italian writers use from birth, but English speakers have no idea what it means, not least because it is in no dictionary I have ever consulted and French and Italians just fling their hands around when asked to explain. Eventually I established it means 'relating to perception by sensory organs', that is, what something looks, smells, feels and tastes like. Why don't they say so?

When the EC introduced such standards of judging in 1992, 60% of Italian olive oils risked being down graded. They had the low acid levels of a superior grade, but not the required standards of authenticity, manufacture, flavour or appearance.

The basic standard for olive oil is virgin olive oil, and that has been defined by the International Olive Oil Council as being: 'obtained solely by mechanical or other physical means under conditions, and particularly thermal conditions, that do not lead to the deterioration of the oil, and which has not undergone any treatment other than washing, decantation, centrifugation and filtration . . .virgin olive oil (must thus be) fit for consumption as it is . . .'

In effect, virgin olive oil is thus made by the traditional mill's first pressing of crushed olives, or by the modern, more common and greater yielding combination of hydraulic press and centrifuge, and the process may use neither heat nor chemical assistance.

The lower an oil's acidity, the more care has to be taken with every aspect of the growing, harvesting and oil making, and the higher its ranking – because low acidity oils keep their integrity, flavour and colour longer.

There are several categories of virgin oil that can be eaten straight from the press, but to include the word virgin in its name an oil must have no more than 3.3 per cent acidity and score at least a 3.5 on the dratted organoleptic scale.

Mediterranean producers all now use fairly much the same standards, and some signal the acidity level of their oils, but some areas have no regular taste panels and others simply get away with what they can. In the end, it's not just the label you should trust, but also your own palate, together with some nod to where you are buying. An expensive shop is no guarantee of quality but should be: a remote hovel is no guarantee of coarseness, but could be.

All things being equal, here is what you need to know about olive oil categories.

Virgin olive oils, fit for consumption as is, and that are normally sold retail:
Extra virgin olive oil: these must reach an organoleptic score of 6.5 or more and have

a maximum acidity of 1%, although most are around 0.5%. They should be impeccable in every way, properly reflecting the individuality of the olives and the time of the year they have been harvested.

Virgin olive oil: with an organoleptic rating of 5.5 or more and a maximum acidity of 1.5%, most of these will be indistinguishable from extra virgin oils.

There is a grade of ordinary virgin olive oil but this is rarely seen.

All the oils so far can be described as natural oils.

Lampante virgin olive oil, refined olive oil, and olive oil are descending grades of olive oil that have been processed in some way to make them palatable. The 'olive oil' category once used to be called 'pure olive oil', and so it is, 100% olive oil, but this is no guarantee of its flavour or, I'm sorry, its organoleptic quality. Some are very lightly flavoured and make excellent commercial oils for mayonnaise, for basic cooking and for the palates of those who are not yet adventurous. 'Light' olive oil is likely to be 'olive oil', for it is not lighter in fat content but lighter in flavour and this will be the result of processing. Its calorie content and imputed health-giving qualities are no different from the finest extra virgin oils.

Almond oil

Best known as a beauty treatment, but edible varieties are bottled and sold, mainly in France. It is pallid in colour and exceptionally fragile in flavour, but if you wait it gradually titillates the mouth with a slight milky greenness, the same after-effects as eating fresh green almonds. Quite what sort of food will stand up to this I do not know, except that its very gentility makes it a good thing to grease baking trays, moisten your hands when moulding sugar, lubricate moulds and so on. Perhaps it is more pleasing outside than inside.

Avocado oil

Long used as a base for cosmetics, cold-pressed avocado oil is currently the handbag, must-have oil in the kitchens of the smart. As with so many good things to eat or drink, its new guise began in New Zealand. The country exports only the best of its avocado crop and thus had a lot of second grade fruit that were virtually useless and valueless – until someone realised the avocado glut happened when there were no grapes to be pressed. After much experimentation a new culinary quality oil was pressed and developed and launched.

Avocado oil has masses of health benefits, unsaturated oils and so on, but it's too expensive to use enough to change your life expectation. It cooks at a higher temperature than olive oil, another great plus, but again it's too expensive to use just for frying. Its uncooked flavour is light and fugitive and thus can't be used as a taste finesser, the way an extra virgin olive oil might be. So what can it do? Where does it actually fit?

Cold-pressed avocado oil is excellent as an extra browning agent in a non-stick pan, when the food you are cooking is light and delicate and doesn't want to be interfered with in any way: thus it's perfect for pan-frying fish or chicken and on grilled or roasted vegetables. It also has the most profound jewel-like colour and so makes a sensational decorative drizzle, particularly on light coloured plates, where it adds sparkle and drama without changing the flavours already there.

The disadvantage of its light flavour gives avocado oil its greatest plus, that of being an elegant, non-intrusive carrier of other tastes. If you want a salad dressing where say, a rose, raspberry, sherry or tarragon vinegar can sing almost solo, with only the slightest underscoring of oil, this is the one.

Realising this some producers are now marketing flavoured avocado oils, offering sometimes new flavours that don't have to fight that of the oil itself. The most interesting use native New Zealand ingredients, notably horopito, a kind of pepper that comes with both unique aroma and a tongue-numbing effect, like Szechuan pepper or Tasmanian pepperbark.

So yes, welcome avocado oil to your kitchen, too. Use it for its vibrancy of colour, for its generous hospitality to other flavours, for its high frying point and, even, for its healthiness. But don't get suckered into using it for its flavour.

Argan oil

A little known oil but which is vital to survival of indigenous Berbers in south-western desert areas of the Souss plain, inland from Agadir in Morocco. It is made from the seed nut of the ancient argan tree, which has adapted to survive in severe conditions that make lesser plants panic. It has been a reliable source of food oil for centuries, but the 20th century began encroaching. Today, after local agitation and the bravery of protesting women, much of its scant habitat is officially protected and argan production is becoming an important source of income. There is nothing better to get at the seed than nimble fingers, even so it can take more than 15 hours work to produce 2½kg of nut to make 1 litre of oil. Cooperatives have been set up to give women jobs – something previously forbidden – and that brings good income back into communities which had little or nothing to spare.

The flavour is light, warm, comforting and, as you might expect, nutty: many think hazelnut oil is the closest. In Morocco it is sprinkled onto couscous, used to dress chargrilled capsicums (bell peppers), used for frying eggs that will be dusted with cumin, even used to finish gorgeous tagines of meat and dried fruits in their typical buttery sauces heightened with ginger and paprika and cumin. Or it makes *amlou* a thick mix of ground almonds, honey and argan oil. *Amlou* is piled onto yeast-raised pancakes, or used as a dip/spread for fresh bread eaten with hot mint tea. . . argan is new territory for most of us, and worth exploring if only to ensure it survives and continues to help support the Berbers of Souss plains. Best used and eaten cold or warmed, and never heated or hot.

Cottonseed

Widely used in vegetable oil mixtures and in oleomargarines, especially in the United States. In these products it has usually been bleached but when used to pack seafood, especially from Japan, it has slight colour and, to me, a rather unpleasant taste and texture, some of which I also think remains in the butter substitutes. It is the second most important seed oil, produced mainly in Russia, the United States and China.

They have been experimenting with a specially produced culinary version of cottonseed oil in Israel; I enjoyed it when I tasted it there some 15 years ago, but it reminded me of sewing machines and the oil used for them.

Grapeseed

Some say delicate, some say dull, but as it is not commonly seen this may not matter. Used for margarine or for salads, but the latter seems wimpish. If you fancy the idea of making your own flavoured oils, then grapeseed works particularly well, absorbing the flavours of herbs, spices, citrus and the like without pushing in where it's not wanted.

Hazelnut/huile de noisettes

Less common than walnut oil, and worth every *centime* – it usually comes from France. It has an affinity with tomatoes, although not as strong as that of walnut oil. Heat ruins it and so it is not a good plan to cook with it; better pretend it is an extra virgin olive oil and pour it lightly over, say, grilled rabbit or game, onto warm artichokes with soft-boiled eggs or green beans into which you have stirred roasted hazelnuts and garlic – that sort of thing. Try flavouring a traditional bread sauce with the oil rather than with butter: just great with game birds.

Hazelnut oil is considered coarser than walnut oil and more strident, and thus it is commonly diluted, with vegetable oil, a lesser olive oil, or, as a sauce, melted butter, but I would always try it neat first, because you might think it just right, as I do.

Not unexpectedly, hazelnut oil works very well with berry fruits and thus with such fruit vinegars as raspberry, especially. When I make fruit vinaigrette, by pureeing soft fruits with a touch of mustard, oil and a suitable vinegar, hazelnut oil adds a perfect finishing touch. Made with blackberries, even those from a freezer, such a vinaigrette is sensational with quickly seared scallops scattered over a salad of autumnal-tinted lettuce leaves; keep the vinegar or acid level minimal. The oil must be kept cool and dark once opened, as it oxidizes very quickly. In extremis I should refrigerate it, even though it thickens and clouds.

Hemp seed oil

A rich green colour and a strongish nutlike flavour that is sometimes diluted with other oils and flavours when retailed. Full of flavour and of goodness for you, highly polyunsaturated, and a definite talking point. Particularly when someone recognises its faint, curious but curiously familiar scent of marijuana; how do they know that? See also Hemp seeds.

Palm and palm kernel oil

The oil palm is native to West Africa and although its existence is barely even suspected by most Europeans it is commonly a part of our diet, especially if you like ice cream products.

The brilliant red fruit of the oil palm grows in bunches averaging 13-18kg/26-32lb in weight and if properly cultivated the tree produces a higher yield than any other oil-producing plant per acre. Each palm fruit is built up like a miniature coconut with a thick fibrous pulp on the outside and a hard kernel inside. Palm oil is obtained from its outer layer and this red substance is an essential ingredient to the food of Brazil and Nigeria, but adds a flavour not readily appreciated by the non-indigenous. More refined palm oils are staples in India and Asia and some edible fats include refined palm oil.

Palm kernel oil is an altogether harder oil, rather like that of the coconut, and it has two uses that some would say are indistinguishable, and others would argue are poles apart. One use is in soap, as Hollywood stars constantly remind us in return for huge fees. If the name is honest, there is olive oil in this soap, too. The other use, as *no one* reminds you, is as a major substitute for milk, butter and cream in 'non-dairy fat' foods. Palm kernel oil, after suitable treatment, can be whipped and frozen into believing it is cream and subsequently ice cream. It is the major fat used in ice creams in Britain and the basis for the *pareve* (dairy-free kosher) whips, creams and ice creams. It comes with very high levels of saturated fats.

Peanut/groundnut oil

The nut has an oil content of 45-50 per cent, which is used in fats, ice cream and margarine. Especially important in the catering trade for, as well as having almost no taste, peanut oil can be used to fry at an extremely high temperature without unpleasant smoking or other side effects. The combination of high temperature and lack of taste means you get crisper food faster and so the oil has had no opportunity to penetrate. By far the best oil for deep-frying and for wok cooking, and also a good basis for making your own flavoured oils.

Pistachio oil

Pistachio oil is almost fluorescent, a profound greeny-yellow, and perfectly but lightly pistachio flavoured: it is such a rare treat it should be used without any chance of confusion, dribbled only onto a guaranteed friend, excellent lettuce or other saladings, perhaps with edible flowers; segments of room temperature blood oranges to accompany duck scattered with roasted pistachios. Or on perfectly poached slices of salmon served just below room temperature. Or on a warm brioche, in which case I might just have whipped some of the oil into an unsalted *beurre cru*, a pretty good idea with all the nut oils incidentally. A minuscule amount of garlic is very good with pistachio oil.

Pine nut oil

Not very immediate in flavour, pine nut oil must be used in greater quantity to be ensured of tasting it, but also with greater restraint and discretion as the slightly resinous flavour can be off-putting. It is good on lightly chilled poached poultry breasts or on salmon, with perfect tomatoes, perhaps dribbled onto small warm rolls to serve with fragrant Moroccan dishes... maybe to finish a Provencal tian of spinach or chard. It's a very good idea to use it as a garnish or dressing with toasted pine nuts.

Poppyseed oil

Another oil popular simply for its lack of taste, an asset in some sorts of cooking. It is sold as *huile blanche* (white oil) in northern France and Paris, where it enjoys greatest popularity.

Pumpkin seed oil

An initial belief in some relationship with motor oil is not unnatural. It is thick, turgid and terribly brown. But it does have an astonishingly rich, nutty flavour – too much to use by itself unless flavouring a soup or a mash or authentic Mexican cooking.

It is said to be very popular in Austria, and so when you are there you might find out what

Salad Dressings

When I have paid a heap for a decent olive oil – or any oil for that matter – I can't think it's right to add many other flavours to it, except those of the foods it is to accompany.

The acidity of a little lemon or lime juice, perhaps a dash of very superior vinegar, and that's it. There's no place for mustard or sugar, for raw onion or bacon bits or cheese or dried herbs or any of the thousand things thought of as 'fixings' to dress a salad. Unless you are using a bland vegetable oil these plebian fancies have no place mixing with the upper classes, extinguishing everything distinguished you have chosen and paid big bucks to enjoy. Garlic is the exception, but even so should be rubbed around the bowl, rather than used in the dressing or salad.

So a salad dressing using good extra virgin oils means only a slosh of oil and a sprinkle of vinegar, usually on to the salad itself, no more than a combined teaspoonful per serving. Then add a very little salt and pepper. The very best way to toss a salad is with your hands, and as soon as the leaves or other ingredients are lightly coated, to then give them a shake and transfer to a second bowl. When a salad is all eaten up there should be no dressing left at the bottom. Your hands and wrists will taste delicious and deserve a good licking. Cook's privilege.

If your salad isn't the type that can be tossed, then dribble, splash or slosh the ingredients directly on to them or allow your guests to do so.

they use it for and tell the rest of us. For salads it very much needs to be diluted with a vegetable oil, and the nicest of these is roasted sunflower and pumpkin seed oil, made in Suffolk, England. This is reputed to make a sensational combination with avocado.

Rape seed oil

Oil-seed rape is now one of Europe's biggest crops and responsible for those sensational blankets of mustard yellow which are not mustard in spring. It is a mixed blessing to say the least. The powdery, musky scent from these fields causes untold agonies of allergy; no laughing matter if you are driving on a motorway. The bitterness of its nectar permeates, and to some palates, ruins honey and its oil must be radically purified and refined to make it useful. Yet, if you buy or use something called mere vegetable oil, this is what it is likely to be, and why it is taking over Britain's fields. However, and it is a big however, cold-pressed rape seed oil is something else, a vigorous rusty red colour and profound roasted-nut flavour that sets the palate racing, with the mind not far behind it. Try it wherever you use walnut oil, but use less of it. Haunting and fascinating and perplexing: how can something so good come from rape seed?

Safflower oil

Safflower, seeds of which have been unmasked in Egyptian tombs of 2000 BC, was originally grown for the colour of its florets, which give a cheap imitation of saffron. When synthetic dyes began to displace safflower it seemed doomed, but then it was discovered that oil from the florets and their seeds has the highest percentage of polyunsaturated oil known – 78 per cent. The major producers are now Mexico and the United States who between them produce over half a million tons of seeds each year.

Sesame seed oil

A very ancient oil, which should be used more as a flavouring than as a frying medium or as an oil by itself. It can be a moody dark red-brown or a less assertive reddish brown, depending on whether the seeds have been first toasted or not. Marco Polo was impressed enough to write about it and it is still widely used in India and the Orient, especially in confectionery and bakery. Add a few drops only when deep-frying tempura or anything else in batter. Add to marinades, especially for microwaving, or sprinkle onto almost anything to which you would add sesame seeds: prawns, green beans, pumpkin purée, chicken joints and baked hams. It very quickly goes rancid so should be stored cool and dark once opened.

Soy bean oil

Although used in China for the past 4,000 years, the first shipment did not arrive in the United Kingdom until 1908. It is one of the top four in the polyunsaturated league and is an extremely good keeper. Soy bean oil also has an elevated smoking point, which means it will fry or deep fry at a temperature high enough to ensure it will not pass what little flavour it has onto the food. As well as margarines and cooking fats the oil is used in paint, printing ink, soap, cosmetics, varnishes and insecticides. And some people's salads.

Sunflower oil

The very high percentage of polyunsaturates in this oil make it very important indeed, and it is widely used as an oil for salads, cooking, fats and margarine. It is very good for frying also but perhaps a little expensive for this use on a regular basis. The sunflower is a native of Mexico but grown in many parts of the world, particularly south Russia. China, Hungary and South Africa also grow enough to be useful but Great Britain, although it has an eminently suitable climate, produces a very small crop indeed. New varieties developed in the old Soviet Union have increased the oil content of seed from 20 to 40 per cent.

Walnut oil/huile de noix

Perigueux, that was the place, on a warm stone wall on the corner of a hot cobbled street. There I first discovered the God-given affinity of tomatoes and walnuts when I poured walnut oil onto a sun-red tomato. Bacon and eggs, gin and tonic, fish and chips? Such are nothing in comparison to this affinity wizardry, and, just as few additions can improve those, you need little else when you have tomatoes and walnut oil. Perhaps some parsley, that's very good, and maybe a little salt and pepper. But no vinegar, no herbs, no garlic or chives, no million-and-one ingredients, clear-out-the-fridge salad. Just two ingredients that work together to make something bigger and better than either. But there's more to walnut oil. It keeps the slight bite of fresh walnuts and together with its inherent sweetness thus both complements and extends the flavours of light meats, from grilled pork chops to pan-seared pheasant breasts. It's terribly good with fruit as you might expect, so grilled peach halves dribbled with walnut oil become a much faster and better tasting accompaniment than grilled stuffed peaches, especially with hot or cold ham. Walnut oil goes well with green salads of course, or add it to mayonnaise made with bland vegetable oil.

Don't cook with it, as most of the flavour goes, but sprinkle it onto cooked foods as you would an extra virgin olive oil. If you have masses of walnut oil and are prepared to experiment, it can be jolly good in breads and scones, but use some of the nuts too, or you might find the flavour so fugitive you will curse.

Keep the oil dark and cool, refrigerated in summer or in centrally heated winter kitchens if you are not using it up quickly, even though it goes thick and cloudy. But most of all be constantly on the alert for really ripe tomatoes.

Flavoured Oils

Truffle oils: they have been called the tomato ketchup of the upwardly mobile, but truffle oils are still the safest way to be overtly sensual in public. You can't help it particularly with white truffle oil, which has one of the world's most arresting, disturbing and irresistible smells, 'redolent of all possible perversity and prohibition, and reeking of every forbidden vice' – see truffle section.

White truffle oil: it would be nice to think some altruistic manufacturer decided to soak a few of his arrestingly expensive white truffles in oil for our benefit, but he didn't, not to make the commercially popular white truffle oils, anyway. They are generally made by flavouring oil with a nature-identical oil, which in this case I whole-heartedly endorse, because it is not there to enhance a feeble dilution. It is what it is.

Just as you should never cook with a white truffle, you should never cook with white truffle oil. Thus instead of shaving white truffle over your risotto you simply sprinkle on some of the oil. You could and should do the same to mashed potato or to scrambled eggs. Adding white truffle oil to the uneasy flavours of artichoke makes the edgiest of combinations. In parts of Italy raw white truffle is shaved over brioches: to emulate this I'd mix the oil into some melted unsalted butter, pull apart a warm brioche, and pour this on to the two halves. You could, of course, have added the oil to some fearfully thin slices of young mushroom, and put these into the brioche, but somehow the texture gets in the way of full abandonment to the flavour.

A white-truffled brioche is not for the faint hearted, but an extraordinary thing to eat late in the morning, perhaps with smoked salmon. If you are dining `a deux, adding a glass of excellent dessert wine would help secure your romantic prospects for the rest of the day.

Once hooked you will think of zillions of ways to use white truffle oil, but beware: the scent plays havoc with some people's finer or coarser sensibilities – they can barely be in the same room as it.

Black truffle oil: this is less immediate than white truffle oil but does have an earthy, meaty flavour the late food writer Jeremy Round bravely described as 'scrotal'. It is also best used without exposure to direct heat, but may be whisked into warm sauces, mashed or scalloped potatoes, poured into eggs just before they scramble, sprinkled onto smoked salmon or worked into whipped cream or butter to go with almost anything – hot or cold ham, the genuine, rather salty ones go orbital. Black truffle oil is just the thing for dressing excellent roasted beef or steaks, sprinkled onto slices of hot, roasted turkey, free-range chicken or game birds or in salads which contain them.

Porcini oil: this is pretty good too, and I make my own with dried porcini (ceps). It keeps its flavour rather well in gentle cooking.

Other flavoured oils

The big growth has been in flavoured olive oils, and most seem to be genuine flavour obtained by maceration of an ingredient with the oil or by pressing the fruit with the olives. The great favourite in New Zealand is an Italian oil flavoured with mandarin, a wonderful flavour that is very stable in cooking as long as it's not too long or too hot. It's wonderful added to anything fishy, hot or cold, or for salads that go with them: I remember scallops and mussels were particularly enhanced. There's a lemon and an orange version, too, and Mas Portell's Catalonian arbequina oils are infused with mushroom, intense basil, chilli, rosemary, oregano and smoked paprika, which is rather less successful than the others.

The other commercially available flavoured oils worth considering are those flavoured with oriental ingredients for wok cooking, like garlic and ginger. But honestly, why pay others to do what is so easily obtained at home? Make flavoured oils the way you would flavoured. vinegar, by macerating. Unwaxed citrus zest, singly or mixed, smoked or plain garlic, any sort of fresh dried or smoked chillies, fresh herbs, fresh or roasted black or green peppercorns etc.

Or think of favourite combinations: fresh lime zest and chillies for a Mexican lift; orange zest, coriander and juniper berries for the flavours of gin; rosemary and thyme; English lavender flower and rose petals with roasted black peppercorns. Or toast some nuts and make your own toasted nut oils too.

Use a light olive oil, like Spanish arbequina oils or an almost flavourless vegetable oil to start, keep them warm but not in sunlight for a few weeks and then test regularly to ensure they are not too strong or need to be strained off and made stronger by adding a fresh batch of the ingredient.

If you really can't be bothered the UK's Castle Aromatics makes outstanding products with sunflower oil and fresh herbs and spices, including startlingly fresh mint, kaffir lime and basil oils plus a smoked garlic, porcini, fresh red chilli and rosemary oil. Yummy.

I see a range of flavoured oils and vinegars as the keys of a piano in your kitchen. With their bright, exact or created flavours plus some zingingly fresh ingredients you can play a favourite or a new flavour tune in the kitchen whenever the mood hits you.

Mayonnaise Magics

A helping of boldly flavoured olive oil can be used to give sophisticated flavour to a mayonnaise made with lesser or vegetable oils. Most of the nut oils and flavoured oils can be used this way, too; a mayonnaise made only with walnut oil would be far too overpowering and needlessly extravagant. Of course, this also applies to mayonnaise you have bought, some of which is inoffensive but hardly tastes of what it says either. Here's the time to be brutal, to override the flavours such mayonnaise came with, and to make the most of its texture by adding your own taste.

So, the magical affinity of walnuts and tomatoes is enhanced by serving them topped with mayonnaise flavoured with walnut oil, and perhaps by also stirring in some roasted and chopped walnuts: with a little crushed garlic such nutty mayonnaise is uber-good on cold vegetables and double that on roasted or grilled fennel. Hazelnut, pistachio and other nut oils work the same magic in greater or lesser amounts, and make an enormous difference to something as simple as cold French beans or asparagus, trout or salmon.

When you make your own mayonnaise it pays to remember you can increase the quantity dramatically by diluting with water or vinegar as you go: when the mayonnaise is very thick keep beating but dribble in water until it is much softer. Then, if you like, change to flavoured vinegar or fruit juice or to a flavoured oil. Now continue with more of the basic oil and the mayonnaise will thicken again. Instead of water you could use an aromatic wine, say gewürztraminer or a gutsy dry rose, a spirit or fruity eau de vie, red or white vermouth or a suitable liqueur.

Fresh herbs and freshly ground spices can also transform ordinary mayonnaise, but it's best to heat the spices a little first, in a dry pan or in the microwave, to encourage them to sing for their supper well before you are due yours. These combinations need a couple of hours to develop out of a refrigerator, or to be refrigerated overnight.

Start on this road of discovery by combining equal parts of ground cinnamon, coriander and cumin and then adding roughly chopped flat leaved parsley: serve that with shelled hard-boiled eggs that have been fried a bright golden brown in a well-flavoured olive oil. Perfect outdoor food, smart enough for a Bentley tailgate at the Melbourne Cup or Ascot.

Minted Waldorf Mayonnaise

All the flavours of the most famous *salade compose*, but easier to enjoy as a mayonnaise that's especially good with cold poultry, tomatoes, a simple pasta salad or to bind boiled and quartered eggs.

150ml/¼ pint mayonnaise
225g/8oz sharp cooking apples, trimmed, cored and peeled
1 tbsp water
optional sugar
2 tbsp walnut oil
1-2 tsp finely chopped celery leaf
1 tbsp fresh mint leaves, chopped

Cook the apple in the water over low heat until soft and fairly dry. Press through a sieve, whisk in the walnut oil and sweeten if you really must – it's better as it is. Mix with the chopped celery leaf and mint and then fold into the mayonnaise. Toasted walnuts would be the right thing if you have a mind to strew.

Olives, Pickles and Sauces

It can't have been long after man first learned to cook food that he looked around for tasty accompaniments or methods to preserve fresh and cooked foods.

The oldest human footprints on earth go to and from saltpans. With salt, with vinegar, with oil and with smoke, man could be sure of excitement, and of something to eat when times were bad. We still look to simple methods of salting and pickling when we want a savoury snack or condiment.

Olives

The olive is one of the foundations of western civilization. Together with wheat and wine it formed the triumvirate of produce for food and for trade in the eastern Mediterranean that supported the first civilizations – Crete was cultivating them at least 5,000 years ago.

There are hundreds of varieties of olives, with infinite variations of flavour and perfume. Rather like apples, some are harvested early in autumn, and some are not ready until the raw depths of winter. Dirk Bogarde's harrowing story of harvesting his Provencal olives in freezing winds rather changes one's view of olives as somehow being a fruit of indolent, sun-sodden pastorality.

Green and black olives are not necessarily different varieties. Some olives are better harvested early and used green, others must be fully ripe and black, and some super-useful trees produce an olive suited to being used as both. Less common are olives harvested half-ripe, usually called violets because of their colour and seen particularly on the North African coast. From all of these come culinary olives, the green, the violet, the natural black and the processed black.

The green olive is generally inedible when knocked or pulled from the tree and must be relieved of its bitterness, if it is to be eaten rather than crushed for oil. The simplest way is to soak the fruits in brine, but there are few varieties inherently sweet enough for such simplicity. Most are first put into a soda (lye) solution, which whilst neutralizing the unpleasantness generates heat and thus also softens and slightly cooks the olives. After washing they are then put into brine and fermented for up to three months.

Ripe olives, which may be anything from violet and purple to brownish but are rarely truly black, are sometimes sterilized but not otherwise processed before going directly into brine. The fermentation of ripe olives is based on yeast action rather than the lactic fermentation of green olives; when they are exposed to air they oxidize, which darkens the skins.

Processed black olives combine something of both the other processes. They do not need to be fully ripe and are alternately immersed in lye and then in water, during which time compressed air is bubbled through to oxidize them throughout. Once you know, you can recognise these, for they are shinier and blacker outside and much more uniformly dark inside.

Each country usually adds another style of olive to its natural green, natural black, assisted black and its violet olives – the old and wrinkly olive. These are the raisins of the olive world, left on the tree over winter so that both cold wind and new season sun desiccate and concentrate their flavours.

Pitted and stuffed olives are a great favourite, if not to eat then for decorative purposes. The most popular are those stuffed with red peppers but there are others. I particularly like those stuffed with an almond and particularly dislike those stuffed with onion or anchovy. Orange and lemon peels are sometimes found in eviscerated olives and both are marvellous but more likely to be encountered at a tapas bar in Spain than in Ilkley or Boise. The stones that have been extracted, mainly by machine nowadays, are often used for low-grade olive oil and the resultant pulp is an animal feed.

Knowing your olives is a lifetime occupation. To that I have no simple solution other than that which is the secret of most really good eating. Shop creatively, taste something new, learn what you don't like and what you do like, and then remember those you liked best.

Spain
Although dozens of olives are used for making Spanish olive oil her soils have a special affinity with edible green olives. The best known are the *manzanilla* and the queen, known as the *gordal* in Seville and the *sevillano* in the rest of Spain. Both are from Andalucia. The queen is large, deep green, and fleshy. The small *manzanilla* is paler, finer textured and silky skinned, especially good for cooking, and as the name suggests has notes of apple. Incidentally, it is only a pitted *manzanilla* olive that properly belongs in a martini cocktail. Pimento, anchovy or almond stuffed, or intact *manzanillas*, are, well, they are just not right.

France
The south of France grows a bewildering number of olives in both colours. And as well as plain black or green the markets of Nimes make a specialty of stuffed olives. The best black olives in brine are from Nyons and Carpentras; Mentons are especially big and luscious. But this is only whence, and local varieties are just as important to know. Amongst green ones, *la picholine* is deliciously savoury and generously fleshed even though small; *lucques* and *petits-lucques* are curved, pointed and part easily from the stone, with a notably rich creaminess; *la salonequo* is often broken and especially good in cooking where a reserved bitterness is welcomed. Round heart-shaped *nyons* (sometimes *tanches*) are the best French black olives, actually a rich plum black. Although rarely seen outside Provence, the *cailletiers* or *olives de Nice* are small but very perfumed, and the proper olive to use in Nicoise cooking.

There is a fascinating museum of olives in a chateau at Cagnes sur Mer and another, private one, at Ampus, open in the afternoons in July and August.

Those olives with DOP status are:
Olives de Nice
Olives cassées de la Vallée des Baux-de-Provence
Olives noires de la Vallée des Baux-de-Provence
Olives noires de Nyons

Greece

The majority of olives are black, and these include some extraordinary varieties sweet enough to eat direct from the trees; the island of Mitilini is reputed to have the best of these. In Greece it is especially easy to detect differences of flavour given by variety, by soil or by micro-climate, however their rather violet-coloured *kalamata* olives are widely thought to be amongst the very best from any source. *Thrumpa* are considered amongst the very best of the wrinkly, over-wintered type of eating olive.

Italy

Amongst Italy's wondrous produce with names we all recognize there is an unsung olive that deserves a wider stage and greater ovations. **The Oliva Nocellara della Belice DOP** is almost red when ripe and has luscious flesh. Grown in the Valle del Belice and in parts of the province of Trapani.

Oliva La Bella della Daunia DOP is voluptuous and big with at least 85% of each fruit offering flesh of outstanding eating.

Flavouring

Flavouring olives your own way is terribly simple. A few minutes in the markets of Fez or a stroll through the Thursday market against the ancient walls of Aigue-Mortes will give you dozens of ideas. Sliced lemon with dried oregano is basically good. Crushed cloves of garlic, crushed coriander seeds (particularly), bay leaves, peppercorns (black, white or green), thyme branches, parsley stalks, sliced peppers, and sliced dried chillies are what I usually use to start. Of course many of the things you would expect to find in olives go with them too, anchovies and crushed nuts particularly. Oils made by soaking dried tomatoes, dried mushrooms and the like give very superior results if you let olives wallow in them a while.

Cooking

If you fancy cooking with olives there are a few tricks. They should have been brined rather than oiled, must be blanched quickly in boiling water, and then stored in cold water for a few hours. They are generally rather better added towards the end of cooking, too. Or you could use prepared olive purées, one of the few really outstanding new products on the market.

Olive purées are often flavoured with nothing much more than a touch of decent vinegar, and all the better for such modesty. I find them terrific with fish – they wonderfully hide the brown membrane that is so difficult to remove from monkfish tails – but are excellent with anything of a Mediterranean persuasion, including roasted chickens and tomato sandwiches. They make an instant all-covering sauce for hot pasta, and might be swirled into mayonnaise for cold pasta salads. If all this is too much trouble, you won't do better than toast fingers spread with black olive pâté, a couple of soft-boiled eggs and something decent on the telly. Incidentally, although olives are important in Provencal *tapenade*, they are not the most important: the word is based on local dialect for capers, *tapeno*, and it is the flavour of capers that should predominate.

Flavoured, oil-enriched, herby or spicy, olives make excellent additions to food to be served warm or cold. Chop them into vegetable purées, sprinkle them on salads, stir them into pasta sauces or toss them on pizza after cooking. They have an unexpected affinity with oranges, with highly flavoured cheeses (think of them with feta in Greek salads) and with many fruits. I remember a plate of black figs, kalamata olives, properly spicy rocket leaves and curls of Parmesan cheese. You would too.

Storing

If you live in a small community where bulk olives are unobtainable, don't hesitate to buy in quantity elsewhere when you can.

Olives sold in bulk look better and more inviting than bottles and jars and are generally cheaper. But there is a paradox. Keeping them dark is more important than keeping them refrigerated; a good display of bulk olives is precisely what puts them at risk. Once at home you should assiduously keep the level of brine or any other preservative just above the olives: a slice or two of lemon usually stops the formation of mould on the brine. It is as well to pop some lemon into large bottles of bulk olives once they have been opened, too.

Cured olives may then be stored in any combination of light brine, oil or vinegar. Generally only the very finest qualities, such as the wondrously fleshy Greek Kalamata, are stored in oil pointed with superior wine vinegar, even though such a ploy would greatly improve the flavour of inferior types.

Even better is to drain the brine and to moisten the olives with olive oil, or a mixture of olive oil and a tasteless vegetable oil, or with vinegar and olive oil. And once you start doing that, the fun really begins.

Pickles and Chutneys

A pickle can mean any food preserved in acid/vinegar or salt, but generally a pickle is based on vegetables and contains little or no sugar, and chutney is more likely to be based on fruits and to contain sugar. The US is particularly fond of a delicious compound style, the sweet pickle.

Salt in solution with water is a preservative, because in strong brine bacteria cannot multiply and cause putrefaction. But too much salt in food can mean an unacceptably hardy flavour to many. Luckily, a process called lactic fermentation can be employed to preserve vegetables with rather less than saturated brine – (See Fruits, Nuts and Vegetables).

All fresh vegetables contain sugars and have a skin covering of micro-organisms, which can be controlled to our advantage. If you quickly put freshly gathered vegetables into brine that contains only 8-11 per cent salt, the putrefactive bacteria will be inhibited but those which act to ferment sugars and make lactic acid develop – it is the same process that sours milk naturally.

Lactic acid is a preservative, too. Usefully, it does not have a marked flavour but it is not powerful enough to be a sole preservative. So once lactic fermentation is complete, the lactic brine is replaced by a brine of 15 per cent salt and about one per cent lactic acid, then neither fermentation nor putrefaction is possible. Lactic acid is often combined with acetic acid, the acid of vinegar, to dilute the latter's sharpness, especially in pasteurized packs.

If vegetables are placed directly into a 15 per cent brine solution or into a mixture of brine and vinegar, this is called non-fermentation brining.

The degree of lactic fermentation, presence of herbs and flavourings, temperature of brining and quality of the initial produce, will all flavour these products. The presence of air causes the growth of bacterial moulds on the top of lactic brines, but these are harmless and can easily be scraped away. The produce, though, should always be kept below the surface of the liquid and away from light as much as possible.

Products pasteurized in liquid are likely to have a lower lactic or salt content, because of the additional sterilizing action of heat treatment.

Preserving in vinegar or acetic acid alone works because it short cuts lactic fermentation by providing from the start a high enough acid level to kill or inhibit all bacterial action. Some items require a mixture of salt and vinegar to control their unique infestation. Onions are pickled by being cooked in vinegar; and when this process also includes fruits, spices and herbs you get spreadable pickles and, by including sugar, chutneys. Make chutneys smooth and you have sauces, and ketchups.

Beetroot: bottles or tins of small pickled beetroots, usually from Scandinavia or Germany, are very useful indeed, cold as a garnish or hot as a vegetable. Drained of their preservative liquid (those from Scandinavia are less sharp) and heated in orange juice and butter, with a little lemon for accent, they become special; a little ground allspice moves them further along. Excellent heated in sour cream spiked with horseradish, with garlic, with parsley or with paprika – or any combination.

Cattails: when they are bigger you know these as bull rushes, which can be boiled and eaten with butter. But when they are young and the tops are hardly 14cm/6in long and no thicker than a small finger they can also be eaten, or pickled. Their flavour is rather green and feral, somewhat like the issue of a marriage between asparagus and artichoke. Pickled cattails are available in specialty food shops in Montreal.

Gherkins: what the French call cornichons. These are usually baby or dwarf cucumbers, and they still make nice decorations when cut almost through their length several times and then fanned out. I find their flavour is often too determined even when they are real gherkins, which are not baby cucumbers at all but a relation, native to the Caribbean.

Capers: Tom Stobart described these as tasting 'goaty' – they can certainly taste very unusual and unusually awful if not used with the greatest care and discretion, for they require a degree of care few bother to understand. Capers are the unopened flowers of a Mediterranean plant that grows like a creeper. Good ones are expensive because the gathering cannot be mechanized – I believe the life of each flower is so short you have to crop them each morning or miss out. Capers are not lactic fermented but put into jars of vinegar brine, which preserves by the joint action of acetic acid and salt. And then there are salted capers.

Once soaked in fresh water or wine to reduce their saltiness, these will give you a gentler and more caper-like flavour. And slowly they seem to be replacing pickled ones on the shelves of delis who care.

Until I learned capers must never be exposed to the air until the very moment you eat them, I had never liked them unless first soaked in milk, and that's something you do only to salted capers, something you are less likely to see. Even then they were used in a sauce rather than as an ingredient to be eaten solo Mr Stobart always combined them with lemon zest and crushed garlic and I always mean to try these with roasted or poached salmon.

I like previously unexposed capers more each time I eat them, and even put them into sandwiches, say chicken with lemon zest and capers, and regularly add them as little balloons of flavour in pasta dishes. They are the most perfect accompaniment to anything smoked, particularly smoked eel, which is increasing in availability and popularity – as it should.

Two things I'm certain about – you should never buy cheap capers, and they must always be covered with liquid, or they develop a taste that makes goats positively fragrant.

Caperberries: these follow the flowers which remain on the caper vine, are like small green footballs, and have rather tough hairy seeds. Once rarely seen they are now widely available. I don't like the contrast between the skin and the seeds, and I don't like the raw woody flavour of the seeds and can't help thinking these have been marketed opportunistically, aimed at those who will buy anything new. But with their slender shape and curved stems they sure look good, like olives that have done well for themselves.

Onions: almost everyone knows more about onions than me, because I dislike them very much. Onions seem to me to represent all the worst of British cooking, onions with everything and vinegar on your chips. I simply do not believe every sauce or stew or soup needs onion as a base and I know that Cheddar cheese, caviar and tomatoes, among other things, are far nicer if they are not massacred by the acidic sharpness of raw onion, which then stays on the palate to disfigure the taste of your wine or pudding. Pickled onions are worse. Eat them if you like, but don't mix them with fine food or wine – and keep your distance.

Chutneys: Indians would not recognize our chutneys, even though the word came from there. Ours are hot and spicy, based on fruits, always contain both vinegar and sugar and should be quite coarse in texture. Often the major fruit has been brined separately, and is added to the cooked base sauce at the end of the cooking process. Mango chutney is the best known, but peach is very good, too. Chutneys mix well with mayonnaise and can also make quick, interesting hot sauces for cold meats; for instance, heat a few spoonfuls of mango chutney, splash in a little citrus juice and the merest touch of brandy.

There is an entirely different type of chutney, which is uncooked and often encountered in countries with an Indian influence. One of the best I tasted was in Mauritius, a whizzed-up mix of coriander leaf, garlic and coconut with a tiny amount of chilli and fresh ginger.

Mustard pickle: what the Americans call piccalilli, a word that almost no one can spell anyway.

Piccalilli: this is a law unto itself. First the vegetable content should be crisp, and so it is lactic fermented or brined rather than being boiled in a sauce like other pickles. The sauce itself is thickened with cornflour and made from onions, garlic, spices, vinegar and, of course, mustard, according to each manufacturer's specific recipe. The usual vegetable content is silverskin onions, gherkins and cauliflower florets. The yellow colour is turmeric, or should be. Some commercial manufacturers use colouring instead, because turmeric fades in sunlight.

Pickles: this is really quite a broad term when you think olives, onion, piccalilli, beetroot and cucumber can be called pickles. Mixed pickles vary from delicious Italian mixtures of crisp vegetables in a light, vinegary brine, which are excellent as hors d'oeuvres, to the Oriental bottles of lime pickle, mango pickle, and so on. As pickles last so well, buy one or two really excellent examples to use from time to time to give a welcome lift to ordinary food. Although I love pickled walnuts, I can't think of a commercially available English mixed pickle that is better than those made by such Indian companies as Patak's or Ferns; but English pickled peaches, oranges or pears, occasionally available, are very good.

Red Cabbage: with or without apple, this is a very cheap canned vegetable that goes a magically long way. Always cured on the day it is gathered, red cabbage can stand a lot of cooking – allowing you to improve it at home so it tastes homemade. Sliced or chopped apple, bacon and spiced vinegar make up the most useful additions – flavour the vinegar by simmering a few spoonsful of good wine vinegar with a dessertspoonful of pickling spice, drain and add. Garlic and orange juice with hot and sweet paprika, smoked or unsmoked, make another wonderful combination; so does garlic and juniper berries and gin, but only stir in the latter as you are serving for it is distressingly fugitive when heated. A touch of molasses gives colour and body. Red cabbage is first choice with any hearty meal, especially for game or fatty continental sausages and is the traditional accompaniment to a true Lancashire Hotpot.

Samphire/salicorne: see under Herbs.

Sauerkraut: the truth about sauerkraut is no less astonishing than that about soft roe or salami. It is made the same way a farmer makes silage for his cattle; indeed the smell can be distressingly similar. Sauerkraut is white cabbage that has been subjected to lactic fermentation but it is rarely drained and rebrined. The sauerkraut you buy in tins is very good but has been cooked, of course. If you are lucky enough to buy sauerkraut uncooked you can eat it as it is, but it's more usual to drain and rinse it and then to flavour it with bacon, onion, garlic, apple, caraway, wine – even champagne. You then cook it for up to an hour; it should not be mushy but have absorbed the cooking liquid you have used, which should have equalled half the original volume of the sauerkraut. Cooked together or separately, sauerkraut and rugged pork sausages, bacon or starchy vegetables all belong to one another. The *choucroutes* that are served in varying ways throughout France are nearly all more filling and rich than expected; and a version into which champagne is poured really does exist. I ate it in Cognac, where they know

Cucumbers

Cucumbers are generally lactic fermented before anything else is done to them. The secret of retaining crispness and developing flavour in all pickled cucumbers is to allow slow fermentation to progress at a low temperature. Only new green cucumbers are cured in a warm spot, and must then be eaten quickly as well as being stored in a very cool or refrigerated environment; if they are not kept cool they soften and then lose colour, flavour and texture.

The techniques and ingredients are accessible to anyone, so when the markets are flooded with such suitable cucumbers as the short Lebanese variety, have a go at making your own.

Salt cucumbers: are treated the most simply of all, and after fermentation are put into a plain brine.

Sweet and sour cucumbers: have extra flavour added to them by mixing vinegar or acetic acid into the second brine. A variety of other herbs and spices might also be included. These are more usual in:

Dill cucumbers: these rely heavily for flavour on fresh fronds of dill, but the brines can also contain peppercorns, red pepper/capsicum and garlic, bay, parsley or horseradish. Grape, blackcurrant, oak and cherry leaves can also be found in the bottle.

New green cucumbers: are not lactic fermented but lightly salted and ready to eat in a few days, whereas dill pickles can take up to three months to taste right.

Traditionally, pickled cucumbers are sliced diagonally or lengthwise and eaten as a relish. Very good with salt beef, as you know, but any hot or cold smoked meat or sausage is transported into a better part of heaven by the addition of crisp slices of pickled cucumber. I particularly like dill cucumber with smoked fish, especially hot-smoked salmon.

a thing or two about food – it was delicious but I don't think I'd do it again; I had a conscience about doing that to champagne.

An unexpected combination is sauerkraut and fish: bake fish steaks on individual nests of sauerkraut and it makes a gratifying but unexpectedly light meal.

Walnuts: picking the young green walnuts that go into pickled walnuts is dangerous work as walnut trees have extremely brittle branches and each nut must be picked individually, unlike ripe walnuts which are shaken from the tree. The green walnuts are hand selected and trimmed before being pickled typically, in malt vinegar, but around Christmas time in particular you may also find them packed in luxuries such as port. Best used the old-fashioned way, as part of a ploughman's lunch – (see Fruits, Nuts and Vegetables).

Sauces

Bean pastes and sauces: beans are the basis of three types of important Chinese ingredients. Brown (sometimes yellow) and black bean sauces are made from different varieties of fermented soy beans and are largely interchangeable as a pungent but generally acceptable flavouring for fish, poultry, meat and vegetable dishes.

Bean paste or Bean sauce: if this is all the label says, it will have been made from a yellowish variety of soy bean, and be rather smooth, thick and brownish, not unlike Japanese miso. The flavour and use is rather like that of soy sauce but the thick texture and rich colour are such that it will change those of a sauce as well as adding distinct savour; very much part of Northern cuisine – a Szechuan variation adds crushed chilli peppers.

Black bean paste or sauce: made from salted and fermented black soy beans and although largely interchangeable with brown bean sauce, seem particularly popular in the West on fish and seafood, for although resolutely savoury, black beans also have a residual sweetness, which is always appreciated with fishy foods. If you buy a bag of the fermented beans, they should be rinsed and chopped before use. They are said to last a very long time without refrigeration. All but the manic purist generally find it simpler to use black bean sauce, in which fermented beans are crushed and extended with soy sauce and other flavourings, particularly orange or tangerine peel and ginger; you may add further ones, sherry or ginger wine, fruit juices, chillies, or garlic, a particular affinity. There is a sweetened version, which may be used instead of Hoisin sauce.

Red bean sauce: made from the adzuki bean and so is likely to be sweet, and used as a filling or flavouring component in sweet baking.

Brown fruit sauce: HP sauce and relations. Date syrup is the base for many, especially HP sauce, but vinegar, onions and fruit of other kinds are also essential. It is easy – and right – to make fun of those who use these and other sauces with no thought for the cook, but like every product that has survived on the market, fruit sauces have their place and time. Give me a good game pie or pork pie and I'd much rather have such a sauce than mustard. I prefer them directly from the refrigerator, too, which lessens unwarranted sweetness. Good for flavouring mayonnaise into which you may wish to incorporate poultry or vegetables.

Chakalaka: this seems like the ultimate African nightmare, but is actually a culinary fairy-godmother. It's made in South Africa with a base of onion, chillies, fresh ginger and curry powder into which you stir tomatoes, green pepper/capsicum and carrots, and then top up with a tin of baked beans – and then the lot is cooked until smooth. Chakalaka was created to sauce *millipap* or *mealie-mealie*, the staple township porridge of cornmeal. And that's the clue to the presence of baked beans in this amazing mixture. By itself cornmeal is unbalanced and a diet based on it exclusively can lead to pellagra and beri beri, terrible diseases of malnutrition. Yet, add bean protein to grain protein and you get a meat protein equivalent and thus a great sustainer of life. Add other vegetables and you have an essentially healthy and varied diet. It could be coming to your local deli soon; South African companies are gearing up to pack and export it.

Fish sauce: although best known as the *nam pla* of Thai cooking, fish sauces are also used throughout south-east Asia and China. They are a result of the fermentation of fish, a direct cousin of the Romans' *garum*. But be calm. None smell or taste of fish if they are any good, but are a lightly coloured and flavoured seasoning, more salty than any other flavour. Used to finish dishes or as a table condiment.

Hoisin sauce: this is the one you use when eating Peking Duck. Also known as Barbecue Sauce even though its name means 'fresh flavour of the sea'. Made from soy beans, flour, sugar, salt, garlic and chilli peppers, it is dark reddish brown in colour, has a creamy consistency and a sweet aftertaste. Particularly associated with roasted duck and pork and the like but, as the name suggests, also with seafood and fish. It may be used as a simple dip, too.

Whatever you do with it, experiment. Make it sweet and sour by adding citrus or vinegars, make it aromatic with sherry or ginger wine, add tomato ketchup to make it more like a western barbecue sauce. With crunchy peanut butter, sesame seeds, sesame oil and a touch of chilli it gives an interesting variation on satay sauces.

Mushroom ketchup: few people make this or any other type of ketchup at home now, but a well stocked larder once always contained a selection of sauces made from ingredients as diverse as cucumbers, oysters, fruit and vegetables. Mushroom ketchup is one of the few that survived and when you can find it (made commercially) buy it more as flavouring than a sauce to lay on the side of your plate. It is made by an interesting process using salt, which when sprinkled on mushrooms will extract the liquid from them. This is heated, flavoured and bottled. Commercial mushroom ketchup often contains soy sauce nowadays, which makes the apparent salt content even higher; it is so high that mushroom ketchup becomes interchangeable with anchovy essence, but that is no bad thing. Use mushroom ketchup only at the end of cooking to strengthen or add interest, in the same way that celery, salt, soy sauce, anchovy essence or garlic and ginger juice might do.

Oyster sauce: a rich brown condiment or dipping sauce made by fermenting oysters and soy sauce, and thus related to fish sauce and soy sauce, but meatier tasting and more expensive than either. Use to finish a dish rather than as a cooking ingredient. Like fish sauce, only poor quality oyster sauces will taste or smell fishy.

Pesto: pesto Genovese, from Genoa of course, has become unavoidable but that's no bad thing. This sauce of fresh basil, pine nuts, garlic, Parmesan and olive oil is bright, pungent and just what tomatoes and pasta need. But it is also an excellent condiment with grilled vegetables, cheese, steak, roast lamb and poultry and fish, particularly oysters – that goes for hot or cold. If you make it yourself you can even consider using it in stuffings or marinades before cooking, which will, it is true, injure much of the special appeal of basil. But take heart, commercial bottles of pesto have been pasteurized and most of them don't taste too bad: otherwise, if you do not have the half-acre field of basil needed to make even a small amount of pesto, buy a jar of commercial pesto and chop into it some fresh leaves and keep your mouth shut. No one will know. If they do, it's because they do it too.

And be bold. Basil pesto is not the only pesto – any sauce pounded together can properly be called a pesto. Use other nuts, other herbs, other cheeses, but if you make pesto in a food processor it just won't have the same flavour because too little of the important oils have been released by the machine's blades, which only cut. You can do two things. You can pound the whizzed up mixture, and this helps. Or you pound the basil or other leaves before you add them to the processor: do this between two sheets of cling film, using a rolling pin, and then be sure you collect the oil left on the film, by rubbing it with fresh breadcrumbs or ground almonds and then putting those into the mixture.

Plum sauce: like smooth plum chutney, made from a particular type of sour yellow Chinese plum. It is essentially sweet and sour and widely used as the start for other sauces: equal amounts of this and tomato ketchup make a basic sweet and sour sauce mix. Sometimes known in America as **duck sauce**, for they were served together rather than the more usual Hoisin sauce. Of course, if you have grown up in Australasia this means something quite different. Spiced plum sauce or plum and tomato sauce, as thick as ketchup but darker in colour and infinitely more nuanced in flavour, is common on dining tables, and usually homemade, too. It adds unjustified life and interest to the dullest cold meats and hot pies, and behaves superbly when offered with the finest fare, including lobster from barbecues, roasted beef or lamb and the best parts of roasted birds.

Rouille: essentially aioli or a garlic mayonnaise with chilli, but it shouldn't be. Sadly chilli-hot rouille is increasingly served with bouillabaisse in the belief this is traditional and correct. It is not, but becoming so. The original, local red pepper that used to be used in rouille is a gentle soul with but the lightest titillation of heat, just enough to tease the palate rather than to injure it.

Chilli-rouille properly belongs to the simple and bland bourrides made west of Marseilles; bourride is mixed white fish poached in stock, which is then thickened with aioli. It is simple and coarse and traditionally a little hot pepper in rouille helped cut the richness.

But bouillabaisse is made from far finer fish and, anyway, flavoured with saffron, the world's most expensive spice. Do you really think traditional cooks used saffron and then added chilli so you couldn't taste it?

The habit of heating up rouille for bouillabaisse apparently arose through restaurants in Marseilles employing chefs and waiters from the poorer west, who brought with them the custom of rouille with everything, and hot coarse chillies. Because they were the ones cooking, that's what they did to the previously gentle rouille of Marseilles.

Once again this shows chillies are a refuge of the poor with nothing but bland food otherwise to eat; and it shows how easily the rest of us can be led. A rouille that is very hot on the tongue may be to your liking, but should have nothing to do with the expense and the universe of fine flavours in a true bouillabaisse.

Soy/shoyu sauce: the quintessential flavouring and condiment of south-east Asian and oriental cooking. Shoyu is the Japanese name and is often used to indicate a naturally brewed rather than artificially produced product, but this can seem precious.

The real thing begins with steamed soy beans mixed with malted wheat kernels, that is wheat grains allowed to sprout and then roasted. Special yeast is added to start a natural fermentation and precisely developed yeasts give this or that manufacturer their particular flavour and style; they are jealously guarded secrets. After three days the mixture grows a mould or culture on the surface, giving aroma and developing new flavours. Some of the sugar and alcohol present transform into acids, which give sharpness to the final flavour. Natural glutamates are also formed, the basis for the sauce's ability to enliven other tastes. After six months maturing, the mixture is drawn off into cloths to be pressed. A deep, reddish brown, clear liquid is funnelled from the pressing machines to be pasteurised and bottled.

Well, that is the classic process, indicated by the words 'naturally brewed' on a label. Commercial processes make an approximation in a few days by hydrolising soy protein using hydrochloric acid, diluting with salt water and then adding corn syrup, colouring and other additives; there is also a process, semi-natural, semi-chemical, which combines both methods.

The Kikkoman Company has been making naturally brewed soy sauce in Japan since 1630 and also makes a special brew just for the Imperial household. The beans for this are hand picked for quality and size and everything else is done the ancient way, including a three-year brew in huge oak casks, which give added complexity of flavour and colour to the result.

Once opened soy sauce keeps its virtues for about a month, and after that it will begin to oxidize and lose most of its subtle complexities; this happens faster and more noticeably if it is exposed to extremes of light or heat. Provided it is well sealed, refrigeration will not harm it. Many oriental ingredients last forever, but not this one.

Light soy sauce: is brewed purposely to give 25 per cent of the usual colour, so it will not discolour dishes when adding flavour; it is often slightly saltier than dark soy sauce.

Dark soy sauce: has a rich dark concentrated flavour that is both sweet and salt. It will colour sauces and foods and this is part of the consideration when using it. Often both dark and light are combined to get precisely the flavour required.

Tamari soy sauce: is made only with soy beans, and is used in sushi restaurants, but rarely in the home.

Low-salt soy sauce: is increasingly marketed.

Sukiyaki sauce: soy sauce mixed with rice wine and sugar, added to water and boiled up as a stock for cooking beef and vegetables: if you make such stock from scratch it's called *warashita*. It's simple to start with soy sauce and then to flavour and sweeten it yourself. Soy sauce and pineapple or orange juice is a very good start. See Teriyaki.

Tabasco: see under Herbs, spices and flavourings.

Teriyaki: a Japanese barbecue and grill marinade, baste or dip. Essentially soy sauce flavoured with wine, sugar and spices; you can make good but individual equivalents by mixing soy sauce with pineapple juice, with mirin and five-spice powder or with plum sauce and ginger wine. Some of these mixtures will be more like sukiyaki sauce.

Worcestershire sauce: this is one of the few good things to come out of the Indian Empire, and is also an echo of everyday life in the Roman Empire. The Romans would have been lost without their *garum*, a sauce made by fermenting and maturing the liquid that small fish give off when salted and left in the sun in barrels. It sounds awful, but after much maturation it ends up being only slightly salty and barely fishy; nothing equivalent remains in the West, but in the East similar fish sauces are used as freely as we use salt.

When such sauces are mixed and matured with extra ingredients – vinegar, molasses, garlic, the bitterness of tamarind and much more that is secret, you get something like Worcestershire sauce. There used to be many of these spicy, hot, salty sauces, made from recipes brought back by gourmand colonels from the India of Empress Victoria. Some were manufactured for distribution and some were kept as private stocks. Lea & Perrins Worcestershire sauce was first made as a private stock but forgotten about by the owner. Eventually the barrel was about to be thrown away by the custodians, some pharmacists, who bravely decided to check on the contents. They discovered the long sojourn in their cellar had transformed a sharp and unpleasant liquid into something with possibilities, and started to make it commercially. Thank goodness.

In Thailand I noticed it used with great abandon by much of the populace, and in Australasia it is used as often as desiccated coconut, which is saying something. But it is extraordinarily good for pepping up boring food and for adding unrecognized piquancy and interest to mayonnaise, soups, aspics, and sauces for fish, herb butters and mince dishes, especially hamburgers and cottage or shepherds' pies. I like to use very little on a lamb chop, rubbed in both sides and left to sit an hour or so before cooking. You know, of course, that a Bloody Mary is bloody awful without Worcestershire sauce.

Lu soy

This is the basic Cantonese simmering sauce or master stock. It gives wonderful colour and flavour to poultry, and is the secret of Lu Shui, the famed Chiu Chow goose dish.

To 300ml/½ pint of light soy sauce add 250g/½ lb each of sugar and of salt, 10 or more slices of fresh ginger plus five-spice powder to taste. Ideally the mixed spice should be bought in pouches that can be removed once the liquid has come to the boil, or soon after if you want a strong but not overpowering flavour. Lu soy does not need to cover the beast or bird you are poaching, but you should turn them from time to time and also regularly spoon over the sauce.

Pasta and Noodles

Even though an Italian word, pasta is about as exclusive to Italy as palaces and royal families are to Great Britain. Marco Polo did not bring it to Europe from China – that is a 19th century American fabrication.

And firm, *al dente* pasta is better for you than well-cooked pasta. Now, having shattered the basic misconceptions, here are some facts.

All pasta is based on a kneaded paste of wheat flour and water for which eggs are sometimes substituted; olive oil can also be included. Fresh pasta is usually made with soft flour, as it is easier to work: dried pasta is more often made from hard (durum) flour, for machinery is more able to stretch the tougher gluten content.

Pasta's origins are the same as those of cheese – no one knows when, where or by whom. Ancient Etruscans, Greeks and Romans enjoyed it – indeed the noodles, *nouilles* and *knudeln* of modern Europe are clearly rooted in the Roman *nodellus*, a word which means little knots and describes what happens to long strands of pasta when on your plate. Even the Arabs have their own noodles, the *trii*, which they introduced to Sicily long ago, in sumptuous recipes. More surprising than pasta's long history is that it was only rarely eaten in post-Roman Italy until the middle of the 19th century, and even then those who ate it all lived in the south. The people of the north used rice as their staple starch.

Pasta products seem spontaneously to have become popular again with pockets of the populace of southern Italy around the 13th century; they had been known there since the Greeks colonized this part of the Mediterranean. This was all well before the appearance of the tomato, so pasta was served with sharp fish or vinegar-pointed sauces or with the voluptuous flower-scented creams and cheeses that dominated European cooking after the return of the Crusaders. When the tomato arrived it was found to flourish most fulsomely near Naples, and soon the inventive proprietors of the rumbustious Neapolitan inns and vermicelli stalls were offering a rich reduced tomato sauce as an optional extra dressing for their pasta products. In 1860, when bearded Garibaldi led the One Thousand into southern Italy from the rice-eating north, this army learned to like the combination and when they returned home they took their new tastes with them, permanently altering the style and flavour of northern Italian cooking. At about the same time, new strains of wheat made wheat flour more readily available and both north and south Italy ate more pasta than ever before and the north can claim to have created two of the most popular pasta sauces –*pesto Genovese* and *salsa Bolognese*.

Many European countries have used long thin noodles in one way or another for centuries, often with or instead of vegetables. The smaller, cut shapes, called macaroni generically, were more often made into sweet puddings. But almost always the pasta was cooked for hours, reducing it to a muciferous mush. This would be horrifying to Neapolitans who like their pasta not *al dente* but *verdi verdi*, which to us would seem barely warmed through, let alone cooked. You are wrong if you think this would be dangerously indigestible; it's quite the reverse. Firm pasta encourages you to chew more, breaking it into small pieces and mixing them with the important digestive enzymes of the saliva. The well-cooked stuff slips down the gullet in great dollops, landing heavily in the stomach with no such enzymic help to assimilation. Thus the digestive trouble begins. If your trouble is other than of stomach, you may care to know a decent meal of spaghetti and tomato sauce is said to supply significant amounts of vitamin E, which is of specific benefit to the reproductive organs (trust the Italians and French to know this). Still, they have given us a clue. Both know the tomato as the 'love apple': *pommo d'amore* and *pomme d'amour* respectively.

In other parts of the world, broadly similar food has been known for aeons. Think of the orientals with their noodles, steamed or fried, and the tiny parcels of dough, the wonton. The Russians' *vareniki* are like ravioli, little pillows of pasta, stuffed with cheese, with cabbage, with fish or strawberries or poppy seeds or almost anything. And in Thailand they make all manner of white or transparent noodles in a fascinating manner, which I first saw being made in a jungle village in the infamous Golden Triangle. They don't make a dough that is rolled out and cut. They make a thick sludge of mixed rice and soy flour, which is ladled into what look like huge icing bags with a much-pierced nozzle. From some height and with considerable dexterity, thin strands are extruded directly into a vat of water a-boil over open charcoal fires, in which they congeal immediately. In seconds they are looped out and hung to drip dry under teak-leaf-thatched roofs in great opalescent skeins. They don't last long in the humidity so the agile villagers had their work and their fortune cut out for them to supply, as they did, nearly all the local district. But the concomitant pigs, scabrous dogs and mucous-choked children cut them right out of my diet. I changed my mind back again on the island of Koh-Samui, off Thailand's east coast.

There I watched rice noodles being made by hand again, starting with the long preparation of a heavy ball of rice flour dough, which was then put into the top of a magnificent brass-bound mill over boiling water. Like the merest whisker of the local buffalo usually used, I was entrusted with pushing the mighty spoke around the great vat of boiling water, and eventually the dough emerged as long translucent strings, directly into the water. After an exact amount of time the fresh noodles were fished out and expertly trimmed and neatly coiled into plastic containers. Customers seemed to know when batches were ready and there seemed hardly anything in stock between cook-ups, not unlike French villagers' regular visits to bakers each day.

There is no end to ingenuity when it comes to making noodles. In Vietnam a particular type of cellophane noodle, thin and transparent, is made with a flour of dried mung bean and in other parts of south-east Asia, gram flour, made from a type of pea, is used. The Chinese make a batter of whatever flour they can get, spread this on an oiled platter and steam until transparent; it is rolled and eaten with chopped green onion and revived dried shrimp. In Japan the great pasta speciality is soba, a spaghetti-type product made with a proportion of buckwheat and usually served cold; you can buy this quite readily where there are Asian shops and it is just as good hot, particularly with anything to do with root vegetables and both summer and winter squash/pumpkin.

Hungarian egg drops, *tarhonya*, are well worth finding. These small pellets of egg pasta should be fried a golden brown in butter before being covered with water to cook. The nuttiness is delicious and once you have eaten them with a paprika-rich goulash, mashed or boiled potatoes will never do again. Orzo, pasta shapes made to look like barley are enjoying great popularity now, as an alternative to rice both in and as part of dishes, chilled salads in particular.

Then there's America. It is the United States that led the march of pasta so steadily to the top of the post-war popularity poll. It was they who popularized the idea of eating Italian pasta as a main course, which it never was: Italian purists would also say pasta should be eaten only as a first course only at lunchtime, and never in the evenings. It was almost certainly someone in the United States who invented *canneloni, tagliatelli* with cream, ham and peas, *carbonara* sauce, and the notion of cold pasta salads. Chances are these innovators were also of Italian extraction, and not all progress is a bad thing. When tens of thousands of Italians emigrated to the United States in the 19th century, a great proportion was from Italy's south, and once they landed in the New World it was pasta they missed and wanted more than anything, and it had to be Neapolitan. It was this export demand that allowed the great pasta families to mechanize and then to sell their products all around the world.

As you might expect, mechanization has had some effect on commercial Italian pasta. Eighty years ago you could find 250-300 different shapes, but now the number is probably closer to only 50 or 60 and that includes new monstrosities like spacemen and flying saucers. The phenomenal amount of pasta sold these days means old standards and quality have had to be forgotten, and there must be many who never having eaten pasta the way it used to be cannot understand the fuss. Take the trouble to buy old-fashioned pasta just once, and you will.

Traditionally made pasta is easy to spot, for it will be dull rather than shiny and, if you can get to it, slightly rough to the touch: often the pack will tell you it is *bronzato*, shaped using bronze die-cuts.

When a paste of high-gluten durum wheat is extruded through bronze shapes, irregularities and defects in the bronze make millions of tiny cuts in the surface of the pasta. This type of pasta is always allowed to dry naturally, although at controlled temperatures. The result is pasta that dries to a dull glow, and the surface always feels rough, the same fine roughness your teeth use to identify a genuine pearl: that roughness is the key to the best pasta eating, for these minute cuts, lumps and bumps dramatically increase the surface of each piece, and thus, once it is cooked and has steamed dry (see Cooking) it is capable of absorbing a great deal of olive oil and sauce. Italians don't actually make sauces for pasta but make dressings, liquids that flavour the pasta.

Most modern commercial pasta is made with softer flour than used to be the case. Modern nylon extrusion moulds then give absolutely smooth surfaces on each piece of pasta and once moulded these are assisted to dry with heat, which adds a give-away glaze. Such pasta is every bit as good nutritionally, but it cannot absorb the sauce.

Other countries tend to use far more sauce than Italy – up to five times more – and to use far less reduced sauces, so the pasta plays second fiddle, becoming added texture to a bowl of sauce. Absorption of flavourings by traditionally made pasta is why it sings in the mouth, and explains why Italians use so comparatively little of their concentrated dressing than someone in the UK might. Italians understand how to combine the two, pasta and sauce or dressing, and to enjoy the flavour of both: we use rather tasteless pasta to bulk out a sauce that is usually far too diluted anyway.

To those who have not been brought up with pasta it can be an extraordinary experience to discover the amazing range of flavours pasta can have, all obtained by varying the thickness and shape of the same combination of wheat flour, water and, possibly, egg. Spinach juice or tomato purée can be added to make green, *verde*, and red, *rosso*, pasta.

Pasta is very simple to make and doubly delicious when fresh rather than dried. The fun of making it can be as addictive as the pleasure of eating it. But before you dash into the kitchen, here's an attempt to guide you through the maze of the most common categories and shapes of Italian pasta.

Pasta Families

Flavoured: with black pepper, beetroot, squid ink, pumpkin purée, orange, walnuts and almost anything else, these have cerebral and visual appeal rather than culinary. Once they are plunged into the requisite boiling water the flavour you have paid for is dissolved away, diluted into insignificance. Obvious if you think about it.

The only way to rescue the flavour you paid over the top for is to flavour the cooking water highly with the same ingredient – pepper, beetroot, squid ink etc. Only in King's Cross, Sydney, have I ever found this, when I enjoyed mussels on saffron linguine, which had been cooked in saffron seafood stock. It's much more rewarding to use decent pasta and to rely for flavouring on a good sauce.

Pasta all'uovo/pasta with egg: here the flour is mixed with a proportion of egg that varies but should never be less than one per 500g/1lb of flour. It is nearly always made into *pasta lunga* products but every type of pasta may be made with eggs.

Pasta corta/short or cut pasta: the best known in these categories are the rounded, hollow pastas, usually cut on the bias and which may be smooth or grooved. These include *macaroni*, *rigatoni*, *penne* and the comparative newcomer, *canneloni*. This category also includes the shapes and shell types so wonderful for holding sauce-juicy chunks of meat or seafood. *Lumache* (snails), *conchiglie* (shells), *gnocchi* and the elbow shapes also come into this category.

Pasta lunga/long pasta: from the tiniest *cappelli d'angelo* (angel's hair) to thick and broad *lasagne*, with every type of *spaghetti*, *vermicelli*, *linguine*, *ziti*, *fettuccine* and *tagliarelli* or *tagliatelli* in between. With or without holes. Once nearly all the thinner *pasta lunga* was made up to 1.5m/5ft in length and looped to dry like wool. Now it's usually cut into 20-32cm/8-12in lengths.

Pasta ripieni/stuffed pasta: *ravioli* in all different sizes is the best known, I suppose, but *tortellini* which look like belly-buttons are much more delicious, I think, as are *cappelletti* which look like head scarves tied on the chin. There are many other varieties of stuffed pastas: *angolotti* and *panzerotti* are seen far more these days as fresh pasta sits firmly beside other easy-to-prepare but inspiring dishes in the supermarket. *Tortelloni* are usually served in cream sauce or tomato sauce, but *ravioli* might be served in butter, especially browned butter.

Pastina: these tiny pieces of dried dough are specially made for serving in soup and are most usually seen as egg drops, squares or bow ties (*farfalli*); then you must also include novelties such as alphabet pasta, tiny animals and the aforementioned visitors from outer space.

Pre-cooked: just what it says, and a special boon when it comes to making lasagne, but make the sauces a little wetter, for the liquid to soften them has to come from somewhere.

Whole wheat: a century ago most pasta would have been rather more 'brown' than white, simply because of milling processes, but by the time it became internationally popular, white flour was universally available. The Veneto, around Venice, still offers *bigoli*, a thick type of spaghetti made from whole flour. People who should know, like Valentina Harris, guffaw at the idea of serving whole wheat pasta, saying it is eaten only by the infirm and the costive, and only when prescribed by doctors. That might be true, but it doesn't mean we shouldn't find other ways to eat whole wheat pasta – if only to show the Italians they don't know everything.

Pasta Shapes

The following can only be arbitrary, and is based more on what you might buy easily rather than what is being made in Italy's village kitchens.

The basic rules about choosing pasta are these: the smooth or ridged shapes are best with smooth but thick and clinging sauces; those with major ridges, crevasses, folds or holes have been planned for very thin sauces or for lumpy sauces, which will be caught and held.

Bella roos: no, neither authentic nor Italian nor one of those new countries. They are new and from Australia, and yes they are kangaroo-shaped, either plain or tomato flavoured. Jumping on the bandwagon?

Bucatini: a thick, hollow version of spaghetti.

Capellini: very thin, flat or round noodles, *capelli d'angelo* being the thinnest.

Cappelletti: 'little hats'. This is a stuffed pasta, like a small peaked and tied head scarf.

Conchiglie: seashells. Available large or small, smooth or ridged. Excellent for trapping the tastiest bits of seafood or meat sauces, and attractive in cold pasta salads. Very big ones can be cooked, stuffed, perhaps with layers of ricotta, spinach and thick tomato sauce and then baked in a sauce.

Couscous: oh yes it is! It's all explained in the section on wheat, page 338.

Farfalli/farfallini etc: a bow-tie shape often with crinkled or diamond-cut edges. Made by pinching the middle of a square of pasta.

Fettuccine: a blood brother of *tagliatelle, fettuccine* originates from Rome, is usually made with egg, and is narrower and thicker than its relation.

Fusilli: a spiral-shaped pasta.

Gnocchi: this should be made with a starch or a thick purée of something other than wheat flour. Dry mashed potato or pumpkin are the most common but wheat flour is almost always also included to get the right texture. The proper shape is a small oval that has been folded over the tines of a fork, and so is ribbed or serrated.

Lasagne: the broadest pasta noodle, smooth or ridged. *Lasagne verdi*, like all green pasta, is coloured with spinach, or it would be nice if it were, but there is no flavour advantage. Lasagne is one of the few pastas not dressed with sauce at the table. Instead it is layered with *bechamel* and *ragu* sauces and returned to the oven to be baked, *lasagne al forno*.

Linguine: another flat, thin noodle.

Macaroni: a generic term for all commercially-made dried pasta. But in general use is often used to mean only the well-known cut, tubular pasta. There are many lengths and sizes of such macaroni.

Mougrabieh: pasta pearls from Lebanon, explained in the section on wheat, page 339.

Orecchiette: these 'little ears' are shaped just like that, and suit salads and chunky sauces.

Pansotti/panzerotti: a triangular, stuffed pasta.

Penne: specially used to indicate a hollow short pasta cut at an acute diagonal angle – up to 25mm/1in long. The shape is reminiscent of the end of a sharpened quill, hence the name.

Quadrucci: these little squares of noodle are used in soup and in today's prosaic times are liable simply to be labelled 'egg squares'.

Ravioli: best known of the stuffed pasta, they are square-shaped and can sometimes be found quite large.

Rigatoni: ridged and tubular, sometimes curved, but without the pointed ends of penne.

Spaghetti: thin strings of pasta, without holes. Called *vermicelli* (little worms) in southern Italy. There are thinner varieties called *spaghettini* and *vermicellini*.

Tagliatelle: a long, thin egg noodle, the speciality of Bologna, one of Italy's greatest food centres. There is also a green one – *tagliatelle verdi*.

Tortellini/Tortelloni/Tortelli: a stuffed pasta, more or less of a twisted ring shape which look like perfect belly-buttons. Can be bought fresh or dried; the dried ones are remarkably good, particularly for a *timbale* – the rich pie of pastry and stuffed pasta in a meat sauce.

Cooking

The manufacturers don't necessarily know best and often tell you to cook your pasta longer than is necessary. The Italians say 'pasta likes friends', meaning you need to keep an eye on it when it cooks. The slightest variation in thickness, humidity or amount of water will affect the time it takes for your pasta to be to your taste. There is a tradition that says some Italians reckoned theirs was ready when a handful flung onto the wall stuck there; I've never been able to find necessary details of type of wall, distance thrown or style of delivery and so have gone for the more mundane tooth test. Boring but effective.

Fresh pasta is supposed to tell you it is cooked by floating to the surface, sometimes in just a few minutes. Don't believe your eyes, for I have rarely found the float test reliable.

You must use as much water as possible so that each pasta piece can swell unhindered, as much as 500ml/18fl oz per serving. The more water you use, the less likely it is pasta will stick together. You know if you're doing it wrong because the cooking water will be cloudy: with the right proportion to pasta it stays fairly clear. Any idea a few spoonfuls of oil on the water will stop pasta sticking is fanciful to say the least, and also continues the calumny pasta will stick anyway. Pasta never sticks to itself if it has been cooked in enough water to disseminate any dissolved starch from the outside.

Classicists say you should never pour pasta into a colander but take it out of the water with a large fork or spoon. Do what you will, but don't rinse it in cold water and then reheat it because that is a recipe for making it sticky.

Now, here is the most important pasta cooking technique. Correctly, cooked pasta should be drained and then allowed to steam dry; it takes a few minutes until you see the pasta shapes becoming a little dull and the steaming is less vigorous. Great, because this now drier surface will suck up and hold the oil or sauce you put on to it: the pasta is now at one with the sauce rather than dog-paddling. If you put pasta into a sauce or mix a sauce into it straightaway you will always be left with puddles on the bottom of plates, and that's not something you see in Italy.

Complicated shapes, like shells, should be drained in a colander, and gently turned so the water caught in the interior drains away.

A good way to ensure you do this is to do what you have seen a thousand times in restaurants but didn't understand. Put the hot pasta into a warm serving dish, let the steaming die down a little and then pour the sauce or dressing onto the top and take it to the table like that. Only mix it together when you are ready to serve; the added time makes the pasta even thirstier.

The exception to the rule is *lasagne*. When *lasagne* is cooked, run cold water into the cooking pot and gently move the lasagne sheets until separate and cool in the running water. Then take them out and lay them on a tea towel to drain and dry. Pre-cooked lasagne is much easier.

Serving

Because it is a simple food, pasta particularly suits simple accompaniments. But which sauce goes with what pasta? Every sauce goes with every pasta, but some are better than others. Thinner sauces are enjoyed more when served with the complicated shapes of *pasta corta*, which can catch the sauce in pools or trap the morsels of flesh. But even this rule can be ignored if you have the wrong type of pasta in the cupboard.

Butter sauces: melted butter flavoured with chopped garlic, herbs and a dash of olive oil makes one of the best and clingiest dressings for *pasta lunga*. If you want to ignore the above advice, some seafood, snippets of cheese, cubes of ham or salami, croûtons or lardons, black olives or cornichons might also be added. It is correct to serve some *ravioli* and *gnocchi* with melted butter; often the former is served with butter that has been allowed to brown slightly.

Cheese: yes, Parmesan and other cheeses do go nicely with pasta dishes. But please don't add it regardless. Such piquant cheese is to be considered an alternative to salt and pepper, and so on some dishes, especially the creamy seafood sauces, the additional flavour of sharp cheese is quite wrong – but not always.

The use of grated Cheddar cheese, spongy and stringy, adds little but bother, unless it is dissolved into a sauce completely. Even so it is pointless using something mild as you spend more trying to get flavour than if you simply bought less of a biting Parmesan, for all its expense. I blame the Italian restaurants themselves for the propagation of Parmesan-with-everything; at least eating chips with everything does not mask flavours which some chef has, or should have, been creating for hours.

Cream sauces: the simplest cream sauce, particularly for *tortellini* or *capelletti*, is simply a reduction of double cream. For two, reduce 300ml/½ pint double cream to half its volume and then flavour according to your store cupboard. An excellent way to proceed now is to add some of the juice from a tin of baby clams or Danish mussels, which have been preserved in brine or their natural juices. Add also some tomato purée, until there is a rosiness rather than ruddiness. Continue reducing until a coating consistency and only then add salt and, if you have some, a teaspoon or two of brandy.

When your pasta shells or *lumachine* or *penne* are cooked and well drained, serve onto hot plates, then quickly toss the clams or mussels in the sauce and let everyone serve themselves. A little oregano is good with this. So is a sprinkle of mixed hot and sweet paprika.

It's bold and Italian to revive good pieces of rinsed and drained dried porcini in a fruity white wine or an amontillado sherry, reducing the liquid until almost disappeared. Stir the porcini and the alcohol essence into the reduced cream, perhaps with some very fresh sweet peas. Yes, Parmesan would be good. Chunks of fresh smoked or hot-smoked salmon with dill and parsley and lemon zest would be just as good.

No-sauce dressing: it is liberating to understand pasta can be served without a sauce. Once pasta is dressed with olive oil, you can add what you like, using the pasta to thread amazing complications of flavour and texture together. I like to think of these as presenting everything as one dish in a pasta bowl, that would otherwise have been served in sorry mounds separately on a plate. Such dishes can be very simple. One of the unexplainably most delicious simply mixes

oiled pasta with quickly cooked small florets of broccoli and tiny cubes of Parmesan. You can be time consuming and add a variety of grilled vegetables, with flat leaf parsley, anchovies and perhaps chopped ham, or add honey-roasted salmon in chunks, black olives, sun-dried tomatoes, *bufala bocconcini* and basil leaves. Strands of chicken mix well with pasta tossed in pesto and any few vegetables. Fried cubes of aubergine fraternize well with bits of bacon, grilled cherry tomatoes and mint leaves. All of them become more operatic with shavings or gratings or tiny cubes of *grana Padano* or Parmesan or a good pecorino. Get the idea? Pasta with no sauce but olive oil can be perfectly heavenly and take ages to sort out, or can be perfectly heavenly and disguise leftovers creatively.

Meat sauces: the basic tomato/meat sauce or *ragù* does not need complication or expense to be good. Gino, who cooked so wonderfully during the first years of Mr Christian's Delicatessen in Notting Hill Gate was properly Italian, temperamental, obsessed with every aspect of his health and more than ready to discuss every detail. Yet his culinary touch was light and from him I learned the secret of so much Italian food; not a lot of ingredients, but very good ingredients cooked in a way that reduces and thus magnifies their flavours. Here's how he made the *ragù* for the shop's *lasagne*, one of the first cooked dishes we prepared and still made to the same recipe as far as I know, thirty years later.

Ideally the meat should be largely a white one, veal or pork, chicken if that is easier and a combination of two of them is best: add some proportion of beef mince if you like but it must not overpower the sweeter meats. Slowly brown the minced meat in olive oil with a little finely chopped onion and a little finely chopped celery, the latter being very important. The meat should cook long enough for all liquid to disappear and to start smelling richly of itself, like a grilling steak might do. You are drying out the meat, so, like pasta, it will then more quickly and completely absorb the flavours of the sauce's other ingredients. Then cover the meat with plum tomatoes canned in tomato juice, including all this juice. Add some bay leaves and then let this simmer gently for several hours – the larger the quantity the longer the time. You can't cook a good *ragù* in 20 minutes, because mince is made from lesser cuts that take a good time to tenderize. No point using sirloin or something like that, because this has none of the sinew and connecting tissue of lesser meats, and you need them for silken texture and deeper flavour.

Note, there is no garlic, no herbs, no red wine and one more time, no expensive cuts of meat. You can add a little white wine but you are as well to do this when the sauce is cooked, for final savour.

At the end of the long cooking the meat will almost have dissolved into the reduced sauce, the flavours will have combined and the colour will be wonderful. It's done when you can crush a piece of the mince against the roof of your mouth with your tongue – that's how tender it should be. Finish with some black pepper and salt if you think it is necessary. Should you wish a higher colour or even stronger tomato flavour then use tomato purée as your cooking liquid, diluted only slightly, or add some, in the way outlined under my piece on that subject, towards the end of the cooking.

Ragù is the sauce used in lasagne making, and for that layered and baked dish, the *ragù* is mixed, swirled rather, with equal quantities of a thick but simply flavoured béchamel sauce. Do not accept as lasagne layers of pasta and undercooked or watery mince with bits of tomato in it, like part-digested vomit and often as sour; without the texture and contrast of the béchamel sauce it is horrid, quite inedible. Once you have a very reduced *ragu* and a thick béchamel you can think about adding other things. Drained spinach, cubes of precooked pumpkin, chunks of chorizo, Polish sausage or cubes of well-flavoured cheese, especially creamy blue cheeses.

Tomato sauces: the simpler the better. If you have tomatoes in your garden which are rugged and red and sun-ripened then simply chop them up and cook them gently with some olive oil, strain them or liquidize and strain, then reduce further. But don't bother to attempt this with the bullets you buy in the guise of tomatoes. If you don't have the goodies in the garden and you can't buy such wonderful varieties as *marmonde* or beefsteak tomatoes, it's always best to open a couple of cans of plum tomatoes and reduce them into a sauce as above, keeping plenty of texture. Olive oil, very little onion and some bay leaf are the only additions to consider. The sauce must boil for a while so the olive oil is emulsified, thus thickening it and making it look better. But you have to be quite patient about reducing the tomatoes enough, and also take care it does not burn or caramelize.

A few minutes before serving, add sprigs of fresh herbs, like basil, thyme or mint, let the flavour draw, fish out the herbs, and serve. Dried herbs that are still vital work as well, particularly a good oregano.

Once you have such a sauce, reduced, emulsified, flavoured and hot and ready to work, you can construct a different pasta dish everyday. As the pasta dries in a serving dish or in individual pasta bowls and before you add the sauce, add chopped olives or anchovies, add chunks of tuna or of any sort of sausage, add crisped bacon, any vegetable or vegetables, chunks of cheese rather than grated cheese, citrus zest – lime particularly – and plenty of fresh parsley or basil and when you have done, only then pour on the tomato sauce. Mix as you serve or as you eat.

Odd Ways with Pasta

I often find myself with some leftover pasta, cooked or uncooked. The latter is often hard to find a use for though but a jar into which these odd leftovers go is an idea and suddenly a pasta meal is more interesting because your plate includes five or six shapes at once.

Here are some ideas for using small amounts of cooked pasta and/or appearing to be creative at the same time.

Casseroles: cooking dried pasta or reheating cooked pasta in the juice of braises, stews and casseroles gives you a meal in one container. And you retain all the vitamins of the dried pasta instead of throwing some away in the cooking water. Liver and bacon is good with pasta in it; so is a *paprikas*, perhaps bumped up with a little extra sweet or smoked sweet paprika and sour cream. Braised steak that is too wet and sloppy can be saved by cooking noodles in the liquid.

Fish: leftover fish incorporated into a rich white sauce with sharp accents of green bell pepper/capsicum, cheese and a light-handed dash of Tabasco is a nice combination with small macaroni shapes. Bake until a crisp golden brown in the oven. Smoked fish would probably be better. Both are, of course, only versions of macaroni cheese.

Flavoured: best of all by a very long way is reflavoured pasta, lime-flavoured pasta particularly: to do this you mix lime oil q.v., with the usual amount of olive oil. When the pasta has almost stopped steaming but is still warm, toss it in the oil. Make sure you have used enough lime for it to be detectable when you have added the other ingredients, first a mixture of seafood or just meaty prawns or hot-smoked salmon and then something green, like peas or sliced artichoke bottoms, something unctuous like soft-boiled quail eggs, or roughly chopped soft-boiled hen's eggs plus flat leaf parsley – and this is where roasted black peppercorns, roughly ground are very good, for they adore being seen out with lime. Do the same thing with other citrus oils, indeed with any other flavoured oil, sesame with restraint, garlic oil with none. You can serve such dishes hot or cold, and flavoured pasta is a favoured salad ingredient.

Fried: it is not only noodles that can be fried. Simply ensure your leftover, unsauced pasta has been well and truly dried and dump it into deep, hot oil, cook until brown, drain and serve. It is particularly good mixed up with masses of fried onion or crisp-fried onion rings. I wouldn't like them like that though; I'd like the pasta fried plain as the basis for a pasta salad to eat outdoors, with smoky flavours, like bacon and sausage with sweet roasted pumpkin, roasted red pepper and a creamy blue cheese or gruyere style. Rugged food, for football players.

Fruit: provided they are not oily, cooked pasta shapes make interesting additions to cooked fruit. Toss the cooked shapes in a little sugar and cinnamon or in some syrup while still warm. They are particularly good with puddings made with dried fruit and with apple – you'd be surprised how good is a layer of small, buttered macaroni at the bottom of, say, an apple crumble. I'd be inclined to pour a little cream or milk over the pasta, so it could be absorbed with the dripping juices of the apple whilst in the oven.

Salads: cold pasta salad is very popular. It can be the basis or an ingredient. As the former, consider adding a few highly flavoured ingredients to pasta tossed in good olive oil and lemon juice whilst still warm - some smoked sausages or frankfurters, some rollmops and sour cream with onion, salami and gherkins, for example. Pasta is especially good in the classic *salade Nicoise*. When incorporating pasta with a poultry salad, use the Polynesian idea of including fruit, too. Mix pasta with chicken, avocado and pineapple, or with turkey, apple, nuts and celery plus some orange segments.

Vegetables: almost any hot vegetable dish that includes a sauce or is in itself rather wet can be extended with pasta shapes. Ratatouille becomes even more filling and nourishing. Lightly cooked (microwaved is best) cauliflower, broccoli, leeks or sliced Brussels sprouts in a cheese sauce over pasta make a snack a perfect lunch or supper dish; this is one place where wholewheat pasta works very well. If you use plain pasta, you can add body by scattering on roughly made wholemeal or white breadcrumbs you have crisped up in butter and then tossed with a very little chili seasoning q.v. Fried pasta shapes are also very good with these vegetables.

Oriental Pasta and Noodles

China and South-east Asia

Noodles of some sort are a staple of most parts of China, where they are made from a variety of flours, reflecting local grains. The further north you move, the more likely you are to find robust wheat noodles, rather than rice noodles. Check the label for cooking times, as they can be part-cooked. Any that are golden brown have been cooked, fried and dried, and can be reconstituted in seconds, or added quickly to stir-fries and served while they retain some texture.

And the slurping noises? Noisy eaters live longer. Slurping when eating noodles is a curious sort of politeness to Fate, because noodles represent longevity, and so to bite them might cut your life expectancy.

Bean thread, glass or cellophane: made from mung beans, these noodles are first soaked and then cooked for up to ten minutes, often with other foods to extend them. They are as transparent as the name suggests, and because of their origin are considered a type of vegetable rather than noodle, or will be described on menus as vegetable noodles. A common filling ingredient in Vietnamese rice wrappers and can be deep-fried directly from the packet.

Egg noodles: even when sold dried, these will have been pre-cooked and so need just a brief rehydration, which can happen directly in a soup or stir-fry.

Handmade: a culinary entertainment as much as anything else, the Chinese equivalent of twirling pizza dough into the air rather than rolling it. Wheat flour is pulled, stretched, thrown and twisted like mad until centrifugal force creates long noodles, very long noodles. It's one of those things one longs to be able to do but is best saved for retirement, like juggling.

Rice noodles: sheets of rice flour batter are steamed and then sliced to make flat rice-sheet noodles, like white *fettucine* or *tagliatelle*. Otherwise, a well-worked ball of steamed rice flour is put through a mill into boiling water, and this makes very thin rice noodles or the even thinner rice vermicelli. If soft and fresh they can sour quickly. Soft or dried rice noodles are already cooked and so need only to be plunged into hot water, or for boiling water to be poured over them, to be heated or re-hydrated. It's obvious, but the fresher the rice noodle, the less time they need in hot water. If they are deep-fried they swell prodigiously, making them very absorbent but curiously unsatisfying to eat. Like Chinese meals.

Rice wrappers: a transparent shape made from a dried cooked batter of rice flour and water, most usually associated with Vietnamese cookery and their splendid notion of wrap 'n roll. They wrap these around light, mixed fillings with plenty of fresh flavoured herbs, including Vietnamese mint, to make see-through spring rolls. Each wrapper is dipped into a bowl of hot water just until they crumple, as though in a lover's arms: they are dry in seconds and while supple are piled with good clean tasting things, rolled and enjoyed. Sold as spring roll wrappers or as *galettes de riz*.

Sweet potato: a Korean type of noodle, translucent when cooked and so like a big brother of cellophane or bean thread noodles. Add to dishes before serving.

Wheat: Hokkien and the even thicker thick Shanghai noodles are made from wheat and eggs and generally sold ready steamed, which you can tell from their rather lollopy state, even in the bag: if so they can be added direct from the package into soups and stir-fries. Thin Shanghai noodles are generally whiter because they contain no eggs, and are most commonly used in soups.

Wonton: stuffed envelopes or money-purse shapes of wheat dough, and so a Chinese ravioli. Served as a major or minor contributor to the ingredients in a Chinese bowl of soup or can be deep-fried. Wonton wrappers can be bought at Chinese supermarkets and kept in the freezer at home. The stuffing can be meat, fish, seafood or vegetable based. A bowl of wonton soup is my favourite comfort food. The best I know are made by the traditional grandmother seated on a stool in the back of a small restaurant in Sandringham, Auckland. The usual sweetness of pork wonton fillings is mere overture for what next happens in your mouth as touches of spices and unrecognised herbs shyly emerge. Apparently the family doesn't find anything special about their grandmother's wonton skills: ' that's the way they are supposed to be!'

Japanese

Ramen: only popular in Japan since the 1950s, a bowl of ramen looks like udon noodles, and may use udon noodles, but the stock is not made of dashi. Ramen is always served to you in the same order. First there's a dab of *tare*, an intense seasoning of miso, soy sauce, rice wine, sugar and, perhaps ginger or fried garlic; every chef has his secret mix and sometimes this will have mellowed in the same pot for decades, subtly changing as more of this or less of that is added. Then comes the soup, not the usual light, seaweed-tuna dashi, but something meaty, made perhaps with ham hocks and roasted bones. Then the noodles, cooked *al dente* or firmer, and then exactly six toppings of meat, vegetables, pickles, fish – even a poached egg. Slurping is allowed, even in New York, where *ramenyas*, ramen shops, are springing up in the best of addresses.

Soba: their gorgeous cream-brown colour gives the clue; they are made from buckwheat flour plus wheat to provide gluten and eggs needed to hold them together. They are most commonly served cold, but dipped into a hot broth and other flavouring agents as you eat.

Somen: fine wheat flour noodles, generally eaten in or with large amounts of either chilled (remarkably good) or hot soup. They are also used for cool noodle salads, something they equally go for in Korea.

Udon: thick wheat noodles, usually with no egg content. Generally these are served in a bowl of hot dashi broth into which anything from sliced roast pork to raw eggs and every imaginable other flavouring might be added. They are a perfect reviver at a street stall at 5.30 am after a freezing visit to Tokyo's cavernous fish market. It takes longer than we had to learn the proper rude slurping way to eat them, so you get more in your mouth than you leave behind. A welcome way to forget the market's whale meat.

New York ways with Noodles

If you are new to noodling, here are ideas from the menu of Republic, a terrific noodle restaurant on Union Square, where you also find New York's original farmer's market.

Noodle dishes

Udon noodles and marinated chicken, cucumber, bean sprouts, peanuts, coconut milk-spinach sauce

Glass noodles and sautéed chicken, vegetables, lime juice, ginger dipping sauce

Rice angel-hair noodles and thinly sliced beef marinaded in soy and galangal, lettuce, cucumber, pickled carrots, daikon, peanuts

Cold Vietnamese vegetable (mung bean) noodles with mint, carrots, broccoli, fried shallots, tofu, bean sprouts, peanuts, egg strips

Cold wheat noodles with bean sprouts, carrots, peanuts, mint, fried shallots, peanut sauce

Egg noodles with curried duck, carrots, celery, scallions (spring onions), bean sprouts, fresh coriander (cilantro)

Noodles in broth

Wheat noodles with beef broth, rare beef, garlic, lemon grass, chilli peppers, bean sprouts

Rice noodles with chicken broth, coconut milk, lime juice, bean sprouts, lemon grass, galangal, fried shallots

Wide rice noodles with salmon stock, shrimp, scallops, squid, watercress, bean sprouts, garlic oil

Udon noodles with miso broth, fried soft and firm tofu, ribbon seaweed, bean sprouts, spinach

Rice noodles with beef broth, tofu, snow peas, straw mushrooms, bean sprouts

Rice noodles with chicken broth, duck curry, taro chips, bean sprouts

Glass noodles with chicken broth, shrimp wontons, watercress, carrots, bean sprouts

Carb Questions

Any diet that excludes a category of food is nonsense.

Pasta is part of the glorious choice we have in the 21st century, just as bread and other grain products are too. To proscribe it is self-righteously perverse, and it's offensive to many millions whose finances mean they have little choice but to rely on bread, rice or pasta as a staple. Neither can we forget teenagers, whose body changes and activities need far more feeding than adults do, and that means super-requirements of concentrated carbohydrate.

Sure, perhaps we ought to think about how often we eat starch-based carbohydrates and we could all eat pasta differently, perhaps with far more raw or cooked vegetables than once might have been the case; we could be more aware and change the balance so pasta is not the major component. It's very easy to make pasta more important than it should be.

For me pasta is important because it is in pasta dishes I use the greatest number of ingredients, far more than I would put on a plate, portion by portion. That variety is probably the single best goal for any diet, that is if you want also to be healthy.

The very best of health comes from consciously eating the broadest variety of foods, so we provide the body with the biggest possible range of micro-nutrients in as many combinations as we can. Science is still pioneering its understanding of micro-nutrients, many of which have not even been identified, so who are we to fiddle? Science doesn't argue that we need them, and that they often work better in combinations with those from other foods.

The resultant thought is simple – try not to eat anything today you ate yesterday, but balance this out over the week rather than meal by meal. The idea of the balanced meal is very counter productive – it's what you eat over the week that really matters.

But then, what about weight control? The simple secret is never to be hungry and to do that by eating six, seven or more times a day. When you are not starving, not aching for the next leaf of lettuce, you are far more likely to eat what's better for you rather than what is not. There is a simple technique, an unequivocal mantra to make sure you don't over eat. . .

Pies, Pâtés and Terrines

Pies have long been a main stay of European culture. Their ancestors were mixtures of meats, herbs, spices and dried fruits baked in coffins or huffs, crusts of varying composition, often painted and gilded, but not meant to be eaten.

Once pastry making was perfected, the idea of baking meats in edible containers quickly became universal, for not only were they easy to store and transport, but the crust gave you more of a meal to enjoy.

Raised Pies

Raised pies, most commonly pork or game pies, are a peculiarly British preserve, and the closest thing left to us of those medieval coffins. They are so called because the unique hot water crust has to be raised or moulded into shape by hand.

The hot water, flour and lard-based cases of raised pies hold a pretty uneasy position between the old and new styles of piecrust – the inedible and the edible. Classically the warm pastry is shaped over a wooden mould and sets in shape: domestically something like a preserving jar is often used as a mould, but I treat it like any other sort of pastry and bake big pies in a loose-bottomed pan.

Pork pies are the best known raised pies, yet even their greatest admirers agree there is commonly a distressing layer of greeny-cream raw pastry between the crisp golden outer crust and the meat. This seems largely to be a matter of commercial compromise, for I have made, been offered, and bought raised pies with thin, beautifully cooked-through crusts, so it is more than possible. But just because the outside was once absolutely inedible and today only just makes it, why must modern contents vie also to be so bland?

The filling of pork or game raised pies is a sort of pâté of minced pork with a high content of fat, vital for flavour and as a guarantee of long life. Life-threatening bacteria generally do not grow on fat. Thus it seems extraordinary to find pork pies so plodding and bleak. Even the beautifully made pies from a famed farm shop, generously packed full of pork and game or duck, taste like damp cardboard, for the meat is utterly unseasoned, and the ill-advised low-fat content means it can only steam in its own juices, inevitably producing the flabby flavour that not even a good stock poured through the cooked crust can balance. A low-fat raised pie is a contradiction of every culinary consideration.

Bad raised pies are a sad opportunity missed, but could be simply recovered. It's not the traditional high fat content driving customers away. There are just too many other things to buy these days that taste better than under-seasoned pork in uncooked pastry cases.

Of course standards vary up and down Britain and perhaps they should. You are more likely to find a good one at a farmers' market. At Notting Hill Gate's Saturday market I bought a game pie from Manor Farm Game that was a revelation: the pastry was cooked all the way through, the filling tasty and tasting of game. I had meant to share it.

And there's the rub. If you too know a tasty raised pie, do you keep it to yourself or should you broadcast its appeal and run the risk of commercialization and all that means? I think you tell, as I have, and hope anyone who starts off so well wants always to excel.

Here is what you might find in stores and how they could be.

Gala: the frenzied pinnacle of British commercial invention, it seems, a pork or veal and ham pie baked in a long oblong with an extruded egg-substitute through the middle. The original, with real eggs, is terrific.

Game pies: ideally, these should contain the coarsely minced dark meat of game birds mixed into a pork farce plus layers of the sliced breast meat. Bacon and fillet or rump steak were once thought essential, too. Old recipes include cayenne and mace with the salt and pepper but unless a really rich stock was made from the bones of the birds and poured into the spaces left by shrinkage after cooking, the result would not have been as tasty and gamey as expected. Because they are meant to be eaten cold, perhaps outdoors, their flavour should be quite marked. When they are good they are fantastic – as above.

If you are making such at home, the raw meat and flavouring mixture should be allowed to rest overnight before cooking; thyme is quite the best herb for these compounds and juniper berries always help. Even a small amount of wine, cognac and garlic make a terrific difference. More of the same must be included in the stock, which should be almost too strong to enjoy by itself. Remember it will be greatly diluted once in the pie and thus no matter how stiffly it might set by itself, will undoubtedly also need extra gelatin added. I use flavoursome aspic rather than plain gelatin and alcohol rather than water and reduce that before use too, so concentrated port might make the aspic for a pheasant and walnut raised pie and so on.

Another version, just as authentic but more domestic, uses just mixed game, first casseroled together (on the bone of course), and then boned, layered and baked in a rich gravy of the cooking stock with added gelatine in a pastry case. Wonderful and even better if you can bear to leave it uncut for several days.

Mutton pie: you'll most likely find these in Scotland, but once they were the wares most commonly hawked by Simple Simon and other itinerant pie sellers. They're small raised pies based on minced mutton (now probably lamb), brown sauce, or stock and such spice as nutmeg or cloves, but minimally. They might once have had red currant jelly poured into them, too, and on market stalls were topped with mint leaves, to prevent a mix up with pork pies. Modern thought finds these also made with short crust pastry, of course, and sometimes topped with mashed potato, like a combination of mutton pie and shepherd's pie.

Pork pies: yes, these could be just minced pork with salt and pepper, and give good porky and peppery results, but only if you are able to get hold of the more flavoursome, naturally raised old breeds of pig. Modern recipes I have suggest mixed spice or allspice but the usual instruction that these should be but a pinch or two for 1.5kg/3lbs of fatty meat is laughable – a good sneeze would give more flavour. There is no good reason for pork pies not to be flavoured with must-ard and herbs, wine and onion and garlic or, best of all, plenty of spices, in the style of British potting.

Pork pies seem to be a major surviving victim of the Puritans' ban on the use of spices and flavourings in food; before that pies were aswirl with all the flavours of Araby and with its dried fruits, too. Even after the ban on spicing was lifted, pork pies had more character than might be garnered from the general standard of today's offerings.

Pork pies have traditionally had a particular association with Leicestershire, Melton Mowbray chiefly, because local pigs were specially well fed on whey, a by-product of cheese making; the bakers of this town also once added butter to the pastry and cayenne to the filling. Dorothy Hartley in *Food in England* says anchovy essence was essential to their mixture because it made the cooked meat pink whereas everyone else's was grey; she put a sage leaf plus marjoram into each pie, which all sounds very encouraging. But there's more. She says the gela-tinous stock which finished each pie, filling the space left by the shrunken cooked meat, was highly flavoured with herbs plus the cores of the apples which had been used for sauces to eat with the other bits of the pig. The cores gave a slight almond flavour plus a welcome acidity. Even that inspired idea would give only a poor reflection of the once commonly manufactured pork and apple raised pie, now rarely seen.

Other centres baked their pork pies in other styles which equally deserve to be better known – Market Harborough used to add apple, sage, onion and sugar; those of Lincolnshire included stock made from the trotters; in Yorkshire they included sage and nutmeg, which sounds good, and in Derbyshire the meat was cooked with its bone before being added to the pies, an even tastier idea.

Although most commonly seen eaten cold, pork pies are very good eaten hot, something you are more likely to find as you travel north in Britain.

Veal and ham pie: this raised pie is usually oblong, having been baked in bread tins. It is properly constructed of layers of chopped veal and about half its weight or less of chopped uncooked ham or gammon. Hard-boiled eggs are always snuggled into the middle. The addition of lemon zest and parsley add extra savouriness and help make this a lighter thing altogether than pork pies. Finer forcemeat may be used instead of chopped veal, and mushrooms, mushroom ketchup, pickled walnuts and pistachio nuts are all traditional additions. If only.

Other Traditional Pies

Cottage and shepherd's pies: easily confused even though only a moment's thought indicates beef goes into the first and sheep meat into the latter – originally it would be stronger tasting mutton but we must make do with lamb. Another old distinction is the beef for cottage pie was always minced or ground, whereas the lamb for shepherd's pie was coarsely chopped or sliced. For both, the inclusion of a good strong meat stock and some Worcestershire sauce, or homemade, spiced ketchup, was essential.

Fidget pie: a rare relation of the squab pie q.v., made of short crust and containing bacon, apple and onion or bacon, potato, apple and onion, and to which a little lamb or mutton would be added if times were good. It was served with sugar in some counties and usually accompanied by cheese, the more common rural protein source. Well made, with far more apples than potato, with very little onion and some fresh thyme (no mixed herbs please) this is well worth resurrecting.

Fruit mincemeat/ mince pies: the ones you eat at Christmas. Originally these would have

Quiche and Savoury Flans

Here's what I do if I have picky or competitive cooks to lunch: I make a quiche, because so few have ever eaten one. Quiche went into the English language and onto the table faster than spaghetti or kebabs ever did. But, woeful to tell, few are quiche at all.

True quiche, the quiche Lorraine, is a wibbly-wobbly savoury custard tart. It's a down-home yet noble celebration of honest backyard fare, just fresh cream lightly set to a silken tremble with fresh eggs in buttery short pastry, and with perhaps some little amount of pre-cooked green bacon and maybe a scattering of finely sliced leek. The pastry should always be blind-baked and there should be no onion; onions are for onion tarts. Quiche should be eaten warm, not hot, not cold, but warm.

It seems quiche might once have been made with puff pastry, for it was the painter who took the name Lorraine (he came from the area) who is said to have brought this style of pastry back from Italy. But quiche didn't originally include cheese, and the only thing oniony was a little white of leek. Eggy mixtures that contained cheese and onion were baked on thick bread slices and called *féouses*.

There are French and German cousins of the quiche absolutely stuffed with bacon and cheese. Like millions of others I have also had salmon quiche, tomato quiche, vegetarian quiche, feta and ham quiche and like most of us, have endured countless spinach quiches awash in their own juices because the chef doesn't know how to drain spinach before baking it in a custard. Even if he or she did, these are not quiche, and each of them diminishes the real thing. Someone somewhere is bound to have refused a genuine quiche, disappointed because it had 'nothing in it'.

The answer is simple. Let's again call these other savoury custard tarts what they used to be – savoury flans. Calling them a French name is pretentious, like saying dentures instead of false teeth, or calling a cake a gateau: these are what *Tiffany's Book of Table Manners for Teenagers* warns against as 'backstairs refained'.

included meat as well as beef suet. The combination of meat with dried fruits, spices and sugar is basic to Bible-land cookery. So, even without the meat, these pies are one of the few things we eat that has relevance to where the events of Christmas are supposed to have happened. Hard sauce, known as rum or brandy butter in the UK, is properly an accompaniment to these and not to Christmas pudding, which is more traditionally served with a light custard sauce; but you'd be foolish not to enhance that with rum or brandy. See squab pie.

Pasty: the true Cornish pasty or pastie should be made with a lard pastry or you are already letting the side down. The raw beef, potato and swede (yellow turnip to Scots, rutabaga in the

US) should all be in thin flakes, not minced or chopped, although the latter is not an absolute heresy: onion doesn't have to be added, but if it is it should be very finely chopped indeed to ensure it melts into the filling and sweetens it, but is not independently detectable. Plenty of pepper is a more important flavouring. Carrot is an abomination in a Cornish pastie to most Cornish men and women, yet personal preference means it is seen.

Squab pie: this should be made with young pigeons, as are many of the greatest pies of the eastern and southern Mediterranean, but these days lamb or mutton is substituted. The importance of squab pie is its descent from the Muslim-influenced style of food that dominated British kitchens longer than any other style, from the 11th century Crusades onwards. Spice is much more traditional than herbs in British food, even though spice came to Britain only when Crusaders returned from campaigning in the Holy Land. Thus it is proper to expect a squab pie to contain apples, onion and sweet spices, but it should also have, and will be more authentic for having, currants or prunes: a little honey helps blend the flavours seductively.

By now I hope you have gathered that a squab pie of lamb, apple and onion plus the dead hand of mixed herbs should be sent back to the chef. Unless a squab pie takes your breath away with bravado flavour and sweet-savoury succulence it is not a squab pie worthy of the name.

Pâtés and Terrines

Well done you if you think pâtés are sausages without skins; you are right. Pâtés and terrines are based on chopped or minced pork usually with a proportion of liver and, sometimes, including salt pork or bacon. They were originally a method of preserving miscellaneous parts of the pig by first sterilizing (baking) and then sealing (with fat).

The difference between pâtés and terrines is now largely eroded and those who manufacture them apply either name arbitrarily. Originally pâtés were the ones that might be turned from the containers in which they were baked and terrines stayed in their earthenware baking dishes, also called terrines.

A well-made and matured pâté was once one of the most certain draws to a delicatessen or specialty food shop, and always a guaranteed winner at a buffet table. When I first worked in Soho in 1966, there was even a shop within a butcher's shop selling nothing but pâté sandwiches – you pointed at one of the appealing pâtés, the woman sliced thickly, slapped the pâté slice between rugged pieces of wonderful white bread and that was lunch – a very good lunch.

Pâtés were a key to the early success of Mr Christian's, my delicatessen, when it first opened in 1974. We built a kitchen in the basement and for many years made 2-300 lbs of pâté a week, not just for our counter but also for others, including Harrods. When I offered a grouse or a game pâté, that's what you tasted. The duck and orange has never been bettered anywhere I've been, and we did a chunky farmhouse terrine, a smooth chicken liver pâté with green peppercorns, and a rich smoked salmon pâté I know was smuggled into New York by Pan Am pilots. And then the fat-fear industry took over and pâté became unfashionable. It stayed that way for over a decade, but look around; I think pâté is back, and if it isn't it should be. One place it never left is the

Chianti area of Tuscany, where they have always made an excellent rustic chicken-liver pâté, so commonly served on toasted bread that the pâté itself has become known as *crostini*.

The distrust of the fat content of pâtés and terrines was unfair – you need the fat for flavour and for keeping quality. The real demon that turned so many from pâté was more likely to be the over-fatty, emulsified and extended 'pâtés' made in Europe, Belgium in particular, that had a longer life at ambient temperatures than most cars. Worse, they never delivered the flavour they promised.

Commercial considerations make the efforts of those big Euro-manufacturers understandable. But when the small kitchens of decent hotels, when the great kitchens of great hotels and of famous restaurants can't put decent flavour into a pâté and onto your palate, something is very wrong. I blame the French, but not without a great deal of thought over many years. Apart from the basic robust farmhouse style of pâté, their technique is wrong.

It's ridiculous to expect the roasted breasts plus a little minced dark meat from ducks or game birds to flavour many times their bulk of fatty pork-based mincemeat, but that is the blindly followed classic way of making pâtés and terrines.

The British way to preserve game birds and such was by potting, that is making a smooth or rough purée of the cooked flesh with butter, perhaps with cognac, rum or calvados but definitely with mace or nutmeg. These are extraordinarily delicious, and easily made at home, but would hardly produce a yield worthwhile enough to support a shop or restaurant.

It took me a few years to work it out, but I finally twigged; the flavour of the bones of the bird was missing from the French method of putting bits of roasted game bird into pork mince and then being baked. I began first to stew the game birds, the ducks or the venison with wine, with herbs, spices and finely chopped bacon – this so its fat rendered completely and could be thoroughly emulsified into the subsequent pâté mixture.

Once the birds were cooked the flesh was removed and mixed with the usual blend of pork belly and liver of some sort. Then came the coup, the cooking liquid was reduced, with the bones back in it, strained and also added to the mixture. This way just two or three small grouse would highly flavour kilos of pork pâté mixture, and a couple of ducks would gorgeously colonise four or five big terrines rather than just a couple. Baked gently and then left at least two days before cutting, these pâtés clearly smelled and tasted at least as much of grouse or duck as of pork. I felt honest about selling them.

There is a second reason for including bacon so early in the pâté making process. Bacon is pink because of nitrates, the benign chemical so excoriatingly good at keeping meat fresh, and that adds a pink tinge to it when cooked. Although infinitesimal in proportion, the nitrate content the bacon gives the pâté mixture encourages a delicious pinkness when the pâté is cut. Grey pâté would be viewed negatively whatever the flavour heights it reached.

There seems to be a light at the end of the tunnel that leads to chilled counters at good delicatessens, specialty shops and food halls. Very few of the pâtés sold now are the dishonest emulsifications of fat with added thickening agents, factory-made flavouring oils, milk fats and gross amounts of monosodium glutamate, all blended and baked into wheels that would survive a Grand Prix. No, they are made the real way, with decent, recognisable ingredients, genuine flavour with the perfectly acceptable adaptations commerce requires and a high fat content. Someone has remembered that if you make pâté and terrines the proper way they have a long life without artificial additives. That's their point.

If you have a food processor or a good old-fashioned mincer/grinder, pâtés and terrines are exceptionally easy to make and very satisfying. The ingredients are cheap and simple to obtain. The pleasure they will give to you, your family and your guests is immeasurable. The fame they will give to your shop is worth pages of advertising.

Pâté de foie gras and *terrine de foie gras* are quite different, and are discussed in the charcuterie section.

Ignore recipes with dozens of steps or with zillions of ridiculous ingredients– there is a catering college in London that recommended mixing choux pastry into chicken liver pâté!

Galantines

Galantines are a triumph of technique over taste. You rarely taste the time spent preparing a recipe: it's the time ingredients spend together, and how, that creates flavour, not knife technique. Galantines take much time and many knife skills, for they are those multi-coloured large sausages or boned birds, made bright with strips and stripes of high energy meats and other ingredients, all in a finely textured mousse held together by gelatine and/or fat. The outer layer might not even be a boned duck or chicken, but merely its skin. I love tradition but these were invented solely to impress, by the highest echelons of *haute cuisine*, for the most *recherché* moments in the bored life of the most privileged rich of earlier times. Based on my less privileged but fascinating career of dining and of judging fine foods, I regrettably know the best looking galantines always have least flavour. Too many fingers.

Storing

It is better to treat all charcuterie products, including pies, pâtés and terrines, as if they were fresh produce; keep them well wrapped and well chilled. Those that contain onion are more likely to go sour quickly, so keep it to a minimum if you must use it.

Making Pâtés and Terrines

Regard these recipes as the most elementary guide to proportion and flavouring, and then do it your way. The first recipe does not include liver, the second always does. You can change the proportion of pork to veal or leave out the veal. Different degrees of mincing give different textures. Chicken liver can be used instead of pig. And so on.

Pork and Veal Pâté

The dried breadcrumbs in this pâté are good home-cookery practice and work well for you if you want to sell pâté, too. They help retain tasty juices in the mixture and give a good slicing texture without the bore of pressing pâtés, a technique commonly recommended, but never once defended on grounds of flavour. Why would you press out the delicious juices of a freshly baked pâté?

Makes about 1kg/2lb
500g/1lb minced fatty pork
500g/1lb minced lean veal
250g/8oz smoked streaky bacon, minced finely
150ml/¼ pint dry white wine
2 large cloves garlic, chopped
1 tsp dried thyme
1 tsp dried rosemary
3 tbsp chopped fresh parsley
2 tbsp dried white breadcrumbs
½ tsp freshly ground allspice
black or white pepper
2 dry bay leaves
To finish: 150ml/¼ pint white wine or stock

First mix together the meats and bacon evenly and then add all the flavourings: it is best to do this with your fingers as stirring tends to break up the meat. If you can, leave to stand at room temperature for a few hours or covered in the refrigerator overnight. If you can't get fresh herbs use twice the amount of any or all of the dried ones. Put into a 1kg/2lb loaf tin or two 500g/1lb tins. Crush the bay leaves, and sprinkle over the top and then pour on the extra wine or stock. Stand the tin in a bain marie and bake at 160C/325F/Gas Mark 3 for – 1½ hours for the large pâté and 1 hour for two smaller ones. If the mixture was refrigerated add 15 minutes. Leave 24 hours before cutting.

Variations: some of the wine could be cognac, of course. Strips of streaky bacon stretched with the back of a knife can be overlapped over the mixture and then tucked down the sides – looks good but does increase both the cost and fat content.
Puréed chicken or pig's liver can be added to this mixture, about 250g/8oz is right, and will give more flavour and a firmer set. For a gamier flavour mix in six crushed juniper berries and ½ teaspoon of ground cloves.

Pork Liver Pâté

Pork liver is a very traditional ingredient in pâtés and terrines, but only because it was available. We have other choices, like chicken or turkey livers, and you could even use calves' liver. To tranquilise the sometimes strong flavour of pork liver the old trick of soaking it in milk overnight works. Otherwise, using sweeter back bacon, fresh pork and just a touch of shallot or onion combats it: too much onion will emphasise the liver flavour. And then, long slow cooking encourages a gentler and more comforting flavour.

Makes about 750g/ 1½ lb
500g/ 1lb pig's liver
25g/ 1oz shallot or onion
1 large garlic clove (or more)
250g/8oz lean pork belly, minced
125g/4oz back bacon, minced
1 tbsp dried white breadcrumbs
½ tsp dried thyme or 1 tsp of fresh leaves
½ large dried bay leaf, finely crushed
½ tsp ground nutmeg
½ tsp ground allspice
½ tsp ground mace
2 tbsp dry white wine
2 tbsp cognac or brandy
plenty of black pepper

Make a very fine purée of the liver, garlic and shallot or onion. Mix with the other ingredients, season highly with freshly ground black pepper and leave to stand for a few hours at room temperature or covered in a refrigerator overnight. Ladle into a suitable loaf tin. Seal tightly with foil and bake in a bain marie for 2-2½ hours at 160C/325F/Gas Mark 3.

My Pork Pie

Although by no means traditional, my recipe for pork pies does at least introduce you to what the possibilities once were and might be. The proportion of meat to fat commonly recommended was two to one. Minced belly of pork approximates this, but if you wish to be more exact, combine lean leg meat with hard back fat. Although sage is more British, thyme is a far better friend to pork and more universally liked. A centre layer of cognac-soaked prunes rolled in cinnamon makes a voluptuous thing to discover as you slice and eat.

To make a 1½kg/3lb pie

For the filling:

875g/1¾ lb minced belly of pork

50g/2oz onion, very finely chopped

150ml/¼ pint dry white wine

2 tsp cognac or brandy

½ tsp dried sage or thyme

1 generous tbsp Dijon mustard

1 small dessert apple, peeled and grated coarsely

½ tsp ground nutmeg

½ tsp ground mace

½ tsp freshly ground black pepper

1 tsp salt

1 packet aspic powder

beaten egg, for glaze

For the case:

375g/12oz plain flour

1 tsp salt

150ml/¼ pint water

125g/4oz lard, cut into small pieces

Mix the pork with all the ingredients, except the aspic powder, and leave at room temperature for a few hours or overnight in the refrigerator, thus ensuring the flavours fully blend.

To make the pastry, first sieve the flour with the salt onto a board and then make a well in the centre. Heat the water with the lard until the lard has melted. Pour the mixture into the flour, mix into a dough and knead until smooth. Keep it covered with cling film when not subsequently working with it, so it keeps warm.

Take a 15cm/6in loose-bottomed cake tin. Reserve about a quarter of the dough and cover with cling film. Press or roll out the remaining dough into a large circle – hands are faster and keep the dough warmer. Fold the dough over a rolling pin and transfer to the tin, and then ease it into shape using your knuckles, ensuring it is neither too thick nor too thin over the base or where the base meets the sides: allow an overlap at the top, all around.

Add the filling, which should be at room temperature. Roll out the reserved pastry so it is just bigger than the tin, transfer and fix in place with a little water. Trim neatly, angling the knife outwards from the tin so there is a slight over hang, and then crimp by hand or by using the handle of a wooden spoon, which gives a deeper, bolder look. Make a slash in the top of the pie and pull back the two edges so there is no chance of them closing during baking.

Bake at 200C/400F/Gas 6 for 30 minutes, and then glaze with the beaten egg and reduce the temperature to 180C/350F/Gas 4 for another 90 minutes.

Let the pie cool and then make up the aspic powder with half the recommended liquid – you could use more white wine rather than water. Pour the liquid in through the hole, slowly and in stages. You need patience for it takes longer and the pie absorbs more than you can imagine. Once the pie is indeed filled, let the aspic set, and then wrap the pie and keep for several days before cutting.

The addition of coarsely chopped parsley or grated lemon zest to the meat mixture, as you would in a veal and ham pie, both work.

Expect the cooked meat to be pale and pork-coloured rather than pink.

For further gold-plated advice on pies, pâtés and terrines look no further than Jane Grigson's matchless *Charcuterie and French Pork Cookery* (Grub Street). Otherwise there's my *Pies, Pâtés and Terrines*, published by Sainsbury's, but now well out of print.

Sugars, Syrups and Honey

Pure sugar is sucrose, a white carbohydrate with a sweet flavour, obtained mainly from sugar cane and the sugar beet, but some countries obtain sugars from palm trees, maple trees and from sorghum, a type of millet.

Before such sugar was discovered by the western world, honey, fruit and such vegetables as parsnip and carrot were the major sources of sweetness.

From a dietary point of view extra sugar, including honey, is unnecessary in an otherwise balanced diet. Enough 'energy fuel' can be obtained from the starch of cereals or from the galactose and fructose of vegetables and fruits respectively, and the advantage of using such sources of sugar is that they are ingested with other vitamins and minerals.

Food manufacturers have got cagey about spelling out sugar contents, and often disguise the sweetness of products by using almost anything but pure sucrose. But the information is there if you know that glucose, laevulose, maltose and fructose (fruit sugar) are all sugars. Invert sugar is a mixture of glucose and laevulose obtained by breaking down sucrose into these simpler sugars. Corn syrup and sorghum syrup are also sweeteners and often used in soft drinks and frozen products.

The one thing to be certain of is that sugar is not a poison, and does not cause disease, no, not even a single one. Impeccable research all round the world has shown the only direct connection sugar has with any negative change to our body is a potential to cause tooth decay. Other than that, an excess of sugar can certainly lead to obesity which in turn causes many a problem – but eating too much of anything or drinking too much alcohol can also make you fat. Sugar is not the enemy.

But don't be fooled by honey. Its sweetness is only sucrose which has been broken down into invert or simpler sugars; the minimal amount of other good things honey contains in no way compensates for eating more sugar than you really need. Honey is not a substitute for sugar – it is an alternative source of something you shouldn't need. Having said that, I also know few people, myself included, can live without either the flavour or the silken texture sugar adds to food. So I'd better stop lecturing and start explaining.

Cane Sugar

Once the white gold of merchants, for whom one cargo load of just 100 tonnes would be worth £1 million, sugar is now simply the world's most common sweetener.

Whence the cane from which it is extracted came no one is quite certain, but it is likely it was the Solomon Islands in the South Pacific. Different cultures produce different sugar-related mythologies, the most titillating of which hails from India. It is said a King Subandu found a sugar cane growing in his bedroom, from which issued a Prince Ilshvaku, reputedly a direct ancestor of the Buddha. I've heard many fine excuses for being found with a sweet young man in your bedroom, but *really*...

As they seem to have been refining sugar since as long ago as 3000 BC, Indian communities also seem to have been the first to cultivate it on any scale. The knowledge spread slowly east to Indo-China and later ebbed west into Arabia and Europe. By the 5th century BC the Persians could both refine sugar and form it into loaves but jealously protected their techniques. Alexander the Great's General Nearchus commented in the 4th century BC on a reed that produced honey without bees and the Arab conquests carried sugar further westwards so that by the 8th century it was being grown and processed in Spain and southern France. But it was not officially mentioned in England until the 12th century, when it was referred to in the Court Rolls. By 1544 there were two refineries in London.

Early sugars had charming names; one was *Zucchero Muccho*, flavoured with musk. This sugar was the highest Egyptian quality and generally available only in the Middle East. *Candi* was, as you might guess, like rock candy – clear chunks made by boiling sugar syrup; five types might be found in the apothecary's shop: simple (unflavoured), rose, violet, lemon and red gooseberry. *Montreal Mill* came not from Canada but from a Syrian town to the south of the Dead Sea. *Caffetin* came from Caffa in the Crimea and was wrapped in palm leaves, which explains its 17th century name, palm sugar, a term now used for something else.

During much of its history, sugar was used as a medicine, for it was far too expensive to use as a food or sweetener. As late as 1736 it was listed alongside the precious gems among the wedding gifts of Maria Theresa, later Empress of Austria and Hungary.

For a long time Venice controlled the sugar trade, but the discovery of the New World radically altered this. In the days of Christopher Columbus, sugar cost at least £20 per lb in modern terms, so on his second voyage west Columbus experimented with growing the cane on Santo Domingo in the Caribbean and found it grew faster and better there than anywhere else. The European crowns fought long, hard and expensively for the new sugar producing areas. At the end of the Seven Years' War in 1763, England had a difficult choice over which French colonies to keep as indemnity, the tiny sugar islands of Martinique and Guadaloupe – or unmeasured Canada. She plumped for the latter only because she was certain she already had the better sugar islands.

In England, rapidly becoming the new hub of the sugar trade, technical developments in refining predated the Industrial Revolution. By 1750 there were more than 150 factories producing over 30,000 tons of white sugar a year, which at an average of something over 15g/ ½oz per cup would sweeten 63 million servings of tea.

By the 18th century you usually bought loaf sugar, refined sugar pressed with syrup into a very hard lump and then shaped into a loaf or cone. It was used with great care, for it was both expensive and highly taxed. In the kitchen books of Mary Senhouse, my grandmother of nine generations ago, you carefully annotated when a loaf was bought, how much was used and when. Sugar didn't come into general use until 1874, when Gladstone removed the tax, a blessing about which dentists have had mixed feelings ever since.

The 3-8m/10-24ft high sugar canes are harvested in tropical sun in ghastly conditions, as any reader of the Australian novel *The Thornbirds* will know; but now this is increasingly done by machine.

The root of each cane is left in the ground to sprout again, a technique known as ratooning and which can be repeated for up to six years. The freshly picked cane deteriorates rapidly, so is processed as quickly as possible.

First the cane is cleaned and shredded to expose the inner core. It is then crushed and sprayed with hot water to form a free running juice. The separated fibres are recycled to fuel the boilers essential to the subsequent process: in Mauritius there is so much of the stuff it feeds local electricity stations, too. Clarification comes next. A range of ingredients must be added to the liquid to encourage pitching of impurities that can then be collected and removed; this sediment is filtered out under vacuum and used as fertilizer in the fields.

Now the process starts in earnest. The clarified liquid is reduced by evaporation and the condensed liquid, a type of treacle or sugar-containing molasses, is seeded to encourage the formation of sugar crystals, which are then extracted by centrifuge. This first extraction gives the biggest crystals, and at this stage they will contain both residual impurities and molasses and also have a very light coating of molasses; this will be golden sugar and demerara. Two more stages of processing and centrifuges result in the extraction of the remaining sucrose in increasingly smaller crystals, which are darkened by greater concentrations of molasses – musc0vado and molasses sugars. Eventually, with almost all the available sucrose extracted, only blackstrap molasses are left.

White sugar is obtained by chemically treating and bleaching the original sucrose-rich syrup, and it is this process that is generally meant by refining.

Beet Sugar

The other source of refined white sugar is the sugar beet, and from the outset you can be assured that the sugar from both is exactly the same thing – pure sucrose. Any differences in taste are the result of the processing technique used – or of imagination. Used as animal fodder and a table vegetable as far back as Roman times, the sugar beet didn't begin to be taken seriously as a sweetening source until the 18th century. In 1575 Olivier de Serres had ascertained beet sugar syrup to be 'very beautiful to see because of its vermilion colour', but he did nothing other than look at it. In 1747 the German Andreas Marggraf extracted sugar from beet and made it solid for the first time and then in 1802 one of his pupils, Achard, set up a sugar factory in Silesia with the help of the King of Prussia; but the quality was low and the price high.

It was Napoleon who finally put beet sugar on the table. Suffering from the British blockade he enlisted the aid of the French Academy of Sciences, and the chemist Delassert finally made sugar from beet into a viable commercial proposition. Nowadays sugar beet is Europe's principal source of sugar. Much of England's comes from Norfolk and thereabouts, and experiments continue to produce better strains that can be grown in more parts of the world more easily.

Sugar beet arrives at the factory to be washed and cut into 'V' shapes, called cosettes. Together with hot water the cosettes are fed into a tower or slowly rotating drum so their sugar can dissolve into the water. Then in other tanks this syrup has lime added to it and then carbon dioxide is bubbled through which forms a precipitate to carry out the impurities. More careful filtration follows, then a sulphur dioxide treatment and then concentration until you have the final syrup, which can be crystallized in the same way as sucrose from cane.

White sugar only can be obtained from beet, which is thus by definition refined. Beet sugar accounts for over half of all the sugar eaten and any coloured sugars made from it, such as *cassonade*, have had the extra colour and flavour added by spraying.

Cane Sugar Products

Demerara sugar: this highly important and delicious natural brown sugar is crystallized from syrup that has been only partly discolorized and filtered during boiling. The large, sparkling, yellow crystals are about 98 per cent pure sucrose and two per cent molasses and thus quite refined, but at least give you some minerals. It takes its name from the county in Guyana where it was first produced. But now there are other types of 'dem' as it is affectionately known, and it can be made by adding cane molasses to refined white sugar, which could thus be beet sugar. It will have exactly the same qualities but you will always know where it has been made for its name must be qualified. Demerara on a packet means it was made from cane sugar in the country in which the cane was grown. Other types, such as London Demerara indicate that it has been artificially made and the qualifying adjective usually indicates this was done in a refinery closer to the point of consumption.

There is almost no nutritional difference between muscovado and demerara sugar.

Demerara is excellent for flavouring cooked or new fruits, and for cereals. It is traditionally used to sprinkle on fruitcakes and biscuits before baking, to give a crunchy topping. It can replace white sugar in virtually every recipe where you do not mind the addition of a little colour.

Light muscovado: is a creamier-coloured muscovado with a lower molasses content than true muscovado. It is ideal for cakes and puddings where you want extra flavour; the darker sugars aren't generally recommended for cake making.

Molasses, Blackstrap molasses: this is the rich concentrated syrup remaining after cane sugar syrup has been through the several boiling and separating processes necessary to extract almost all the pure sucrose. It contains some sucrose and other types of sugar as well as everything that refined white sugar is missing, in fact 8-10 per cent of molasses is vital minerals including iron, copper, calcium, magnesium, chromium, phosphorous, potassium and zinc.

There are various colours and grades, depending on how much sugar is left in the liquid. The darker the molasses the less sugar it contains. All types can also contain sulphur, which is used in some refineries – unsulphured molasses is usually light coloured and better flavoured. Some cane growing areas will simply reduce cane syrup over heat and call this sweet golden liquid molasses; but this is never sold commercially that I know of. Molasses is mainly used these days to flavour baking, in Creole cooking and to add flavour to the water when boiling hams.

Molasses sugar, Black Barbados, Demerara molasses: this is fairly difficult to find outside sugar cane processing areas. It is a very strong tasting sugar with high molasses content and a rich, almost black colour. The sticky texture and taste are similar to good treacle toffee.

Muscovado or Barbados sugar: the most common naturally dark sugar, this is extracted after the mother liquor has made three trips through the centrifuge. It is the last time the producer can extract sugar from the almost exhausted source. Thus the crystals are very small and one-seventh of their weight is molasses, which forms a coating on each crystal.

The rich flavour is very similar to that of dark rum and can substitute for it. One of the best ways to use this is on Dusky Virgins, a simple, delicious and quick way to make something as good as crème brûlée in minutes. Mix equal volumes of plain yoghurt and whipped cream together and pile into ramekins, over fresh fruit if you like. The acidity of the yoghurt will stiffen and set the cream. On top of each, sprinkle muscovado sugar and leave to chill for several hours, during which time the sugar will melt, looking like a crust of caramelized white sugar but tasting very much better.

Treacle: this is much sweeter than molasses for it is actually the full syrup that has only had a proportion of the sucrose removed from it, and again can only be made from cane sugar, although golden syrup might also be added to it – the label will tell you. Used mainly for puddings.

Turbinado: a raw sugar which has been steam cleaned and is thus lighter in colour and flavour. A term found rather more often in the United States where true raw sugar is considered unfit for human consumption because of its impurities, turbinado falls somewhere between light muscovado and demerara in appearance and flavour and thus either of these or light soft brown sugar may be substituted when you are using American cookbooks.

Other than those natural brown sugars from the cane, it's all sweetness and white, for further refining produces a crystal that is practically 100 per cent pure sucrose, and it is this white granulated sugar which is usually demanded and to which the refineries and factories are basically geared. There is no proof that refined white sugar is in itself more fattening than the natural brown sugars, but the latter are nutritionally more valuable and balanced, relatively.

White Sugars

These are classified according to grain size, and may be made from cane or beet.

Caster sugar: useful for cake making, drinks and decorating where the smaller grain either dissolves faster or looks prettier – usually under 25mm in Britain. In the United States the grain is even smaller and called superfine or Baker's Special.

Cube sugar: this is produced by moulding and pressing selected granulated sugar with sugar syrup which cements the crystal. On drying, it is very hard and this is presumably based on the process which formed loaf sugar.

Granulated sugar: although varying from country to country each grain is usually about 1mm. One can be substituted for the other.

Icing sugar: called confectioner's sugar in the United States, this is made by grinding small crystals, and cornflour is usually added to prevent caking.

Jam sugar: a useful, relatively new product which blends granulated sugar with apple pectin and citric acid and thus guarantees a good set when making preserves.

Preserving sugar: specially suited to such work as its large crystals dissolve slowly and do not settle in a dense layer on the bottom of the pan – therefore there is less stirring and less chance of your jam burning.

Rock or Candy sugar: huge sugar crystals, often strung together. It is used for sweet making as it does not burn easily.

Brown Sugars

Light brown and dark brown soft sugars are usually granulated white beet sugar that has been coloured and flavoured with sugar cane molasses. If you hold these sugars under running water the applied coating will be seen to dissolve. They are not just artificially created alternatives to demerara or muscovado sugars but have been carefully planned to have very specific culinary uses.

Cassonade: few French people believe it but this is white beet sugar coloured and flavoured with sugar cane molasses as explained above. The molasses equivalent of sugar beet is utterly inedible.

Light brown: this is rather fine grained, designed to dissolve easily, and specially recommended for creaming with butter (or margarine if you must) for cake making or for making brown sugar meringues. It will give marginally more flavour and a little more colour than white sugar.

Dark brown: also planned with baking in mind, when rich colour and dark flavour is wanted, in ginger breads, rich fruit cakes or other mixtures containing vine fruits. Like muscovado sugars, you can almost pretend it is dark rum you have used.

Golden Sugars

Golden sugars are made in Mauritius and sit in a culinary oasis of their own between white sugar and demerara. They may be sold as unrefined because the crystals naturally contain a slight amount of molasses and thus offer a certain amount of the original vitamins and minerals, at the same time there is little molasses flavour and they may be used as though white sugar, even in tea.

Essentially, steam cleaning and careful manipulation of the processing cleverly leaves less molasses in the crystals than in a demerara, but has stopped short of complete refining.

Golden sugars tend to create anything but sweetness in the mouths of white sugar refiners who say any sugar which has been processed in some way is by definition a refined sugar and that it is deceptive of the producers to say these are unrefined. In the end, it matters little. The difference in nutrition, colour and flavour is minimal unless you are eating sugars by the spoonful, in which case you are unlikely to care anyway.

Golden Syrup

Terribly popular but, like 'brown sugars', a little dishonest. It is a syrup of refined sugar plus something called invert sugar plus colouring from the original sugar syrup. Invert sugar is sucrose, a complex sugar, broken down into its components, the two simple sugars called dextrose and laevulose. If you must have syrup, treacle is probably a marginally better choice; but I wouldn't put anybody off a golden-syrup flavoured steamed pudding.

If you are American you cannot easily buy British golden syrup so you must use corn syrup and, if you like, colour it with some brown sugar of one kind or another.

Coffee Crystals

These stupid, over expensive, maddening things, thought to be the height of sophistication in far too many restaurants and houses, seem carefully planned to ensure you either enjoy the complete cup of coffee in all its bitterness before the crystals begin to dissolve, or that you drink it stone-cold, by which time some of the crystals might have dissolved. I can't think why anybody buys them.

Flavoured Sugars

There are many other flavoured sugars you might find useful to make and use. They should be allowed to sit for at least two weeks in a cool dark place before you can expect the flavours to have been absorbed. Even quite small amounts make nice gifts when prettily presented.

Citrus sugar: wonderful on fruit, in cream or sprinkled over hot or cold puddings of almost any type. This may be flavoured with lemon, lime, bitter (Seville) or sweet oranges, tangerines or any of the new citrus styles marketed. Rub the zest with sugar lumps, but stop before you get to the bitter pith. As the outer layer of the cube collects the zest and oils and thus slightly dissolves, scrape it off onto a plate; keep everything well away from absorbent wooden chopping boards. When you have enough, dry the flavoured sugar and zest residue very gently in a low oven, and then crush it and store in an air-tight jar.

You might find it easier to mix a few tablespoons of finely grated zest with each 250g/8oz of granulated sugar and to dry that before storing. Do the grating directly over the sugar or on to a plate or you will lose the zest, and remember rub sugar over the inside of the grater to collect the zest there: even so citrus sugar made this way will not be as elegantly flavoured as the cube method.

Floral sugar: rose petals, jasmine flowers, rose geranium, lavender and orange blossom are the best. Violet is a terrific idea too, but where can you find strongly scented ones these days? The flowers should be perfectly dry and used in quite large amounts. Take extra special care to store away from heat and light and then use on berry fruits, or in cream cheeses, yoghurts, whipped cream, sponges and the like. It takes one or two weeks for the sugar to absorb the oils and fragrances of the flowers.

Spice sugars: cinnamon, ginger, aniseed, cardamom, clove or mixed spice sugars are suddenly invaluable once you have them, for pancakes and batters, toast, yoghurts, cake toppings or flavourings, fruit pies, hot chocolate and coffee or the whipped cream which might top them. Use very freshly ground spices and about two tablespoons of white or brown sugar per 250g/8oz.

Vanilla sugar: perhaps the most useful sweet flavouring in any kitchen is vanilla sugar, caster sugar which has been stored with vanilla beans in a screw-top jar. The beans may also be removed and used several times for flavouring sauces etc, simply being dried properly before returning to the sugar; and the sugar can be topped up as it is used.

Cooking

The important contributions to cooking made by sugar are its preservative qualities and its lightening of cake mixtures, accompanied by an irreplaceable satiny mouth feel.

Sugar's preservative role gives us jams, jellies and preserves, for a high sugar level prevents the growth of bacteria or the action of enzymes. It is important that sugar is used when freezing fresh fruits and some vegetables, as the temperatures of a freezer are not low enough to kill or dissuade the attentions of enzymic actions that putrefy such goods. In addition the presence of sugar or sugar syrup in frozen soft fruits or berries prevents the formation of ice particles that break up the structure of the fruit and cause them to disintegrate when defrosted. Cream, butter and egg yolks all freeze better if sugar is added and cakes and biscuits will freeze well if they have a high sugar content.

Sugar in a cake mixture helps keep the gluten of the flour soft and pliable, allowing it to expand thereby giving volume and lightness.

I know it is popular but I cannot bring myself to use sugar when cooking peas or tomatoes. If you need sugar either you have been soaking the peas, which removes their own sugar, or are using unripe or English salad tomatoes, for which there is no cure – or perhaps you have used too much salt.

Other Sweeteners

The usual substitute for sugar is honey, another natural sweetener that was replaced by refined sugar when it became generally available. However you are also likely to find these in shops and recipes:

Corn syrup: made by hydrolysis of the corn starch, that is, a chemical splitting into component sugars together with the addition of water. Regularly used in baking in the United States; it adds sweetness and notably more suppleness in the mouth. Indeed it's the key to success of many American specialty cakes. If you find a recipe that calls for corn syrup, you can replace it with golden syrup, but remember it will give added colour and flavour but not the all important mouthfeel.

Maple syrup: the reduced, sweet sap of the North American sugar maple (*Acer saccharum*) varies in sweetness, colour and flavour depending on how much it is boiled. Use hot, especially on pancakes and waffles or with bacon; otherwise as a flavouring for ices, sauces, icings and baking. Sometimes crystallized to make maple sugar. Be very, very careful when buying maple sugar as all kinds of smarty-pants tricks are played on the labels. The world 'flavor' warns something other than the real thing is included, and other tricky word combinations hope to hide from you that the bottle contains only a small portion of the real thing, made up with sugar syrup and 'flavors'. If a bottle seems too cheap to be the real thing, it is too cheap to be the real thing.

Palm sugar: also known as **jaggery** among countless local names, this is made from the boiled sap of a number of varieties of palm tree. Moist and tawny and only slightly crystalline, it has a truly delicious fudgy flavour that is less sweet than cane and beet sugars. Available packed in many forms, including frozen, and is always a sensation when used instead of cane or beet sugars. In Sri Lanka jaggery is melted over heat, lightly spiced and then thickened with desiccated coconut as a stuffing for small sweet pancakes, served as a Small Eat, the specialty sweet and savoury foods served there, with tea in the afternoon. Baked apples, pears and peaches are transformed, baked bananas double their ambrosial appeal and a mixture of toasted nuts and warmed palm sugar on ice cream is almost too good to eat. Almost...

Sorghum syrup: a relatively natural product made by concentrating the stalk juice of sorghum, which is a type of millet. Less common nowadays.

Honey

You may safely dismiss most claims made for honey as sweet nothings. Honey is essentially a concentrated solution of water and sucrose which has been predigested into simpler sugars, laevulose and dextrose, which will make up 75 per cent of the bulk. To be stored and sold in the retail market honey has been strained to take from the solution of sugar all traces of wax debris, but leaving pollen and other minutiae including colloids. It is only these minimal ingredients that could remotely give honey magical qualities. There do seem to be substantiated claims that it helps wounds to heal, but essentially, honey is sugar and sugar is calories.

Even without claims for it as an elixir of life, honey has long been one of the world's most important foods. Together with the lowly parsnip and carrot it was the world's main sweetener until sugar dropped in price to become more universally available in the late 19th century. Honey is recognizable in Egyptian pyramid burials at least 5000 years old and has been relied upon, as sugar syrup is today, as a preservative. But it is not entirely safe or as sterile as so commonly believed; untreated honey contains many spores including that of fatally dangerous botulism. The exact strain is weak enough to be destroyed internally by children and adults but babies under a year old should not be fed untreated honey or honeycomb.

The greatest marvel of honey is the extraordinary industry which goes into its manufacture: to call bees busy is a phenomenal understatement. It all starts with nectar, the sugary syrup that collects in the base of flowers. In some cases – the Australian eucalyptus for instance – a bee might obtain a full load of nectar from one blossom but it is more usual to have to visit up to 1500. It commonly takes 300 bees up to a month to make 500g/1lb of honey from nectar.

First they store it in a special nectar stomach, whence the bee can siphon off supplies to keep it going, the bee is so well designed it can carry its own weight whereas jets have to settle for a 25 per cent payload. It has been estimated the bee is efficient enough to fly four million miles at a steady 7 mph on a gallon of nectar.

Back at the hive the nectar is transferred from mouth to mouth of worker bees. This digests the original complicated sugars to simple invert sugar, that combination of laevulose and dextrose, and reduces the moisture content from 70 per cent to between 15 and 20 per cent: because the hive is kept at a constant 32C further reduction is unavoidable. The point of the effort is to give the bees food for winter. It is sometimes said feeding bees sugar syrup that they then convert makes cheap honey, but this is incorrect. Because the bees' natural food has been taken from them, bee keepers must artificially feed the bees during winter. None of the sugar syrup is converted and stored as honey.

Once the honeycombs are harvested the cells are decapped, usually by a heat process, and the honey extracted by centrifugal force. If the solid particles of wax and pollen are not removed, crystallization will begin more quickly than required. Sometimes new honeys are stored unstrained or part-refined and later heated to 52C for several days to liquidize them before further treatment. Once bottled, the honey is usually heated again which helps promote a shelf life of 6-9 months.

Even such strained and pasteurized honey will contain enough oils and essences from its origins to present an enormous range of flavours and styles. This is the real point of honey today, spectacular natural flavours in a natural product.

Most commercial honeys are blended for uniformity and from year to year will contain honey from a number of countries. China is a major source, and so are America, Russia, Australia and Africa, some honeys giving colour, some fragrance, some texture and some sheer economy.

The aristocrats are honeys made from the nectar of a single flower and the rarer the flower the more expensive the honey. Like good olive oils, these should never be used in cooking but enjoyed solo.

If you like a medium richness and fullness of flavour, clover honey is a marvellous middle range choice but even this will vary according to the country. Generally, the hotter the country the richer the flavour of any honey and thus Australian clover honey will be more robust than an English one.

The queen of honeys is generally thought to be Greek Hymettus, flavoured with the nectar of wild thyme from the mountain of that name; others argue Middle European acacia honey is better. Yet honeys from Galicia in north-west Spain come with IGP status: *azamora* is a variety including multifloral, eucalyptus, chestnut and two local specialties, which is a dark amber and has a strong fruity flavour, *brezo* has a reddish amber and a curious bitterness accompanied by light floral notes. Honey from Granada *miel de Granada DOP* also offers a varity of flavours including avocado, rosemary, thyme, French lavender and perhaps best of all orange blossom honey. Mono-source honey, only from rosemary or from Spanish lavender is offered by equally noted *miel de La Alcarria DOP*.

The range of single flower honeys increases every year and some shippers will be able to offer specials on a once only basis. There is a huge choice – over 300 single flower honeys in the United States alone – with some of the best coming from the Balkans and Mediterranean;

lavender honey and rosemary honey have their addicts and there are supposed to be rose and raspberry blossom honeys but I have never yet spotted them. My absolute favourite is orange blossom honey, and it is a lifetime of pleasure to compare those of each country which makes it, which includes Central American countries as well as the Middle East. Linden (usually called lime) blossom honey is also exceptionally delicious.

English honey is properly famed for its elegance but single flower varieties are terribly expensive, presumably because there is so little harvested in most summers. Scottish heather honey is an exception to the hot weather/robust honey rule for in this the cool moors have produced a very tasty, rather direct honey which is particularly well thought of for desserts and cooking in general. A great deal of British and European honey making is blighted by the ever-increasing acreage of rape, the nectar of which gives an overbearing muskiness and bitterness which many find destroys their enjoyment of honey, even when in minute quantities.

New Zealand supplies some outstandingly individual honey from its native trees, many of which have supportable claims to being truly organic. Manuka (or ti-tree) is a dark, full, sharpish honey; pohutukawa honey is made from the gorgeous red flowers of a tree that lines the beaches and blooms at Christmas time.

New Zealand Honeydew is not really a honey in that it is not made by bees but by aphids which live on the bark of black beech trees in the country's virgin Southern Alps: it is untreated and also guaranteed organic. It has a slightly yeasty nose and flavour with a stunning aftertaste of orange flower water.

But it is to Australia you must buzz if you want to taste extraordinary honey with truly independent and often challenging flavours. The country is said to have the widest range of any, with an amazing variation of flavour, sweetness and colour. The eucalyptus honeys – blue gum, white gum etc – are a great place to start as you work up to Tasmanian Leatherwood honey. This spicy, complex honey is unlike anything you have ever thought of as honey, and some people simply can't abide its confrontational flavour; it's widely exported.

Clear honey: even the most carefully refined and pasteurized honey will crystallize eventually. It depends very much on the type and some heather honeys may not begin for up to two years. If you have honey that has crystallized and you prefer it not to be, stand the sealed pot in cold water and slowly bring it to a temperature into which you can just put your fingertips. Keep the water at this temperature until the honey is clear. Do not think of clear honey which is crystallized as 'off'.

Comb honey: if you can bear to chew the wax, this is the most nutritious of honeys, and, being complete, is more likely to contain whatever is said to be one of life's elixirs. But don't make the mistake of storing comb honey lying down. The bees don't. Examine a comb closely and you will see each cell slopes back slightly, so it can stand upright without leakages. This is how you should keep it too. It is always untreated and increasingly expensive. Generally you find you buy a square cut from a larger comb, but sometimes the bees have been persuaded to make combs in smaller, plastic squares – an expensive but practical ploy.

Set honey: the real term is crystallized honey, an effect which is perfectly natural, but which can be helped by stirring or whipping clear honey.

Cooking

The individual oils and perfumes of specialist honeys are lost in baking, so it is pointless using anything but the most basic blends. Indeed if you want the best of honey flavour in cooking it is far better to add it to cooked fruits, exotic sweetmeats and pastries after they are cooked. For the latter, typically in Greek and Middle Eastern pastries using filo pastry, diluted honey is much better than syrup, but you must always use a cold honey or syrup on hot pastry: hot syrup on hot pastry, or cold on cold, or hot on cold will always give sogginess.

To convert recipes using sugar, calculate that sugar and honey have the same sweetening capacity weight for weight. But by volume honey is almost twice as sweet; one tablespoon of honey is as sweet as two tablespoons of sugar. You must also use slightly less liquid to mix the original recipe.

Storing

Like most natural products, honey does not stand up to light and heat. It also frosts in very cold conditions, caused by bubbles of air being forced out as the honey shrinks. When it expands again on reheating the bubbles remain and are virtually impossible to remove.

Sushi and Sashimi

The take-away sushi shop is with us, and now there is sushi in supermarkets too.

There are even books telling us how to make it at home, none of which recreates the pleasure of the sort of sushi restaurant where irresistible little plates jog past your eyes on a continuous circle of temptation, like Hornby trains for big boys.

The West has taken to sushi with as much gusto as Japanese girls took to ankle sox and myriad hair clips. But how many of us know what it should be?

Sushi is meant to be eaten the very moment it is made, or pdq afterwards. The special, slightly sticky rice, gently acidified with rice vinegar, will still be warm, so that when the raw fish or other ingredients are put upon it, as with nigiri-style sushi, the rice will draw the coldness into itself and then both rice and topping will be at an equal, optimum room temperature, for maximum flavour. Only ocean fish and salt water seafood are used raw, as fresh water fish are more likely to harbour parasites.

It's a magnificent, wonderfully ephemeral oriental concept and the goal of perfect mutual temperature is why sushi chefs work so very fast: the mystic moment can be missed in a heartbeat.

This goal is the defence of countless sushi restaurants that display take-away packs of sushi at ambient temperature – one, in Three Lamps, Auckland going so far as to position them directly in the sun's rays. 'They look more so pretty for you in the sun! Refrigerator muchly bad bad.'

What Ms Butterfly didn't know is that warm rice is a number one food poisoning agent, and that in cities that bother to count, sushi is Tummy Enemy Number 1. Those who do know the danger sell their sushi lightly chilled, like wasabi, which now glitters on Piccadilly, London. But if sushi is chilled, the rice loses it tenderness and both rice and topping lose some of their flavour. So are they really selling sushi, or selling what they think they can get away with? Hard one to solve? Not at all. Only eat sushi you have seen it made in front of you. If you must buy it chilled, then wait a good ten minutes for it to warm up a little, which helps but the rice never regains its original texture. While you wait, you might like to think about this: How many Japanese do you see buying sushi from a supermarket or from chilled self-service shelves?

As a tick list, here are the main types you should see steaming past your station:
Maki sushi: a sheet of nori seaweed is spread with warm sushi rice, which is then topped (usually) with vegetables. It's rolled up using the *makisu* mat, the edge of the seaweed is wetted so it sticks together, and then the roll is cut into slices.
Californian sushi: the same as maki, with the addition of avocado to the filling, which is more likely to be fish or seafood than vegetables. Sometimes the rice is flavoured with sesame seeds or similar and sometimes the rice is rolled without a nori outer.
Nigiri sushi: a handful of rice is pressed together and shaped in the palm, so one surface is subtly arched and then is topped with fish of some sort, often with a dab of wasabi between the two. Sometimes the two elements are bound together by a thin strip of seaweed. Once *nigiri* were more likely to be made with cooked fish, as this was safer, but now there is both raw and

cooked and an ultimate destination of sushi – and sashimi – eaters is *toro*, the raw, incredibly creamy belly flesh of bluefin tuna. Popular, and cheaper, *unagi-nigari* are made with freshwater eels, *anago-nigari* will be the salt-water species.

Temaki sushi: this time the nori sheet is rolled into a cone and filled with rice and other goodies. Too big to be eaten with chopstiscks, and so is eaten in the hand, like an ice cream cone.

Inari sushi: sushi rice is wrapped in a thin slice of tofu that has been flavoured with sugar, mirin and soy sauce and then fried. Rectangular or triangular.

Chirashi/bara sushi: a family style sushi made by mixing sushi rice with fish, seafood, vegetables and thin slices of egg.

Oshi sushi: invented in Osaka, this is sushi rice, vinegared fish and other ingredients layered and pressed in a mould. It is sliced to serve.

Sashimi is simpler to judge for it is largely raw fish, anything from sea slug to lobster, via clams, shark, tuna and *fuju*, the one that first paralyses and then kills you if you're served the wrong sliver. The curious thing about sashimi to occidentals is the better the quality of fish, the less it tastes of fish – there should be no smell louder than a faint mumble of an ocean sound.

One wonders what the point is, but then the West is less tuned into eating texture for its own sake and is far less easy to excite with the intellectual appeal of otherwise tasteless food, unless it is fearfully expensive; then we are right up there.

With both sushi and sashimi the tradition is to eat with soy sauce into which nose-runningly hot, green wasabi q.v. has been stirred, the thinking behind which battles me.

Some of the best meals I have ever had were from a sushi train, where the dishes were replaced only a whistle-stop faster than the diners ate them. And I have been a guest at restaurants in Tokyo where a simple sushi meal equalled the cost of a small car. Superb flavours and fascinating textures eaten as soon as they were made meant an ever-changing spectrum of challenges to the palate, and with such stimulation the conversation sparkled too. But then, I had suggested my companions eat with almost no soy sauce and something less than an injury of wasabi. Much of the conversation was about the lingering aftertastes they were discovering, when they had been used only to the hot, salt-lick of soy/wasabi.

I know it's worse than teaching a grandmother a new way to suck eggs (not that my grandmother would: that's another story) but sushi and sashimi without the extra loadings become edible masterpieces. With the usual drenchings of soy and wasabi they might as well be half-chewed, sliced white bread: with a little, they are sublime; with none at all, food for gods.

Like the shop assistant who was told graphically what he could do with a too-expensive cucumber, I am already overloaded with coarse suggestions from those I've told not to eat exaggerated amounts of chillies, and from those I've tried to convince not to eat raw onion with oysters or smoked salmon or caviare. Torture me, martyr me. I know I'm right about sushi, too.

But there's more to disturb the dreams of sushi lovers. Do you know about Ren Chin, or what those two contracted words might mean? They are read as 'microwave' and 'zap', and if you are to believe *Gourmet* magazine (I do) this is deep frozen *nigiri*-style sushi that has been used by the food-service industry in Japan for ten years, and could be going retail. The frozen sushi comes in a patented container that allows microwaves to reheat the rice, but not touch the fish, which is defrosted by transferred heat. Raw fish, like salmon, is just as melting and tender, soy-grilled eel every bit as good as Momma-san might make.

Someone better rewrite the words of that old song, you know the one: If you knew sushi, like I (once) knew sushi. Oh! Oh! Oh! etc.

Tea

What must we do to make tea as fashionable as coffee?

It is infinitely more variable in flavour, much harder to ruin in the making, and so naturally flexible in caffeine content it is kid's play to match your tea to your mood – an Assam to startle the senses, an oolong to refresh, and a green tea to soothe. If only we could be asked which tea we would like, rather than being offered what is to hand.

Britain was one of the pioneers of tea drinking in the non-oriental world, and yet with few exceptions it remains a very difficult country in which to get a decent cup of tea. You would think there are only low-grade blends, chosen for instant colour and quick harsh flavours, which must be mollified with milk and sugar to be remotely palatable. How sad, when merchants and blenders offer a remarkable range of quality teas, and amongst even the nationally known brands there are truly outstanding products at bargain prices – if they are made and served properly.

Tea is a liquor made by steeping the dried, top-leaf shoots of a type of camellia, *camellia sinensis*: black teas should be made with boiling water but for some specialist green tea even 50C is too hot.

The habit of drinking the result began in China, where tea was certainly used as a beverage by the sixth century. By the eighth century it was popular enough to have been taxed; about the same time the Japanese adopted it and began to ritualise tea making and drinking.

It was not until the mid-17th century that tea was seen in England, first imported via Holland. There wasn't much of it, even though Queen Catherine, the Portuguese wife of Charles II, had popularized it in court and aristocratic circles. But by 1689 the East India Company had begun direct importation and in 1721 was given a monopoly in the trade by Parliament. In the mid-18th century tea had become universal, the principal drink of all classes. It was perhaps the first hot drink the poor had ever had and, as with white bread, they were determined to keep up with the nobs, even though 450g/1lb of the very cheapest tea probably cost a third of a man's weekly wage. There was plenty of it, however, because England had the ships to bring it from China.

Russia became a tea drinking nation early in the 17th century and their tea came overland by caravan, which was considered a better way to transport tea than by exposing it to salt air, protection from which is why tea chests were always lined with metallic foil.

The taxes on tea imported into the UK were exorbitant and led to an enormous trade in smuggled tea. Anxious about the lost revenue, Prime Minister Pitt compelled the East India Company to import enough tea to supply all needs without raising prices, and smuggling ceased. Some would say the drinking of tea is also what finally ended London's gin era, when there were twice as many burials as baptisms.

The unhealthy close liaison between Parliament and the East India Company was an important contributor to the loss of America to the Empire. In 1765 Parliament decided to tax the colonies and their imports, but not to use the taxes to improve or assist the colonies. After they refused to pay the tax on tea, the colonists quickly generated a smuggling trade from Holland. The East India Company forced Parliament, who acted like a subsidiary company, to give them absolute rights to the tea trade with the American colonies – they were to take tea direct, cutting out the European exporters and the American importers.

Resentment and self-interest erupted and the colonists decided to forgo tea. In December 1773 the first East India Company tea ships arrived in Boston. On the night of the 16th a group of colonists dressed as native Americans threw the tea into the water. Tea parties at other ports were quickly organized. Parliament closed Boston's port… and it was war.

Fifty years later the great Indian tea plantations were established, and so supplies and opportunities to deal direct multiplied. But the huge, growing market of America was not interested and by and large is still not: ask for tea and you are still likely to get a forlorn tea bag beside a cup of barely tepid water. Will they ever forgive? American tea blends remain far paler and more fragrant than those of England, a clear memory of the style of China tea their forefathers would have known, before India's stronger brews were on the market.

The tea bush *camellia sinensis* is native to a fan-shaped area that starts in Vietnam and expands westwards to Assam and eastwards into China. It has a fragrant white flower and if not kept plucked would grow into a 12m/40ft tree. In the last 20 years, more and more tea has been grown in East Africa, so much so these countries are now major exporters and Kenya grows tea of notably high quality. The plant is remarkably free with its affections and cross-breeds within its own species with abandon, so, like humans, almost every new bush is different from all others. In an effort to keep up quality, notably successful individual bushes have for some years been cloned, giving a more predictable and consistent product than the usual lottery of quality. It sounds like a good idea, but no-one knows what curious ancestral behaviour a cloned bush may suddenly display in ten or 20 years. On the one hand many plantations are going strongly for all clonal replanting: but older hands are timid, perhaps properly, and say every plantation should be a mixture of clonal and naturally bred tea. Watch this space.

Like coffee, the height above sea level at which tea is grown is a major influence on its body and flavour. Low-grown and 'mid-country' teas flourish furiously in the lush, humid foothills, giving large volumes of leaves with plenty of colour and body and straightforward, robust flavour without finesse. High-grown teas produce more slowly in the cooler days and cold nights at 4000 to 6000ft; the crop is very much smaller but has greatly superior flavour, fragrance and delicacy – high-grown Darjeelings from such single estates as Castleton or Margaret's Hope retail in London for close to £150/$US275 a kilo.

Only the top two, very new leaves and the emerging leaf bud between them are plucked to make tea, something never successfully mechanized. I first stood in a tea garden during plucking in Sri Lanka. The colourfully clothed women spoke little, yet one all-pervasive sound bound them into a sisterhood; the combined pinching and picking of the tea leaves sounded like the too-close munching of a dairy herd.

In some areas gathering can continue year round, in others there are dormant periods. But there are always better and worse times for picking. The best are called the flushes; the first flush is early in spring, the second a little later, and the third flush, after summer, gives the autumnal teas. In between is when the standard teas are collected.

There are three types of curing process, giving green, semi-fermented/oolong tea or black tea. Each technique gives a distinctive and easily recognizable type of leaf and flavour. The essential processes are first withering, to reduce the moisture content of the leaf, and then crushing or tearing to release internal juices and then fermenting or oxidizing those juices to develop colour and flavour and, finally, firing to dry the leaves: as with wine or cheese the slightest difference in technique makes more or less of particular characteristics given by soil or climate.

Basic Tea Styles

Black tea: the withered leaf is crushed and fermented fully until it is all brown before it is fired, thus offering greater colour, flavour and tannin; the Chinese often call this red tea, referring to its colour when brewed.

Brick tea: finely powdered tea leaves compacted under great pressure. Can be green or black and you grate or chip a little into a mug or teapot. Its claims to popularity are you can carry it in your pocket and the drink it makes is hot. Tibetans believe it is improved when they whisk rancid yak butter into it, which gives you some idea. However, the shiny pressed bricks, usually squares or oblongs, often sport illustrations and calligraphy of the highest standard; they make marvellously useless gifts, unless to a homesick Tibetan.

Brocade teas: very fancy green teas – see page 528.

CTC tea: once, all tea was large leafed, or orthodox; quality, unblended or green teas will still be like this and need up to eight minutes to brew properly. Now we also have CTC tea. This is a process invented in 1928 that cuts, tears and curls the leaf into smaller pieces, and these give a faster, stronger brew – two to three minutes – because boiling water can penetrate all of each particle without delay.

Green tea: the original tea. Most teas that first came to Europe and what is now the USA would have been this style. Once the leaves are gathered they are withered and dried immediately. This preserves their green colour and means the tea will have a definite taste of green vegetation. Originally this drying or firing was done by hand in very large woks, and some of the highest grades are still finished like this: they are known as pan-fired teas and the process can also shine the leaf giving it a metallic sheen, hence gunpowder green tea. They are graded according to the size and shape of the fired leaf; the highest grades of the rolled leaves, sometimes helped into shape by steaming, are the smallest and called pin head. Country green teas are generally the brightest and freshest tasting green teas.

Green teas have a great deal less caffeine and tannin content than semi-fermented or fermented (black) teas and are thus ideal for later in the day and to soothe rather than stimulate; this is also why the Chinese can put tea leaves directly into a covered mug, to which they add water again and again. You could not do that to black teas for the tannin extraction would be unpalatable.

Green tea is credited with enormous health benefits, often to do with its high proportion of anti-oxidants. The buzz is such that today green tea or its sometimes imaginary fragrance is found in everything from candles to scents; unfortunately almost everything is also found in green tea. In furious bids to be seen to keep up with trends green tea mixtures are being created for even the most august brands. But look at the label – are the added flavours made from natural ingredients, or are they yet another repository for so-called nature-identical oils? It seems such a defeat for good sense, such an undeserved success for opportunistic marketing teams, to proclaim green tea's health benefits and then to sell it riddled with industrial chemistry.

Whatever green tea you buy, but particularly if you buy some of the rare and wonderful specialties from China, take great care to read the brewing instructions. Some green teas must be brewed at only 50°C or 60°C, and for no more than a minute.

Monkey picked: often made oolong style, and I'm still not certain the tale is true about the leaf tips being picked by monkeys; they reckon only monkeys can get to tea bushes growing wild in difficult terrain. Whenever I've bought it I've thought it was cheaper than I expected and then better tasting than I expected. So, plenty to talk about over a cup or two.

Oolongs/ semi-fermented tea: the most common are Formosa and China oolongs. After the initial withering, leaves for oolong tea are slightly crushed, and the exposure of the interior juices begins the fermentation or oxidation of the leaf. This chemical change is what develops the character and flavour of the tea, creating tannins and so on, and is accompanied by an obvious change from green to brown. Oolong teas are allowed only to part-ferment, and this is stopped when the leaves are fired, leaving them still part-green, part-brown.

The flavour most associated with oolongs is that of peaches and there are indeed often memories of this fruit, particularly in the aroma. If you detect a little bitterness, this is part of the acceptable flavour spectrum, and oolongs are too good to drink with milk or lemon. Lesser grades of China oolong sometimes benefit from sugar. They are all exceedingly good after-dinner teas – elegant, soothing, refreshing without being too stimulating, as the caffeine count is low.

Orthodox: this means the tea leaf has been treated the original way, rather than the modern CTC method. The leaves will be very much the same size they were when picked or only minimally torn or cut: such tea is generally only the higher and highest qualities and should be brewed for up to eight minutes to get maximum flavour.

Tea bags: invented early in the 20th century by an American tea broker, who started taking his tea samples around in silk envelopes. If you treat tea bags properly you will get a very good cup of tea, but most people do not: as usual it's a matter of reading the label and doing as it says. Tea bags should be brewed for at least two minutes – if you want stronger tea, use less water, if you want weaker tea, use more, but without the full brewing time you get only a speck of what you have paid for, and are throwing money away.

White tea: rare and expensive, this tea is made only from the smallest and newest leaf shoot, which is covered with a silvery fur. The Chinese usually call it white tea, but when the style is produced in other tea areas it is more likely to be called silver tips.

Choosing your Tea

It is a very broad view, but if you start with the green teas of China and Japan, move ever westwards to Sri Lanka and then up to Assam, you follow a pattern of tea styles and relative tannin/caffeine content: the further west and then north you go, the stronger the tea and the more tannin/caffeine it will offer.

Chinese and Japanese green teas are the mildest of them all, and almost all the Chinese ones grow in Fujian province in the south east of China. Move south someway, and teas become mild, fruity oolongs and if you then move westwards you find Chinese black teas, all of which are milder in caffeine and tannin than anything from the Indian continent, but stronger than oolongs or green tea.

Now go further west to Sri Lanka for liquory teas with exceptional fragrance and firm fresh body that comes from a move up the rungs of caffeine and tannin. On up through India until you find Assam, the malty-strong heavyweight of teas.

The exceptions to this pattern are the aristocratic high-grown Darjeelings of northern India and the world-class teas now coming from Kenya, which are close to Sri Lankans in fragrance, flavour and colour. Within this broad-stroke picture there are thousands of variations, but it's very useful for assessing a tea you've not met before. With this knowledge you might start the day with a strong black Indian tea and as the day progresses, move down to a Ceylon or Kenyan, on to Darjeeling or a China Black, then to oolongs and finish the day calmly with no caffeine or tannin at all, with green tea.

China

China's greatest tea gardens are in the east and Fuzhou (Fuchow) in the south east was the great port whence stirring tea clippers raced to Europe. China is by far the biggest of the world's few producers of green teas: only Japan and Taiwan also grow them. Fujian province is the only area producing oolongs other than Taiwan.

Chinese black teas are divided between north China blacks and south China blacks, sometimes called reds from the colour of their liquor. These black teas never have the astringency or bite of Indians and some are so rounded and full in the mouth they can remind one of aromatic chocolate. The Chinese have a well organized and carefully observed system of numbered quality standards, and thus if you find a tea you like a lot, try to find its number so you can get it again.

Bohea: an old, broad term for China black teas in Britain.

Brocades/ fancy leaf teas: intricately woven, sewn or folded green tea leaves that are good to look at when dried, and then swell into evocative shapes when brewed often into flowers; hence their alternative name Flowering Teas. Some are created specifically to be brewed in a glass, so the unfolding can be watched and enjoyed as part of the tea experience. They can be searingly expensive, but some can be brewed up to five times, which helps. Butterfly in Love from Yunnan is one such, which does look rather like butterflies when brewed. Yu Huan Jade

Ring tea comes in hand-rolled circles and is said to have a 'meadow' flavour. From Anhui comes Jin Shang Tian Hua and here leaves are sewn together as a chrysanthemum blossom that when brewed releases the flower, suspended: this is one of the teas that should be brewed in a glass. Top price, over £550/$US880 a kilo at Fortnum & Masons, goes to Fairy Lady's Golden Rings from the Tai Pu Mountains in Fujian province. Made in the shape of the earrings of the local fairy who persuaded tea to grow all year round, it has a natural jasmine flavour. There are more brocade teas, and most are available at the Rare Tea counter of Fortnum & Masons, in London. See Semi-fermented, page 527.

Ching Wo: a South China Black or Red Congou, and considered amongst the very best. Gives a reddish liquor, as the type suggests, which is very aristocratic and even the look of the tightly rolled leaves is high class. Like gunpowder green teas it has the gift of lending its superior flavour to lesser teas in blends, rather than being overwhelmed.

Chrysanthemum: the only infusion or tisane commonly encountered in China, made from chrysanthemum petals, and rather less acrid than you might expect. Sometimes mixed with Pu-erh tea.

Chun Mee: a common green tea made from young, medium-sized leaves, which roll peculiarly neatly and thinly. Because they then curve to look like pencilled brows it is known colloquially as eyebrow tea. It is the best grade of a style called Young Hyson, all rather sharper tasting than gunpowder teas.

Dragon's Well or Longjing: one of the best, branded green teas, fired flat and with a rich green colour and flavour. It should be made only with the top shoot, hand picked with no accompanying leaf, no matter how small. Made near Hangzhou.

English Breakfast Teas: once another name for north China black teas that include the well known Keemuns, and which are fragrant, full-bodied and naturally sweet when of high quality. English Breakfast tea blends of today rarely contain North China blacks but are constructed from Indian and African tea, becoming a brighter, brisker thing altogether.

Gunpowder: is the best known of the green teas and instantly recognizable because the leaves are always rolled into balls with a metallic sheen. The smallest and highest grades are known as pinhead. A sprinkle of gunpowder in the pot encourages greatness in Ceylon tea particularly, and the combination of gunpowder with China black was the most common offering when hostesses still mixed tea leaves from a precious tea caddy into a personal blend in front of their guests. By itself it is especially good after a chilli-hot meal.

Gunpowder green is the base of mint teas in Morocco, although elsewhere mint teas are made of the herb alone.

Hyson: an old generic name for all green teas in Britain, but actually a style made from bigger leaves than the previous tea and thus rather coarser.

Keemun: from Anhui province and generally thought the best of north China black teas although they were always made as greens until the 1880s. The best have a naturally sweet, mouth-filling flavour that has variously been described as orchidaceous, winey or like chocolate.

I think they are all those things and thus are always great with such very un-Chinese comforts as cream sponges, cup cakes, chocolate cakes, ginger cake and shortbread.

Oolong teas: these are a world unto themselves, and have their own grading system. Basically they divide into Formosa oolongs from Taiwan/Formosa and mainland China oolongs, which are usually from Fujian province.

Formosas are generally finer and more delicious than China oolongs: the very highest qualities have a distinct fruitiness and a beguiling sweetness, sometimes reminiscent of peaches. **China oolong** teas are noticeably coarser, with a distinct earthiness, but are just as refreshing. A rather expensive one I bought in Hong Kong was thought by a food-wise MP of my acquaintance to smell of fish paste. I wish he had not said so, for on reflection it was undoubtedly true; but we never established if this was intrinsic or there had been some contagion.

The difference in leaf picked for oolongs in spring and in autumn is greater than with any other type of tea, and the early summer teas picked from late May to mid-August are generally thought the tops. Freak conditions producing one-off results and complicated intermediary gradings make oolongs a lifetime study, so it is really worth taking advice – and spending good money.

Oolongs are always orthodox tea, with a rather large leaf that thus requires a good long brew – up to seven or eight minutes. In Chiu Chow restaurants, where goose is a great specialty, China oolongs are brewed by a contrasted Gung Fu method, in which small teapots are stuffed with leaves and then a quick, very strong brew is made from them. More often than not they also use a tea known as Iron Goddess of Mercy, which created many a snigger when Margaret Thatcher was UK Prime Minister. It is served curiously too. Very small cups are arranged on a tray and the tea is poured from a height so it splashes in and out of the cups and on to the tray as the pot is moved back and forth and round and round, supposedly so everyone gets the same flavour. It is as well the cups are so small, for the tea is very bitter and metallic.

Generally only the top few of the eight main categories are exported. Formosa oolongs rise from Fine grades to Finest, which are also sometimes called Poppy or Peony oolongs. Then it's on to Fancy or Peach Blossom and to Top Fancy oolong, often sold as Silver Tips. Peach Blossom and Silver Tips are the teas with the fruitiest nose and flavour, a wonderful way to finish a special meal whether heavy or light, for oolongs always manage to assail and astonish the senses.

China oolongs are graded differently from Formosa oolongs, taste earthier and are much more an acquired taste: Kwai Flower is one you might enjoy. With a little more effort and a lot more money you might find **Osmanthus tea**, oolong leaves blended with the fragrant flowers of *osmanthus fragrans*, but for only ten days during October, which gives some idea of why it costs the earth to drink something so heavenly.

The highest grades of tea grown in other regions of the world are sometimes made the oolong way, in Darjeeling particularly, usually indicated by using 'silver tips' in the tea's name.

Pai Ma Tan: very large leafed green tea, which is also very slightly fermented, and thus looks like the aftermath of weeding the herbaceous border. A very acquired taste, but some do. This is often sold as white tea, but is not.

Panyong: one of the best known of the south China black teas, traditionally also called red teas. These teas from Fujian province are less immediate than Keemuns, more clarets than Burgundies – (see Ching Wo).

Pu-erh: this is a warning rather than a description, and may very well be onomatopoeic for a common reaction to it. Pu-erh, from Yunnan, has a challenging earthy flavour that can seem disgustingly mouldy; indeed it is purposely kept a long time and can be so. Just as some palates are devastated by the tiniest amount of goat milk cheese, pu-erh might target some people's tastebuds differently, seeming interesting to some, horrid to others. It can be so strongly flavoured I find it nauseating even to have on the table, but this might be my peculiar sensory organs. Certainly, the Cantonese like it enormously and describe old ones as having a velvety feel on the tongue.

Pu-erh is the most common tea served with dim sum in Hong Kong, but you can always ask for an oolong or jasmine tea.

Souchong: like Congou and Pouchong, descriptive of a style of large leaf in China teas.

Yunnan: these teas from a western province are generally of a very high grade and often glow with golden leaf tips. They have a bold earthiness and to some have overtones of lapsangs: a single leaf of lapsang in a potful of Yunnan will magically enhance this.

India

The country has three main styles, south Indian that are similar to Sri Lankans, north Indian which are amongst the world's strongest, and Darjeeling, also northerly but producing a light and fragrant style found nowhere else in the world.

Assam: the most important tea producing area of India, in the Brahmaputra valley in the north east. Strong, heavy-liquoring, malty teas which cream massively, a daunting phrase which means the tannin extraction is so high the teas go creamy and cloudy as they cool. Assams are generally used in blends as the solid base for all the breakfast blends you have ever drunk, good or bad.

Assams do have excellent flavour if you brew them properly – subsequently dilute with more water if you like, but it's not an Assam if you have merely dunked a bag or brewed for a few seconds. The finest grades show a lot of golden tips and may even contain stalk, a characteristic of the teas produced late in the season. Any tea sold as an Assam will mean it has the character of Assam and will contain Assam teas, but has usually been extended and tempered by teas from other areas and countries.

Constantly improved standards and processing techniques now mean it is also possible to buy single estate Assam teas. Mokalbari is typical of the vigorous Assam style, Hazelbank is thought to be particularly rich in flavour and both Mohukutie and Mangalam give the ideal 'malty' Assam flavour.

Darjeeling: the only Indian teas that are universally self-drinkers, that is, all of them are fine enough not to require blending. They grow in the Himalayan foothills of Bengal at up to 6500ft and have long been the highest priced teas sold in quantity. There are three main seasons, first flush, second and autumnal.

Most first flushes are semi-fermented, but the tea gardens would rather say they are lightly fermented; whatever you call it the leaf has not been fully fermented and shows quite green yet gives a liquor that is darker and richer than you would expect, combining body with a unique astringent, grassy freshness and fragrance. The leaf is not as big as either of the oolongs but will still require up to five minutes to brew perfectly.

Darjeeling tea is specially famous for having a muscatel flavour, but few drunk in Britain have this character, most commonly found in second flush and mid-season teas (July to September). Virtually all these go to Germany, where they are prepared to pay the premium prices. I have drunk a perfect one just once, in Germany, and it was indeed like sipping a bunch of grapes.

Autumnal teas are delicious, floral, syrupy and with a heavier liquoring: unfortunately they lose their character very quickly and must be cared for with great skill. Although self-drinkers, Darjeelings have a famed ability to add to other teas and if you are blending at home this is a good place to begin. I was secretly given a canister of tea said to be HM the Queen's private blend. It was clearly Assam based, strong, rich and immediate, but Darjeelings added a wine-like fragrance and sweetness and it was excellent without milk and sugar or with both. Twinings Queen Mary tea, the blend of the present Queen's grandmother, is based on second growth Darjeelings and has a true muscatel flavour, but is not available in all their markets.

Darjeelings offer tremendous opportunities to taste individual estates: Castleton and Margaret's Hope are famous and expensive. But even in Auckland and Adelaide I have seen teas from other single estates offered. Some names to trust are Bannockburn, Chamong, and Jungpana, grown at a particularly high level, has one of the finest and most exceptional of muscatel flavours. A Darjeeling Raritat is a blend of fine Second Flush Darjeelings, all said to be grown within sight of Mt Everest.

Harder to find are other styles. A Darjeeling Phoobsering is a true white tea, made only with the downy tips and, unusually, dried naturally under the sun – June-picked is best. The Singbulli and Margaret's Hope estates both produce an oolong style: the former gives a green liquor with a rose petal character, the latter is floral, peachy and retains its characteristic Darjeeling notes. Fortnum & Mason stock them, of course.

Nilgiris: this is the best known of teas grown in southern India, possibly because it grows at up to 6000ft and thus is a higher quality than teas from the Madras district. It is quite like Ceylon teas and can sometimes taste pleasantly citric.

Indonesia

Generally found only in blends, but highly thought of in the tea trade, and could throw up some individual stars, in the same way coffee does in this region. Sumatran teas are very similar to Assams, but cheaper, and most find their way to Ost Friesland where they like their tea even darker and stronger than the Irish.

Japan

There is much more to tea in Japan than the ritualized tea ceremony, as much about porcelain and frocks as the drink itself. Pan-fired teas have been polished in an iron drum giving a whitish sheen; basket-fired tea is a more careful process and gives better taste.

Ban-cha: the least of teas, the prunings from shaping bushes at the end of the plucking season. Particularly low in caffeine. You use boiling water and drink directly. Ban-cha Hougicha or Hoji-cha includes fragrant stems and has been toasted to turn it brown, giving a coffee-coloured drink which is light in every other way.

Genmai-cha: an extraordinary mixture of green tea with brown and puffed rice, rather like tipping all your breakfast into a pot, and thus thought very gratifying.

Gyokuro-cha: the best. Specially selected leaves from reed-mat shaded bushes make a naturally sweet and fragrant green tea. Terribly expensive, too, like anything of quality in Japan. It should be brewed for 90 seconds to two minutes with freshly boiled water that has first been allowed to cool in a bowl for 90 seconds and is thus 60-65C.

Matt-cha: powdered *ten-cha* for the tea ceremony; the water should be only 60-65C, you use about 2g per teacup and there's a lot of whisking involved to encourage a froth on top. The longer that lasts the better your chance of remaining in top kimono circles. Modern Japanese without a Tea House in their minuscule apartments also make *matt-cha* with hot or cold milk and with iced water. It is an excellent base for unusual sweet and savoury sauces (pheasant is a common victim), sorbets and ice creams. *Hiki-cha* is a high grade of ceremonial powdered tea

Sen-cha: basic green tea. Three teaspoons will make enough tea for three people and it should be brewed for 30 seconds with water that is just below boiling.

Ten-cha: a lesser *Gyokuro* and dried as flat leaves rather than rolled. Usually powdered to make *matt-cha*.

Kenya

Now one of the most important of tea producers. Most of the production is CTC tea for blending and the characteristics are very similar to high-grown Sri Lankan tea – brisk, clean, red-liquoring and very refreshing. Blends of Kenyan tea alone are now sold and Twinings Afternoon Tea blend is largely Kenyan teas and very good indeed; the best tea is now so good some of the highland gardens are producing orthodox-leaf self-drinkers. Individual estates worth seeking are Marinyn and Subukia.

Sri Lanka

The country has changed its name but the teas are still commonly called Ceylon teas. Many British judge a good cup of tea by the look of the brew and generally think a thick dark brew a promise of decent tea – until they are presented with a good Sri Lankan or Ceylon tea. For even though the liquor remains clear and brilliant they offer wonderfully brisk and fully flavoured teas with none of the harshness or aggressive punch of Assams. The best pluckings are February and March and then in August and September, but other months produce greater quantities, except January which is disappointing from every aspect. Unusually, some of the coarsest looking leaves produce some of the finest drinking teas.

Ceylon Silver Tips is a very particular tea, made from a special tea bush with maroon leaves. The buds of the leaf are either sun-dried or dried naturally in a heated room. Small amounts only are made, and together with exquisite flavour it comes also with the reputation of being an aphrodisiac.

There are four major growing regions in Sri Lanka and all produce teas that may be drunk unblended.

Kandy: the lowest-grown teas generally used in blends to give Ceylon character without great finesse. Commonly thought to be a better all-round drink than many mid-level teas.

Uva   Dimbula: these similar mid-level regions give a stronger, bitter liquor which is typically reddish and fragrant. They offer good-looking leaves for orthodox teas, which make long elegant twists. Single estates with good reputations are Rosita, Shawlands and Kenilworth, but there are dozens worth noting.

Nuwara Eliya: wonderfully fragrant high-grown teas with light liquor, great sweet fragrance and a clean, refreshing and very long finish. Lover's Leap and Tommagong are highly rated.

Blends

Once, most people blended their own, usually combining black and green teas from either side of their prized caddy. When commerce took over, many merchants blended tea suited to the water of individual districts. There are still merchants in the UK who will do this, even for individual stores, but not many.

As with coffee, when you see a country or area name on a tea blend, it is most likely to be indicative of a style rather than of origin.

Tea Blends

Afternoon blends: Indian or Ceylon, often with lots of Kenyan. The big straightforward sort of flavour many call 'builders', imagining it is what these labourers drink from tin mugs.

Breakfast blends: usually based on Assam teas to give a kick start to the system. Irish Breakfast is probably the strongest, fiercely Assam in content, yet if brewed properly has fragrance of flavour and nose. With a heavy breakfast of fried or fatty foods, and with eggs, it clears the palate quickly. English Breakfast used to be largely China blacks and gentler but this is less usual these days, when it is Assam plus others.

Caravan: sometimes called Russian Caravan. Usually a blend of orthodox China black teas, imitating the style of tea that went overland to Russia rather than by sea, and which was thus thought less likely to have been affected by tropical heat or salt sea air.

China black: can be almost anything, and as it is fairly easy to get teas from identified areas and specialist blends that tell you what they contain, I should avoid this catch-all style – but you could be lucky.

Prince of Wales: Twinings' Prince of Wales blend is a very fine example of Keemun-based tea, in this case with a little added oolong. Warm, smooth mouthfeel and typical chocolate notes in the aftertaste. Blended for the Duke of Windsor when he was Prince of Wales the blend was once available only outside Britain whilst there was a living Prince of Wales, but it is now sold there with impunity. What will be next to crumble?

Royal: a tea blended by Fortnum & Mason for another of the British royal family, this time for King Edward VII, who also being Emperor of India, wanted a blend of Indian and Ceylon teas. It is Fortnums' best seller.

Staff: a somewhat derogatory term for a mix of Indian tea with Earl Grey, that tastes more like tea with a lift than the scented brew alone and so is thought less aristocratic.

Flavoured Teas

Apple: a staple tea in Turkey, comforting, addictive, delicious.

Chai: a sudden new darling of cafés and people with a yen for the exotic. Created in India, it's a strong but ordinary blend of tea complemented by a mixture of spices, and usually drunk with milk and sugar, or made with condensed milk, as is common in India. Good ones are fabulous but because you don't know how long the spices have been ground or kept, the flavour most people profess to like has little to do with the potential. It's easier to see this if you buy a chai mixture in tea bags, which easily absorb the spices' oils, and thus exposed they oxidize faster.

Chai spice mixtures include three or four of the expected sweet spices plus ginger and black pepper, at the very least. Frankly, if you are going to drink a lot of this, it's best to make it fresh each time, and to use whole rather than ground spice: for starters, a crushed cardamom or two, perhaps a couple of cloves, a piece of cinnamon stick, a blade of mace, a couple of crushed peppercorns and if you have some, a sprinkle of dried orange peel. Make sure you can still taste the tea. See: Spiced tea.

Earl Grey: if this tea flavoured with oil of bergamot – the citrus, not the flower – really was once a secret recipe given to an earlier Earl Grey in China, it follows it should be made only with China teas. There is only one company I know that bases theirs on Keemuns and it is so marvellously superior I cannot imagine why everyone does not follow suit. It seems that it's just as likely the tea was invented in London by Sir Joseph Banks and his cronies, but it doesn't matter: it was a good idea then and can be a great one now.

There was no such thing as commercial protection in the 18th century and the secret of the flavour soon got out. Now each company has a different idea of how Earl Grey tea should taste and suddenly there is an ever-increasing range of Earl Grey teas.

One company in Portobello Road Market makes it with a stronger tea base, some tea shops offer an Earl Grey with rose petals, there is an oolong Earl Grey that's light and delicate and green tea versions too. In Auckland New Zealand, Tea Lovers Ltd offers 10 choices including Earl Grey Cream with vanilla and caramel flavours, Earl Grey Special with citrus pieces, lemon grass and jasmine flowers, Earl Grey Orange with orange pieces, Smoky Earl Grey with Lapsang Souchong and Earl Grey Imperial, this time blending bergamot oil with Darjeeling tea, a combination also flavouring a most superior chocolate by *chocolatier* Pierre Marcolini. They might not all seem like tea to you, or to me, but they'll make terrific sorbets and ice creams.

It is crass to choose Earl Grey and then to add lemon slices that smother most of its scent and flavour. Add milk if you must, and a little sugar enhances the citric fruitiness, but it is blended to be drunk with neither.

If the bergamot flavour is too aggressive for you, Earl Grey may be mixed with other decent black teas, particularly a Keemun I think. Unless you drink it up quickly, Earl Grey tea should be stored in an air-tight container because the flavouring oils are fugitive and oxidize quickly, so you are soon deprived of the very flavour for which you bought the tea.

Elderflower: the light muscatel flavour of dried elderflowers is just one of the many new ideas mixed into green tea by Fortnum and Masons; a little 'flavouring' is added too. Up to you.

Fruit teas and blends: fruit-*flavoured* teas increase in popularity and the choice is amazing – pineapple and coconut, passion fruit with vanilla, mango, wild strawberry. I know they give a lot of pleasure, but is still seems a very curious thing to want to drink something as simple and natural as tea with a factory-composed flavouring, no matter how much they bleat about them being 'nature-identical'. When your sense of fun and adventure takes over, the wild strawberry one is outstanding.

Another type of fruit tea is a tannin- and caffeine-free blend of dried-fruit pieces, rose hips, hibiscus blossoms and flavouring oils, and thus not really teas. The best I ever made, quite by accident, was done by pouring boiling water over glacé pineapple pieces. There's one made in New Zealand called Autumn Gold that's basically a chopped mixed salad of dried autumn fruits with dried strawberries: unusual and very popular.

Jasmine: traditionally made in the green tea gardens of eastern China. Jasmine flowers are harvested early each morning and strewn onto long flat rows of withered green tea leaves, which are turned with pitchforks as they absorb the flowers' oils and scents. Every 24 hours the flowers are sifted out and replaced by more; the number of times depends on the quality of the flowers. The amount of labour involved makes the low cost of these teas remarkable. F9301 is the usual standard sold in the United Kingdom, but if you can find it, FS904 is very much better – it is sometimes known as Chun Feng. Some gardens used to use a much faster steaming process, but this is said to be on the wane.

For tea freaks, there are finer and finer, rarer and rarer jasmine teas made in China. For over a century Tai Mu Long Zhu, has been rolled by hand in the mountains of Fujian, and is a green tea with only subtle jasmine flavour: it's perhaps the most expensive. Fujian Finest Jasmine, as sold by Fortnum and Mason's Rare Tea counter, is made with jasmine picked in the morning but allowed to open and intensify in a warm room for a day before being mixed with the green tea leaves: the orange-gold colour is particularly striking.

Jasmine tea is a very good digestive, indeed, and if made strong enough also the basis for sensational ice creams and sorbets – (see Cooking with Tea).

Lapsang souchong: large leaf tea that is smoked over a type of pine after firing. It is one of the few teas better when under-brewed. It may be mixed to a greater or lesser degree with plain black teas, and a small amount mixed into Earl Grey tea tastes rather good when drunk in the open air, where sturdier flavours are appreciated. There are two basic styles; Mainland or China Lapsang and Formosa Souchongs. In direct contrast to oolongs, the China Lapsangs are of higher quality. The ragged leaf and size of Formosa Lapsangs absorb so much smoke they would be undrinkable in a sane world, yet they are most popular. Like Darjeelings, the best China Lapsangs are found in Germany. Funny old world.

Lichee couchong: flavoured with lichee fruit. Rather less known than jasmine and rose teas and rather more delicate of flavour. A delicious and haunting change.

Osmanthus: one of the rarest teas, made only for ten days in the year; see under Flavoured tea.

Rose pouchong or **congou:** a large leaf China black tea made the same way as jasmine tea but imbued with the natural scent and oils of fresh roses. Extraordinarily delicious, soothing and calming. The rose flavour is specially good with the best baking, especially cream scones and strawberry or raspberry jam. The alternate names given merely indicate minor technical differences in leaf appearance. Available loose or in tea bags, and both must be transferred to an air tight container immediately or the virtue of the rose goes within days. Wonderful for making ice creams and sorbets, of course. There are imposters merely 'flavoured' with rose.

Although sold by some of the grandest names in the business, including Twinings and Fortnums, rose pouchongs and couchongs can also be bought from Chinese supermarkets. Buy the leaf tea in packets rather than loose from a self-serve bin, or buy the tea bags. Like Earl Grey and jasmine tea, this one must be kept very well sealed.

Spiced: flavoured more gently than chai q.v. and seen rather more in the United States, but increasingly popular in Britain during winter: some are called Christmas teas and the best tea joke I know is one made in the UK from white tea and thus called White Christmas tea.

Tea made with a piece of cinnamon stick in the pot, or a crushed cardamom pod or two is wonderfully stimulating and warming. Fresh or dried orange peel is good too, and so when I am in the United States I stock up on Constant Comment, a tea blend with sweet spices and orange that is calming and delicious.

Vanilla: when it's good it's great, when it's not it's awful. This should be excellent tea in which you find ground up or chopped vanilla beans. If you don't it has been 'flavoured'. Fauchon of Paris makes the best, and visitors to Mauritius will discover more economical ways to buy such tea, for it is made widely there.

High quality vanilla teas are exceptionally soothing, with a velvety mouthfeel and long aftertaste. Marriage Frères of Paris offer a caffeine-free mixture of *roiboos* q.v. and vanilla, highly recommended by those who discuss tea on the Internet.

The king and queen of flavoured teas must be Marriage Freres of Paris, a brand also sold in good shops – and dedicated tea shops – throughout the UK, USA and in Australia and New Zealand. Rare and wonderful fruit oils and ingredients are mixed with equally wonderful teas and tisane ingredients to offer flavours you won't find elsewhere, and many make superb iced teas. Are all the added flavours natural – or nature-identical oils? If these don't interest you, Marriage Freres also sell exceptional specialty teas, too.

Tisanes

A brew-up of leaves or flowers, often herbal, and generally with some medical properties or claims.

Camomile: a natural tranquillizer, but if you don't like its flavour, use it to add sparkle to blonde hair as a rinse conditioner. Related to fever-few which is supposedly an aid in avoiding and treating migraine. Honey is a better sweetener than sugar.

Hibiscus: not the exotic bloom of the South Pacific but a related mallow flower, much appreciated in Egypt and some Caribbean islands (as roselle) and used as the bright base for many commercial brews and blends of exotic 'natural' things with every possible type of health, wealth and wisdom claim: sort of sweet and roseate and very red. The *mauve* found in Corsican and Provencal markets is a mallow.

Lemon balm/melisse: (but sometimes, *citronelle*, confusingly) also good as a relaxing sleep inducer and calmer of migraines. Famous as an enlivener of bath times: you could bathe and brew at the same time.

Lemon grass/citronelle: used extensively as a tea in some parts of the Caribbean and as a way of life in Mauritius. Everything is claimed for it, but none of that matters as much as how delicious and refreshing it is. For food, only the fleshy base is used, but for a tea much more of the woody stem can be included, but it should be bashed to crush it, and also requires a longer brew.

Lime blossom/tilleul: the flowers of the linden tree – muscle relaxer and inducer of sweating.

Mate/yerba mate: the leaves of a South American shrub dried, roasted and then brewed like tea to produce a caffeine-rich drink that tastes like wet haystacks. It's usually served and carried about in hollowed gourds and sucked through a straw with a strainer incorporated somewhere. Those who think themselves better than gauchos and gourds sip through silver straws or *bombillas*.

Mint: dried or fresh mint of all kinds makes a very calming and refreshing hot drink and is especially good as a digestive. All Arab mint teas are not the same; in Morocco the pot will always include gunpowder green tea too, but as you move eastwards towards Egypt this or other tea disappears until only fresh mint is used.

Raspberry leaf: is said to aid giving birth.

Roiboos: the word means red bush, and this is a brew made from the leaves of a bush from South Africa that is taking over the world, so much so it's often espoused by classic tea drinkers who think even Earl Grey a travesty. Caffeine free, but a stimulating flavour that does the job just as nicely. Very easy to take into other worlds by adding spices, herbs, dried fruit and so on.

Rose hip/gratte-cul: an important aid for those who retain water, for it is a reliable diuretic.

Rosemary/romarin: reduces summery headaches and is good for the liver. May be fresh or dried and is generally combined with black tea: fresh sprigs give by far the better flavour and work better too, I think.

Rose petal: immensely calming – when you are in Hong Kong or China buy masses of unsprayed dried pink rose buds and brew them for five or more minutes in covered cups or bowls to retain the fragile scent. Quite the most sensuous way to finish a meal. While guests are still there, anyway.

Verbena/verveine: a sharp citric digestive and nerve soother.

Making tea

You draw it, mash it, stand it or brew it. In Australasia you might boil it in a billy can over an open fire, and you certainly boil it in Turkey and such places. But, apart from *not* boiling it European tea making is simple:

- Boil water that is as freshly drawn as possible. It must never be taken from the hot water supply, especially if that is from a tank for it will have lost much of its brew capabilities by being depleted of oxygen. As we rarely have teas blended for individual water supplies, you might well have to invest in a filter jug or filtered water supply system. These get rid of unwanted minerals etc from hard waters that add unwanted flavour and form a hideous scum on pots and cups.
- Warm the tea pot thoroughly with hot water and then pour it out.
- Add the tea, using rather more or less than one teaspoon per person according to your taste and forget the one for the pot, a marketing ploy if ever I heard one.
- Take the pot to the kettle – never the other way around – and the second it comes to the boil, pour the boiling water into the pot. The water should only just boil because then it is richest in oxygen, which is what works so hard on your behalf to extract the flavour from tea leaves. The longer water is boiled or kept hot the less oxygen it contains: this is why tea

made from reboiled water really never tastes as good as you hoped.
- Let the tea infuse. The importance of knowing the size of the tea leaf in your pack is paramount, for this determines how long it should be brewed – *the larger the leaf the longer the brew*. Interestingly, a brown leaf of any size gives a stronger brew than a black one.

Most people do not leave tea long enough, confusing colour with strength. Orthodox leaves require five to seven or even eight minutes to develop flavour and colour, and the CTC blends need at least two minutes. Naturally this gives stronger colour and flavour than when you only brew for one minute, so you can thus use less tea and get a finer flavour. That is real economy and true value for money. This includes tea bags, which are rarely allowed to give of their best.

The colour that comes quickly from most modern teas, and especially from tea bags, is from teas called Bright Colouring Africans, included simply because they colour water so quickly. To dip tea bags in and out of hot water a few times is to retrieve only a small percentage of the flavour and colour that is inside. One tea bag can make two or three delicious flavourful cups of tea if allowed to brew for two or three minutes – either do it in a tea pot, or brew in one cup or mug, divide the brew between the others, then top up with more water. When I gave this advice on BBC TV's Pebble Mill at One, a woman wrote to say I had all but saved her marriage as until she allowed tea bags to brew, she was constantly insulted by her husband about her tea.

The most important guarantee of a decent cup of tea is to get the brew off the leaves or to get the tea bags out as soon as the time is up. It was common well into the mid-20th century to make tea in two pots, one of them for brewing, one for pouring. It was only on the second pot, in which there are no leaves, a tea cosy should have been used. If you put a cosy onto tea while it is brewing, the temperature is kept too high and the nasty tannins get extracted too soon and you get bitter tea. If that is the sort of flavour you like, buy Assam tea and throw away the cosy.

Happily, more and more manufacturers make tea pots with removable baskets, which can be taken out with the leaves once brewing is over. They make a brilliant difference if like me you drink two or three cups at a time: with the tea leaves gone, each cup will taste as fresh and good as the first, even if you do put on a cosy when the leaves have been removed.

Cooking with Tea

The flavour of tea is fragile when cooked and quickly disappears. Thus soaking dried fruit in cold tea is quite pointless; water will do as well but doesn't sound as good. I expect the habit began when tea was very expensive and none could be thrown away. If you really want tea flavour in fruit loaves or other baking the brew must be really strong, at least 25g/1oz of tea leaves or tea bags to 600ml/1 pint of boiling water, milk or orange juice; such strong fruit-juice teas may be sweetened and thus turned into a highly individual syrup to be poured hot or cold as a sauce for ice creams, cakes, desserts – even with fresh fruit. If you want such syrups to be crystal clear, you should steep the tea in cold water overnight, as you must when making iced tea.
Storing

Natural black, oolong and green teas have quite a long life if protected from too much heat and light – they do not contain oils which will oxidize, the way coffee does. But the oils and fragrances of flavoured teas are fairly fugitive and so it is always best to keep these and any tisanes in air-tight containers in a cool place. This also means a container not very much bigger than the tea or tea bags themselves. I try never to let them become less than half full, then add a new pack and shake it all about, whether tea bags or leaf tea.

Tea Matching

It should be no surprise; teas can be matched to food as successfully as can wine. The rules are those for wines – match like weight with like weight, thus a heavy bodied Assam with big red-meat dishes, aromatic Ceylon teas with poultry and fish.

In summer, the tea can be iced, but note the instructions for making this on page 543

All the following recommendations are from either Sam or Stephen Twining, and based on the tea being drunk without milk, and with little or no sugar.

Red Meats: Assams or English Breakfast. They have the clean, acid finish of a good red wine. Chinese Yunnans and Keemuns have the velvety mouth feel and fruitiness of clarets and better match subtler meats, like lamb or veal, or chicken cooked in red wine.

Bacon & Eggs: a full bodied blend, like English or Irish Breakfast is the thing, but an Assam does just the same trick for lovers of really strong tea: the cleaner, clearer style of Ceylon teas work as well, but differently, for those who like a more aromatic cup to clear the palate of bacon fat or egg.

Curries: Darjeelings. Their elegance and muscatel-like flavour has unexpected empathy with the spices. The flavour nicely suits tuna and trout too but in all cases under brew rather than over brew to retain the special fruitiness.

Fish and Poultry: Ceylons. They have exactly the right balance of natural fragrance and floral character and a clean long finish; particularly good with oily fish, salmon perhaps. The naturally sweet floral notes of Oolongs, Keemuns and Yunnans also work well.

Seafood: Green teas, or very special Ceylons.

Desserts and Sweet Dishes: Earl Grey. Nothing quite like it to refresh the palate, with or after a good old-fashioned steamed pudding or a creamy, fruity trifle. Its perfumed acidity is sensational, hot or iced, with crème brulee, particularly one including passion fruit – in fact you could make a strong brew and use this to flavour an Earl Grey crème brulee. At tea time match Earl Grey with honey sandwiches, gingerbreads and sweet cakes. Keemuns and blends in which they predominate, like Prince of Wales, have a distinct chocolate-base note, something to pick up with chocolate cakes or biscuits, or to use as a complement to anything with summer's red berries.

Fruit and Fruit Desserts: Formosa oolongs. With or after anything made with berry fruits, their distinct peachy fragrance and natural sweetness seem to extend the flavours in your mouth. Rose pouchong, rose-petal-scented black China tea, is stronger, but with its exotic and comforting rose scent is just as good.

Digestive: Jasmine tea, flower-scented green tea. The Chinese know what they are doing to serve jasmine tea during banquets. Just as good after a meal too, but run a very close thing by a rose pouchong, sometimes called a China rose tea or rose black tea.

End of the Day: Rose pouchong again. Mild, fragrant and a wonderful digestive – it's also very good with the creams and jams of a decent afternoon tea. Unless you serve . . .

Cucumber Sandwiches: The tarry smoky flavour of lapsang souchong, made very weak, adds something magical to a cucumber sandwich. Indefinable and utterly delicious. You get the same effect if you add a little lapsang to your favourite black tea and brew them together well, but with plenty of water to keep it weak. Stephen Twining also recommends lapsang souchong with blue cheeses.

Tea Sorbet and Ice Creams

Wonderfully refreshing tea sorbets and fascinating tea ice creams can be made with dozens of different flavours, although they will all be the same colour. Rose Pouchong, Earl Grey and jasmine tea make most elegant versions. Victorians preferred ices made with green tea but you can use any fragrant tea or tisane and should experiment with a mixture of tea and fruit juice – Ceylon tea and pineapple juice, for instance. Choose a quality tea with large leaves if you make it just with water. If you use fruit juice, to make the brew a lesser quality tea with smaller leaves can be used. Tea sorbets seem especially suited for serving with tropical fruits.

Serves four to six
50g/2oz tea leaves or tea bags, dry weight
600ml/1pint /1¼ pints US, boiling water or fruit juice
150g/6oz /1¼ cups US white sugar
(optional) 2 egg whites

Pour the boiling water onto the tea leaves and brew up to seven minutes for large whole leaves and up to five minutes for medium leaves, according to recommendations or instructions. Quality tea bags are suitable and need only brew for three minutes. Do not over brew or too much tannin will be released.

If you are using leaves pour the brew off carefully or strain the brewed tea through fine muslin, and then, either way, make the liquid back up to the original volume with more water or juice. Add most of the sugar but finish sweetening when the liquid is cool: it will taste less sweet when it is cold and much less sweet when it is frozen.

Freeze in a covered container until mushy, beat back to a consistent texture quickly and fold in 1-2 beaten egg whites. Return to the tray and freeze without further interference.

For ice creams, make the tea with boiling milk, brew it very well, strain through muslin and then make up to the original quantity of liquid again, allow this to cool and then sweeten it according to your ice cream base. The simplest of these is made by whisking together a very cold 200g can of sweetened condensed milk and 150ml/¼ pint very cold double (heavy) cream. Once this is the consistency of a custard it will hold up to 300ml/¼ pint of a fruit purée or flavoured liquid. Blend in this amount only of cold, strong milk tea and then freeze; it does not usually need to be whisked during the freezing, but you can.

Tea-flavoured ice cream is much admired when you use jasmine, Rose Pouchong or a tea that includes natural vanilla; green tea gives an intriguing flavour, sometimes found in old books as stone cream, perhaps because of the colour.

Flavoured fruit teas and tisanes do make wonderful ices if you want to eat such things: Fortnum and Mason's wild strawberry tea makes such a superb ice cream I can almost forgive the flavour subterfuge. There are dozens more that do just as magically.

Tea Smoking

The most extraordinary use of tea leaves is to smoke food in a wok. You need only basic tea leaves, nothing scented or special, plus rice or barley. Because the food is sealed in the wok, this is a hot-smoking process, which will cook as well as smoke. Fish is the best possible choice, particularly the oily ones, mackerel, salmon and so on. You can also use the technique quickly, to add smoke flavour to food that is already cooked, anything from duck, the usual Chinese target, to chicken or breakfast sausages. Shelled hard-boiled eggs turn out looking the same colour as brown shells, and the reaction when anyone not in the know picks up one is usually hilarious, well, it is if you're watching.

- Mix together 125g/4oz rice, barley, wheat or rye grains and 50g/2oz black tea leaves. Line a wok and its cover with aluminium foil, and then put the smoking mixture in the base.
- Add a rack of metal and put onto that the food, leaving plenty of space for the smoke to circulate.
- Jam on the lid, and seal with tea towels you have wet, wrung out and then twisted. The smoke smells delicious but is incredibly permeating and will make everything smell for days if it escapes.
- Some add 50g/2oz of sugar to the mixture, but this only makes a more acrid smoke more quickly and adds nothing good to the effect or the flavour. Ditto any sort of alcohol, which gives no advantage. The idea of adding herbs seems appealing but they add nothing unless they contain high levels of oil: juniper berries and rosemary work but you are better having such flavours already in the food, from a marinade for instance. A flavoursome sawdust or wood chips, from camphor wood, sandalwood or cedars, can be substituted for a third of the tea.

To flavour cooked food: put the well-sealed wok containing the items over maximum heat for ten minutes, remove from the heat and let stand for ten minutes before removing the lid.

To smoke and cook at the same time: put the well-sealed wok containing the food to be cooked and smoked over maximum heat for ten minutes. For large amounts of food, reduce the heat to low and continue smoking for up to five minutes: for small and thin foods, remove from the heat after the ten minutes. In both cases, leave at least ten minutes before removing the lid. The seal keeps food warm and very moist for ages, up to an hour.

The only thing you might do wrong at first is over smoking, but you soon learn and it is one of the most impressive of techniques for entertaining. I have been doing it since 1980 and it has never palled.

Vinegars

The basis of vinegar is acetic acid, and thus a vinegar-like flavour could be obtained by diluting man made acetic acid with water.

But it would be of little culinary use, for real vinegars can be as complicated of flavour as the finest wines or ales, from which they should be made.

The souring of wine or ale is a natural process and is the result of the oxidizing of alcohol to form natural acetic acid, which will happen to any alcoholic liquid with less than 18 per cent alcohol when exposed to air. It is not enough simply to open a bottle of wine or ale and wait for vinegar. The process must be controlled of speed and temperature, or the original liquid will go off in its own direction losing flavour or picking up others before the acetic acid level is high enough to inhibit further bacteria-activated flavour change.

Modern techniques make modern vinegars in less than 24 hours. But the best vinegars, wine vinegars that is, are made by the Orleans process. First wine is converted to basic vinegar over three weeks or so, which promotes the development of bouquet and perfume. It is then drawn off to mature in oaken casks for three or four months. Look for some indication that the Orleans process has been used on the label; if you find it and compare the contents with ordinary wine vinegar you'll taste a very sharp difference indeed.

Balsamic: balsamic vinegar became a buzzword of the greedy and flash 80s. Certainly, if it was the real thing you had to flash plenty of cash, for it can cost £100 or more for quite a small bottle. Other stuff called balsamic vinegar sells for 5% of this in supermarkets.

The real thing must say **Aceto Balsamico di Modena tradizionale DOP** on the label: the *tradizionale* is what separates the aristos from the wannabees. This is as much a guarantee as you can expect. Such a label guarantees what is in the bottle will have been made only in Modena by an extraordinary method and be at least 12 years old; any matured for over 25 years will be marked *extra vecchio*. The label should also tell you it is registered as a DOP product. Although internationally known it is not the only product of this kind protected by DOP status.

Aceto Balsamico Tradizionale di Reggio Emilia DOP is made exactly the same way and stands out because it's sold in bottles with the shape of an upturned tulip. Different ages and qualities are indicated by label – gold, silver etc. A good thing for shopkeepers and shoppers bored with Modena.

These are not true vinegars but made with cooked and concentrated must or pressed juice of the white trebbiano grape; the reduction by boiling means the grape juice will not ferment. The must is aged in fragrant wooden vessels, sometimes just of juniper or oak, sometimes a progression of different woods also including cherry, mulberry, birch and others. It becomes progressively more deeply flavoured, deeply coloured and concentrated as it ages – often it will be many decades old. Its appeal is a balance of sour and sweet, a complex richness to enjoy just by itself, with only minimal intrusion of oils, salt and pepper. A true balsamic is best used with no additions, for its complexity serves far better than anything else you might think of adding.

Traditional balsamic vinegar is credited with magical restorative properties and certainly has the same ability as very ancient sherry, a tiny amount of which transforms huge quantities of younger stuff in the solera system. Thus you need use only small amounts on food. Or so I thought until I spoke to a manufacturer. 'No no,' he said, 'we only use it in small amounts because it is so expensive – it is wonderful when you use lots of it!'

I suppose that is why other companies make cheaper non-traditional balsamic vinegars all over Italy. They use the same trebbiano must and the colour is as likely to be caramel, but it's not the real thing or is the real thing diluted with wine vinegar. Sure, this addition might be aristocratic wine vinegar of some age, and the balsamic might well be 10 or 20 or more years old, but somehow this is not what the label promises. The real thing does not have vinegar added. Yes, I know it brings the price down and makes it more accessible, but it is also adding acidity and nuances that are far from traditional. If you put a motorcycle engine into a Rolls-Royce, could you sell it as a Rolls-Royce without being thought fraudulent? These mixtures of balsamic and wine vinegar should be honest and call themselves something else, and do it on the front of the label, rather than skulking their secret on the back label; just dropping *tradizionale* puts too much of the onus on the shopper.

Cod balsamics do have great gulping helpings of the flavour of their grander relations and are a much more useful thing for general salading and cooking. And yet…frankly I find solera-style sherry vinegar quite as entrancing, and sometimes better.

There is a white balsamic vinegar on the market but this is so transparently an opportunistic modern creation, and has little merit.

Chinese: Chinese vinegars are usually based on rice wine, have a great spectrum of flavour from very mild to defiant pungency, and divide into four main groups. Many are aged in wood and the best are often compared to Italian balsamic vinegar. Those from colder northern provinces, where vinegar is very extensively used in cooking, are considered China's finest. All offer tremendous scope for experimenters, taking a flavour you already use with confidence, and then shooting it upwards or sideways into new brilliancy.

White: very much milder than any western vinegar, so if you are substituting with white wine or brewed vinegar in a recipe you must dilute them.

Red: the best known is Chinkiang, made from glutinous rice and malt. It is powerful, aromatic and very dark red or brown; specially used in the Chiu Chow and Hakka kitchens of Cantonese cooking and particularly good with seafood. Yan-Kit So likened it to a lesser balsamic vinegar, which explains its frequent use as a condiment. European red wine vinegar is a waif-like substitute, even though often recommended; old solera sherry vinegar would be closer.

Black: very dark and deeply flavoured, these may be made from rice or from sorghum: but like white vinegars, some may be diluted, so shop with care.

Sweet: this is the richest style of black vinegar and is used in braising and stewing, to balance and enhance the fattiness. Once you use it with pork or duck you will be enslaved.

Cider: people drink it, prescribe it – almost worship it. Cider vinegar is the elixir of life if you believe only half of what people say. Well… some people don't even like the flavour and generally I find it a little intrusive, appley and honey-like, which is not unexpected I suppose. But it does come into its own when you are pickling fruit – peaches, pears, plums and so on. Then it is wonderful. It is made, of course, from 'soured' cider.

Cider vinegar is the best one to use with pickling spice when sousing fish. Just a teaspoon or less adds resonant interest to an apple sauce for duck or goose or pork.

Malt: this is made from 'soured' ale that is an unhopped beer. Brown malt vinegar is coloured, usually with caramel. It is actually less sharp than wine vinegars but does not carry with it the advantages of other aromas and flavours and is usually distilled to increase its strength.

Spirit vinegar and distilled vinegar are almost always made from malt vinegar and are thus the same thing. White malt vinegar, distilled or otherwise, has simply been decolorized by a charcoal process.

Sherry: one of the wonders of the world, much more reasonably priced than a decent balsamic and easier to buy than Chinese varieties. Sherry vinegar is a rich, full golden brown, and when you pull the cork of the bottle a balloon of truly mellow fruitfulness makes the senses swoon. Well, it does mine.

Sherry is made from wines that are not very drinkable in their young and unfortified state. Some are too acidic even for the mellowing sherry process, and it is these that are made into vinegar. Two processes give unique flavour to the finest sherry vinegars: they age in oaken or chestnut sherry casks, and they are aged and blended by the solera system, just as is sherry. This means the ageing vinegar is blended with progressively older vinegars and with a magic only nature manages, the older the vinegar the less you need to make an extraordinary difference. A teaspoonful will often change the flavour of an entire barrel.

The procedure is generally known as that of *criaderas* and *soleras* and this should be specified on the label. The next quality is *anadas*, in which the sherry is aged with no additions of other older ones. Least of the Jerez sherries, but which can have excellent quality are those made in the *cabeco* style in which a vinegar makers blends from various sources, and not necessarily with aged ones, and these are usually just labelled *Vinagre de Jerez/* Sherry Vinegar. A Vinagre de Jerez DOP has been aged over 6 months if it says 'Sherry Vinegar' and for more than two years if it says 'Sherry Reserve Vinegar'.

If you sip a teaspoonful of sherry vinegar the flavour should fill your mouth with an arching spectrum of flavour, and remain there for a good long time. You might get a hit of brown sugar flavour at the start but this should be followed with flashes of unsuspected floral and grape memories, and sweetness.

The rich, full flavour of sherry vinegar means you need comparatively little, and its floral sweetness means I often use it unassailed by the temperance of oil, on tomatoes or on buffalo milk mozzarella. It is by far the best to use in such cold Spanish soups as gazpacho, lifting them well beyond the realms of liquid salad and making the inclusion of raw onion even more suspect.

Whether solo or with oil, sherry vinegar clearly exposes the shallow wickedness of making salad dressings with mustard and sugar and such excess. Use decent ingredients and additions are unnecessary. Oh yes, and you can also throw away the dratted jam jar in which such concoctions are traditionally shaken, and jolly good riddance too. Pour oil and vinegar separately on to salad and mix well, or sprinkle on to your tomatoes and such, marvelling at the way the vinegar clusters in defiant camps amidst the thicker oil, so you can dip or swirl and make a thousand flavours as you eat. What did everyone do before screw-top jars?

Best bet is to buy only a Vinagre de Jerez DOP.

You will also find vinegar made from sherry grapes away from the Xeres area that has the lien on true sherry: nearby areas even age a Pedro Ximinez vinegar as much as 25 years. Equally interesting are Montilla vinegars, made from the delicious grapes that make a wine rather like sherry, but cheaper.

Wine: do not take it for granted all wine vinegar will reward you with a kaleidoscope of wondrous flavour. It will only be as good as the wine from which it was made, and only if it was also made by the slow, expensive Orleans process, which protects all the natural aromas of the wine. Most wine vinegar is not made this way; like most ingredients of excellence, Orleans vinegar costs more, but it really is worth buying this if you care about your food, and want wine vinegar. If you can't, then buy something that has individuality.

The range of wine-based vinegars seems to increase by the vintage. Chardonnay, cabernet and riesling vinegars can all be bought, as can a vermouth vinegar. None offers as much true flavour difference as a muscatel vinegar I first tasted at Brindisa in London's scintillating Borough Market – a typically boisterous, over-flowing continental food market, yet just a footstep away from London Bridge Underground. The vinegar was made in Catalonia, and the perfumed appeal of muscatel grapes somehow survives acidification, to give immediately identifiable difference. Muscatel vinegar gives amazing lift to a simple salad to go with salmon, lobster or other rich seafood; perhaps you might flavour a mayonnaise, or an aioli with some, for the sweetness of muscatel is a particularly good mate of fish. It would be good on any salad including fresh fruit or such salad flowers as nasturtium and rose petals, or on a salad just of crushed cherry tomatoes, blood oranges and flat leaf parsley. Really worth tracking down by the time next summer is here.

It could have something to do with the perception of glamour its name suggests; yet champagne vinegar also has individuality you can taste and trust. As with sherry, the basic wines of Champagne are close to undrinkable in their natural state, and so the most difficult are encouraged to become vinegar. Champagne vinegar has a fresh, clean taste lost when combined with strong oils, and can be used just by itself, but in small quantities of course.

Vinagre del Condado de Huelva DOP is made west of Seville and is a very superior wine vinegar indeed. Made only with wine from grapes grown in the DOC Huelva area, it is prepared by the same criaderas y soleras or anada methods of sherry vinegars. There are more categories from which to choose:

Vinegar from County of Huelva: has not been aged.

Old vinegar from the County of Huelva has three age categories:

Solera: a criaderas y soleras vinegar aged between six months and one year

Reserva: a criaderas y soleras vinegar aged at least one year

Ananda: an añadas sherry aged without blending for at least three years

Cooking

Very reduced vinegars, especially the flavoured ones, are the key to finishing, say, the cooking juices of some quickly fried liver or fish, emulsified with the cooking butter or oil by a quick fast boil up. Sweet and sour sauces are nothing without vinegar; but they are improved if you use a good quality one. The mere whisper of vinegar can miraculously transform the flavour of a lifeless casserole, especially if it is a rather fatty one. The use of vinegar in bread dough is a cheat's way to emulate the flavour of real sourdough. You only need 25ml/1fl oz of cider vinegar for 500g/1lb of flour.

. . . and something very special

Of the hundreds of new products I discover and taste each year, few are as exciting as the fruit vinegar essences I found at London's Great Taste Awards recently. This small range of very reduced vinegars flavoured with fruit and flowers is something anyone could make, but don't, and so is welcomed just for that. It is a traditional product rethought, rather than something created in the hope of profit. Use these in small amounts to flavour and finish everything from an oxtail stew to a raspberry ice cream, via marinades, salad dressings, glazes or simple condiments. Sweet gooseberry and elderflower fruit vinegar essence won a gold medal at the show, and the range also includes gold-medal winner raspberry vinegar essence, elderberry, black currant, strawberry, blackberry and red currant. They should be in every kitchen.

Flavoured Vinegars

Red or white wine vinegar has long been flavoured after manufacture with a variety of herbs, petals or fruit, but if you have the choice cider vinegar is probably a more grateful foundation for them. Best known and most useful is tarragon-flavoured vinegar, which adds classic complementary flavours to chicken salads – including Waldorf and Chicken Caesar salads – and is equally good when fresh pears are included. Dill vinegar is just about as good and a winner with shellfish and seafood, but shallot, chilli and garlic vinegars are rather coarse, useful in marinades rather than dressings. Any idea of putting shallot vinegar or vinegar and shallots onto raw oysters must be stifled, for this is a vulgar way of allowing culinary cowards to gag down something they'd otherwise eschew.

You can make a vinegar flavoured with almost anything by infusing almost anything in a bottle of vinegar in a warm place, checking how the flavour develops every few days. The zest of lemon, mandarin, orange, blood orange, kumquat and lime all make superior and useful vinegar.

Spiced vinegars usually get no further than peppercorns in a chilli vinegar; the best I ever made was using only roughly cracked roasted black peppercorns with a little garlic and orange peel, but it would actually have been more useful if I had macerated these in an oil. Most herbs can also be infused in vinegar, especially basil, bay and thyme, but be careful making a rosemary vinegar as it can get too strong very quickly. The creative will soon be combining citrus zests and fresh herbs to make something their very own.

Floral vinegars are rather less usual, but take the time to make a rose vinegar, which will take several weeks and might need you to strain out and replace the fragrant petals more than once, and you will be richly rewarded. Haunting and somehow smoky it should be used only with the lightest of oils or just by itself. Or you can sweeten it and then dilute with sparkling water for great refreshment. This was more traditionally done with raspberry vinegar.

Vinegars flavoured with raspberries, strawberries, black currants, red currants, blackberries and blueberries are the basis of a style of refreshing summer drink that has largely been buried without trace but which deserves to be unearthed. Some commercial raspberry vinegar is sweetened, so it can be used thus, but it's then useless in dressings. Unsweetened raspberry vinegar has a knockout affinity with raw cauliflower and with raw spinach and other saladings. If you purée summer berries with a little oil and then a fruit vinegar you get an extravagantly coloured and flavoured dressing for a chunky salad or for cold poultry, game and fish; a squeeze of juice from fresh ginger will tip it into greater savouriness.

To make any of these berry vinegars, start with 500g/1lb of berries (they can be a mixture) and 600ml/1 pint of decent vinegar, ideally cider vinegar. Combine and leave on a warm window ledge for five days and then strain out the fruit and replace with another 500g/1lb. After another 5-7 days, again strain out the fruit and store the vinegar in a cool place. Sometimes you will want to start with more fruit or to macerate more times to get deeper colour and flavour. It's best to sweeten it only when needed. I once used my raspberry vinegar, together with some of the pickled raspberries and some fresh ones, to make a sweet and sour raspberry sauce to serve with duck for HE the Chinese Ambassador when he stayed at a house in which I was cooking in Scotland. He asked if I had learned to cook in Beijing, his home town, which I took to be a great compliment. It did look and taste exceptionally good.

Postscript

For anyone with access to the internet, the culinary world is your oyster. But beware – just because information is on the internet it doesn't mean it is authoritative or, even, correct. You need at least three sites to agree on a fact before you can believe it, and even then local word use, ethnic mix and experience can skew things very weirdly. As an example, an *entrée* is a main course in the UK, Europe and US but is a first course in Australasia: a spring onion in the UK is a scallion or green onion in the US but is a shallot in Australia. If you are cooking from the internet, remember a proper UK cup is 10 fluid ounces but that a US cup is 8 fluid ounces – the UK pint is 25% bigger than the US pint, ditto quart etc. Curiously, Australia has taken to the US measure and NZ equivocates between UK and US.

Of the many newspapers worth reading on the internet, the *New York Times* is way up amongst the best and doesn't cost you anything. Their food pages are published on a Wednesday.

When you are travelling, an interest in food ingredients, in markets and shops, supermarkets and restaurants and cafes will probably bring far greater enjoyment to a day than visiting a famous church. Thus it's always worthwhile buying a guide to local food or food establishments, ideally one based on food shops, outlets and markets rather than on restaurants.

Food and wine tourism is one of the world's fastest growing industries, and in all the big beautiful cities, from Sydney to London, you'll find focused guide books easily available; often they are free publications from the local tourist organisation. Elsewhere it'll be a state wine and food trail guide, something done particularly well by South Australia, or a country-wide guide like *Cuisine* magazine's publication *Wine Country in NZ*. This is a complete guide to wine, wineries, markets, delis, artisan producers, specialty shops and restaurants and where to stay during your explorations.

The most direct experience of new or authentic ingredients has always been in markets, but that was something you once expected only in Europe. Today, farmers' markets have changed that. There are thousands in the US, hundreds in the UK and they have rapidly become essential to life in Australia and NZ.

Wherever you are, in New York or Hawke's Bay, ask about the local farmers' markets as soon as you can. They always make somewhere new a delicious experience.